ISSA

Fundamentals of Information Systems Security

THIRD EDITION

David Kim | Michael G. Solomon

JONES & BARTLETT
LEARNING

World Headquarters
Jones & Bartlett Learning
5 Wall Street
Burlington, MA 01803
978-443-5000
info@jblearning.com
www.jblearning.com

Jones and Bartlett's books and products are available through most bookstores and online booksellers. To contact Jones and Bartlett Publishers directly, call 800-832-0034, fax 978-443-8000, or visit our website www.jbpub.com.

Substantial discounts on bulk quantities of Jones & Bartlett Learning publications are available to corporations, professional associations, and other qualified organizations. For details and specific discount information, contact the special sales department at Jones & Bartlett Learning via the above contact information or send an email to specialsales@jblearning.com.

Production Credits

VP, Executive Publisher: David D. Cella
Executive Editor: Matt Kane
Acquisitions Editor: Laura Pagluica
Editorial Assistant: Mary Menzemer
Production Manager: Carolyn Rogers Pershouse
Associate Production Editor: Juna Abrams
Director of Marketing: Andrea DeFronzo
Marketing Manager: Amy Langlais
Manufacturing and Inventory Control Supervisor: Amy Bacus

Composition: S4Carlisle Publishing Services
Cover Design: Scott Moden
Director of Rights & Media: Joanna Gallant
Rights & Media Specialist: Merideth Tumasz
Media Development Editor: Shannon Sheehan
Cover and Header Image: © Zffoto/Shutterstock
Printing and Binding: Edwards Brothers Malloy
Cover Printing: Edwards Brothers Malloy

Library of Congress Cataloging-in-Publication Data
Names: Kim, David (Information technology security consultant), author. |
    Solomon, Michael (Michael G.), 1963- author.
Title: Fundamentals of information systems security / David Kim and Michael G. Solomon.
Description: Third edition. | Burlington, Massachusetts : Jones & Bartlett
    Learning, 2016. | Includes bibliographical references and index.
Identifiers: LCCN 2016038356 | ISBN 9781284116458 (pbk.)
Subjects: LCSH: Computer security. | Information resources--Security measures.
Classification: LCC QA76.9.A25 K536 2016 | DDC 005.8--dc23
LC record available at https://lccn.loc.gov/2016038356

6048

Printed in the United States of America
22 21 20 19 18   10 9 8 7 6 5 4

Contents

CHAPTER 7

Auditing, Testing, and Monitoring   216

Preface

Purpose of This Book

This book is part of the Information Systems Security & Assurance (ISSA) Series from Jones & Bartlett Learning (*www.issaseries.com*). Designed for courses and curriculums in IT Security, Cybersecurity, Information Assurance, and Information Systems Security, this series features a comprehensive, consistent treatment of the most current thinking and trends in this critical subject area. These titles deliver fundamental information security principles packed with real-world applications and examples. Authored by Certified Information Systems Security Professionals (CISSPs) and experienced cybersecurity consultants, they deliver comprehensive information on all aspects of information security. Reviewed word for word by leading technical experts in the field, these books are not just current, but forward-thinking—putting you in the position to solve the cybersecurity challenges not just of today, but of tomorrow, as well.

Part I of this book on information security fundamentals focuses on new risks, threats, and vulnerabilities associated with the transformation to a digital world and the Internet of Things (IoT). Individuals, students, educators, businesses, organizations, and governments have changed how they communicate, share personal information and media, and do business. Led by the vision of the IoT, the Internet and broadband communications have entered into our everyday lives. This digital revolution has created a need for information systems security. With recent compliance laws requiring organizations to protect and secure private data and reduce liability, information systems security has never been more recognized than it is now.

Part II is adapted from CompTIA's Security+ professional certification. CompTIA's Security+ is the most widely accepted foundational, vendor-neutral IT security knowledge and skills professional certification. As a benchmark for foundational knowledge and best practices in IT security, the Security+ professional certification includes the essential principles for network security, operational security, and compliance. Also covering application, data, and host security, threats and vulnerabilities, access control, identity management, and cryptography, the Security+ certification provides a solid foundation for an IT security career.

Part III of this book provides a resource for readers and students desiring more information on information security standards, education, professional certifications, and recent compliance laws. These resources are ideal for students and individuals desiring additional information about educational and career opportunities in information systems security.

Learning Features

The writing style of this book is practical and conversational. Step-by-step examples of information security concepts and procedures are presented throughout the text. Each chapter begins with a statement of learning objectives. Illustrations are used both to clarify the material and to vary the presentation. The text is sprinkled with Notes, Tips, FYIs, Warnings, and Sidebars to alert the reader to additional helpful information related to the subject under discussion. Chapter Assessments appear at the end of each chapter, with solutions provided in the back of the book.

Chapter summaries are included in the text to provide a rapid review or preview of the material and to help students understand the relative importance of the concepts presented.

Audience

The material is suitable for undergraduate or graduate computer science majors or information science majors, students at a 2-year technical college or community college who have a basic technical background, or readers who have a basic understanding of IT security and want to expand their knowledge.

Acknowledgments

This is the flagship book of the Information Systems Security & Assurance (ISSA) Series from Jones & Bartlett Learning (*www.issaseries.com*). The ISSA series was designed for IT security and information assurance curriculums and courseware for those colleges and universities needing a hands-on approach to delivering an information systems security and information assurance degree program whose graduates would be ready for the work force.

The entire ISSA series was developed by information systems security professionals, consultants, and recognized leaders in the field of information systems security, all of whom contributed to each word, sentence, paragraph, and chapter. The dedication and perseverance displayed by those involved was driven by a single passion and a common goal: "to help educate today's information systems security practitioner" by creating the most up-to-date textbooks, courseware, and hands-on labs to ensure job and skill-set readiness for information systems security practitioners.

Thank you to Jones & Bartlett Learning for having the vision and patience to champion this effort and build the world's best information systems security content and curriculum. Thank you to Michael Solomon and Jeff Parker and the entire Jones & Bartlett Learning team who contributed to this book and entire ISSA Series during the past 6 months of development.

And last but not least, I would like to thank my wife, MiYoung Kim, who is and always will be by my side. I love you more each day.

David Kim

I would like to thank David Kim and the whole Jones & Bartlett Learning team for providing pertinent editorial comments and for helping to fine tune the book's content. All of you made the process so much easier and added a tremendous amount of value to the book. And thanks so much to Stacey and Noah for your help in researching the many diverse topics.

Michael G. Solomon

The Authors

David Kim is the president of Security Evolutions, Inc. (SEI; *www.security-evolutions.com*), located outside the Washington, DC, metropolitan area. SEI provides governance, risk, and compliance consulting services for public and private sector clients globally. SEI's clients include healthcare institutions, banking institutions, governments, and international airports. SEI's IT security consulting services include security risk assessments, vulnerability assessments, compliance audits, and designing of layered security solutions for enterprises. In addition, available services include developing business continuity and disaster recovery plans. Mr. Kim's IT and IT security experience encompasses more than 30+ years of technical engineering, technical management, and sales and marketing management. This experience includes LAN/WAN, internetworking, enterprise network management, and IT security for voice, video, and data networking infrastructures. He is an accomplished author and part-time adjunct professor who enjoys teaching cybersecurity to students across the United States.

Michael G. Solomon, CISSP, PMP, CISM, is a full-time security and OpenEdge speaker, consultant, author, and gamification evangelist who specializes in leading teams in achieving and maintaining secure IT environments. As an IT professional and consultant since 1987, he has led projects for many major organizations and has authored and contributed to numerous books and training courses. From 1998 until 2001, he was an instructor in the Kennesaw State University's Computer Science and Information Sciences (CSIS) department, and currently teaches graduate Computer Science and Security courses at the University of the Cumberlands. Michael is also a PhD candidate in Computer Science and Informatics at Emory University.

PART I

The Need for Information Security

Information Systems Security

THE INTERNET HAS CHANGED DRAMATICALLY from its origins. It has grown from a tool used by a small number of universities and government agencies to a worldwide network with more than 3 billion users. As it has grown, it has changed the way people communicate and do business, bringing many opportunities and benefits. Today the Internet continues to grow and expand in new and varied ways. It supports innovation and new services such as IP mobility and smartphone connectivity. When the Internet started, the majority of connected devices were solely computers, whether for personal use or within a company. In the most recent years, however, an increasing variety of devices beyond computers, including smartphones, smart cars, appliances, vending machines, smart homes, and smart buildings, can connect and share data.

The Internet as we know it today is expanding rapidly as the **Internet of Things (IoT)** takes over and impacts our day-to-day lives. Although the Internet officially started back in 1969, the extent to which people depend on the Internet is new. Today, people interact with the Internet and cyberspace as part of normal day-to-day living. This includes personal use and business use. Users must now address issues of privacy data security and business data security. Security threats can come from either personal or business use of your Internet-connected device. Intelligent and aggressive cybercriminals, terrorists, and scam artists lurk in the shadows. Connecting your computers or devices to the Internet immediately exposes them to attack. These attacks result in frustration and hardship. Anyone whose personal information has been stolen (called **identity theft**) can attest to that. Worse, attacks on computers and networked devices are a threat to the national economy, which depends on **e-commerce**. Even more important, cyberattacks threaten national security. For example, terrorist attackers could shut down electricity grids and disrupt military communication.

You can make a difference. The world needs people who understand computer security and who can protect computers and networks from criminals and terrorists. Remember, it's all about securing your sensitive data. If you have sensitive data, you must protect it. To get you started, this chapter gives an overview of information systems security concepts and terms that you must understand to stop cyberattacks.

Chapter 1 Topics

This chapter covers the following topics and concepts:

- What unauthorized access and data breaches are
- What information systems security is
- What the tenets of information systems security are
- What the seven domains of an IT infrastructure are
- What the weakest link in an IT infrastructure is
- How an IT security policy framework can reduce risk
- How a data classification standard affects an IT infrastructure's security needs

Chapter 1 Goals

When you complete this chapter, you will be able to:

- Describe how unauthorized access can lead to a data breach
- Relate how availability, integrity, and confidentiality requirements affect the seven domains of a typical IT infrastructure
- Describe the risk, threats, and vulnerabilities commonly found within the seven domains
- Identify a layered security approach throughout the seven domains
- Develop an IT security policy framework to help reduce risk from common threats and vulnerabilities
- Relate how a data classification standard affects the seven domains

Information Systems Security

Today's **Internet** is a worldwide network with more than 3 billion users. It includes almost every government, business, and organization on Earth. However, having that many users on the same network wouldn't solely have been enough to make the Internet a game-changing innovation. These users needed some type of mechanism to link documents and resources across computers. In other words, a user on computer A needed an easy way to open a document on computer B. This need gave rise to a system that defines how documents and resources are related across network machines. The name of this system is the **World Wide Web (WWW)**. You may know it as **cyberspace** or simply as the Web. Think of it this way: The Internet links communication networks to one another. The Web is the connection of websites, webpages, and digital content on those networked computers. Cyberspace is all the accessible users, networks, webpages, and applications working in this worldwide electronic realm.

Recent Data Breaches in the United States (2013–2015)

The past couple of years have seen a dramatic increase in the number of reported **data breaches** in the United States. Both the public sector and the private sector have fallen victim. **TABLE 1-1** lists a summary of recent data breaches, the affected organization, and the impact of the data breach to that organization.

TABLE 1-1 Recent data breaches in the United States, 2013–2015.

ORGANIZATION	DATA BREACH	IMPACT OF DATA BREACH
Adobe Systems Incorporated: Software subscription database	In a breach on October 3, 2013, Adobe announced that hackers had published data for 150 million accounts and had stolen encrypted customer credit card data. Logon credentials were also compromised for an undetermined number of Adobe user accounts.	The hackers stole 3 million credit card records and accessed 160,000 Social Security numbers (SSNs). Adobe has offered a year's worth of credit monitoring to customers affected by the breach.
Anthem, Inc.: Blue Cross Blue Shield customer database	On February 4, 2015, Anthem disclosed that criminal hackers had broken into its servers and potentially stolen from its servers over 37.5 million records that contain personally identifiable information. On February 24, 2015, Anthem raised the number of victims to 78.8 million people whose personal information was affected. The data breach extended into multiple brands Anthem uses to market its health care plans, including Anthem Blue Cross, Anthem Blue Cross and Blue Shield, Blue Cross and Blue Shield of Georgia, Empire Blue Cross and BlueShield, Amerigroup, Caremore, and UniCare.	Individuals whose data was stolen could have problems resulting from identity theft for the rest of their lives. Anthem had a $100 million insurance policy covering cyberattacks from American International Group One.

ORGANIZATION	DATA BREACH	IMPACT OF DATA BREACH
Excellus BlueCross BlueShield: Blue Cross Blue Shield customer database	Personal data from more than 10 million members became exposed after the company's IT systems were breached, beginning as far back as December 2013. Among the affected individuals in the Excellus breach are members of other Blue Cross Blue Shield plans who sought treatment in the 31-county upstate New York service area of Excellus, according to the company. Compromised data includes names, addresses, birthdates, SSNs, health plan ID numbers, and financial account information, as well as claims data and clinical information.	The suit against Excellus alleges that the health insurer failed to fulfill its legal duty to protect the sensitive information of its customers and those customers whose data were stored in its systems. In addition, the suit alleges that Excellus knew about the security breach for over one month before it publicly disclosed the incident.
Hilton Hotels & Resorts: Travel industry customer and credit card database	After multiple banks suspected a credit card breach at Hilton properties across the country, Hilton acknowledged an intrusion involving malicious software had been found on some point-of-sale systems. Hilton said the stolen data included cardholder names, payment card numbers, security codes, and expiration dates, but no addresses or personal identification numbers.	Hilton identified and took action to eradicate unauthorized malware that targeted payment card information and strengthened its security. The company offered one year of free credit monitoring to affected customers.
Target Corp.: Customer and credit card database of the nationwide retailer	In December 2013, a data breach of Target's systems affected up to 110 million customers. Compromised customer information included names, phone numbers, email, and mailing addresses.	Target agreed to reimburse some costs that financial institutions incurred as a result of the breach, but the retailer has failed to reach a settlement with MasterCard over the resulting dispute.

(*continues*)

TABLE 1-1 Recent data breaches in the United States, 2013–2015. (*Continued*)

ORGANIZATION	DATA BREACH	IMPACT OF DATA BREACH
Experian Information Solutions, Inc., and T-Mobile USA, Inc.: Database of T-Mobile customers applying for credit	On September 15, 2015, Experian discovered that attackers had breached one North American business unit server containing the personal data of about 15 million T-Mobile customers who had applied for credit. T-Mobile shared this information with Experian to process credit checks or provide financing. Social Security and credit card information was compromised. The Internal Revenue Service (IRS) has confirmed that 13,673 U.S. citizens have been victimized through the filing of $65 million in fraudulent individual income tax returns as a result of this data breach.	T-Mobile is suffering reputational and financial damage because of the actions of a third-party partner and not its own, notwithstanding the carrier's choice of business partners.
Sony Pictures Entertainment: Confidential files, emails, and employee data	On November 24, 2014, a hacker group identifying itself with the name Guardians of Peace leaked confidential data from the Sony Pictures film studio. The data leak included personal information about Sony Pictures employees and their families, emails between employees, information about Sony executive salaries, copies of then-unreleased Sony films, and other information. In December, the FBI identified the Guardians of Peace as acting on behalf of the North Korean government.	On January 2, 2015, U.S. President Barack Obama issued an executive order enacting additional sanctions against the North Korean government and a North Korean arms dealer, specifically citing this cyberattack and ongoing North Korean policies. Obama also issued a legislative proposal to Congress to update current laws to better respond to cybercrimes like the Sony hack and to be able to prosecute such crimes compatibly with similar offline crimes while protecting citizens' privacy.

ORGANIZATION	DATA BREACH	IMPACT OF DATA BREACH
U.S. Office of Personnel Management : Agency of the U.S. Federal government	In June 2015, the U.S. Office of Personnel Management (OPM) announced that it had been the target of a data breach impacting approximately 22 million people. The data breach was noticed by the OPM in April 2015. Federal officials described it as among the largest breaches of government data in the history of the United States. Information targeted in the breach included personally identifiable information such as SSNs as well as names, dates, and places of birth and addresses. The hack went deeper than initially believed and likely involved theft of detailed security clearance-related background information.	The data breach has created a massive counterintelligence threat that could easily last 40 years. For every nonmarried federal employee in the background investigation database, at least four out of five people will require monitoring. For those who have been married or married more than once, the number of affected people is at least 12 out of 14.
The Wendy's Co.: Customer and credit card database of the nationwide fast-food retailer	After becoming suspicious in December 2015, the Ohio-based burger chain began looking into reports of unusual activity on credit cards used at Wendy's locations across the country. The company hired a team of cybersecurity experts to help assess the damage and is cooperating with law enforcement in a criminal investigation. Customers at as many as 6,000 Wendy's locations may have been affected.	The investigation is new and ongoing, but card breaches are becoming more and more common in the restaurant industry. Restaurant chains are especially susceptible, likely because of their use of outdated technology.

Unfortunately, when you connect to cyberspace, you also open the door to a lot of bad guys. They want to find you and steal your data. Every computer or device that connects to the Internet is at risk, creating an Internet of Things (IoT) that supports users in all aspects of their lives. Like outer space, the maturing Internet is a new frontier. There is no Internet government or central authority. It is full of challenges—and questionable behavior. This questionable behavior is evident given the data breaches we've seen in the past three years alone. In the United States, public and private sectors have been compromised through unauthorized access and data breach attacks. These recent attacks have been committed by individuals, organized cybercriminals, and attackers from other nations. The quantity of cyberattacks on U.S. interests is increasing.

With the Internet of Things (IoT) now connecting personal devices, home devices, and vehicles to the Internet, there are even more data to steal. All users must defend their information from attackers. **Cybersecurity** is the duty of every government that wants to ensure its national security. Data security is the responsibility of every organization that needs to protect its information assets and sensitive data (e.g., SSNs, credit card numbers, and the like). And it's the job of all of us to protect our own data. **FIGURE 1-1** illustrates this new frontier.

The components that make up cyberspace are not automatically secure. These components include cabling, physical networks, operating systems, and software applications that computers use to connect to the Internet. At the heart of the problem is the lack of security in the **Transmission Control Protocol/Internet Protocol (TCP/IP)** communications protocol. This protocol

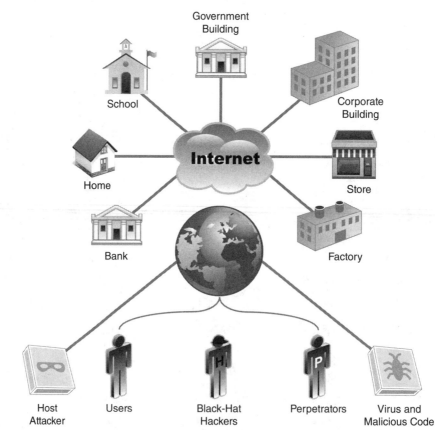

FIGURE 1-1

Cyberspace: the new frontier.

is the language that computers most commonly use to communicate across the Internet. (A **protocol** is a list of rules and methods for communicating.) TCP/IP is not just one protocol but a suite of protocols developed for communicating across a network. Named after the two most important protocols, TCP/IP works together to allow any two computers to communicate. Connecting two or more computers creates a network. TCP/IP breaks messages into chunks, or packets, to send data between networked computers. The problem lies in the fact that data are readable within each IP packet using simple software available to anyone. This readable mode is known as **cleartext**. That means you must hide or encrypt the data sent inside a TCP/IP packet to make the data more secure. **FIGURE 1-2** shows the data within the TCP/IP packet structure.

All this raises the question: If the Internet is so unsafe, why did everyone connect to it so readily? The answer is the huge growth of the Web from the mid-1990s to the early 2000s. Connecting to the Internet gave anyone instant access to the Web and its many resources. The appeal of easy worldwide connectivity drove the demand to connect. This demand and subsequent growth helped drive costs lower for high-speed communications. Households, businesses, and governments gained affordable high-speed Internet access. And as wireless and cellular connections have become more common and affordable, it has become easier to

FIGURE 1-2

TCP/IP communications are in cleartext.

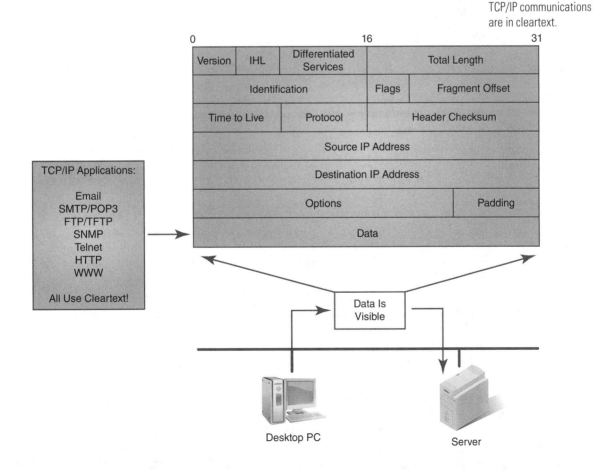

FIGURE 1-3

Internet of Things (IoT) supports any-to-any connectivity.

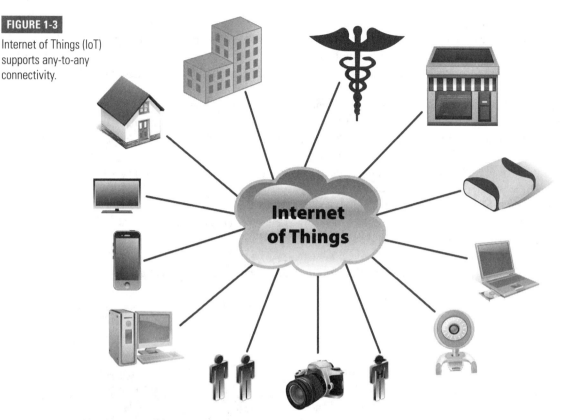

stay connected no matter where you are and what devices you need to connect. **FIGURE 1-3** shows how the IoT is making the world a digitally connected one. The IoT magnifies the risk, threat, and vulnerability issues, given that a hacker or attacker can gain unauthorized access to any IP-connected device. Once access to an IP-connected device is granted, data can be stolen or damage can be done if the attacker desires. It's this "dark villain" nature of a hacker that helped label hackers as "black hats."

Internet growth has also been driven by generational differences. **Generation Y**'s culture is taking over as baby boomers begin to retire. This new generation grew up with cell phones, **smartphones**, and "always-on" Internet access. These devices provide real-time communication. Today's personal communications include Voice over IP (VoIP), text messaging, instant messaging (IM), and chatting as well as audio and video conferencing. These real-time, Session Initiation Protocol-enabled (SIP-enabled) applications are commonly known as **unified communications**. Examples of unified communication applications include Google Chat™ instant messaging service, Yahoo!® Messenger, WebEx,™ GoToMeeting,™ and Skype™ for Business's online meeting features.

Meanwhile, an **information security** war is raging. The battlefield is cyberspace and the enemies are already within the gates. To make matters worse, the enemy is everywhere—both in the local area and around the world. The enemy seeks your sensitive data. Thus, the name of the game for an attacker is to gain unauthorized access. **Unauthorized access** means that the attacker obtains your authorized logon ID and password without your permission.

Using those logon credentials, the attacker gains access to the same systems and applications that your access permits. If unauthorized access is granted, then depending on that user's access controls, sensitive data may be accessible and can be downloaded. For this reason, information technology infrastructures need proper security controls. This information security war has created a great demand for information systems security and information assurance professionals—for a new kind of cyberwarrior to help defend security and business interests.

Risks, Threats, and Vulnerabilities

This book introduces the dangers of cyberspace and discusses how to address those dangers. It explains how to identify and combat the dangers common in **information systems** and IT infrastructures. To understand how to make computers more secure, you first need to understand the concepts of risks, threats, and vulnerabilities.

Risk is the likelihood that something bad will happen to an asset. It is the level of exposure to some event that has an effect on an asset. In the context of IT security, an asset can be a computer, a database, or a piece of information. Examples of risk include the following:

- Losing data
- Losing business because a disaster has destroyed your building
- Failing to comply with laws and regulations

A **threat** is any action that could damage an asset. Information systems face both natural and human-induced threats. The threats of flood, earthquake, or severe storms require organizations to create plans to ensure that business operation continues and that the organization can recover. A **business continuity plan (BCP)** gives priorities to the functions an organization needs to keep going. **A disaster recovery plan (DRP)** defines how a business gets back on its feet after a major disaster such as a fire or hurricane. Human-caused threats to a computer system include viruses, malicious code, and unauthorized access. A **virus** is a computer program written to cause damage to a system, an application, or data. **Malicious code**, or **malware**, is a computer program written to cause a specific action to occur, such as erasing a hard drive. These threats can harm an individual, business, or organization.

A **vulnerability** is a weakness that allows a threat to be realized or to have an effect on an asset. To understand what a vulnerability is, think about lighting a fire. Lighting a fire is not necessarily bad. If you are cooking a meal on a grill, you will need to light a fire in the grill. The grill is designed to contain the fire and should pose no danger if used properly. On the other hand, lighting a fire in a computer data center will likely cause damage. A grill is not vulnerable to fire, but a computer data center is. A threat by itself does not always cause damage; there must be a *vulnerability* for a threat to be realized.

Vulnerabilities can often result in legal liabilities. Any vulnerability that allows a threat to be realized may result in legal action. Since computers must run software to be useful, and since humans write software, software programs inevitably contain errors. Thus, software vendors must protect themselves from the liabilities of their own vulnerabilities with an **End-User License Agreement (EULA)**. A EULA takes effect when the user opens the package and installs the software. All software vendors use EULAs. That means the burden of protecting IT systems and data lies on internal information systems security professionals.

End-User License Agreements (EULAs)

EULAs are license agreements between a user and a software vendor. EULAs protect the software vendor from claims arising from the behavior of imperfect software. EULAs typically contain a warranty disclaimer. This limits their liability from software bugs and weaknesses that hackers can exploit.

Here is an excerpt from Microsoft's EULA, stating that the company offers only "limited" warranties for its software. The EULA also advises that the software product is offered "as is and with all faults."

DISCLAIMER OF WARRANTIES. THE LIMITED WARRANTY THAT APPEARS ABOVE IS THE ONLY EXPRESS WARRANTY MADE TO YOU AND IS PROVIDED IN LIEU OF ANY OTHER EXPRESS WARRANTIES (IF ANY) CREATED BY ANY DOCU-MENTATION OR PACKAGING. EXCEPT FOR THE LIMITED WARRANTY AND TO THE MAXIMUM EXTENT PERMITTED BY APPLICABLE LAW, MICROSOFT AND ITS SUPPLIERS PROVIDE THE SOFTWARE PRODUCT AND SUPPORT SERVICES (IF ANY) AS IS AND WITH ALL FAULTS, AND HEREBY DISCLAIM ALL OTHER WARRANTIES AND CONDITIONS....

Microsoft's EULA also limits its financial liability to the cost of the software or US$5, whichever is greater:

LIMITATION OF LIABILITY. ANY REMEDIES NOTWITHSTANDING ANY DAMAGES THAT YOU MIGHT INCUR FOR ANY REASON WHATSOEVER (INCLUDING, WITHOUT LIMITATION, ALL DAMAGES REFERENCED ABOVE AND ALL DIRECT OR GENERAL DAMAGES), THE ENTIRE LIABILITY OF MICROSOFT AND ANY OF ITS SUPPLIERS UNDER ANY PROVISION OF THIS EULA AND YOUR EXCLUSIVE REMEDY FOR ALL OF THE FOREGOING (EXCEPT FOR ANY REMEDY OF REPAIR OR REPLACEMENT ELECTED BY MICROSOFT WITH RESPECT TO ANY BREACH OF THE LIMITED WARRANTY) SHALL BE LIMITED TO THE GREATER OF THE AMOUNT ACTUALLY PAID BY YOU FOR THE SOFTWARE PRODUCT OR U.S.$5.00. THE FOREGOING LIMITATIONS, EXCLUSIONS AND DISCLAIMERS (INCLUDING SECTIONS 9, 10 AND 11 ABOVE) SHALL APPLY TO THE MAXIMUM EXTENT PERMITTED BY APPLICABLE LAW, EVEN IF ANY REMEDY FAILS ITS ESSENTIAL PURPOSE.

What Is Information Systems Security?

The term *security* is easiest to define by breaking it into pieces. An information system consists of the hardware, operating system, and application software that work together to collect, process, and store data for individuals and organizations. Thus **information systems security** is the collection of activities that protect the information system and the data stored in it. Many U.S. and international laws now require this kind of security assurance. Organizations must address this need head-on. **FIGURE 1-4** reviews the types of information commonly found within an IT infrastructure.

U.S. Compliance Laws Drive Need for Information Systems Security

Cyberspace brings new threats to people and organizations. People need to protect their privacy. Businesses and organizations are responsible for protecting both their intellectual property and any personal or private data they handle. Various laws require organizations to use security controls to protect private and confidential data. Recent U.S. laws related to information security include the following:

- **Federal Information Security Management Act (FISMA)**—Passed in 2002, FISMA requires federal civilian agencies to provide security controls over resources that support federal operations.

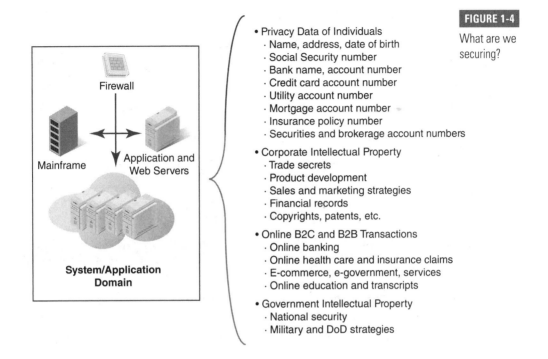

FIGURE 1-4

What are we
securing?

- Privacy Data of Individuals
  · Name, address, date of birth
  · Social Security number
  · Bank name, account number
  · Credit card account number
  · Utility account number
  · Mortgage account number
  · Insurance policy number
  · Securities and brokerage account numbers

- Corporate Intellectual Property
  · Trade secrets
  · Product development
  · Sales and marketing strategies
  · Financial records
  · Copyrights, patents, etc.

- Online B2C and B2B Transactions
  · Online banking
  · Online health care and insurance claims
  · E-commerce, e-government, services
  · Online education and transcripts

- Government Intellectual Property
  · National security
  · Military and DoD strategies

- **Federal Information Security Modernization Act (FISMA)**—Passed in 2014, FISMA was enacted to update FISMA 2002 with information on modern threats as well as security controls and best practices.
- **Sarbanes-Oxley Act (SOX)**—Passed in 2002, SOX requires publicly traded companies to submit accurate and reliable financial reporting. This law does not require securing private information, but it does require security controls to protect the confidentiality and integrity of the reporting itself.
- **Gramm-Leach-Bliley Act (GLBA)**—Passed in 1999, GLBA requires all types of financial institutions to protect customers' private financial information.
- **Health Insurance Portability and Accountability Act (HIPAA)**—Passed in 1996, HIPAA requires health care organizations to have security and privacy controls implemented to ensure patient privacy.
- **Children's Internet Protection Act (CIPA)**—Passed in 2000 and updated in 2011, CIPA requires public schools and public libraries to use an Internet safety policy. The policy must address the following:
  - Restricting children's access to inappropriate matter on the Internet
  - Ensuring children's security when using email, chatrooms and other electronic communications
  - Restricting hacking and other unlawful activities by children online
  - Disclosing and distributing personal information about children without permission
  - Restricting children's access to harmful materials
  - Warning children on the use and dangers of social media

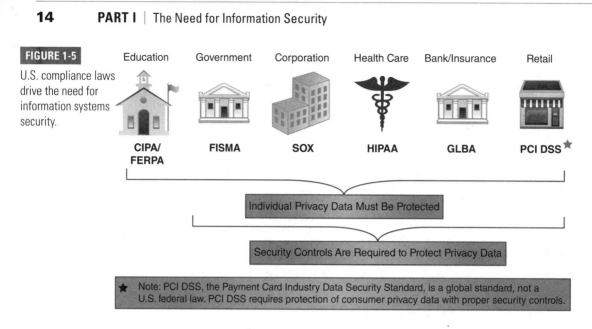

- **Family Educational Rights and Privacy Act (FERPA)**—Passed in 1974, FERPA protects the private data of students and their school records.

FIGURE 1-5 shows these laws by industry.

Tenets of Information Systems Security

Most people agree that private information should be secure. But what does "secure information" really mean? Information that is secure satisfies three main tenets, or properties, of information. If you can ensure these three tenets, you satisfy the requirements of secure information. The three tenets are as follows:

- **Confidentiality**—Only authorized users can view information.
- **Integrity**—Only authorized users can change information.
- **Availability**—Information is accessible by authorized users whenever they request the information.

FIGURE 1-6 illustrates the three tenets of information systems security. When you design and use security controls, you are addressing one or more of these tenets.

When finding solutions to security issues, you must use the C-I-A triad. You have to define your organization's security baseline goals using this triad for a typical IT infrastructure. Once defined, these goals will translate into security controls and requirements based on the type of data you are protecting.

> **Technical TIP**
>
> Some systems security professionals refer to the tenets as the A-I-C triad to avoid confusion with the U.S. Central Intelligence Agency, commonly known as the CIA.

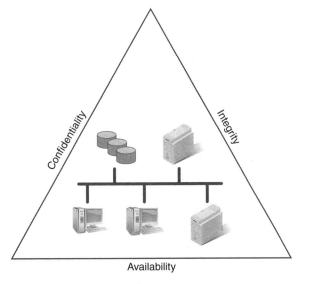

FIGURE 1-6

The three tenets of information systems security.

Identity Theft

Identity theft affects about 15 million U.S. citizens each year, with financial losses costing upward of $50 billion. Identity theft is a major threat to U.S. consumers. Many elements make up a person's identity. These include but are not limited to the following:

- Full name
- Mailing address
- Date of birth
- Social Security number
- Bank name
- Bank account number
- Credit card account number
- Utility account number
- Medical record number
- Mortgage account number
- Insurance policy number
- Securities and investment account numbers

For example, an impostor can access your accounts with just your name, home address, and Social Security number. Paper statements and account numbers tossed in the garbage can be retrieved by an unscrupulous person, making it easier for your privacy data and financial account information to be compromised. Shredding those documents before discarding them reduces the possibility of loss.

This threat extends beyond mere financial loss. Identity theft can damage your Fair Isaac Corp. (**FICO**) personal credit rating. This could stop you from getting a bank loan, mortgage, or credit card. It can take years to clean up your personal credit history. FICO is a publicly traded company that provides information used by Equifax, Experian, and TransUnion, the three largest consumer credit-reporting agencies in the United States.

Confidentiality

Confidentiality is a common term. It means guarding information from everyone except those with rights to it. Confidential information includes the following:

- Private data of individuals
- Intellectual property of businesses
- National security for countries and governments

U.S. compliance laws that protect citizens' private data require businesses and organizations to have proper security controls to ensure confidentiality.

With the growth in e-commerce, more people are making online purchases with credit cards. This requires people to enter private data into e-commerce websites. Consumers should be careful to protect their personal identity and private data. Laws require organizations to use security controls to protect customers' private data. A **security control** is something an organization does to help reduce risk. Examples of such controls include the following:

- Conducting annual security awareness training for employees. This helps remind staff about proper handling of private data. It also drives awareness of the organization's framework of security policies, standards, procedures, and guidelines.
- Putting an **IT security policy framework** in place. A policy framework is like an outline that identifies where security controls should be used.
- Designing a layered security solution for an IT infrastructure. The more layers or compartments that block or protect private data and intellectual property, the more difficult the data and property are to find and steal.
- Performing periodic security risk assessments, audits, and penetration tests on websites and IT infrastructure. This is how security professionals verify that they have properly installed the controls.
- Enabling security incident and event monitoring at your Internet entry and exit points. This is like using a microscope to see what is coming in and going out.
- Using automated workstation and server antivirus and malicious software protection. This is the way to keep viruses and malicious software out of your computer.
- Using more stringent access controls beyond a logon ID and password for sensitive systems, applications, and data. Logon IDs with passwords are only one check of the user. Access to more sensitive systems should have a second test to confirm the user's identity.
- Minimizing software weaknesses in your computers and servers by updating them with patches and security fixes. This is the way to keep your operating system and application software up to date.

Protecting private data is the process of ensuring data confidentiality. Organizations must use proper security controls specific to this concern. Some examples include the following:

- Defining organization-wide policies, standards, procedures, and guidelines to protect confidential data. These are instructions for how to handle private data.
- Adopting a **data classification standard** that defines how to treat data throughout your IT infrastructure. This is the road map for identifying what controls are needed to keep data safe.
- Limiting access to systems and applications that house confidential data to only those authorized to use that data.

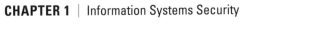

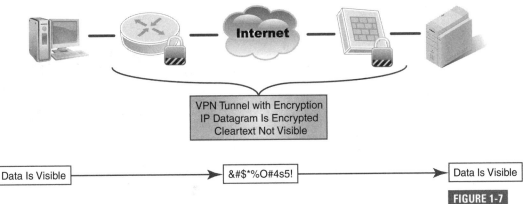

VPN Tunnel with Encryption
IP Datagram Is Encrypted
Cleartext Not Visible

Data Is Visible &#$*%O#4s5! Data Is Visible

FIGURE 1-7

Encryption of cleartext
into ciphertext.

- Using cryptography techniques to hide confidential data and keep that data invisible to unauthorized users.
- Encrypting data that cross the public Internet.
- Encrypting data that are stored within databases and storage devices.

Sending data to other computers using a network means you have to take special steps to keep confidential data from unauthorized users. **Cryptography** is the practice of hiding data and keeping it away from unauthorized users. **Encryption** is the process of transforming data from cleartext into **ciphertext**. Cleartext data are data that anyone can read. Ciphertext is the scrambled data that are the result of encrypting cleartext. An example of this process is shown in **FIGURE 1-7**.

Data privacy is so important that local and state governments are starting to pass laws to protect it by extending federal laws.

Integrity

Integrity deals with the validity and accuracy of data. Data lacking integrity—that is, data that are not accurate or not valid—are of no use. For some organizations, data and information are intellectual property assets. Examples include copyrights, patents, secret formulas, and customer databases. This information can have great value. Unauthorized changes can undermine the data's value. This is why integrity is a tenet of systems security. **FIGURE 1-8** shows what is meant by data integrity and whether that data are usable. Sabotage and corruption of data integrity are serious threats to an organization, especially if the data are critical to business operations.

Availability

Availability is a common term in everyday life. For example, you probably pay attention to the availability of your Internet service, TV service, or cell phone service. In the context of information security, availability is generally expressed as the amount of time users can

> ⚠ **WARNING**
>
> Never enter private data in an email in cleartext. Remember, email traffic transmits through the Internet in cleartext. This means your data are completely visible to whomever sees the email. Also, never enter private data in a website if that site is not a trusted host that can be checked by telephone or other means. Never enter private data into a website or web application that does not use encryption (e.g., look for the lock icon in your browser to verify if **Hypertext Transfer Protocol Secure (HTTPS)** encryption is enabled on that website or application).

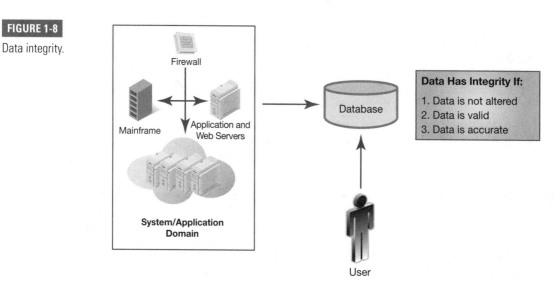

use a system, application, and data. Common availability time measurements include the following:

- **Uptime**—Uptime is the total amount of time that a system, application, and data are accessible. Uptime is typically measured in units of seconds, minutes, and hours within a given calendar month. Often uptime is expressed as a percentage of time available, e.g., 99.5 percent uptime.

- **Downtime**—Downtime is the total amount of time that a system, application, and data are not accessible. Downtime also is measured in units of seconds, minutes, and hours for a calendar month.

- **Availability**—Availability is a mathematical calculation where A = (Total Uptime) / (Total Uptime + Total Downtime).

- **Mean time to failure (MTTF)**—MTTF is the average amount of time between failures for a particular system. Semiconductors and electronics do not break and have an MTTF of many years (25 or more years, etc.). Physical parts such as connectors, cabling, fans, and power supplies have a much lower MTTF (five years or less), given that wear and tear can break them.

- **Mean time to repair (MTTR)**—MTTR is the average amount of time it takes to repair a system, application, or component. The goal is to bring the system back up quickly.

- **Mean time between failures (MTBF)**—MTBF is the predicted amount of time between failures of an IT system during operation.

- **Recovery time objective (RTO)**—RTO is the amount of time it takes to recover and make a system, application, and data available for use after an outage. Business continuity plans typically define an RTO for mission-critical systems, applications, and data access.

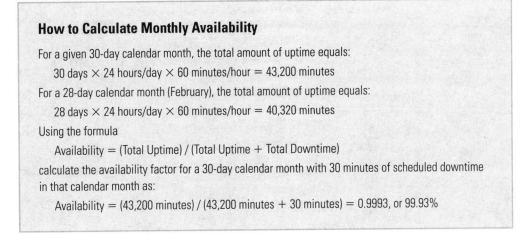

How to Calculate Monthly Availability

For a given 30-day calendar month, the total amount of uptime equals:

30 days $\times$ 24 hours/day $\times$ 60 minutes/hour = 43,200 minutes

For a 28-day calendar month (February), the total amount of uptime equals:

28 days $\times$ 24 hours/day $\times$ 60 minutes/hour = 40,320 minutes

Using the formula

Availability = (Total Uptime) / (Total Uptime + Total Downtime)

calculate the availability factor for a 30-day calendar month with 30 minutes of scheduled downtime in that calendar month as:

Availability = (43,200 minutes) / (43,200 minutes + 30 minutes) = 0.9993, or 99.93%

Telecommunications and Internet service providers offer their customers **service-level agreements (SLAs)**. An SLA is a contract that guarantees a minimum monthly availability of service for wide area network (WAN) and Internet access links. SLAs accompany WAN services and dedicated Internet access links. Availability measures a monthly uptime service-level commitment. As in the monthly availability example discussed in the sidebar, 30 minutes of downtime in a 30-day calendar month equates to 99.993 percent availability. Service providers typically offer SLAs ranging from 99.5 percent to 99.999 percent availability.

The Seven Domains of a Typical IT Infrastructure

What role do the three tenets of systems security play in a typical IT infrastructure? First, let's review what a typical IT infrastructure looks like. Whether in a small business, large government body, or publicly traded corporation, most IT infrastructures consist of the seven domains shown in **FIGURE 1-9**: User, Workstation, LAN, LAN-to-WAN, WAN, Remote Access, and System/Application Domains.

A typical IT infrastructure usually has these seven domains. Each one requires proper security controls. These controls must meet the requirements of the C-I-A triad. The following is an overview of the seven domains and the risks, threats, and vulnerabilities you will commonly find in today's IT environments.

User Domain

The User Domain defines the people who access an organization's information system.

User Domain Roles, Responsibilities, and Accountability

Here's an overview of what should go on in the User Domain:

- **Roles and tasks**—Users can access systems, applications, and data depending upon their defined access rights. Employees must conform to the staff manual and policies.

FIGURE 1-9

The seven domains of a typical IT infrastructure.

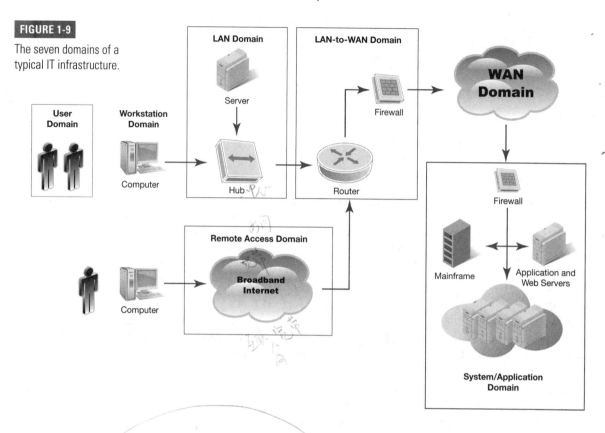

The User Domain is where you will find an **acceptable use policy (AUP)**. An AUP defines what users are allowed and not allowed to do with organization-owned IT assets. It's like a rule book that employees must follow. Violation of these rules can be grounds for dismissal. This is where the first layer of defense starts for a layered security strategy.

- **Responsibilities**—Employees are responsible for their use of IT assets. New legislation means that for most organizations it's a best practice to introduce an AUP. Organizations may require staff, contractors, or other third parties to sign an agreement to keep information confidential. Some require a criminal background check for sensitive positions. The department manager or human resources manager is usually in charge of making sure employees sign and follow an AUP.

- **Accountability**—Typically, an organization's human resources department is accountable for implementing proper employee background checks. These should be performed for individuals who will be accessing sensitive data.

Risks, Threats, and Vulnerabilities Commonly Found in the User Domain

The User Domain is the weakest link in an IT infrastructure. Anyone responsible for computer security must understand what motivates someone to compromise an organization's system, applications, or data. **TABLE 1-2** lists the risks and threats commonly found in the User Domain as well as plans you can use to prevent them.

TABLE 1-2 Risks, threats, vulnerabilities, and mitigation plans for the User Domain.

RISK, THREAT, OR VULNERABILITY	MITIGATION
Unauthorized access	Users must be made aware of phishing emails, pretexting or cons, keyboard loggers, and perpetrators impersonating an IT or delivery person in an attempt to obtain logon ID and password credentials.
Lack of user awareness	Conduct security awareness training, display security awareness posters, insert reminders in banner greetings, and send email reminders to employees.
User apathy toward policies	Conduct annual security awareness training, implement acceptable use policy, update staff manual and handbook, discuss during performance reviews.
Security policy violations	Place employee on probation, review AUP and employee manual, discuss during performance reviews.
User insertion of CDs and USB drives with personal photos, music, and videos	Disable internal CD drives and USB ports. Enable automatic antivirus scans for inserted media drives, files, and email attachments. An antivirus scanning system examines all new files on your computer's hard drive for viruses. Set up antivirus scanning for emails with attachments.
User downloads of photos, music, and videos	Enable **content filtering** and antivirus scanning for email attachments. Content-filtering network devices are configured to permit or deny specific domain names in accordance with AUP definitions.
User destruction of systems, applications, or data	Restrict users' access to only those systems, applications, and data needed to perform their jobs. Minimize write/delete permissions to the data owner only.
Attacks on the organization or acts of sabotage by disgruntled employees	Track and monitor abnormal employee behavior, erratic job performance, and use of IT infrastructure during off-hours. Begin IT access control lockout procedures based on AUP monitoring and compliance.
Employee romance gone bad	Track and monitor abnormal employee behavior and use of IT infrastructure during off-hours. Begin IT access control lockout procedures based on AUP monitoring and compliance.
Employee blackmail or extortion	Track and monitor abnormal employee behavior and use of IT infrastructure during off-hours. Enable intrusion detection system/intrusion prevention system (IDS/IPS) monitoring for sensitive employee positions and access. IDS/IPS security appliances examine the IP data streams for inbound and outbound traffic. Alarms and alerts programmed within an IDS/IPS help identify abnormal traffic and can block IP traffic as per policy definition.

Workstation Domain

A **workstation** can be a desktop computer, a laptop computer, a special-purpose terminal, or any other device that connects to your network. Workstation computers are generally thin clients or thick clients. A **thin client** is software or an actual computer with no hard drive that runs on a network and relies on a server to provide applications, data, and all processing. Thin clients are commonly used in large organizations, libraries, and schools. In contrast, a **thick client** is more fully featured hardware that contains a hard drive and applications and processes data locally, going to the server mainly for file storage. An ordinary PC is an example of a thick client. Other devices that can be considered workstations are **personal digital assistants (PDAs)**, smartphones, and tablet PCs. You can find more details about mobile devices in the "Remote Access Domain" section.

Workstation Domain Roles, Responsibilities, and Accountability

Here's an overview of what should go on in the Workstation Domain:

- **Roles and tasks**—An organization's staff should have the access necessary to be productive. Tasks include configuring hardware, hardening systems, and verifying antivirus files. **Hardening** a system is the process of ensuring that controls are in place to handle any known threats. Hardening activities include ensuring that all computers have the latest software revisions, security patches, and system configurations. The Workstation Domain also needs additional layers of defense, a tactic referred to as **defense in depth**. Another common defense layer is implementing workstation logon IDs and passwords to protect this entry into the IT infrastructure.
- **Responsibilities**—An organization's desktop support group is responsible for the Workstation Domain. Enforcing defined standards is critical to ensuring the integrity of user workstations and data. The IT security personnel must safeguard controls within the Workstation Domain. Typically, human resources departments define proper access controls for workers based on their jobs. IT security personnel then assign access rights to systems, applications, and data based on this definition.
- **Accountability**—An organization's IT desktop manager is typically accountable for allowing employees the greatest use of the Workstation Domain. The director of IT security is generally in charge of ensuring that the Workstation Domain conforms to policy.

Risks, Threats, and Vulnerabilities Commonly Found in the Workstation Domain

The Workstation Domain requires tight security and access controls. This is where users first access systems, applications, and data. The Workstation Domain requires a logon ID and password for access. **TABLE 1-3** lists the risks, threats, and vulnerabilities commonly found in the Workstation Domain, along with ways to protect against them.

LAN Domain

A **local area network (LAN)** is a collection of computers connected to one another or to a common connection medium. Network connection mediums can include wires, fiber-optic cables, or radio waves. LANs are generally organized by function or department. Once

TABLE 1-3 Risks, threats, vulnerabilities, and mitigation plans for the Workstation Domain.

RISK, THREAT, OR VULNERABILITY	MITIGATION
Unauthorized access to workstation	Enable password protection on workstations for access. Enable auto screen lockout for inactive times. Disable system admin rights for users.
Unauthorized access to systems, applications, and data	Define strict access control policies, standards, procedures, and guidelines. Implement a second level or layer of authentication to applications that contain sensitive data (e.g., **two-step authentication**).
Desktop or laptop computer operating system software vulnerabilities	Define a workstation operating system **vulnerability window** policy and standard. The vulnerability window is the gap in time a workstation is exposed to a known vulnerability until patched. Perform frequent **vulnerability assessment** scans as part of ongoing security operations.
Desktop or laptop application software vulnerabilities and software patch updates	Define a workstation application **software vulnerability** window policy. Update application software and security patches according to defined policies, standards, procedures, and guidelines.
Infection of a user's workstation or laptop computer by viruses, malicious code, or malware	Use workstation antivirus and malicious code policies, standards, procedures, and guidelines. Enable an automated antivirus protection solution that scans and updates individual workstations with proper protection.
User insertion of CDs, digital video discs (DVDs), or universal serial bus (USB) thumb drives into the organization's computers	Deactivate all CD, DVD, and USB ports. Enable automatic antivirus scans for inserted CDs, DVDs, and USB thumb drives that have files.
User downloads of photos, music, or videos via the Internet	Use content filtering and antivirus scanning at Internet entry and exit. Enable workstation auto-scans for all new files and automatic file quarantine for unknown file types.
User violation of AUP, which creates security risk for the organization's IT infrastructure	Mandate annual security awareness training for all employees. Set up security awareness campaigns and programs throughout the year.
Employees and users want to use their own smartphone or tablets, driving the need to support Bring Your Own Device (BYOD)	Develop a BYOD policy and procedure that allows employees to use their personal smartphones or mobile devices. BYOD policies and procedures typically permit the organization to data-wipe the user's smartphone or mobile device if it is lost or the employee is terminated.

connected, your computer can access systems, applications, possibly the Internet, and data. The third component in the IT infrastructure is the LAN Domain.

The physical part of the LAN Domain consists of the following:

* **Network interface card (NIC)**—The interface between the computer and the LAN physical media. The NIC has a 6-byte Media Access Control (MAC) layer address that serves as the NIC's unique hardware identifier.
* **Ethernet LAN**—This is a LAN solution based on the **IEEE 802.3 CSMA/CD** standard for 10/100/1,000Mbps Ethernet networking. **Ethernet** is the most popular LAN standard. Today's LAN standard is the **Institute of Electrical and Electronics Engineers (IEEE)** 802.3 **Carrier Sense Multiple Access/Collision Detection (CSMA/CD)** specification. Ethernet is available in 10-Mbps, 100-Mbps, 1-Gbps, 10-Gbps, 40-Gbps, and now 100-Gbps speeds for campus and metro Ethernet backbone connections.
* **Unshielded twisted-pair cabling**—This is the workstation cabling that uses RJ-45 connectors and jacks to physically connect to a 100Mbps/1Gbps/10Gbps Ethernet LAN switch. Today, organizations use Category 5 or Category 6 UTP transmission media to support high-speed data communications.
* **LAN switch**—This is the device that connects workstations into a physical Ethernet LAN. A switch provides dedicated Ethernet LAN connectivity for workstations and servers, providing maximum throughput and performance for each workstation. There are two kinds of LAN switch. A **Layer 2 switch** examines the MAC layer address and makes forwarding decisions based on MAC layer address tables. A **Layer 3 switch** examines the network layer address and routes packets based on routing protocol path determination decisions. A Layer 3 switch is the same thing as a router.
* **File server and print server**—These are high-powered computers that provide file sharing and data storage for users within a department. Print servers support shared printer use within a department.
* **Wireless access point (WAP)**—For **wireless LANs (WLANs)**, radio transceivers are used to transmit IP packets from a WLAN NIC to a **wireless access point (WAP)**. The WAP transmits WLAN signals for mobile laptops to connect. The WAP connects back to the LAN switch using unshielded twisted-pair cabling.

Ethernet switches typically provide 100-Mbps or 1-Gbps connectivity for each workstation. Today, Ethernet LAN switches support 100-Mbps and 1-GigE desktop speeds and backbone connections at 10-Gbps and 40-Gpbs speeds. These backbone connections commonly use fiber-optic cabling.

The logical part of the LAN Domain consists of the following:

* **System administration**—Setup of user LAN accounts with logon ID and password access controls (that is, user logon information).
* **Design of directory and file services**—The servers, directories, and folders to which the user can gain access.
* **Configuration of workstation and server TCP/IP software and communication protocols**—This involves IP addressing, the **IP default gateway router**, **subnet mask address**, etc. The IP default gateway router acts as the entry/exit to the LAN. The subnet mask address defines the IP network number and IP host number.

- **Design of server disk storage space; backup and recovery of user data**—Provision for user data files on LAN disk storage areas where data are backed up and archived daily. In the event of data loss or corruption, data files can be recovered from the backed-up files.
- **Design of virtual LANs (VLANs)**—With Layer 2 and Layer 3 LAN switches, Ethernet ports can be configured to be on the same VLAN, even though they may be connected to different physically connected LANs. This is the same thing as configuring workstations and servers to be on the same Ethernet LAN or broadcast domain.

Users get access to their department's LAN and other applications according to what their job requires.

LAN Domain Roles, Responsibilities, and Accountability

Here's an overview of what should go on in the LAN Domain:

- **Roles and tasks**—The LAN Domain includes both physical network components and logical configuration of services for users. Management of the physical components includes:
  - Cabling
  - NICs
  - LAN switches
  - Wireless access points (WAPs)
    LAN system administration includes maintaining the master lists of user accounts and access rights. In the LAN Domain, two-step authentication might be required. Two-step authentication is like a gate whereby the user must confirm his or her identity a second time. This mitigates the risk of unauthorized physical access.
- **Responsibilities**—The LAN support group is in charge of the LAN Domain. This includes both the physical component and logical elements. LAN system administrators must maintain and support departments' file and print services and configure access controls for users.
- **Accountability**—The LAN manager's duty is to maximize use and integrity of data within the LAN Domain. Typically, the director of IT security must ensure that the LAN Domain conforms to policy.

Risks, Threats, and Vulnerabilities Commonly Found in the LAN Domain

The LAN Domain also needs strong security and access controls. Users can access company-wide systems, applications, and data from the LAN Domain. This is where the third layer of defense is required. This defense protects the IT infrastructure and the LAN Domain. **TABLE 1-4** lists the risks, threats, and vulnerabilities commonly found in the LAN Domain, along with appropriate risk-reducing strategies.

LAN-to-WAN Domain

The LAN-to-WAN Domain is where the IT infrastructure links to a wide area network and the Internet. Unfortunately, connecting to the Internet is like rolling out the red carpet for bad guys. The Internet is open, public, and easily accessible by anyone. Most Internet traffic

TABLE 1-4 Risks, threats, vulnerabilities, and mitigation plans for the LAN Domain.

RISK, THREAT, OR VULNERABILITY	MITIGATION
Unauthorized access to LAN	Make sure wiring closets, data centers, and computer rooms are secure. Do not allow anyone access without proper ID.
Unauthorized access to systems, applications, and data	Define strict access control policies, standards, procedures, and guidelines. Implement a second-level identity check to gain access to sensitive systems, applications, and data. Restrict users from access to LAN folders and read/write/delete privileges on specific documents as needed.
LAN server operating system software vulnerabilities	Define server/desktop/laptop vulnerability window policies, standards, procedures, and guidelines. Conduct periodic LAN Domain vulnerability assessments to find software gaps. A vulnerability assessment is a software review that identifies bugs or errors in software. These bugs and errors go away when you upload software patches and fixes.
LAN server application software vulnerabilities and software patch updates	Define a strict software vulnerability window policy requiring quick software patching.
Unauthorized access by rogue users on WLANs	Use WLAN **network keys** that require a password for wireless access. Turn off broadcasting on WAPs. Require second-level authentication prior to granting WLAN access.
Compromised confidentiality of data transmissions via WLAN	Implement encryption between workstation and WAP to maintain confidentiality.
LAN servers with different hardware, operating systems, and software make them difficult to manage and troubleshoot	Implement LAN server and configuration standards, procedures, and guidelines.

is cleartext. That means it's visible and not private. Network applications use two common transport protocols: Transmission Control Protocol (TCP) and User Datagram Protocol (UDP). Both TCP and UDP use port numbers to identify the application or function; these port numbers function like channels on a TV, dictating which station you're watching. When a packet is sent via TCP or UDP, its port number appears in the packet header. Because many services are associated with a common port number, knowing the port number essentially reveals what type of packet it is. This is like advertising to the world what you are transmitting.

Examples of common TCP and UDP port numbers include the following:

- **Port 80: Hypertext Transfer Protocol (HTTP)**—HTTP is the communications protocol between web browsers and websites with data in cleartext.
- **Port 20: File Transfer Protocol (FTP)**—FTP is a protocol for performing file transfers. FTP uses TCP as a connection-oriented data transmission but in cleartext, including

the password. *Connection-oriented* means individual packets are numbered and acknowledged as being received, to increase integrity of the file transfer.

- **Port 69: Trivial File Transfer Protocol (TFTP)**—TFTP is a protocol for performing
file transfers. TFTP utilizes UDP as a connectionless data transmission but in cleartext.
This is used for small and quick file transfers, given that it does not guarantee individual
packet delivery.
- **Port 23: Terminal Network (Telnet)**—Telnet is a network protocol for performing
remote terminal access to another device. Telnet uses TCP and sends data in cleartext.
- **Port 22: Secure Shell (SSH)**—SSH is a network protocol for performing remote
terminal access to another device. SSH encrypts the data transmission for maintaining
confidentiality of communications.

A complete list of well-known port numbers from 0 to 1023 is maintained by the Internet
Assigned Numbers Authority (IANA). The IANA helps coordinate global domain name services, IP addressing, and other resources. Well-known port numbers are on the IANA website
at *www.iana.org/assignments/service-names-port-numbers/service-names-port-numbers.xml.*

Because the TCP/IP suite of protocols lacks security, the need is greater for security controls in dealing with protocols in this family. The LAN-to-WAN Domain represents the fourth
layer of defense for a typical IT infrastructure.

LAN-to-WAN Domain Roles, Responsibilities, and Accountability

Here's an overview of what should go on in the LAN-to-WAN Domain:

- **Roles and tasks**—The LAN-to-WAN Domain includes both the physical pieces and
logical design of security appliances. It is one of the most complex areas to secure
within an IT infrastructure. You need to maintain security while giving users as much
access as possible. Physical parts need to be managed to give easy access to the service.
The security appliances must be logically configured to adhere to policy definitions.

   This will get the most out of availability, ensure data integrity, and maintain confidentiality. The roles and tasks required within the LAN-to-WAN Domain include managing and
configuring the following:

  - **IP routers**—An IP router is a network device used to transport IP packets to
and from the Internet or WAN. Path determination decisions forward IP packets.
Configuration tasks include IP routing and access control lists (ACLs). Like a filter,
ACLs are used to permit and deny traffic.
  - **IP stateful firewalls**—An **IP stateful firewall** is a security appliance used to
filter inbound IP packets based on various ACL definitions configured for IP, TCP,
and UDP packet headers. A stateful firewall can examine IP, TCP, or UDP packet
headers for filtering.
  - **Demilitarized zone (DMZ)**—The DMZ is a LAN segment in the LAN-to-WAN
Domain that acts as a buffer zone for inbound and outbound IP traffic. External
servers such as web servers, **proxy servers**, and email servers can be placed here
for greater isolation and screening of IP traffic.
  - **Intrusion detection system (IDS)**—An IDS security appliance examines
IP data streams for common attack and malicious intent patterns. IDSs are passive,
going only so far as to trigger an alarm, but they will not actively block traffic.

- **Intrusion prevention system (IPS)**—An IPS does the same thing as an IDS but can block IP data streams identified as malicious. IPSs can end the actual communication session, filter by source IP addresses, and block access to the targeted host.
- **Proxy servers**—A proxy server acts as a middleman between a workstation and the external target. Traffic goes to the intermediary server that is acting as the proxy. Data can be analyzed and properly screened before they are relayed into the IT infrastructure by what are called **proxy firewalls** or **application gateway firewalls**.
- **Web content filter**—This security appliance can prevent content from entering an IT infrastructure based on filtering of domain names or of keywords within domain names.
- **Email content filter and quarantine system**—This security appliance can block content within emails or unknown file attachments for proper antivirus screening and quarantining. Upon review, the email and attachments can be forwarded to the user.
- **Security information and event management (SIEM)**—This includes monitoring the IT assets within the LAN-to-WAN Domain, including the DMZ VLAN, firewalls, IDS/IPS, and other security appliances to maximize confidentiality, integrity, and availability and monitor for security incidents and alarms triggered by specific events.
- **Responsibilities**—The network security group is responsible for the LAN-to-WAN Domain. This includes both the physical components and logical elements. Group members are responsible for applying the defined security controls.
- **Accountability**—Your organization's WAN network manager has a duty to manage the LAN-to-WAN Domain. Typically, the director of IT security ensures that the LAN-to-WAN Domain security policies, standards, procedures, and guidelines are used.

Risks, Threats, and Vulnerabilities Commonly Found in the LAN-to-WAN Domain

The LAN-to-WAN Domain requires strict security controls, given the risks and threats of connecting to the Internet. This domain is where all data travel into and out of the IT infrastructure. The LAN-to-WAN Domain provides Internet access for the entire organization and acts as the entry and exit point for the WAN. This is also known as the Internet ingress/egress point. The LAN-to-WAN Domain is where the fourth layer of defense is required. **TABLE 1-5** lists the risks, threats, and vulnerabilities commonly found in the LAN-to-WAN Domain, along with appropriate risk-reduction strategies.

WAN Domain

The Wide Area Network (WAN) Domain connects remote locations. As network costs drop, organizations can afford faster Internet and WAN connections. Today, telecommunications service providers sell the following:

- **Nationwide optical backbones**—Optical backbone trunks for private optical backbone networks.
- **End-to-end IP transport**—IP services and connectivity using the service provider's IP networking infrastructure.

TABLE 1-5 Risks, threats, vulnerabilities, and mitigation plans for the LAN-to-WAN Domain.

RISK, THREAT, OR VULNERABILITY	MITIGATION
Unauthorized network probing and port scanning	Disable **ping**, probing, and port scanning on all exterior IP devices within the LAN-to-WAN Domain. Ping uses the Internet Control Message Protocol (ICMP) echo-request and echo-reply protocol. Disallow IP port numbers used for probing and scanning and monitor with IDS/IPS.
Unauthorized access through the LAN-to-WAN Domain	Apply strict security monitoring controls for intrusion detection and prevention. Monitor for inbound IP traffic anomalies and malicious-intent traffic. Block traffic right away if malicious.
Denial of service (DoS)/distributed denial of service (DDoS) attacks on external public-facing IP's and Internet link	Upstream Internet service providers (ISPs) must participate in DoS/DDoS attack prevention and discarding of IP packets when a stream of half-open TCP SYN packets start to flood the ISP link.
IP router, firewall, and network appliance operating system software vulnerability	Define a strict zero-day vulnerability window definition. Update devices with security fixes and software patches right away.
IP router, firewall, and network appliance configuration file errors or weaknesses	Conduct postconfiguration penetration tests of the layered security solution within the LAN-to-WAN Domain. Test inbound and outbound traffic and fix any gaps.
The ability for remote users to access the organization's infrastructure and download sensitive data	Apply and enforce the organization's data classification standard. Deny outbound traffic using source IP addresses in access control lists. If remote downloading is allowed, encrypt where necessary.
Download of unknown file type attachments from unknown sources	Apply file transfer monitoring, scanning, and alarming for unknown file types from unknown sources.
Unknown email attachments and embedded URL links received by local users	Apply email server and attachment antivirus and email quarantining for unknown file types. Stop domain-name website access based on content-filtering policies.
Lost productivity due to local users surfing the Web and not focusing on work tasks	Apply domain-name content filtering at the Internet entry/access point.

- **Multisite WAN cloud services**—IP services and connectivity offered for multisite services such as **Multiprotocol Label Switching (MPLS)** WAN services. MPLS uses labels or tags to make virtual connections between endpoints in a WAN.
- **Metropolitan Ethernet LAN connectivity**—Ethernet LAN connectivity offered within a city's area network.
- **Dedicated Internet access**—A broadband Internet communication link usually shared within an organization.

- **Managed services**—Router management and security appliance management $24 \times 7 \times 365$.
- **Service-level agreements (SLAs)**—Contractual commitments for monthly service offerings such as availability, packet loss, and response time to fix problems.

The WAN Domain represents the fifth layer of security for an overall IT infrastructure. WAN services can include dedicated Internet access and managed services for customers' routers and firewalls. Management agreements for availability and response times to outages are common. Networks, routers, and equipment require continuous monitoring and management to keep WAN service available.

WAN Domain Roles, Responsibilities, and Accountability

Here's an overview of what should go on in the WAN Domain:

- **Roles and tasks**—The WAN Domain includes both physical components and the logical design of routers and communication equipment. It is the second most complex area to secure within an IT infrastructure. Your goal is to allow users the most access possible while making sure what goes in and out is safe. The roles and tasks required within the WAN Domain include managing and configuring the following:
  - **WAN communication links**—These are the physical communication links provided as a digital or optical service terminated at your facility. Broadband connection speeds can range among the following:
    - DS0 (64 Kbps) to DS1 (1.544 Mbps) to DS3 (45 Mbps) for digital service
    - OC-3 (155 Mbps) to OC-12 (622 Mbps) to OC-48 (2,488 Mbps) for optical service
    - 10/100/1000 Mbps Metro Ethernet LAN connectivity, depending on physical distance
  - **IP network design**—This is the logical design of the IP network and addressing schema. This requires network engineering, design of alternate paths, and selection of IP routing protocol.
  - **IP stateful firewall**—This is a security appliance that is used to filter IP packets and block unwanted IP, TCP, and UDP packet types from entering or leaving the network. Firewalls can be installed on workstations or routers or as standalone devices protecting LAN segments.
  - **IP router configuration**—This is the actual router configuration information for the WAN backbone and edge routers used for IP connections to remote locations. The configuration must be based on the IP network design and addressing schema.
  - **Virtual private networks (VPNs)**—A VPN is a dedicated encrypted tunnel from one endpoint to another. The VPN tunnel can be created between a remote workstation using the public Internet and a VPN router or a secure browser and a **Secure Sockets Layer virtual private network (SSL-VPN)** website.
  - **Multiprotocol Label Switching (MPLS)**—MPLS is a WAN software feature that allows customers to maximize performance. MPLS labels IP packets for rapid transport through virtual tunnels between designated endpoints. This is a form of Layer 1/Layer 3 overlay network and bypasses the routing function's path determination process once a long-lived flow is configured or dynamically determined.

- **Simple Network Management Protocol (SNMP) network monitoring and management**—SNMP is used for network device monitoring, alarm, and performance.
- **Router and equipment maintenance**—A requirement to perform hardware and firmware updates, upload new operating system software, and configure routers and filters.
- **Responsibilities**—The network engineer or WAN group is responsible for the WAN Domain. This includes both the physical components and logical elements. Network engineers and security practitioners set up the defined security controls according to defined policies. Note that because of the complexities of IP network engineering, many groups now outsource management of their WAN and routers to service providers. This service includes SLAs that ensure that the system is available and that problems are solved quickly. In the event of a WAN connection outage, customers call a toll-free number for their service provider's **network operations center (NOC)**.
- **Accountability**—Your organization's IT network manager must maintain, update, and provide technical support for the WAN Domain. Typically, the director of IT security ensures that the company meets WAN Domain security policies, standards, procedures, and guidelines.

Some organizations use the public Internet as their WAN infrastructure. Although it is cheaper, the Internet does not guarantee delivery or security.

Risks, Threats, and Vulnerabilities Commonly Found in the WAN Domain (Internet)

Telecommunication service providers are in the business of providing WAN connectivity for end-to-end communications. Service providers must take on the responsibility for securing their network infrastructure first. Customers who sign up for WAN communication services must review the terms, conditions, and limitations of liability within their service contract. This is important because organizations must figure out where their duties start and end regarding router management and security management.

The most critical aspect of a WAN services contract is how the service provider supplies troubleshooting, network management, and security management services. The WAN Domain is where the fifth layer of defense is required. **TABLE 1-6** lists the risks, threats, and vulnerabilities found in the Internet segment of the WAN Domain and appropriate risk-lowering strategies.

Telecommunications service providers sell WAN connectivity services. Some providers now also provide security management services. The following section presents WAN connectivity risks, threats, and vulnerabilities and risk-reducing strategies.

Risks, Threats, and Vulnerabilities Commonly Found in the WAN Domain (Connectivity)

Telecommunications companies are responsible for building and transporting customer IP traffic. Sometimes this IP traffic is bundled with dedicated Internet access, providing shared broadband access organization-wide. If organizations outsource their WAN infrastructure, management and security must extend to the service provider. Organizations must define security policies and needs for their managed security provider to put in place. **TABLE 1-7** lists the risks, threats, and vulnerabilities related to connectivity found in the WAN Domain and appropriate risk-lowering strategies.

TABLE 1-6 Risks, threats, vulnerabilities, and mitigation plans for the WAN Domain (Internet).

RISK, THREAT, OR VULNERABILITY	MITIGATION
Open, public, easily accessible to anyone who wants to connect	Apply acceptable-use policies in accord with the document "RFC 1087: Ethics and the Internet." Enact new laws regarding unauthorized access to systems, malicious attacks on IT infrastructures, and financial loss due to malicious outages.
Most Internet traffic sent in cleartext	Prohibit using the Internet for private communications without encryption and VPN tunnels. If you have a data classification standard, follow the policies, procedures, and guidelines specifically.
Vulnerable to eavesdropping	Use encryption and VPN tunnels for end-to-end secure IP communications. If you have a data classification standard, follow the policies, procedures, and guidelines.
Vulnerable to malicious attacks	Deploy layered LAN-to-WAN security countermeasures, DMZ with IP stateful firewalls, IDS/IPS for security monitoring, and quarantining of unknown email file attachments.
Vulnerable to DoS, DDoS, TCP SYN flooding, and IP spoofing attacks	Apply filters on exterior IP stateful firewalls and IP router WAN interfaces to block TCP SYN "open connections" and ICMP (echo-request) ping packets. Alert your Internet service provider (ISP) to put the proper filters on its IP router WAN interfaces in accordance with CERT Advisory CA-1996-21. This can be found here: *www.cert.org /advisories/CA-1996-21.html.*
Vulnerable to corruption of information and data	Encrypt IP data transmissions with VPNs. Back up and store data in offsite data vaults (online or physical data backup) with tested recovery procedures.
Inherently insecure TCP/IP applications (HTTP, FTP, TFTP, etc.)	Refer to your data classification standard for proper handling of data and use of TCP/IP applications. Never use TCP/IP applications for confidential data without proper encryption. Create a network management VLAN and isolate TFTP and SNMP traffic used for network management.
Email of **Trojans**, **worms**, and malicious software by hackers, attackers, and perpetrators	Scan all email attachments for type, antivirus, and malicious software at the LAN-to-WAN Domain. Isolate and quarantine unknown file attachments until further security review is conducted. Provide security awareness training to remind employees of dangers, such as embedded URL links and email attachments from unknown parties, and to urge them to be careful when clicking on links and opening files.

Remote Access Domain

The Remote Access Domain connects remote users to the organization's IT infrastructure. Remote access is critical for staff members who work in the field or from home—for example, outside sales reps, technical support specialists, or health care professionals. Global access makes it easy to connect to the Internet, email, and other business applications

TABLE 1-7 Risks, threats, vulnerabilities, and mitigation plans for the WAN Domain (connectivity).

RISK, THREAT, OR VULNERABILITY	MITIGATION
Commingling of WAN IP traffic on the same service provider router and infrastructure	Encrypt confidential data transmissions through service provider WAN using VPN tunnels.
Maintaining high WAN service availability	Obtain WAN service availability SLAs. Deploy redundant Internet and WAN connections when 100 percent availability is required.
Maximizing WAN performance and throughput	Apply WAN optimization and data compression solutions when accessing remote systems, applications, and data. Enable access control lists (ACLs) on outbound router WAN interfaces, in keeping with policy.
Using SNMP network management applications and protocols maliciously (ICMP, Telnet, SNMP, DNS, etc.)	Create separate WAN network management VLANs. Use strict firewall ACLs allowing SNMP manager and router IP addresses through the LAN-to-WAN Domain.
SNMP alarms and security monitoring 24 × 7 × 365	Outsource security operations and monitoring. Expand services to include managed security.

anywhere you can find a **Wireless Fidelity (Wi-Fi)** hotspot. The Remote Access Domain is important to have but dangerous to use. It introduces many risks and threats from the Internet.

Today's mobile worker depends on the following:

- **Highly available cell phone service**—Mobile workers need cell phone service to get in touch with office and support teams.
- **Real-time access for critical communications**—Use of text messaging or **instant messaging (IM) chat** on cell phones provides quick answers to short questions and does not require users to completely interrupt what they are doing.
- **Access to email from a mobile device**—Integration of email with cell phones, smartphones, tablets, PDAs, or **BlackBerry** devices provides users the ability to quickly respond to important email messages.
- **Broadband Wi-Fi Internet access**—Some nationwide service providers now offer Wi-Fi broadband access cards. They allow wireless access in major metro areas.
- **Local Wi-Fi hotspot**—Wi-Fi hotspots are abundant, including in airports, libraries, coffee shops, and retailers. Most are free, but some require that users pay for access.
- **Broadband Internet access to home office**—Staffers who work from home require broadband Internet access. This service is usually bundled with VoIP telephone and digital TV services.
- **Secure remote access to a company's IT infrastructure**—Remote workers require secure VPN tunnels to encrypt all IP data transmissions through the public Internet. This is critical if private data are being accessed remotely.

The scope of this domain is limited to remote access via the Internet and IP communications. The logical configuration of the Remote Access Domain requires IP network engineering and VPN solutions. This section addresses individual remote access and large-scale remote access for many remote users. The Remote Access Domain represents the sixth layer of defense for a typical IT infrastructure.

Remote Access Domain Roles, Responsibilities, and Accountability

Here's an overview of what should go on in the Remote Access Domain:

- **Roles and tasks**—The Remote Access Domain connects mobile users to their IT systems through the public Internet. The mobile user must have a remote IP device able to connect to the Internet. Besides laptop computers, mobile users can use smartphones, tablets, and PDAs as handheld computers. The mobile software on these devices makes possible phone calls, voicemail, email, text messaging, and web browsing remotely.

The roles and tasks required within the Remote Access Domain include managing and designing the following:

- **Cell phones, smartphones, PDAs, and BlackBerry units**—Company-issued devices should be loaded with up-to-date firmware, operating system software, and patches according to defined policies. Policy should require use of passwords on this equipment.
- **Laptop VPN client software**—When organizations use VPN tunnels between the LAN-to-WAN Domain and remote-user laptop computers, you must select VPN software that meets your organization's specific needs and that works with your other software.
- **Secure browser software**—Webpages that use Hypertext Transfer Protocol Secure (HTTPS) need secure browsers. HTTPS encrypts the data transfer between secure browsers and secure webpages.

The Risk from Backdoor Analog Phone Lines and Modems

Some maintenance vendors use analog phone lines and modems to reach equipment. That means they do not use IP or SNMP protocols. Although this is convenient, it allows an insecure backdoor into the IT system. Attackers use tools that can get around an analog modem's password. Be alert for user workstations that are equipped with an analog modem connected to a backdoor analog phone line. Your company might not know that IT staff and software developers have set up these backdoors. This can be a risk because analog modems generally have few security controls.

The following are some of the best ways to reduce these risks and threats:

- Do not install single analog phone lines without going through a private branch exchange (PBX) or VoIP phone system.
- Work with local phone service companies to make sure no single analog phone lines are installed.
- Block unidentified calls (i.e., calls that appear on caller ID screens as "unknown") from entering your phone system.
- Watch call-detail record (CDR) reports from PBX and VoIP phone systems for rogue phone numbers and abnormal call patterns.

- **VPN routers, VPN firewalls, or VPN concentrators**—Remote access VPN tunnels end at the VPN router, VPN firewall or VPN concentrator, usually within the LAN-to-WAN Domain. All data are encrypted between the VPN client (remote laptop) and the VPN router, firewall, or concentrator—hence the name *tunnel*.
- **Secure Sockets Layer (SSL)/VPN web server**—SSL uses 128-bit encryption between a safe HTTPS webpage and a safe browser. This encrypted VPN tunnel gives end-to-end privacy for remote webpage data sharing.
- **Authentication server**—A server that performs a second-level authentication to verify users seeking remote access.
- **Responsibilities**—The network engineer or WAN group is usually in charge of the Remote Access Domain. This includes both the hardware components and logical elements. Network engineers and security practitioners are in charge of applying security controls according to policies. These include maintaining, updating, and troubleshooting the hardware and logical remote access connection for the Remote Access Domain. This requires management of the following:
  - IP routers
  - IP stateful firewalls
  - VPN tunnels
  - Security monitoring devices
  - Authentication servers
- **Accountability**—Your organization's WAN network manager is accountable for the Remote Access Domain. Typically, the director of IT security must ensure that the Remote Access Domain security plans, standards, methods, and guidelines are used.

Risks, Threats, and Vulnerabilities Commonly Found in the Remote Access Domain

Remote access is dangerous yet necessary for mobile workers. This is true for organizations that rely on a mobile workforce such as sales reps, consultants, and support staff. As organizations cut costs, many urge staff to work from home. The WAN in this case is the public Internet. Making those connections secure is a top job. You will use your organization's strict data classification standard to verify users and encrypt data.

Remote access security controls must use the following:

- **Identification**—The process of providing identifying information, such as a username, a logon ID, or an account number.
- **Authentication**—This is the process for proving that a remote user is who the user claims to be. The most common authentication method is supplying a password. Many organizations use second-level verifying services, such as a **token** (hardware or software), **biometric** fingerprint reader, or smart card. A token can be a hardware device that sends a random number or a software token that text-messages a number to the user. A biometric fingerprint reader grants access only when the user's fingerprint is matched with one stored in the system. A smart card is like a credit card that acts similar to a token. It has a microprocessor chip that verifies the user with a smart-card reader.
- **Authorization**—The process of granting rights to use an organization's IT assets, systems, applications, and data to a specific user.

TABLE 1-8 Risks, threats, vulnerabilities, and mitigation plans for the Remote Access Domain.

RISK, THREAT, OR VULNERABILITY	MITIGATION
Brute-force user ID and password attacks	Establish user ID and password policies requiring periodic changes (i.e., every 30 or 60 days). Passwords must be used, passwords must have more than eight characters, and users must incorporate numbers and letters.
Multiple logon retries and access control attacks	Set automatic blocking for attempted logon retries (e.g., block user access after three logon attempts have failed).
Unauthorized remote access to IT systems, applications, and data	Apply first-level (i.e., user ID and password) and second-level (i.e., tokens, biometrics, and smart cards) security for remote access to sensitive systems, applications, and data.
Private data or confidential data compromised remotely	Encrypt all private data within the database or hard drive. If data are stolen, the thief cannot use or sell it because it will be encrypted.
Data leakage in violation of existing data classification standards	Apply security countermeasures in the LAN-to-WAN Domain, including data leakage security-monitoring tools and tracking, as per your organization's data classification standard.
A mobile worker's laptop is stolen	Encrypt the data on the hard drive if the user has access to private or confidential data. Apply real-time lockout rules when told of a lost or stolen laptop by a user.
Mobile worker token or other authentication stolen	Apply real-time lockout procedures if a token is lost or a device is compromised.

- **Accountability**—The process of recording user actions. The recorded information is often used to link users to system events.

    TABLE 1-8 lists Remote Access Domain risks, threats, and vulnerabilities as well as risk-mitigation strategies.

System/Application Domain

The System/Application Domain holds all the mission-critical systems, applications, and data. Authorized users may have access to many components in this domain. Secure access may require second-level checks.

Examples of applications that may require second-level authentication include the following:

- **Human resources and payroll**—Only staff who work on payroll services need access to this private data and confidential information.
- **Accounting and financial**—Executive managers need access to accounting and financial data to make sound business decisions. Securing financial data requires unique security controls with access limited to those who need it. Publicly traded companies are subject to Sarbanes-Oxley (SOX) compliance law requiring security.
- **Customer relationship management (CRM)**—Customer service reps need real-time access to information that includes customer purchasing history and private data.

> **Technical TIP**
>
> Security controls keep private data and intellectual property safe. Encrypting data can stop bogus users. Hackers looking for data know where people hide it and how to find it. Encrypting the data within databases and storage devices gives an added layer of security.

- **Sales order entry**—Sales professionals need access to the sales order-entry and order-tracking system. Private customer data must be kept safe.
- **U.S. military intelligence and tactics**—U.S. military commanders who make decisions on the battlefield use highly sensitive information. Access to that information must meet U.S. Department of Defense (DoD) data classification standards.

The System/Application Domain represents the seventh layer of defense.

System/Application Domain Roles, Responsibilities, and Accountability

Here's an overview of what should go on in the System/Application Domain:

- **Roles and tasks**—The System/Application Domain consists of hardware, operating system software, applications, and data. This domain includes hardware and its logical design. An organization's mission-critical applications and intellectual property assets are here. It must be secured both physically and logically.

    We limited the scope of the System/Application Domain to reducing risks. These include the following:

    - **Physical access to computer rooms, data centers, and wiring closets**—Set up procedure to allow staff to enter secured area.
    - **Server architecture**—Apply a converged server design that employs server blades and racks to combine their use and reduce costs.
    - **Server operating systems and core environments**—Reduce the time that operating system software is open to attack by installing software updates and patches.
    - **Virtualization servers**—Keep physical and logical virtual environments separate and extend layered security solutions into the cloud. Virtualization allows you to load many operating systems and applications using one physical server.
    - **System administration of application servers**—Provide ongoing server and system administration for users.
    - **Data classification standard**—Review data classification standards, procedures, and guidelines on proper handling of data. Maintain safety of private data while in transport and in storage.
    - **Software development life cycle (SDLC)**—Apply secure software development life cycle tactics when designing and developing software.
    - **Testing and quality assurance**—Apply sound software testing, penetration testing, and quality assurance to fill security gaps and software weaknesses.
    - **Storage, backup, and recovery procedures**—Follow data storage, backup, and recovery plans as set by the data classification standard.

- **Data archiving and retention**—Align policies, standards, procedures, and guidelines to digital storage and retention needs.
- **Business continuity plan (BCP)**—Conduct a business impact analysis (BIA) and decide which computer uses are most important. Define RTOs for each system. Prepare a BCP focused on those things that are most important for the business to keep going.
- **Disaster recovery plan (DRP)**—Prepare a disaster recovery plan based on the BCP. Start DRP elements for the most important computer systems first. Organize a DRP team and a remote data center.
- **Responsibilities**—The responsibility for System/Application Domain lies with the director of systems and applications and the director of software development. This domain includes the following:
  - Server systems administration
  - Database design and management
  - Designing access rights to systems and applications
  - Software development
  - Software development project management
  - Software coding
  - Software testing
  - Quality assurance
  - Production support
- **Accountability**—The directors of systems and applications and software development are accountable for the organization's production systems and uses. Typically, the director of IT security is accountable for ensuring that the System/Application Domain security policies, standards, procedures, and guidelines are in compliance.

Risks, Threats, and Vulnerabilities Commonly Found in the System/Application Domain

The System/Application Domain is where the organization's data are like treasure. They can be private customer data, intellectual property, or national security information. They are what attackers seek deep within an IT system. Protecting this treasure is the goal of every organization. Loss of data is the greatest threat in the System/Application Domain.

With a data classification standard, types of data can be isolated in like groups. The more important the data, the deeper you should hide and store them. Consider encrypting data to be stored for a long time. **TABLE 1-9** lists common System/Application Domain risks, threats, and vulnerabilities as well as risk-mitigation strategies.

Weakest Link in the Security of an IT Infrastructure

The user is the weakest link in security. Even information systems security practitioners can make mistakes. Human error is a major risk and threat to any organization. No group can completely control any person's behavior. For these reasons, every organization must be prepared for malicious users, untrained users, and careless users.

TABLE 1-9 Risks, threats, vulnerabilities, and mitigation plans for the System/Application Domain.

RISK, THREAT, OR VULNERABILITY	MITIGATION
Unauthorized access to data centers, computer rooms, and wiring closets	Apply policies, standards, procedures, and guidelines for staff and visitors to secure facilities.
Downtime of servers to perform maintenance	Create a system that brings together servers, storage, and networking.
Server operating systems software vulnerability	Define vulnerability window for server operating system environments. Maintain hardened production server operating systems.
Insecure cloud computing virtual environments by default	Implement virtual firewalls and server segmentation on separate VLANs. A virtual firewall is a software-based firewall used in virtual environments.
Susceptibility of client/server and web applications	Conduct rigorous software and web application testing and penetration testing prior to launch.
Unauthorized access to systems	Follow data classification standards regarding stringent use of second-level authentication.
Data breach where private data of individuals are compromised	Separate private data elements into different databases. For archiving purposes, encrypt sensitive data at rest within databases and storage devices.
Loss or corruption of data	Implement daily data backups and offsite data storage for monthly data archiving. Define data recovery procedures based on defined recovery time objectives (RTOs).
Loss of backed-up data as backup media are reused	Convert all data into digital data for long-term storage. Retain backups from offsite data vaults based on defined RTOs.
Recovery of critical business functions potentially too time-consuming to be useful	Develop a business continuity plan for mission-critical applications providing tactical steps for maintaining availability of operations.
Downtime of IT systems for an extended period after a disaster	Develop a disaster recovery plan specific to the recovery of mission-critical applications and data to maintain operations.

The following strategies can help reduce risk:

- Check the background of each job candidate carefully.
- Give each staff member a regular evaluation.
- Rotate access to sensitive systems, applications, and data among different staff positions.
- Apply sound application and software testing and review for quality.
- Regularly review security plans throughout the seven domains of a typical IT system.
- Perform annual security control audits.

To build a respected and effective profession, information systems security professionals must operate ethically and comply with a code of conduct. This section explains why this tenet is the basis of the profession.

Request for Comments (RFC) 1087: Ethics and the Internet

IAB Statement of Policy

The Internet is a national facility, of which the utility is largely a consequence of its wide availability and accessibility. Irresponsible use of this critical resource poses an enormous threat to its continued availability to the technical community. The U.S. government sponsors of this system have a fiduciary responsibility to the public to allocate government resources wisely and effectively. Justification for the support of this system suffers when highly disruptive abuses occur. Access to and use of the Internet are privileges and should be treated as such by all users of this system.

The IAB strongly endorses the view of the Division Advisory Panel of the National Science Foundation Division of Network, Communications Research and Infrastructure, which, in paraphrase, characterized as unethical and unacceptable any activity which purposely:

(a) seeks to gain unauthorized access to the resources of the Internet,

(b) disrupts the intended use of the Internet,

(c) wastes resources (people, capacity, computer) through such actions,

(d) destroys the integrity of computer-based information, and/or

(e) compromises the privacy of users.

Ethics and the Internet

Imagine if there were no air traffic controllers and airplanes flew freely. Trying to take off and land would be extremely dangerous. There would probably be many more accidents. Such a situation would wreak havoc.

Incredibly, cyberspace has no authorities that function like air traffic controllers. To make matters worse, human behavior online often is less mature than in normal social settings. Cyberspace has become the new playground for today's bad guys. This is why the demand for systems security professionals is growing so rapidly.

The U.S. government and the Internet Architecture Board (IAB) has defined a policy regarding acceptable use of the Internet geared toward U.S. citizens. It is not a law or a mandate, however; because cyberspace is global and entirely without borders, this policy cannot be enforced. Its use is based on common sense and personal integrity. The sidebar presents the IAB's standard of ethics and the Internet.

Ethics are a matter of personal integrity. The systems security profession is about doing what is right and stopping what is wrong. Use of the Internet is a privilege shared by all. It is a communications medium with no borders, no cultural bias, and no prejudice. Users have the privilege to connect. This is something to be thankful for. Unfortunately, bad guys use cyberspace to commit crimes and cause trouble. This has created a global need for systems security professionals.

IT Security Policy Framework

Cyberspace cannot continue to flourish without some assurances of user security. Several laws now require organizations to keep personal data private. Businesses cannot operate effectively on an Internet where anyone can steal their data. IT security is crucial to any organization's ability to survive. This section introduces you to an IT security policy framework. The framework consists of policies, standards, procedures, and guidelines that reduce risks and threats.

Definitions

An IT security policy framework contains four main components:

- **Policy**—A policy is a short written statement that the people in charge of an organization have set as a course of action or direction. A policy comes from upper management and applies to the entire organization.
- **Standard**—A standard is a detailed written definition for hardware and software and how they are to be used. Standards ensure that consistent security controls are used throughout the IT system.
- **Procedures**—These are written instructions for how to use policies and standards. They may include a plan of action, installation, testing, and auditing of security controls.
- **Guidelines**—A guideline is a suggested course of action for using the policy, standards, or procedures. Guidelines can be specific or flexible regarding use.

FIGURE 1-10 is an example of a hierarchical IT security policy framework. Policies apply to an entire organization. Standards are specific to a given policy. Procedures and guidelines help define use. Within each policy and standard, identify the impact for the seven domains of a typical IT infrastructure. This will help define the roles, responsibilities, and accountability throughout.

Foundational IT Security Policies

The focus of your organization's IT security policy framework is to reduce your exposure to risks, threats, and vulnerabilities. It is important to relate policy definition and standards to practical design requirements. These requirements will properly apply the best security controls and countermeasures. Policy statements must set limits as well as refer to standards, procedures, and guidelines. Policies define how security controls and countermeasures must be used to comply with laws and regulations.

Examples of some basic IT security policies include the following:

- **Acceptable use policy (AUP)**—The AUP defines the actions that are and are not allowed with respect to the use of organization-owned IT assets. This policy is specific to the User Domain and mitigates risk between an organization and its employees.

FIGURE 1-10

Hierarchical IT security policy framework.

- **Security awareness policy**—This policy defines how to ensure that all personnel are aware of the importance of security and behavioral expectations under the organization's security policy. This policy is specific to the User Domain and is relevant when you need to change organizational security awareness behavior.
- **Asset classification policy**—This policy defines an organization's data classification standard. It tells what IT assets are critical to the organization's mission. It usually defines the organization's systems, uses, and data priorities and identifies assets within the seven domains of a typical IT infrastructure.
- **Asset protection policy**—This policy helps organizations define a priority for mission-critical IT systems and data. This policy is aligned with an organization's **business impact analysis (BIA)** and is used to address risks that could threaten the organization's ability to continue operations after a disaster.
- **Asset management policy**—This policy includes the security operations and management of all IT assets within the seven domains of a typical IT infrastructure.
- **Vulnerability assessment and management**—This policy defines an organization-wide vulnerability window for production operating system and application software. You develop organization-wide vulnerability assessment and management standards, procedures, and guidelines from this policy.
- **Threat assessment and monitoring**—This policy defines an organization-wide threat assessment and monitoring authority. You should also include specific details regarding the LAN-to-WAN Domain and AUP compliance in this policy.

Organizations need to tailor their IT security policy framework to their environment. After conducting a security assessment of their IT setup, many organizations align policy definitions to gaps and exposures. Policies typically require executive management and general legal counsel review and approval.

Data Classification Standards

The goal and objective of a data classification standard is to provide a consistent definition for how an organization should handle and secure different types of data. Security controls protect different data types. These security controls are within the seven domains of a typical IT infrastructure. Procedures and guidelines must define how to handle data within the seven domains of a typical IT infrastructure to ensure data security.

For businesses and organizations under recent compliance laws, data classification standards typically include the following major categories:

- **Private data**—Data about people that must be kept private. Organizations must use proper security controls to be in compliance.
- **Confidential**—Information or data owned by the organization. Intellectual property, customer lists, pricing information, and patents are examples of confidential data.
- **Internal use only**—Information or data shared internally by an organization. Although confidential information or data may not be included, communications are not intended to leave the organization.
- **Public domain data**—Information or data shared with the public such as website content, white papers, and the like.

U.S. Federal Government Data Classification Standard

The U.S. government, under Executive Order 13526, defines a data classification standard for all federal government agencies, including the Department of Defense (DoD). President Barack Obama signed this executive order on December 9, 2009. Although the U.S. government and its citizens enjoy the free flow of information, securing information is essential for national security, defense, or military action.

The following points define the U.S. federal government data classification standards:

- **Top secret**—Applies to information that the classifying authority finds would cause grave damage to national security if it were disclosed.
- **Secret**—Applies to information that the classifying authority finds would cause serious damage to national security if it were disclosed.
- **Confidential**—Applies to information that the classifying authority finds would cause damage to national security.

Whereas public-domain information is considered unclassified, it is not part of the data classification standard.

The U.S. government does have rules for handling unclassified (posing no threat to national security if exposed) and controlled unclassified information (for official use only, sensitive but unclassified, and law enforcement sensitive). Note that these rules are not included in Executive Order 13562 and were based on previous standards put into use by the administration of President George W. Bush.

Depending on your organization's data classification standard, you may need to encrypt data of the highest sensitivity even in storage devices and hard drives. For example, you may need to use encryption and VPN technology when using the public Internet for remote access. But internal LAN communications and access to systems, applications, or data may not require use of encryption.

Users may also be restricted from getting to private data of customers and may be able to access only certain pieces of data. Customer service reps provide customer service without getting to all of a customer's private data. For example, they may not be able to see the customer's entire Social Security number or account numbers; only the last four digits may be visible. This method of hiding some of the characters of the sensitive data element is called **masking**.

Technical TIP

Organizations should start defining their IT security policy framework by defining an asset classification policy. This policy, in turn, aligns itself directly to a data classification standard. This standard defines the way an organization is to secure and protect its data. Working from your data classification standard, you need to assess whether any private or confidential data travels within any of the seven domains of a typical IT infrastructure. Depending on how you classify and use the data, you will need to employ appropriate security controls throughout the IT infrastructure.

CHAPTER SUMMARY

This chapter introduced information systems security and the systems security profession. You saw a common definition for a typical IT infrastructure. You learned about risks, threats, and vulnerabilities within the seven domains. Each of these domains requires the use of strategies to reduce risks, threats, and vulnerabilities. You saw how IT security policy frameworks can help organizations reduce risk by defining authoritative policies. You also learned that data classification standards provide organizations with a road map for ways to handle different types of data. But who is going to implement the security controls?

Qualified IT security professionals are required to design and implement the appropriate security controls and countermeasures. As an IT security professional, you must have the highest human integrity and ethics. There are several professional security certifications available to security professionals. CompTIA's Security+ professional certification is foundational to entry level IT security professionals. (ISC)^2, the **International Information Systems Security Certification Consortium**, offers the **Certified Information Systems Security Professional CISSP®** certification for more experienced professionals. Obtaining the CISSP® professional certification requires the following: passing a certification exam, having at least five years of experience working in the information system security field, adhering to a code of ethics, and submitting continuing professional education (CPE) credits to maintain your certification.

KEY CONCEPTS AND TERMS

Acceptable use policy (AUP)

Application gateway firewalls

Availability

Biometric

BlackBerry

Business continuity plan (BCP)

Business impact analysis (BIA)

Carrier Sense Multiple Access/Collision Detection (CSMA/CD)

Certified Information Systems Security Professional (CISSP)

Children's Internet Protection Act (CIPA)

Ciphertext

Cleartext

Confidentiality

Content filtering

Cryptography

Cybersecurity

Cyberspace

Data breach

Data classification standard

Defense in depth

Demilitarized zone (DMZ)

Disaster recovery plan (DRP)

Downtime

E-commerce

Encryption

End-User License Agreement (EULA)

Ethernet

Family Educational Rights and Privacy Act (FERPA)

Federal Information Security Management Act 2002 (FISMA)

Federal Information Security Modernization Act 2014 (FISMA)

FICO

File Transfer Protocol (FTP)

Generation Y

Gramm-Leach-Bliley Act (GLBA)

Hardening

Health Insurance Portability and Accountability Act (HIPAA)

Hypertext Transfer Protocol (HTTP)

Hypertext Transfer Protocol Secure (HTTPS)

Identity theft

IEEE 802.3 CSMA/CD

Information security

Information systems

Information systems security

KEY CONCEPTS AND TERMS, *continued*

Instant messaging (IM) chat

Institute of Electrical and
Electronics Engineers (IEEE)

Integrity

International Information
Systems Security Certification
Consortium (ISC)^2

Internet

Internet of Things (IoT)

Intrusion detection system/
intrusion prevention system
(IDS/IPS)

IP default gateway router

IP stateful firewall

IT security policy framework

Layer 2 switch

Layer 3 switch

Local area network (LAN)

Malicious code

Malware

Masking

Mean time between failures
(MTBF)

Mean time to failure (MTTF)

Mean time to repair (MTTR)

Multiprotocol Label Switching
(MPLS)

Network interface card (NIC)

Network keys

Network operations center (NOC)

Personal digital assistant (PDA)

Ping

Protocol

Proxy firewalls

Proxy server

Recovery time objective (RTO)

"RFC 1087: Ethics and the Internet"

Risk

Sarbanes-Oxley Act (SOX)

Secure Sockets Layer virtual
private network (SSL-VPN)

Security control

Service level agreement (SLA)

Simple Network Management
Protocol (SNMP)

Smartphone

Software vulnerability

Subnet mask address

Telnet

Thick client

Thin client

Threat

Token

Transmission Control Protocol/
Internet Protocol (TCP/IP)

Trivial File Transfer Protocol
(TFTP)

Trojan

Two-step authentication

Unified communications

Uptime

Virtual LAN (VLAN)

Virtual private network (VPN)

Virus

Vulnerability

Vulnerability assessment

Vulnerability window

Wireless access point (WAP)

Wireless Fidelity (Wi-Fi)

Wireless LAN (WLAN)

Workstation

World Wide Web (WWW)

Worm

CHAPTER 1 ASSESSMENT

1. Information security is specific to securing information, whereas information systems security is focused on the security of the systems that house the information.

A. True

B. False

2. Software manufacturers limit their liability when selling software using which of the following?

A. End-User License Agreements

B. Confidentiality agreements

C. Software development agreements

D. By developing error-free software and code so there is no liability

E. None of the above

3. The _____ tenet of information systems security is concerned with the recovery time objective.

A. Confidentiality

B. Integrity

C. Availability

D. All of the above

E. None of the above

4. If you are a publicly traded company or U.S. federal government agency, you must go public and announce that you have had a data breach and must inform the impacted individuals of that data breach.

A. True

B. False

5. Organizations that require customer service representatives to access private customer data can best protect customer privacy and make it easy to access other customer data by using which of the following security controls?

   A. Preventing customer service representatives from accessing private customer data
   B. Blocking out customer private data details and allowing access only to the last four digits of Social Security numbers or account numbers
   C. Encrypting all customer data
   D. Implementing second-tier authentication when accessing customer databases
   E. All of the above

6. The _____ is the weakest link in an IT infrastructure.

   A. System/Application Domain
   B. LAN-to-WAN Domain
   C. WAN Domain
   D. Remote Access Domain
   E. User Domain

7. Which of the following security controls can help mitigate malicious email attachments?

   A. Email filtering and quarantining
   B. Email attachment antivirus scanning
   C. Verifying with users that email source is reputable
   D. Holding all inbound emails with unknown attachments
   E. All of the above

8. You can help ensure confidentiality by implementing _____.

   A. An acceptable use policy
   B. A data classification standard
   C. An IT security policy framework
   D. A virtual private network for remote access
   E. Secure access controls

9. Encrypting email communications is needed if you are sending confidential information within an email message through the public Internet.

   A. True
   B. False

10. Using security policies, standards, procedures, and guidelines helps organizations decrease risks and threats.

    A. True
    B. False

11. A data classification standard is usually part of which policy definition?

    A. Asset protection policy
    B. Acceptable use policy
    C. Vulnerability assessment and management policy
    D. Security awareness policy
    E. Threat assessment and monitoring policy

12. A data breach is typically performed after which of the following?

    A. Unauthorized access to systems and application is obtained
    B. Vulnerability assessment scan
    C. Configuration change request
    D. Implementation of a new data center
    E. Implementation of a web application update

13. Maximizing availability primarily involves minimizing _____.

    A. The amount of downtime recovering from a disaster
    B. The mean time to repair a system or application
    C. Downtime by implementing a business continuity plan
    D. The recovery time objective
    E. All of the above

14. Which of the following is not a U.S. compliance law or act?

    A. CIPA
    B. FERPA
    C. FISMA
    D. PCI DSS
    E. HIPAA

15. Internet IP packets are to cleartext what encrypted IP packets are to _____.

    A. Confidentiality
    B. Ciphertext
    C. Virtual private networks
    D. Cryptography algorithms
    E. None of the above

The Internet of Things Is Changing How We Live

THE INTERNET OF THINGS (IOT) is a new topic in today's connectivity and communications vision. This vision has many privacy, security, technical, social, and legal challenges. The Internet first brought global connectivity. This connectivity transformed the way people and businesses communicate. Today, users are "always on" and always connected (i.e., *hyperconnected*) to the Internet. **Social media** is driving real-time connectivity and communications. Facebook®, Twitter®, LinkedIn®, Pinterest®, Google+®, Instagram®, and other services and applications have changed the way people communicate. The Internet today provides a medium for all types of personal and business communications, whether they be:

- **VoIP**—Real-time voice communications between people.
- **IM chat**—Instant messenger for real-time chat messaging.
- **Audio conferencing**—Real-time audio conference calling among multiple people.
- **Video conferencing**—Real-time video conference calling among multiple people.
- **Collaboration**—Real-time document sharing and editing with audio and video conference calling among multiple remote people.
- **Digital media**—Audio recordings, pictures, videos for social media uploading and sharing.

The Internet changed the way people and businesses communicate. Now, with the emergence of the IoT, comes a tsunami of devices that users want to connect. This is driven by the expectation for near real-time access to things deemed important, including consumer products, household items, cars, trucks, traffic lights, building and facility sensors, industrial monitoring and control systems, and critical infrastructure device connectivity.

There are both advantages and disadvantages to the promise of the IoT. The IoT is transforming the way we live, work, and play. Remember when you used to use the telephone to make a restaurant reservation? Now you can do it online with email confirmation. Remember having to meet with a travel agent to make travel plans and arrangements for a family vacation? Now you can research and book your own family vacation online with access to real reviews and critiques from other vacationing families. Remember having to travel for a company strategy session or meeting? Now you can collaborate remotely with real-time audio, video, and collaboration applications. These changes allow businesses to save money and time by not having to pay for travel to group meetings.

The IoT has five critical challenges to overcome:

- **Security**—The Internet is already the Wild West, with plenty of bad guys and little law enforcement, yet there is an increasing demand to connect more things to the Internet.
- **Privacy**—Whose data are they? Who owns the intellectual property of personal information, data, and media? What is a privacy policy statement, and why is that important to you?
- **Interoperability**—How do we define standards and protocols such that all IoT-connected devices can communicate and be accessible?
- **Legal and regulatory compliance**—The IoT vision presents legal and regulatory compliance issues that typically have not always kept pace with the speed of IoT implementations.
- **Emerging social and economic issues**—The countries of the world and their citizens must quickly learn to understand and overcome any political, environmental, and economic issues presented by the IoT vision.

Chapter 2 Topics

This chapter covers the following topics and concepts:

- How the Internet of Things (IoT) has evolved from the late 1990s to present
- How the Internet transformed personal and business communications in a TCP/IP world
- What the effects of IoT will be on people, businesses, and the way we live
- How businesses evolved from bricks-and-mortar to e-commerce to IoT
- Why today's businesses need an Internet and IoT marketing strategy
- How IP mobility is helping to drive an IoT world
- What are the key issues created by the IoT

Chapter 2 Goals

When you complete this chapter, you will be able to:

- Describe the evolution of the Internet of Things (IoT) from the late 1990s to present
- Recognize the impact that the Internet and IoT have on human and business life
- Understand how bricks-and-mortar businesses transform into e-business models with e-commerce and an IoT strategy
- Explain how IP mobility is driving IoT to include both personal and business environments
- List the new challenges created by the IoT

Evolution of the Internet of Things

The evolution and rapid growth of the Internet was possible with the deployment of nation-wide optical fiber backbone networks. Faster speeds and greater bandwidth deliver more opportunities for humans to interact with connected things. With high-speed networks now extending to the mobile user, the opportunities are limitless. Today's consumer and business user benefits from broadband connectivity, thanks to nationwide cellular and wireless Internet service providers (ISPs). Fueled by the optical fiber backbone infrastructure growth of the late 1990s, ISPs extended their reach by connecting to cellular networks throughout the United States. This led to a surge in connecting mobile endpoints such as smartphones and tablets. People, businesses, and now their devices are connecting to the Internet. Parents can keep an eye on their children through a secure webcam connection monitoring their living room or day care center. Businesses are using the Internet to conduct secure transactions. Vending machines are now equipped with a cellular phone network antenna for secure credit card transaction processing. Smartphones and tablets that are cellular or Wi-Fi connected can be equipped with secure credit card transaction software. Credit card swiping attachments are also available for mobile payments. Rural healthcare services can be provided using telemedicine, secure video communications, and collaboration. Any device that can connect to the Internet can be accessed by the owner of that device.

The term **Internet of Things (IoT)** was first used in 1999. Kevin Ashton, a British technology visionary, first used it to describe objects connected to the Internet—any type of objects. Mr. Ashton's IoT describes objects in the physical world connecting to the Internet and allowing for any-to-any connectivity as long as the use is authorized by its owner. At the same time, **radio frequency identification (RFID)** was being implemented within supply chain management processes to track the movement of goods and their delivery. Today, the term *IoT* is used to describe how a wide variety of objects, devices, sensors, and everyday items can connect and be accessed. Connecting IP devices and other objects to the Internet is not a new idea, but the vision of what's possible with IoT is gaining momentum. The speed of IoT implementations is not slowing down; in fact, it is rapidly increasing. This creates the issues and challenges described previously.

Technology and market trends laid the foundation for IoT and are driving where IoT is headed. The danger in this system lies in the fact that these drivers push development and con-nectivity ahead of the security, privacy, and regulatory compliance that might govern it. How can we protect all of these IP-connected devices? Is it a good idea to connect all your objects and devices to the Internet? The following technology and market trends are drivers for IoT:

- **IP-based networking is globally adopted**—The Internet provides global connectivity for any user, business, or device.
- **Connectivity is everywhere**—Broadband Internet connectivity is provided free in many public areas and as a benefit for customers (e.g., bars, restaurants, etc.) in cities globally.
- **Smaller and faster computing**—Smaller semiconductors and faster chips results in faster computing and smaller device sizes.
- **Cloud computing is growing**—Cloud services allow for faster and easier access to data and content.

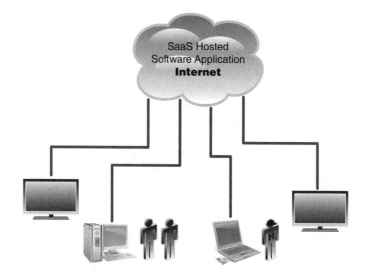

FIGURE 2-1

Software as a Service
(SaaS) application
delivery model.

- **Data analytics feeds the growth**—Capturing and studying the analytics of what, how, when, and why devices connect and communicate on the Internet feed analytics for enhancing service and performance.

   The IoT provides an avenue for things to connect. This connectivity encompasses both personal and business life. IoT applications are being developed and hosted in secure cloud infrastructures. This can support a one-to-many delivery model via the Internet. **Application service providers (ASPs)** are software companies that build applications hosted in the cloud and on the Internet. Users don't have to buy software and install it on their workstations or laptop computers; rather, they run the applications hosted in a cloud using a secure browser. This is sometimes referred to as **Software as a Service (SaaS)** computing. FIGURE 2-1 depicts the SaaS hosted application delivery model.

   With the growth in cloud hosting companies such as Amazon Web Services (AWS) came the growth in cloud application development. IoT applications for both personal and business scenarios were born. With ASPs building SaaS applications, new online e-businesses were born. The days of needing a bricks-and-mortar storefront are gone. Today you must have a storefront on the World Wide Web. Without an online presence, businesses have no access to global users and suppliers. Internet marketing, having a World Wide Web presence, and maximizing **search engine optimization (SEO)** are all important business requirements in today's IP-connected world.

Converting to a TCP/IP World

How did email become the foremost personal and business communication tool? How did iTunes become the number-one online music distribution site on the Internet? How did cell phones and the Internet impact the way we communicate? How did these changes affect

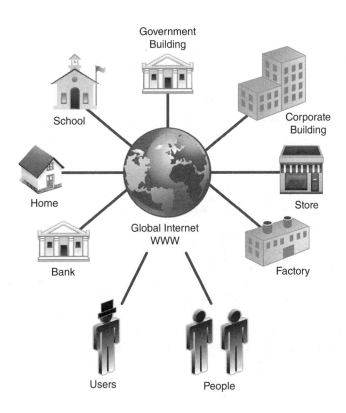

FIGURE 2-2

How the Internet and TCP/IP transform our lives.

businesses? The quick answer is that the transition to a Transmission Control Protocol/ Internet Protocol (TCP/IP) world changed our way of life. People, families, businesses, educators, and government all communicate differently than they did before, and nearly everyone has easy access to the Internet. **FIGURE 2-2** shows how the Internet and TCP/IP transform everyday life.

IoT's Impact on Human and Business Life

People choose to use technology and be connected to the Internet. This choice has transformed our day-to-day lives personally, socially, and professionally. The Internet impacts our personal, social, and business lives. When we awake in the morning, we use an Internet device to check the weather, the news, and social media sites. When we get to the office, we check our business emails and respond accordingly. Prior to the widespread use of the Internet—in the "dark ages," about 30 years ago—people seemed content to talk on landline telephones and watch TVs that used analog equipment. There was no World Wide Web to provide instant access to information. News was available in newspapers, on television, or on the radio. To talk to people in real time, you had to get them to a landline telephone. The advent of pagers and voice-messaging systems helped with real-time access and with storing and forwarding information. Eventually, cell phones replaced pagers, allowing people to reach practically anyone, no matter where they were.

In the mid- to late 1990s, as use of the Internet and World Wide Web became common-place, access across the information superhighway began to change everyone's lives. People-to-people communication switched to the Internet, with commerce close behind.

How People Like to Communicate

Social media drive how we as individuals communicate with family members, friends, and business associates. The prevalence of social media sharing (e.g., LinkedIn for professional contacts and Facebook for personal contacts) blurs the line between business and personal. Today's hyperconnected individual communicates in two basic ways:

- **Real-time communications**—When you need to talk to someone right now, real-time communication is the preferred mode, whether you are reacting to a life-threatening situation, conducting financial transactions such as buying stock or securities, or responding to a security breach.
- **Store-and-forward communications**—When you do not need an immediate response from someone you choose to contact, store-and-forward communications may be used. Store-and-forward communication occurs in near real time. Voicemail and email are examples of store-and-forward communications. Both forms of communication store the message for later retrieval. Voicemail can even be converted into audio files and sent to your email inbox. This is an example of **unified messaging (UM)** in which all of your messages (both voice and email) can be accessed via email.

IoT Applications That Impact Our Lives

Once the foundation for people-to-people communications was laid, opportunities for IoT applications rode on top of that. The following sections list some common IoT applications that can impact our daily lives.

The IoT's Impact on Humans

- **Health monitoring and updating**—Sensors can monitor human vital statistics and securely send data analytics to a bedside application or mobile application. New human IoT applications will provide near real-time monitoring of human performance (e.g., monitoring performance health indicators for athletes in training, tracking blood sugar levels for diabetics with a mobile application, or monitoring a patient's high cholesterol that submits a recommended menu for what to eat that day).
- **Home security and smart home control systems**—Homeowners can have near real-time access to home security systems, access to home surveillance video camera feeds, and full control over home heating and air-conditioning settings to maximize energy efficiency. Parents can even keep an eye on their children while they are away from home. Monitoring household use of water, electric, gas, and energy can help with water and energy savings and help keep costs down.
- **Online family member calendars**—Families can use tools to help plan shared rides and other activities that require parent/child coordination. This is especially vital if parents are acting as chauffeurs for their children during the school year. Family dinners, vacations, and children's transportation needs can be scheduled and coordinated more efficiently.

- **Near real-time tracking and monitoring of family members via global positioning systems (GPS)**—Parents concerned about where their children are can enable GPS tracking and monitoring through their smartphone and cellular phone service provider. GPS tracking applications and mobile applications provide parents with near real-time location finding of their children using their smartphone as the tracking device.
- **Online banking, bill paying, and financial transactions**—Homeowners can now fully automate bill payments using online banking systems and applications via autopay deductions directly from their checking accounts. No more paper bills, no more writing checks, and no more mailing a payment through the U.S. postal delivery system. Today most vendors and businesses accept secure, online e-payments, whether via an electronic checking account, credit card, or electronic wire transfer.
- **Online e-commerce purchases for household goods, food, services**—Homeowners now have the ability to purchase goods and services online and pick them up at a retail store or have them drop-shipped to their front door. Online grocery stores now deliver groceries, providing maximum efficiency for on-the-go parents who have no time to shop. Holiday shopping is done primarily online, allowing shoppers to avoid long checkout lines and stress at the shopping mall. Today, with government, businesses, and individuals moving to a completely online and digital world, individuals can interact and transact business from their homes or places of business, as long as they are connected to the Internet. Even ordering a pizza for home delivery has advanced to restaurants now providing delivery services for entire family meals delivered hot and ready to eat.
- **Automobiles with smart computers and "always-on" Wi-Fi Internet access**—Car shopping must-haves have evolved beyond miles per gallon and now include many advanced features and functions, such as:
  - "Always-on" Wi-Fi Internet access
  - Hands-free Bluetooth connectivity
  - Lojack® car locator
  - Remote control ignition starter
  - Automobile diagnostics that can be securely uploaded to the manufacturer prior to a car service appointment for preassessment analysis

The IoT's Impact on Businesses

Now that we know more about the impact that the IoT has on our day-to-day personal lives, what about the IoT's impact on businesses? The IoT is changing how businesses must sell and market their products and services. More important, businesses are looking for new opportunities the IoT brings. ASPs are the new wave of Internet startup companies providing IoT-based business products, services, and solutions. Cloud-based applications with mobile applications for end users to interact with from their smartphones or tablet devices are where IoT applications are headed. Here are some interesting IoT applications that businesses are beginning to adopt:

- **Retail stores**—Stores, banks, restaurants, and manufacturers must have a World Wide Web presence direct to their customers. Coupled with an online catalog system and ability to accept secure electronic payments with self-pickup or delivery to your front door,

The Internet Society

The Internet Society (*www.internetsociety.org/who-we-are/mission*) has captured the human essence of the Internet in its vison and mission statements:

Vision Statement: The Internet is for everyone.

Mission Statement: To promote the open development, evolution, and use of the Internet for the benefit of all people throughout the world.

To help achieve our mission, the Internet Society:

- Facilitates open development of standards, protocols, administration, and the technical infrastructure of the Internet.
- Supports education in developing countries specifically, and wherever the need exists.
- Promotes professional development and builds community to foster participation and leadership in areas important to the evolution of the Internet.
- Provides reliable information about the Internet.
- Provides forums for discussion of issues that affect Internet evolution, development and use in technical, commercial, societal, and other contexts.
- Fosters an environment for international cooperation, community, and a culture that enables self-governance to work.
- Serves as a focal point for cooperative efforts to promote the Internet as a positive tool to benefit all people throughout the world.
- Provides management and coordination for on-strategy initiatives and outreach efforts in humanitarian, educational, societal, and other contexts.

customers can make purchases anytime from their Internet-connected smartphones, tablets, or computers. The cost to deliver goods and services is significantly reduced when consumers shop online. This has created a paradigm shift from traditional bricks-and-mortar retail stores to implementing an online e-commerce portal. Customers can see and purchase products and services anytime, anywhere. Portals that have self-service are now supported with live IM chat with a customer service representative while shoppers are on the website. Businesses can benefit from streamlined sales order entry linked directly to inventory management. The supply chain can be optimized throughout the manufacturing and distribution process flow, given near real-time sales order access.

- **Virtual workplace**—Businesses and companies that are in the people or professional services business line do not need to come to a physical office unless it is for important meetings or presentations. Today, the IoT supports all communication types, including full two-way video conferencing and collaboration with colleagues that are located remotely or teleworking from home. Today's IoT provides working or single parents with an opportunity to be productive while at home, especially if they have child care or other obligations. Workers can save time on commuting, maximize productivity, save on transportation and food costs, and collaborate effectively with colleagues.
- **Remote sensors for utility/environmental/infrastructure monitoring**— Businesses that require monitoring of things such as electric meters, water usage, pH

balance of water, carbon monoxide meters, or gas leak sensors can all benefit from the IoT. Imagine having near real-time access to sensor and meter readings, especially if alerts or alarm indicators are exceeded for safety reasons. Any business involved in utilities, critical infrastructure, or environmental services can benefit from Internet-connected sensors and meter-reading devices. This access can replace the need for a human to physically visit the location and obtain a meter reading.

- **City and public service traffic-monitoring applications**—Smart cities can monitor and report on real-time traffic conditions and redirect traffic flow during rush-hour conditions with near real-time updates to mobile applications accessible to smart cars. City parking garages can pinpoint available parking spots.

- **The IoT is transforming the B2C service delivery model**—Companies are transforming the way they deliver customer service via the Internet. This **business-to-consumer (B2C)** transformation is led by new web applications, mobile applications, that are providing online access to their products and services. No matter what you need or want, businesses are transforming how they package, deliver, and sell it to you, the consumer. Prior to the digital revolution, remember going to the record or CD store? There is no more record or CD store! Digital music distribution is now done online through various music distribution sites. Training companies have transformed instructor-led training courses into online e-learning delivery with videos, audio recordings, and student interaction. Training for consumer products is typically provided via a YouTube video, with step-by-step instructions showing consumers how to assemble a product. This type of customer experience is what the IoT is driving. It's a better, faster, more effective way to train your customers on using your product or service. Using YouTube videos also brings the cost of delivery to nearly zero. This increases the customer experience by providing fast and easy installation instructions for the product. IoT applications use the Internet to create an entire customer experience and offering. This includes a complete Internet and social media marketing campaign, with frequent buyer coupons and incentives sent via email. Sales and other special services send near real-time Short Message Service (SMS) text messages for those who register online.

- **New "Anything as a Service" IoT applications**—As new IoT applications and mobile applications are developed, businesses can latch onto the **Anything as a Service (AaaS)** delivery model, which allows businesses to transform themselves into an IoT service offering. Anything as a Service means that whatever you are currently doing can be transformed into a hosted, secure cloud solution where you access your content and information from a website. Calendars, healthcare reminders, dry cleaning, grocery shopping, babysitting, tax preparation services, finding products or services, or finding anything, for that matter, are possible with the Internet. Businesses that can convert or invent new products or new services will win the IoT as a service offering in tomorrow's IoT commerce environment.

Evolution from Bricks and Mortar to E-Commerce

The Internet changed more than how people communicate. It also revolutionized business. Bricks-and-mortar businesses now have global reach. E-commerce changed how businesses sell, and the Internet changed how they market.

What is e-commerce? It is the sale of goods and services on the Internet. Online customers buy goods and services from a vendor's website. They enter private data and checking account or credit card information to make payment.

E-commerce supports two business models: **business-to-consumer (B2C)** and **business-to-business (B2B)**:

- **Business-to-consumer (B2C)**—Businesses create an online storefront for customers to purchase goods and services directly from their website, such as *www.amazon.com.*
- **Business-to-business (B2B)**—Businesses build online systems with links for conducting sales with other businesses, usually for integrated supply-chain purchases and deliveries.

E-commerce systems and applications demand strict **confidentiality, integrity, and availability (CIA)** security controls. Organizations must use solid security controls to protect their information from all attackers on the Internet. This is especially true if private data and credit card information cross the Internet. To comply with the **Payment Card Industry Data Security Standard (PCI DSS)**, businesses must conduct security assessments and use the correct controls to protect cardholder data. The Internet created a global online marketplace nearly overnight. No one foresaw such a large change—or the resulting impact. Once the Internet became ubiquitous, advertising, sales, and marketing were no longer confined to television, radio, newspapers and magazines, and direct mail. Marketing is about finding new customers, keeping them, and providing better goods and services. The Internet made these activities possible with online convenience. The Internet has realigned business challenges. These new challenges include the following:

- Growing the business through the Internet
- Changing an existing conventional business into an e-business
- Building secure and highly available websites and e-commerce portals
- Building a web-enabled customer-service strategy
- Finding new customers with Internet marketing

Companies such as Amazon, Dell, Apple, Western Union, eBay, Priceline.com, Domino's Pizza, and UPS have all created e-business models. Each uses websites as the main way to reach global customers. Their customers make purchases with enhanced customer-service delivery built into the websites. Self-service is the name of the game. Many online activities, such as account management, can be self-serve. Real-time access to customer service agents via VoIP and IM chat can enhance the experience for high-value customers.

What is an e-business strategy? It changes business functions and operations into web-enabled applications. E-business strategies include marketing and selling goods and services on the Internet. An e-business strategy typically includes these elements:

- **E-commerce solution**—This might be an online catalog and system for purchasing goods and services in a secure transaction.
- **Internet marketing strategy**—Internet marketing strategies involve search engine optimization (SEO), which uses embedded meta tags and keywords to help search engines sort results; customer lead generation, in which marketers request customer information from information websites and white-paper downloads; email blasts, in which

advertisements and discount coupons are emailed directly to prospects; and push marketing, which involves direct sales and marketing based on user interest.

- **E-customer service-delivery strategy**—This is a self-serve and online customer service strategy.
- **Payment and credit card transaction processing**—Secure online payment processing and credit card transaction processing must be encrypted with strict back-end system security controls to prevent unauthorized access to private customer data.

Why Businesses Must Have an Internet and IoT Marketing Strategy

Building an e-business strategy involves more than simply building a website. An e-business owner must understand how to find new business partners and new customers globally through the Internet. Without an e-business strategy or migration plan to get there, a business will lose to Internet-savvy competitors. An Internet marketing strategy is a key part of a business's success. It is all about getting more eyeballs to your websites and keeping them there. Internet marketing strategies use search engine strategies, joint marketing agreements, and content that is fresh and in demand. Bricks-and-mortar business models are out of date as the sole model in today's global market. Businesses must have an online e-business presence that provides customers with continuous access to information, products, and services. **FIGURE 2-3** shows the process of transforming to an e-business model on the World Wide Web.

As businesses include the Internet in their business models, they increase their exposure to online risks, threats, and vulnerabilities. Remember, connecting to the Internet means exposing yourself to hackers and cyberthieves. Secure web applications, secure front-end and back-end systems, and encryption of private customer data are critical security controls that each organization must implement to reduce risk.

This is not to say that bricks-and-mortar stores are not needed or are wholly obsolete. Almost ironically, the massive online store Amazon quietly opened its first real-world retail

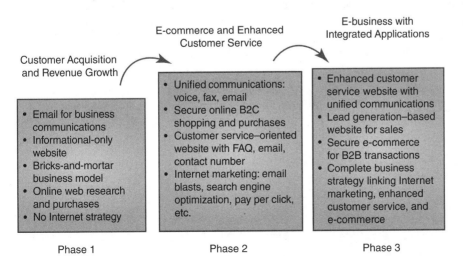

FIGURE 2-3

Transforming to an e-business model on the Web.

Phase 1 — Phase 2 — Phase 3

presence in late 2015. Purported plans to open several hundred more bricks-and-mortar stores in upcoming years speak to how bricks-and-mortar stores will continue to coexist with an online e-commerce presence and the overall customer experience.

IP Mobility

Communication devices have changed as much as the techniques people use to communicate. Previous changes to communicating involved adopting newer computers and connecting to networks. Voice communication generally occurred using telephones. For many years, telephones did little more than support voice communication. Over the past several years, personal communication devices and mobile phones have become very powerful. Use of cell phones exploded in the 1990s as people began to use them to extend their mobility. Today's mobile phones, smartphones, and PDAs have grown to match the power and flexibility of many small computers. A PDA is a lightweight, handheld, usually stylus-driven computer used as a personal organizer, with calendar, address book, and the like. Software publishers have responded with many programs targeted for the portable device market. Tablets, smartphones, and netbooks have emerged to fill a need for lightweight portable devices. A growing number of people carry these devices instead of larger laptops for everyday use.

Mobile Users and Bring Your Own Device

One of the big trends affecting organizations of all sizes is the growing use of personal communication devices. As users came to rely on their personal devices, employees came to expect to keep connectivity while at work. Organizations able to permit the devices still had to employ some control over the use of these devices through policy. This policy popularly became known as **Bring Your Own Device (BYOD)**. Organizations with such a policy can allow their employees and contractors to use their own personally chosen and personally procured devices to connect to the network at their office. This practice often replaces the need for the organization to procure limited model options and issue them to employees for individual use. Some advisers will support the "business sense" of such a move as it relates to lower purchase price, lower operational costs, and supportability of users and applications, but others recognize that BYOD opens the door to considerable security issues.

Users want small devices that are multifunctional and connected. In the past decade, laptops got smaller, lighter, and more powerful. They became powerful enough to match the performance of many desktop computers. Users began to rely on their laptops and enjoy the mobility of taking work away from their desks. They also enjoyed being able to leave their offices and still be connected to email and a growing number of office

---

Mobile Phone, Smartphone, or PDA?

As mobile devices have matured, so have the terms to describe them. Today a mobile device that allows the user to place and receive telephone calls and text messages is a *mobile phone*. Other devices that lack telephone abilities but can run programs using a mobile operating system are called *PDAs*. Devices that combine the capabilities of mobile phones and PDAs are commonly called *smartphones*.

applications. The user community began to expect mobility and freedom from desktop computers. Computer manufacturers began to offer smaller and lighter laptops to appeal to a growing desire to be connected everywhere without having to carry a heavy device around.

The smartphone and PDA manufacturers paid attention as well. They began to make their devices faster and more powerful—more computer-like. One of the leaders in increasing market share among business users was BlackBerry. The first BlackBerry device was released in 1999. It allowed users to use a single device to make phone calls, access email, and manage schedules. Users could also run some applications and perform some of their work without a laptop. Apple followed with its iOS products, starting with the popular iPhone®. The first iPhone was released in 2007. The first Android phone, the T-Mobile G1™, using the brand-new Android operating system, was released in 2008. With these three heavy hitters in the market, the race was on to win the most mobile users.

The question was: "Who really wants to use mobile devices?" The answer was: "Almost everyone!" People wanted mobile devices for their personal and professional lives. This trend pointed to the importance of BYOD. The supply of mobile devices, software, and services barely kept up with demand. Mobile users discovered more uses for mobile technology with each new device or software release. Mobile computing began to approach the power and convenience of traditional computing. But at least three issues remained: network speed, usability, and security.

There are many uses for mobile devices and applications. Some of the earliest applications were really just lightweight web apps. Users connected to the web server using a lightweight browser on their mobile device. Later smartphones and PDAs supported native applications that did not require continuous network connections. Some applications must be connected at all times, but others do not need to be. One example is an application that stores employee timesheet information on a central server. The mobile device must connect to a network to synchronize data with the server but does not need to maintain a constant connection. Applications that do not require continuous network connection make it possible to work with mobile data aboard, for example, an aircraft or other remote location.

One of the earliest uses of mobile devices was to take work away from the workplace. Mobile workers quickly became the drivers for migrating applications to mobile devices. General applications that help manage email and schedules were among the first to be made available. Medical professionals quickly realized the advantages of mobile computing to meet their specific needs. Medical treatment and medical information management have long been related tasks. Medical personnel need to access patients' charts and files filled with their private medical information, and they need to do so quickly, to provide the best treatment. Hospitals, clinics, and practices have invested substantial amounts of time and money in managing patient data. The recent push to store medical records electronically makes accessing those data much more important. Mobile devices make it possible for doctors, nurses, and other authorized medical personnel to access and update patient records on demand.

Mobile Applications

Many organizations tried to meet the needs of new mobile user demands by simply enabling their applications for the Web. Most mobile devices included limited web browsers and could run a few applications. This approach opened many applications to users who could previously access the applications only by using in-house computers. Unfortunately, functionality often suffered. Applications that were not written for web browsers often end up being confusing and frustrating for users. Many applications failed due to bad interface design for mobile users.

Once mobile device manufacturers, software developers, and service providers began to support mobile users, the main questions they began to ask were: "Who is using mobile applications?" and "Who wants to use mobile applications?" They found that many users from multiple domains found uses for mobile applications. Among the most aggressive early adopters were medical personnel.

Medical applications were a good fit for mobile applications from the early days of mobile devices. Medical personnel need to interact with patients and their data continually. For example, a hospital patient may see several doctors, nurses, and other practitioners each day. Each medical staffer needs to have access to some of the patient's information. Patient information can include demographics, history, diagnosis, and treatment. Each caregiver who interacts with a patient must have access to the patient's information to provide appropriate care. It is difficult and expensive to place a computer in every room, so medical practices and hospitals realized early on that mobile devices provide the ability to grant access to the necessary information without having to invest in many computers and network infrastructure. Each caregiver can carry a mobile device and have easy access to the required information on demand.

IP Mobile Communications

Today's 4G networks provide true IP communications. This is a significant improvement over previous technologies. Each 4G device has a unique IP address and appears just like any other wired device on a network. This allows mobile devices to interact with any other IP device without having to translate addresses. The only limitation on capabilities is in the processing power of the mobile device. As mobile devices become faster and faster, the differences are decreasing.

Mobile devices can now operate like wired devices without being restricted by a physical boundary. This is both an advantage and a potential danger. Traditional network management is often based on the knowledge of where devices are located. Devices that move around freely can be more difficult to track down, let alone to secure.

Mobile users want to connect to networks just as if they were physically plugged into the network in their office. **Mobile IP** makes this possible. Using Mobile IP, users can move

Selecting Multiple Items from a List

One example of the difficulties in mapping an application to a mobile device deals with lists. Suppose your legacy application asks the user to select the toppings he or she wants on a pizza. A classic web application using a full-featured web browser application makes it easy for users to select more than one topping. The standard method for Microsoft Windows users is to hold down the Control key and click on each topping. This simple action is difficult on iPhones, iPads®, or Android devices because there is no Control key, so software developers must find different ways to allow mobile device users to select multiple toppings for their pizzas.

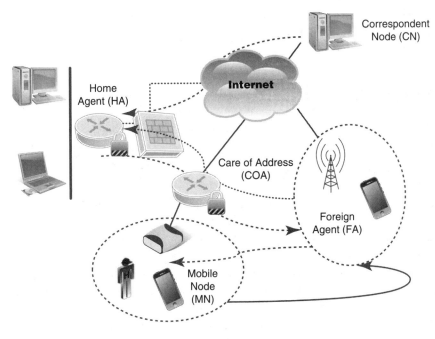

FIGURE 2-4

IP mobile communications.

1. Mobile node (MN) connects to foreign agent (FA).
2. FA assigns care of address (COA) to MN.
3. FA sends COA to home agent (HA).
4. Correspondent node (CN) sends message to MN.
   a. CN's message for MN goes first to HA.
   b. HA forwards message to COA.
   c. FA forwards message to MN.

between segments on a LAN and stay connected without the interruption that would normally happen using standard TCP/IP. Users will not even realize that their devices might move from one network to another as they move about. Users can maintain a connection to the network as long as the mobile device stays within network coverage. The network device can switch between cellular and Wi-Fi and still provide transparent connections.

FIGURE 2-4 demonstrates how Mobile IP provides connection transparency for several entities working together to ensure that mobile devices can move from one network to another without dropping connections:

- **Mobile node (MN)**—The mobile device that moves from one network to another. The MN has a fixed IP address regardless of the current network.

- **Home agent (HA)**—A router with additional capabilities over standard routers, the HA keeps track of the MNs it manages. When an MN leaves the local network, the HA forwards packets to the MN's current network.

- **Foreign agent (FA)**—A router with additional capabilities connected to another network (not the HA network), the FA assigns the MN a local address. When the MN connects to another network that supports Mobile IP, it announces itself to the FA.

- **Care of address (COA)**—The local address for the MN when it connects to another network, the FA assigns the COA to the MN and sends it to the HA when the MN connects. In many cases, the COA is actually the FA address. The HA forwards any packets for the MN to the COA. The FA receives the packets and forwards them to the MN.

- **Correspondent node (CN)**—This is the node that wants to communicate with the MN.

Suppose an MN leaves the home network and connects to some other network. When the MN connects to a new network, the FA sends the COA to the HA. Then a CN wants to communicate with the MN. The CN sends a message to the MN's IP address. The network routes the packet to the MN's home network. The HA receives the packet and forwards it to the COA. The FA forwards the packet to the MN.

New Challenges Created by the IoT

In the introduction to this chapter, you learned about the five key challenges that the IoT must overcome:

- **Security**—How do you keep the bad guys out if you enable the IoT for your personal and professional life?
- **Privacy**—How do you protect your family's identity and privacy data from theft or unauthorized access that can lead to identity theft?
- **Interoperability and standards**—How well do IoT manufacturers and ASP developers ensure that devices communicate securely?
- **Legal and regulatory compliance**—What role do the international, federal, and state levels contribute toward legal, tax, and regulatory requirements regarding IoT-related business transactions that involve payment for goods and services?
- **E-commerce and economic development issues**—What are the economic rules of engagement for conducting business on the World Wide Web? How is IoT connectivity and information sharing to be deployed globally?

Security

Remember, the security triad consists of confidentiality, integrity, and availability (CIA). What if an individual or a business connects something to the Internet without security in mind? What if there is nothing of value or of a sensitive nature to steal; do you still connect? What should a user or a business do before connecting to the Internet? These same questions hold true for devices that connect via the IoT. You, the user, are the owner of your asset and the information contained in that asset, so it is critical that you decide what is at risk if you connect your personal life, home, and business content to the Internet. You have to have a high degree of trust to connect your identity, social and family life, home, and professional life to the Internet. Or you have to have a high degree of trust that you can enable your own security controls as a defense strategy for connecting your assets to the IoT. Regardless of your defense strategy, there are risks, threats, and vulnerabilities everywhere. So, where does trust come into play? As an individual user of the Internet, do the same human protocols and human etiquette apply online? What is acceptable or unacceptable behavior, and who or what organization defines what is acceptable or unacceptable?

The Internet is already filled with hackers and bad guys. Security and data breaches are occurring every day. Now people and businesses want to connect more devices via the IoT phenomenon? It is already happening. Each day there are more Internet-connected devices and people. Businesses continue to expand their online presence, and new applications are being developed and sold via the Internet. Software products and distribution are no longer done via CD or DVD. Once software licensing is paid for online, you can immediately download the software to your device and install it. People are becoming more dependent on their electronic devices and real-time connectivity. This increasing level of dependency on Internet connectivity and IoT device access is not going away. It is increasing. As people and businesses become even more dependent on the IoT, so will the opportunities for bad guys to attack, steal, and damage. This is why security is the greatest challenge for the IoT to overcome. Who will act as the governing body? What policies and procedures or code of conduct should people and businesses abide by when interacting with the IoT? Security has global issues that impact all humans, governments, and businesses.

The following summarizes the security challenges of IoT devices:

- IoT devices such as sensors or consumer items (Internet-connected TV) are deployed in large quantities. Depending on the criticality of the application, an outage could impact many endpoints if attacked.

- IoT devices are ubiquitous and can have wide reach into the user or household population. For example, electrical meters that are Internet connected introduce a critical infrastructure vulnerability if an attack could be replicated and pushed to individual endpoints.

- IoT devices that are not updated or maintained properly may permit vulnerabilities to become entry points into your network or organization. This is the equivalent of a vendor announcing an **End of Life (EOL)** support timeline for a product or software application.

- IoT upgrades can be difficult to distribute and deploy, leaving gaps in the remediation of IoT devices or endpoints. Cars that have Wi-Fi access and onboard computers require software patches and upgrades from the manufacturer. This maintenance must be performed for all cars requiring the upgrade to remediate a software vulnerability.

- IoT devices typically do not provide the user or owner with any inside visibility or knowledge of how the device works and connects to the Internet. Vendors or service providers that have remote access to an IoT device may be able to pull information or data from your IoT device without your permission. Review of the product warranty and IoT communications and data sharing with a service provider may be part of your use agreement.

- IoT devices typically are not physically secure and can be located anywhere in public areas or outside your house. Your home's electrical panel, cable TV, or fiber optic cable points of entry are typically not that secure. Security is lacking for Wi-Fi-connected IoT devices on public or open Wi-Fi networks.

- Environmental IoT devices are typically out in the open capturing readings and measurements for scientific reasons or research reasons. If an IoT device can act as a point of entry into an IP data network, a vulnerability in one device is compounded if there are many IoT devices out there.

Privacy

How do you protect your family's identity and privacy data from theft or unauthorized access that can lead to identity theft? Do you even know what your privacy rights are as an individual living in your state and country? Are those same privacy rights extended to the Internet and IoT devices? Who owns the data in your IoT devices? Privacy has many layers. First is you and your own identity and private data. Then you extend privacy to your spouse or other family members. Families require a privacy strategy to ensure that all family members' privacy data are kept confidential. Leakage of one family member's private data may be the opportunity for other family members' private data to be compromised.

Users must have a level of trust to use the Internet and IoT devices. More important is a respect for privacy. A user's rights must be clearly defined, and a user's private data must also be clearly defined for all IoT devices. The IoT is creating new concerns for privacy and what private data are and who owns those data. Who owns the actual data within an IoT device, the owner of the device (you) or the manufacturer? What about **metadata** of the data itself? Does metadata belong to the owner of the IoT device or the manufacturer that is collecting it via the Internet, as defined in the warranty and software license agreement that is assumed when the device user purchased the product? Metadata about the use patterns and information about the IoT device are beneficial to the manufacturer. But are these data yours? The definition of data and who owns data must be clearly understood before you purchase and connect the device to the Internet.

The IoT introduces new and interesting privacy challenges. These challenges must be fully understood and vetted by both the manufacturer of the IoT device and the individual user of that device. The following privacy challenges must be addressed by manufacturers and defined in the right-of-use and end user software licensing agreement:

- **Privacy policy statement**—An actual legal definition of the user's privacy rights as documented in the manufacturer's privacy policy statement. This privacy policy statement must accompany any online form where privacy data is input by an individual.
- **Definition of data, metadata, or analytical data use and rights**—This is an actual definition that defines what data, metadata, or analytical data are and what they may be used for, and if permission is required by the user for use of those data.
- **Ability for a user to provide consent to a manufacturer's or application service provider's privacy policy statement**—Users must be able to read the statement online and accept or decline the privacy policy's terms and conditions. Once a

---

FYI

What if you are a health fanatic and you subscribe to an online calorie and health performance tracking service via a mobile application? Your refrigerator, which is IoT-connected, along with your online grocery store purchases, work together to track what you are eating and convert it to calories. You also decide to link the online restaurant reservation system you use to your calorie and health performance tracking application. When you order at a restaurant, the food and calories are automatically calculated into your daily calorie calculator. On top of all that, your IoT fitness calorie monitor feeds real-time updates to your online calorie and health performance tracking application as you exercise and burn calories. The calorie and health performance ASP that hosts your calorie and health performance data performs analytics on your data and creates new metadata about your data. These metadata are sold to healthcare researchers or manufacturers of healthy foods. If they include demographics, such as your age, weight, and geographical location, they have a lot of information about you, even though it is considered **de-identified data**.

This concern about who owns the metadata, or data about the data, is very common within the privacy arena. This is probably the number-one privacy challenge that has yet to be fully vetted. In general, people do not know their privacy rights, and it is important for users to fully understand those rights. This introduces a fine line between what a user is comfortable doing and how much trust the user has in the manufacturer of his or her IoT device.

user provides consent, it is typically more painful to remove that consent. Some companies make you write a formal written removal of consent with no online capability.

- **Determine the domain of privacy**—If you permit geolocation tracking of you and your smartphone or IP mobile device and another application service provider uses that information about you and where you go, is that infringing on your privacy rights? What if you didn't even know those data were being collected? Invasion of privacy in your own home makes sense, but does that extend to the IoT devices within your home that are Internet connected? Domains of privacy become blurred when your privacy data or metadata are aggregated or correlated with other data to create new data. Remember, IoT devices can collect information about people with granular specificity. Data profiles can be created, thus creating new threats and patterns of behavior that you, the owner, may not want leaked or used by another party.

In addition to these privacy challenges, the following questions are presenting new areas for exploration and understanding among IoT legal experts and privacy consultants:

- How do we address the data source and the data collectors' rights and use of data?
- Is there a happy medium that includes de-identification of private data, with no ability to link those data to a person?
- How will an individual or business even know what a good privacy posture or preference is?
- Will current social contexts and acceptable behavior extend to the IoT?
- Can we develop privacy by design (with a set of core requirements) and put in place a standard implementation of privacy for all of the IoT?

Questions like these require careful analysis and risk-mitigating solutions, especially from a legal and regulatory compliance perspective. U.S. federal and state privacy laws are meant to protect the private data of citizens while requiring entities that use, handle, store, and transmit private data to abide by certain security and privacy requirements.

Interoperability and Standards

Interoperability and standards are key to implementing a consistent IoT device, connectivity, and communications environment. Without it, application service providers, IoT device manufacturers, and customers would be discouraged from implementing and connecting IoT devices. ISPs and end-user customers all adopted the use of TCP/IP version 4 communications protocol to ensure interoperability for end-to-end IP communications. Following a common theme of interoperability and standards for IoT device connectivity, security is critical to ensure device-to-device functionality. As long as the **Internet Engineering Task Force (IETF)** is involved, interoperability and standards can be pursued for IoT solutions. Following the Internet Society's four fundamental principles—connect, speak, share, and innovate—is key to driving the success of IoT innovation.

A fully interoperable IoT environment is desired to allow any IoT-connected device to talk to another IoT-connected device. This communication can occur either directly or indirectly through a shared server or application acting as a central point of communication. The key here is, how is information being collected, stored, and used? Interoperability requires similar operating systems (OSs), communication protocols, and methods for transmitting data in a secure manner to a server or application server hosted in a secure cloud. Standardization and adoption of common protocols and transmission schemas including encryption/ decryption are all important requirements that require standardized implementations.

Interoperability has significant financial impacts if not properly addressed. This is what manufacturers and application software vendors do not want. They want to bring the cost of IoT devices and applications that support IoT devices way down so that they are affordable, given the masses of users and businesses that can benefit from the IoT. Interoperability drives down the cost of IoT implementation for users and businesses. Implementation of open standards and interoperability requirements will allow for more IoT devices to connect. This increases the economic value, or return on investment, for IoT deployments as benefits are derived to pay for the cost of IoT deployment. Interoperability will drive economic benefits and financial impact into the trillions into 2025, according to a 2015 McKinsey Global Institute report.

Interoperability, standards, protocols, and definitions are needed for early development and implementation of IoT devices. The following are key challenges that must be addressed with interoperability and standards:

- **Some manufacturers want to design and deploy proprietary IoT devices and solutions**—This is a strategy to lock in early adopter customers and businesses to their own solutions. This creates technology silos that do not permit for information sharing and requires a gateway or intermediary solution to share information. If the data are in a shareable format, it is possible for applications to share IoT device data. Application program interfaces (APIs) or other software interfaces may be needed for noncompatible IoT devices and applications to share information between them. This hinders the implementation and acceptance of IoT.

- **Cost factors to implement functional, operational, technical, and security capabilities into IoT devices and applications**—Cost is always a key consideration in designing and implementing an IoT go-to-market strategy. Price points must be low and affordable, knowing that the masses will drive volume purchases for IoT device connectivity. Vendors and manufacturers must weigh the cost of interoperability into the IoT device itself versus getting the product out in the marketplace with immediate adoption.

- **Time-to-market risk**—There is no doubt that a first-to-market advantage exists for the global-scale IoT device marketplace. Vendors and manufacturers have been playing this game ever since technology was invented. How fast you get ahead of the interoperability and standards curve is based on where most of the user and business community is regarding use of proprietary or open standards-based IoT technology deployments. Without a time-to-market stress point, there would be no issue of going out on a limb regarding building product and releasing product before interoperability and standards can be globally adopted and accepted.

- **Technology outdated risk**—IoT vendors, manufacturers, and software developers each take risks when developing IoT technical solutions and products without interoperability and standards definitions fully defined and adopted. This situation forces an early design to use open and widely available standards or proprietary solutions and techniques. Obviously, the more open and flexible your architecture, the easier it is to adapt and alter technical interoperability and standard technology decisions during the design phase of IoT device and solutions development.

- **A void in interoperability and standards for IoT devices can create an environment of bad IoT devices**—Without interoperability and standards among IoT devices, there will be a lack of communication and information sharing. This may cause multiple IoT environments in which the devices may not be able to communicate or share data. This creates more issues with multiple IoT devices and IoT disparate networks that only those devices can connect to and share information with. What's the point of the IoT vision if the devices that connect don't communicate and share information with one another? Herein lies the ultimate challenge for IoT interoperability and standards adoption. Configuration updates must be automated, simple, and fully interoperable among IoT devices. Without an ability to send updated firmware, OS software, and other IoT device software, devices will become outdated. This will increase the risk of having vulnerable or outdated IoT devices connected to a production IP network. A remote configuration capability is what can drive interoperability and standards for all IoT devices and systems.

Legal and Regulatory Issues

The deployment of IoT devices on the public open Internet introduces some immediate concerns from a regulatory and legal perspective. Some of these concerns have never existed before. With regulatory compliance throughout the United States now in full effect for many vertical industries, how are users and businesses to deploy IoT-centric devices and solutions in a compliant manner? This poses an interesting question for those vertical industries under a compliance law such as HIPAA for healthcare, FERPA for higher education, FISMA for the federal government, the **Federal Financial Institutions Examination Council (FFIEC)** for banking and finance, and PCI DSS v3.1.1 as a standard to follow for secure credit card transaction processing.

With regulatory compliance, we are concerned about properly handling sensitive data and ensuring its confidentiality. Sensitive data are uniquely defined for users and individuals under these compliance laws. But what about IoT device data? IoT devices use the Internet to communicate. Depending on where the server or IoT application resides, your IoT data are traversing physical networks and crossing state boundaries. That means your private data are subject to the privacy laws of the state you live in as well as the state that the IoT hosting company resides in. It is this movement of data that can quickly cause a legal issue. If the IoT data are classified to be private data or sensitive data protected under regulatory compliance, that IoT vendor or solutions provider is required to adhere to security control requirements and data protection laws as needed. This cross-border data movement is not new to the Internet. What is new is that IoT devices can share and communicate your IoT device data to other systems and applications without your authorization or knowledge. This complicates the privacy issue because the data can cross state borders without your knowledge or approval at times.

Who is collecting your IoT device data? Who is collecting your behavior patterns throughout your IoT devices? What is the collector doing with your IoT device and behavior data? This is a brand-new legal and privacy issue with IoT data discrimination. The data collected from your IoT devices tell a specific story about you and your use of that IoT device. These data can be used for good things as well as used against you in a discriminating manner. Depending on the third-party right-to-use clauses, IoT vendors and ASPs may be using your data or metadata in a manner that may be discriminatory toward you. These can even include data about where you travel or eat and what you do for entertainment. Metadata can be accumulated and sold to other companies seeking demographic marketing data about you and your spending habits. How valuable is this information to the other company? Does the IoT or device-tracking application vendor have the right to sell your metadata information? When engaging globally with other individuals from other countries, which laws apply to that person's privacy such that security controls may or may not be required?

Finally, what about IoT device liability? What if your IoT device is used for healthcare monitoring and alerts/alarms, but there is a malfunction? If someone is injured or killed as a result of a faulty IoT device, does the limitation of liability come from the IoT device manufacturer, the ASP, or whom? Manufacturers have no way of knowing how that IoT device will be used by the owner. What if that device is used to commit or aid in a crime or robbery? If a hacker can compromise a home IoT security system and video camera system and then rob that house while the owners are away, who is liable for this actual robbery and loss of possessions? What if an IoT device is used to compromise access to other IT systems, applications, and data using the vulnerable IoT device as a launch pad? These examples demonstrate the potential liabilities that may occur using IoT devices in the real world. Current liability laws and protection may or may not address IoT devices connected to the public Internet. How can we stay ahead of this legal and regulatory compliance curve? This is not an easy task. Assessing legal implications of IoT devices and their implementations must address privacy rights of individuals first. This must be followed by an understanding of what is acceptable and unacceptable from a liability perspective for businesses involved in IoT device manufacturing or solutions.

E-Commerce and Economic Development Issues

IoT is an e-commerce and economic enabler for less developed countries seeking to connect to the Internet. IoT technology has a significant impact on developing economies, given that it can transform countries into e-commerce-ready nations.

Industrial and critical infrastructure solutions that incorporate the IoT may help underdeveloped countries accelerate their global Internet and e-commerce presence. This includes implementation of IoT critical infrastructure solutions that monitor agriculture, energy, water availability, industrialization, and management of the environment and natural resources. The IoT can help cities, counties, and countries deploy critical infrastructure technologies to accelerate economic development and growth.

Food, water, agriculture, and farming all can be supported with IoT devices, sensors, and monitors to help countries build new foundations for agriculture and food processing.

Using the IoT to track and monitor progress is a viable solution for governments to deploy as they build critical infrastructure and provide basic necessities for their people and businesses. The following are examples that the IoT brings to e-commerce and economic development for countries:

- **Infrastructure resources**—Foundational to the deployment of the IoT, a communication infrastructure and broadband Internet network are needed within that country. This is the foundation for IoT device connectivity and communications in a global marketplace.

Critical-Infrastructure IoT

Countries implementing new water supply management systems require proper sensor monitoring and tracking to ensure fresh water supplies are maintained and water supplies are reaching the people that need it. Agriculture and farming are dependent on water irrigation and can also benefit from the IoT. Sensors can monitor water supplies as well as water quality, providing near real-time data back to water management systems and personnel. Using this IoT infrastructure to manage an entire region's fresh water supply can support proper population and agricultural growth. Using the IoT to help with water management system planning, including capacity planning, can benefit human and agricultural growth. Once implemented for water management, other similar critical infrastructure services (e.g., waste water management, etc.) can follow a similar implementation path. This IoT foundation can support that country's economic development and e-commerce road map. Agriculture and other natural resources can become part of that country's IoT and international trade e-commerce strategy. Whether that natural resource is water, agriculture, natural resources, or minerals, an IoT foundation can help drive that country's economic development and e-commerce strategy.

- **Foundational investments**—Countries seeking to invest in critical infrastructures may be able to leapfrog past other countries that are struggling with regulatory and legal issues in regard to accelerating deployments.
- **Technical and industry development**—New skills are needed to bring new technologies and economic solutions to bear using the Internet and the IoT as a key economic driver. As IoT technology and industry interoperability and standards mature, so will IoT device deployment and user and business adoption.
- **Policy and regulatory definitions**—Countries and emerging economies are positioned to create and implement policies and regulations to help ensure that security and privacy become part of the deployment.

Other considerations emerge when dealing with international e-commerce. When engaging in foreign or international e-commerce, who is responsible for paying taxes and submitting those taxes? Questions like these require answers, especially when the IoT expands beyond countries and international borders.

CHAPTER SUMMARY

In this chapter, you learned about changes in communication and the impact the Internet has had on people and business. This impact has led us to an Internet of Things (IoT) whereby any IP-connected device is able to connect to the Internet. This evolution was created by the Internet and its explosive growth and popularity. This evolution has transformed our personal and professional lives and the way we conduct business. As more users and their devices connect to the Internet, there are more opportunities for sharing and using information across the IoT universe. This may include human or personal interaction with the IoT and professional or business interaction with the IoT where businesses are transforming into application service providers, providing new innovative products and services. We learned that the IoT is not without business challenges and issues that must be overcome.

These new IoT business challenges and issues include all aspects of human interaction with the Internet and IoT-connected devices, including security, privacy, interoperability and standards, legal and regulatory issues, and e-commerce and economic development. Global cooperation and participation in the IoT interoperability and standards area will ensure that IoT vendors, manufacturers, and ASPs are all on a common platform to build and implement IoT devices and solutions for tomorrow's marketplace. Without this global cooperation, the IoT vision as described by the Internet Society will have difficulty getting implemented.

KEY CONCEPTS AND TERMS

Anything as a Service (AaaS)
Application service provider (ASP)
Audio conferencing
Bring Your Own Device (BYOD)
Business-to-business (B2B)
Business-to-consumer (B2C)
Collaboration
Confidentiality, integrity, and availability (C-I-A)
De-identified data
Digital media
End of life (EOL)

Federal Financial Institutions Examination Council (FFIEC)
IM chat
Internet Engineering Task Force (IETF)
Internet of Things (IoT)
Interoperability
Metadata
Mobile IP
Payment Card Industry Data Security Standard (PCI DSS)
Privacy

Radio frequency identification (RFID)
Real-time communications
Search engine optimization (SEO)
Security
Social media
Software as a Service (SaaS)
Store-and-forward communications
Unified messaging
Video conferencing
Voice over IP (VoIP)

CHAPTER 2 ASSESSMENT

1. The Internet is an open, public network shared by the entire planet. Anyone can connect to the Internet with a computer and a valid Internet connection and browser.

A. True
B. False

2. Which of the following are challenges that IoT industry must overcome?

A. Security and privacy
B. Interoperability and standards
C. Legal and regulatory compliance

D. E-commerce and economic development
E. All of the above

3. Which phenomenon helped drive near real-time, high-speed broadband connectivity to the endpoint device?

A. Internet connectivity
B. Email
C. VoIP
D. Social media sharing
E. All of the above

4. Which of the following requires an IoT-connected automobile?

A. Near real-time access to household controls and systems
B. Ability to track the whereabouts of your children through location finder GPS applications
C. Real-time alerts regarding reminders to pay bills on time
D. Online e-commerce and online shopping with direct delivery
E. Traffic monitoring sensors that provide real-time updates for traffic conditions

5. Which of the following are impacts of the IoT on our business lives?

A. E-commerce
B. Integrated supply chain with front-end sales order entry
C. Companies now offering delivery services for products and services with real-time updates
D. Customer reviews providing consumers with product and service reviews online and with more information about customer satisfaction
E. All of the above

6. Which of the following helps support remote teleworking?

A. Presence/availability
B. IM chat
C. Video conferencing
D. Collaboration
E. All of the above

7. Which is a security challenge that IoT deployments must overcome?

A. Congestion of mobile IP traffic
B. Secure communication with other IoT devices
C. Liability of an IoT device failing to send an update message
D. Pricing for software licensing in the IoT device
E. Privacy data use sharing agreement

8. Unified messaging provides what functionality for users on the go?

A. Voice messages that are converted to audio files and emailed to the user's emailbox for playback while on the road
B. One-to-many communications
C. Many-to-many communications
D. VoIP communications and messaging
E. SIP communications and messaging

9. Which of the following applications can eliminate the need for face-to-face training?

A. Audio/video conferencing
B. Collaboration
C. IM chat
D. Presence/availability
E. All of the above

10. Why do e-commerce systems need the utmost in security controls?

A. It is a PCI DSS standard.
B. Private customer data is entered into websites.
C. Credit card data is entered into websites.
D. Customer retention requires confidence in secure online purchases.
E. All of the above

11. Which of the following is *not* a challenge that must be overcome by IoT deployments?

A. Security
B. Availability
C. Legal and regulatory
D. E-commerce and economic development
E. Privacy

12. Typically, data must be _____ to be shared or used for research purposes.

A. Encrypted
B. Hashed
C. De-identified
D. Masked out
E. In cleartext

Malicious Attacks, Threats, and Vulnerabilities

I N THIS CHAPTER, YOU WILL LEARN about the software used to conduct a malicious **attack**. This software is called **malware**. You will also learn about different types of attacks. The Internet is an untamed new frontier. There are many bad people wanting to steal your data. If your device and sensitive information are connected to the Internet, there is potential for loss or damage. Unlike in your everyday life, in cyberspace there is no real law of the land. Criminal acts that lead to destruction and theft occur regularly. These acts affect businesses, individuals, and governments. The criminals often go unpunished, as was the case with the Sony Pictures Entertainment hack that occurred in late 2014.

Malicious attacks result in billions of dollars in damages each year. Fortunately, many companies and individuals like you are working hard to protect IT assets from attacks. In this chapter, you will learn how to identify security vulnerabilities, protect your organization from threats, and keep your computers safe from malicious attacks.

Chapter 3 Topics

This chapter covers the following topics and concepts:

- What the global scope of cyberattacks is
- What you are trying to protect
- Whom you are trying to catch
- What kinds of tools are used to attack computer systems
- What a security breach is
- What risks, vulnerabilities, and threats are
- What malware is
- What a malicious software attack is
- What a social engineering attack is
- What a wireless network attack is
- What a web application attack is
- What countermeasures are

Chapter 3 Goals

When you complete this chapter, you will be able to:

- Identify malicious software and implement countermeasures
- Identify common attacks and develop appropriate countermeasures
- Recognize social engineering and reduce the risks associated with it
- Recognize threats and types of attacks on wireless networks
- Recognize threats and types of attacks on web applications

Malicious Activity on the Rise

You have probably seen the stories on the news, viewed the humorous ads on TV, or read the headlines about cyberattacks. A case in point: Recently, authorities sent a college student to prison for 20 years for hacking the email account of a U.S. vice presidential candidate. In a similar incident, clothing retailer TJX Companies admitted to carelessness in allowing the theft of millions of payment card numbers of its customers. In addition, in a humorous prime-time commercial, a clueless employee sets off a company-wide virus attack by clicking a "harmless" email link. Everywhere around you, you find examples of the malicious attacks that security professionals face every day. Headlines are abundant with news of recent data breaches. Data breaches are occurring in the public sector and the private sector. No organization or individual is safe from the risk of stolen digital data or a loss of your digital identity.

Although these attacks grabbed the attention of the news media and the public, most victims of cyberattacks don't publicize the incidents at all. Every day, systems around the world are under threat. In most cases, the only people who ever know about these attacks are security professionals and IT personnel. Security professionals are responsible for protecting their systems from threats and for handling malicious attacks when they do occur. One of the most effective ways to protect computer systems is to ensure that vulnerabilities are mitigated throughout the IT infrastructure, quickly and efficiently.

TABLE 3-1 shows the top 10 hacking countries, as identified by Bloomberg Business in April 2013. In 2013, China was the top country of origin for cyberattacks, at 41 percent. The United States was second at 10 percent. Remember, the country of origin may be difficult to pinpoint. This is particularly true if **botnets** are used to perform the actual attack. A botnet is a bunch of Internet-connected computers under the control of a remote hacker. The remote hacker can control these botnet-connected computers and launch an attack even though the hacker himself may live in a different country. This makes it difficult to find and capture the perpetrator.

> **NOTE**
>
> Attackers sometimes use **transitive access** to gain the trust of a targeted system or user. When transitive access is pursued by the attacker, the desired target system or service is indirectly attacked by first compromising a system trusted by the target. This creates a false sense of security, given that the target system is familiar with and trusts the source device or user. Attackers can use this trust to their advantage by planning an attack from this trusted device or user.

TABLE 3-1 Top 10 hacking countries, 2013.

SOURCE	SHARE OF ATTACKS (%)
China	41%
United States	10%
Turkey	4.7%
Russia	4.3%
Taiwan	3.7%
Brazil	3.3%
Romania	2.8%
India	2.3%
Italy	1.6%
Hungary	1.4%

Data from Bloomberg Business, Top 10 Hacking Counties, 2013.

What Are You Trying to Protect?

In a word, you are trying to protect assets. An **asset** is any item that has value. Although all items in an organization have some value, the term *asset* generally applies to those items that have substantial value. An organization's assets can include the following:

- **Customer data**—Name, address, phone, Social Security number (SSN), date of birth, cardholder data, protected health care information.
- **IT assets and network infrastructure**—Hardware, software, and services.
- **Intellectual property**—Sensitive data such as patents, source code, formulas, or engineering plans.
- **Finances and financial data**—Bank accounts, credit card data, and financial transaction data.
- **Service availability and productivity**—The ability of computing services and software to support productivity for humans and machinery.
- **Reputation**—Corporate compliance and brand image.

Let's look at each of these types of assets individually and discuss how they are at risk from malicious attacks.

Customer Data

News sources love to report on the quantity of data elements stolen in a data breach. Loss of customer private data, cardholder data, or electronic protected health care data elements rise to top of newsworthy headlines because of the impact. In the digital era of today, customer private data is vulnerable to theft and abuse by another individual. When private data is used to impersonate an individual, the outcome is called **identity theft**. Customer private data may include first and last name, home address, phone number, date of birth, SSN, or cardholder data.

IT and Network Infrastructure

Hardware and software are key pieces of any organization's infrastructure. **FIGURE 3-1** shows the seven domains of a typical IT infrastructure framework. Components in each domain may connect to a network or to the Internet. Threats can exist, both internal to the IT infrastructure and external, given that the IT infrastructure is connected to the Internet.

Damage to data caused by new threats includes **armored virus**, **ransomware**, and **cryptolocker** malware, which can cost corporations time and money to fix or replace. Armored viruses have hardened code that makes it difficult to reverse-engineer and build an antivirus for the malware. Ransomware is a new form of malware linked to a time clock, forcing the victim organization to pay a ransom to prevent its data from being deleted. Cryptolocker is a specific form of ransomware that encrypts critical files or data until the victim pays a ransom to obtain the decryption keys. Malicious attacks on critical hardware and software systems can also lead to more widespread problems within organizations. These problems can include loss of critical data or theft of financial information or intellectual property. Unprotected IT and network infrastructure assets can offer attackers and cybercriminals the widest opening to access sensitive resources. The ease of access makes assets that are connected to the Internet the most common first point of attack. That means you should put

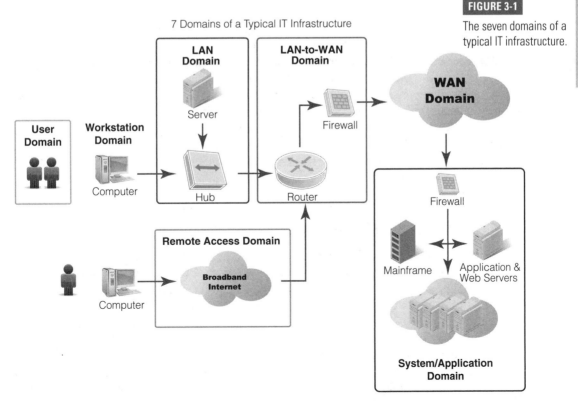

7 Domains of a Typical IT Infrastructure

FIGURE 3-1

The seven domains of a typical IT infrastructure.

Malicious Attacks, Threats, and Vulnerabilities

3

your most valuable assets deep inside your IT infrastructure to enable a layered security defense. Layered security defenses are critical given the sophistication of new, **polymorphic malware** software. Polymorphic malware is harmful given that it can morph, or change, making it difficult to see and be remediated with antivirus or anti-malware applications.

Intellectual Property

Intellectual property is the center of many organizations. Intellectual property is an asset of an organization. It can be a unique business process or actual data such as customer data. Examples of intellectual property include such things as patents, drug formulas, engineering plans, scientific formulas, and recipes. Suppose a restaurant chain has a unique process for quickly preparing and delivering food. If the rest of the industry knew about that process, it would remove the restaurant's competitive advantage. In a digital world, data constitute the most valuable asset. The more data you have, the more valuable you are. And, if you have metadata for your data, that can add additional value to your data.

> **NOTE**
>
> In February 2016, Hollywood Presbyterian Medical Center was a victim of ransomware using a cryptolocker malware application. The cryptolocker malware locks systems by encrypting critical files and demanding a ransom to obtain the decryption key. Hollywood elected to pay the ransom of $17,000 using Bitcoin to obtain the decryption keys. The hospital made the decision to pay the ransom and return to normal operations. In this case, no data breach occurred, but the incident resulted in a complete loss of control of all computer systems, given that critical files were encrypted and thus rendered unusable.

What have you been reading in the news headlines? That data breaches or data losses are occurring every day in every aspect of life. This type of loss includes identity theft, business theft, or intellectual property theft. Data breaches occur frequently. As an information systems security professional, it is your mission to prevent a data breach from occurring to your assets. *That* is your number-one objective.

The core issue from an IT security perspective is protecting the theft of intellectual property and preventing its release to competitors or to the public. The theft of intellectual property can nullify an organization's competitive advantage. Imagine that a company called Alpha Drug Company invested $2 billion to develop a new prescription drug, with the expectation that it would earn $10 billion when it releases the drug. Now imagine that just as Alpha Drug Company was set to bring its medication to market, Beta Drug Company obtained Alpha's formulas and rushed its own version to market. Alpha would lose the first-to-market advantage, given that it invested in R&D and a big chunk of the revenue associated with the new drug. Protecting intellectual property is a top-of-mind consideration for any organization.

Finances and Financial Data

Financial assets are among the highest-profile assets in any organization. These assets can take various forms. They can be real financial assets, such as bank accounts, trading accounts, purchasing accounts, corporate credit cards, and other direct sources of money or credit. Alternatively, they can be data that allows access to real financial assets. Financial data can include customer credit card numbers, personal financial information, or usernames and passwords for banking or investment accounts. Other examples include the transaction data that companies and banks use to transfer financial data between themselves. This can include electronic data interchange (EDI) numbers or automated clearinghouse (ACH) transactions used for electronic payments or transfer of funds.

Loss of financial assets due to malicious attacks is a worst-case scenario for all organizations. Not only does it represent significant physical loss, but it can also have long-term effects on a company's reputation and brand image.

Service Availability and Productivity

Computer applications provide specific services that help organizations conduct business operations. It is important that critical services be available for use when organizations need them. *Downtime* is the time during which a service is not available due to failure or maintenance. Downtime can be intentional or unintentional. Often administrators will schedule

Operation Get Rich or Die Tryin'

In May 2010, a court sentenced 28-year-old Albert Gonzalez to 20 years in federal prison for breaching security at several well-known retailers and stealing millions of credit card numbers. After stealing the numbers, Gonzalez resold them using a variety of shadow "carding" websites. Using a simple packet sniffer, Gonzalez managed to steal payment card transaction data in real time. He then parked the card numbers on blind servers in places like Latvia and Ukraine (formerly part of the Soviet Union). Gonzalez, who named his activities "Operation Get Rich or Die Tryin'," enjoyed a lavish lifestyle through the sale of the stolen credit card information. Although the Secret Service eventually tracked him down, Operation Get Rich or Die Tryin' lasted for more than two years. During that period, it cost major retailers like TJX, Office Max, Barnes & Noble, Heartland, and Hannaford more than $200 million in losses and recovery costs. This was the largest computer crime case ever prosecuted.

At first glance, Operation Get Rich or Die Tryin' seems like an open-and-shut case. An attacker committed a series of cybercrimes, investigators caught the perpetrator, and the authorities successfully prosecuted him. Mr. Gonzalez bore the fault and blame, and the corporations and the millions of cardholders received justice. Not all the blame belongs to the cybercriminal, however. In most cyberattacks, the victim plays a part in the success of the attack. Nearly all cyberattacks use known techniques, and organizations can protect their systems from known attacks. Failing to prevent an attack all but invites an attack.

To make this point, shareholders, banking partners, and customers of TJX have filed a series of class-action lawsuits against the company. These lawsuits claim that the "high-level deficiencies" in TJX's security practices made the company at least partially responsible for the damages caused by Albert Gonzalez and his accomplices. The lawsuits point out, for example, that the packet sniffer Gonzalez attached to the TJX network went unnoticed for more than seven months. Court documents also indicate that TJX failed to notice the transfer of more than 80 GB of stored data from its servers using TJX's own high-speed network. Finally, an audit performed by TJX's payment card-processing partners found that TJX failed to comply with nine of the 12 requirements for secure payment card transactions. TJX's core information security policies were so ineffective that the company was unable to place sole blame on Gonzalez and have subsequently settled several lawsuits against them.

Along with the lawsuits, TJX faced a serious backlash from customers and the media when the details of the scope of the breaches trickled out. Customers reacted angrily when they learned that nearly six weeks had passed between the discovery of the breach and the company notifying the public. News organizations ran headline stories that painted a picture of TJX as a clueless and uncaring company. Consumer organizations openly warned people not to shop at TJX stores. TJX's reputation and brand image were shattered in the wake of Operation Get Rich or Die Tryin'. In the end, the real lesson of Operation Get Rich or Die Tryin' might not be the crime itself but how a lackluster security policy was chiefly responsible for the crime happening in the first place.

intentional downtime in advance. For example, when servers need operating system up-grades or patches, administrators take them offline intentionally so they can perform the necessary work without problems. When administrators schedule intentional downtime, they try to do it so that it has little impact on the rest of the organization. Administrators care-fully manage any impact that downtime does have so that it does not disrupt critical business operations. You might be familiar with intentional downtime scenarios such as weekend up-grades of critical software or overnight application of patches to such things as email systems.

Unintentional downtime is usually the result of technical failure, human error, or attack. Technical failure and human error are the most common causes of unintentional down-time. Although downtime caused by malicious attacks is less common, research indicates that it is growing rapidly. Malicious attacks can occur and cause downtime in any of the seven domains of an IT infrastructure. Typically, malicious attacks are targeted on the User, Workstation, LAN, and LAN-to-WAN domains.

Opportunity cost is the amount of money a company loses due to downtime. Downtime can be either intentional or unintentional, but either kind directly affects system availability. Some organizations refer to opportunity cost as **true downtime cost**. Opportunity cost usu-ally measures the loss of productivity experienced by an organization due to downtime. For example, suppose a major airline's reservation servers fail. While the servers are down, no customers can book flights. You can measure the opportunity cost of that downtime in the dollar amount of the unsold tickets. The opportunity cost of unintentional downtime is usually much higher than the opportunity cost of intentional downtime. Opportunity cost is a serious concern for information security professionals. It comprises a large portion of the $1 trillion estimated yearly cost of dealing with cybercrime and malicious attacks.

> **NOTE**
>
> A data breach policy and procedure will prepare your organization for handling a data breach. This includes communicating to the customers, regulatory bodies, and insurance underwriters. If your organization is under regulatory compliance requirements, you may be subject to legal requirements for data breach notification. Executive management, including legal staff, are typically involved in making specific recommendations regarding a data breach to the organization's board of directors. Proper handling of a data breach must be done with relevant legal advice.

Reputation

One of the most important things that information security pro-fessionals try to protect is their organization's reputation and brand image. Companies that suffer from security breaches and malicious attacks that expose any assets are likely to face serious negative consequences in the public eye. For example, a security breach that allows attackers to steal customer credit card data and distribute those data internationally would do significant harm to that company's reputation and brand image. Even if the com-pany's response were swift and solved the problem effectively, the negative public perception of the company and its brands could remain for the long term. Among other consequences, this could lead to a decline in the organization's revenue, net worth, and market capitalization.

Whom Are You Trying to Catch?

In popular usage and in the media, the term **hacker** often describes someone who breaks into a computer system without authorization. In most cases that means the hacker tries to take control of a remote computer through a network or by software cracking. The media and the general public also use the word *hacker* to describe anyone accused of using technology for terrorism, vandalism, credit card fraud, identity theft, intellectual property theft, or one of many other forms of crime. In the computing community, the term *hacker* generally describes a person who enjoys exploring and learning how to modify something, particularly related to computer systems. Hackers, for good or bad, are considered to be experts and tinkerers, but because of the way the media megatively protrays the term, hackers are often the subject of some controversy.

This book attempts to address the confusion surrounding this term by categorizing hackers as follows:

NOTE

Another type of attacker is a **script kiddie**—a **wannabe** hacker, a person of any age with little or no skill. This person simply follows directions or uses a "cookbook" approach to carrying out a cyberattack, without fully understanding the meaning of the steps he or she is performing.

- **Black-hat hackers**—A **black-hat hacker** tries to break IT security and gain access to systems with no authorization in order to prove technical prowess. Black-hat hackers generally develop and use special software tools to exploit vulnerabilities. Black-hat hackers generally exploit holes in systems, but they generally do not attempt to disclose vulnerabilities they find to the administrators of those systems. They tend to promote the free and open use of computing resources as opposed to the notion of security.
- **White-hat hackers**—A **white-hat hacker**, or **ethical hacker**, is an information systems security professional who has authorization to identify vulnerabilities and perform penetration testing. The difference between white-hat hackers and black-hat hackers is that white-hat hackers will identify weaknesses for the purpose of fixing them, and black-hat hackers find weaknesses just for the fun of it or to exploit them.
- **Gray-hat hackers**—A **gray-hat hacker** is a hacker with average abilities who may one day become a black-hat hacker but could also opt to become a white-hat hacker. Another common definition is a hacker who will identify but not exploit discovered vulnerabilities, yet may still expect a reward for not disclosing the vulnerability openly. There is no common definition for this type of hacker.

Hackers are different from crackers. A **cracker** has a hostile intent, possesses sophisticated skills, and may be interested in financial gain. Crackers represent the greatest threat to networks and information resources. These threats usually involve fraud, theft of data, destruction of data, blockage of access, and other malicious activity. However, the activities of hackers can also cause damage and loss.

Attack Tools

Protecting an organization's assets and IT infrastructure requires that you have some idea of how attackers think. Knowing how an attack is conducted and what tools are used will help you build a defense plan. In fact, many organizations use the same tools that attackers use to help identify weaknesses they need to address. It is always better to find weaknesses in your own environment before an attacker does, but it is even more important to quickly remediate that weakness.

Computer criminals and cyberattackers use a number of hardware and software tools to discover exploitable weaknesses and other tools to perform the actual attack. These tools and techniques can include the following:

- Protocol analyzers
- Port scanners

- OS fingerprint scanners
- Vulnerability scanners
- Exploit software
- Wardialers
- Password crackers
- Keystroke loggers

Protocol Analyzers

A **protocol analyzer** or **packet sniffer** (or just **sniffer**) is a software program that enables a computer to monitor and capture network traffic, whether on a LAN or a wireless network. Attackers can capture and compromise passwords and cleartext data. Protocol analyzers come in both hardware versions and software versions, or a combination of both. Sniffers operate in **promiscuous mode**, which means that every data packet can be seen and captured by the sniffer. Sniffers decode the frame and IP data packet, allowing you to see data in cleartext if it has not been encrypted.

Port Scanners

A **port scanner** is a tool used to scan IP host devices for open ports that have been enabled. Think of a port number as a channel commonly associated with a service. For example, Port 80 is for HTTP web traffic, Port 21 is File Transfer Protocol (FTP), and Port 23 is Telnet, and so on. Request for Comments (RFC) 1700, now superseded by RFC 3232, lists the most common TCP/UDP port numbers and services. (For a complete list of port numbers, refer to the Internet Assigned Numbers Authority [IANA].) Port scanners are used to identify open ports or applications and services that are enabled on the IP host device. This provides attackers with valuable information that can be used in the attack.

OS Fingerprint Scanners

An **operating system (OS) fingerprint scanner** is a software program that allows an attacker to send a variety of packets to an IP host device, hoping to determine the target device's operating system (OS) from the responses. Whereas network protocols are generally standard, different operating system vendors are free to implement them as they see fit. The packets sent from the OS fingerprint scanner will recognize differences from the various operating systems used in workstations, servers, and network devices. When an IP host device responds, then the OS fingerprint scanner can guess what operating system is installed on the device. Once an attacker knows what OS and version is installed, the better chance he has to use applicable software vulnerabilities and exploits. A software *vulnerability* is a bug or weakness in the program. An *exploit* is something that an attacker can do once a vulnerability is found.

Vulnerability Scanners

A **vulnerability scanner** is a software program that is used to identify and, when possible, verify vulnerabilities on an IP host device. From this information, a vulnerability scanner compares known software vulnerabilities in its database with what it has just found. The vulnerability scanner lists all known software vulnerabilities and prioritizes them as critical, major, or minor.

For a complete and up-to-date list of known software vulnerabilities and exposures, visit https://cve.mitre.org. The Common Vulnerabilities & Exposure (CVE) list is maintained and managed by the Mitre Corporation on behalf of the U.S. Department of Homeland Security. This list is now referred to as the **National Vulnerability Database (NVD)**.

> **NOTE**
>
> The NVD (https://nvd.nist.gov) is the U.S. government repository of standards based vulnerability management data represented using the Security Content Automation Protocol (SCAP). This data enables automation of vulnerability management, security measurement, and compliance. The NVD includes databases of security checklists, security-related software flaws, misconfigurations, product names, and impact metrics.

Exploit Software

Exploit software is an application that incorporates known software vulnerabilities, data, and scripted commands to "exploit" a weakness in a computer system or IP host device. It is a program that can be used to carry out some form of malicious intent. This includes things like a denial of service attack, unauthorized access, a brute-force password attack, or buffer overflow. Remember, software vulnerabilities create a weakness in the system such as a software bug, glitch, or backdoor vulnerability.

An attacker will use exploit software when performing vulnerability assessments and **intrusive penetration testing**. Vulnerability assessments might identify a weakness; penetration testing positively verifies the weakness by working to exploit it. Therefore, intrusive testing generates malicious network traffic. Penetration testing is what a black-hat or white-hat hacker performs to penetrate a computer system or IP host device. This can lead to gaining system access as well as access to data, which are the prize that most black-hat hackers are seeking. A white-hat hacker, given permission, performs penetration testing to confirm that a discovered vulnerability is legitimate, resulting in critical risk exposure. White-hat hackers then recommend ways to mitigate the risk exposure as part of the post-mortem penetration testing report.

Wardialers

A **wardialer** is a computer program that dials telephone numbers, looking for a computer on the other end. The program works by automatically dialing a defined range of phone numbers. It then logs and enters into a database those numbers that successfully connect to the modem. Wardialers are becoming more archaic and less often used due to the rise of digital telephony, IP telephony, or Voice over IP (VoIP). Prior to VoIP, attackers would use wardialers to gain access to private branch exchange (PBX) phone systems in an attempt to obtain dial tone or international dialing capability to commit toll fraud. In addition, an attacker would use a wardialer to identify analog modem signals and gain access to the remote system within an IT infrastructure.

Some wardialers can also identify the operating system running on a computer, as well as conduct automated penetration testing. In such cases, the wardialer runs through a predetermined list of common usernames and passwords in an attempt to gain access to the system.

A network intruder can use a wardialer to identify potential targets. If the program does not provide automated penetration testing, the intruder can attempt to hack a modem with unprotected logons or easily cracked passwords. A network system administrator can use a commercial wardialer to identify unauthorized modems on an enterprise network. These unauthorized modems can provide attackers with easy access to an organization's internal network and must be controlled or eliminated.

Although wardialing is a rather old attack method, it is still useful for finding access points to computers. Many computer networks and voice systems have modems attached to phone lines. These modems are often attached either for direct access for support purposes or by people attempting to bypass network-access restrictions. Even today's Internet-connected environments may have a few modems out there, ready to answer another computer that calls. Successfully connecting to a computer using a modem provides a possible access point to the rest of the organization's network.

Password Crackers

The purpose of password cracking is to uncover a forgotten or unknown password. A **password cracker** is a software program that performs one of two functions: a **brute-force password attack** to gain unauthorized access to a system or recovery of passwords stored as a cryptographic hash on a computer system. A **cryptographic hash** is an algorithm that converts a large amount of data to a single (long) number. Once mathematically hashed, the hash value can be used to verify the integrity of those data. In a brute-force password cracking attempt, an attacker tries every possible character combination until the "cracked" password succeeds in granting acccess. Dictionary attacks are a subset of brute-force attacks. In a **dictionary password attack**, hackers try shorter and simpler combinations, including actual words (hence the name of the attack), because such passwords are so common.

Keystroke Loggers

A **keystroke logger** is a type of surveillance software or hardware that can record to a log file every keystroke a user makes with a keyboard. The keystroke logger might store the log file locally for later retrieval or send it to a specified receiver. Employers might use keystroke loggers to ensure that employees use work computers for business purposes only. However, spyware can also include keystroke logger software, hoping to transmit information such as a password to an unknown third party. (You'll learn about spyware later in this chapter.) As a piece of hardware, a keystroke logger is typically a battery-sized plug that serves as a connector between the user's keyboard and computer. Because the device resembles an ordinary keyboard plug, it is relatively easy for someone who wants to monitor a user's behavior to hide such a device in plain sight. Besides, workstation keyboards usually plug into the back of the computer, which makes the keystroke logger even harder to detect. As the user types on the keyboard, the keystroke logger collects each keystroke and saves it as text in its own miniature hard drive. Later, the person who installed the keystroke logger must return and physically remove the device in order to access the information the device has gathered.

A keystroke logger software program is usually disguised as a Trojan malicious software program. This malicious software can be delivered by a URL link, PDF file, or ZIP file. As long as an attacker has network access to a computer, he or she can transfer any file, including executable files, to the target computer. Many attackers then use social engineering to trick users into launching the downloaded programs. Users can also unwittingly download keystroke loggers as spyware, which an attacker can then execute as part of a rootkit. (You'll learn more about rootkits later in this chapter.) The keystroke logger program records each keystroke the user types and periodically uploads the information over the Internet to whomever installed the program.

What Is a Security Breach?

In spite of the most aggressive steps to protect computers from attacks, attackers sometimes get through. Any event that results in a violation of any of the confidentiality, integrity, or availability (CIA) security tenets is a **security breach**. Some security breaches disrupt system services on purpose. Others are accidental and may result from hardware or software failures. Regardless of whether a security breach is accidental or malicious, it can affect an organization's ability to conduct business as well as affecting the organization's credibility.

Activities that can cause a security breach include the following:

- Denial of service (DoS) attacks
- Distributed denial of service (DDoS) attacks
- Unacceptable web-browsing behavior
- Wiretapping
- Use of a backdoor to access resources
- Accidental data modifications

Denial of Service Attacks

Denial of service (DoS) attacks result in downtime or inability of a user to access a system. DoS attacks impact the availability tenet of information systems security. A DoS attack is a coordinated attempt to deny service by occupying a computer to perform large amounts of unnecessary tasks. This excessive activity makes the system unavailable to perform legitimate operations. When a disk fills up, the system locks an account out, a computer crashes, or a CPU slows down, the result is denial of service—hence the name. DoS attacks generally originate from a single computer. Once you detect a DoS attack, you can stop it easily.

Two common types of DoS attacks are as follows:

- **Logic attacks**—Logic attacks use software flaws to crash or seriously hinder the performance of remote servers. You can prevent many of these attacks by installing the latest patches to keep your software up to date.
- **Flooding attacks**—Flooding attacks overwhelm the victim computer's CPU, memory, or network resources by sending large numbers of useless requests to the machine.

One of the best defenses against DoS attacks is to use intrusion prevention system (IPS) software or devices to detect and stop the attack. Intrusion detection system (IDS) software and devices can also detect DoS attacks and alert you when such attacks are in progress. Without a defense against DoS attacks, they can quickly overwhelm servers, desktops, and network hardware, slowing computing in your organization to a grinding halt. In some cases, these attacks can cripple an entire infrastructure.

Most DoS attacks target weaknesses in the overall system architecture rather than a software bug or security flaw. Attackers can launch DoS attacks using common Internet protocols such as TCP and Internet Control Message Protocol (ICMP). A DoS attack launched through one of these protocols can bring down one or more network servers or devices by flooding it with useless packets and providing false information about the status of network services. This is known as a *packet flood.*

One popular technique for launching a packet flood is a **SYN flood**. SYN is a TCP control bit used to initialize TCP/IP communication with another device. Normally, to establish communication, the host receiving the SYN bit immediately responds (with both the SYN and ACK bits) and awaits a confirmation. In a SYN flood, the attacker sends a large number of packets requesting connections to the victim computer; however, the ACK bit is never received. The victim computer records each request and reserves a place for the connection in a local table in memory. The victim computer then sends a confirmation back to the attacker, but the attacker never acknowledges the confirmation. All these reserved bits of memory are small, but as they accrue, the amount eventually fills the victim's connections table to capacity until it runs out of memory for other operations. In the meantime, no legitimate users can connect to the victim computer, because the SYN flood has filled the connection table. The victim computer will remain unavailable until the connection requests time out.

Another popular technique is **smurfing**. The smurf attack uses a directed broadcast to create a flood of network traffic for the victim computer.

Both internal attackers and external attackers can launch DoS attacks. However, most attacks come from anonymous outsiders. Network intrusion detection (IDS/IPS) is usually effective at detecting these attacks.

> **NOTE**
>
> RFC 2827 is a useful source of information for the security administrator. It provides a method for using ingress traffic filtering to prohibit DoS attacks, which often use forged IP addresses.

Security personnel routinely take aggressive steps to ensure that attackers cannot use their systems for malicious purposes. In addition, some web content providers and network device manufacturers now include new rules designed to prevent DoS attacks in their default configuration tables. Preventing attackers from gaining access to your computers is a full-time effort, but it's one that is worth the expense.

Distributed Denial of Service Attacks

The **distributed denial of service (DDoS)** attack is a type of DoS attack that also impacts a user's ability to access a system. A DDoS attack overloads computers and prevents legitimate users from gaining access. DDoS attacks differ from regular DoS attacks in their scope. In a DDoS attack, attackers hijack hundreds or even thousands of Internet computers, planting automated attack agents on those systems. The attacker then instructs the agents to bombard the target site with forged messages. This overloads the site and blocks legitimate traffic. The key here is strength in numbers. The attacker does more damage by distributing the attack across multiple computers.

Larger companies and universities tend to be attractive targets for attackers launching DDoS attacks. Researchers have estimated that attackers issue thousands of DDoS attacks against networks each week. This threat is so serious that preventing such attacks is a top priority in many organizations, including security product vendors. DDoS attacks are more difficult to stop than DoS attacks because they originate from different sources. Protecting computers from DDoS attacks requires several layers of security. Both DoS and DDoS attacks come in many forms and different levels of severity and can cost millions of dollars in lost revenue.

Unacceptable Web Browsing

A violation of an organization's acceptable use policy (AUP), such as an employee's unacceptable web browsing, can itself be a security breach. Organizations should have an AUP that clearly states what behavior is acceptable and what is not. Unacceptable use can include unauthorized users searching files or storage directories for data and information they are not supposed to read, or users simply visiting prohibited websites. The AUP defines the actions that are security breaches.

Wiretapping

Attackers can tap telephone lines and data communication lines. **Wiretapping** can be *active*, where the attacker makes modifications to the line. It can also be *passive*, where an unauthorized user simply listens to the transmission without changing the contents. Passive intrusion can include the copying of data for a subsequent active attack.

Two methods of active wiretapping are as follows:

- **Between-the-lines wiretapping**—This type of wiretapping does not alter the messages sent by the legitimate user but inserts additional messages into the communication line when the legitimate user pauses.
- **Piggyback-entry wiretapping**—This type of wiretapping intercepts and modifies the original message by breaking the communications line and routing the message to another computer that acts as a host.

Although the term *wiretapping* is generally associated with voice telephone communications, attackers can also use wiretapping to intercept data communications. When referring to the interception of data communications, however, the more commonly used term is *sniffing* (although sniffing extends beyond simple wiretapping to include intercepting wireless transmissions).

Backdoors

Software developers sometimes include hidden access methods, called **backdoors**, in their programs. Backdoors give developers or support personnel easy access to a system without having to struggle with security controls. The problem is that backdoors don't always stay hidden. When an attacker discovers a backdoor, he or she can use it to bypass existing security controls such as passwords, encryption, and so on. Where legitimate users log on through front doors using a user ID and password, attackers use backdoors to bypass these normal access controls.

Attackers can also compromise a system by installing their own backdoor program on it. Attackers can use this type of backdoor to bypass controls that the administrator has put in place to protect the computer system. The **netcat** utility is one of the most popular backdoor tools in use today.

Rootkits are malicious software programs designed to be hidden from normal methods of detection. They allow an attacker to gain access to a computer system. Rootkits are installed by attackers once they obtain root or system administrator access privileges. Rootkits commonly include backdoors. Traditional rootkits replace critical programs to give attackers backdoor access and enable them to hide on the host system. Because they replace system software components, rootkits can be more powerful than application-level Trojan horse backdoors. You'll learn more about rootkits later in this chapter.

> **🛈 NOTE**
>
> Almost every network vendor ships devices with a default username and password, which you must change when setting up the device. Your failure to change these default usernames and passwords when new equipment is deployed will result in a known backdoor in your system—a serious vulnerability!

Data Modifications

Data that are purposely or accidentally modified impact the integrity tenet of information systems security. This is also considered a security breach. An incomplete modification can occur when multiple processes attempt to update data without observing basic data integrity constraints. Another example is truncating data because the record field is not large enough to hold the complete data. This can occur with most programming languages and can be difficult to detect. However, the results can be significant. The best way to avoid data modification issues is to validate data before storing that data and to ensure that your programs adhere to strict data integrity rules.

Additional Security Challenges

Additional challenges to ensuring safe and secure communications can originate from spam, hoaxes, spyware, and even local information stored by web browsers. A combination of these challenges is also possible.

Spam and Spim

Spam is unwanted email. **Spim** consists of instant messages or IM chats. Most spam and spim are commercial advertising—often for get-rich-quick schemes, dubious products, or other services. Sending spam costs very little because the recipient covers most of the costs associated with spam. It costs money for ISPs and online services to transmit spam. Processing large volumes of unwanted messages is expensive. ISPs transfer these costs directly to subscribers. In addition, spamming forces the receiving user to waste administrative time on cleanup and monitoring of their received messages.

Email spam and IM chat spim target individual users with direct-mail messages or IM chat accounts. Often spammers and spimmers send messages to members of mailing lists associated with public or private email discussion forums or IM chat forums. Another popular technique for spammers is to use software to construct email addresses from common usernames and domain names and to send messages to those addresses. For example, a spam program might send an email message to the address aaron@yahoo.com as well as to all other addresses in the yahoo.com domain containing names that start with the letter *A*. Spim follows the same approach but uses instant messages instead of email.

A favorite technique of spammers is to send messages containing an "unsubscribe" link to a set of email addresses. The idea is to use the link to determine whether an email address is valid. That is, instead of unsubscribing users who click the link, spammers simply determine that the email address is valid and therefore an even more attractive target. On a similar note, spam-generating software often includes lists of email addresses. The software makers often assert that these are addresses for people who have "opted in," but in fact they are typically random addresses from newsgroups or mailing lists. Although spammers often claim to remove addresses from their rolls on request, they almost never do.

Spam is no longer merely a nuisance. The ability to block it is critical for IT security. Recently, spam has become a way for criminals to solicit individual and company information and to plant

> **NOTE**
>
> If you suspect that a message you received is a hoax, you can visit a website called Snopes (*www.snopes.com*) to research it. Often you will find an entry in Snopes that matches the message you received. Snopes isn't the final word on every hoax, but it can provide you with a convenient way to start your research.

Trojan horses and other malware onto user computers. In addition, possession of some kinds of spam—for example, spam related to child porn—is illegal.

To fight cybercrime, organizations must tackle spam. A **phishing** email is a fake or bogus email to trick the recipient into clicking on an embedded URL link or opening an email attachment. As described in the previous section, malicious software, Trojans, or keystroke loggers can be embedded in a phishing email. A user who receives this email may unknowingly enable malicious software by clicking on a URL link or opening an email attachment. Antivirus, anti-spyware, and anti-malicious-software applications are needed to combat this type of incident.

Hoaxes

A **hoax** is some act intended to deceive or trick the receiver. In this context, hoaxes normally travel in email messages. Often these messages contain warnings about devastating new viruses. Although hoaxes do not automatically infect systems the way viruses or Trojan horses do, dealing with them is time consuming. In fact, you may wind up spending much more time disproving hoaxes than handling real virus and Trojan horse incidents.

The best way to handle hoaxes is to ask users not to spread them by forwarding them to others. Forwarding a cute message to one or two friends is not a problem. However, sending an unconfirmed warning or plea to everyone in your address book and asking all those recipients to forward it to everyone in *their* address books, just adds to the clutter that already fills everyone's inboxes. Recipients of this kind of email should not pass it to everyone they know.

Cookies

To help a web server track a user's history, web browsers allow the web server to store a cookie on the user's hard drive. A **cookie** is simply a text file that contains details gleaned from past visits to a website. Cookies have value, since HTTP is a stateless protocol (one that can't retain data from one visit to the next), so a data file cookie is used to keep a small record of the last visit. These details might include the user's username, credit card information the user has entered, and so on. Later, when the user sends a request to the web server, the server can access the cookie instead of requiring that the user reenter the information.

Cookies are sometimes controversial because they allow a web server to transmit files to a person's computer for storage on that person's hard drive. Because cookies are text files, though, they generally cannot cause immediate harm. Cookies do not directly perform malicious acts. Cookies cannot spread viruses, nor can they access additional information on the user's hard drive. This does not mean that cookies do not pose a security issue, however. Although cookies cannot gather information from a user's hard drive, as mentioned, they sometimes do store information that is sensitive, such as credit card details.

The problem with cookies is that they store information in cleartext files. That means anyone with access to your computer can potentially read the contents of your cookies. Although a cookie might offer some level of convenience, such as remembering what flight you were researching earlier, it can easily compromise your privacy as well. Although websites developed in a secure manner would never store information like credit card numbers in a cookie, some sites are sloppy. You never really know what information is stored in the cookies on your computer. The best way to avoid having personal information stored in cookies is to restrict the cookies you allow to websites you trust.

As you visit more and more websites, you will likely find more and more cookies on your computer. In fact, users may well end up with hundreds of cookies on their computers, which can become a nuisance. Fortunately, you can delete these cookies at any time. In addition, you can prevent your web browser from allowing cookies in the first place. Check your browser's help information for instructions.

What Are Risks, Threats, and Vulnerabilities?

Risks, threats, and vulnerabilities go together. *Risk* is the probability that something bad is going to happen. A *threat* is any action that can damage or compromise an asset. A *vulnerability* is a weakness in the design or software code itself. A vulnerability that can be exploited is a threat.

If a vulnerability exists in a system, so does the possibility of a threat. Any threat against a vulnerability creates a risk that a negative event may occur. You can't eliminate threats, but you can protect against vulnerabilities. That way, even though a threat still exists, it cannot exploit the vulnerability. The key to protecting assets from the risk of attack is to eliminate or address as many vulnerabilities as possible.

You can find many threats and vulnerabilities within an IT infrastructure. **TABLE 3-2** lists some of the common ones found within each of the seven domains of an IT infrastructure.

TABLE 3-2 Common threats and vulnerabilities in the seven domains of an IT infrastructure.

DOMAIN	COMMON THREATS AND VULNERABILITIES
User domain	Lack of awareness or concern for security Accidental acceptable use policy violation Intentional malicious activity Social engineering
Workstation domain	Unauthorized user access Malicious software introduced Weaknesses in installed software
LAN domain	Unauthorized network access Transmitting private data unencrypted Spreading malicious software
LAN-to-WAN domain	Exposure and unauthorized access to internal resources from the outside Introduction of malicious software Loss of productivity due to lack of Internet access
WAN domain	Transmitting private data unencrypted Malicious attacks from anonymous sources Denial of service attacks Weaknesses in software
Remote Access domain	Brute-force password attacks on access and private data Unauthorized remote access to resources Data leakage from remote access or lost storage devices
System/Application domain	Unauthorized physical or logical access to resources Weaknesses in server operating system or application software Data loss from errors, failures, or disasters

> **FYI**
>
> Identifying and responding to threats and vulnerabilities can be a complicated process. In some cases, a threat may be too expensive or time-consuming to eliminate. Your goal should be to reduce the occurrence of as many threats as possible, but you should also carefully assess whether the cost of protecting some assets is greater than the value of the assets themselves. You do not want to spend more time and money identifying and responding to threats than the assets are actually worth.

Threats can come from an individual, a group of individuals, or an organization. A threat to a computing device is any action, either accidental or malicious, that can have a negative effect on the assets and resources of an individual or organization. The asset might be hardware, software, databases, files, data, or the physical network itself.

A threat is significant from a security viewpoint. The goal of computer security is to provide insights, methodologies, and techniques that deal with threats. You can achieve this goal by developing policies that help computer and network system administrators, designers, developers, and users avoid undesirable system characteristics and weaknesses.

You can identify threats and rank them according to their importance and impact. You can rank threats by their potential for dollar loss, negative reputation created, monetary liability, or how often they are likely to occur. Each organization may rank a threat higher or lower than another organization does based on its impact to that organization.

The most common threats, in no particular order, include the following:

- Malicious software
- Hardware or software failure
- Internal attacker
- Equipment theft
- External attacker
- Natural disaster
- Industrial espionage
- Terrorism

Not all threats are malicious. Although some threats may be intentional, others may be accidental. Accidental threats might include hardware failure or a software problem caused by a lack of controls. The results of accidental threats can be just as damaging as malicious threats, however. You must make every effort to minimize all security breaches, whether they are malicious or accidental. The overall goal is to protect the network and computer system from any attack and to prevent the theft, destruction, and corruption of individual or organizational assets.

Threat Targets

Using his or her favorite search engine, an attacker can find precise instructions for breaching nearly any protocol, operating system, application, device, or hardware environment. For this reason, you must monitor all threats very closely. You never know where one might come from next. It may be a professional cybercriminal or someone within your own four walls. The safest bet is to monitor all threat targets constantly and carefully.

The first step in developing a monitoring plan is to identify where in the seven domains of an IT infrastructure threats are likely to occur. **TABLE 3-3** lists many common threat targets and where they are found in an IT infrastructure.

From this list, it should be clear that there are many opportunities for an attacker to cause big problems. You should also notice that many of the threat targets appear in different categories. The need for a comprehensive security plan across all domains should be clear.

Threat Types

To secure information, you must protect its confidentiality, integrity, and availability (CIA). The three major threat types directly threaten each of the CIA tenets. They are as follows:

* Disclosure threats
* Alteration threats
* Denial or destruction threats

Disclosure Threats

Disclosure occurs any time unauthorized users access private or confidential information that is stored on a network resource or while it is in transit between network resources. Disclosure can also occur when a computer or device containing private or confidential data, such as a

TABLE 3-3 Threat targets in the seven domains of an IT infrastructure.

DOMAIN	THREAT TARGET
User domain	Employees' own human traits and behavior. Violations of the acceptable use policy are targeted.
Workstation domain	Workstations, laptops, and mobile devices are the target, along with their vulnerabilities. This domain is the point of entry into the IT infrastructure.
LAN domain	Windows Active Directory/Domain Controllers, file servers, print servers. In addition, the IP data network is part of the LAN domain and is a target for ID and authentication attacks.
LAN-to-WAN domain	DMZ VLANs or dedicated remote connections are typically terminated here. Public-facing IP devices, including perimeter security with firewalls, IDS/IPS, and remote VPN terminations, reside here.
WAN domain	IP routers, TCP/IP stacks and buffers, firewalls, gateways, switches, and WAN service providers are targeted.
Remote Access domain	Virtual private networks (VPNs), two-factor authentication, and remote access for mobile workers and teleworkers are typically supported and targeted.
System/Application domain	Web and application servers, operating systems, and applications. Back-end database servers and database tables with sensitive data are the target.

database of medical records, is lost or stolen. Two techniques that attackers employ to illegally obtain or modify data are as follows:

- **Sabotage**—Sabotage is the destruction of property or obstruction of normal operations. Technically, sabotage attacks the availability property of information security.
- **Espionage**—Espionage is the act of spying to obtain secret information, typically to aid another nation state. Terrorists and enemy agents might well be involved in activities to obtain sensitive government information that they can use to perpetuate future attacks.

 NOTE

An *information leak* is any instance of someone who purposely distributes information without proper authorization.

Sabotage is not a silent attack, but espionage can occur without any obvious trace.

In many organizations, a great deal of stored information is unavailable to the public. This information can include personal information on a user's computer or confidential records stored in a massive database. The effects of the disclosure of this information can vary. For example, where the disclosure of a user's personal information could cause embarrassment, public disclosure of a citizen's private records could result in severe repercussions. In addition, disclosing information could cause even more problems if government secrets or intelligence files are involved.

Information security personnel devote much time and effort to combating disclosure threats. In particular, the U.S. government focuses very closely on disclosure threats because of their potential to cause problems for critical security areas. One of the most difficult things about combating these types of threats, however, is that unauthorized users can intercept unprotected data without leaving any trace of their activities. For this reason, security research and development have focused on the disclosure threat and its countermeasures.

Alteration Threats

An alteration threat violates information integrity. This type of attack compromises a system by making unauthorized changes to data on a system, either intentionally or unintentionally. This change might occur while the data are stored on a network resource or while they are moving between two resources. Intentional changes are usually malicious. Unintentional changes are usually accidental. People can, and often do, make mistakes that affect the integrity of computer and network resources. Even so, unintentional changes still create security problems.

Modifications to the system configuration can also compromise the integrity of a network resource. Such a modification can occur when an unauthorized party tampers with an asset or when an authorized user makes a change that has unintended effects. For example, a user might modify database files, operating systems, application software, and even hardware devices. Modifications might include creating, changing, deleting, and writing information to a network resource. It's a good idea to put techniques in place that enable you to track or audit these changes as they happen. That way, you can have a record of who, what, when, where, and how modifications were made. In addition, change management systems limit who can make changes, how they make changes, and how they document changes. It is very important that only authorized parties change assets, and only in authorized ways.

Is It Really a DoS Threat?

Poor response time is not always due to a DoS attack. It might be because of oversubscription of network facilities. *Oversubscription* just means that more computers or processes are using a network than the intended network load. In other words, users are overusing the network. Network vendors use this technique to increase revenue at the user's expense. Alternatively, the provider may be causing a user's inability to reach some network resource. For example, the provider may have taken key resources offline to perform a system update or website modifications. Yet another culprit might be *throttling*, a technique some administrators use to reduce network traffic. On the other hand, the problem could be simple user error.

Advance preparation can reduce the severity of alteration threats. For example, if you have a backup or copy of the data, then the impact of a breach may be less severe than if a backup is not available. However, data recovery should always be the last resort. A far better approach is to avoid an alteration attack in the first place. Protecting your information is always better than repairing or recovering it.

Denial or Destruction Threats

Denial or destruction threats make assets or resources unavailable or unusable. Any threat that destroys information or makes it unavailable violates the availability tenet of information security. A denial or destruction attack is successful when it prevents an authorized user from accessing a resource either temporarily or permanently.

A DoS attack is an example of a denial or destruction threat. As you learned earlier in this chapter, a DoS attack, which is usually malicious, prevents authorized users from accessing computer and network resources. Many organizations are potential victims of DoS attacks. In fact, any computer connected to the Internet is a DoS threat candidate. This type of attack can represent a minor problem or a great danger, depending on the importance of the blocked asset or resource. For example, suppose an attacker floods a specific port on a server. If the port is not for a critical resource, the impact may be minimal. However, if the port supports authorized user access to your company's website, it could prevent customers from accessing it for minutes or hours. In that case, the impact could be severe.

> ⚠️ **WARNING**
>
> Even if a DoS attack floods a noncritical port, the excess traffic could cause the server to crash or become so slow it cannot service legitimate requests in a timely manner. In this case, the DoS attack is still successful.

What Is a Malicious Attack?

An **attack** on a computer system or network asset succeeds by exploiting a vulnerability in the system. There are four general categories of attack. An attack can consist of all or a combination of these four categories:

- **Fabrications**—Fabrications involve the creation of some deception in order to trick unsuspecting users.
- **Interceptions**—An interception involves eavesdropping on transmissions and redirecting them for unauthorized use.

- **Interruptions**—An interruption causes a break in a communication channel, which blocks the transmission of data.
- **Modifications**—A modification is the alteration of data contained in transmissions or files.

As you learned earlier, security threats can be active or passive. Both types can have negative repercussions for an IT infrastructure. An active attack involves a modification of the data stream or attempts to gain unauthorized access to computer and networking systems. An active attack is a physical intrusion. In a passive attack, the attacker does not make changes to the system. This type of attack simply eavesdrops on and monitors transmissions.

Active threats include the following:

- Birthday attacks
- Brute-force password attacks
- Dictionary password attacks
- IP address spoofing
- Hijacking
- Replay attacks
- Man-in-the-middle attacks
- Masquerading
- Social engineering
- Phishing
- Phreaking
- Pharming

Such attacks are widespread and common. A growing number of them appear on information systems security professionals' radar screens every year. Following is a description of several of the most common types of malicious attacks.

Birthday Attacks

Once an attacker compromises a hashed password file, a **birthday attack** is performed. A birthday attack is a type of cryptographic attack that is used to make brute-force attack of one-way hashes easier. It is a mathematical exploit that is based on the birthday problem in probability theory.

Brute-Force Password Attacks

One of the most tried-and-true attack methods is the brute-force password attack. In a brute-force password attack, the attacker tries different passwords on a system until one of them is successful. Usually the attacker employs a software program to try all possible combinations of a likely password, user ID, or security code until it locates a match. This occurs rapidly and in sequence. This type of attack is called a *brute-force password attack* because the attacker simply hammers away at the code. There is no skill or stealth involved—just brute force that eventually breaks the code.

With today's large-scale computers, it is possible to try millions of combinations of passwords in a short period. Given enough time and using enough computers, it is possible to crack most algorithms.

Dictionary Password Attacks

A *dictionary password attack* is a simple attack that relies on users making poor password choices. In a dictionary password attack, a simple password-cracker program takes all the words from a dictionary file and attempts to log on by entering each dictionary entry as a password.

Users often engage in the poor practice of selecting common words as passwords. A password policy that enforces complex passwords is the best defense against a dictionary password attack. Users should create passwords composed of a combination of letters and numbers, and the passwords should not include any personal information about the user.

IP Address Spoofing

Spoofing is a type of attack in which one person, program, or computer disguises itself as another person, program, or computer to gain access to some resource. A common spoofing attack involves presenting a false network address to pretend to be a different computer. An attacker may change a computer's network address to appear as an authorized computer in the target's network. If the administrator of the target's local router has not configured it to filter out external traffic with internal addresses, the attack may be successful. IP address spoofing can enable an attacker to access protected internal resources.

Address resolution protocol (ARP) poisoning is an example of a spoofing attack. In this attack, the attacker spoofs the MAC address of a targeted device, such as a server, by sending false ARP resolution responses with a different MAC address. This causes duplicate network traffic to be sent from the server. Another type of network-based attack is the **Christmas (Xmas) attack**. This type of attack sends advanced TCP packets with flags set to confuse IP routers and network border routers with TCP header bits set to 1, thus lighting up the IP router like a Christmas tree.

> **NOTE**
>
> A CERT advisory on IP spoofing reports that the CERT Coordination Center has received reports of attacks in which intruders create packets with spoofed source IP addresses. This exploit leads to user impersonation and escalated privilege access on the target system. This means that the intruder can take over logon connections and create havoc.

Hijacking

Hijacking is a type of attack in which the attacker takes control of a session between two machines and masquerades as one of them. There are a few types of hijacking:

- **Man-in-the-middle hijacking**—In this type of hijacking, discussed in more detail in a moment, the attacker uses a program to take control of a connection by masquerading as each end of the connection. For example, if Mary and Fred want to communicate, the attacker pretends to be Mary when talking with Fred and pretends to be Fred when talking to Mary. Neither Mary nor Fred know they are talking to the attacker. The attacker can collect substantial information and can even alter data as they flow between Mary and Fred. This attack enables the attacker to either gain access to the messages or modify them before retransmitting. A man-in-the-middle attack can occur from an insider threat. An insider threat can occur from an employee, contractor, or trusted person within the organization.
- **Browser or URL hijacking**—In a browser or **URL hijacking** attack, the user is directed to a different website than what he or she requested, usually to a fake page that the attacker

FYI

Session hijacking reveals the importance of identifying the other party in a session. It is possible for an intruder to replace a legitimate user for the remainder of a communication session. This calls for a scheme to authenticate the data's source throughout the transmission. In fact, authenticating both ends of a connection, a process called *mutual authentication*, could reduce the potential of an undetected hijack. However, even the strongest authentication methods are not always successful in preventing hijacking attacks. That means you might need to encrypt all transmissions.

has created. This gives the user the impression that the attacker has compromised the website when in fact the attacker simply diverted the user's browser from the actual site. This type of attack is also known as **typo squatting**. Attackers can use this attack with phishing to trick a user into providing private information such as a password. (You'll learn about phishing in a moment.)

- **Session hijacking**—In **session hijacking**, the attacker attempts to take over an existing connection between two network computers. The first step in this attack is for the attacker to take control of a network device on the LAN, such as a firewall or another computer, in order to monitor the connection. This enables the attacker to determine the sequence numbers used by the sender and receiver. After determining the sequence numbering, the attacker generates traffic that appears to come from one of the communicating parties. This steals the session from one of the legitimate users. To get rid of the legitimate user who initiated the hijacked session, the attacker overloads one of the communicating devices with excess packets so that it drops out of the session.

Replay Attacks

Replay attacks involve capturing data packets from a network and retransmitting them to produce an unauthorized effect. The receipt of duplicate, authenticated IP packets may disrupt service or have some other undesired consequence. Systems can be broken through replay attacks when attackers reuse old messages or parts of old messages to deceive system users. This helps intruders to gain information that allows unauthorized access into a system.

Man-in-the-Middle Attacks

A **man-in-the-middle attack** takes advantage of the multihop process used by many types of networks. In this type of attack, an attacker intercepts messages between two parties before transferring them on to their intended destination.

Web spoofing is a type of man-in-the-middle attack in which the user believes a secure session exists with a particular web server. In reality, the secure connection exists only with the attacker, not the web server. The attacker then establishes a secure connection with the web server, acting as an invisible go-between. The attacker passes traffic between the user and the web server. In this way, the attacker can trick the user into supplying passwords, credit card information, and other private data.

Attackers use man-in-the-middle attacks to steal information, to execute DoS attacks, to corrupt transmitted data, to gain access to an organization's internal computer and network resources, and to introduce new information into network sessions.

Masquerading

In a **masquerade attack**, one user or computer pretends to be another user or computer. Masquerade attacks usually include one of the other forms of active attacks, such as IP address spoofing or replaying. Attackers can capture authentication sequences and then replay them later to log on again to an application or operating system. For example, an attacker might monitor usernames and passwords sent to a weak web application. The attacker could then use the intercepted credentials to log on to the web application and impersonate the user.

Eavesdropping

Eavesdropping, or sniffing, occurs when a host sets its network interface on promiscuous mode and copies packets that pass by for later analysis. Promiscuous mode enables a network device to intercept and read each network packet, even if the packet's address doesn't match the network device. It is possible to attach hardware and software to monitor and analyze all packets on that segment of the transmission media without alerting any other users. Candidates for eavesdropping include satellite, wireless, mobile, and other transmission methods.

Social Engineering

Attackers often use a deception technique called **social engineering** to gain access to resources in an IT infrastructure. In nearly all cases, social engineering involves tricking authorized users into carrying out actions for unauthorized users. The success of social engineering attacks depends on the basic tendency of people to want to be helpful.

Social engineering places the human element in the security breach loop and uses it as a weapon. A forged or stolen vendor or employee ID could provide entry to a secure location. The intruder could then obtain access to important assets. By appealing to employees' natural instinct to help a technician or contractor, an attacker can easily breach the perimeter of an organization and gain access.

Personnel who serve as initial contacts within an organization, such as receptionists and administrative assistants, are often targets of social engineering attacks. Attackers with some knowledge of an organization's structure will often also target new, untrained employees as well as those who do not seem to understand security policies.

Eliminating social engineering attacks can be difficult, but here are some techniques to reduce their impact:

- Ensure that employees are educated on the basics of a secure environment.
- Develop a security policy and computer use policy.
- Enforce a strict policy for internal and external technical support procedures.

- Require the use of identification for all personnel.
- Limit the data accessible to the public by restricting the information published in directories, Yellow Pages, websites, and public databases.
- Be very careful when using remote access. Use strong validation so you know who is accessing your network.
- Teach personnel the techniques for sending and receiving secure email.
- Shred all documents that may contain confidential or sensitive information.

Phreaking

Phone phreaking, or simply **phreaking**, is a slang term that describes the activity of a subculture of people who study, experiment with, or explore telephone systems, telephone company equipment, and systems connected to public telephone networks. Phreaking is the art of exploiting bugs and glitches that exist in the telephone system.

Phishing

Fraud is a growing problem on the Internet. **Phishing** is a type of fraud in which an attacker attempts to trick the victim into providing private information such as credit card numbers, passwords, dates of birth, bank account numbers, automated teller machine (ATM) PINs, and Social Security numbers.

A phishing scam is an attempt to commit identity theft via email or instant message. The message appears to come from a legitimate source, such as a trusted business or financial institution, and includes an urgent request for personal information. Phishing messages usually indicate a critical need to update an account (banking, credit card, etc.) immediately. The message instructs the victim to either provide the requested information or click on a link provided in the message. Clicking the link leads the victim to a spoofed website. This website looks identical to the official site but in fact belongs to the scammer. Personal information entered into this web page goes directly to the scammer, not to the legitimate organization.

A variation of the phishing attack is spear phishing. **Spear phishing** uses email or instant messages to target a specific organization, seeking unauthorized access to confidential data. As with the messages used in regular phishing attempts, spear-phishing messages appear to come from a trusted source.

The best way to protect against phishing of any kind is to avoid clicking on a link directly provided by a suspect email. Supplying personal information when prompted to do so by an email or instant message is too easily done once the website is in front of you. If you believe the request might be legitimate, call the company's customer service department to verify the request before providing any information. If you do call the company, do not use any phone numbers contained in the suspect message. Even if the URL displayed in the

> **NOTE**
>
> Many social engineering activities occurring today have their basic roots in strategies developed by phreakers. In fact, several current social engineering attacks bear names that begin with the letters "ph" to pay homage to these social engineering pioneers.

> **NOTE**
>
> Anti-malware programs and firewalls cannot detect most phishing scams because they do not contain suspect code. Some spam filters even let phishing messages pass because they appear to come from legitimate sources.

How to Identify a Phishing Scam

It may be difficult to identify a phishing scam simply by looking at the web page that opens when you click a link in an email message. However, clues in the sender's address can sometimes reveal the deception. Look for the following:

- Phishers often substitute similar-looking characters for the real characters in a URL. For example, they might use a 1 (numeral one) in place of a lowercase *L*—think *paypa1.com* rather than *paypal.com*.
- Phishing scams have become so sophisticated that phishers can appear to use legitimate links, including the real site's security certificate. Before clicking a link, you should preview it to see where it will take you. If you notice that the domain name looks odd, do not click the link. Instead, contact the legitimate website's customer service or technical support group and ask whether the link is valid. This approach takes more time, but it is far safer than just clicking through links without checking them.
- Some phishers purchase domain names that are similar to those of legitimate companies—for example, *walmartorder.com*. The real company is Wal-Mart, but the company does not include *order* in its domain name.
- One ploy is to use the same domain name but with .org rather than .com. The con artists who use these domain names then send out millions of emails requesting that consumers verify account information, birth dates, Social Security numbers, and so on. Inevitably, some computer users will respond. Carefully examine the entire domain name!

message is legitimate, manually enter the web address in your browser rather than clicking on a link in the message.

The Anti-Phishing Working Group (APWG) is a global, pan-industrial law enforcement association focused on eliminating fraud and identity theft resulting from email spoofing of all types. For more information, visit the APWG website at *www.antiphishing.org*. In addition, the Federal Trade Commission (FTC) website (*www.ftc.gov*) offers advice for consumers and an email address for reporting phishing activity, plus a form to report identity theft.

Pharming

Pharming is another type of attack that seeks to obtain personal or private financial information through domain spoofing. A pharming attack doesn't use messages to trick victims into visiting spoofed websites that appear legitimate, however. Instead, pharming "poisons" a domain name on the domain name server (DNS), a process known as **DNS poisoning**. The result is that when a user enters the poisoned server's web address into his or her address bar, that user navigates to the attacker's site. The user's browser still shows the correct website, which makes pharming difficult to detect—and therefore more serious. Where phishing attempts to scam people one at a time with an email or instant message, pharming enables scammers to target large groups of people at one time through domain spoofing.

What Is Malicious Software?

Not all software performs beneficial tasks. Some software infiltrates one or more target computers and follows an attacker's instructions. These instructions can include causing damage, escalating security privileges, divulging private data, or even modifying or deleting data. This type of software is **malicious software**, or **malware** for short. The purpose of malware is to damage or disrupt a system. The effects of malware can range from slowing down a PC to causing it to crash, enabling the theft of credit card numbers, and worse. Simply surfing the Internet, reading email, or downloading music or other files can infect a personal computer with malware—usually without the user's knowledge.

Malware exists in two main categories: infecting programs and hiding programs. Infecting programs actively attempt to copy themselves to other computers. Their main purpose is to carry out an attacker's instructions on new targets. Malware of this type includes the following:

- Viruses
- Worms

As their name implies, hiding programs hide in the computer, carrying out the attacker's instructions while avoiding detection. Malware that tends to hide includes the following:

- Trojan horses
- Rootkits
- Spyware

The following sections describe each type of malware.

Viruses

A computer *virus* is a software program that attaches itself to or copies itself into another program on a computer. The purpose of the virus is to trick the computer into following instructions not intended by the original program developer. Users copy infected files from another computer on a network, from a flash drive, or from an online service. Alternatively, users can transport viruses from home and work on their portable computers, which have access to the Internet and other network services.

A computer virus acts in a similar fashion to a biological virus. It "infects" a host program and may cause that host program to replicate itself to other computers. The virus cannot exist without a host, and it can spread from host to host in an infectious manner.

The first virus recorded was the Creeper virus, written by researcher Bob Thomas in 1971. The Creeper copied itself to other networked computers, displaying the message "I'm the creeper, catch me if you can!" Thomas designed the virus as an experimental self-replicating program to see how such programs would affect computers on a network. Shortly after the Creeper virus was released, researchers unleashed the Reaper program to find and eradicate the Creeper.

Today, hundreds of thousands of known viruses infect programs of all types. The main concern with viruses is that they often attach themselves to common programs. When users run these infected programs, they are actually running virus code with their user credentials and authorization. The virus doesn't have to escalate privileges; the user who runs the infected program provides the virus with his or her authenticated credentials and permissions.

Over time, viruses have grown smarter. For example, some viruses can combat malware-detection programs by disabling their detection functions. Others compensate for the fact that files infected by a virus typically increase in size, making them relatively easy to detect, by spoofing the preinfected file's size. That way, it appears that nothing has changed.

Worms

A *worm* is a self-contained program that replicates and sends copies of itself to other computers, generally across a network, without any user input or action. The worm's purpose may be simply to reduce network availability by using up bandwidth, or it may take other nefarious actions. The main difference between a virus and a worm is that a worm does not need a host program to infect. The worm is a standalone program.

The first worm reported to spread "in the wild" was the Morris worm. Robert Tappan Morris wrote the Morris worm in 1988. The Morris worm attacked a buffer overflow vulnerability. The original intent of the Morris worm was to estimate the size of the Internet by spreading across the Internet and infecting computers running versions of the UNIX operating system. The worm spread faster than its author expected, however. In the end, the worm infected computers multiple times, eventually slowing each infected computer to the point it became unusable. The Morris worm was the first malware incident to gain widespread media attention and resulted in the first conviction under the U.S. 1986 Computer Use and Fraud Act.

> **NOTE**
>
> A *buffer overflow* is a condition in which a running program stores data in an area outside the memory location set aside for the data. By storing more data than a program expects, you can insert instructions into a program that alter the program's behavior at runtime. Buffer overflows are numerous and always result from a programmer neglecting to validate input data.

Trojan Horses

A *Trojan horse*, also called a **Trojan**, is malware that masquerades as a useful program. Its name comes from the fabled Trojan horse in *The Aeneid*. In the poem, the Greeks, who had been at war with Troy for 10 years, construct a large wooden horse and offer it as a "gift" to the Trojans. The Trojans, viewing the gift as a peace offering, bring the horse into the city. That night, as the Trojans sleep, Greek soldiers hiding in the belly of the hollow horse climb out and open the city gates to admit the rest of the Greek army into the city. The Greeks soundly defeat Troy that night.

Similarly, Trojan horse programs use their outward appearance to trick users into running them. They look like programs that perform useful tasks, but actually, they hide malicious code. Once the program is running, the attack instructions execute with the user's permissions and authority.

The first known computer Trojan was Animal, released in 1974. Animal disguised itself as a simple quiz game in which the user would think of an animal and the program would ask questions to attempt to guess the animal. In addition to asking questions, however, the program copied itself into every directory to which the user had write access.

Today's Trojans do far more than just save copies of themselves. Trojans can hide programs that collect sensitive information, open backdoors into computers, or actively upload and download files. The list of possibilities is endless.

Rootkits

Rootkits are newer than other types of malware. They did not appear until around 1990. A rootkit modifies or replaces one or more existing programs to hide traces of attacks. Although rootkits commonly modify parts of the operating system to conceal traces of their presence, they can exist at any level—from a computer's boot instructions up to the applications that run in the operating system. Once installed, rootkits provide attackers with easy access to compromised computers to launch additional attacks.

> ▶ **TIP**
>
> Rootkits often work with other malware. For example, suppose a program, malware.exe, is running on a Windows system. A simple rootkit might replace the Windows Task Manager with a modified version that does not list any program named malware.exe. Administrators would not know the malware program is running.

Rootkits exist for a variety of operating systems, including Linux, UNIX, and Microsoft Windows. Because there are so many different types of rootkits, and because they effectively conceal their existence once installed on a machine, they can be difficult to detect and remove. Even so, identifying and removing rootkits is crucial to maintaining a secure system. A host-based IDS can help detect rootkit activity.

If you do detect a rootkit on your system, the best solution is often to restore the operating system from the original media. This requires rebuilding and restoring user and application data from backups, assuming these exist. This becomes more difficult if you have not completely documented the system. Preventing unauthorized access that can enable an attacker to install a rootkit is far more effective than attempting to remove an installed rootkit.

Spyware

Spyware is a type of malware that specifically threatens the confidentiality of information. It gathers information about a user through an Internet connection, without his or her knowledge. Spyware is sometimes bundled as a hidden component of freeware or shareware programs that users download from the Internet, similar to a Trojan horse. Spyware can also spread via peer-to-peer file swapping. Spyware has been around since the late 1990s, increasing in popularity after 2000. The rapid growth of the Internet enabled attackers to collect useful information from more and more unsuspecting users.

> ▣ **NOTE**
>
> Licensing agreements that accompany software downloads sometimes warn users that a spyware program will be installed along with the requested software. Often, however, because they are composed in dense legal language, these licensing agreements go unread.

Once installed, spyware monitors user activity on the Internet. Spyware can also gather information such as email addresses and even passwords and credit card numbers. The spyware can relay these data to the author of the spyware. The author might use the data simply for advertising or marketing purposes but could employ it to facilitate identity theft.

In addition to stealing information, spyware steals from users by using their Internet bandwidth to transmit this information to a third party, as well as by consuming their

3

Malicious Attacks, Threats, and Vulnerabilities

Adware

Adware is similar to spyware but does not transmit **personally identifiable information (PII)**. PII is any information that can help identify a specific person. Examples of PII include driver's license numbers, Social Security numbers, credit card numbers, and so on. Instead, information collected by adware is meant to optimize marketing campaigns. For example, adware can help deliver popups tailored to purchasing habits or can be used for market research purposes.

A **popup** is a type of window that appears on top of the browser window. Popups generally contain ads. Although popups are not strictly adware, many adware programs use them to interact with users. Some software products include an option for blocking popups.

Spyware and adware have rapidly become increasingly common threats to computers, with some experts estimating that more than 90 percent of computers are already infected. Fortunately, a number of software suppliers make anti-spyware and anti-adware software. In fact, many antivirus and general anti-malware software programs also detect and remove spyware and adware. Sorting through these programs to find the right offering for your organization is a challenging task—but an important one.

computers' memory resources. Computers running multiple spyware programs often run noticeably more slowly than clean computers. Furthermore, because spyware uses memory and other system resources, it can cause system instability or even crashes.

Because spyware exists as independent executable programs, it can perform a number of operations, including the following:

- Monitoring keystrokes
- Scanning files on the hard drive
- Snooping other applications, such as chat programs or word processors
- Installing other spyware programs
- Reading cookies
- Changing the default homepage on the web browser

What Are Common Types of Attacks?

Depending on the attacker's goal and objective, many different types of attacks can suit their needs and abilities. These attacks can be summarized in three categories:

- **Attacks on availability**—These attacks impact access or uptime to a critical system, application, or data.
- **Attacks on people**—These attacks involve using coercion or deception to get another human to divulge information or to perform an action (e.g., clicking on a suspicious URL link or opening an email attachment from an unknown email address).
- **Attacks on IT assets**—These attacks include penetration testing, unauthorized access, privileged escalation, stolen passwords, deletion of data, or performing a data breach.

Social Engineering Attacks

Social engineering is the art of one human attempting to coerce or deceive another human into doing something or divulging information. We do this all the time in our day-to-day lives. Children social engineer their parents into giving permission or providing something they want. As a spouse, you may social engineer your partner into doing a chore you're responsible for. Criminals and hustlers are no different: They use social engineering tactics to get humans to divulge information about themselves or someone else. This is key in order to obtain private data to perfect identity theft. Hackers also attempt to social engineer targeted employees into divulging information about IT systems or applications so that the hackers can gain access.

Hackers and perpetrators use many different tactics to attempt to social engineer their victims. Here is a summary of social engineering attacks that may be used on you or your organization:

- **Authority**—Using a position of authority to coerce or persuade an individual to divulge information.
- **Consensus/social proof**—Using a position that "everyone else has been doing it" as proof that it is okay or acceptable to do.
- **Dumpster diving**—Finding unshredded pieces of paper that may contain sensitive data or private data for identity theft.
- **Familiarity/liking**—Interacting with the victim in a frequent way that creates a comfort and familiarity and liking for an individual (e.g., a delivery person may become familiar to office workers over time) that might encourage the victim to want to help the familiar person.
- **Hoaxes**—Creating a con or a false perception in order to get an individual to do something or divulge information.
- **Impersonation**—Pretending to be someone else (e.g., an IT help desk support person, a delivery person, a bank representative).
- **Intimidation**—Using force to extort or pressure an individual into doing something or divulging information.
- **Scarcity**—Pressuring another individual into doing something or divulging information for fear of not having something or losing access to something.
- **Shoulder surfing**—Looking over the shoulder of a person typing into a computer screen.
- **Tailgating**—Following an individual closely enough to sneak past a secure door or access area.
- **Trust**—Building a human trust bond over time and then using that trust to get the individual to do something or divulge information.
- **Urgency**—Using urgency or an emergency stress situation to get someone to do something or divulge information (e.g., claiming that there's a fire in the hallway might get the front desk security guard to leave her desk).
- **Vishing**—Performing a phishing attack by telephone in order to elicit personal information; using verbal coercion and persuasion ("sweet talking") the individual under attack.
- **Whaling**—Targeting the executive user or most valuable employees, otherwise considered the "whale" or "big fish" (often called *spear phishing*).

Wireless Network Attacks

Wireless network attacks involve performing intrusive monitoring, packet capturing, and penetration tests on a wireless network. Given the rapid deployment of wireless network connectivity in both public and private places, the mobile user is under constant threat. Wireless networks may be compromised as a network access point into your IT infrastructure. Implementation of proper wireless networking security controls is the key to mitigate the risks, threats, and vulnerabilities that arise from wireless networks. Many different tactics are used by hackers and perpetrators as they attempt to penetrate and attack wireless networks.

Here is a summary of wireless network attacks:

- **Bluejacking**—Hacking and gaining control of the Bluetooth wireless communication link between a user's earphone and smartphone device.
- **Bluesnarfing**—Packet sniffing communications traffic between Bluetooth devices.
- **Evil twin**—Faking an open or public wireless network to use a packet sniffer on any user who connects to it.
- **IV attack**—Modifying the initialization vector of an encrypted IP packet in transmission in hopes of decrypting a common encryption key over time.
- **Jamming/interference**—Sending radio frequencies in the same frequency as wireless network access points to jam and interfere with wireless communications and disrupting availability for legitimate users.
- **Near field communication attack**—Intercepting, at close range (a few inches), communications between two mobile operating system devices.
- **Packet sniffing**—Capturing IP packets off a wireless network and analyzing the TCP/IP packet data using a tool such as Wireshark®.
- **Replay attacks**—Replaying an IP packet stream to fool a server into thinking you are authenticating to it.
- **Rogue access points**—Using an unauthorized network device to offer wireless availability to unsuspecting users.
- **War chalking**—Creating a map of the physical or geographic location of any wireless access points and networks.
- **War driving**—Physically driving around neighborhoods or business complexes looking for wireless access points and networks that broadcast an open or public network connection.

In addition to these specific attacks, hackers may also attempt to exploit weaknesses in the wireless encryption method used by the target: WEP (Wireless Encryption Protocol), WPA (Wi-Fi Protected Assets), or WPS (Wi-Fi Protected Setup).

Web Application Attacks

Web **application attacks** involve performing intrusive penetration tests on public-facing web servers, applications, and back-end databases. Given the rapid deployment of e-commerce and customer or member portals and websites, access to private data, sensitive data, and intellectual property is abundant. Many different tactics are used by hackers and perpetrators when attempting to penetrate and attack web applications.

Web applications that are public facing on the Internet are subject to a host of web application attacks, including:

- **Arbitrary/remote code execution**—Having gained privileged access or sys admin rights access, the attacker can run commands or execute a command at will on the remote system.
- **Buffer overflow**—Attempting to push more data than the buffer can handle, thus creating a condition where further compromise might be possible.
- **Client-side attack**—Using malware on a user's workstation or laptop, within an internal network, acting in tandem with a malicious server or application on the Internet (outside the protected network).
- **Cookies and attachments**—Using cookies or other attachments (or the information they contain) to compromise security.
- **Cross-site scripting (XSS)**—Injecting scripts into a web application server to redirect attacks back to the client. This is not an attack on the web application but rather on users of the server to launch attacks on other computers that access it.
- **Directory traversal/command injection**—Exploiting a web application server, gaining root file directory access from outside the protected network, and executing commands, including data dumps.
- **Header manipulation**—Stealing cookies and browser URL information and manipulating the header with invalid or false commands to create an insecure communication or action.
- **Integer overflow**—Creating a mathematical overflow which exceeds the maximum size allowed. This can cause a financial or mathematical application to freeze or create a vulnerability and opening.
- **Lightweight Directory Access Protocol (LDAP) injection**—Creating fake or bogus ID and authentication LDAP commands and packets to falsely ID and authenticate to a web application.
- **Local shared objects (LSO)**—Using **Flash cookies** (named after the Adobe Flash player), which cannot be deleted through the browser's normal configuration settings. Flash cookies can also be used to reinstate regular cookies that a user has deleted or blocked.
- **Malicious add-ons**—Using software plug-ins or add-ons that run additional malicious software on legitimate programs or applications.
- **SQL injection**—Injecting Structured Query Language (SQL) commands to obtain information and data in the back-end SQL database.
- **Watering-hole attack**—Luring a targeted user to a commonly visited website on which has been planted the malicious code or malware, in hopes that the user will trigger the attack with a unknowing click.
- **XML injection**—Injecting XML tags and data into a database in an attempt to retrieve data.
- **Zero-day**—Exploiting a new vulnerability or software bug for which no specific defenses yet exist.

What Is a Countermeasure?

There are no simple measures to protect your organization from computer attacks. You must focus on countermeasures that detect vulnerabilities, prevent attacks, and respond to the effects of successful attacks. This is not easy—but it is better than the alternative. Dealing with computer and network attacks is a cost of doing business in the IT field.

Although smart attackers and intruders continue to invent new methods of attacking computer and network resources, many are well known and can be defeated with a variety of available tools. The best strategy is to identify vulnerabilities and reduce them to avoid attacks in the first place.

Avoiding attacks should be the highest priority. Even so, some attacks will succeed. Your response to attacks should be as aggressive, proactive, and reactive as the attack itself. You can respond to attacks by developing plans to rapidly restore computer and network resources if they are attacked, closing holes in your organization's defenses, and obtaining evidence for prosecution of offenders. Of course, you should use the lessons learned from an attack to protect the network from similar attacks.

Responding to attacks involves planning, policy, and detective work. Fortunately, law enforcement agencies, forensic experts, security consultants, and independent response teams are available to assist you in responding to a security incident as well as prosecuting offenders. In addition, many organizations have special teams to handle security incidents when they occur. These **security incident response teams (SIRTs)** know how to recognize incidents and respond to them in a way that minimizes damage and preserves evidence for later action.

As you read the following chapters, you will learn about many countermeasures. To get you started, this section introduces you to a few of the most common countermeasures you can take to protect your IT infrastructure. You may also need to use some of them to respond to threats, vulnerabilities, and malicious attacks in progress.

Countering Malware

Malware provides a platform for attacks on both personal and business networks. Anti-malware measures are the first line of defense against these attacks. You must take steps to prevent the introduction of malware into your environment. It's always better to prevent malware than to have to fix damage caused by malware. You must develop a security program for preventing malware.

Following are six general steps for preventing malware:

- Create an education (information security awareness) program to keep your users from installing malware on your system.
- Post regular bulletins about malware problems.
- Never transfer files from an unknown or untrusted source unless the computer has an anti-malware utility installed. (You'll learn more about anti-malware utilities in a moment.)
- Test new programs or open suspect files on a quarantine computer—one that is not connected to any part of your network—before introducing them to the production environment.

- Install anti-malware software, make sure the software and data are current, and schedule regular malware scans to prevent malicious users from introducing malware and to detect any existing malware.
- Use a secure logon and authentication process.

Another important tactic for countering malware is staying abreast of developments in malware. Keep up with the latest malware information by reading weekly computer journals or joining organizations like the National Cyber Security Alliance (NCSA) or US-CERT. In addition, you should frequently check the following websites for information about malware:

- **National Cyber Security Alliance (NCSA)**—*www.staysafeonline.org.*
- **United States Computer Emergency Readiness Team (US-CERT)**—*http://us-cert.gov.*

In addition, you should use anti-malware software on your system to scan all files introduced to workstations and on mail servers. (Note that the more common name for this type of software is *antivirus software*. However, because today's antivirus software generally addresses more than just viruses, the term *anti-malware software* is more accurate.) Most administrators use anti-malware software at many points throughout the network.

Many anti-malware products are available to prevent the spread of all types of malware as well remove malware from infected computers. These include the following:

- **BitDefender**—*www.bitdefender.com.*
- **Kaspersky Anti-Virus**—*www.kaspersky.com.*
- **Webroot Antivirus**—*www.webroot.com.*
- **Norton AntiVirus**—*www.symantec.com/norton/antivirus.*
- **ESET Nod32 Antivirus**—*www.eset.com.*
- **AVG Antivirus**—*www.avg.com.*
- **G DATA Antivirus**—*www.gdatasoftware.com.*
- **Avira Antivirus**—*www.avira.com.*
- **McAfee Endpoint Protection**—*www.mcafee.com.*
- **Trend Micro**—*www.trendmicro.com.*
- **Microsoft Security Essentials**—*www.microsoft.com/ security_essentials.*

Some anti-malware software works by examining the activity generated by a file to determine whether it is malware. These types of anti-malware programs use an approach called *heuristic analysis* to see whether programs "act" like malware. Other types of anti-malware software detect malware by comparing programs and files to signatures of known types of malware. The problem is, these programs may not immediately recognize and counteract newly created malware signatures. The anti-malware software must update its signature database to include these new signatures before the software can detect it. Because attackers constantly invent new viruses, it's imperative that you keep your anti-malware software up to date. An effective approach is to run an anti-malware program update and scan with every logon.

> **NOTE**
>
> You can find reviews of anti-malware programs on the Web. Two popular review sites that provide feedback from other users are *www.star-reviews.com* and *http://anti-virus-software-review.toptenreviews.com.* Checking reviews written by others whose requirements and scenarios are similar to yours can help you select the best products for your organization.

3

Malicious Attacks, Threats, and Vulnerabilities

Note that even if you detect and eliminate a malware infection on a system, there is still a chance that malware is lurking elsewhere in the organization, ready to reinfect or attack the system. This is especially true in collaborative environments; files containing viruses may be stored in central servers and distributed throughout the network. This cycle of infection, disinfection, and reinfection will continue until you completely purge the malware from the entire system. If you detect malware anywhere in your system, you must scan all your systems, including storage devices, for its existence.

Protecting Your System with Firewalls

A **firewall** is a program or dedicated hardware device that inspects network traffic passing through it and denies or permits that traffic based on a set of rules you determine at configuration. A firewall's basic task is to regulate the flow of traffic between computer networks of different trust levels—for example, between the LAN-to-WAN domain and the WAN domain, where the private network meets the public Internet.

There are numerous firewall solutions available. Prominent firewall vendors include the following:

- **Palo Alto Networks**—*www.paloaltonetworks.com.*
- **Cisco Systems**—*www.cisco.com.*
- **SonicWALL**—*www.sonicwall.com.*
- **WatchGuard Technologies**—*www.watchguard.com.*
- **Check Point**—*www.checkpoint.com.*
- **ZyXEL**—*www.zyxel.com.*
- **Netgear**—*www.netgear.com.*
- **Juniper Networks**—*www.juniper.net.*
- **DLink**—*www.dlink.com.*
- **MultiTech Systems**—*www.multitech.com.*

CHAPTER SUMMARY

Risks, threats, and vulnerabilities in the seven domains of an IT infrastructure and its assets are an everyday menace. It is essential that organizations and individual users identify their own risks, threats, and vulnerabilities and implement a plan to mitigate them.

There are many types of threats. These include confidentiality threats, integrity threats, and availability threats. In addition, there is the threat of a malicious attack. Malicious attacks can originate from active threats that include brute-force, masquerading, IP address spoofing, session hijacking, replay, man-in-the-middle, and dictionary password attacks. Passive threats can include eavesdropping and monitoring. Viruses are the most common and frequent type of attack. Anti-malware software is the most effective method of countering a virus attack. The easiest target are users unaware of the security threats.

Threat targets are increasing as more users join the Internet community. Common targets include computer systems, network components, software, electrical systems, and databases. Black-hat hackers, white-hat hackers, gray-hat hackers, script kiddies, and crackers can launch attacks.

KEY CONCEPTS AND TERMS

Adware
Application attacks
Arbitrary code execution
Armored virus
Address resolution protocol (ARP) poisoning
Asset
Attack
Backdoor
Birthday attack
Black-hat hacker
Bluejacking
Bluesnarfing
Botnets
Brute-force password attack
Buffer overflow
Christmas attack
Client-side attack
Command injection
Cookie
Cracker
Cross-site scripting (XSS)
Cryptographic hash
Cryptolocker
Denial of service (DoS)
Dictionary password attack
Directory traversal
Disclosure
Distributed denial of service (DDoS)
DNS poisoning
Dumpster diving
Ethical hacker

Evil twin
Exploit software
Familiarity
Firewall
Flash cookies
Gray-hat hacker
Hacker
Header manipulation
Hijacking
Hoax
Identity theft
Impersonation
Insider threat
Integer overflow
Intellectual property
Intrusive penetration testing
IV attack
Jamming
Keystroke logger
LDAP injection
Local shared objects (LSO)
Malicious add-ons
Malicious software
Malware
Man-in-the-middle attack
Masquerade attack
National Vulnerability Database (NVD)
Near field communication attack
Netcat
Operating system (OS) fingerprint scanner
Opportunity cost

Packet sniffer
Password cracker
Personally identifiable information (PII)
Pharming
Phishing
Phreaking
Polymorphic malware
Popup
Port scanner
Promiscuous mode
Protocol analyzer
Ransomware
Remote code execution
Replay attack
Rogue access points
Rootkit
Scarcity
Script kiddie
Security breach
Security incident response team (SIRT)
Session hijacking
Shoulder surfing
Smurfing
Sniffer
Social engineering
Spam
Spear phishing
Spim
Spoofing
Spyware
SQL injection

KEY CONCEPTS AND TERMS, *continued*

SYN flood	URL hijacking	Whaling
Tailgating	Vishing	White-hat hacker
Transitive access	Vulnerability scanner	Wiretapping
Trojan	Wannabe	Xmas attack
True downtime cost	War chalking	XML injection
Trust	War driving	Zero-day
Typo squatting	Wardialer	
Urgency	Watering hole attack	

CHAPTER 3 ASSESSMENT

1. The main goal of a hacker is to steal or compromise IT assets and potentially steal data.

A. True
B. False

2. Which of the following best describes intellectual property?

A. The items a business has copyrighted
B. All patents owned by a business
C. The unique knowledge a business possesses
D. Customer lists
E. All of the above

3. Which of the following terms best describes a person with very little hacking skills?

A. Hacker
B. Script kiddie
C. Cracker
D. Wannabe
E. All of the above

4. A(n) _____ is a software tool that is used to capture packets from a network.

5. Which type of attacks result in legitimate users not having access to a system resource?

A. DDoS
B. Social engineering
C. Man in the middle
D. Phishing emails
E. SQL injection

6. A SYN flood attack floods a target with invalid or half-open TCP connection requests.

A. True
B. False

7. Which of the following is an example of social engineering?

A. SQL injection
B. XML injection
C. Security design
D. Impersonation
E. All of the above

8. Which of the following security countermeasures is best for end-point protection against malware?

A. Antivirus/anti-malware protection
B. Data leakage prevention
C. Standardized workstation and laptop images
D. Security awareness training
E. All of the above

9. War driving involves looking for open or public wireless networks.

A. True
B. False

10. Which of the following impacts availability?

A. Cross-site scripting
B. SQL injection
C. DDoS
D. Packet sniffing
E. None of the above

11. Which type of attack involves capturing data packets from a network and transmitting them later to produce an unauthorized effect?

    A. Man in the middle
    B. SYN flood
    C. Replay
    D. Smurf
    E. SQL injection

12. A(n) _____ is any action that could damage an asset.   *threat*

13. A(n) _____ is any weakness that makes it possible for a threat to cause harm to a computer or network.   *vulnerability*

14. Which type of malware is a self-contained program that replicates and sends copies of itself to other computers, generally across a network?

    A. Virus
    B. Worm
    C. Trojan
    D. Rootkit
    E. Cookie manipulation

15. Which type of malware involves extorting the user or organization into paying money to release a decryption key?

    A. Virus
    B. Trojan
    C. Logic bomb
    D. Cryptolocker malware
    E. Your worst nightmare virus

3

The Drivers of the Information Security Business

EVERY ORGANIZATION CARRIES OUT TASKS to satisfy business objectives. Without objectives, organizations have no purpose. You must identify the elements in your organization that support your business objectives.

These elements are your organization's **business drivers.** Business drivers include people, information, and conditions that support business objectives. Information security activities directly support several common business drivers, including compliance and efforts to protect intellectual property. Security activities can also negatively affect business drivers, making it more difficult to satisfy your business objectives.

Some outside requirements direct how your organization carries out its tasks. These requirements can come from legislation, regulation, industry demands, or even your own standards. Every organization has some requirements with which it must comply. There are multiple ways that your organization can meet requirements. Most regulations require that you develop plans to handle business interruptions or disasters. In fact, most activities that restore operations after an interruption support several requirements.

Always consider different controls to satisfy compliance requirements. It's important that you balance security activities with their impact on your business drivers to protect your information's security. In this chapter, you will learn about security-related business drivers and how they support your overall business drivers.

Chapter 4 Topics

This chapter covers the following topics and concepts:

- What risk management is
- How BIA, BCP, and DRP differ from one another and how they are the same
- How to describe the impact of risks, threats, and vulnerabilities on an organization
- How to close the information security gap
- How to mitigate risk and achieve compliance with laws, regulations, and requirements
- How to keep private data confidential
- How to mitigate the risk of mobile workers and use of personal devices

Chapter 4 Goals

When you complete this chapter, you will be able to:

- Define risk management and the way organizations should approach risk management
- Distinguish BIA, BCP, and DRP from one another and compare them with one another
- Describe the impact of risks, threats, and vulnerabilities on the IT infrastructure
- Define an acceptable level of risk or liability
- Shrink the information security gap based on risk mitigation strategies
- Adhere to compliance laws and governance (policies, standards, procedures, and guidelines)
- Manage and mitigate risk as part of ongoing security operations
- Determine how to comply with CIA goals that are defined for your IT infrastructure
- Identify risks associated with mobile workers and use of personally owned devices

Defining Risk Management

Risk management is the process of identifying, assessing, prioritizing, and addressing risks. Any organization that is serious about security will view risk management as an ongoing process.

Risk management is not something you do just once. Each part of the risk management process is separate but can and will occur many times. Risk management ensures that you have planned for risks that are most likely to have an effect on your organization. A secure organization has plans in place to address risks *before* events occur. Thus, organizations that align security with their strategic business objectives can drive business success with risk mitigation.

Every business possesses assets or resources, whether intellectual property, infrastructure and facilities, or employees. Risk is the probability that an uncertain event will affect one or more of those resources. Most people view risks only in terms of negative effects. However, the **Project Management Body of Knowledge (PMBOK)**, a best practices guide for project management maintained by the **Project Management Institute (PMI)**, states that the effects of risk can be positive or negative. PMI bases its risk management philosophy on a proactive approach, which simultaneously does the following:

- Minimizes the effects of negative risks
- Maximizes the effects of positive risks

Consider the classic view of risks. **FIGURE 4-1** shows the classic relationship among risks, threats, and vulnerabilities.

As shown in the figure, the risk equation is as follows:

$$\text{Risk} = \text{Threats} \times \text{Vulnerabilities}$$

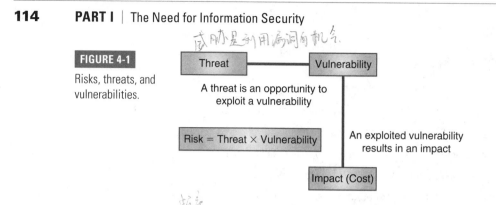

FIGURE 4-1

Risks, threats, and vulnerabilities.

A *threat* is the frequency of any event. In most cases, the events in the threat equation are negative or adverse events. *Vulnerability* is the likelihood that a specific threat will successfully be carried out. Multiplying the probability of a threat and the likelihood of a vulnerability yields the *risk* of that particular event. Risks apply to specific assets or resources. If you multiply the risk probability by the value of the resource, the result is the expected loss from exposure to a specific risk.

Many people have never thought of risk as a positive thing. However, uncertainty can result in events that have negative *or* positive effects. For example, suppose your organization plans to deploy new software to your end users based on projected availability from your software vendor. Your risk-management plan should address the responses to both an early and a late software delivery. If you receive the software early, you can either perform more exhaustive testing or begin deployment early. If your software vendor is late delivering software to you, you may miss your projected deployment date. You should have plans in place to address both the positive and negative effects of a delivery date that does not match your schedule.

A **risk methodology** is a description of how you will manage risk. The risk methodology that your organization adopts should include the approach, the required information, and the techniques to address each risk. The approach defines how you will carry out the steps of the risk methodology process. For example, the approach could state that risk analysis will be conducted at specified intervals. The tools for conducting this analysis can include the documents that define, categorize, and rank risks. This approach is consistent with the PMI's PMBOK. While the PMI approach isn't the only way to do things, it does provide a prescriptive approach to project management in general, including risk management.

The result of the risk identification process is a list of identified risks. PMI calls this list the **risk register**. The risk register can contain many different types of information but should contain at least the following:

- A description of the risk
- The expected impact if the associated event occurs
- The probability of the event occurring
- Steps to mitigate the risk
- Steps to take should the event occur
- Rank of the risk

Your organization's ability to respond to any risk starts with how well you identify potential risks. Be creative when asking for risk register input. Using multiple perspectives will give you a more complete response plan. You can solicit input for the risk register in several ways, including the following:

* Risk identification brainstorming meetings
* Formal surveys
* Informal polls and requests for comments
* Incentived events, such as "lunch and learn" sessions that include a forum for collecting comments and feedback

It's crucial to ensure that you have the support of your organization's upper management. Without management's support, you'll likely lack the authority to carry out the steps needed to develop a good risk management plan. You will enjoy the benefits of having full management support from the very beginning in these risk identification activities. Don't bring in management as an afterthought.

As the process of collecting information continues, more and more people should become involved. However, larger groups can discourage participants from speaking up about weaknesses within your organization. They may fear reprisal or fear that others will view them as complainers. You may find that one technique in particular, the **Delphi method**, produces the candid results you need. This is an approach to using formal anonymous surveys in multiple rounds to collect opinions and information. Because the surveys are anonymous, the method encourages candid responses. A panel reviews each round of survey responses and creates a new survey based on the results of the previous round. Multiple rounds allow you to focus on areas of concern and assemble detailed information from a number of subject matter experts.

Now that you know what risk management is, it is important to consider how risks would apply to each of the seven domains of an IT infrastructure. This process starts with a risk, threat, and vulnerability analysis or assessment of the User, Workstation, LAN, LAN-to-WAN, WAN, Remote Access, and System/Application domains. Performing a risk analysis and risk assessment is described in a later chapter.

Implementing a BIA, a BCP, and a DRP

The primary focus of risk management is to preempt realized threats. It's not possible to foresee and prevent every event that results in loss. That means that the likelihood still exists that any organization will encounter an event that will interrupt normal business operations. Information security requires all information to be available when any authorized user needs it. You'll have to develop and implement methods and techniques for protecting the organization's IT resources and ensuring that events do not interrupt normal business functions.

Business Impact Analysis

The first step in developing plans to address interruptions is to identify those business functions that are crucial to your organization. Some of your organization's activities are critical to the operation of the business, and some aren't. When an event interrupts your

organization's ability to conduct operations, it's important to restore the most crucial opera-
ons first. Before you can do this, you have to identify what those functions are.

A *business impact analysis* (BIA) is a formal analysis of an organization's functions and
activities that classifies them as critical or noncritical. A BIA helps define a road map for
business continuity and disaster recovery. Critical functions are required to run the business. If you cannot carry out a critical function, it causes unacceptable damage. Noncritical
functions may be important, and you might miss them if they did not exist, but their absence
would not stop an organization from conducting business. A BIA arranges critical activities
based on importance and helps an organization determine which functions to restore in
what order if there is a major interruption. BIAs also assist organizations with risk management and incident response planning.

In the BIA, each critical function is fully described in its own section, including a description of recovery goals and requirements for each function. Recovery goals and requirements
are expressed as follows:

- **Recovery point objective (RPO)**—Measured in time, the RPO is the maximum amount of
  data loss that is acceptable. Depending on the nature of the function, staff members may
  be able to recreate or reenter data. RPO provides direction on how to back up data, policies on recovery, and whether loss prevention or loss correction is a better option.
- **Recovery time objective (RTO)**—The RTO expresses the maximum allowable time
  to recover the function. Many less formal recovery plans overlook RTO. Time may be
  a critical factor, and specifying the requirements for recovery time helps determine
  the best recovery options.
- **Business recovery requirements**—These requirements identify any other business
  functions that must already be in place for the specified recovery function to occur.
  Business recovery requirements help in determining the recovery sequence.
- **Technical recovery requirements**—Technical recovery requirements define the technical
  prerequisites that are needed to support each critical business function. In most cases, technical recovery requirements dictate which IT infrastructure components must be in place.

Ensuring that operations and functions that are critical to an organization are able to continue is crucial to the organization's survival. The BIA will help identify not only which
functions are critical, but also how quickly essential business functions must return to full
operation following a major interruption. The BIA will also identify resource requirements
for returning each function to full operation. BIAs generally assume a worst-case scenario in
which the physical infrastructure supporting each activity or function has been destroyed,
along with any data. You can choose to plan for any interruption timeframe, but in many
BIAs, restoration plans assume that access to primary resources will not be possible for at
least 30 days. In other words, a solid BIA will indicate the requirements necessary to conduct business for an extended period when the normal infrastructure is unavailable.

Business Continuity Plan

A *business continuity plan* (BCP) is a written plan for a structured response to any events
that result in an interruption to critical business activities or functions. Performing a BIA is

an important first step toward generating a BCP in that the BIA identifies the resources for which a BCP is necessary.

There is generally no reason to develop a BCP for resources that aren't crucial to an organization's survival. The BCP primarily addresses the processes, resources, equipment, and devices needed to continue conducting critical business activities when an interruption occurs that affects the business's viability.

The most important part of any BCP is setting priorities, with the understanding that people always come first. There are no exceptions. Any plan that addresses business interruptions and disasters must place the safety and well-being of the organization's people as the highest priority. All other concerns are secondary. The order of priorities for a well-balanced BCP should be as follows:

- Safety and well-being of people
- Continuity of critical business functions and operations, whether onsite or offsite, manual, or dependent upon IT systems
- Continuity of IT infrastructure components within the seven domains of an IT infrastructure

You must address the needs of each category before continuing to the next category. If conditions are hazardous for humans, those humans can't do anything productive. If your people are safe but your building is damaged, you can't replace servers or network hardware. You must wait for the damage to be repaired or for the organization to be relocated to restore infrastructure components. Keep the order of resource priority in mind as you develop plans to avoid business process interruptions.

A formal BCP isn't just helpful for many organizations—in some circumstances, it's required. Legislation and regulations often require a BCP to ensure that systems are safe. Today's organizations increasingly rely on IT resources and require a solid IT infrastructure to conduct business. The cost for system downtime for these companies can be extreme. Direct and indirect costs associated with downtime can exist in several categories, including:

- Lost customers
- Lost revenue
- Lost market share
- Additional expenses
- Damaged reputation

Organizations must consider contingency and recovery plans from a comprehensive perspective. Plans cannot focus on individual resources to the exclusion of others. Although each of the components of contingency and recovery plans do generally address specific resources, they must do so within a larger context. Keeping the larger context in view during plan development enables you to address the risks to an organization as opposed to merely fixing a broken resource.

> **█ NOTE**
>
> Direct costs are immediate expenditures that reduce profit. Indirect costs, such as losing a customer, affect the overall revenue stream but are harder to calculate because there is no expenditure record. In the case of indirect costs, the impact is that potential sales just never happen.

Elements of a complete BCP should include the following:

- Policy statement defining the policy, standards, procedures, and guidelines for deployment
- Project team members with defined roles, responsibilities, and accountabilities
- Emergency response procedures and protection of life, safety, and infrastructure
- Situation and damage assessment
- Resource salvage and recovery
- Alternate facilities or triage for short-term or long-term emergency mode of operations and business recovery

Briefly, a BCP directs all activities required to ensure that an organization's critical business functions continue with little or no interruption. The BCP assumes that the infrastructure components needed to support operations are in place. Unfortunately, that is not always the case after a disaster. What happens when a fire destroys your data center? How can you continue business operations in that case? The answer is, you need another plan: a *disaster recovery plan* (DRP).

Disaster Recovery Plan

A **disaster recovery plan (DRP)** directs the actions necessary to recover resources after a disaster. A DRP is part of a BCP. It is necessary to ensure the restoration of resources required by the BCP to an available state. The DRP extends and supports the BCP by identifying events that could cause damage to resources that are necessary to support critical business functions. The BCP already contains a list of the resources necessary to support each business function. The next step in developing a DRP is to consider what could happen to each resource.

BCP Versus DRP: What's the Difference?

What is the difference between a BCP and a DRP? A BCP does not specify how to recover from disasters, only interruptions. In general, an *interruption* is a minor event that may disrupt one or more business processes for a short period. In contrast, a *disaster* is an event that affects multiple business processes for an extended period. Disasters often also cause substantial resource damage that you must address before you can resolve the business process interruption.

Threat Analysis

A threat analysis involves identifying and documenting threats to critical resources. Before you can recover from a disaster, you need to consider what types of disasters are possible and what types of damage they can cause. For example, recovering from a data-center fire is different from recovering from a flu epidemic. Some common threats include the following:

- Fire
- Flood

- Hurricane
- Tornado
- Disease
- Earthquake
- Cyberattack
- Sabotage
- Utility outage
- Terrorism

With the exception of disease, each of these threats has the potential to damage an organization's infrastructure. In contrast, disease directly affects personnel. You can address disease with various solutions. If, however, the disease affects people charged with carrying out the recovery plans, the recovery may be unsuccessful.

Note that these threats do not necessarily occur one at a time. One threat may lead to another threat. For example, a flood that introduces contaminated water into an office may lead to disease that incapacitates your staff. As another example, a tornado or earthquake could result in a fire. Always assume that disasters may occur in groups, not only as single events.

Impact Scenarios

After defining potential threats, the next step in creating a comprehensive DRP is to document likely impact scenarios. These form the basis of the DRP. In most organizations, planning for the most wide-reaching disaster rather than focusing on smaller issues results in a more comprehensive plan. Narrowing the focus on smaller issues can result in a DRP that fails to consider a broader strategy. A broader strategy is necessary to recover from the loss of multiple resources simultaneously. An impact scenario such as "Loss of Building" will likely encompass all critical business functions and the worst potential outcome from any given threat. A DRP may include additional impact scenarios if an organization has more than one building.

A solid DRP might also contain additional, more specific impact scenarios. For example, your plan may include a scenario that addresses the loss of a specific floor in a building. Many plans underestimate the resources necessary to move from one location to another. Don't neglect the resources necessary to execute each step of your plan. A recovery plan that fails just because you didn't have access to a truck large enough to move your equipment to an alternate site isn't a very solid plan.

Recovery Requirement Documentation

Once you complete the analysis phase, you should document the business and technical requirements to initiate the implementation phase. You'll likely need access to asset information, including asset lists and their availability during a disaster. Each asset has an owner. The owner of an asset must grant access to it to the disaster relief team. Typically, the BCP and DRP have team leaders who have full authority to conduct their tasks and functions to enable business continuity or recovery of business functions and operations. BCP and DRP teams typically include executive management, legal, and public relations staff members to address all aspects of internal and external communications.

The asset information must already be identified and provided in the BCP. This information must be readily available for the disaster recovery team and includes the following:

- Complete and accurate inventory of all facility assets
- Complete and accurate inventory of IT assets, hardware, software, licenses, contracts, and maintenance agreements
- Complete and accurate list of alternative office facilities and triage locations
- Complete and accurate list and contact details for business partners, vendors, service providers, and suppliers
- Disaster recovery team member contact information—work and personal
- Critical business functions and operations and required IT systems, applications, resources, and data recovery
- Retrieval of backed-up data for recovery and use
- Detailed IT system, application, and data recovery procedures
- Disaster recovery team members and resources needed for manual and workaround solutions
- Recovery time objectives (RTO) and steps required to achieve this metric

Disaster Recovery

It's important to train all personnel on the proper response to any disaster. A common mistake is for personnel to be too eager to begin the recovery process. Even though your organization has devoted substantial time and resources to developing a DRP, you must ensure that you react to the disaster, not the plan. The critical steps in responding to a disaster include the following:

- **Ensure everyone's safety first**—No other resource is as important as people.
- **Respond to the disaster before pursuing recovery**—Required response and containment actions depend on the nature of the disaster and may not have anything to do with the recovery effort.
- **Follow the DRP, including communicating with all affected parties**—Once your people are safe and you have responded to the disaster, you can pursue recovery actions.

Disaster recovery is an extension of the DRP. It addresses recovering from common system outages or interruptions. A disaster is generally larger than a common outage, and the resources may not be available to enact simple recovery solutions. For example, most database management systems enable you to quickly recover the primary database from a replicated copy. However, if a disaster has resulted in the destruction of your database server computer, you'll have to restore the server to a stable state before you can restore your database data.

A disaster may render your data center unusable, forcing you to relocate your operations. Careful planning for such a move makes it viable. Although moving your data center to another location may not sound like a major undertaking, it involves many details—which is why you should devote so much effort

> **NOTE**
>
> In some industries, cooperative agreements are mandatory. For example, banks are required to maintain cooperative agreements with other banks. They are also required to regularly test their ability to use other banks' facilities to ensure uninterrupted service to their customers.

TABLE 4-1 Data center alternatives for disaster recovery.

OPTION	DESCRIPTION	COMMENTS
Hot site	Facility with environmental utilities, hardware, software, and data that closely mirrors the original data center	Most expensive option, least switchover time
Warm site	Facility with environmental utilities and basic computer hardware	Less expensive than a hot site but requires more time to load operating systems, software, data, and configurations
Cold site	Facility with basic environmental utilities but no infrastructure components	Least expensive option but at the cost of the longest switchover time, since all hardware, software, and data must be loaded at the new site
Mobile site	Trailer with necessary environmental utilities that can operate as a warm site or cold site	Very flexible, fairly short switchover time and widely varying costs based on size and capacity

to planning. You must install hardware and software, and there are network and telecommunications requirements. **TABLE 4-1** lists several common data center options for disaster recovery.

It may be to your advantage to work out a mutual aid agreement with another company whereby each organization agrees to provide backup resources in the event of a disaster. The agreement could include after-hours access to computing resources or physical space to use as a temporary data center. Carefully examine all the requirements when considering a cooperative agreement. Providing basic critical functionality for a data center may seem straightforward, but some resources, such as telecommunications service, may not be easy to switch from one location to another. Also, consider how close any alternate location is to your existing location. If your proposed alternate location is too close to your main location, a large disaster such as a flood or an earthquake could affect both.

Disaster recovery is rapidly becoming an increasingly important aspect of enterprise computing. As business environments become more complex, more things can go wrong. Recovery plans have become more complex to keep up. DRPs vary from one organization to another, depending on many factors. These include the type of organization, the processes involved, and the level of security needed. Most enterprises remain unprepared or underprepared for a disaster. And despite recurrent reminders, many companies do not have a DRP at all. Of those that do, nearly half have never tested their plan—which is essentially the same as not having one.

It's crucial to validate your DRP for effectiveness and completeness and test it for accuracy. It's rare that the first version of a DRP is complete and correct. You must test your DRP to identify gaps. Once the gaps are identified, you need to further refine the DRP. You can engage a disaster recovery firm to assist in such tests. These tests can range from simple reviews to complete disaster simulations. The most effective tests simulate real disasters,

4

The Drivers of the Information
Security Business

including transferring software between computer systems and ensuring that you can establish communications at an alternate location. The following are various types of DRP tests:

- **Checklist test**—This is the simplest type of DRP test. In a checklist test, each participant follows steps on the DRP checklist and provides feedback. You can use checklist tests for DRP training and awareness.
- **Structured walk-through**—A structured walk-through is similar to a checklist test, but the DRP team uses role playing to simulate a disaster and evaluate the DRP's effectiveness. This type of test is also called a *tabletop exercise* or a *conference room test*.
- **Simulation test**—A simulation test is more realistic than a structured walk-through. In a simulation test, the DRP team uses role playing and follows through with as many of the effects of a simulated disaster as possible without affecting live operations.
- **Parallel test**—A parallel test evaluates the effectiveness of the DRP by enabling full processing capability at an alternate data center without interrupting the primary data center.
- **Full-interruption test**—This is the only complete test. Full-interruption tests interrupt the primary data center and transfer processing capability to an alternate site.

Not all aspects of DRPs are reactive. Some parts of a DRP are preventive and intended to avoid the negative effects of a disaster in the first place. Preventive components of a DRP may include some of the following:

- Local mirroring of disk systems and use of data protection technology, such as a redundant array of independent disks (RAID) or storage area network (SAN) storage system
- Surge protectors to minimize the effect of power surges on delicate electronic equipment
- Uninterruptible power supply (UPS) and/or a backup generator to keep systems going in the event of a power failure
- Fire prevention systems
- Antivirus software and other security controls

Assessing Risks, Threats, and Vulnerabilities

One of the first steps in developing comprehensive BCPs and DRPs is to fully assess the risks, threats, and vulnerabilities associated with your organization's critical resources. You can't protect your environment from every possible threat, so it's necessary to prioritize. Until you know the risks, you can't know which remedies are necessary.

There are many approaches to assessing risk. Each organization conducts the process in its own unique way. Instead of starting from scratch in the risk assessment process, you can use one of the many methodologies that are available. At least one of these is likely a good fit for your organization. Investing the time to research the various offerings can make the whole process more effective and efficient. **TABLE 4-2** lists common risk assessment methodologies.

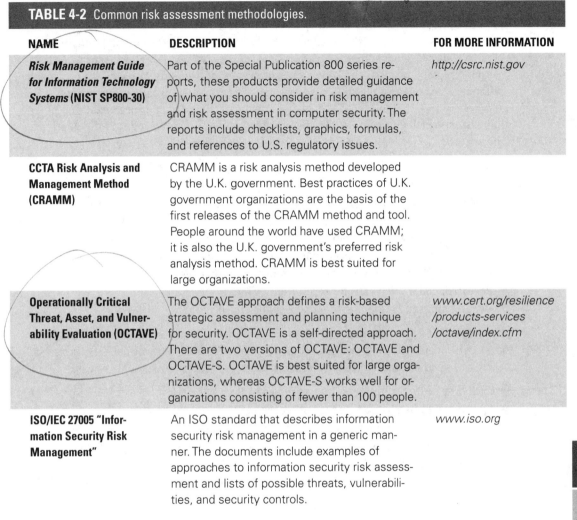

TABLE 4-2 Common risk assessment methodologies.

NAME	DESCRIPTION	FOR MORE INFORMATION
Risk Management Guide for Information Technology Systems (NIST SP800-30)	Part of the Special Publication 800 series reports, these products provide detailed guidance of what you should consider in risk management and risk assessment in computer security. The reports include checklists, graphics, formulas, and references to U.S. regulatory issues.	http://csrc.nist.gov
CCTA Risk Analysis and Management Method (CRAMM)	CRAMM is a risk analysis method developed by the U.K. government. Best practices of U.K. government organizations are the basis of the first releases of the CRAMM method and tool. People around the world have used CRAMM; it is also the U.K. government's preferred risk analysis method. CRAMM is best suited for large organizations.	
Operationally Critical Threat, Asset, and Vulnerability Evaluation (OCTAVE)	The OCTAVE approach defines a risk-based strategic assessment and planning technique for security. OCTAVE is a self-directed approach. There are two versions of OCTAVE: OCTAVE and OCTAVE-S. OCTAVE is best suited for large organizations, whereas OCTAVE-S works well for organizations consisting of fewer than 100 people.	www.cert.org/resilience /products-services /octave/index.cfm
ISO/IEC 27005 "Information Security Risk Management"	An ISO standard that describes information security risk management in a generic manner. The documents include examples of approaches to information security risk assessment and lists of possible threats, vulnerabilities, and security controls.	www.iso.org

Closing the Information Security Gap

In spite of all best efforts, no collection of security controls is perfect. There are always some vulnerabilities for which there are no controls. The difference between the security controls you have in place and the controls you need in order to address all vulnerabilities is called the **security gap**.

A valuable tool to help ensure you are satisfying your organization's **security policy** is a **gap analysis**. From an IT security perspective, a security policy defines a risk-mitigating definition or solution for your organization. A gap analysis is a comparison of the security controls you have in place and the controls you need in order to address all identified threats. Gap analysis activities should be ongoing. They should consist of regular reviews of day-to-day practices vis-à-vis the latest threat assessment. Threats that you do not address through at least one control indicate gaps in your security.

Performing gap analysis is an effective method for gauging the overall security of an organization's IT environments. In addition, a gap analysis can provide assurances that security implementations are consistent with real requirements. You can conduct many different types of gap analysis activities. They can be formal investigations or informal surveys. Factors that influence the analysis include the size of your organization, the industry in which you operate, the cost involved, the efforts involved, and the depth of the analysis.

- Identifying the applicable elements of the security policy and other standards
- Assembling policy, standard, procedure, and guideline documents
- Reviewing and assessing the implementation of the policies, standards, procedures, and guidelines
- Collecting inventory information for all hardware and software components
- Interviewing users to assess knowledge of and compliance with policies
- Comparing the current security environment with policies in place
- Prioritizing identified gaps for resolution
- Documenting and implementing the remedies to conform to policies

One important aspect of a gap analysis is determining the cause of the gap. The fact that a gap exists means there is a lack of adequate security controls, but *why* does the gap exist? There are several common reasons for security gaps in any organization, such as:

- Lack of security training, resulting in noncompliant behavior
- Intentional or negligent disregard of security policy
- Unintended consequence of a control or policy change
- Addition or modification of hardware or software without proper risk analysis
- Configuration changes that lack proper risk analysis
- Changes to external requirements, such as legislation, regulation, or industry standards that require control changes

As you can see, most security gaps relate closely to user actions. One of the first steps you can take to close gaps is to ensure that you fully train personnel on security issues. Well-trained people are your best allies in securing your IT environment. As your security efforts become more sophisticated and your organization's personnel become more security savvy, you should encounter fewer security gaps.

Adhering to Compliance Laws

The last 30 years have seen an explosion in computing power and in the number of ways computers are used. The increased reliance on networked resources, hardware, and software has created many new opportunities for the malicious use of resources. Information has become a valued asset to organizations and an attractive target of attackers. As information-related crime has grown, so has legislation and regulation to protect organizations and individuals from criminal activity.

Today's organizations are increasingly subject to various laws enacted
vacy of electronic information. Each organization must comply with law'
although the specific laws and regulations to which an organization is s
the organization's location, the type of information it handles, and the
operates.

The following list summarizes many of the most far-reaching law'
affect how organizations conduct IT operations:

- **Sarbanes-Oxley Act (SOX)**—Sarbanes-Oxley, which became law in July 2002, introu...
  sweeping changes to the way corporate governance and financial practices are regulated.
  As a direct result of several public financial scandals, SOX established the Public Company
  Accounting Oversight Board (PCAOB), which is responsible for overseeing, regulating, inspecting, and disciplining accounting firms in their roles as auditors of public companies.
  SOX also dictates policies that address auditor independence, corporate governance, internal control assessment, and enhanced financial disclosure.

- **Health Insurance Portability and Accountability Act (HIPAA)**—HIPAA, which took
  effect on April 14, 2006, governs the way doctors, hospitals, and other health care
  providers handle personal medical information. HIPAA requires that all medical records, billing, and patient information be handled in ways that maintain the patient's
  privacy. HIPAA also guarantees that all patients be able to access their own medical
  records, correct errors or omissions, and be informed of how personal information
  is used. To ensure every affected person is aware of HIPAA's requirements, patients
  must receive notifications of privacy procedures any time they submit medical
  information.

- **Federal Financial Institutions Examination Council (FFIEC)**—FFIEC has established
  a standard for security controls and maturity assessments. This includes an inherent
  risk profile assessment and a cybersecurity maturity assessment. Using these two
  benchmarks, financial organizations can assess their current risk profile and their
  current cybersecurity maturity level based on performing these self-assessments
  internal to their organization.

- **Federal Information Security Management Act (FISMA)**—FISMA officially recognizes the importance of information security to the national security and economic
  health of the United States. FISMA was enacted in 2002 and required every federal
  agency to develop and maintain formal information security programs, including security awareness efforts; secure access to computer resources; strict acceptable use
  policies; and formal incident response and contingency planning.

- **Federal Information Security Modernization Act (FISMA)**—FISMA 2014 is the update to the original FISMA enacted in 2002. This is the first amendment to the original FISMA. Updates to FISMA 2014 include these:

  - Reasserts the authority of the director of the Office of Management and Budget
    (OMB) with oversight while authorizing the Secretary of the Department of Home-
    land Security (DHS) to administer the implementation of security policies and
    practices for federal information systems

- Requires agencies to notify Congress of major security incidents within seven days. OMB will be responsible for developing guidance on what constitutes a major incident

- Places more responsibility on agencies looking at budgetary planning for security management, ensuring that senior officials accomplish information security tasks and that all personnel are responsible for complying with agency information security programs

- Changes the reporting guidance focusing on threats, vulnerabilities, incidents, the compliance status of systems at the time of major incidents, and data on incidents involving personally identifiable information (PII)

- Calls for the revision of OMB Circular A-130 to eliminate inefficient or wasteful reporting

- Provides for the use of automated tools in agencies' information security programs, including periodic risk assessments, testing of security procedures, and detecting, reporting, and responding to security incidents

- **Gramm-Leach-Bliley Act (GLBA)**—GLBA addresses information security concerns in the financial industry. GLBA requires that financial institutions provide their clients a privacy notice that explains what information the company gathers about the client, where the information is shared, and how the company protects that information. Companies must provide clients with this privacy notice prior to entering into an agreement to do business.

- **Payment Card Industry Data Security Standard (PCI DSS v3.2)**—Although not a law, PCI DSS v3.2 affects any organization that processes or stores credit card information. The founding payment brands of the PCI Security Standards Council—including American Express, Discover Financial Services, JCB, MasterCard Worldwide, and Visa International—developed PCI DSS v3.2 to foster consistent global data security measures. The PCI DSS v3.2 is a comprehensive security standard that includes requirements for security management, policies, procedures, network architecture, software design, and other critical protective measures.

- **The Family Education Rights and Privacy Act (FERPA)**—This federal law protects the privacy of student education records. The law applies to all schools that receive funds under an applicable program of the U.S. Department of Education. Under FERPA, schools must receive written permission from a parent or eligible student before releasing any information contained in a student's education record.

- **The USA Patriot Act of 2001**—Passed 45 days after the September 11, 2001, attacks on the World Trade Center in New York City and on the Pentagon in Washington, D.C., the Patriot Act substantially expanded the authority of U.S. law enforcement agencies to enable them to fight terrorism in the United States and abroad. It expands the ability of law enforcement agencies to access information that pertains to an ongoing investigation.

- **Children's Online Privacy Protection Act of 1998 (COPPA)**—The COPPA Rule restricts how online information is collected from children under 13 years of age. COPPA was made effective in 2000 and gained additional consent requirements in

2013. It dictates what a website operator must include in a privacy policy, when and how to seek verifiable consent from a parent, and what responsibilities an operator has to protect children's privacy and safety online.

- **Government Information Security Reform Act (Security Reform Act) of 2000**— This act focuses on management and evaluation of the security of unclassified and national security systems. It formalized existing OMB security policies and restated security responsibilities contained in the Computer Security Act of 1987.

- **California Database Security Breach Act (SB 1386) of 2003**—This California act, SB 1386, along with several other similar state acts, requires any company that stores customer data electronically to notify its customers any time there is a security breach. The company must immediately notify any affected customers if someone breaches its computer system and steals unencrypted information. Other similar bills limit the ability of financial institutions to share nonpublic personal client information with affiliates and third parties.

> **NOTE**
>
> A **privacy policy** defines what an organization does with the data it collects about you and why it collects those data. Privacy policies also explain what you must do if you do not want your data to be shared or sold to third parties.

It's the responsibility of each organization to understand which laws and regulations apply to them and to employ necessary controls to comply. This effort often requires frequent attention and results in audits and assessments to ensure that the organization remains compliant.

Keeping Private Data Confidential

Many of the compliance requirements you saw in earlier sections address data confidentiality. One of the most important classes of security controls is those that keep information confidential. Ensuring availability and integrity is important, but confidentiality gets the most attention. That's because you cannot undo a confidentiality violation. That is, once someone views confidential data, there is no way to remove those data from his or her memory. You must pay careful attention to each of the three tenets of information security to protect your organization's data assets. **FIGURE 4-2** shows the three tenets of information security.

You will learn different techniques to ensure the confidentiality, integrity, and availability of data. At the highest level, data are secure when they are available to authorized users and not available to unauthorized users. You will have to cover many details before you can fully ensure your data's security. Maintaining confidentiality will certainly be a recurring theme. In fact, many controls to ensure confidentiality also ensure other aspects of data security.

As you learn more about various security controls, you will see how they work together to protect data from unauthorized use. Most strategies to secure data use a three-pronged approach that includes the techniques of authentication, authorization, and accounting. These three techniques help ensure that only authorized users can access resources and data. They also ensure that enough information is captured to troubleshoot access issues after the access

> **NOTE**
>
> In the context of monitoring information system activity, the term **accounting** means recording events in log files. You can use computer event accounting to trace users' actions and determine a sequence of events that is helpful with investigating incidents.

FIGURE 4-2

The three tenets of
information security.

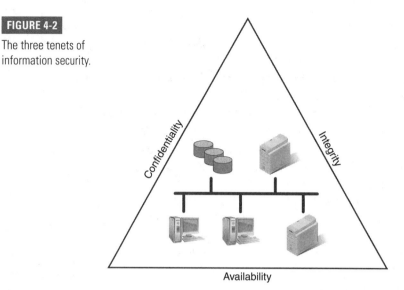

occurs. Investigations into security incidents rely on accounting information to reconstruct
past events.

The basic purpose of the three-pronged approach is to maintain security by preventing
unauthorized use of any protected resource. Many authentication and access controls can
help accomplish this task. Some of the authentication controls you will learn about include
the following:

- Passwords and personal identification numbers (PINs)
- Smart cards and tokens
- Biometric devices
- Digital certificates
- Challenge-response handshakes
- Kerberos authentication
- One-time passwords

> **NOTE**
>
> Businesses and organizations under a
> regulatory compliance law must address
> regulated data versus non regulated data.
> Data that are under a regulatory compli-
> ance requirement typically mean that
> those data must have incorporated proper
> security controls, including stringent
> access controls, real-time monitoring, and
> data encryption at rest, in storage, and
> in transit. Data confidentiality is a top-of-
> mind business challenge for organizations
> under a regulatory compliance law. Proper
> data confidentiality security controls can
> mitigate the threat of a data breach or
> data loss. Any organization not employing
> proper controls to comply with regulations
> might be subject to fines levied against
> them or even to criminal prosecution.

Once you have authenticated a user, access controls help ensure
that only authorized users can access the protected resource. Authorization controls you will learn about include the following:

- Authentication server rules and permissions
- Access control lists
- Intrusion detection and prevention
- Physical access control
- Connection and access policy filters
- Network traffic filters

These two lists give a brief overview of some of the security controls that help to ensure your organization's data security.

Mobile Workers and Use of Personally Owned Devices

Another emerging business driver for companies and organizations is mobility. **Mobility** allows remote workers and employees to be connected to the IT infrastructure in almost real time. This means that speed and effective communications can help businesses increase productivity, sales, revenue, and profit. The hyperconnected mobile worker is now "always on." This helps drive productivity throughout the organization. The prevalence of these mobile road warriors, such as outside sales representatives who visit clients, introduces a critical risk element for businesses, given that the point of entry into the organization's IT infrastructure is performed by the user within the User Domain connecting via the Workstation Domain with their endpoint device. Depending on the given situation, the endpoint device can be anything from a laptop or tablet to a smartphone. Each of these devices introduces its own risks, threats, and vulnerabilities. Mobility is the business driver that is leading businesses and organizations to adopt a Bring Your Own Device (BYOD) strategy. BYOD is a term that addresses employees using their personally owned devices, such as a laptop computer or smartphone, for business use as well as personal use.

BYOD Concerns

The acceptance of BYOD into corporate environments and government environments has created a unique business challenge that must be solved. This challenge is based on the fact that the IT asset is owned by the employee. Regardless, that IT asset and its user must still abide by the organization's mobility, BYOD, and acceptable-use policy. The following elements are commonly addressed in a BYOD policy definition:

- **Data ownership**—Personal data such as contacts, pictures, or emails are the intellectual property of the employee. Business emails and all attachments are the intellectual property of the organization. This distinction must be clearly defined in a BYOD policy.
- **Support ownership**—The employee owns the IT asset and all support and maintenance responsibilities unless reimbursement is approved by the organization.
- **Patch management**—Software updates and **patches** are recommended and should be performed by the employee on his or her own device, as defined by the organization through policy definition.
- **Antivirus management**—Any IT asset that accesses the organization's intellectual property must have proper (as defined by the BYOD policy) **antivirus**/anti-malware protection installed.

> **NOTE**
>
> Businesses and organizations must make a decision regarding use of personal IT assets for business purposes. This includes employees using personal smartphones for business emails that may or may not contain sensitive data as an email attachment. Mobility is driving the convergence of business and personal-use IT assets. The use of social media is driving the convergence of business and personal communications and information sharing. The investment needed to provide laptops and smartphones for employees may be cost-prohibitive for some businesses or organizations. Many organizations are now implementing policies and procedures to ensure the confidentiality of business information on personally owned devices such as laptops or smartphones. Employees using personal IT assets typically must still abide by the organization's acceptable-use policy, email and Internet usage policy, and BYOD policy. The BYOD policy may require authorization to perform data wiping or data deletion in the event of loss or theft of the device.

4

The Drivers of the Information
Security Business

- **Forensics**—Employees must agree that if their personally owned IT asset is part of a formal incident response investigation, the IT asset may be confiscated to conduct a thorough forensics investigation on the asset.

- **Privacy**—Employees are entitled to retain and maintain their privacy; however, the organization's acceptable-use policy and definitions for data wiping and data deletion must be fully understood by employees prior to agreeing to use their personally owned devices to conduct business.

- **Onboarding/offboarding**—The BYOD policy should be explained and agreed to during the HR onboarding process. The policy also should include handling (e.g., data wiping, data deletion, etc.) of the personally owned IT asset during offboarding prior to employee termination and removal of access controls.

- **Adherence to corporate policies**—The use of personally owned IT assets requires employees to abide by all other policies and procedures, including the acceptable-use policy.

- **User acceptance**—The employee must agree to data wiping and data deletion (as required by the BYOD policy) in addition to a separation of private data versus business data.

- **Architecture/infrastructure considerations**—The use of any personally owned IT asset must meet the organization's IT standards and may require installation of new software to assist with security.

- **Legal concerns**—Employees must agree to abide by the organization's policies and procedures, particularly if a legal issue or incident investigation is involved (for example, a forensics investigation).

- **Acceptable-use policy**—Employees must abide by all organizational policies and procedures, in particular the organization's acceptable-use policy.

- **Onboard camera/video**—The BYOD policy should address the use of camera and video capabilities of any personally owned IT asset. The content of those pictures and videos must abide by the acceptable-use policy. Typically, employees are responsible for all personal data backups, including pictures and videos.

Endpoint and Device Security

With mobility and BYOD comes the need to enable endpoint or device security controls. The following discussion presents endpoint device security controls that can mitigate the risks, threats, and vulnerabilities commonly associated with mobility and BYOD environments:

- **Full device encryption**—Require that laptops, tablets, and smartphones are equipped with data encryption, thus mitigating the risk of a lost or stolen device.

- **Remote wiping**—Install software that will enable organizations to initiate remote wiping of data or email in the event of loss or theft of the device.

- **Lockout**—Require device screen savers with lockout timers that conform to the organization's Workstation Domain security policies and procedures.

- **Screen locks**—Require a password-protected screen-lock function that requires the owner to enter a password to gain access to the device.
- **Global positioning system (GPS)**—Install a GPS that uses satellite and/or cellular communications to pinpoint the physical location of the device if it is connected to a communications network.
- **Application control**—Install software that allows for application control or device control.
- **Storage segmentation**—Require that devices that are shared for personal and business use have segmented storage to physically separate personal data from business data.
- **Asset tracking**—Require that all IT assets that are connected to the IT infrastructure, whether personally owned or owned by the organization, be tracked as IT assets by the organization.
- **Inventory control**—Require that all mobile devices owned by employees be IT–asset inventoried such that proper change management and incident response can be performed to all endpoint devices.
- **Mobile device management**—Require that a **mobile device management (MDM)** software agent (a software application that allows organizations to monitor, control, data wipe, or data delete business data from a personally owned device) be installed on any mobile device.
- **Device access control**—Require that all personally owned devices conform to the organization's BYOD policy and have proper device access controls to access the IT asset itself, access controls for email access, and access controls for remote access to the IT infrastructure.
- **Removable storage**—Require the use of **removable storage** or data backups as defined in the organization's BYOD policy and acceptable-use policy. Data backups of personal data are the responsibility of the employee. Data backups of business data are the responsibility of the employee or the organization, according to policy definition.
- **Disabling unused features**—Depending on the BYOD policy and acceptable-use policy definition, disallow the use of specific applications and features, such as the use of text messaging of sensitive data.

CHAPTER SUMMARY

In this chapter, you learned that security is much more than a way to keep data secret. Security is an integral part of any organization. BCP and DRP readiness ensures that an organization can perform its primary business functions, even in the event of a disaster, and that it will do so by protecting all of its assets, including its data. A sound security infrastructure provides the assurance that the organization has employed the necessary controls to comply with all necessary laws, regulations, and other security requirements. In short, security keeps an organization viable and allows it to conduct business.

In addition, this chapter presented business drivers for information systems security. Depending on the type of business or vertical industry you are in, compliance, security, and privacy are all driving requirements for implementing proper security controls. Confidentiality of regulated data is a top-of-mind business driver. Mobility and the use of personally owned IT assets are also driving the way organizations permit the use of BYOD assets for their employees.

KEY CONCEPTS AND TERMS

Accounting

Antivirus

Business drivers

California Database Security Breach Act (SB 1386)

Children's Online Privacy Protection Act (COPPA)

Delphi method

Disaster recovery plan (DRP)

Gap analysis

Government Information Security Reform Act (Security Reform Act)

Mobile device management (MDM)

Mobility

Patch

Privacy policy

Project Management Body of Knowledge (PMBOK)

Project Management Institute (PMI)

Recovery point objective (RPO)

Recover time objective (RTO)

Remote wiping

Removable storage

Risk management

Risk methodology

Risk register

Security gap

Security policy

USA Patriot Act

User acceptance

CHAPTER 4 ASSESSMENT

1. Risk management is responding to a negative event when it occurs.

A. True

B. False

2. With respect to IT security, a risk can result in either a positive or a negative effect.

A. True

B. False

3. According to PMI, which term describes the list of identified risks?

A. Risk checklist

B. Risk register

C. Risk methodology

D. Mitigation list

E. All of the above

4. What is the primary purpose of a business impact analysis (BIA)?

A. To identify, categorize, and prioritize mission-critical business functions

B. To provide a road map for business continuity and disaster recovery planning

C. To assist organizations with risk management

D. To assist organizations with incident response planning

E. All of the above

5. Which of the following terms defines the amount of time it takes to recover a production IT system, application, and access to data?

- A. Recovery point objective
- B. Recovery time objective
- C. Risk exposure time
- D. Production recovery time
- E. None of the above

6. The recovery point objective (RPO) defines the last point in time for _____ recovery that can be enabled back into production.

- A. System
- B. Application
- C. Production
- D. Data
- E. None of the above

7. Which of the following solutions are used for authenticating a user to gain access to systems, applications, and data?

- A. Passwords and PINs
- B. Smart cards and tokens
- C. Biometric devices
- D. Digital certificates
- E. All of the above

8. Which risk management approach requires a distributed approach with business units working with the IT organization?

- A. OCTAVE
- B. CRAMM
- C. NIST SP800-33
- D. ISO 27005
- E. None of the above

9. The NIST SP800-30 standard is a _____ management framework standard for performing risk management.

- A. Risk
- B. Threat
- C. Vulnerability
- D. Security
- E. None of the above

10. Which term indicates the maximum amount of data loss over a time period?

- A. RAI
- B. ROI
- C. RTO
- D. RPO
- E. None of the above

11. Organizations that permit their employees to use their own laptops or smartphone devices and connect to the IT infrastructure describe a policy referred to as:

- A. RTO
- B. MDM
- C. BYOD
- D. AUP
- E. None of the above

12. Which of the following are organizational concerns for BYOD and mobility?

- A. Data ownership
- B. Privacy
- C. Lost or stolen device
- D. Data wiping
- E. All of the above

13. ____ is the U.S. security-related act that governs regulated health care information.

14. Which U.S. security-related act governs the security of data specifically for the financial industry?

- A. GLBA
- B. COPPA
- C. HIPAA
- D. FERPA
- E. None of the above

15. Which of the following business drivers are impacting businesses' and organizations' security requirements and implementations?

- A. Mobility
- B. Regulatory compliance
- C. Productivity enhancements
- D. Always-on connectivity
- E. All of the above

4

The Drivers of the Information Security Business

PART II

Securing Today's Information Systems

Access Controls

ACCESS CONTROLS are methods used to restrict and allow access to certain items, such as automobiles, homes, computers, and even your smartphone. Your first experience with access controls might have been as a child when you locked a brother or sister out of your room or used a locker at school. Similarly, the key to your car fits *only* your car, so only you can unlock and start it. The same is true of your house or apartment. Many people also use a special code to unlock a smartphone or tablet. No one can unlock the phone or tablet without the code. Or maybe you can't view certain channels on your television without a security code.

Access control is the process of protecting a resource so that it is used only by those allowed to use it. Access controls protect a resource from unauthorized use. Just as the lock-and-key systems for your house or car are access controls, so are the **personal information numbers (PINs)** on your bank or credit cards. Another way to define access controls is that they are mitigations put into place to protect a resource from a threat. However you think of access controls, they are tools to make sure that only "allowed" users can access a resource.

Businesses use access controls to manage what employees can and cannot do. Access controls define who users (people or computer processes) are, what users can do, which resources they can reach, and what operations they can perform. Access control systems use several methods to achieve this goal, including passwords, hardware tokens, biometrics, and certificates. Access can be granted to physical assets, such as buildings or rooms. Access can also be granted to computer systems and data.

Chapter 5 Topics

This chapter covers the following topics and concepts:

- What the four parts of access control are
- What the two types of access control are
- How to define an authorization policy
- What identification methods and guidelines are

- What authentication processes and requirements are
- What accountability policies and procedures are
- What formal models of access control are
- What threats there are to access controls
- What some effects of access control violations are
- What centralized and decentralized access controls are

Chapter 5 Goals

When you complete this chapter, you will be able to:

- Define access control concepts and technologies
- Describe the formal models of access control
- Describe how identity is managed by access control
- Develop and maintain system access controls

Four-Part Access Control

Before an asset can be protected, the protector must know some information about the intended user. The four parts of **access control** are as follows:

- **Identification**—Who is asking to access the asset?
- **Authentication**—Can the requestor's identity be verified?
- **Authorization**—What, exactly, can the requestor access? And what can they do?
- **Accountability**—How can actions be traced to an individual? We need to ensure that a person who accesses or makes changes to data or systems can be identified. This process of associating actions with users for later reporting and research is known as **accountability**.

These four parts are divided into two phases:

- **The policy definition phase**—This phase determines who has access and what systems or resources they can use. The authorization definition process operates in this phase.
- **The policy enforcement phase**—This phase grants or rejects requests for access based on the authorizations defined in the first phase. The identification, authentication, authorization execution, and accountability processes operate in this phase.

Two Types of Access Controls

Access controls generally fall into one of two categories:

> **NOTE**
>
> Sometimes the difference between *access control* and *access controls* can be confusing. Just remember that *access control* is something that you do to protect resources. The way you protect resources from unauthorized access is by using different types of *access controls*.

- **Physical access controls**—These control access to physical resources. They could include buildings, parking lots, and protected areas. For example, you probably have a key to the door of your office. This key controls the *physical* access to your office.

- **Logical access controls**—These control access to a computer system or network. Your company probably requires that you enter a unique username and password to log on to your company computer. That username and password allow you to use your organization's computer system and network resources.

Physical Access Control

An organization's facilities manager is often responsible for **physical access control**. This person might give you a security card (also known as a **smart card**) programmed with your employee ID number. You might need to swipe this card through a card reader to open a gate to the parking lot and swipe it in the elevator to be let off on your floor. You might also need to swipe this card to unlock a door leading to your office. This card allows you to enter these locations because you are an employee. The organization's authorization policy grants you, as an employee, physical access to certain places. People without an authorized card shouldn't get past the front gate. If your organization shares your office building with other organizations, you might even have a second card that grants access into the building after hours. These cards control access to *physical* resources.

Logical Access Control

Security administrators use **logical access controls** to decide who can get into a system and what tasks they can perform. A system manager can also use logical access controls to influence how staff personnel use a system. Examples of system controls for a human resources (HR) system include the following:

- **Deciding which users can get into a system**—HR employees may be the only employees who are allowed to reach sensitive information stored on an HR server.

- **Monitoring what the user does on that system**—Certain HR employees might be allowed to view documents, but other HR employees might be able to actually edit those documents.

- **Restraining or influencing the user's behavior on that system**—An HR staffer who repeatedly tries to view restricted information might be denied access to the entire system.

These permissions control access to logical (or system) resources.

The Security Kernel

The **security kernel** is the central part of a computing environment's hardware, software, and firmware that enforces access control for computer systems. The security kernel provides a central point of access control and implements the **reference monitor** concept. It mediates all access requests and permits access only when the appropriate rules or conditions are met. For example:

1. The subject requests access to an object. The security kernel intercepts the request.
2. The security kernel refers to its rules base, also known as the **security kernel database**. It uses these rules to determine access rights. Access rights are set according to the policies your organization has defined.
3. The kernel allows or denies access based on the defined access rules. All access requests handled by the system are logged for later tracking and analysis.

FIGURE 5-1 shows a request for access coming from the subject to a particular object—in this case, a file. The reference monitor intercepts the access request. The access is granted according to the rules in the security kernel database. This rule base might be an **access control list (ACL)**, a directory, or another repository of access permissions. If the rules permit the access request, the reference monitor permits access and creates a log entry.

It is easy to see that the overall security of any system's access control depends on the security of the operating system. Most of the popular computer operating systems (e.g., Windows®, Linux®/UNIX®, OS X®) provide extensive security features. These features allow administrators to create very secure systems. However, the popular operating systems for many mobile devices (e.g., Android™ and iOS®) lack some of these security features. One argument is that mobile devices do not need the same level of security features as servers or full-featured client computers. However, as mobile devices become more and more powerful, the need for tighter security increases. Some computing environments need even more security guarantees than most operating systems provide. Systems that handle

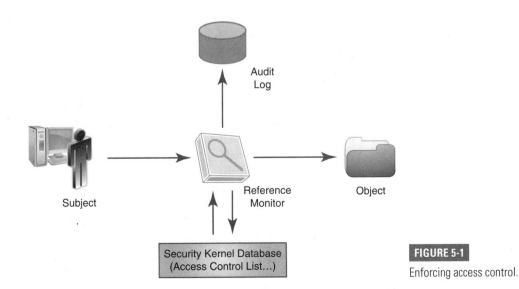

FIGURE 5-1

Enforcing access control.

extremely sensitive information, such as classified information on government servers, need more security controls. Several operating systems have included additional controls to address the additional security needs of such systems. These operating systems, referred to as **trusted operating systems (TOS)**, provide features that satisfy specific government requirements for security. One of the most widely used set of criteria for TOS design is the Common Criteria, which you will read about later in this chapter.

Access Control Policies

An **access control policy** is a set of rules that allows a specific group of users to perform a particular set of actions on a particular set of resources. If users aren't authorized, they don't have access to system functions or system resources. You use access control policies to reduce and control security risks. Both automated processes and humans use access control policies.

You must understand the four central components of access control to manage access control policies well:

- **Users**—These are the people who use the system or processes that perform some service for other people or processes. A more general term for users is *subjects*.

- **Resources**—Protected objects in the system. Resources can be accessed only by authorized subjects. Resources can be used only in authorized ways.

- **Actions**—Activities that authorized users can perform on the resources.

- **Relationships**—Optional conditions that exist between users and resources. Relationships are permissions granted to an authorized user, such as *read*, *write*, *execute*.

> ▶ **TIP**
>
> Many discussions of access control concepts use the terms *subject* for the user and *object* for the resource. You may also see the term *request*, which refers to an access action a subject tries to carry out.

Authorization Policies

The first step to controlling access is to create a policy that defines authorization rules. **Authorization** is the process of deciding who has access to which computer and network resources. In most organizations, authorization is based on job roles, background screening, and any government requirements. These conditions or policies are decided primarily by either a group membership policy or an authority-level policy.

The most detailed authorization policy is based on each individual user. In this type of policy, each user has specific assigned privileges. These **user assigned privileges** allow administrators to define approved resource access at a very detailed level. However, maintaining a user-based authentication approach is very difficult. This type of authentication requires a lot of administration time to stay current.

In a **group membership policy**, authorization is defined by what group(s) users are in. Assigning group-based privileges reduces the administrator workload by grouping similar users together. For example, perhaps only the security cards of members of the IT department give access to the room where computer equipment is stored. If you're not a member of this IT group, your security card does not let you enter this room to retrieve a new monitor. If you want to access the computer equipment storage room, you must first contact the IT department, which likely assigns a member of the IT group to help you.

In an **authority-level policy**, you need a higher degree of authority to access certain resources. For example, perhaps only a senior-level member of the IT group has permission to enter the room that houses servers. Servers are often more valuable than computer monitors, so a policy might specify that only a senior staff member can enter the server room.

Methods and Guidelines for Identification

Once you define authorization rules in an authorization policy, you can enforce the rules. Each time a user requests access for a resource, the access controls grant or deny access based on the authorization policy.

The first step in enforcing an authorization policy is identification. **Identification** is the method a subject uses to request access to a system or resource. A subject can be a user, a process, or some other entity. There are several methods commonly used to identify subjects. The method you choose depends on your security requirements and the capabilities of your computing environment. In the next section, you'll learn about various methods and guidelines for how a subject identifies itself to a system.

Identification Methods

A **username** is the most common method to identify a user to a system. A username can be in the form of a user ID, an account number, or some other assigned identifier. Some applications identify a user through the use of a **smart card**, which often takes the form of a plastic credit card. Smart cards make it easy for subjects to provide complex identification credentials without having to remember long passwords. Just as you might slide your credit card through an electronic card reader to make a purchase, you can swipe a smart card through a card reader that grants access to parking facilities, buildings, and rooms.

Biometrics are another access control method for identifying subjects. Biometrics are used to recognize humans based on one or more physical or behavioral traits. Examples of biometrics include fingerprints, face or voice recognition, DNA matching, handwriting, retina scans, and even the way a person types.

> **NOTE**
>
> The U.S. Customs and Border Protection (CBP) program uses two different types of biometrics to identify authorized members of the program. The CBP defines several different programs that preauthorize frequent travelers to bypass regular customs lines and use faster automated kiosks. The NEXUS kiosks at select U.S. and Canadian border crossings use retina scans to identify users. The Global Entry kiosks at many international airports in the United States use fingerprint scanners to identify users.

Identification Guidelines

To ensure that all **actions** carried out in a computer system can be associated with a specific user, each user must have a unique identifier. That means that it is important for each user to have a different user account from any other user. Your account policy should prohibit generic accounts and user account sharing. A unique identifier (an ID) makes it possible to tell the difference between multiple users with the same name. The process of associating an action with users for later reporting or analysis is called

accounting. You should keep current the data used to identify subjects and monitor those data closely. You should disable the IDs of users who leave the organization or who are inactive for an extended time. You should apply standard naming conventions; these should not relate to job functions. The process for issuing IDs should be documented and secure.

Processes and Requirements for Authentication

So far in this chapter, you have learned about methods to define authorization rules and identify users. The next step is authentication. In this part of access control, a user validates, or proves, the identity he or she provided during identification. **Authentication** answers the question, Are users who they say they are? Authentication proves that the subject requesting access is the same subject who has been granted access. Without authentication, you could never really know if users are who they say claim to be.

Authentication Types

There are five types of authentication:

- **Knowledge**—Something you know, such as a password, passphrase, or personal identification number (PIN).

- **Ownership**—Something you have, such as a smart card, key, badge, or token.

- **Characteristics**—Some attribute that is unique to you, such as your fingerprints, retina, or signature. Since the characteristics involved are often physical, this type of authentication is sometimes defined as *something you are.*

- **Location**—Somewhere you are, such as your physical location when you attempt to access a resource.

- **Action**—Something you do or how you do it, such as the way you type on a keyboard.

> **⚠ WARNING**
>
> A combination of username and password is considered single-factor authentication even though it requires two steps. This might or might not be adequate for access to more sensitive systems, applications, or data. In this case, you might be required to provide two-factor or multifactor authentication, in which you would swipe a card (something you have) to enter a building, then type a PIN (something you know) to ensure the security of a valuable resource.

Each type of authentication can be easily compromised on its own. The use of controls from only one category is known as **single-factor authentication**. Systems containing sensitive or critical information should use at least two of these authentication types. The use of techniques from two or more of these categories is called **two-factor authentication** and provides a higher level of security than using only one.

Authentication by Knowledge

Authentication by **knowledge** is based on something you know, such as a password, passphrase, or PIN. Static passwords are those that are seldom, if ever, changed. Passwords are the oldest and most common method of authentication for computer systems. They are also the weakest. You should not use passwords alone to protect valuable resources. As the value of a resource increases, so should the strength of the access controls protecting it. Two-step authentication should be the minimum requirement for valuable resources.

Attackers often use brute-force or dictionary attacks to crack passwords. These methods can easily crack weak passwords, such as those that are very short or contain dictionary words.

- A **brute-force attack** involves trying every possible combination of characters. Modern password crackers don't try every combination of letters, numbers, and special characters in alphabetic order. Rather, they first measure the entropy (a measure of randomness) of characters. Then they test low-entropy words first, medium-entropy words next, and then high-entropy words last.

> ▶ **TIP**
>
> A shorter password life span means more protection for the user. To create stronger password controls for users, consider a 30-day password-change policy. A shorter password life span means a lower chance that an attacker can compromise and use the password before it expires.

- A **dictionary attack** works by hashing all the words in a dictionary (often supplemented with suffixes such as 01, 02, 4u, and so on) and then comparing the hashed value with the system password file to discover a match. Hackers are familiar with all the usual tricks, such as spelling a name backward or simple substitution of characters (such as 3 for e, 0 for o, $ for s, and so on).

- Because most systems store a hash of the password, attackers first precompute these dictionary words and build a table. Then they look up the stored hashed version of the password in the table to discover the word that generated it. These tables, known as **rainbow tables**, are widely available. For example, AccessData's forensic investigator's tool known as the Forensic Toolkit® (FTK®) features a rainbow table with a million words. According to FTK's website, the table detects 28 percent of user passwords.

Password Account Policies: In addition to encouraging password best practices, your account policy should include clear password requirements. Following is a list of suggested account policy password requirements. (You can, and should, change the specifics of these items for your organization.)

- Complexity
  - Passwords must contain at least eight alphanumeric characters.
  - Passwords must contain a combination of uppercase and lowercase letters and numbers.
  - Passwords must contain at least one special character within the first seven characters of the password.
  - Passwords must contain a nonnumeric letter or symbol in the first and last character positions.
  - Passwords must *not* contain the username.
  - Passwords must never include the name of the user or the names of any close friends or relatives.
  - Passwords must never use an employee's ID number, Social Security number, birth date, telephone number, or any personal information that can be easily guessed.
  - Passwords must never include common words from an English dictionary (or a dictionary of another language with which the user is familiar).

Password Best Practices

One of the most visible security policies is the user account policy. This is a policy that each user must encounter. A good user account policy sets clear requirements for user accounts and passwords. You have already seen that an account policy should prohibit generic user accounts. Your account policy should also include password best practices:

- **Create strong passwords**—Your password must be complex enough to be unlikely to be compromised. It must meet minimum length requirements. You should never use a word that appears in the dictionary as your password. Passwords should not be based on personal information. Hackers have easy access to powerful password-cracking tools that use extensive word and name dictionaries. More secure passwords use words that don't make any sense but that are easy to remember. For example, you might create a password using letters from the first words of a poem or song. Or you might substitute obscure characters, such as asterisks (*), dollar signs ($), "at" symbols (@), brackets ({}), mathematical symbols (+), and the like. These can be extremely difficult to guess or crack. Remember: Cracking tools check for simple tricks such as words spelled backward or simple substitutions for certain characters (for example, where mouse becomes m0us3).

- **Don't store a written copy of the password unless absolutely necessary**—If you must store a written copy, keep it in a secure place. Alternatively, write down a hint for your password instead of the actual password. Destroy any written copies when they are no longer needed.

- **Never share your passwords with anyone**—Even if it is someone you trust, your password should be kept private.

- **Use different passwords for different important user accounts**—Using a single password for all your accounts is like using a single key for your car, your house, your mailbox, and your safety deposit box. If you lose the key, an attacker has access to everything. When you use different passwords for different systems, if one of your passwords is stolen, only that one system is compromised. This strategy prevents intruders from gaining access to accounts and data on other systems. Also, avoid using passwords that are similar to one another—for example, passwords that use the names of your children. If you use the same or similar passwords for more than one system, it makes it easier for an intruder who obtains one of your passwords to figure out the rest.

- **If you think a password is compromised, change it immediately**—Also, the first time you use them, change passwords that are assigned to you. Ideally, you should change passwords at least once every 30 days.

- **Be careful when saving passwords on computers**—Some dialog boxes (such as those for remote access and other telephone connections) present options to save or remember passwords. Selecting these options poses a potential security threat because the password is automatically listed when someone opens the dialog box.

- Passwords must never employ commonly used proper names, including the name of any fictional character or place.
- Passwords must never contain any simple pattern of letters or numbers, such as *qwertyxx*.
- Expiration. Passwords expire every 30 days and must be changed.
- Recovery. Forgotten passwords can be recovered after providing alternate authentication credentials via the organization's internal password recovery utility.

- Disablement. User accounts will be disabled immediately when a user no longer is ~~ ated with the organization or no longer requires provided access.
- History. Password history is stored, and you cannot change your password to any ⌐ 10 previous passwords you used.

Passphrase Usage: A **passphrase** is a bit different from a password. It is longer and generally harder to guess, so it's considered more secure. Because it usually contains more than one word, a passphrase is more secure against dictionary attacks. Most often, passphrases are used for public and private key authentication. The user uses a passphrase that is known only to the user, and the user uses that passphrase to unlock a private key that gives the user access to information. In most cases, the user converts the passphrase to a password. However, a system can be programmed to automatically convert the passphrase to a password according to an algorithm. A passphrase is stronger than a password, but the downside is that it takes a bit longer to type. Although passphrases are static, they aren't as susceptible to brute-force attacks as passwords.

> **NOTE**
>
> It's okay to reuse a password for resources that aren't considered critical—for example, to access articles on an online news site. Just don't use that same password for any logons for critical resources.

Account Lockout Policies: Many systems are configured to disable a user ID after a certain number of consecutive failed logon attempts. In many cases, user accounts are disabled after three to five attempts. The number of failed logon attempts that trigger an account action is called the **threshold**. The user may be locked out for a few minutes, a few hours, or until the account is reset by a security administrator. This practice helps guard against attacks in which attackers make many attempts to guess a password. It also enables an intruder to lock out users, however—a form of denial of service (DoS) attack—by entering groups of incorrect passwords.

FYI

Unless your organization uses an automated password-reset process, your help-desk personnel will likely find that password-reset requests are the most common type of request they receive. When help-desk personnel receive such a requests, they should require the user to provide information that verifies his or her identity. For example, the user should provide proof in the form of a driver's license or employee ID. If the request is not made in person, help-desk personnel should use a form of questioning that verifies the user's identity—for example, "What is your mother's maiden name?" A lack of strong identity validation can allow an attacker to request a password change for any user's account and access the account at will.

Although auditing logon events can be helpful for your intrusion detection efforts, be careful. Failure auditing can also expose your systems to a DoS attack. A DoS attack occurs in one of two ways:

- Attackers fill the security log, possibly causing a system crash or preventing other users from logging on.
- Attackers cause events to be overwritten. They do this by continuously attempting to log on to your network with incorrect usernames or passwords. Purposely overwriting audit events can effectively erase evidence of attack activity.

Be cautious when you're defining an account-lockout policy. A restrictive policy increases the probability of preventing an attack on your organization. But with a stringent account-lockout policy, you can also unintentionally lock out authorized users, which can be frustrating and costly. When you apply an account-lockout policy, set the threshold to a high enough number that authorized users aren't locked out due to mistyped passwords.

Audit Logon Events: You will learn more about auditing later in the chapter, but it is worth mentioning here as well. One method of keeping track of who is accessing your computing environment is to **audit** logon events. This practice provides you with a record of when every user logs on or off a computer. If an unauthorized user steals a user's password and logs on to a computer, you can determine when that security breach occurred. When you audit failure events in the logon event category (also known as **failure auditing**), you can see whether the failure event was due to unauthorized users or attackers attempting to log on to a computer or system. This is an example of intrusion detection.

Authentication by Ownership

Authentication by **ownership** is the second type of verification. This is based on something you have, such as a smart card, a key, a badge, or a token. Tokens can be synchronous or asynchronous.

Synchronous Tokens: A **synchronous token** uses an algorithm that calculates a number at both the authentication server and the device. It displays the number on the device's screen. The user enters this number as a logon authenticator, just as he or she would use a password.

In a **time-based synchronization system**, the current time is used as the input value. The token generates a new dynamic password (usually every minute) that is displayed in the window of the token. To gain access, the password is entered with the user's PIN at the workstation. No token keyboard is required. This system requires that the clock in the token remains in sync with the clock in the authentication server. If the clocks drift out of sync, the server can search three or four minutes on each side of the time to detect an offset. If the difference becomes too great, you must resynchronize the clocks.

> **⬛ NOTE**
>
> Synchronous tokens can be used in proximity devices that cause both the PIN and the password to be entered automatically.

An **event-based synchronization system** avoids the time-synchronization problem by increasing the value of a counter with each use. The counter is the input value. The user presses a button to generate a one-time password, and then enters this password with his or her PIN at the workstation to gain access. One common problem with event-based synchronization systems occurs when a user creates a password using the token but doesn't use the password to log on, and the counter in the server and the counter in the token become out of sync.

Continuous authentication is used by systems that continuously validate the user's identity. This is often done with proximity cards or other devices that continuously communicate with the access control system. If the user walks away from the desktop and steps outside the range of the access control detector, the system locks the desktop.

Asynchronous Tokens: The **asynchronous token** is the second of two types of token-based devices. It looks like a credit card-sized calculator. The authentication server issues a challenge number that the user enters. The token computes a response to the value provided by the authentication server. The user then replies to the server with the value displayed on the token. Many of these systems also protect the token from misuse by requiring the user to enter a PIN along with the initial challenge value.

An asynchronous token device uses challenge-response technology that involves a dialogue between the authentication service and the remote entity that it's trying to authenticate. This requires a numeric keyboard. **FIGURE 5-2** shows an asynchronous token challenge-response process.

1. User requests access via authentication server (i.e., UserID)
2. Authentication server issues challenge number to user
3. User enters challenge number with PIN in smartphone
4. Smartphone calculates cryptographic response (i.e., "password").
5. User sends "password" to authentication server
6. Authentication server grants access to application server

Here are the steps in an asynchronous challenge-response session:

1. The user initiates a logon request.
2. The authentication server provides a challenge (a random number that is the input value) to the user.
3. The user enters the challenge received from the server and a secret PIN known only to the user into the calculation device (a credit card-sized calculator or a software program on a computer or smartphone).
4. The token (or program) generates the response (the password) to the challenge, which appears in the window of the token.
5. The user provides the correct password to the authentication server.
6. Access is granted. Without the asynchronous token device and the correct PIN, a correct answer to the challenge cannot be generated.

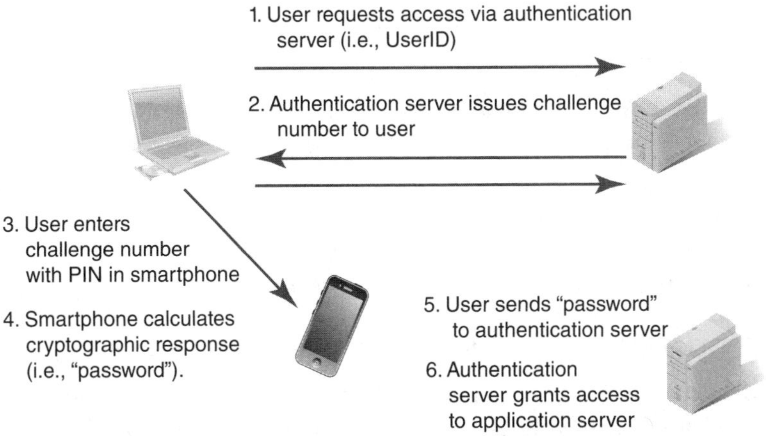

1. User requests access via authentication server (i.e., UserID)

2. Authentication server issues challenge number to user

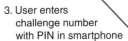

3. User enters challenge number with PIN in smartphone

4. Smartphone calculates cryptographic response (i.e., "password").

5. User sends "password" to authentication server

6. Authentication server grants access to application server

FIGURE 5-2

Asynchronous token challenge-response.

5

Access Controls

USB tokens use **public key infrastructure (PKI)** technology—for example, a certificate signed by a trusted certification authority—and don't provide one-time passwords. A **USB token** is a hardware device that you plug into your computer's USB port. The device is encoded with your digital signature. With it, you don't have to type anything in. The presence of the digital signature on the token is enough to provide proof of possession (something you have).

A smart card is a token shaped like a credit card that contains one or more microprocessor chips that accept, store, and send information through a reader. The information contained within the smart card provides authentication information. Most smart cards need a reader to power the embedded microprocessor. The user inserts the card into the reader to begin communication.

A significant advantage of a smart card is that the user authentication process is completed at the user location between the smart card and the reader. IDs and authentication data are not transmitted to a remote server, thereby avoiding the "trusted path" problem (that is, the fact that when IDs and authentication information are transmitted to a remote server, sensitive information can be exposed to sniffers or tappers). With a smart card, the reader maintains a handshake with the authentication server and directly vouches for the authentication. It then establishes a trusted path in accord with the **Common Criteria for Information Technology Security Evaluation**, also known simply as **Common Criteria**. The Common Criteria framework allows users, vendors, and testing laboratories to collaborate and share efforts to formally specify, implement, and evaluate information system products.

Finally, many organizations use several varieties of magnetic stripe cards (also known as *memory cards*) to control access to restricted areas, such as sensitive facilities or parking areas.

> ■ **NOTE**
>
> One problem with smart cards is that some users leave them unattended in the reader. That means any user is authorized as long as the smart card remains in the reader.

> ■ **NOTE**
>
> Not all smart cards must be physically inserted into a reader. A contactless, or proximity, smart card contains an embedded radio frequency (RF) transceiver that works when the card is near the reader.

> ■ **NOTE**
>
> For more information about the Common Criteria, visit *www.commoncriteriaportal.org*.

Authentication by Characteristics/Biometrics

Biometrics can be used for both identification (physical biometrics) and authentication (logical biometrics). Biometrics involves measuring various unique parts of a person's anatomy or physical activities. The common biometric measures you'll learn about in this chapter can be broken into two categories:

- **Static (for example, physiological) measures**—What you are. Physiological biometrics include recognizing fingerprints, iris granularity, retina blood vessels, facial looks, hand geometry, and so on.

- **Dynamic (for example, behavioral) measures**—What you do. Behavioral biometrics include voice inflections, keyboard strokes, and signature motions. Note that biometrics of this type are sometimes separated into their own category (authentication by action).

Concerns Surrounding Biometrics: There are three primary concerns with biometrics:

- **Accuracy**—Biometric devices are not perfect. Each has at least two error rates associated with it. The false rejection rate (FRR) is the rate at which valid subjects are rejected.

The false acceptance rate (FAR) is the rate at which invalid subjects are accepted. There is a tradeoff between the FRR and the FAR. The point at which the two rates are equal is called the **crossover error rate (CER)**. The CER is the measure of the system's accuracy expressed as a percentage. In practice, biometric devices that protect very sensitive resources are generally configured to accept a high level of false rejections. Systems that protect less sensitive resources may grant access to potentially unauthorized personnel so as not to excessively slow down access.

- **Acceptability**—Certain biometric measurements, such as retinal scans, are more objectionable to some users than other biometric measurements such as signature dynamics. It's important to note that if users are not comfortable using a system, they may refuse to submit to it.

- **Reaction time**—Each biometric device requires time for the system to check an identity and give a response. A system that takes too long may not work. For example, consider facial recognition at security airports. If the system needs five minutes to identify a passenger, then passenger checkpoint lines will become far longer than they already are. Reaction time must be fast for most checkpoints. Anything too slow hinders productivity and access.

Types of Biometrics: There are many types of biometrics, including:

- **Fingerprint**—This records the pattern of ridges and valleys on the tip of a finger.

- **Palm print**—This examines the physical structure of the palm. Both palm prints and fingerprints are considered highly accurate for verifying a user. The system reaction time is 5–7 seconds, and people tend to accept them.

- **Hand geometry**—With this type of biometric, a camera takes a picture of the palm of the hand and, using a 45-degree mirror, the side of the hand. An analysis is made using the length, width, thickness, and contour of the fingers. Hand geometry measurements are highly accurate. System response time is 1–3 seconds, and people tend to accept these, too.

- **Retina scan**—This type of biometric analyzes the blood-vessel pattern of the rear portion of the eyeball area, known as the *retina*, using a low-level light source and a camera. A retina scan is very accurate for identification and authentication. However, a retina scan is susceptible to changes in a person's physical condition, such as those caused by diabetes, pregnancy, and heart attacks. The emergence of these conditions requires users to enroll in the system again. Many people don't like retina scans because they feel they are intrusive and unsanitary and because they fear they will have to reveal private medical data. Response time averages 4–7 seconds.

- **Iris scan**—This type of biometric uses a small video recorder to record unique patterns in the colored portion of the eye, known as the *iris*, caused by striations, pits, freckles, rifts, fibers, and so on. Iris scans are very accurate for identification and authentication. Iris-scan devices provide the capability for continuous monitoring to prevent session hijacking. Response time is 1–2 seconds. Iris scans are well accepted.

- **Facial recognition**—With facial-recognition biometrics, video cameras measure certain features of the face, such as the distance between the eyes, the shape of the chin and jaw, the length and width of the nose, the shape of cheekbones and eye sockets, and so on. Fourteen common features are selected from about 80 or so features that can be measured. These features are used to create a facial database. Facial recognition is accurate for authentication because face angle can be controlled. However, it's not as accurate for identification in a moving crowd. Because facial recognition is passive and nonintrusive, it can give continuous authentication.

- **Voice pattern**—With voice-pattern biometrics, audio recorders and other sensors capture as many as seven parameters of nasal tones, larynx and throat vibrations, and air pressure from the voice. Voice pattern isn't accurate for authentication, because voices can be too easily replicated by computer software. Accuracy can be further diminished by background noise. Most users accept this type of biometric. Response time varies up to 14 seconds. Because of this long response time, it's not popular for everyday use.

- **Keystroke dynamics**—Here a user types a selected phrase onto a reference template. The keystroke dynamics measure each keystroke's dwell time (how long a key is held down) and flight time (the amount of time between keystrokes). Keystroke dynamics are considered very accurate. They lend themselves well to two-factor authentication. Because the technology is easy to use when someone is logging on, it combines the ID processes of something you should know with something you own. Keystroke dynamics are well accepted and can give constant authentication.

- **Signature dynamics**—With this type of biometric, sensors in a pen, stylus, or writing tablet are used to record pen-stroke speed, direction, and pressure. Signature dynamics are accurate and users accept them.

Advantages and Disadvantages of Biometrics: Biometrics offer these advantages:

- A person must be physically present to authenticate.
- There is nothing to remember.
- Biometrics are hard to fake.
- Lost IDs or forgotten passwords are not problems.

Biometrics do have negatives. These include the following:

- Physical characteristics might change.
- Physically disabled users might have difficulty with systems based on fingerprints, hand geometry, or signatures.
- Not all techniques are equally effective, and it is often difficult to decide which technique is best for a given use.
- Response time may be too slow.
- The required devices can be expensive. With methods that require lots of time to authenticate, the organization may have to provide a large number of authentication machines so as not to cause bottlenecks at entry and access.

Privacy Issues: Biometric technologies don't just involve collecting data *about* a person. Biometrics collects information *intrinsic* to people. Every person must submit to an examination, and that examination must be digitally recorded and stored. Unauthorized access to this data could lead to misuse. Biometrics also can be used to watch a person's movement and actions. Lastly, recorded and replayed ID data might be used to allow a person to pretend to be someone else, creating a risk for identity theft.

Authentication by Location

A user's physical location can also be a strong indicator of authenticity. Location can provide additional information to suggest granting or denying acess to a resource. For example, suppose a user provides a PIN, along with a debit card number, to a card reader. The card reader is located in a fuel pump in Topeka, Kansas. However, the IP address of the user providing the PIN is located in Tampa, Florida. The separate locations may raise enough suspicion to deny the necessary access to the funds. On the other hand, a taxi scheduling application may use the customer's smartphone location to validate that a request for pickup is valid. As with other methods, authentication by location should only be used in multifactor authentication.

Authentication by Action

One of the newest authentication methods is based on a user's actions. There is confusion as to whether this is really a subset of biometrics. We already covered the details in the biometrics section, but be aware that authentication by action is sometimes set aside as a separate authentication category. It is also called *something you do*. This type of authentication stores the patterns or nuances of how you do something. The most common use is to record typing patterns. Most people type with predictable speed and pauses between different keys. These patterns can be stored and used during authentication.

Single Sign-On

A **single sign-on (SSO)** strategy allows users to sign on to a computer or network once and have their identification and authorization credentials allow them into all computers and systems where they are authorized. They don't need to enter multiple user IDs or passwords. SSO reduces human error, which is a major part of system failures. It is highly desirable but difficult to put in place.

Advantages and Disadvantages of SSO

Advantages of SSO include the following:

- It's an efficient logon process. The user has to log on only once.
- It can provide for stronger passwords. With only one password to remember, users are generally willing to use stronger passwords.
- It provides continuous, clear reauthentication. The SSO server remains in contact with the workstation and monitors it for activity. This allows timeout thresholds that can be enforced consistently throughout the system near the user entry point. When a workstation or endpoint device is not active for a certain period, it can be disconnected. This protects

The Kerberos Key Distribution Center Server

The Kerberos key distribution center (KDC) server serves two functions:

- **It serves as the authentication server (AS)**—An authentication server confirms a user through a pre-exchanged secret key based on the user's password. This is the symmetric key that is shared with the KDC and stored in the KDC database. After getting a request for service from the user, all further dialogue with the user workstation is encrypted using this shared key. The user does not send a password to the KDC. Instead, the authentication occurs at the time the Kerberos software on the user's workstation requests the password to create the shared key to decrypt the ticket from the authentication server. The ticket contains the session key for use in communicating with the desired application server. If the wrong password is supplied, the ticket can't be decrypted, and the access attempt fails.

- **It serves as the ticket-granting server (TgS)**—The ticket-granting server (TGS) provides a way to get more tickets for the same or other applications after the user is verified, so that step doesn't need to be repeated several times during a day. Tickets usually expire daily or after a few hours.

the system from a user leaving a workstation open to an unauthenticated person who could pretend to be the original user.

- It provides failed logon attempt thresholds and lockouts. This protects against an intruder using brute force to obtain an authentic user ID and password combination.
- It provides centralized administration. It ensures consistent application of policy and procedures.

Disadvantages of SSO include the following:

- A compromised password lets an intruder into all areas open to the password owner. Using dynamic passwords and/or two-factor authentication can reduce this problem.
- Static passwords provide very limited security. Two-factor authentication or at least a one-time (dynamic) password is required for access by the user using SSO.
- Adding SSO to unique computers or legacy systems in the network might be difficult.
- Scripts make things easier to administer, but they expose data. Scripting doesn't provide two-factor authentication to sensitive systems and data.
- The authentication server can become a single point of failure for system access.

Authentication systems share some common service requirements. They all provide some method for users (subjects) to request access to some resources (objects). Then they provide some way for the request to be either granted or denied. One way to handle SSO authentication is using a central server. The user contacts the central server for all requests. Another approach is called **federation**. Federated authentication systems share user credentials among several servers. Users only see the initial sign-on process. Credential sharing after sign-in happens behind the scenes among trusted servers. Another related approach is **transitive trust** authentication. In this model the initial sign-on credentials are forwarded by request to other trusted servers. An authentication server will only share user credentials with another server that it trusts. This is only slightly different from federation. In a federated system, the group of authentication servers is static. With transitive trust environments, the group of trusted servers builds over time and can be different for each user and request. The servers in the trusted group depend on the access request path a user follows.

SSO Processes

Examples of SSO processes include the Kerberos, SESAME, and LDAP methods.

Kerberos: Kerberos is a computer network authentication protocol that allows nodes communicating over a nonsecure network to prove their identity to one another in a secure manner. Kerberos is also a suite of free software published by the Massachusetts Institute of Technology (MIT) that applies the Kerberos protocol. Its design is aimed primarily at a client/server model, and it provides mutual authentication—the user and the server each verify the other's identity. Kerberos protocol messages are protected against eavesdropping and replay attacks.

To get started, the user sends his or her ID and access request through the Kerberos client software on the workstation to the **key distribution center (KDC)**. The authentication server of the KDC verifies that the user and the requested service are in the KDC database and sends a ticket. The ticket is a unique key for the user that is time-stamped for the requested service. If time expires before the ticket is used, it won't work. Included in the ticket are the user ID and the session key as well as the ticket for the object encrypted with the object's key shared with the KDC.

With Kerberos, security depends on careful execution and maintenance. Lifetimes for authentication credentials should be as short as possible, using time stamps to reduce the threat of replayed credentials. The KDC must be physically secured because it—particularly the authentication server—is a potential single point of failure. Redundant authentication servers can reduce the risk. The KDC should be hardened, meaning it should have a secured operating system and application. It should not allow any non-Kerberos network activity.

> **NOTE**
>
> Smart cards can provide SSO services. The presence of a smart card in a continuous authentication system can appear to the user as SSO. All authentication exchanges are transparent to the user. As long as the smart card is available to the authentication system, the user doesn't have to provide any credentials to access resources.

SESAME: The **Secure European System for Applications in a Multi-Vendor Environment (SESAME)** is a research and development project funded by the European Commission. SESAME was developed to address some weaknesses in Kerberos. SESAME supports SSO. Unlike Kerberos, it improves key management by using both symmetric and asymmetric keys to protect interchanged data. It is essentially an extension of Kerberos. It offers public key cryptography and role-based access control abilities.

LDAP: The **Lightweight Directory Access Protocol (LDAP)** is a protocol for defining and using distributed directory services. One of the core services LDAP provides is handling access control credentials. LDAP makes it easy for administrators to manage logon and access credentials on computers and devices across a network. LDAP is open source and doesn't rely on any specific vendor's product. Although LDAP doesn't provide a complete SSO solution, you will find the protocol is used in many SSO solutions. Since LDAP routinely exchanges sensitive information across networks, it is essential to secure the messages. One of the most common ways to ensure LDAP messages are secure is to use **Secure LDAP**, or LDAP over SSL (LDAPS). This version of LDAP just uses SSL/TLS for all message exchanges across the network.

Policies and Procedures for Accountability

At this point, you have learned about how users are identified (step 1), authenticated (step 2), and authorized (step 3). Now it's time for the last part of the access control process: accountability. **Accountability** is tracing an action to a person or process to know who made the changes to the system or data. This is important for audits and investigations as well as for tracing errors and mistakes. Accountability answers the question, "Can you hold users responsible for what they do on the system?"

Log Files

Log files are a key ingredient to accountability. Log files are records that detail who logged on to the system, when they logged on, and what information or resources they used. In the early days of computing, logs were used on systems that were shared by several users. It was necessary to charge users for their time using the systems, so logs tracked that data. Log files were also used by companies such as CompuServe and AOL when Internet use was charged by the hour. On today's networks, most billing is either a fixed fee or based on bandwidth usage. Time-based billing has become uncommon. Logging now is used for more than just billing. It is also a valuable tool to detect, prevent, or monitor access to a system.

Monitoring and Reviews

One of the main reasons to track user access activities is to detect questionable actions and respond to them. That means you should use software that monitors your activity logs and generates alerts when it finds suspicious activity. Continuous monitoring is an important part of a secure access control system. But not all suspicious activity is obvious. At times the only way to detect account policy violations is to review user actions over a period of time. Your account policy should include a requirement for periodic user account reviews. Such reviews help to validate that user access definitions are correct. They also help to find inappropriate activity or excessive permissions. Of course, every policy should outline steps to take to respond to any violations. Knowing how to respond to violations is just as important as finding them in the first place.

Data Retention, Media Disposal, and Compliance Requirements

Many current laws require that organizations take measures to secure many types of data. The Health Insurance Portability and Accountability Act (HIPAA) is one example of legislation that requires data security. It protects the privacy of personal health data and gives patients certain rights to that information. Another example is the Fair and Accurate Credit

Transactions Act (FACTA). FACTA requires any entity that keeps consumer data for business purposes to destroy personal data before discarding them.

These and similar laws require the protection of privacy data with proper security controls. These laws outline the right ways to handle, store, and dispose of data. If these rules and regulations aren't followed, intruders can, for example, simply dive into dumpsters to get sensitive data.

Procedures

Organizations can apply access controls in various forms, providing different levels of restriction and at different places within the computing system. A combination of access controls provides a system with layered, defense-in-depth (DiD) protection. A DiD approach makes it harder for attacks to succeed, because the attacker must compromise multiple security controls to reach a resource. An attacker who successfully beats one security control should run into several other controls in a layered system. Security personnel should ensure that they protect every critical resource with multiple controls. Never rely on a single control to protect a resource.

Security Controls

A **security control** is any mechanism intended to avoid, stop, or minimize a risk of attack for one or more resources. There are several types of security controls; these perform differently based on their purpose. Most organizations need a diverse mix of security controls to protect their systems from all types of attacks. **TABLE 5-1** lists the most common types of security controls.

Media Disposal Requirements

Most security attention tends to focus on securing active resources. Many organizations tend to overlook the fact that data still exist on retired media or even in the trash. It is important to ensure that no data leak out of an organization on discarded media. Media-disposal requirements prevent attackers from getting their hands on files, memory, and other protected data. Many organizations allow media to be used again, but only if the original data were not sensitive. As an extreme example, media that contains plans for a nuclear weapon would not qualify for reuse. You could violate the law if you do not destroy data before discarding the media.

> **NOTE**
>
> Methods of destruction include shredding, burning, or grinding of CD-ROMs, hard drives, USB drives, DVDs, paper documents, flash memory, and other forms of media.

It is not always necessary that you physically destroy media. Another method is to use a **degausser**. A degausser creates a magnetic field that erases data from magnetic storage media. Once data go through a degausser, the data cannot be recovered. When you use a degausser, not enough magnetic material is left to rebuild the data. If the media-stored information wasn't extremely sensitive, you can use some media to store other data. However, if the media held very sensitive data, it should be destroyed.

Another method used to destroy data without harming the media that stores them is repeated writing. Repeatedly writing random characters over data usually will destroy the data. This practice is called **overwriting**. This process works well if the amount of data to be overwritten is fairly small and the overwriting is fairly fast. Large amounts of data or

TABLE 5-1 Types of security controls.

CONTROL TYPE	DESCRIPTION
Administrative	These are policies approved by management and passed down to staff in the form of rules. They are a first line of defense to inform users of their responsibilities. Examples include policies on password length.
Logical/technical	These are additional policies that are controlled and enforced automatically. This reduces human error. For example, a computer can check passwords to make sure they follow the rules.
Hardware	This includes equipment that checks and validates IDs, such as Media Access Control (MAC) filtering on network devices, smart card use for two-step authentication, and security tokens such as radio frequency identification (RFID) tags. In this instance, MAC is a hardware address that uniquely identifies each node of a network. Media Access Control is not the same as the mandatory access controls discussed later in the chapter.
Software	These controls are embedded in the operating system and application software. They include the Microsoft Windows standard NTFS permissions, user accounts requiring logon, and rules restricting services or protocol types. These items are often part of the ID and validation phase.
Physical	These are devices that prevent physical access to resources, including such things as security guards, ID badges, fences, and door locks.

slow writing devices can make this type of data destruction too slow to be useful in a production environment.

Formal Models of Access Control

Some of the most visible types of technical controls are those protecting access to computer resources. Most users have encountered access control restrictions. For example, any user who has typed an incorrect password should have been denied access.

Because there are many ways to restrict access to different resources, it is helpful to refer to models to help design good access controls. There are several formal models of access control, including the following:

- **Discretionary access control (DAC)**—With DAC, the owner of the resource decides who gets in and changes permissions as needed. The owner can give that job to others.

- **Mandatory access control (MAC)**—With MAC, permission to access a system or any resource is determined by the sensitivity of the resource and the security level of the subject. It cannot be given to someone else. This makes MAC stronger than DAC.

- **Nondiscretionary access control**—Nondiscretionary access controls are closely monitored by the security administrator, not the system administrator.

- **Rule-based access control**— A list of rules, maintained by the data owner, determines which users have access to objects.

Other models are based on the work of Biba, Clark-Wilson, and Bell-La Padula. These models describe the use of access controls and permissions to protect confidentiality or integrity.

Discretionary Access Control

The Common Criteria define **discretionary access control (DAC)** as follows:

[A] means of restricting access to objects based on the identity of subjects and/or groups to which they belong. The controls are discretionary in the sense that a subject with certain access permission is capable of passing that permission (perhaps indirectly) on to any other subject.

The Common Criteria also note the following:

[S]ecurity policies defined for systems used to process classified or other sensitive information must include provisions for the enforcement of discretionary access control rules. That is, they must include a consistent set of rules for controlling and limiting access based on identified individuals who have been determined to have a need to know for the information.

These definitions apply equally to both public and private sector organizations processing sensitive information.

Operating Systems-Based DAC

Operating systems have primary responsibility for controlling access to system resources such as files, memory, and applications. One of the main jobs for security administrators is to maintain access controls. Access controls are effective when they ensure that only authorized users can access resources. They are efficient when they ensure that users can access all the resources they need. Creating access controls that are both effective and efficient can be challenging. Organizations must decide how they will design and maintain access controls to best meet their needs. Here are a few points organizations must consider in developing access control policies:

* **Access control method**—Today's operating systems contain access control settings for individual users (rule-based) or for groups of users (role-based). Which method you use depends on the size of the organization and the way specific access rights need to be for individuals or roles.

* **New user registration**—When new users are brought into an organization, their user accounts must be created. This can take a lot of time. It must be done quickly, however, so new people can do their jobs. User registration must be standardized, efficient, and accurate.

* **Periodic review**—Over time, users often get special permission to complete a particular project or perform some special task. These permissions need to be reviewed from time to time to make sure they stop when they are no longer needed. This review solves problems of compliance and auditing by making sure people can access only required areas.

Defeating Least Privilege, Separation of Duties, and Need to Know

Least privilege means granting the minimum access that allows a user to accomplish assigned tasks. Stated another way, it means to grant just enough authorization for users to do their jobs, but nothing else. Least privilege is difficult to maintain, but it does protect data from excessive authorization.

Separation of duties is the process of dividing a task into a series of unique activities performed by different people, each of whom is allowed to execute only one part of the overall task. This principle prevents people from both creating and approving their own work. Separation of duties can be a valuable tool to prevent fraud or errors by requiring the cooperation of another person to complete a task. Dual control is an example of separation of duties. Examples include a safe with two combination locks on the door or a missile-control system that requires the simultaneous turning of keys in consoles too far apart for one person to manage.

Need to know is the concept of preventing people from gaining access to information they don't need to carry out their duties. Providing access on the basis of need to know can reduce the chance of improper handling of data or the improper release of information.

Least privilege, separation of duties, and need to know can be defeated by the following:

- **Collusion**. Users work together (**colluding**) to avoid the controls, aggregate their authority, and assist each other in performing unauthorized tasks. Job rotation reduces the risk of collusion.
- **Covert channels**. These are hidden (covert) ways of passing information against organizational policy. There are two main types of covert channels: timing (signaling from one system to another) and storage (the storing of data in an unprotected or inappropriate place).

Application-Based DAC

Application-based DAC denies access based on context or content. The application presents only options that are authorized for the current user. For example, an automatic teller machine (ATM) menu limits access by displaying only the options that are available to a particular user. You can apply security controls using these types of DACs based on user context or resource contents:

FYI

The **Trusted Computer System Evaluation Criteria (TCSEC)** provides definitions of both DAC and MAC. These definitions fit the needs of public and private sector organizations that need to protect sensitive information. TCSEC was a prominent standard in the U.S. Department of Defense's Rainbow Series. The Rainbow Series was a collection of computer-security standards and guidelines published in the 1980s and 1990s. Each book in the series had a different-colored cover, which led to the nickname for each book. The TCSEC had an orange cover and is often called simply *The Orange Book*. The Common Criteria superseded *The Orange Book* in 2005.

- In a context-based system, access is based on user privileges as defined in the user's own data records. This is usually granted to persons acting in a certain job role or function.
- In a content-dependent system, access is based on the value or sensitivity of data items in a table. This system checks the content of the data being accessed and allows, for example, a manager of Department A to see employee records for personnel that contain an A in the Department field but not records containing any other value in that field.

Permission Levels

Permission levels indicate a subject's rights to a system, application, network, or other resources. In a DAC environment, the authorization system uses permission levels to determine what objects any subject can access. Permission levels can be any of the following:

- **User-based**—The permissions granted to a user are often specific to that user. In this case, the rules are set according to a user ID or other unique identifier.
- **Job-based, group-based, or role-based access control (RBAC)**—Permissions are based on a common set of permissions for all people in the same or similar job roles.
- **Project-based**—When a group of people (for example, a project team) are working on a project, they are often granted access to documents and data related just to that project.
- **Task-based**—Task-based access control limits a person to executing certain functions and often enforces mutual exclusivity. In other words, if a person executes one part of a task, he or she might not be allowed to execute another related part of the task. This is based on the concepts of separation of duties and need to know.

Mandatory Access Control

Mandatory access control (MAC) is another method of restricting access to resources. You determine the level of restriction by how sensitive the resource is. This is represented by a classification label. Individuals must then be formally authorized (i.e., obtain clearance) to access sensitive information. Security policies defined for systems that are used to process classified information (or any other sensitive information) must include provisions for enforcing MAC rules. That is, they must include a set of rules that controls who can access what information.

> **NOTE**
>
> Remember: Sensitivity labels, or classifications, are applied to all objects (resources). Privilege- or clearance-level labels are assigned to all subjects (users or programs).

Under mandatory access control, the system and the owner jointly make the decision to allow access. The owner gives the need-to-know element. Not all users with a privilege or clearance level for sensitive material need access to all sensitive information. The system compares the subject and object labels that go with the terms of the Bell-La Padula confidentiality model, which is covered later in the chapter. Based on that comparison, the system either grants or denies access.

Temporal isolation restricts access to specific times. It first classifies the sensitivity level of objects. Then it allows access to those objects only at certain times. Temporal isolation is often used in combination with role-based access control. You may see temporal isolation more commonly described as **time-of-day restrictions**. Regardless of the term used, they both simply mean restricting access to specific time windows.

Nondiscretionary Access Control

In nondiscretionary access control, access rules are closely managed by the security administrator. They are not managed by the system owner or by ordinary users for their own files.

Nondiscretionary access control can be used on many operating systems. This strategy is more secure than discretionary access control. The system doesn't rely only on users' compliance with organizational policies. For example, even if users obey well-defined file protection policies, a Trojan horse program could change the protection to allow uncontrolled access. This kind of exposure isn't possible under nondiscretionary access control.

Security administrators have enough control in nondiscretionary access control to make sure sensitive files are write-protected for integrity and readable only by authorized users, to preserve confidentiality. The chances that a corrupted program will be used are reduced because users can run only those programs they are expressly allowed to run.

Nondiscretionary access control helps ensure that system security is enforced and tamperproof. If your organization needs to manage highly sensitive information, you should seriously consider using nondiscretionary access control. It does a better job of protecting confidentiality and integrity than DAC. The data owner, who is often the user, does not make access decisions. This allows you to enjoy some of the benefits of MAC without the added administrative overhead.

Rule-Based Access Control

In a rule-based system, access is based on a list of rules that determine who should be granted access. Data owners make or allow the rules. They specify the privileges granted to users, such as read, write, execute.

The success of rule-based access control depends on the level of trust you have with the data owners. This type of access control pushes much of the administration down to the data owner. For technical and security-conscious users, this type of access control tends to work well. It doesn't work as well in environments with many users or where users lack the necessary technical skills and training. **FIGURE 5-3** shows how individual rules control each user's permissions.

Access Control Lists

Most operating systems provide several options to associate lists or permissions with objects. These lists are called **access control lists (ACLs)**. Different operating systems provide different ACL-enabling options. For example, Linux and OS X have read, write, and execute permissions. These can be applied to file owners, groups, or global users. Windows has both share permissions and security permissions, both of which enable ACLs to define

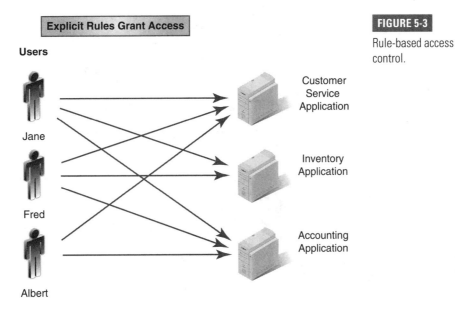

FIGURE 5-3

Rule-based access control.

access rules. Share permissions are used to get to resources by a network share. Security permissions are used to get to resources when the user is logged on locally. Some Windows permissions include the following:

- **Share permissions**—Full, change, read, and deny.
- **Security permissions**—Full, modify, list folder contents, read-execute, read, write, special, and deny.

In both share and security permissions, deny overrides every other permission. But what happens if no ACL exists for a resource? Most authorization systems use *implicit deny*, which means that if no rule to grant access exists, access is automatically denied. This approach is more restrictive but more secure.

Because of the greater number of choices, Windows ACLs are said to be more fine-grained, because they allow a greater level of control. **FIGURE 5-4** shows an ACL.

Role-Based Access Control

Another type of access control is **role-based access control (RBAC)**. An RBAC policy bases access control approvals on the jobs the user is assigned. The security administrator assigns each user to one or more roles. Some operating systems use groups instead of roles. The resource owner decides what roles have access to which resources. Microsoft Windows uses global groups to manage RBAC. **FIGURE 5-5** shows RBAC.

Before you can assign access rules to a role, you must define and describe the roles in your organization. The process of defining roles, approvals, role hierarchies, and constraints is called **role engineering**. Starting with a clear list of role definitions that fit your organization is key to RBAC. The real benefit of RBAC over other access control methods is

5

Access Controls

FIGURE 5-4

An access control list.

Hal	
User Hal Directory	Full Control
User Kevin Directory	Write
User Kara Directory	No Access
Printer 001	Execute

Kevin	
User Hal Directory	Write
User Kevin Directory	Full Control
User Kara Directory	No Access
Printer 001	No Access

Kara	
User Hal Directory	Write
User Kevin Directory	Full Control
User Kara Directory	No Access
Printer 001	Execute
Printer 002	Execute

its ability to represent the structure of the organization and force compliance with control policies throughout it.

Suppose that Jane and Fred in Figure 5-5 should have access to the Inventory application, but Albert should not. As shown in the figure, however, Albert *does* have access to this application—a need-to-know violation. This error is due to the overgeneralizing of roles. Overgeneralizing roles can result in providing more access to individuals

FIGURE 5-5

Role-based access control.

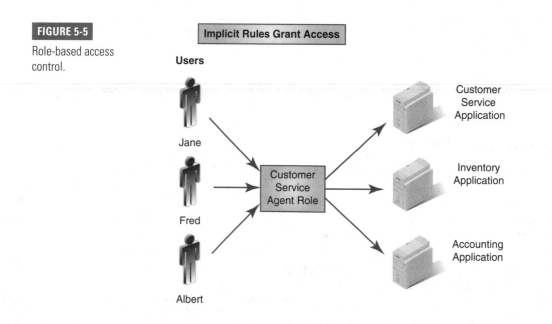

Implicit Rules Grant Access

Users

Jane

Fred

Albert

Customer Service Agent Role

Customer Service Application

Inventory Application

Accounting Application

than was intended. When you assign roles, consider creating one role for every user or one role for a very small number of users. Windows' "deny permission" option makes it possible to create a rule that overrides a role. That would fix Albert's excessive permission. This decision is dependent on risk. A user might be given a role with similar privileges and might be granted access above his need to know in order to reduce administrative costs.

Content-Dependent Access Control

FIGURE 5-6 shows how content-dependent access control can protect data. Content-dependent access control is based on what is contained in the data. It requires the access control mechanism (the arbiter program, which is part of the application, not the operating system) to look at the data to decide who should get to see it. The result is better granularity than other access control methods you have seen. Access is controlled to the record level in a file rather than simply to the file level. The cost of doing this is higher, however, because it requires the arbiter program. The arbiter program uses information in the object being accessed—for example, what is in a record. The decision usually comes to a simple if-then question—for example, "If high-security flag equals yes, then check security level of user." Managers might have access to the payroll database to review data about specific employees, but they might not have access to the data about employees of other managers.

Constrained User Interface

With a **constrained user interface**, a user's ability to get into—or interface with—certain system resources is restrained by two things: The user's rights and permissions are restricted, and constraints are put on the device or program providing the interface. A device such as an ATM or software such as on a public-access kiosk browser lets users reach only specific functions, files, or other resources. It limits their access by restricting their ability to request access to unauthorized resources. For example, some systems gray out icons that are not available. Several methods of constraining users are as follows:

Access Based on Values in Data (i.e., Department)

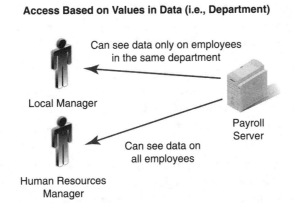

Can see data only on employees in the same department

Local Manager

Payroll Server

Can see data on all employees

Human Resources Manager

FIGURE 5-6

Content-dependent access control.

- **Menus**—One way to keep users out of certain data is to simply not give them any idea that the data exist. When the user logs on, the menu that comes up does not include closed areas.

- **Database views**—Also called **view-based access control (VBAC)**, this approach is often used with relational databases. The database system creates a view for each user that limits the data that he or she is able to see. Although there may be more data in the database, the user can access only the data defined in the view. Many current databases provide a way to partition a database into several slices. This feature, called **multitenancy**, allows different groups of users to access a database without being able to access each other's data. This ability is important to organizations that want to use the cloud for their shared applications and databases.

- **Physically constrained user interfaces**—The user interface mechanism presents the user with a limited number of options. For example, an ATM offers only a certain number of buttons to push. This makes it a **physically constrained user interface**.

- **Encryption**—This approach constrains users because it requires them to have the decryption key to reach or read information stored on the system. Encryption also hides information such as credit card details from the user.

Other Access Control Models

Other access control models have helped shaped today's access controls. The most prominent access models include the Bell-La Padula model, the Biba integrity model, the Clark and Wilson integrity model, and the Brewer and Nash model. You will learn about each model in the following sections.

Bell-La Padula Model

The **Bell-La Padula model** focuses on the confidentiality of data and the control of access to classified information. This model is different from the Biba integrity model, covered in the next section, which describes rules to protect data integrity. In the Bell-La Padula model, the parts of a system are divided into subjects and objects, and the current condition of a system is described as its **state**. The model defines a secure state. The model guarantees that each state transition preserves security by moving from secure state to secure state. This process makes sure the system meets the model's security objectives. The Bell-La Padula model is built on the concept of a state machine that features a set of allowable states in a computer network system. The transition from one state to another state is defined by what are known as **transition functions**.

Biba Integrity Model

In 1977, Kenneth J. Biba defined the first model to address integrity in computer systems based on integrity levels. The **Biba integrity model** fixed a weakness in the Bell-La Padula model, which addresses only the confidentiality of data. The Biba integrity model consists of three parts:

- The first part says a subject cannot read objects that have a lower level of integrity than the subject does. A subject at a given integrity level can read only objects at the same integrity level or higher. This is known as a simple **integrity axiom**.

- The second part says a subject cannot change objects that have a higher level.
- The third part says a subject may not ask for service from subjects that have a higher integrity level. A subject at a given integrity level can call up only a subject at the same integrity level or lower.

Clark and Wilson Integrity Model

Published in 1987 by David Clark and David Wilson, the **Clark and Wilson integrity model** focuses on what happens when users allowed into a system try to do things they are not permitted to do. It also looks at internal integrity threats. These two components were missing from Biba's model. This model looks at whether the software does what it is designed to do. That is a major integrity issue. The Clark and Wilson integrity model addresses three integrity goals:

- It stops unauthorized users from making changes. (Biba addressed only this integrity goal.)
- It stops authorized users from making improper changes.
- It keeps internal and external consistency.

The Clark and Wilson integrity model defines well-formed transactions and constraints on data. For example, a commercial system should allow a new luxury car sale to be entered only at a price of $40,000. It should not be possible to enter the sale at $4,000 or at $400,000. This keeps internal consistency. Internal consistency makes sure the system operates as expected every time.

> **NOTE**
>
> This model is considered a commercial integrity model. Unlike the earlier models, which were designed for military uses, this model was designed to be used by businesses.

In the Clark and Wilson integrity model, a subject's access is controlled by the permission to execute the program (a well-formed transaction). Therefore, unauthorized users cannot execute the program (first integrity rule). Authorized users can access different programs that allow each one to make specific, unique changes (separation of duties). Two important parts of this model are as follows:

- These three access entities—subject, program, and object—combine to form the access triple.
- Integrity is enforced by binding. Subject-to-program and program-to-object binding enforces integrity. This creates separation of duties. It makes sure only authorized transactions can be performed.

Brewer and Nash Integrity Model

The **Brewer and Nash integrity model** is based on a mathematical theory published in 1989 to ensure fair competition. It is used to apply dynamically changing access permissions. It can separate competitors' data within the same integrated database to make sure users don't make fraudulent changes to objects that belong to a competing organization. It's also used to stop users or clients from using data when they have a conflict of interest.

A **Chinese wall** security policy defines a wall, or barrier, and develops a set of rules that makes sure no subject gets to objects on the other side of the wall. **FIGURE 5-7** shows a Chinese wall in action. It illustrates the way an audit company handles audits for competing businesses.

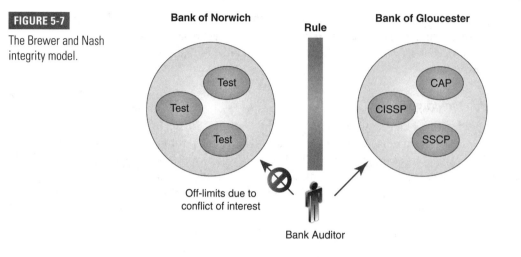

FIGURE 5-7

The Brewer and Nash integrity model.

In this example, an auditor allowed to work on data related to the Bank of Gloucester is prohibited from getting to any data belonging to the Bank of Norwich. Even though the auditor works for a company that performs the audits for both banks, internal controls at the audit company prevent access between areas that would create a conflict of interest.

This model makes sure conflicts of interest are recognized and that people are prevented from taking advantage of data to which they should not have access. For example, if a user is allowed into one company's data, the data belonging to that company's competitors can automatically be deemed off-limits.

 NOTE

Controls can't prevent conflicts of interest. Conflicts of interest have to do with individuals' positions, not with the data themselves.

Effects of Breaches in Access Control

Your failure to control access can give your opposition an advantage. That opposition might be a military force, a business interested in competitive intelligence, or even your neighbor. The following list details some of the losses that can occur:

- Disclosure of private information
- Corruption of data
- Loss of business intelligence
- Danger to facilities, staff, and systems
- Damage to equipment
- Failure of systems and business processes

Not all incidents have the same effect. Some are easier to spot than others. For example, losses due to disclosure of business secrets, including business intelligence, often go unnoticed for quite some time. Losses due to corruption of data might make a database and all its backups useless by the time it is discovered. Data corruption can easily cause failures in systems and business processes.

Some types of denial of service (DoS) attacks are short-lived. They are found quickly and can be stopped before they cause serious damage. Other types of DoS attacks take longer to evolve. They can affect the ability of a business to serve its customers. Customers might then take their business elsewhere. This type of DoS attack inflicts more severe damage on an organization.

Threats to Access Controls

The challenges of access control come in many forms. This list can never be complete. New threats evolve all the time. An example is the peer-to-peer (P2P) risk in which P2P users share their My Documents folder with each other by accident. This can expose sensitive documents to other users.

Access controls can be compromised in several ways, including the following:

- **Gaining physical access**—If an intruder has physical access to a device, logical access control is basically worthless. Data can be copied or stolen outright. Someone with physical access can install hardware or software keystroke loggers or can damage equipment. For example, this person could start a DoS attack. Small removable media, such as writable CDs, DVDs, USB memory sticks, or hard drives, create a physical access risk. It's easy to copy data to one of these devices. Smartphones and mobile devices are another common risk. Today's mobile devices include cameras and capability for audio and video recording.

- **Eavesdropping by observation**—Sometimes security staff misses the most obvious breach, allowing information to be seen. Data on papers on an authorized user's desk or screen are open to a spy. Enforcing the right policies and procedures can prevent this kind of data loss.

- **Bypassing security**—Any means of accessing data can lead to a security breach. Developers might think about access via only one method, such as through a website. But attackers might easily bypass the security measures in place. The information security team must consider other access paths, such as attackers mapping a drive or logging on at the server's keyboard.

- **Exploiting hardware and software**—Attackers often try to install programs on a system they control. These programs are often called **Trojan horses**. The network administrator or workstation owner may not even know the attacker is there.

- **Reusing or discarding media**—Attackers can recover erased or altered information from discarded or reused media. It is safer and cheaper to shred documents and physically destroy media than to simply throw them out.

- **Electronic eavesdropping**—Attackers can eavesdrop by wiretapping network cables. Some media are more resistant to eavesdropping than others. For example, fiber-optic cable is safer than copper. However, no medium provides complete protection. The increased interest in mobile devices and wireless access points has increased the risk of eavesdropping. Users who connect their mobile devices to insecure access points are easy targets for attackers.

- **Intercepting communication**—Another variation of eavesdropping is the physical interception of data communications. This is called **sniffing**. With sniffing, attackers capture network traffic as it passes by. Sniffing is often used in a **man-in-the-middle (MITM)** attack. The attacker inserts himself between two victims and relays messages between them. The attacker makes it seem as if the two victims are talking directly to each other over a private connection. In fact, the attacker is in control of the entire conversation.

- **Accessing networks**—Networks often include unprotected connections. Many organizations build their networks with more drops (female connectors at wall plates) than they need. This allows the organization to add more users in the event of future growth. These unused connection points are often active connections. Intruders can use these connections to gain network access. Network access risks increase as organizations add wireless access points. Making network access easier often benefits attackers as well as legitimate users. Organizations must carefully monitor and restrict all network access points.

- **Exploiting applications**—Several programs and modules have a common programming weakness known as **buffer overflow**. This happens when an attacker enters more characters than expected into an input field, which allows malicious code throughout the application. There are many other ways to exploit weaknesses in applications, and attackers are always on the lookout to find new ways to compromise applications.

Effects of Access Control Violations

You have seen some of the ways attackers can compromise access controls. But what happens if an attacker is successful? What is the impact of an access control violation? An access control violation can have the following harmful effects on an organization:

- Loss of customer confidence
- Loss of business opportunities
- New legislation and regulations imposed on the organization
- Bad publicity
- More oversight
- Financial penalties

> **NOTE**
>
> You can find a state-by-state summary of disclosure laws at the following URL: *www.ncsl.org/research/ telecommunications-and-information- technology/security-breach-notification- laws.aspx.*

For example, Egghead Software voluntarily reported a breach in the summer of 2000 and was sold to Amazon within a year of the disclosure. After the breach, customers didn't trust the company with their credit cards. They hesitated to purchase Egghead's products. The corporate world took notice. As a result, other companies stopped reporting violations. Finally, the government stepped in with new laws that force companies to reveal financial data access breaches.

In 2003, California passed a mandatory disclosure law that affects all companies that do business in California or with that state's residents. The law protects its residents from disclosure of their **personally identifiable information (PII)**. PII is often the information that bad guys use to steal identities. Note, however, that this law doesn't cover other intrusions, such as theft of intellectual property. But new laws haven't stopped the violations. Data breaches still happen, and some of them make the news headlines. Some of the most newsworthy data breaches in the recent past include Target, Home Depot, Blue Cross Blue Shield, Harvard University, the U.S. Army National Guard, and the U.S. Office of Personnel Management. The problem of access violations affects many organizations.

Credential and Permissions Management

As you have learned about access control, you probably have thought about how to store all the information needed to support access control decisions. You need to allow users to register and provide valid identification and authentication credentials. Then you have to define access permissions, associate permissions with users, and allow for maintenance. In fact, all these tasks are part of **credential management**. Credential management systems provide the ability to collect, manage, and use the information associated with access control. But managing credentials is only the first step. It is also necessary to manage permissions and access rules. In a dynamic system with many users, this task can easily become overwhelming. Microsoft offers a feature called **Group Policy** to help administrators manage access controls. A **Group Policy Object (GPO)** is a collection of settings for users or computers that can be applied efficiently to a group of computers. GPO features allow Windows administrators to define settings in one place that can easily apply to many users or computers.

Centralized and Decentralized Access Control

Centralized access control is an access control approach in which a single common entity— such as an individual, department, or device—decides who can get into systems and networks. The access controls are managed centrally rather than at the local level. Owners decide which users can get to which objects. The central administration supports the owners' directives. Centralized authentication services are applied and enforced through the use of **authentication, authorization, and accounting (AAA)** servers.

The benefits of using AAA servers include the following:

> **NOTE**
>
> Centralized access control is generally simpler to manage, but the drawback is that if it fails, large numbers of user can be affected and unable to get into the computer system.

- It involves less administration time because user accounts are maintained on a single host.
- It reduces design errors because different access devices use similar formats.
- It reduces security administrator training because only one system is learned.
- It improves and eases compliance auditing because all access requests are handled by one system.
- It reduces help-desk calls because the user interface is consistent.

Types of AAA Servers

In the following sections, you'll read about leading types of AAA servers: RADIUS, the most popular, along with TACACS+, DIAMETER, and SAML.

RADIUS

Remote Authentication Dial-In User Service (RADIUS) is the most popular AAA service. It is an authentication server that uses two configuration files:

- A client configuration file that contains the client address and the shared secret for transaction authentication
- A user configuration file that contains the user identification and authentication data as well as the connection and authorization information

RADIUS follows these steps in the authentication process:

1. The network access server (NAS) decrypts the user's UDP access request.
2. The NAS authenticates the source.
3. The NAS validates the request against the user file.
4. The NAS responds by allowing or rejecting access or by requesting more information.

TACACS+

Terminal Access Controller Access Control System Plus (TACACS+) is an Internet Engineering Task Force (IETF) standard that uses a single configuration file to:

- Control server operations
- Define users and attribute/value pairs
- Control authentication and authorization procedures

TACACS+ was originally developed by Cisco Systems before being released as an open standard. Cisco had previously extended the original **Terminal Access Controller Access Control System (TACACS)** protocol to develop its own proprietary version called **Extended TACACS (XTACACS)**. TACACS+ was the next step in the evolution after XTACACS. An Options section contains operation settings, the shared secret key, and the accounting filename. TACACS+ follows these steps in the authentication process:

1. Using TCP, the client sends a service request with the header in cleartext and an encrypted body containing the user ID, password, and shared key.
2. The reply contains a permit/deny as well as attribute/value pairs for the connection configuration, as required.

DIAMETER

DIAMETER (not an acronym) is based on RADIUS. However, RADIUS works only in a highly fluid or mobile workforce. DIAMETER is not restricted in that way. It works well with a stable or static workforce. DIAMETER consists of the following:

- **Base protocol**—The base protocol defines the message format, transport, error reporting, and security used by all extensions.
- **Extensions**—The extensions conduct specific types of authentication, authorization, or accounting transactions.

DIAMETER also uses **User Datagram Protocol (UDP)**. Computer applications that use UDP send messages, known as **datagrams**, to other hosts on an Internet Protocol (IP) network. UDP does this without requiring special transmission channels or data paths. As such, UDP's service is somewhat unreliable because datagrams can arrive out of order. They can also seem to be duplicated or even missing. UDP simply relies on applications to fix those issues. That spares UDP the trouble of wasting valuable time and resources fixing those issues itself. That makes UDP faster, which is why it's often used for streaming media and online gaming.

DIAMETER uses UDP in a P2P mode rather than client/server mode. In a P2P mode, a user provides another user with direct access to his hard drive. The second user also has access to the first user's hard drive. No centralized structure exists. **FIGURE 5-8** shows an example of computers connected in P2P mode.

In a client/server mode, the structure is centralized. A client—for example, a user—connects to a server to request access to certain information. **FIGURE 5-9** shows an example of computers connected in client/server mode.

This allows servers to initiate requests and handle transmission errors locally, which reduces the time a data packet takes to move across a network connection (latency) and improves performance. The user sends an authorization request containing the request command, a session ID, and the user's user ID and password. This authorization request is sent to a network-attached storage (NAS) device. The NAS approves the user's credentials. If it is approved, the NAS returns an answer packet. The answer packet contains attribute/value pairs for the service requested. The session ID uniquely identifies the connection and resolves the RADIUS problem with duplicate connection identifiers in high-density installations.

SAML

Security Assertion Markup Language (SAML) is an open standard used for exchanging both authentication and authorization data. SAML is based on XML and was designed to support access control needs for distributed systems. SAML is often used in web application access control. SAML is not a complete centralized AAA system. It is a data format specification. We include it in this section because systems that use SAML do depend on a central trusted authority to issue security tokens.

FIGURE 5-8

P2P mode.

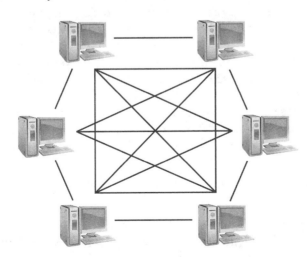

FIGURE 5-9

Client/server mode.

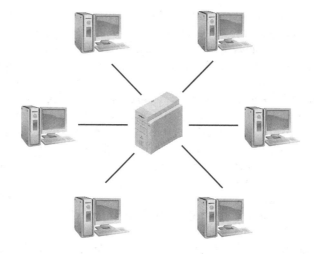

Decentralized Access Control

Another access control approach is to handle access control decisions and administration locally. This approach is called **decentralized access control**. That means access control is in the hands of the people, such as department managers who are closest to the system users. Access requests are not processed by one centralized entity.

On one hand, decentralized access control often results in confusion. Why? Because it can lead to loss of standardization and to overlapping rights. This might cause gaps in the access control design. On the other hand, a decentralized approach eliminates the single-point-of-failure problem. It ends the perception that a central controlling body cannot respond effectively to local conditions.

The two most common examples of decentralized access control are the **Password Authentication Protocol (PAP)**, which uses cleartext usernames and passwords, and the **Challenge-Handshake Authentication Protocol (CHAP)**. CHAP is more secure than PAP since it hashes the password with a one-time challenge number to defeat eavesdropping-based replay attacks. As the explosion in the number of smartphones and tablets continues, so does the need to provide secure access. Access controls for mobile devices are evolving. There are two relatively new approaches designed for mobile use. The **Initiative for Open Authentication (OATH)** is an ongoing effort to develop a reference architecture for strong authentication. Over 30 organizations contribute to the OATH project. OATH developed several standards to support mobile device authentication. The first is the **HMAC-based one-time password (HOTP)** algorithm. HOTP provides a very secure method to authenticate a user using an authentication server. The **time-based one-time password (TOTP)** algorithm is an example of HOTP. It combines a time stamp with a hashed value to reduce vulnerability to replay attacks. OATH proposes a reference framework that supports both centralized and decentralized access control models.

Privacy

One of the most visible security concerns is that of **privacy**. The growing awareness of identity theft and the importance of protecting privacy have resulted in new laws and standards to ensure privacy. Personal privacy is only one aspect of this growing issue. Organizations are becoming more and more aware of the dangers of privacy violations. Organizations often monitor their staff electronically because they are worried about the following:

- Liability in harassment suits
- Skyrocketing losses from employee theft
- Productivity losses from employees shopping or performing other nonwork-related tasks online

Electronic monitoring creates its own privacy issues in the workplace. Depending on the country or jurisdiction, the legal levels of staff monitoring might vary widely. The current thinking is that for employees to have a reasonable expectation of privacy, they must establish two things:

- They have a subjective expectation of privacy.
- This subjective expectation of privacy is reasonable.

If either element is missing, no protected interest is established. This means that if an employee is led to expect that something, such as an email message, is private, his or her employer cannot legally violate that privacy. If, however, the company informs employees that email sent over the company's network is monitored, then the employee can no longer claim to have an expectation of privacy. In other words, once the company stakes its claim over its cyberdominion, its employees have no right to privacy there.

Companies must clearly communicate their policies for what is acceptable for employees to do and what will be monitored. In many cases, employees cannot expect *any* privacy while using corporate systems. An organization's acceptable use policy (AUP) is an important document to set the appropriate expectations for, among other things, privacy.

Logon banners are messages that provide notice of legal rights to users of systems and devices. These should be used on your systems and devices. Logon banners are used to gain the following:

- Employee consent to monitoring
- Employee awareness of potential disciplinary action in the event of misuse of the account
- Employee consent to the retrieval of stored files and records

Logon banners are used to legally eliminate any expectation of privacy for employees using corporate systems.

Monitoring in the Workplace

A 2007 American Management Association (AMA) survey titled "Electronic Monitoring & Surveillance" found that "73% of organizations use technology tools to automatically monitor email, and 40% of employers assign an individual to manually read and review email." In addition, "66% [monitor] Internet connections," while "fully 65% of companies use software to block connections to inappropriate websites."

Monitoring in the workplace includes but is not limited to the following:

- Opening mail or email
- Using automated software to check email

- Checking phone logs or recording phone calls
- Checking logs of websites visited
- Getting information from credit-reference agencies
- Collecting information through point-of-sale (PoS) terminals
- Recording activities on closed-circuit television (CCTV)

Employers monitor their staff to check the quality and quantity of their employees' work. Employers are often liable for the actions of their employees, so they need to be sure that their employees are behaving properly.

To make sure the staff understands monitoring, an employer should have a clear code of conduct or policy. Employees should know that they could be disciplined if they do not follow the policy.

Cloud Computing

One of the strongest trends in enterprise development is incorporating shared services into computing environments. **Cloud computing** is the practice of using computing services that are delivered over a network. The computing services may be located within the organization's network or provided by servers that belong to some other network. There are several cloud models to meet the needs of a diverse user environment. Cloud services generally fall into one of the following categories:

- **Private cloud**—All the hardware and software required to provide services, including the network infrastructure, is operated for a single organization. The components may be managed by the organization or by a third-party provider. The actual infrastructure can be located within the organization's network or outside it.

- **Community cloud**—This type of infrastructure provides services for several organizations. The different organizations share the cloud environment and use it for their specific needs. The infrastructure can be managed by one of the participating organizations or by a third party.

- **Public cloud**—This type of cloud infrastructure is available to unrelated organizations or individuals. Public clouds are generally available for public use and are managed by a third-party provider.

- **Hybrid cloud**—This type of cloud infrastructure contains components of more than one type of cloud, including private, community, and public clouds. Hybrid clouds are useful to extend the limitations of more restrictive environments. They often are used

FYI

Cloud computing introduces new security concerns. The Payment Card Industry Data Security Standard (PCI DSS) publishes a document that directly addresses cloud security concerns. This document is a good resource for cloud computing in general and cloud security concerns. You can find this document at *https://www .pcisecuritystandards.org/pdfs/PCI_DSS_v2_Cloud_Guidelines.pdf.*

to provide resiliency and load balancing by distributing workload among several infrastructures or segments.

In the most general case, a **cloud service provider (CSP)** maintains several data centers with racks of server computers. Each server runs multiple virtual machines and is able to provide services to many clients simultaneously. CSPs offer different services to their customers over the Internet. Common cloud services include:

- **Infrastructure as a Service (IaaS)**—IaaS provides users with access to a physical or virtual machine. Users must select and load their own operating systems. They then manage all aspects of the machine, just as though it were a local computer.

- **Platform as a Service (PaaS)**—PaaS provides the user with access to a physical or a virtual machine running any of a number of popular operating systems. Unlike IaaS, with PaaS, the CSP manages the operating system and the underlying hardware. Instead of connecting to a local server, the user connects to a virtual server in the cloud. Once the connection is made, the user treats the cloud instance just like any other computer. The user can install and run software as though the server were in the local data center.

- **Software as a Service (SaaS)**—In the SaaS model, users access software from cloud clients. The most basic type of cloud client is the web browser. Users do not need to install or manage any software. All they have to do is connect to the correct server and use the software as though it were running in their local network. Some popular examples of SaaS are Google Apps™ service, Microsoft Office 365™, and SalesForce®.

There are several advantages to using cloud services over traditional in-house software. Most of the advantages include some cost savings. Such advantages include the following:

- **No need to maintain a data center**—The CSP maintains multiple data centers and handles all the logistics and details of making services available anywhere on the Internet.

- **No need to maintain a disaster recovery site**—Since the CSP already maintains services and data at multiple sites, multiple copies of data in the cloud are always available.

- **Outsourced responsibility for performance and connectivity responsibility**—All clients must do is have access to the Internet. The CSP is responsible for making sure everything works as promised in its contracts.

- **On-demand provisioning**—Cloud customers can increase and decrease the computing power and storage space they purchase based on current needs. This can save organizations substantial amounts of money over maintaining unused hardware. It also means that the organization can respond to increased demand without having to buy and set up new servers.

Cloud computing does have its disadvantages. For example, moving services outside the organization makes it more difficult to control the entire environment. Cloud disadvantages include the following:

- **Greater difficulty in keeping private data secure**—Data stored in the cloud is more accessible—to both authorized users and attackers. Cloud environments are essentially untrusted. Data owners must enforce extra precautions to ensure access controls are sufficient to protect their data.

- **Greater danger of private data leakage**—One of the advantages of cloud computing is that the CSP ensures that your data are always available. One way it does this is by keeping multiple current copies of data in different locations. Every additional copy of private data increases the possibility that data may leak to unauthorized users.

- **Greater demand for constant network access**—Access to cloud services depends on the network connection to those services. That means a user who doesn't have reliable or fast Internet access may encounter difficulties with cloud services. This concern is greatest for mobile users who travel in and out of areas of reliable coverage or users who do not have reliable Internet access.

- **Greater need for clients to trust outside vendors**—Releasing private data to a CSP requires some level of trust in that provider. Trusting a third party with sensitive data may violate some laws, regulations, or vendor requirements. Before you move data to a cloud, you must carefully examine all constraints due to outside requirements. Although the safest policy is to treat the cloud as an untrusted environment, there has to be some basic level of trust with your CSP.

One of the most difficult problems organizations encounter today is keeping private data secure in the cloud. The main difficulty is that data move from a trusted location inside an organization's infrastructure to an untrusted cloud environment. Since users can connect to cloud services, the question is, who should be responsible for identification, authorization, and authentication? The **Cloud Security Alliance (CSA)** is a nonprofit organization with a mission to promote best practices for using cloud computing securely. CSA has published a guide on cloud security, *Security Guidance for Critical Areas of Focus in Cloud Computing*. The report describes the challenges of cloud computing this way:

> Managing information in the era of cloud computing is a daunting challenge that affects all organizations; even those that aren't seemingly actively engaged in cloud-based projects. It begins with managing internal data and cloud migrations and extends to securing information in diffuse, cross-organization applications and services. Information management and data security in the cloud era demand both new strategies and technical architectures.

> There is no easy solution to the problem of managing access control in cloud environments. Researchers are exploring novel ways to ease the burden on organizations. Today the best approaches are to extend the existing concepts you have learned in this chapter. Some of the access controls will likely exist in cloud environments. The most important rule is always to use a defense-in-depth strategy. Never rely on only a single control to protect any resource.

CHAPTER SUMMARY

In this chapter, you learned that access controls are ways to permit or deny access to certain resources. Organizations use access controls to manage what staff can and can't do. Access controls specify who users are, what they can do, which resources they can get to, and what operations they can carry out. Access control systems use several technologies, including passwords, hardware tokens, biometrics, and certificates. Access can be granted to physical assets, such as buildings or rooms. Access can also be granted to information systems.

You learned that the four parts of access control are identification, authorization, authentication, and accountability. These four parts create an access control process that can be divided into two phases: the policy-definition phase and the policy-enforcement phase. You learned how you first need to decide who is authorized for access and what systems or resources they are allowed to use. Then you learned how access is granted or rejected based on the authorizations defined in the first phase. You also learned about the formal models of access control, access control methodologies and challenges, and the effects of access control breaches.

KEY CONCEPTS AND TERMS

Access control
Access control list (ACL)
Access control policy
Accountability
Accounting
Actions
Asynchronous token
Audit
Authentication
Authentication, authorization, and accounting (AAA)
Authority-level policy
Authorization
Bell-La Padula model
Biba integrity model
Biometrics
Brewer and Nash integrity model
Brute-force attack
Buffer overflow

Challenge-Handshake Authentication Protocol (CHAP)
Characteristic
Clark and Wilson integrity model
Cloud computing
Cloud Security Alliance (CSA)
Cloud service provider (CSP)
Colluding
Collusion
Common Criteria for Information Technology Security Evaluation (Common Criteria)
Constrained user interface
Continuous authentication
Covert channels
Credential management
Crossover error rate (CER)

Datagrams
Decentralized access control
Degausser
DIAMETER
Dictionary attack
Discretionary access control (DAC)
Event-based synchronization system
Federation
Group membership policy
Group Policy
Group Policy Object (GPO)
HMAC-based one-time password (HOTP)
Identification
Initiative for Open Authentication (OATH)
Key distribution center (KDC)

5

KEY CONCEPTS AND TERMS, *continued*

Knowledge

Least privilege

Lightweight Directory Access Protocol (LDAP)

Log files

Logical access control

Man-in-the-middle (MITM)

Mandatory access control (MAC)

Multitenancy

Need to know

Overwriting

Ownership

Passphrase

Password Authentication Protocol (PAP)

Personal identification numbers (PINs)

Physical access control

Physically constrained user interface

Privacy

Public key infrastructure (PKI)

Rainbow tables

Reference monitor

Relationships

Remote Authentication Dial-In User Service (RADIUS)

Resources

Role-based access control (RBAC)

Secure European System for Applications in a Multi-Vendor Environment (SESAME)

Secure LDAP

Security Assertion Markup Language (SAML)

Security control

Security kernel

Security kernel database

Separation of duties

Single sign-on (SSO)

Single-factor authentication

Smart card

Sniffing

State

Synchronous token

Temporal isolation

Terminal Access Controller Access System (TACACS)

Terminal Access Controller Access System Plus (TACACS+)

Threshold

Time-based one-time password (TOTP)

Time-based synchronization system

Time of day restrictions

Transition functions

Transitive trust

Trojan horses

Trusted Operating Systems (TOS)

Two-factor authentication

USB token

User assigned privileges

User Datagram Protocol (UDP)

Username

View-based access control (VBAC)

XTACACS (Extended Terminal Access Controller Access System)

CHAPTER 5 ASSESSMENT

1. Access controls are policies or procedures used to control access to certain items.

A. True

B. False

2. Which answer best describes the authorization component of access control?

A. Authorization is the method a subject uses to request access to a system.

B. Authorization is the process of creating and maintaining the policies and procedures

necessary to ensure proper information is available when an organization is audited.

C. Authorization is the validation or proof that the subject requesting access is indeed the same subject who has been granted that access.

D. Authorization is the process of determining who is approved for access and what resources they are approved for.

3. Which answer best describes the identification component of access control?

   A. Identification is the validation or proof that the subject requesting access is indeed the same subject who has been granted that access.
   B. Identification is the method a subject uses to request access to a system.
   C. Identification is the process of determining who is approved for access and what resources they are approved for.
   D. Identification is the process of creating and maintaining the policies and procedures necessary to ensure proper information is available when an organization is audited.

4. Which answer best describes the authentication component of access control?

   A. Authentication is the validation or proof that the subject requesting access is indeed the same subject who has been granted that access.
   B. Authentication is the process of creating and maintaining the policies and procedures necessary to ensure proper information is available when an organization is audited.
   C. Authentication is the process of determining who is approved for access and what resources they are approved for.
   D. Authentication is the method a subject uses to request access to a system.

5. Which answer best describes the accountability component of access control?

   A. Accountability is the validation or proof that the subject requesting access is indeed the same subject who has been granted that access.
   B. Accountability is the method a subject uses to request access to a system.
   C. Accountability is the process of creating and maintaining the policies and procedures necessary to ensure proper information is available when an organization is audited.
   D. Accountability is the process of determining who is approved for access and what resources they are approved for.

6. Physical access controls deter physical access to resources, such as buildings or gated parking lots.

   A. True
   B. False

7. When you log on to a network, you are presented with some combination of username, password, token, smart card, or biometrics. You are then authorized or denied access by the system. This is an example of _____.

   A. Physical access controls
   B. Logical access controls
   C. Group membership policy
   D. The Biba integrity model
   E. None of the above

8. Access controls cannot be implemented in various forms, restriction levels, or different levels within the computing environment.

   A. True
   B. False

9. Which of the following is an example of a formal model of access control?

   A. Discretionary access control (DAC)
   B. Mandatory access control (MAC)
   C. Nondiscretionary access control
   D. The Clark and Wilson integrity model
   E. All of the above

10. Physical access, security bypass, and eavesdropping are examples of how access controls can be _____.

    A. Stolen
    B. Compromised
    C. Audited
    D. Authorized

11. Challenges to access control include which of the following?

    A. Laptop loss
    B. Exploiting hardware
    C. Eavesdropping
    D. Exploiting applications
    E. All of the above

12. When the owner of the resource determines the access and changes permissions as needed, it's known as _____.

A. Mandatory access control (MAC)
B. Discretionary access control (DAC)
C. Nondiscretionary access control
D. Content-dependent access control
E. Role-based access control

13. The process of identifying, quantifying, and prioritizing the vulnerabilities in a system is known as a _____.

A. Vulnerability policy
B. Vulnerability deterrent
C. Vulnerability authorization
D. Vulnerability assessment

14. The security kernel enforces access control of computer systems.

A. True
B. False

15. When it comes to privacy, organizations are concerned about which of the following?

A. Liability in harassment suits
B. Skyrocketing losses from employee theft
C. Productivity losses from employees shopping or performing other nonwork-related tasks online
D. All of the above

Security Operations and Administration

SECURITY PROFESSIONALS MUST UNDERSTAND how security operations and administration create the foundation for a solid security program. Your role as a security professional is similar to that of a coach. You work with staff to identify the strengths and weaknesses of your "players," or assets. Your goal is to win the game. In the world of the security professional, the "game" is to secure your organization's resources. Your "opponents" are unauthorized users trying to steal your data and use it against you.

As a coach, you have a playbook of strategies. You need to keep these strategies out of the hands of your opponents. You also need to make sure your strategies abide by the rules and regulations of the industry. To prepare them for the challenge, you must educate and train your players. You must give them the skills they need to work together as a team and win the game.

If you are successful, your organization will run as smoothly as a championship team. Everybody will understand the mission and how to work together to complete it. If you fail, your team will appear confused. Each player will seem to do his or her own thing, regardless of the consequences. The next thing you know, your organization's information will fall into the hands of your opponents. Your trade secrets will no longer be secret, your organization will spend a lot of money fixing what's broken, and you and your employees might find yourselves "on the bench" or even looking for other jobs.

In this lesson, you'll learn the skills you'll need to develop a strong security administration team.

Chapter 6 Topics

This chapter covers the following topics and concepts:

- What security administration is
- What compliance is
- What professional ethics are
- What the infrastructure for an IT security policy is
- What data classification standards are
- What configuration management is
- What the change management process is

- What the system life cycle (SLC) and system development life cycle (SDLC) are
- How software development relates to security

Chapter 6 Goals

When you complete this chapter, you will be able to:

- Manage the security infrastructure
- Create and support policies
- Classify data
- Develop and maintain security programs
- Manage major and minor changes to systems
- Promote user awareness of security
- Understand and use professional ethics

Security Administration

Security administration within an organization refers to the group of individuals responsible for planning, designing, implementing, and monitoring an organization's security plan. Before you can form an administrative team, your organization must identify its information assets. After your organization identifies and documents the assets, you should assign responsibility of each one to a person or position. Once you have a list of assets and know who is responsible for each one, you can form the team. This administrative team then determines the sensitivity of each asset so that it can plan how to secure each one accordingly.

Controlling Access

The primary task of an organization's security administration team is to control access to systems or resources. There are four aspects of access control:

- **Identification**—Assertions made by users about who they are.
- **Authentication**—The proving of that assertion.
- **Authorization**—The permissions a legitimate user or process has on the system.
- **Accountability**—Tracking or logging what authenticated and unauthenticated users do while accessing the system.

The security administration team leads these efforts by determining the best security controls to put in place to secure your organization's resources.

Documentation, Procedures, and Guidelines

The security administration team handles the planning, design, implementation, and monitoring of your organization's security program. Several types of documentation are necessary to provide the input the security administration team needs to make the best decisions to secure assets. The most common documentation requirements include the following:

- **Sensitive assets list**—What assets must the organization take measures to secure? The list can include computers, network components, databases, documents, and any other assets that could be vulnerable to attack.
- **The organization's security process**—How does it all work?
- **The authority of the persons responsible for security**—Which administrator is responsible or authorized for what assets and what actions?
- **The policies, procedures, and guidelines adopted by the organization**—What information needs to be communicated, how is it communicated, and when is it communicated?

The security administration team puts together all the pieces of a puzzle to ensure your organization complies with stated policies. An organization must comply with rules on two levels:

- **Regulatory compliance**—The organization must comply with laws and government regulations.
- **Organizational compliance**—The organization must comply with its own policies, audits, culture, and standards.

As a result, the security administration team's documentation, procedures, and guidelines focus on compliance and compliance monitoring. They have to make sure the organization follows the various rules and regulations.

Disaster Assessment and Recovery

The security administration team's responsibilities include handling events that affect your computers and networks. These include incidents, disasters, and other interruptions. The security administration team forms an incident response team to handle any security incidents. This team is composed of individuals who are responsible for responding to incidents and investigating security breaches. Another team managed by the security administration team is the **emergency operations group**. This group is responsible for protecting sensitive data in the event of natural disasters and equipment failure, among other potential emergencies.

Despite the best efforts of the incident response team, the emergency operations group, and system administrators, all systems are subject to failure or attack. The security administration team ensures that an organization can respond rapidly and effectively to any event.

Security Outsourcing

Many organizations rely on outside firms to handle security monitoring and analysis. This means you might need to monitor the work of the outsourcing firm or work with it when handling incidents. This approach has both advantages and disadvantages:

- **Advantages**—A security management firm has a high level of expertise because it focuses on security—and security only—every day. Simply put, it will have expertise and experience that your own organization might not have.

- **Disadvantages**—Outsourcing has two primary disadvantages. First, the outsourcing firm might not know your organization well and might not possess internal knowledge. Second, by outsourcing, you won't develop in-house capability or talent and will therefore need to continue to pay for these services indefinitely.

Outsourcing Considerations

The security administration team must work closely with an outside firm to make sure both agree to specific security requirements. Integrating data or processing with third parties introduces new threats. Relocating data or processes (or both) outside your own data centers raises trust questions. How can you trust another organization to protect your intellectual property? Though there are many concerns to address when outsourcing, the main concerns include:

- **Privacy**—Does the third party agree to uphold your privacy policy? How do they plan to control how data are collected, stored, handled, and destroyed?

- **Risk**—What additional risks exist by transferring data over a trust boundary? How are any new risks addressed? Who is responsible for managing new outsourcing risks?

- **Data security**—What controls protect data confidentiality and integrity from unauthorized access? Are access controls consistent with internal controls? How is data availability protected? Are backups and redundancy measures in place to minimize downtime? How are backups and redundant data copies protected?

- **Ownership**—Who owns the data, the infrastructure, and the media? Who is responsible for each component?

- **Adherence to policy**—Does each third party commit to upholding your security policies and procedures?

Several types of agreements are common when outsourcing to external organizations. These agreements help to formalize answers to the preceding questions. A list of the most common agreements that define how an outsourcing relationship works would include:

- **Service-level agreement (SLA)**—This type of agreement is a a formal contract between your organization and the outside firm that details the specific services the firm will provide. Some examples of security-related services detailed in an SLA can include:
  - How and when potential security breaches are communicated
  - How logs and events are reported
  - How confidential data are handled
  - What the security system uptime requirements are (for example, you might require that all critical security systems have 99.99 percent reliability)

The SLA should communicate the expectations of both the organization and the outside firm. The SLA should anticipate the needs of both parties. Each member of the security administration team must thoroughly analyze his or her department's risks. Any unaccounted risk is likely to cost your organization in terms of either data loss or expenses to fix it. Think of this as similar to maintaining an automobile: Regular oil changes are less expensive than blown head gaskets. Maintaining an engine is cheaper than fixing one.

- **Blanket purchase agreement (BPA)**—A streamlined method of meeting recurring needs for supplies or services, a BPA creates preapproved accounts with qualified suppliers to fulfill recurring orders for products or services. BPAs can be very helpful in simplifying the process of recurring purchases.

- **Memorandum of understanding (MOU)**—Also called a letter of intent, a MOU is an agreement between two or more parties that expresses areas of common interest that result in shared actions. MOUs are generally less enforcable than a formal agreement but still more formal than an oral agreement.

- **Interconnection security agreement (ISA)**— Often an extension of a MOU, the ISA serves as an agreement that documents the technical requirements of interconnected assets. This type of document is most often used to specify technical needs and security responsibilities of connected organizations.

The negotiation process and creation of agreements is one of the first steps in the business partner **onboarding** process. Any time your organization decides to outsource data or processing, you must carefully consider the security impact and responsibilities. The onboarding process provides time to plan for contingencies before a problem occurs. It also provides the opportunity to clearly communicate goals and expectations for all parties. Likewise, you should specify an **offboarding** process to follow when you terminate relationships with outsourced resources. The offboarding process defines how to transfer control of data and other assets, terminate communications, and complete any open transactions. This process is necessary to ensure that no remnants of data or processing remain once an outsourcing relationship ends.

Compliance

Your organization's security policy sets the tone for the way you approach security activities. It also states the rules with which you must comply. Think of a security policy in terms of traffic laws. Traffic laws maintain a certain degree of order and safety on the roads. If these laws aren't enforced, the roads become dangerous. An information security policy is no different. Your security policy isn't much good if it isn't enforced. This is where compliance enters the picture. When policies are enforced, the organization complies with those policies. Three primary means are used to ensure compliance:

- Event logs
- Compliance liaison
- Remediation

Event Logs

Event logs are records of actions that your operating system or application software create. An event log records which user or system accessed data or a resource and when. You can think of event logs as being similar to the system a public library uses to keep track of who checks out books. When a book is late or missing, the library checks its records to determine who last checked out the book. When an information security breach occurs in your organization, an event log helps determine what happened to the system and when. It can help you track down the culprit or help you fix the problem. You can change the amount of information that event logs record. Recording every event requires a tremendous amount of disk space and can actually slow down your computers. It also means that reading through the log files is more difficult. On the other hand, logging too few events may cause you to miss recording some important details. It is important to record all the actions that you may need in the future to investigate security problems. It is also important to ensure that access to your event logs is controlled. You don't want an attacker to be able to compromise your system and then erase any trace of the attack.

Compliance Liaison

As organizations and security policies become larger and more complex, it becomes difficult to stay compliant. A **compliance liaison** makes sure all personnel are aware of—and comply with—the organization's policies. Different departments within an organization might have different security ideas or needs. A compliance liaison works with each department to ensure it understands, implements, and monitors compliance. A compliance liaison can also help departments understand how to include information security in their daily operations. Another important role of a compliance liaison is dealing with outsourcing service providers. After going through the trouble of creating interoperability documents, you need to ensure the rules you've set down are being followed. The compliance liaison reviews agreement requirements throughout any outsourcing engagement. This review helps validate whether or not a service provider is in compliance with current agreements.

Remediation

Mitigating vulnerabilities reduces the risk of attacks against your computers and networks. In some cases, the best solution is to block an intruder and deny access to a resource. In other cases, it is possible to remove the vulnerability. **Remediation** involves fixing something that is broken or defective. With computer systems, remediation refers to fixing security vulnerabilities.

Of course, some problems are more important than others. You should fix high-risk issues before lower-risk ones. When possible, the best option is to remove vulnerabilities. If you cannot effectively remove a vulnerability, the next best step is to remove the ability of an attacker to exploit the vulnerability. You should always design security policies to protect your assets from attack. Compliance is extremely important in securing information technology systems.

Professional Ethics

One of the most important roles security professionals assume is that of leadership in compliant behavior. People won't follow the rules if they don't trust the leaders. Every respected profession has its own code of ethics and conduct. Adhering to such a code fosters the respect of any profession's practitioners. The security profession is no different from other professions in this regard. It is important that security professionals have a definite code of ethics that governs their behavior. Most security certification organizations publish their codes of ethics. In fact, most certifications require candidates to adhere to a specific code of ethics before qualifying for the certification. For example, both (ISC)^2 and CompTIA provide solid ethical guidelines. However, guidelines aren't effective unless you adopt and practice them. Here are some tips for practicing strong ethics:

- **Set the example**—Demonstrate strong ethical principles in your daily activities. Users will follow your lead. If you are serious about ethics, your users will be more serious about ethics.

- **Encourage adopting ethical guidelines and standards**—Security professionals must know their ethical boundaries and set an example by adhering to them. This often means making difficult decisions and setting a good example. You must push the organization to define its code of ethics. This helps the staff operate ethically and responsibly.

- **Inform users through security awareness training**—Make sure users are aware of and understand their ethical responsibilities.

Common Fallacies About Ethics

Simply writing down a list of ethics-oriented rules is not enough. It is important that security professionals actually use ethics in their everyday lives. The first step in adhering to ethics rules is to understand the most common assumptions many computer users hold that may lead them to unethical behavior. Here are some of these common assumptions:

- Users assume that computers should prevent abuse. If they can gain unauthorized access, it's the organization's fault—not theirs.
- Users believe that in some legal systems, they have the right to explore security vulnerabilities as a form of free speech or expression.
- Users think their actions may cause only minor damage. They think that a little damage won't bother anyone.
- Users think that if it's easy to break in, it must be all right to do so.
- Users think that hacking is okay if their motives are not damaging. They think if they are not making any money or otherwise advancing themselves by hacking into a system, they must not be committing a crime.
- Users think information should be free. They think it's okay to look through somebody's system to obtain information.

Codes of Ethics

A code of ethics helps ensure professionalism. Several published codes apply to information security. For example, published statements from the **Internet Architecture Board (IAB)** summarize the tone of most security-related codes of ethics. These statements explain what the IAB considers ethical and appropriate behavior.

Internet Architecture Board (IAB) Statement of Policy

The IAB has provided a list of unethical and unacceptable practices. In 1989, the IAB issued a statement of policy about Internet ethics. The title of this document is RFC 1087. Although it was one of the first statements on the ethics of Internet use, it still applies today. RFC 1087 (*https://tools.ietf.org/html/rfc1087*) states that any activity is unethical and unacceptable that purposely does any of the following:

"Seeks to gain unauthorized access to the resources of the Internet"
"Disrupts the intended use of the Internet"
"Wastes resources (people, capacity, computer) through such actions"
"Destroys the integrity of computer-based information"
"Compromises the privacy of users"
"Involves negligence in the conduct of Internet-wide experiments"

The key point of the document is this: Access to the Internet is a *privilege*, not a right.

Professional Requirements

In any profession, rules and regulations enforce professional ethics. Those rules might come from the certifying agencies. If you violate the rules, you risk losing your certification or license.

In other contexts, laws and regulations require ethical behavior. For example, the Organization for Economic Cooperation and Development (OECD) is an organization of more than 30 countries. Its goal is economic cooperation and growth. In 1980, it created eight privacy principles. These principles have formed the basis for much of the world's privacy legislation. In summary, the principles state the following:

- An organization should collect only what it needs.
- An organization should not share its information.
- An organization should keep its information up to date.
- An organization should use its information only for the purposes for which it was collected.
- An organization should properly destroy its information when it is no longer needed.

> **NOTE**
>
> For more information about the OED, visit *www.oecd.org*. You can find a report on the original OECD Privacy Guidelines and their application in today's environments at *www.oecd.org/sti/ieconomy/49710223.pdf*.

Technical TIP

As you have learned, many certification organizations require adherence to a code of ethics. You can find the (ISC)^2 Code of Ethics at *https://www.isc2.org/ethics/default.aspx*. The CompTIA Candidate Code of Ethics is available at *https://certification.comptia.org/testing/test-policies/continuing-education-policies/candidate-code-of-ethics*.

Personnel Security Principles

For all the technical solutions you can devise to secure your systems, the human element remains your greatest challenge. You might be surprised how far a little education can go. If your staff are aware of how security risks can hurt both themselves and the organization, they'll be more likely to help you run a tight ship.

It's important to know what a user should and shouldn't do. The best way to accomplish this goal is to create well-defined job descriptions, job roles, and responsibilities. When you know what people should be doing, it's easier to identify activities they aren't supposed to do. If their roles or responsibilities are vague, it's more difficult to flag bad behavior—which means people are more likely to get away with things.

Minimizing access to information and assets is an important security control. You have already learned about some concepts related to personnel security. These concepts are very important and bear revisiting. Pay careful attention to any security concepts that directly affect personnel. People are the most important assets in your organization. It is vital that they know how to contribute to maintaining your organization's security.

Limiting Access

When deciding how to grant access to users, one of the core concepts is limiting access. The idea that users should be granted only the levels of permissions they need in order to perform their duties is called the principle of *least privilege*. Always use this principle. Otherwise, you run the risk of allowing unauthorized users access to information they shouldn't be able to access. For example, weak access controls may allow a sales clerk to view employee salaries.

The *need-to-know* requirement is another concept that relates to the principle of least privilege. This states that people should have access only to information they need to perform their jobs, regardless of the employee's clearance level. So, even though users might have a top-secret security clearance, it doesn't mean they should have access to *all* top-secret information. They need access to only that information they need to do their jobs.

Separation of Duties

Separation of duties breaks a task into subtasks that different users must carry out. This means a single user cannot carry out a critical task without the help or approval of another user. To put it another way: A user who plans to harm a system must get help from others. A conspiracy is hard to organize and to hide. For example, separation of duties helps ensure that an employee cannot create a new vendor *and* cut a check to that vendor. That prevents an employee from opening a bank account for Acme Consulting, going into the system at work to create a new vendor named Acme Consulting, and then cutting a check for $1,000 to Acme Consulting.

Job Rotation

Another way to protect your organization from personnel-related security violations is to use **job rotation**. Job rotation minimizes risk by rotating employees among various systems or duties. This prevents collusion, where several employees conspire to commit fraud. It also gives managers a chance to track which users were authorized to take what actions and when. If other security measures have failed, job rotation provides an opportunity to find the security breach before it inflicts more harm. Job rotation also provides trained backup, since several employees learn the skills of specific jobs.

Mandatory Vacations

Much like job rotation, mandatory vacations provide the chance to detect fraud. When users are on vacation, you should suspend their access to your environment. This prevents them from working from home, where they might attempt to cover their tracks. Under U.S. banking rules, for example, certain bank employees must take two consecutive weeks of vacation. Until recently, the law forbade managers from contacting these vacationing employees with work-related matters. That rule has been relaxed to allow for read-only access to systems so that employees can at least keep up with their email correspondence. However, they still cannot participate in work-related activities while on vacation.

Security Training

Because personnel are so important to solid security, one of the best security controls you can develop is a strong security training and awareness program. Security training helps gain the support of all employees. They become security advocates who are motivated to comply with policies that relate to their jobs. They are careful to avoid security breaches. You should train employees, then train them again at specified intervals. This repeated training refreshes employees' knowledge and reminds them of the importance of security. Well-trained personnel can make the difference between a secure environment and a collection of attacks and mistakes.

Employees should be aware of security threats to an organization, especially from human factors. These threats include installing rogue technologies, selecting weak passwords, and phishing attacks. These types of threats are common because so many organizations fail to train their personnel on the importance of recognizing them. Simply explaining how weak passwords can endanger personal and business information can often encourage users to create stronger passwords.

Security Awareness

A security awareness program should address the requirements and expectations of your security policy. The security policy requires actions and provides authority for security controls. It's one of the best forms of defense. Employees are more likely to comply with a security control if they realize the policy mandates it. In addition to explaining why each part of your policy is necessary, the program should explain the penalties for policy violations.

An awareness program is different from a formal training program. Most users don't understand what security is and why it's necessary. You can use security awareness programs—including posters, emails, and employee newsletters, among other tools—to do the following:

- Teach users about security objectives
- Inform users about trends and threats in security
- Motivate users to comply with security policies

Employees generally want to do what's best for the company. When security seems to get in the way of their productivity, however, they'll often bypass security measures to complete their work more quickly. For example, suppose an employee, Bob, is home for the weekend and receives a call from another employee, Sue, at the office. Sue says she needs Bob's password to get to a file or system so she can finish a project. No matter how often you remind employees of the risks of sharing passwords, most people will still be quick to give up their passwords in this situation. It's your job to reinforce the importance of following security policies. It's also your job to teach them how to solve productivity problems and still maintain a high level of security.

Awareness programs can remind staff about security policies. These programs can also measure how well the staff follows the security policy. The programs provide staff with practical advice on how to deal with security incidents. A good program convinces staff that security is their personal duty. You can help employees change their behavior such that security becomes a part of their daily routine.

Make note of employees who aren't following policies. Use this information in a training session to present employees with scenarios that are specific to their work. Ask employees, "What would you do when . . . ?" The information you gather helps identify gaps in your awareness program. Tailor your program with this information.

Social Engineering

One of the most popular types of attack on computer systems involves social engineering. Social engineering is deceiving or using people to get around security controls. Because most people want to be helpful, it is not too hard for an attacker to convince someone with system access to do something he or she shouldn't do. It is one of the most critical areas of security. As you grant more employees access to systems and data, the risk of security breaches goes up. Technical solutions will not stop an authorized user from calling an unauthorized person and reading sensitive data over the phone. The best way to avoid social engineering is to ensure that you train your personnel to recognize social engineering attempts and know how to handle such attacks. Your security training should cover the most common types of social engineering attacks, including:

- **Intimidation**—Using threats or harassment to bully another person for information.
- **Name-dropping**—Using the names of managers or superiors to convince another person that a higher authority has allowed access to information.
- **Appeals for help**—Tugging at a person's sense of compassion or understanding of a difficult, and perhaps unreasonable, situation. The goal of the emotional appeal is to bypass normal procedures or gain special consideration. When combined with an incentive, such as a reward, this type of engineering is very effective. For example, consider the scam in which the scammer promises to send you money if you'll help him transfer money to a disadvantaged person. Unfortunately, this type of emotional appeal fools many people every year.
- **Phishing**—Technology works quite well in social engineering. Take, for example, phishing. In a phishing attack, scammers create an email or webpage that resembles the work of a reputable organization. The scammers want you to believe it's a reputable organization so you'll share sensitive information with them. They use this information to gain access to your financial information or to steal your identity. A phishing attack can also take the form of a survey that asks questions in an effort to capture sensitive information.

> ### ▋ NOTE
>
> For more information about the latest phishing techniques and fraud alerts, see *www.fraudwatchinternational .com/phishing*.

The Infrastructure for an IT Security Policy

Every company operates within a complex combination of laws, regulations, requirements, competitors, and partners. In addition, morale, labor relations, productivity, cost, and cash flow affect how a company operates. Within this environment, management must develop and publish an overall security statement and directives. From the security team's perspective, a security program addresses these directives through policies and their supporting elements, such as standards, procedures, baselines, and guidelines. **FIGURE 6-1** shows the elements of a security policy environment.

Each element has a specific requirement for security professionals, who are involved with compliance monitoring, security awareness, training, access control, privacy, incident response, log analysis, and more.

Your security policy sets the organization's tone and culture. As a security professional, you're often required to apply policy intent. You must understand the details of your organization's security policy. The policy is the high-level statement of values and direction. Your organization's standards, baselines, procedures, and guidelines implement your security policy.

The role of the security professional is to provide support for these elements. This support includes informing staff of policies, training, and enforcement. You have a role in any updates or changes. **FIGURE 6-2** shows a typical security policy hierarchy.

Policies

Written security policies document management's goals and objectives. They explain the company's security needs and their commitment to meeting those needs. A security policy should read like a short summary of key facts. If the policy is too complex, management has trouble embracing and approving it.

For example, a good organizational security policy might read simply, as in "Security is essential to the future of our organization" or "Security in our products is our most important task." This type of statement provides managers with guidance they need to make decisions. The security policy also helps your organization evaluate how well it is complying with laws, regulations, and standards of due care and due diligence. The primary purpose of any security-related policy is to reduce risk. The policy helps the organization focus its efforts in a particular area.

Policies aren't of much value if they're not read, available, enforced, and updated. You must post policies in a location available to every employee. For example, you'll often see policies posted in break rooms. Policies must be current, especially in keeping with new

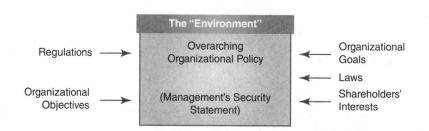

The security policy environment.

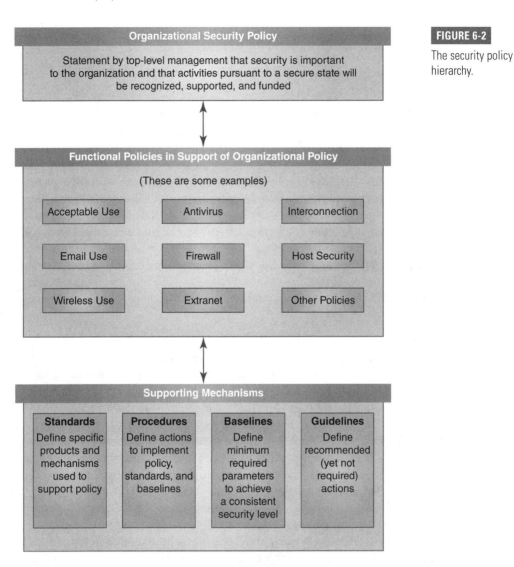

Organizational Security Policy

Statement by top-level management that security is important
to the organization and that activities pursuant to a secure state will
be recognized, supported, and funded

Functional Policies in Support of Organizational Policy

(These are some examples)

Acceptable Use	Antivirus	Interconnection
Email Use	Firewall	Host Security
Wireless Use	Extranet	Other Policies

Supporting Mechanisms

Standards	**Procedures**	**Baselines**	**Guidelines**
Define specific products and mechanisms used to support policy	Define actions to implement policy, standards, and baselines	Define minimum required parameters to achieve a consistent security level	Define recommended (yet not required) actions

FIGURE 6-2

The security policy
hierarchy.

laws and regulations. You should meet with employees at least once a year to ensure they
are up to date on the latest policies. Maintain a record of this review with each employee.

A security policy helps all employees understand the assets and principles the organization values. With a clear policy, your staff is more likely to respect the organization's assets.
Remember, staff will take policies only as seriously as the organization takes them.

A **functional policy** declares an organization's management direction for security in such
specific functional areas as email, remote access, and Internet surfing. The departments responsible for these functional policies write them. For example, human resources, information technology, operations, and facilities would each produce their own specific functional
policies. A functional policy should use strong language, such as *will* and *must*. Most people
consider a term such as *should* as merely a suggestion, not a mandate. Weak word choices

don't demand as much attention as strong words. For example, a good access control functional policy reads as follows:

"All authorized users must be allowed to do *only* their authorized tasks. Unauthorized users must not have access to the company systems or resources."

One example of a functional policy is the **privacy policy.** A privacy policy specifies how your organization collects, uses, and disposes of information about individuals. Most consumers who provide personal information demand a strong privacy policy. It gives the organization an opportunity to clearly state how they will handle their customers' personal information. Another example of a functional policy is an acceptable use policy (AUP). This type of policy sets clear limits on how the organization will allow its assets to be used. The most common focus of this type of policy dictates the way personnel must use the organization's computer resources. The policy may include guidance on the acceptable use of social media or even specific websites.

Policies allow organizations to state different goals at very high levels. These goals may be intended for their own employees, business partners, customers, or perhaps all of these groups. They set the organization's tone and communicate commitment in different areas. All decisions that an organization's personnel make should flow from the high-level policies.

Standards

Standards are mandated requirements for hardware and software solutions used to address security risk throughout an organization. Standards might refer to a specific antivirus product or password-generation token. Simply put, when a standard is in place, it means the organization has selected a solution—and that solution only—to fulfill a policy goal.

Adopting standards carries many advantages. Often, standards save an organization money because it can negotiate bulk purchases with vendors. A vendor might sell a single-user license for $29.95. However, that same vendor might sell multiple licenses for only $24.95 per license. If that organization needs multiple licenses to comply with a standard, bulk purchasing can save the company several thousand dollars. In addition, many vendors offer free training with bulk purchases. This can save the organization the time and trouble of training its staff on how to use the product.

You don't have to develop your own standards for each situation. You can adopt standards created by government, industry, or other sectors and use them as your own. Standards also establish a common basis throughout an organization. This helps keep all departments on the same page. They ensure that each department has the blueprints it needs to stay compliant.

The main disadvantage of standards is vulnerability. If the selected product is flawed, the entire organization will be at risk after it installs the product. A single standard cannot work if a vendor doesn't support the product or if it is too expensive to maintain or license. Examine alternatives when evaluating products for standards. Ensure that each selection you make comes with a guarantee of support if problems arise.

Procedures

Procedures are step-by-step systematic actions to accomplish a security requirement, process, or objective. They are one of the most powerful tools available to you. They can provide documentation of the way you do business and ensure that no employee's critical

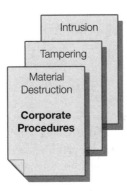

FIGURE 6-3

Systematic actions.

knowledge remains only in his or her head. Procedures cover things such as changing passwords, responding to incidents, and creating backups. **FIGURE 6-3** shows a few sample procedures.

Procedures ensure that you enforce the intent of a policy. They require you to follow a series of steps to complete a task. The following are all true of procedures:

- They reduce mistakes in a crisis.
- They ensure you don't miss important steps.
- They provide for places within the process to conduct assurance checks.
- They are mandatory requirements, like policies and standards.

Baselines

In many cases, it is helpful to define basic configurations for specific types of computers or devices. For example, having a document that lists the components and configuration settings for a standard workstation makes it easy to ensure that all new workstations are the same. Security personnel often create such basic configurations, called **baselines**, to ensure that they enforce the security minimums. Baselines are the benchmarks that help make sure a minimum level of security exists across multiple applications of systems and across different products. Baselines are helpful in configuring new computers or devices as well as for comparing with existing systems to see if they still meet the minimums. **FIGURE 6-4** shows a basic baseline corporate configuration.

Baselines tell how to apply security devices to make sure that they create a constant level of security throughout the organization. Different systems or platforms have different ways of handling security issues. Baselines tell system administrators how to set up the security for each platform. This helps achieve a constant level of security.

Baselines are the great leveler of options offered through different security products, operating systems, and applications. This is becoming more important as more hybrid products enter the security market. These products combine services into multifunctional

Baseline Corporate Configuration		
VPN Setup	IDS Configuration	Password Rules

FIGURE 6-4

Baseline corporate configuration.

devices. Organizations often create baseline standards for each operating system in use. You might have different baselines for Windows 8, Windows 10, Windows Server 2012 R2, Windows Server 2016, Mac OS X, Linux, and so on.

Guidelines

Organizations often use **guidelines** to help provide structure to a security program. They outline recommendations for the purchase and use of acceptable products and systems. Guidelines are simply actions that the organization recommends. These guidelines usually exist in the form of white papers, best practices, or other formats defined by an organization's security program.

You must carefully select the language you use in guidelines. A few wrong words can transform a guideline into a company standard. For example, consider the following example of an overarching statement as dictated by the company CEO:

"This company will follow the recommendations of the ISO 27001 standard."

That statement makes ISO 27001 mandatory within that organization. Make sure that's the intent before you make such a bold statement.

Data Classification Standards

Mandatory access control (MAC) involves assigning each object a specific classification. Classifying information often relies on the regulations that apply to the specific type of data. Examples include the protection of personal information, financial information, and health information.

Classifying data is the duty of the person who owns the data or of someone the owner assigns. You can refer to this person as the *data owner*. A similar term, *system owner*, refers to the person or group that manages the infrastructure. System owners are often in control of change or configuration management. System owners are *not* in control of data classification.

It's important to understand the difference between clearance and classification. The authorization grants clearance to *users*. The data owner assigns a classification to *data*. Systems enforce access control by determining that a subject has the right clearance to access a classified object. Operating systems usually enforce access restrictions along with the principles of least privilege or need to know.

Organizations take into account three criteria in classifying information:

- **Value**—You can define the value of information by several different measures: the value to the organization, the value to competitors, the cost of replacement or loss, and the value to the organization's reputation.
- **Sensitivity**—Sensitivity is the measure of the effect that a breach of the integrity or the disclosure of information would have on the organization. Organizations can measure sensitivity in many ways, including liability or fines, reputation, credibility, or loss of market share.
- **Criticality**—Criticality is the measure of the importance of the information to the mission of the organization. What would happen to the organization if the information were lost?

Information Classification Objectives

The objectives of classifying information are as follows:

* To identify information protection requirements, which are based on the risk the business faces if the information is disclosed or the data or system are corrupted
* To identify data value in accordance with organization policy
* To ensure that sensitive and/or critical information is provided appropriate protection/ controls
* To lower costs by protecting only sensitive information
* To standardize classification labeling throughout the organization
* To alert employees and other authorized personnel to protection requirements
* To comply with privacy law and regulations

Organizations can derive many benefits from classifying information:

* Data classified as sensitive or critical get a level of protection that matches that data's classification.
* The organization gets more value for its costs because it applies increased controls only where it needs them most. Compare, for example, costs of physical security at an expensive jewelry store, an inexpensive jewelry store, and a costume-jewelry store. None of those stores would operate efficiently using the security system of another. All organizations have data that are of high, medium, and low value. Each classification value warrants a different security level.
* Appropriate markings enable staff to recognize the need to protect classified data.

Examples of Classification

The U.S. government uses a hierarchical series of classifications that include Unclassified, Restricted, Confidential, Secret, and Top Secret. The private sector uses various categories such as public (low), private (medium), and confidential (high).

Government classifications are well known and standardized. Company-related classifications are less well known and are not standard. This creates issues for the private sector. For example, when an employee changes jobs, the new employer might value "private" above "confidential." In his old job, his employer valued "private" below "confidential." That's confusing. It's even more confusing when this happens within the same company. Part of a security professional's job is to identify these inconsistencies and make recommendations to correct them.

> **NOTE**
>
> Compartmentalized information is data that require special authorization beyond the normal classification system. It is important that your procedures include steps to properly handle this type of information.

Classification Procedures

Classification procedures are critical to effective data classification. Before implementing these procedures, it's vital that you first determine their scope and process. Classification *scope* determines what data you should classify; classification *process* determines how you handle classified data. You must label and mark all resources properly. By adhering to strong procedures, you'll be ready for any upcoming audits.

To determine the scope of your classification plan, you should do a business impact analysis to evaluate all your organization's data. This determines the data's value and criticality to your organization's operations. Data value is determined according to the following:

- Exclusive possession (trade secrets)
- Utility (usefulness)
- Cost to create or recreate the data
- Liability (protection regulations)
- Convertibility/negotiability (financial information)
- Operational impact (if data are unavailable)
- Threats to the information
- Risks

Based on the results of the business impact analysis, you must identify the necessary number of classification levels. You will also standardize the title of each level for use throughout your organization. Send this information to the information owners responsible for assigning the initial classifications. These classifiers must understand the related regulations, customer expectations, and business concerns. The goal is to achieve a consistent approach to handling classified information.

You might find it useful to create a training program so that your classifiers handle all data in a consistent manner. The owner is also responsible for a periodic review of classifications to ensure they are still current. This review is particularly critical any time legislators or regulators introduce new government regulations. Finally, the owner is responsible for declassifying information that no longer requires special handling. Government organizations often declare information automatically declassified after a certain number of years.

You must mark all media containing sensitive information according to the organization's classification policy and procedures. That is the only way staff will know what special handling measures to use. You should label magnetic and optical media both electronically and with simple labels. Documents in hard-copy form require labels externally on the cover and internally on the pages.

Assurance

Internal and external auditors should review the organization's information-classification status as a component of their regular audit process. They also should evaluate the level of compliance with the classification policy and procedures. This ensures that all parts of the organization adhere to the process. This review might reveal situations in which information is overclassified.

Information security personnel should regularly visit workstations and other areas where users might leave unprotected classified materials. They also should make sure that when violations occur, they submit appropriate reports to supervisors and managers. Ideally, employee performance evaluations should include any instances when employees mishandle information. This helps staff understand the importance of this process. The organization should consider implementing a **clean desk/clear screen policy**, which states that users must *never* leave sensitive information in plain view on an unattended desk or workstation.

Configuration Management

It is unusual for any component in a networked computer environment to remain un-
changed for a long period. Organizations commonly make modifications to the hardware,
software, firmware, documentation, test plans, and test documentation of an automated
system throughout the system life cycle. It's important that all configuration changes occur
only within a controlled process. Uncontrolled configuration changes often result in conflicts
and even new security vulnerabilities. The process of managing all changes to computer and
device configurations is called *configuration management*.

From the perspective of a security professional, configuration management evaluates the
impact a modification might have on security. Will it affect the confidentiality, integrity, or
availability of the system, application, or documentation? As a security professional, your
job is twofold:

- Ensure that you adequately review all system changes.
- Ensure that the change to the configuration will *not* cause unintended consequences for
  security.

You must control all modifications to ensure that the change will affect your environment as
expected and that your environment will operate as authorized.

Hardware Inventory and Configuration Chart

Many organizations lack a hardware inventory that tells them what they have, who has ownership or possession of it, and which departments or systems are using it. This is a serious gap
in a security program. In the event of a fire, equipment failure, or theft, this lack of documentation can slow the response and extend operational loss. It also makes proper configuration
management extremely difficult, if not impossible. A decision to roll out a new patch, service
pack, or release will be complicated if you can't find, update, and test every affected device.

Hardware Configuration Chart

You must have an up-to-date map or layout of the configuration of the hardware components. This helps ensure that you configure all systems according to the baseline. It also
ensures that you properly review the work completed on a system or network so that you
can make the correct changes without bypassing any security features. A hardware configuration chart should include the following:

- An as-built diagram of the network, to help you plan the sequence of a change and see the
  ripple effects it might generate.
- Copies of all software configurations so that you can examine changes and updates
  planned for one device in terms of their impact on other devices. These configurations
  should include items such as router, switch, and firewall configurations.

Patch and Service Pack Management

You should regularly check for any available vendor upgrades and service packs. This process may be an involved one if you have many types of software and hardware from different
vendors. Nevertheless, it is necessary to address all known vulnerabilities. The organization

must have a patch-management process to ensure that it rolls out patches to all computers and devices without causing system outages. You should test every patch prior to rollout to ensure that it will not disable other systems or functions.

The Change Management Process

It is common to discuss change and configuration control as a pair of activities, but they are really two ends of a spectrum. The confusion, of course, lies where a particular activity crosses from one to the other. Drawing a sharp line between the two is difficult because different organizations of different complexities will draw the line in different places:

- **Configuration control** is the management of the baseline settings for a system device. The baseline settings meet security requirements. They require that you implement them carefully and only with prior approval.

- **Change control** is the management of changes to the configuration. Unmanaged changes introduce risk, because they might affect security operations or controls. An improper change could even disable the system or equipment. Change control ensures that any changes to a production system are tested, documented, and approved. The change itself must follow a change control process that ensures that you make the change correctly and report it to management.

FIGURE 6-5 shows the balance between change control and configuration control.

Change Control Management

Change control management develops a planned approach to controlling change by involving all affected departments. The objective is to maximize the benefits for all people involved in the change and minimize the risk of failure.

To be effective, change management should be multidisciplinary, touching all aspects of the organization. Nevertheless, an organization should not be constrained so much that it loses all flexibility. Change management should allow organizations to adopt new technologies, improvements, and modifications.

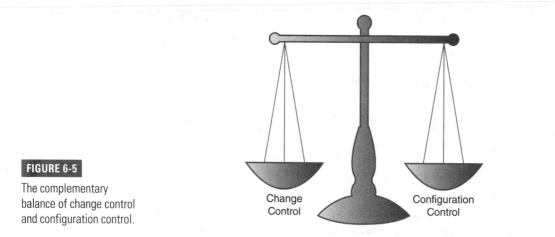

FIGURE 6-5

The complementary balance of change control and configuration control.

Change Control   Configuration Control

Change management requires a written policy approved by the chief information officer or the IT director and the business information security manager. The policy must define all roles, responsibilities, and procedures related to change management. Here are some important things to remember:

- You should communicate change management procedures and standards effectively. They should define the techniques and technologies you'll use throughout the enterprise in support of the policy.
- Change management can be either reactive or proactive. With **reactive change management**, management responds to changes in the business environment. The source of the change is external. Some examples are changes in regulations, customer expectations, and the supply chain. With **proactive change management**, management initiates the change to achieve a desired goal. In this case, the source of the change is internal, such as the adoption of new technology.
- Your organization can conduct change management in several ways. It can occur on a continuous basis, a regularly scheduled basis, a release basis, or when you deem it necessary on a program-by-program basis.

Reviewing Changes for Potential Security Impact

Change creates risk for a business. It might circumvent established security features and it could result in outage or system failure. It might require extensive retraining for employees to learn how to use the new systems. Because of the risk involved, you must include security personnel in the change control process.

The formal change control process should protect the integrity of the IT systems and ensure that all changes in the production environment are properly tested, scheduled, and communicated. Members of the change control committee attend meetings and forums to estimate, plan, review, and prepare for the organization's production environment.

Change Control Committees

A senior manager or business-process owner should lead a **change control committee**. This committee oversees all proposed changes to systems and networks. The committee approves changes and the schedule for implementing the changes. In this manner, you cannot make changes to a system, application, or network without the proper review, funding, and documentation.

In cooperation with IT, the change control committee—in some cases called a *change control board*—provides the oversight to protect the computing resources and the data contained within those applications and databases. As part of the change process, key members meet with counterparts from the IT organizations to review upcoming plans and ensure that you properly evaluate all changes. They also make sure that the necessary security controls have been applied and evaluated. They communicate their findings to all parts of the organization.

In brief, the primary objectives of the change control committee are to ensure all changes are as follows:

- Properly tested
- Authorized

- Scheduled
- Communicated
- Documented

When you use solid change control, identifying recent changes that might have caused a production problem is easy. That simplifies the problem resolution process and makes your environment more secure.

Change Control Procedures

Change control procedures ensure that a change does not happen without following the right steps. This helps you avoid problems such as scope creep, which allows unauthorized changes to sneak into a system. It also helps avoid problems caused by lack of oversight, by lack of testing, or by making changes without proper authorization. **FIGURE 6-6** shows a sequence of change control procedures.

1. **Request**—In the request stage, you should describe all proposed changes in writing and submit the change request to the change control committee for review. You should never make a change to a system without approval.
2. **Impact assessment**—The impact assessment stage evaluates the effect of the change on the budget, resources, and security of the system or project.
3. **Approval**—The approval (or, in some cases, disapproval) stage is the formal review and acceptance (or rejection) of the change by the change control committee.
4. **Build/test**—The build/test stage is the actual development or building of the change according to the approved change document. You then must test the change to ensure that it does not cause unexpected problems for other systems or components. This testing might include regression testing and an in-depth review of the security of the modified product.
5. **Implement**—Once you test the change and approve it for release, you can schedule the installation process. This is where adequate separation of duties ensures that no one person can make the change without proper review and oversight. The final hurdle is notifying management that you have made the change successfully.
6. **Monitor**—In this stage, you must monitor all systems to ensure that the system, program, network, and other resources are working correctly. You should address any user issues or requests using your organization's problem resolution procedures. Monitoring might identify the need for future changes. This restarts the change control process.

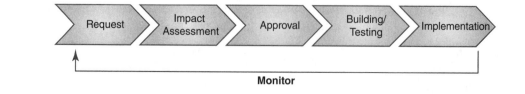

FIGURE 6-6

Change control
procedures.

Change Control Issues

Solid change control procedures include the components that tend to identify issues and provide recovery avenues if needed. A successful change control program should include the following elements to ensure the quality of the change control process:

- **Peer review**—This ensures that a peer or another expert double-checks all changes before you put them into production. Peers can often catch problems before they make it to the testing phase.
- **Back-out plans**—These ensure that if the change doesn't work properly, a plan exists to restore the system to a known good condition. In spite of the best control procedures, you may accidentally release changes that have unintended effects. You must know how to undo, or back out of, a destructive change.
- **Documentation**—You must keep documentation current to reflect the true system's design. You should keep backup copies off-site as well. Documentation is necessary to understand how the system is supposed to operate.

Application Software Security

One critical area of concern is application software. Attackers know that the software development process is complex and that the result of the process is often an application that contains weaknesses. Secure software can be difficult to write. It requires attention to security at every stage of the process as well as a structured process to ensure that the software does just what it is supposed to do. There are several popular methods to describe and control the systems and software development process. Understanding the process of software development is important in developing software with very few weaknesses. You should be familiar with two of the most popular methods, the **system life cycle (SLC)** and the **system development life cycle (SDLC)**. The steps in these processes are very similar except that the SLC includes operations and disposal and the SDLC ends with the transition to production.

For some organizations, maintenance and new development are done by developers, making them part of SDLC. For others, specialized maintenance teams handle maintenance and development, making them part of SLC. More and more organizations use the term SDLC to describe the entire change and maintenance process for application and system software.

The System Life Cycle

This section covers the common steps used in the SLC. The more the security professional can be involved in each step, the more likely the needed security will be built into the system from the start. The main justification for SLC—and for building security in at the start—is reducing or avoiding cost:

- Consumers of commercial software products will see lower costs because you will need to deliver fewer patches and fixes. In addition, there will be fewer losses due to weaknesses in the software that attackers find and exploit.
- Vendors of commercial software will see lower costs because they require smaller support staffs and have lower warranty and product maintenance costs.

The common steps used in the SLC are as follows:

1. **Project initiation and planning**—One of the first requirements of a successful project is to have all the necessary resources available. The resources you will need should represent the areas that you need to consider and integrate into the project. Your role is to provide advice on building security into the project from the very beginning. This includes project budgets, system design, maintenance, and the project timeline. You should address threats, vulnerabilities, risks, and controls here first.

2. **Functional requirements and definition**—This is the "what-if?" phase. Always state requirements using positive terms: The program must handle some data or perform some function. You will need to think about what the program should or will do when the data don't meet the specifications. What happens when the software receives unexpected input? Are there too many characters? Are fields missing? Are users seeing delayed transmissions? Failure to consider these factors creates a great number of security mishaps.

3. **System design specification**—In this phase, a project is broken into functions and modules. For that, you must consider the type of hardware on which the system is going to run. Security issues here include physical security of the hardware and network. Security also has to account for all the possible platforms. It isn't enough to say the project is limited to Linux or Windows, for example. Each platform features a wide variety of versions and runs on an almost infinite combination of peripherals, chipsets, and drivers.

4. **Build (develop) and document**—Coding standards should include standard libraries of function calls. They should also include industry-standard solutions for items such as cryptography, hashing, and access control. You need to secure code in development so that only developers have access and so that you grant access only on a need-to-know basis. Even developers should have access only to the parts they need to see. You should not leave copies lying around in printed or machine-readable form, such as on CDs or USB memory sticks.

5. **Acceptance testing**—You should create a test plan during the functional design stage. This plan must include testing to make sure the new programs provide necessary security and, where applicable, privacy. The people responsible for the tests should not be the developers. In addition, past-due delivery dates for developers should *not* affect the time allotted for testing.

6. **Implementation (transition to production)**—During this transition, developers will be working on delivery of training and assistance to users and help desk personnel. Security features need to be carefully explained to both groups. In some organizations, developers also will help manage the turnover of code to maintenance staff.

7. **Operations and maintenance**—When there are problems with the system, it's likely that maintenance, operations, and help desk personnel will be the first to know. They need to track the issues that come in and be ready to report their results to management. This procedure fuels the change management process. These personnel require training to understand the differences between a request for change, a software malfunction, and a security weakness or breach. In addition, they need to know how to handle each of those events.

8. **Disposal**—Over time, component parts will reach the end of their life span. You will need to upgrade a backup system or procure a larger disk to replace a smaller one. You should ensure that you have procedures to sanitize the media and then dispose of it in a cost-effective way. In years past, organizations would wipe a disk and resell it. Today, the value of a small used disk is often less than the cost to securely wipe it with a tool such as DBAN and then simply dispose of the disk.

Testing Application Software

Security professionals often help test new systems or upgrades to existing systems. These tests should be thorough enough to ensure that you test for all expected and unexpected actions and that you handle errors correctly. You should also perform tests to test the maximum load on the system, including transaction volume, memory allocation, network bandwidth, and response times. If you use production or sensitive data in testing, make sure you take steps to keep those data secure.

Since input validation attacks are so common, your security personnel should work with software testing personnel to make sure tests catch any input vulnerabilities. One type of testing for input vulnerabilities is called **fuzzing**. Fuzzing is the practice of providing random input to software to see how it handles unexpected data. Fuzzing can help identify input vulnerabilities better than testers trying to think of bad input.

Systems Procurement

One common way new vulnerabilities make their way into an environment is through a change that causes unintended side effects. You should thoroughly evaluate any change to your environment to ensure that it doesn't introduce new vulnerabilities. Do this with new hardware and software as well. Procuring new equipment is a critical role of the security professional, but doing so can decrease your overall security if the process is not handled well. Any time you need to procure new equipment, you should carefully evaluate which products will meet your requirements. To ensure that new equipment does not expose your environment to any new vulnerabilities, you must do the following:

- Evaluate the various solutions that are available.
- Evaluate the vendors in terms of maintenance, support, and training.
- Use the Common Criteria to ensure that you simplify the evaluation process.
- Monitor vendor contracts and service-level agreements (SLAs).
- Correctly install equipment and formally accept it at the end of the project.
- Follow the organization's procurement procedures to ensure a fair purchasing process.
- Monitor systems and equipment to identify equipment that is reaching the end of its life span so that you can schedule it for replacement.

The Common Criteria

Because procuring new equipment can lead to security vulnerabilities, it makes sense to formalize the process. The need for a formal approach to evaluate systems and equipment gave rise to several different sets of standards. The U.S. government created a series of computer security standards documents known as the Rainbow Series due to the bold colors on the covers of the documents. *The Red Book* describes components of a trusted network infra-structure (TNI). *The Orange Book* talks about maintaining access control and confidentiality in a classified system. Both used a series of evaluative levels (C2, B3, and so on), and vendors had their products evaluated against these levels. The developers of the Rainbow Series for-mally called it TCSEC.

Other governments created their own equivalents. Some started with TCSEC and made modifications. Eventually, these merged into what became ITSEC. The governments of the United States, the United Kingdom, Canada, Germany, France, and the Netherlands used ITSEC as a starting point. Then they developed a new procurement standard called the Common Criteria.

The Common Criteria have a series of increasingly more difficult evaluation assurance levels (EALs) numbered from 1 (lowest) to 7 (highest). Evaluation labs are scattered all over the world. Leading vendors within an industry (for example, vendors of firewalls) collectively create a standard, ideal, and perfect solution. Any vendor can have its product evaluated against the standard. An EAL rating assures that the vendor's claims match the collective standard to a defined level of testing. The product's documentation, development, and performance must all match the evaluation claims.

Data Policies

All data reach their end of usefulness at some point. What do you do when you no longer need or can use data? The best action is to simply follow the guidance in your data policies. Of course, that means you must already have data policies in place. Policies that cover data man-agement should cover transitions throughout your data's life cycle. A solid data policy should contain sections or even full documents that cover retention and storage as well as disposal.

Retention and storage sections of your data policies should state how long you will keep different types of data. Some data items have longer lifetimes of usefulness than others. If you need to keep historical data for research purposes, your policy should address how to store it. Your security policy should extend to cover stored data as well.

But what do you do when you no longer need data? You can either overwrite the data on the media to ready the data for reuse, a process called *wiping*, or destroy the media. Your choice depends on the usefulness of the media and the sensitivity of the data. For extremely sensitive data it is safer to erase the data and destroy the media to keep it out of the hands of someone who may be able to recover all or part of the erased data.

Whenever you need to dispose of equipment, you should ensure that you dispose of it in a secure way so that you do not expose any confidential data. Several options are available to you, including the following:

- **Degaussing**—Applying a strong magnetic force to magnetic media usually makes all elec-tronics unusable.

- **Physical destruction**—Physically destroying the media on which data are stored guarantees that you eliminate any confidential material.

- **Overwriting data**—This option does not destroy the media at all. It is included here as a viable alternative to actual media destruction. Repeatedly overwriting data on media re-duces the chance that any data can be recovered. However, the possibility still remains that a determined person may be able to recover some of the deleted data.

| **Technical TIP** |

The formal name for the Common Criteria is ISO/IEC 15408.

Certification and Accreditation

Between procurement and disposal, you will need to ensure that the components in your computing environment are sufficient for your requirements. **Certification** is the process of reviewing a system throughout its life cycle to ensure that it meets its specified security requirements. **Accreditation** is the formal agreement by the authorizing official to accept the risk of implementing the system. The process includes the following players:

- **Authorizing official**—The senior manager who must review the certification report and make the decision to approve the system for implementation. The **authorizing official (AO)** officially acknowledges and accepts the risk that the system may pose to agency mission, assets, or individuals.

- **Certifier**—The individual or team that is responsible for performing the security test and evaluation (ST+E) for the system. The **certifier** also prepares the report for the AO on the system's operating risk.

- **System owner**—The person responsible for the daily operations of the system and ensuring that the system continues to operate in compliance with the conditions set out by the AO is the **system owner**.

Certification: Certification is the technical evaluation of a system to provide assurance that the organization implemented the system correctly. The system should meet the initial design requirements to ensure that the security controls are working effectively. A certifier or team of certifiers does this task. The certifier should have the skill to perform the verification process and the tests necessary to prove compliance. Certification of a system means the following:

- The system meets the technical requirements.
- The system meets the functional requirements.
- The system provides assurance of proper operation.

In order to certify, the person (or people) involved in the process must first know the technical and functional requirements. They also must know the capabilities of the system they are recommending for purchase or for approval to move into production. These might be software or hardware requirements. You might evaluate them in terms of quantity or quality, such as the ability to authenticate 100 users a minute or to ensure 99.99 percent uptime. You might base the requirements on non-IT factors, such as weight or energy consumption. The accreditors must examine all the requirements. Whether conducting or managing these tasks, many of them will fall to you as a security professional.

Finally, the certifiers must match these lists to make sure the new system meets or exceeds each specification. When they're sure that it does, they recommend management approval. This doesn't mean the system is right for your organization or that it is the best solution available. Certification means only that the product meets its technical and functional specifications and operates as promised.

Accreditation: Accreditation occurs after you certify a system. Accreditation is the process of management officially accepting the system. The accreditor or designated approving authority reviews the certification reports and, based on the operational environment, accepts the system for operation. You can define this process in two ways:

- Accreditation is management's formal acceptance of risk.
- Accreditation is management's permission to implement.

Triggers for New Certification: The certification and accreditation processes ensure that a system not only meets the security requirements today but that it continues to meet them through the operations and maintenance phases of its life cycle. The post-accreditation phase lists the activities required to continue to operate and manage the system so that it maintains an acceptable level of risk. You must continually assess risk to meet this requirement for the following reasons:

- Business needs change due to new products, new processes, mergers, or divestitures.
- Products (solutions) that were once accredited might no longer meet the needs of the business.
- Vendors often upgrade or replace products, and these replacements need to be recertified and reaccredited.

Software Development and Security

You learned earlier in this chapter about the importance of developing secure software. Software development requires specal attention from a security perspective. Applications represent the most common avenue for users, customers, and attackers to access data. That means you must build the software to enforce the security policy and to ensure compliance with regulations, including the privacy and integrity of both data and system processes. Regardless of the development model your organization adopts, you should make sure that the application properly performs the following tasks:

- Checks user authentication to the application.
- Checks user authorization (privilege level).
- Has procedures for recovering database integrity in the event of system failure.
- Handles errors and exceptions consistently and does not allow any error or exception to go unhandled. Unhandled exceptions can reduce an application's security. Plan for approaches to handle all errors and exceptions with standard responses. Give users a consistent error response and provide clear explanations and instructions. Empower your users to make the right choices.
- Validates all input (never accepts any input from a source without validating it first). If the data fails validation, throw it away; do not try to sanitize it! That means you have to validate data on the client and on servers. Attackers can often change data as the data travels from a client to the server. Validating it on the server again is the only way to be sure that the data are valid. Some attacks that depend on weak validation include:

- **Cross-site scripting (XSS)**—This is an attack in which an attacker inputs client-side script code to a web application. The code would then be viewed by other users, and their client software would execute the script instructions. The XSS attack exploits the trust users have for a server.
- **Cross-site request forgery (XSRF)**—Similar to the XSS attack, an attacker provides script code that causes a trusted user who views the input script to send malicious commands to a web server. The XSRF attack exploits the trust a server has in a user.
- **Structured Query Language (SQL) injection**—An attack technique in which an attacker provides malicious SQL statements to access unauthorized data or carry out unauthorized commands.
- Defines secure configuration baselines. When you release your application to end users, provide a documented set of configuration settings that define a secure baseline, or starting point.
- Provides guidance on hardening your application. In addition to providing a secure baseline, offer guidance on changing configuration settings that will keep your application secure. It should also provide guidance on further configuration settings or the addition of external controls that will increase your application's security.
- Provides and applies frequent patches. Ensure that you apply the latest security patches for your environment. It should also provide frequent security patches to the users of your application, along with a convenient method of applying patches and managing the patching process.

Software developed in-house will have source code, object code, and runtime executables. You need to manage and protect these with policies, standards, and procedures. For example:

- You should protect source code from access by unauthorized users.
- You should track changes to source code by version control systems so that rollback to a previous version is error free.
- Programmers should not be able to update production systems directly (programmers to test, then test to production).

Software Development Models

Secure software development requires a formal model for creating and modifying software. This process is known as the software development life cycle, or SDLC, which uses industry best practices to guide software development activities as projects with specific start and end dates and a set of required deliverables. At this time, the two most widely accepted models for software development include:

- The waterfall model. Based on traditional project management practices in which extensive planning precedes any development. Progress through a project moves forward along a well-defined path.
- Agile development method. A newer family of project management approaches that depend on very short sprints of activity. Agile works well in very dynamic environments where requirements change and are often revisited.

Technical TIP

You may recognize SQL injection as a common attack. According to the Open Web Application Security Project, *www.owasp.org*, SQL injection vulnerability is one of the most common recurring vulnerabilities in web applications. Growing databases and a need for faster data have led to a growth in nonrelational databases, called *NoSQL databases*. Although NoSQL databases are not specifically vulnerable to SQL injection attacks, that doesn't mean you should consider them any more secure. Even NoSQL databases are vulnerable to injection attacks.

Waterfall Model

Many current software development methods base their models on the **waterfall model**, illustrated in **FIGURE 6-7**. This is a sequential process for developing software. It includes the SDLC and the SLC you learned about earlier. In the waterfall model, progress flows downward, like a waterfall. The essence of the waterfall model is that no phase begins until the previous phase is complete. The phases are as follows:

1. Requirements specification
2. Design
3. Construction
4. Integration
5. Testing and debugging
6. Installation
7. Maintenance

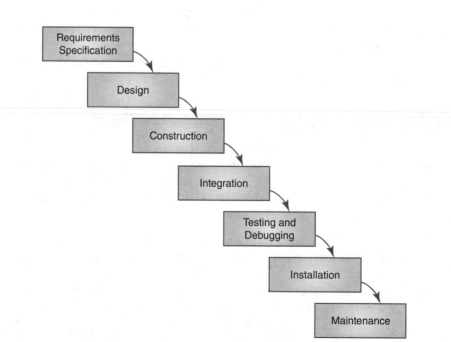

FIGURE 6-7

The waterfall model.

The basic waterfall model originated in the manufacturing and construction industries. It's a feature of highly structured physical environments in which late revisions are very costly, if not entirely cost prohibitive. When Winston W. Royce devised this model in 1970, no formal software development methods existed. This hardware-oriented model was adapted to software development.

Because of perceived shortcomings of this model, you'll find modifications of the waterfall model. Most software development models use at least some phases similar to the waterfall model. The importance of the model is in its focus on ensuring that each phase is complete before moving on. Though this may be quite difficult in large development environments, always invest the time to properly plan and design your software. Don't just start writing programs!

Agile Software Development

Traditional software development management is still based largely on some variation of the waterfall method. During the 1990s, some organizations began to realize that the software industry was changing in different ways. Increasing demands to develop more complex software more efficiently led to new methods of managing software development. Instead of managing large projects with long delivery schedules, many organizations looked for ways to be more responsive. They wanted to be able to develop their software in smaller pieces. This move toward smaller development cycles eventually became known as the **agile development** method.

Agile loosely describes a method of developing software that is based on small project iterations, or **sprints**, instead of long project schedules. Organizations that use agile produce smaller deliverables more frequently and can evaluate a large project in terms of its individual pieces as they are completed. Sprints are generally one to four weeks in duration. That means there is some deliverable once or more frequently each month. This focus on frequent delivery makes it possible to see and use pieces of a large software product as it matures over time.

The first organized meeting of agile enthusiasts was in 2001. Several organizations that were exploring this new type of software development sent representatives to a meeting in Snowbird, Utah, to collaborate and exchange ideas. The attendees created the foundational document of the agile movement—the *Manifesto for Agile Software Development.* It is a concise document that reflects its writers' affection for simple methods. Here is the *Manifesto for Agile Software Development* (*http://www.agilemanifesto.org/*) in its entirety:

> We are uncovering better ways of developing software by doing it and helping others do it. Through this work we have come to value:
>
> * Individuals and interactions over processes and tools
> * Working software over comprehensive documentation
> * Customer collaboration over contract negotiation
> * Responding to change over following a plan
>
> That is, while there is value in the items on the right, we value the items on the left more.

FIGURE 6-8 shows the basic idea behind the agile method. Unlike the waterfall method, agile is designed to be iterative. Each time around the cycle is a single sprint. It takes many sprints to create a complete software project. Each sprint ends at a specific point in time and should have some deliverable. A deliverable should be something, such as working software, that the team can demonstrate. The focus on working software helps focus the team on results.

FIGURE 6-8

The agile software
development method.

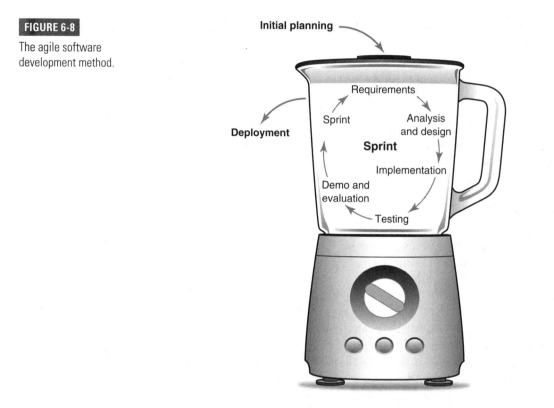

Agile is a popular technique of managing software development projects. It tends to perform well in organizations that
encourage ongoing communication and value short development
cycles. It is important to begin developing software with security
in mind from the very beginning. Agile methods encourage developers to plan for security and then test for security at the end of
each sprint. Developing secure software can become an integral
part of the overall development effort—that is, if the organization
values and encourages security. Regardless of the development
method an organization uses, attention to security is more important than any method.

NOTE

You can find more information on the
Manifesto for Agile Software Development
and the agile method in general at *http://
agilemanifesto.org*. Another good starting
point to learn about agile is *www.agile-
process.org*.

CHAPTER SUMMARY

In this chapter, you learned that security professionals must understand that security operations and administration are the basis of any solid security program. You
learned how security administration works to plan, design, implement, and monitor
an organization's security plan. You learned that professional ethics are essential for

every solid security plan. You learned what you have to do to make sure your security program is compliant. You learned how the policies, standards, guidelines, and procedures of your plan work together to shape your security program. You learned how data classification standards affect the decision-making process. You learned how to use configuration management to manage system modifications, and how configuration control and change control affect the change management process. You explored the eight common steps of the system life cycle (SLC), the system development life cycle (SDLC), and how these steps reduce costs. You learned why software development methods require special security considerations. Finally, you learned how user awareness is pivotal to the success of your security program.

KEY CONCEPTS AND TERMS

Accreditation	Emergency operations group	Proactive change management
Agile development	Event logs	Procedure
Authorizing official (AO)	Functional policy	Reactive change management
Baseline	Fuzzing	Remediation
Blanket purchase agreement (BPA)	Guideline	Security administration
Certification	Interconnection security agreement (ISA)	Service-level agreement (SLA)
Certifier	Internet Architecture Board (IAB)	Sprint
Change control	Job rotation	SQL injection
Change control committee	Memorandum of understanding (MOU)	Standard
Clean desk/clear screen policy	Offboarding	System development life cycle (SDLC)
Compliance liaison	Onboarding	System life cycle (SLC)
Configuration control	Privacy policy	System owner
Cross-site request forgery (XSRF)		Waterfall model
Cross-site scripting (XSS)		

CHAPTER 6 ASSESSMENT

1. Security administration is the group of individuals responsible for the planning, design, implementation, and monitoring of an organization's security plan.

   A. True
   B. False

2. The security program requires documentation of:

   A. The security process
   B. The policies, procedures, and guidelines adopted by the organization
   C. The authority of the persons responsible for security
   D. All of the above
   E. None of the above

3. An organization does not have to comply with both regulatory standards and organizational standards.

   A. True
   B. False

4. A(n) _____ is a formal contract between your organization and an outside firm that details the specific services the firm will provide.

   A. Security event log
   B. Incident response
   C. Service-level agreement (SLA)
   D. Compliance report

5. Which software testing method provides random input to see how software handles unexpected data?

   A. Injection
   B. Fuzzing
   C. Valid error input
   D. Boundary input

6. In 1989, the IAB issued a statement of policy about Internet ethics. This document is known as _____.

   A. OECD
   B. RFC 1087
   C. (ISC)² Code of Ethics Canons
   D. CompTIA Candidate Code of Ethics
   E. None of the above

7. _____ is the concept that users should be granted only the levels of permissions they need in order to perform their duties.

   A. Mandatory vacations
   B. Separation of duties
   C. Job rotation
   D. Principle of least privilege
   E. None of the above

8. Which of the following is an example of social engineering?

   A. An emotional appeal for help
   B. A phishing attack
   C. Intimidation
   D. Name-dropping
   E. All of the above

9. Policy sets the tone and culture of the organization.

   A. True
   B. False

10. _____ involve the standardization of the hardware and software solutions used to address a security risk throughout the organization.

    A. Policies
    B. Standards
    C. Procedures
    D. Baselines

11. Which of the following is true of procedures?

    A. They increase mistakes in a crisis.
    B. They provide for places within the process to conduct assurance checks.
    C. Important steps are often overlooked.
    D. None of the above
    E. All of the above

12. Data classification is the responsibility of the person who owns the data.

    A. True
    B. False

13. The objectives of classifying information include which of the following?

    A. To identify data value in accordance with organization policy
    B. To identify information protection requirements
    C. To standardize classification labeling throughout the organization
    D. To comply with privacy law, regulations, and so on
    E. All of the above

14. Configuration management is the management of modifications made to the hardware, software, firmware, documentation, test plans, and test documentation of an automated system throughout the system life cycle.

    A. True
    B. False

15. The change management process includes _____ control and _____ control.

    A. Clearance, classification
    B. Document, data
    C. Hardware inventory, software development
    D. Configuration, change

16. More and more organizations use the term _____ to describe the entire change and maintenance process for applications.

    A. System development life cycle (SDLC)
    B. System life cycle (SLC)
    C. System maintenance life cycle (SMLC)
    D. None of the above

17. When developing software, you should ensure the application does which of the following?

    A. Has edit checks, range checks, validity checks, and other similar controls
    B. Checks user authorization
    C. Checks user authentication to the application
    D. Has procedures for recovering database integrity in the event of system failure
    E. All of the above

18. There are several types of software development methods, but most traditional methods are based on the _____ model.

    A. Modification
    B. Waterfall
    C. Developer
    D. Integration

Auditing, Testing, and Monitoring

PLANNING FOR SECURE SYSTEMS doesn't stop once you've deployed controls. If you really want to protect yourself from data breaches, you have to make sure you're ready for any type of attack. To do that, you evaluate your systems regularly. One crucial type of evaluation to avoid a data breach is a *security audit*. When you audit a computer system, you check to see how its operation has met your security goals. Simply put, when you audit a system, you see if things on the system work according to plan. Audits also often look at the current configuration of a system as a snapshot in time to verify that it complies with requirements.

You can audit a system manually or you can do it using automated computer software. Manual tests include the following:

- Interviewing your staff
- Performing vulnerability scans
- Reviewing application and operating system access controls
- Analyzing physical access to the systems

With automated tests, the auditing software creates a report of any changes to important files and settings. These files and settings might relate to computing devices, operating systems, or application software. Computing devices can include personal computers, mobile devices, servers, network routers, and switches. Application software includes any software that runs on any computing device that provides services to users.

Of course, long before you can audit a system, you need to create the policies and procedures that establish the rules and requirements of the system. That is, before you can determine whether something has worked, you must first define how it's *supposed* to work. This is known as *assessing* your system. You evaluate all the components of your system and determine how each should work. This sets your baseline expectations. Once you have that, you can audit the system. You compare the system's performance to your baseline expectations to see whether things worked as planned.

Chapter 7 Topics

This chapter covers the following topics and concepts:

- What security auditing and analysis are
- How to define your audit plan
- What auditing benchmarks are
- How to collect audit data
- Which post-audit activities you need to perform
- How to perform security monitoring
- Which types of log information you should capture
- How to verify security controls
- How to monitor and test your security systems

Chapter 7 Goals

When you complete this chapter, you will be able to:

- Describe the practices and principles of security audits
- Review ways to monitor systems, including log management and the use of an intrusion detection system (IDS) or intrusion prevention system (IPS)
- Set metrics for system performance
- Assess an organization's security compliance

Security Auditing and Analysis

The purpose of a security audit is to make sure your systems and security controls work as expected. When you review your systems, you should check for the following:

- **Are security policies sound and appropriate for the business or activity?** The purpose of information security is to support the mission of the business and to protect it from the risks it faces. With respect to security, one of the most visible risks is that of data breach. Your organization's policies and supporting documents define the risks that affect it. Supporting documents include your organization's procedures, standards, and baselines. When you conduct an audit, you are asking the question, "Are our policies understood and followed?" The audit itself does not set new policies. Auditors might, however, make recommendations based on experience or knowledge of new regulations or other requirements.

:ontrols supporting your policies? Are the security controls aligned cor-
'our organization's strategies and mission? Do the controls support your poli-
ure? If you cannot justify a control by a policy, you should probably remove
a control is explained as "for security" but with no other explanation, you
e it. Security is not a profit center, and it should never exist for its own sake.
department. Its purpose is to protect the organization's assets and revenue

- **Is there effective implementation and upkeep of controls?** As your organization evolves and as threats mature, it is important to make sure your controls still meet the risks you face today.

If you can answer yes to these questions, you're in good shape. If you can't answer yes, don't worry. You'll develop these skills in this chapter.

Security Controls Address Risk

Security controls place limits on activities that might pose a risk to your organization. You must review security regularly to make sure your controls are current and effective. This security review includes the following activities:

- **Monitor**—Review and measure all controls to capture actions and changes on the system.
- **Audit**—Review the logs and overall environment to provide independent analysis of how well the security policy and controls work.
- **Improve**—Include proposals to improve the security program and controls in the audit results. This step applies to the recommended changes as accepted by management.
- **Secure**—Ensure that new, and existing, controls work together to protect the intended level of security.

Although security controls protect your computers and networks, you should ensure that each one is necessary and is effective. Each control should protect your organization from a specific threat. A control without an identified threat is a layer of overhead that does not make your organization any more secure. Carefully ensure that all security controls you have in place address specific threats. It is fine to have multiple controls that address the same threat—just ensure that each control does address at least one threat.

Recall that risk is defined as the probability that a threat will be realized. You can calculate the expected loss by multiplying the risk probability by the asset cost. Identifying risks enables you to measure the validity of the control. When you use a control that costs more than the potential loss if a threat is realized, you may be wasting your organization's resources. One of the best ways to avoid wasting your organization's resources is to ensure that you follow the security review cycle. **FIGURE 7-1** shows how the steps in the security review cycle all fit together.

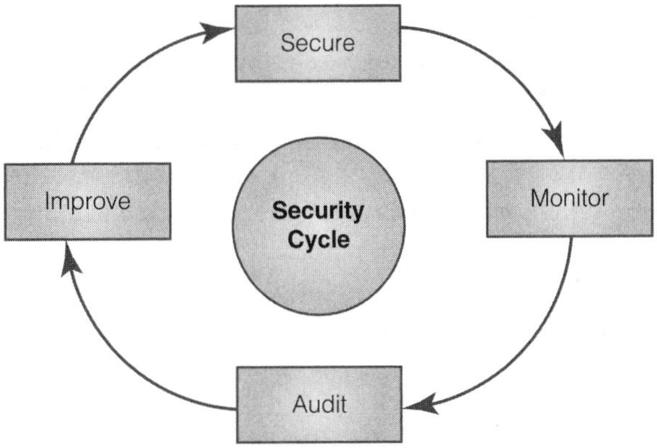

FIGURE 7-1

The security review cycle.

Determining What Is Acceptable

Your first step toward putting the right security controls in place is to determine what actions are acceptable:

- Your organization's security policy should define acceptable and unacceptable actions.
- Your organization might create its own standards based on those developed or endorsed by standards bodies.
- Communications and other actions permitted by a policy document are *acceptable*.
- Communications and other actions specifically banned in your security policy are *unacceptable*. Other communications or other actions may be unacceptable as well. Any action that may reveal confidential information, cause damage to a system's integrity, or make the system unavailable is also unacceptable, even if the policy does not specifically ban it.

Permission Levels

The proper permission level for your organization depends on your organization's needs and policies. It's essential to match your organization's required permission level with its security structure. If you don't, you might lose a lot of data, and your reputation could suffer. You could also find that users simply attempt to bypass your security controls if your security controls are tougher than is necessary. The most common permission levels are as follows:

- **Promiscuous**—Everything is allowed. This permission level is used by many home users but makes it easier for attackers to succeed.
- **Permissive**—Anything not specifically prohibited is OK. This permission level is suitable for most public Internet sites, some schools and libraries, and many training centers.
- **Prudent**—A reasonable list of things is permitted; all others are prohibited. This permission level is suitable for most businesses.
- **Paranoid**—Very few things are permitted; all others are prohibited and carefully monitored. This permission level is suitable for secure facilities.

Regardless of the levels of permission you use, it is important to "inspect what you expect." This phrase applies to all aspects of auditing. It simply means that if you expect a computer to use prudent permission levels, look closely at its user rights and permissions. Make sure that the controls in place do what you expect them to do. User rights and permissions reviews are an integral part of any security audit. If you have great security controls in place but you give your users unlimited permissions, you really aren't keeping your systems very secure.

Areas of Security Audits

Audits can be very large in scope and cover entire departments or business functions. On the other end of the spectrum, they can be narrow and address only one specific system or control. An audit provides management with an independent assessment of whether the best controls are in place and how well they work. This helps management understand and address the risks.

For example, a high-level security policy audit is a review of your security policy to ensure it is up to date, relevant, communicated, and enforced. This type of audit also helps ensure that your policy reflects the culture of your organization. These audits may also determine whether users or customers accept the controls or whether they try to bypass the controls they view as unrealistic. In addition, this type of audit tests how well your infrastructure protects your application's data. It ensures that the application limits access to authorized users only and that it hides (encrypts) data that unauthorized users should not see.

You must also audit all your organization's firewalls, routers, gateways, wireless access points, and other network devices to ensure that they function as intended and that their configurations comply with your security policy. Finally, audits can test the technologies themselves. They detect whether all your networked computers and devices are working together according to your policy. They help ensure that your rules and configurations are up to date, documented, and subject to change control procedures.

Purpose of Audits

An audit gives you the opportunity to review your risk management program and to confirm that the program has correctly identified and reduced (or otherwise addressed) the risks to your organization.

An audit checks whether controls are:

- **Appropriate**—Is the level of security control suitable for the risk it addresses?
- **Installed correctly**—Is the security control in the right place and working well?
- **Addressing their purpose**—Is the security control effective in addressing the risk it was designed to address?

The audit report that auditors create should recommend improvements or changes to the organization's processes, infrastructure, or other controls as needed. Audits are necessary because of potential liability, negligence, and mandatory regulatory compliance. Audits can expose problems and provide assurance of compliance. Many jurisdictions require audits by law.

How often should you conduct audits?

Audit frequency is an important consideration. Some audits only need to occur on demand. These include post-incident audits or any audit required by an external authority, such as a regulatory agency. Other audits should be conducted according to a schedule. Many regulations require annual or quarterly audits. Internal requirements may call for audits even more frequently. For example, diligent organizations often audit their server logs on a weekly basis and IDS/IPS logs on a daily basis. Your security policy should include the audit categories and frequency requirements to direct your audit schedule.

Laws and regulations require some companies that employ a certain number of employees or are in a particular industry to have both internal and external audits. Industries that must conduct these required audits include financial services organizations and any organization that handles personal medical records. Federal laws or vendor standards that require internal and external audits include the Sarbanes-Oxley Act (SOX), the Health Insurance Portability and Accountability Act (HIPAA), and the Payment Card Industry Data Security Standard (PCI DSS). The Personal Information Protection and Electronic Documents Act (PIPEDA) is a Canadian law that protects how organizations collect, use, or disclose personal information in e-commerce transactions. It also includes audit requirements.

An audit might find that an organization lacks sufficiently trained and skilled staff. It might show that the company does not do enough to oversee security programs and manage assets. An audit might encourage an organization to provide better staff training. On the other hand, an audit might validate that an organization is meeting or exceeding its requirements.

Many new regulations make management personally responsible for fraud or mismanagement of corporate assets. In the past, corporations were mostly accountable for these failings; now individuals are responsible. It is in the organization's best interests to make every effort to be compliant with all necessary requirements to protect itself and its people.

Customer Confidence

Customers will generally do business only with organizations they trust. If customers know you consistently audit your systems for security, they may be more willing to share their sensitive information with you.

Many business-to-business service providers use auditing standards to build customer confidence. The Auditing Standards Board of the American Institute of Certified Public Accountants issued the Statement on Auditing Standards Number 70 (SAS 70) in 1993. This was the first standard of its kind and provided audit guidance for many service organizations. SAS 70 was developed for organizations such as insurance and medical claims processors, telecommunication service providers, managed services providers, and credit card transaction processing companies. There were two types of SAS 70 audits: Type I and Type II. An SAS 70 Type I audit encompasses the service auditor's assessment of the service organization's description and implementation of controls to achieve the environmental control objectives. An SAS 70 Type II audit includes the information in a Type I audit as well as the service auditor's assessment of whether or not the identified controls were implemented and operating effectively. Although SAS 70 was general in its scope, the standard did not address many of the emerging issues encountered in today's service organizations. For example, SAS 70 does not address supporting colocation or providing cloud-based services. SAS 70 was officially retired in June 2011.

In 2011, the Statement on Standards for Attestation Engagements Number 16 (SSAE 16) superseded SAS 70. SSAE 16 expanded the scope of SAS 70 and is the predominant auditing and reporting standard for service organizations. SSAE 16 provides guidance to auditors when verifying controls and processes. It also requires that the reports include descriptions of the design and effectiveness of the audited controls. These reports provide details that describe the organization's specific controls. For example, a company seeking to lease space in a data center might ask the data center to provide the results of an SSAE 16 or SAS 70 audit to get an independent assessment of the security controls in that data center.

Reliance on the results of SAS 70, and now SSEA 16, has increased across many organizations. The AICPA has recognized the increased complexities of service organizations and created three different levels of audit reporting for service organizations. The Service Organization Control (SOC) framework defines the scope and contents of three levels of audit reports. **TABLE 7-1** lists the SOC reports and characteristics of each one.

SOC 1, SOC 2, and SOC 3 reports are important tools for an organization's auditors. The SOC 1 report primarily focuses on internal controls over financial reporting (ICFR). This type of report is often used to prepare financial statements for the user organization and to implement proper controls to ensure the confidentiality, integrity, and availability of the data generated by the financial reporting requirements. SOC 2 and SOC 3 reports both address primarily security-related controls. The security-related controls in these reports are critical to the success of today's technology service provider organizations. The primary difference between SOC 2 and SOC 3 reports is their audience. SOC 2 reports are created for internal and other authorized stakeholders; SOC 3 reports are intended for public consumption.

> **NOTE**
>
> For more information about SAS 70, see *http://sas70.com*. For more information about SSAE 16, see *http://ssae16.com*. For more information on SOC 1, SOC 2, and SOC 3 reports, see *www.ssae16.org/white-papers*.

TABLE 7-1 Service Organization Control (SOC) reports.

REPORT TYPE	CONTENTS	AUDIENCE
SOC 1	Internal controls over financial reporting	Users and auditors. This is commonly implemented for organizations that must comply with Sarbanes-Oxley (SOX) or the Gramm-Leach-Bliley Act (GLBA).
SOC 2	Security (confidentiality, integrity, availability) and privacy controls	Management, regulators, stakeholders. This is commonly implemented for service providers, hosted data centers, and managed cloud computing providers.
SOC 3	Security (confidentiality, integrity, availability) and privacy controls	Public. This is commonly required for the customers of SOC 2 service providers to verify and validate that the organization is satisfying customer private data and compliance law requirements (such as HIPAA and GLBA).

Defining Your Audit Plan

In planning the activities for an audit, the auditor first must define the objectives and determine which systems or business processes to review. The auditor should also define which areas of assurance to check.

An auditor must also identify the personnel—both from his or her own team and from the organization being audited—who will participate in the audit. These people will gather and put together information to move the audit along. The auditor must be sure that everyone has the right skills, is prepared to contribute, and is available when they are needed.

Some auditors include a review of previous audits to become familiar with past issues. Other auditors choose not to review previous audits to avoid being prejudiced by prior conclusions.

Defining the Scope of the Plan

You must define the boundaries of the review at the beginning of the project. It is critical to determine which areas the audit will review and which it will not. You must be sure that the areas not reviewed in the current audit will be subject to another audit and you must set responsibility for those areas. All systems and networks must have a clearly designated owner. In some cases, the scope of an audit extends beyond a single organization. If your organization outsources data or processing, you may need to include assets that exist outside your organization. You may need to audit components that you access through an interoperability agreement. Determining the scope of an audit may require interaction with external organizations.

At this point, you need to decide whom to inform that an audit is under way. In many cases, if users know you are auditing them, they may start to follow rules they had previously ignored. If knowing about an audit changes user behavior, your audit will not be accurate. On the other hand, trying to perform an audit without telling staff makes the job more difficult by limiting access to critical information. You have to consider this tradeoff on a case-by-case basis. **FIGURE 7-2** shows how the scope of an audit can span all seven domains in the IT infrastructure.

> **NOTE**
>
> Auditing every part of an organization and extending into all outsourcing partners may not be possible because of resource constraints. Auditors should give the highest-risk areas the top priority.

An auditor should take the time to properly plan an audit before conducting any audit activities. Planning is far more than just listing the files and documents to inspect. In fact, auditors often do a substantial amount of work preparing for an audit. Here's what you can expect from an auditor throughout the planning and execution phases:

- **Survey the site(s)**—An auditor will want to understand the environment and the interconnections between systems before starting the audit activities.
- **Review documentation**—An auditor will want to review system documentation and configurations, both during planning and as part of the actual audit. Reviewing interoperability agreement requirements is necessary when audits include external partners. These documents specify agreed-upon compliance requirements for outsourcing partners.

FIGURE 7-2

Audit scope and the seven domains of the IT infrastructure.

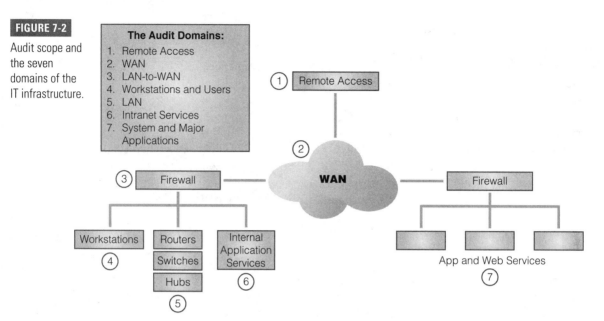

The Audit Domains:
1. Remote Access
2. WAN
3. LAN-to-WAN
4. Workstations and Users
5. LAN
6. Intranet Services
7. System and Major Applications

- **Review risk analysis output**—An auditor will want to understand system criticality ratings that are a product of risk analysis studies. This helps rank systems into the appropriate order for mitigation in the reporting phase.
- **Review server and application logs**—An auditor might ask to examine logs to look for changes to programs, permissions, or configurations.
- **Review incident logs**—An auditor might ask to review security incident logs to get a feel for problem trends.
- **Review results of penetration tests**—When an organization conducts penetration tests, the tester prepares a report listing weaknesses that were found. The auditor needs to review this report and make sure that the audit addresses all items.

Auditing Benchmarks

A **benchmark** is the standard to which your system is compared to determine whether it is securely configured. One technique in an audit is to compare the current setting of a computer or device with a benchmark to help identify differences.

In this section, you will find common ways to audit or review systems, business processes, or security controls. All of these examples are best practices. They often are used as guidelines for auditing a business or business process. Your organization's management may have formally adopted one of the following examples. This can be especially true if your organization is subject to government regulation or legislation. If so, then the benchmark directs the main course of your audit. Otherwise, the auditor, with senior management's approval, decides how an audit is carried out.

- **ISO 27002**—ISO 27002 is a best-practices document that gives good guidelines for information security management. For an organization to claim compliance, it must perform an audit to verify that all provisions are satisfied. ISO 27002 is part of a growing suite of standards, the ISO 27000 series, that defines information security standards.

- **NIST Cybersecurity Framework (CSF)**—NIST CSF, first released in 2014, is a response to a U.S. Presidential Executive Order calling for increased cybersecurity. It focuses on critical infrastructure components but is applicable to many general systems. The road map provides a structured method to securing systems that can help auditors align business drivers and security requirements. NIST also publishes a series of special publications that cover many aspects of information systems. For example, NIST SP 800-37 is a standard that describes best practices, including auditing, for U.S. government information systems.

- **ITIL (Information Technology Infrastructure Library)**—This is a set of concepts and policies for managing IT infrastructure, development, and operations. ITIL is published in a series of books, each covering a separate IT management topic. ITIL gives a detailed description of a number of important IT practices, with comprehensive checklists, tasks, and procedures that any IT organization can tailor to its needs.

Other organizations, such as ISACA and the Institute of Internal Auditors, have developed commonly used audit frameworks. Your organization might develop a set of guidelines in house or adopt and customize an audit framework developed elsewhere. Here are two examples of these types of frameworks:

> **NOTE**
>
> NIST SP 800 is a series of best-practices documents. The website, *http://csrc.nist.gov/*, is organized with the newest documents listed first. Lower-numbered items might still be current because revisions don't change the number.

- **COBIT**—The Control Objectives for Information and related Technology (COBIT) is a set of best practices for IT management. It was created by the Information Systems Audit (ISA), the Control Association (ISACA), and the IT Governance Institute (ITGI) in 1996. COBIT gives managers, auditors, and IT users a set of generally accepted measures, indicators, processes, and best practices. You can use COBIT to help obtain the most benefit from the use of information technology and to develop appropriate IT governance and control in a company.

- **COSO**—The Institute of Internal Auditors (IIA) produces the Committee of Sponsoring Organizations (COSO) of the Treadway Commission. This volunteer-run organization gives guidance to executive management and governance entities on critical aspects of organizational governance, business ethics, internal control, enterprise risk management, fraud, and financial reporting. COSO has established a common internal control model. Many companies and other organizations use it to assess their control systems.

Unless a law or regulation prohibits it, organizations are free to choose whatever audit methods make the most sense to them. They might use one of the options mentioned here, or they might use guidelines from another organization or trade group. They might even develop their own document. Whichever method fits your requirements best, ensure you have an audit method to follow before conducting your first audit.

Audit Data Collection Methods

Before you can analyze data, you need to identify and collect those data. There are many ways to collect data, including:

- **Questionnaires**—You can administer prepared questionnaires to both managers and users.
- **Interviews**—These are useful for gathering insight into operations from all parties. Interviews often prove to be valuable sources of information and recommendations.
- **Observation**—This refers to input used to differentiate between paper procedures and the way the job is really done.
- **Checklists**—These prepared documents help ensure that the information-gathering process covers all areas.
- **Reviewing documentation**—This documentation assesses currency, adherence, and completeness.
- **Reviewing configurations**—This review involves assessing change control procedures and the appropriateness of controls, rules, and layout.
- **Reviewing policy**—This review involves assessing policy relevance, currency, and completeness.
- **Performing security testing**—This testing, **vulnerability testing** and **penetration testing**, involves gathering technical information to determine whether vulnerabilities exist in the security components, networks, or applications.

Areas of Security Audits

Part of the auditing process is to ensure that policy statements exist for all key areas. Auditors document any key areas that your policy does not address. After that, they check to see if all personnel are following policies, procedures, and standards.

You will need a password standard (minimum characters and complexity) and a password procedure (guidelines for setting, changing, and resetting passwords) to support your access control policy. Many organizations use their password policies as their system access policies. This is a dangerous mistake. You should develop a separate access control policy that says something similar to the following:

> Authorized users should be able to do only that which they are authorized to do. Unauthorized users should be prohibited from doing anything.

> **NOTE**
>
> The audit process should be a cooperative arrangement in which all parties work together to make your organization more secure. You should not view it as "us versus them." The auditors and the audited organization should both be working toward the same goal: a more secure environment.

Because passwords are so often the targets of attacks, the use of passwords is declining. Instead, many organizations are starting to use tokens, smart cards, or biometrics for authentication. (Of course, a combination of these authentication types is even better, as you learned in an earlier chapter.) As your IT environment changes, make sure your policies change, too. You don't want all access control policies to dictate password strength when half your systems are using smart cards. A thorough audit ensures that your security policy is up to date and reflects your current environment. You should identify and remove any policies that are out of date.

TABLE 7-2 shows several of the critical areas that you should include in a security audit.

Control Checks and Identity Management

It is important to ensure that your security controls are effective, reliable, and functioning as you intended. Without monitoring and reviewing, you have no assurance that your information security program is effective or that personnel are exercising due diligence. When auditing an identity management system, you should focus on these key areas:

- **Approval process**—Who grants approval for access requests?
- **Authentication mechanisms**—What mechanisms are used for specific security requirements?
- **Password policy and enforcement**—Does the organization have an effective password policy and is it uniformly enforced?
- **Monitoring**—Does the organization have sufficient monitoring systems to detect unauthorized access?
- **Remote access systems**—Are all systems properly secured with strong authentication?

 NOTE

Auditors routinely talk with management during the audit to check what they are finding. Auditors are capable of making mistakes, and this gives management the chance to correct misunderstandings and state their case before the auditors issue their final report.

TABLE 7-2 Areas that you should include in an audit plan.

AREA	AUDIT GOAL
Antivirus software	Up-to-date, universal application
System access policies	Current with technology
Intrusion detection and event-monitoring systems	Log reviews
System-hardening policies	Ports, services
Cryptographic controls	Key management, usage (network encryption of sensitive data)
Contingency planning	Business continuity plan (BCP), disaster recovery plan (DRP), and continuity of operations plan (COOP)
Hardware and software maintenance	Maintenance agreements, servicing, forecasting of future needs
Physical security	Doors locked, power supplies monitored
Access control	Need to know, least privilege
Change control processes for configuration management	Documented, no unauthorized changes
Media protection	Age of media, labeling, storage, transportation

Post-Audit Activities

After audit activities are completed, the auditors still have more work to do. Additional auditor tasks include exit interviews, data analysis, generation of the audit report, and a presentation of findings to management.

Exit Interview

The auditor performs an exit interview with key personnel to alert them to major issues and recommendations that will come later in the audit report. This enables management to respond quickly and act on serious issues. Aside from these early alerts, auditors should not provide details before the final report. If they do, they might give a false view of the organization's security preparedness.

Data Analysis

Auditors commonly analyze data they collect away from the organizational site, when such data removal is permitted. This enables the auditor to review everything learned and to present observations using a standard reporting format. Offsite analysis also enables auditors to remove themselves from the pressure often encountered while on site. Every organization wants to receive a positive audit report, and that desire sometimes translates into subtle pressure for an auditor. Performing data analysis at a different location from the audited organization can help encourage unbiased analysis.

Generation of Audit Report

Audit reports generally contain at least three broad sections:

- **Findings**—These are often listed by level of compliance to the standard benchmark. The comparison of audit findings with a stated policy or with industry best practices gives a picture of where the organization must improve.
- **Recommendations**—Auditors recommend how to fix the risks they have found. They also tell how the staff might not be complying with a policy or process. In most reports, the recommendations address the most important issues first. Audit recommendations should include the following:
  - **Timeline for implementation**—Change recommendations should not be open-ended. Each recommendation should have a suggested deadline.
  - **Level of risk**—The audit should make clear the level of risk the organization faces from each finding.
  - **Management response**—Auditors should give management an opportunity to respond to a draft copy of the audit report. They should then put that response in the final report. This response often clarifies issues and explains why controls were not used or why recommendations

> **NOTE**
>
> Most audit reports get right to the point. An audit report often begins with a summary followed by the details. The summary often finds its way outside the organization's leadership, so be careful not to expose security weaknesses in it. You should include private or confidential information only in the details section of the report, and always label such information appropriately.

in the draft copy are not necessary. The response can also include action plans for fixing gaps in controls.

- **Follow-up**—When necessary, auditors should schedule a follow-up audit to ensure the organization has carried out recommendations.

Presentation of Findings

When the auditors complete the audit report, they present their findings to the organization. Depending on your organization's structure and size, the findings presentation could be a formal meeting or it could involve simply delivering the report to a single person. Regardless of how you receive the audit findings, it is important that the audited organization examine the report and make the necessary changes. The findings might lead to changes based on regulatory requirements or available budget.

Security Monitoring

The first goal of a security program is to set the security posture of an organization. The security policy defines the security posture, but the security program carries out the policy in actions. A security posture defines how an organization documents initial configurations, monitors activity, and remediates any detected issues. Monitoring is an important part of any security program. The primary purpose of monitoring is to detect abnormal behavior. After all, you can't remediate behavior that you can't detect! Security monitoring systems might be technical in nature, such as an intrusion detection system (IDS), or they might be administrative—for example, observing employee or customer behavior on a closed-circuit TV.

When you detect abnormal or unacceptable behavior, the next step is to stop it. Stopping both overt and covert intrusive acts is both an art and a science. **Overt acts** are obvious and intentional. **Covert acts** are hidden and secret.

Many attackers will attempt to avoid detection controls you have in place. In fact, just the presence of security-monitoring controls can deter many attackers. On the other hand, it is possible to have too many monitoring devices. Security monitoring must be obvious enough to discourage security breaches but adequately hidden so as not to be overbearing.

Some tools and techniques for security monitoring include the following:

- **Baselines**—In order to recognize something as abnormal, you first must know what normal looks like. Seeing a report that says a system's disk space is 80 percent full tells you nothing unless you know how much disk space was used yesterday or even last week. That is, a system that used an additional 1 percent of disk every week and just tipped the alarm is very different from a system that was at 40 percent for the last month but suddenly doubled in usage. Baselines are essential in security monitoring.
- **Alarms, alerts, and trends**—Alarms and alerts are responses to security events that notify personnel of a possible security incident, much like a door-open alert or a fire alarm. Reporting detected security events is necessary to maintain secure information systems. The difference between an alarm and an alert depends on the asset state. Opening a door generates an alert if an alarm is not set. However, once an alarm is set,

opening the door generates an alarm. This works like your home alarm system. During the day, opening a door may just cause the system to create a tone (alert), but at night, opening the door triggers an alarm. Be aware that employees will quickly ignore repeated false alarms. For example, if your neighbor's car alarm goes off repeatedly, you don't run to the window each time. That means employees will likely not respond to a real incident. For this reason, storing alerts and alarms makes it possible to show how events occur over time. This type of analysis helps identify trends. Trend analysis helps auditors focus on more than just individual events.

- **Closed-circuit TV**—Properly using a closed-circuit TV involves monitoring and recording what the TV cameras see. You must ensure that the security officers monitoring the cameras are trained to watch for certain actions or behaviors. Your staff must also be trained in local law; many jurisdictions prohibit profiling based on race or ethnicity.
- **Systems that spot irregular behavior**—Examples include IDSs and honeypots—that is, traps set to capture information about improper activity on a network.

Security Monitoring for Computer Systems

Just as there are many types of physical monitoring controls, there are also many ways to monitor computer and network system activity. You must select the controls that monitor the many aspects of your computing environment to detect malicious activity. Many tools exist to help you monitor your system's activities, both as they are occurring and after the fact.

Real-time monitoring provides information on what is happening as it happens. This type of monitoring is important in maintaining a proactive security posture. You can use the information from real-time monitoring controls to contain incidents and preserve your organization's business operations. A network intrusion detection system is one example of a real-time monitoring control. It monitors and captures network traffic as it travels throughout your network. Examples of this type of control include the following:

- **Host IDS**—A host intrusion detection system (HIDS) is excellent for "noticing" activity in a computer as the activity is happening. IDS rules help identify suspicious activity in near real time.
- **System integrity monitoring**—Systems such as Tripwire enable you to watch computer systems for unauthorized changes and report them to administrators in near real time.
- **Data loss prevention (DLP)**—DLP systems use business rules to classify sensitive information to prevent unauthorized end users from sharing it. Data that DLP protects are generally data that could put an organization at risk if they were disclosed. For example, DLP systems prevent users from using external storage services, such as Dropbox, for sensitive data.

Non-real-time monitoring keeps historical records of activity. You can use this type of monitoring when it's not as critical to detect and respond to incidents immediately. Examples of this type of control include the following:

- **Application logging**—All applications that access or modify sensitive data should have logs that record who used or changed the data and when. These logs support proof of compliance with privacy regulations, investigation of errors or problems with records, and tracking of transactions.

- **System logging**—This type of logging provides records of who accessed the system and what actions they performed on the system.

Following is a partial list of activities that you need to log:

- **Host-based activity**—This includes changes to systems, access requests, performance, and startups and shutdowns.
- **Network and network devices**—These include access, traffic type and patterns, malware, and performance.

Monitoring Issues

Logging does have its costs. Any time you choose to log system or application activity, you have to store that information somewhere. Many organizations turn off logs because they produce too much information. After all, without enough staff to review the logs, what's the point of gathering all those data? Without a way to analyze log data automatically, logging simply uses up disk space. It doesn't provide any value. Other challenges include the poor quality of the log data and the complexity of attacks. Often it's difficult to see the value in eating up staff time to analyze logs.

> **NOTE**
>
> Organizations should monitor traffic to ensure that all sensitive data are encrypted as the data are transmitted through the network.

 Other monitoring issues that scare off some organizations from aggressive monitoring include the following:

- **Spatial distribution**. Attacks are difficult to catch with logs if they come from a variety of attackers across a wide area. To make matters worse, attackers can use a number of computers managed by different administrators and spread over a large area.
- **Switched networks**. It can be harder to capture traffic on networks that are very segmented through the use of switches and virtual LANs. It will take more work to reconstruct what actually happened from segmented log files.
- **Encryption**. Encrypting data makes logging more difficult because monitors can't see all the data to decide if they are suspicious. Unencrypted parts can be logged, but the rest is virtually invisible. You can encrypt data at various levels:
  - **Data Link Layer encryption (wireless Wired Equivalent Privacy [WEP] and Wi-Fi Protected Access [WPA])**. With this type of encryption, you encrypt everything above the Data Link Layer. WEP encryption should never be used for wireless security; instead, use WPA.
  - **Network Layer encryption (IPSec and some other tunneling protocols)**. With this type of encryption, you encrypt everything above the Network Layer.
  - **Application Layer encryption (SSL and SSH and others)**. This type of encryption encrypts above the Transport Layer.

Logging Anomalies

One important aspect of monitoring is determining the difference between real attacks in log entries and activity that is merely noise or a minor event. In doing this, monitors of all types make two basic types of mistakes:

- **False positives**—Also known as Type I errors, **false positives** are alerts that seem malicious yet are not real security events. These false alarms are distractions that waste administrative effort. Too many false alarms cause the administrator to ignore real attacks. To combat this, you might decide not to record infrequent or human-error "attacks." You can do this by creating **clipping levels** that ignore an event unless it happens often or meets some other predefined criteria. For example, a failed logon attempt should not be of much interest unless it occurs several times in a short period. A common clipping level for failed logons is five. That means the system will trigger an alarm any time a user logon fails five times in a row. Clipping levels help reduce the number of false-positive errors.
- **False negatives**—The other type of monitoring error is a failure of the control to catch suspicious behavior. **False negatives**, also known as Type II errors, are the failure of the alarm system to detect a serious event. Perhaps the event went unnoticed, or maybe the alarm was fooled into thinking the event was not serious when in fact it was. In some monitoring controls, false negatives are a result of the control being configured incorrectly. The control should be more sensitive to the environment and report more suspect activity.

Log Management

Logging is a central activity for security personnel. Log files can help provide evidence of normal and abnormal system activity. They can also provide valuable information on how well your controls are doing their jobs. The security and systems administrators must consider several things to ensure you are keeping the right information and that information is secure.

First, you should store logs in a central location to protect them and to keep them handy for thorough analysis. Have lots of storage space and monitor your log file disk space requirements. If a log file fills up, you're faced with three bad choices:

- Stop logging
- Overwrite the oldest entries
- Stop processing (controlled or crash)

Attackers sometimes purposely fill a log to cause one of these failures. The storage device for your log files must be large enough to prevent this possibility. In addition, your logging settings must not impose artificially low log file size constraints.

 NOTE

To find a list of NTP servers, see *http://tf.nist.gov/tf-cgi/servers.cgi.*

To link activities between systems and logs, computers and devices on your network must have synchronized clocks. Network Time Protocol (NTP) synchronizes time for all computers and devices that support it. Most modern routers and servers do this. International government-run NTP servers provide an unbiased third party to supply the time.

Keeping Log Files

Regulation, policy, or log volume might dictate how much log information you keep. If a log file is subject to litigation, you must keep it until the case is over. If litigation is not under way, a company can make its own decisions about log quantity and retention. Exceptions to that rule may be based on laws or regulations. Once litigation begins, providing the data in those logs is a costly process that the company must bear. A company can lower litigation costs by limiting the quantity of data collected in logs to only what is needed and keeping those data for only as long as they are likely to be useful.

In some cases, regulations may specify how long you must keep data. For example, the Payment Card Industry Data Security Standard (PCI DSS) requires that logs be kept for at least one year. It's best to have a written retention standard. That way, if necessary, you can explain in court that you deleted logs as part of your normal business practice rather than appearing to have done so in an attempt to destroy evidence.

To prevent overwriting or modification, some systems write logs to a CD-ROM or other write-only device. Protecting logs from modification or read access makes it hard for an attacker to clean up traces of the attack. Log files that are easy to access make it easy for an attacker to remove log file entries linked to the attack. Log files also often contain confidential information about users or information, which you might need. You must ensure that you protect all your log files from unauthorized access, deletion, or changes.

Types of Log Information to Capture

Your organization might need a large number of logs to record all the activity on your systems, networks, and applications. The four main types of logs that you need to keep to support security auditing include:

- **Event logs**—General operating system and application software events.
- **Access logs**—Access requests to resources.
- **Security logs**—Security-related events.
- **Audit logs**—Defined events that provide additional input to audit activities.

As shown in **FIGURE 7-3**, you should record all suspicious activity, errors, unauthorized access attempts, and access to sensitive information. As a result, you will not only track incidents, you'll also keep your users accountable for their activities.

The **Security Information and Event Management (SIEM) system** helps organizations manage the explosive growth of their log files. It provides a common platform to capture and analyze entries. Organizations collect log data from sources such as firewalls, IDSs and IPSs, web servers, and database servers. In addition, many organizations have multiple brands or versions of these systems. SIEM collection and analysis devices take the log data in whatever format they are created, from whatever device creates them, and standardize that data into a common format. The system stores the standard log messages in a database for easy access. You can run SIEM vendor-supplied reports or custom reports against those databases to access and analyze your log file information.

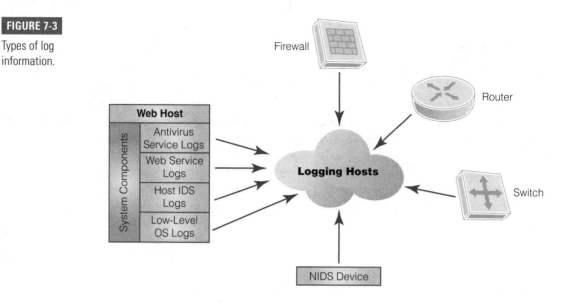

FIGURE 7-3

Types of log
information.

As operating system, application software, and network device vendors change products, the new log file formats may be different from previous products. If your organization uses a SIEM system to handle your log files, such format changes aren't critical. You can merge files from the new products into the same database without limiting the ability to produce reports that cover the before-and-after time period.

SIEM systems monitor user activity and ensure that users act only in accordance with policy. That means SIEM systems are a valuable method of ensuring regulatory compliance. They can also integrate with identity management schemes to ensure that only current user accounts are active on the system.

How to Verify Security Controls

One specific class of monitoring controls can provide a very good layer of security. This class of controls monitors network and system activity to detect unusual or suspicious behavior. Some controls in this class can even respond to detected suspicious activity and possibly stop an attack in progress. Controls that monitor activity include intrusion detection systems (IDSs), intrusion prevention systems (IPSs), and firewalls.

> **NOTE**
>
> The two types of the primary security control types are preventative and detective controls. IDS and IPS represent each type of control. A *detective control* simply detects when a defined event occurs, whereas a *preventative control* prevents the event of ever happening. Both types of controls are important.

Intrusion Detection System (IDS)

Layered defense requires multiple controls to prevent attacks. One of the most common layered-defense mechanisms is to place an IDS behind a firewall to provide increased security. A network intrusion detection system (NIDS) monitors traffic that gets through the firewall to detect malicious activity. A host-based

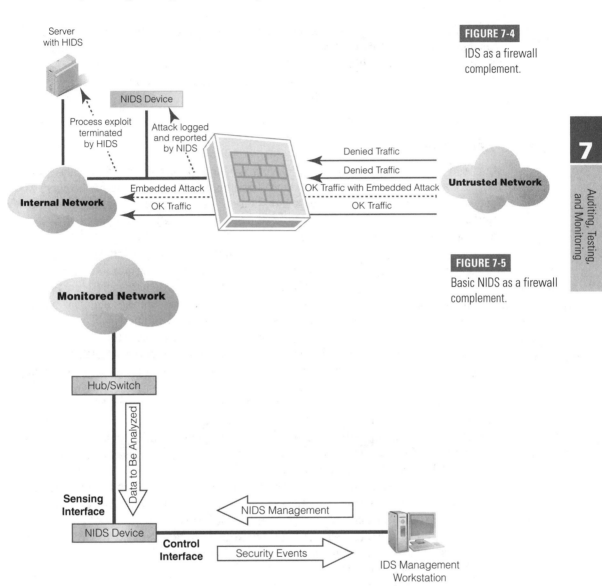

FIGURE 7-4

IDS as a firewall
complement.

FIGURE 7-5

Basic NIDS as a firewall
complement.

intrusion detection system (HIDS)—covered later in this chapter—
does the same for traffic aimed at a particular computer or device.
Because the HIDS sees a narrower view, you can tune it to detect very
specific activities. Unlike the NIDS, the HIDS will also see traffic that
originates inside the perimeter. **FIGURE 7-4** shows a network with a
NIDS and a HIDS device.

As shown in **FIGURE 7-5**, you can connect a NIDS to a switch or
hub. The IDS then captures all traffic on the switch and analyzes it to
detect unauthorized activity. You can do this analysis in several ways,
depending on the type of engine in the IDS.

> **NOTE**
>
> Administrators commonly configure
> a NIDS without an IP address on
> its monitoring port. That makes it
> extremely difficult for the outsider to
> send packets to or otherwise directly
> address the NIDS. Administrators
> reach the device via another interface,
> which should be on a different subnet.

You connect the IDS to a management console that lets the administrator monitor and manage it. Ideally, the IDS will not be detectable from the network. That means attackers will not be able to determine where the IDS is positioned on the network. The administration port on the IDS is not accessible from the network, which prevents an attacker from altering the configuration of the IDS.

Analysis Methods

Monitoring and detection devices must examine and analyze activity to know when to raise an alarm or alert. Devices can use several methods to analyze traffic and activity. Some methods compare network packets or addresses to rules, whereas others look at the frequency and type of activity. These two methods are called pattern- or signature-based and anomaly- or statistical-based IDSs.

Pattern- or signature-based IDSs, using what's known as rule-based detection, rely on pattern matching and stateful matching to compare current traffic with activity patterns (signatures) of known network attacks. Pattern-matching systems scan packets to see whether specific byte sequences, known as *signatures*, match the signature of known attacks. Often the patterns are related to a certain service and port (source or destination). To avoid this type of control and attempt to escape detection, many attackers change their attacks. You must frequently update your signature files to ensure that you can detect the latest known attacks. **Stateful matching** improves on simple pattern matching. It looks for specific sequences appearing across several packets in a traffic stream rather than just in individual packets. Although more detailed than pattern matching, stateful matching can still produce false positives. Like pattern matching, stateful matching can detect only known attacks. It needs frequent signature updates.

> **NOTE**
>
> False positives are a problem with pattern matching because these systems report close matches, particularly if the pattern lacks granularity—for example, if it's not unique.

Anomaly-based IDSs, sometimes called *profile-based systems*, compare current activity with stored profiles of normal (expected) activity. These are only as accurate as the accuracy of your definition of "normal activity." Once you define normal system operation, the IDS compares current activity to what you consider normal activity. Anything the IDS considers abnormal is a candidate for analysis and response. The more common methods of detecting anomalies include the following:

- **Statistical-based methods**—These develop baselines of normal traffic and network activity. The device creates an alert when it identifies a deviation. These can catch unknown attacks, but false positives often happen because identifying normal activity is hard.
- **Traffic-based methods**—These signal an alert when they identify any unacceptable deviation from expected behavior based on traffic. They can also detect unknown attacks and floods.
- **Protocol patterns**—Another way to identify attacks without a signature is to look for deviations from protocols. Protocol standards are provided by Request for Comments (RFC) memorandums published by the Internet Engineering Task Force (IETF). You can get more information on RFCs at *www.ietf.org/rfc.html*. This type of detection works for well-defined protocols but may cause false positives for protocols that are not well defined.

HIDS

HIDS technology adds to your entire system's protection by keeping watch over sensitive processes inside a computer, also called a *host*. HIDS systems generally have the following qualities:

- They are usually software processes or services designed to run on server computers.
- They intercept and examine system calls or specific processes (database and web servers, for example) for patterns or behaviors that should not normally be allowed.
- HIDS daemons can take a predefined action such as stopping or reporting the infraction.

HIDSs also have a different point of view than NIDSs. A HIDS can detect inappropriate traffic that originates inside the network. It can also recognize an anomaly that is specific to a particular machine or user. For example, a single user on a high-volume mail server might originate 10 times the normal number of messages for a user in any day (or hour). The HIDS will notice and issue an alert, but a NIDS may not notice a reportable event. To the NIDS, it just looks like increased network traffic.

Layered Defense: Network Access Control

The best defense is to have multiple layers of controls in place. This increases the chances that you'll protect your systems from more attacks than with just a single control. **FIGURE 7-6** shows how network devices work in multiple layers to try to prevent an attack on the internal protected network. The router detects and filters out some traffic, and the firewall detects and stops unwanted traffic.

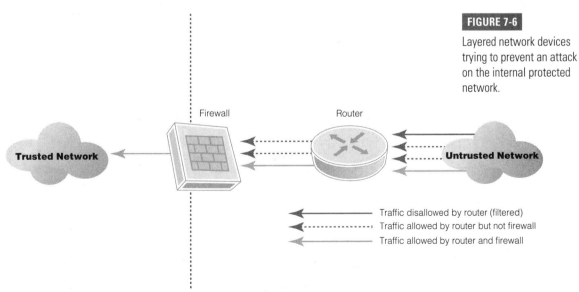

FIGURE 7-6

Layered network devices trying to prevent an attack on the internal protected network.

Control Checks: Intrusion Detection

A NIDS is an important component in any multilayered defense strategy. **FIGURE 7-7** shows how a NIDS can monitor outside attacks as well as insider misuse. A NIDS outside the network gives some idea of the types of attacks faced by the firewall. The internal NIDS detects the types of attacks that may get by the firewall. You can also install this device as an IPS. That way, the device not only can detect a potential attack, it can also change its rules to filter traffic to stop the attack. These devices also work well with HIDS devices. While the NIDS helps protect your system from malicious network traffic, the HIDS will see the types of activity being attempted on the host itself.

Host Isolation

Some servers, or hosts, must be open to the Internet. Web servers are examples of such hosts. You want any user to be able to access your web server—but you don't want everyone to be able to get to your internal network. A simple solution is to isolate the hosts connected to the Internet from the rest of your network. Host isolation isolates one or more host computers from your internal networks and creates a demilitarized zone (DMZ). **FIGURE 7-8** shows a DMZ with two isolated hosts. A DMZ is a physical or logical subnetwork that contains and exposes an organization's external services to a larger untrusted network, usually the Internet. Outside traffic from the untrusted Internet is allowed only into the DMZ, where it can get to certain company services. The web applications in the DMZ then access the trusted internal network but prevent the outside user from getting directly to the internal network.

System Hardening

No computer is completely secure. In fact, very few operating systems or application software packages are secure when you install them. It is important that security administrators go through a process, called **hardening**, to change hardware and software configurations

Using NIDS devices to monitor outside attacks.

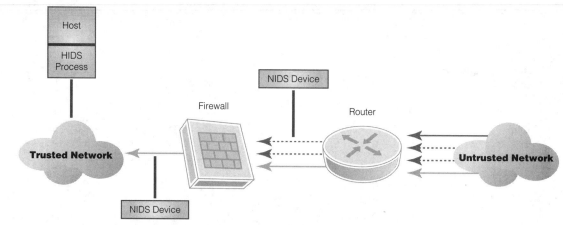

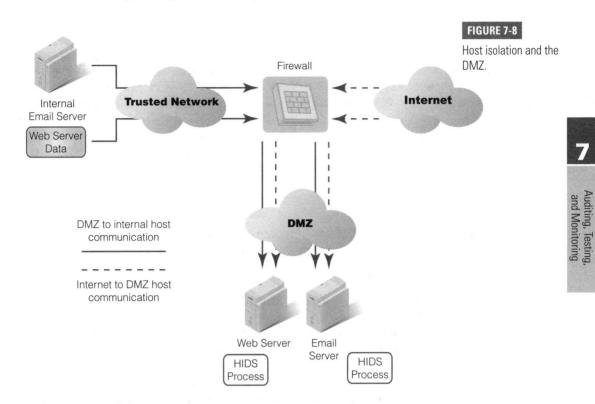

FIGURE 7-8

Host isolation and the DMZ.

7

Auditing, Testing, and Monitoring

to make computers and devices as secure as possible. A computer or device with a **hardened configuration** is one on which you have carried out the following minimal actions:

- Turned off or disabled unnecessary services and protected the ones that are still running.
- Secured management interfaces and applications.
- Protected passwords through aggressive password policies.
- Disabled unnecessary user accounts.
- Applied the latest software patches available.
- Secured all computers and devices from any unauthorized modification.

In addition to hardening systems, it is important to harden your network as well. There are many opportunities to harden networks, but just a few steps go a long way toward making your networks (and network devices) more secure. Those steps include:

- Disabling unused network interfaces
- Disabling unused application service ports
- Using MAC filtering to limit device access
- Implementing 802.1x, port-based Network Access Control (PNAC)

Harden all systems before implementing them. Failure to harden a system before you put it into production almost certainly will result in its compromise.

Set a Baseline Configuration

After hardening a computer or device, you must record the hardened configuration settings. That way you can compare the hardened configuration against known secure configurations. You can also compare the configuration settings in the future with the original settings to see if anything has changed. Creating a baseline makes it easy to ensure that security is consistent between the various systems. When it is easy to define standard settings, you can more easily control individual system differences. For example, you can decide whether to allow certain services or applications on an individual computer if you know that its basic configuration meets your standards.

Disable Unnecessary Services

One of the easiest and most effective steps to harden computers is to shut down unneeded services and programs. Attackers know that most computers run more services and programs than they really need. For example, many server computers run web servers even if they don't host a website. Attackers search for these unneeded services and try to exploit vulnerabilities in them. You should disable unnecessary services. Even better, uninstall services you don't need. Attackers can't attack programs that aren't there. Close unneeded firewall ports and restrict certain services, such as mobile code, telnet, and FTP. You should configure firewalls to deny anything not specifically allowed. This will stop attackers from secretly adding new and unexpected services.

You should harden all routers and other network devices, too. Protect against unauthorized administrator access and changes to router tables. Network devices ship with either no passwords or default passwords. You should change the default passwords before connecting any device to your network. You manage these device passwords like all passwords. They should be complex and changed regularly. You must document any changes to network devices and log the user ID of the administrator making the changes. You should examine all configuration logs on a regular basis, perhaps by a SIEM implementation.

Servers and network devices aren't the only items you need to harden; don't forget about workstations. Workstations need a standard configuration and access controls. Organizations should have a hardened image for workstations. You can create a standard image by installing a fresh copy of an operating system and hardening it. Remove unnecessary services and add security products such as antivirus software and personal firewalls. The image also should contain company-standard software such as a word processor, spreadsheet, and browser plug-ins. When you verify that the image meets your organization's standards for workstations, you can use the image as a starting point for all new desktops and laptops. This process can help ensure security compliance and reduce maintenance time.

Physically protect servers, perhaps behind locked doors. Make sure all computers and devices have the latest patches applied. You can use third-party patch management software to track patches issued by all vendors of all products installed on a company's computers and devices. Some products even have automatic "phone-home" patch management.

In most cases, the best solution for servers exposed to the Internet is to make sure you don't use those servers for any other purpose. For example, a computer that is located in your DMZ and functions as a web server should not provide any other services.

Review Antivirus Programs

An audit of the system should include a review of the antivirus and other anti-malware programs your organization uses. This review should ensure that all software products and their data are up to date. Perform antivirus scans periodically on all network devices and computers. Schedule a full scan of all systems on a regular basis. Scan all application servers, workstations, and gateways.

Monitoring and Testing Security Systems

Securing a closed environment is difficult. Your main goal as a security professional is to protect your organization's sensitive data from attackers. As hard as it is to secure a closed system, the job becomes far more difficult when your network connects to the Internet. Just by connecting to the Internet, you roll out a red carpet for attackers. Your job is to deploy strategies to control access to your systems. Keep in mind that completely securing your system is impossible. Although there are many risks associated with information security, two of the most common risks are:

- Attackers who come in from outside, with unauthorized access, malicious code, Trojans, and malware
- Sensitive information leaking from inside the organization to unauthorized people who can damage your organization

Monitoring

How can you prevent the leakage of sensitive information from your organization? There is no fail-safe method, but monitoring is key. Of course, you can't watch every IP packet on your system. Even if you could train humans to do this mind-numbingly boring work, you wouldn't be able to put enough people on it to keep up. Instead, you must monitor your traffic with an intrusion detection system, or IDS. The premise behind an IDS is that you identify abnormal traffic for further investigation. Intrusion protection systems, or IPSs, go a step beyond IDSs by actively blocking malicious traffic. An IDS alerts you to potentially unauthorized activity; an IPS blocks it. Of course, before you can use an IDS or an IPS, you must create a baseline definition of normal traffic.

Testing

In addition to monitoring your system, you must test it. The main purpose of any security test is to identify uncorrected vulnerabilities on a system. A system might have been secure at one time, but the addition of a new service or application might have made the system vulnerable. The point of testing is to discover new vulnerabilities so you can address them. **FIGURE 7-9** shows the main goals of security testing.

The frequency of your testing depends on such factors as the volatility (rate of changes) of the system and the sensitivity or criticality of the system. Also, policy and regulation often mandate tests. A few of the most common test schedule trigger points are as follows:

- During the security certification phase
- After major system changes (new technology upgrades, application changes)

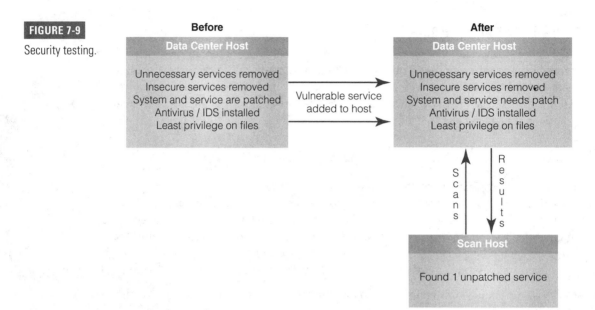

FIGURE 7-9

Security testing.

- New threats
- During system audits
- Periodically, depending on the nature of the system
- Once a year on critical systems

If none of the other items on the list triggers a test, you should do one at least once a year. Some companies might choose shorter or longer testing intervals, depending on a risk analysis.

A Testing Road Map

No perfect solution exists when it comes to testing, and not every security professional will follow the same path. **FIGURE 7-10** shows a road map for security testing. As shown in the figure, security testing consists of a few common activities that give you a complete view of your system's security. The most common activities include the following:

- **Reconnaissance**—This activity involves reviewing the system to learn as much as possible about the organization, its systems, and its networks. Public resources for the job, such as Whois and Dig, are invisible to network administrators—and this is a problem when they are used by attackers instead of penetration testers.
- **Network mapping**—This phase uses tools to determine the layout and services running on the organization's systems and networks.

> **NOTE**
>
> *Vulnerability testing* tries to find a system's weaknesses. *Penetration testing* is a focused attack to exploit a discovered vulnerability. Attackers follow the same steps as penetration testers; the difference between the two is that attackers don't have your consent to penetrate the system. The following is a brief overview of each testing type to help point out their differences.
>
> The goals of vulnerability testing include:
> - Identify vulnerability (passively)
> - Document lack of security control or misconfiguration
> - Examine vulnerabilities related to credentialed and noncredentialed users
>
> The goals of penetration testing include:
> - Identify threats
> - Bypass controls
> - Exploit vulnerabilities

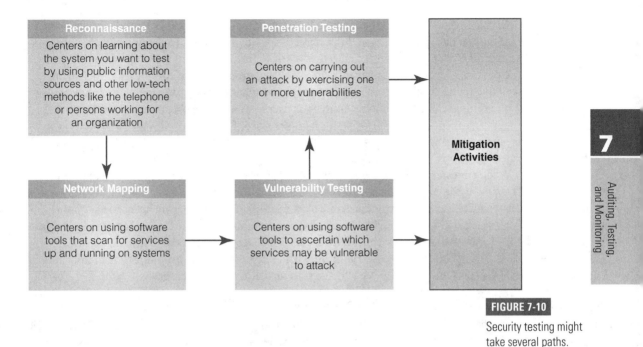

FIGURE 7-10

Security testing might take several paths.

- **Vulnerability testing**—Vulnerability testing involves finding all the weaknesses in a system and determining which places may be attack points.
- **Penetration testing**—In this phase, you try to exploit a weakness in the system and prove that an attacker could successfully penetrate it.
- **Mitigation activities**—Any actions intended to reduce or address vulnerabilities found in either penetration tests or vulnerability tests.

Establishing Testing Goals

Before you run your testing procedures, it's important that you establish your testing goals. Security testing is most concerned with evaluating how well your controls address vulnerabilities. First, identify vulnerabilities and rank them according to how critical they are to your systems. Next, document a point-in-time (snapshot) test for comparison to other time periods. You want to ensure that your security controls are working properly regardless of the time of day or volume of activity. Then prepare for auditor review. This enables your IT staff to tune and test their own procedures using vulnerability analysis in preparation for real audits. Finally, find the gaps in your security. This step enables covert testers (discussed in a moment) to determine the likelihood of system compromise and intrusion detection.

Reconnaissance Methods

Reconnaissance is the first and most basic of many tests. In the reconnaissance phase, you gather information through techniques such as social engineering or by researching the organization's website. Attackers use as many types of reconnaissance as possible to gather information about an organization. You should understand what these attackers are doing and then limit their ability to gather information about you.

Social engineering is a fancy phrase for lying. It involves tricking someone into sharing confidential information or gaining access to sensitive systems. In many cases, the attacker never comes face to face with the victim. Instead, the attacker might phone an employee and pose as a system administrator. All too often, attackers trick employees into sharing sensitive information. After all, employees think, what's wrong with giving your password to an administrator? You should train your users to recognize social-engineering attacks.

Another reconnaissance tool is the Whois service. This service provides information, such as names and phone numbers of administrators, that can help attackers. **FIGURE 7-11** shows the output from a Whois request.

A **zone transfer** is a unique query of a DNS server that asks it for the contents of its zone. The zone is the domain that the server manages. Administrators often use this tool to synchronize DNS servers within the same organization. If you allow zone transfers without restriction, attackers can use this information to try to figure out the names and types of servers that reside both inside and outside your network. The best defense from this type of information leakage is to lock down your DNS server.

> **NOTE**
>
> Organizations should be very careful to avoid letting their domain name registration lapse. Someone else might scoop it up and use it as his or her own. Such an action could cause great cost to the organization's reputation. This type of social engineering is a bit more sophisticated than the run-of-the-mill variety.

Network-Mapping Methods

Network mapping is an extended type of reconnaissance. Network mapping discovers details about a network, including its hosts and host addresses as well as available services. This might enable attackers to identify certain types of systems, applications, services, and configurations. **FIGURE 7-12** shows some of the information network mapping may provide.

An attacker can use Internet Control Message Protocol (ICMP; also known as *ping*) packets to discover a network layout. This gives the attacker an advantage in setting up an attack. As shown in **FIGURE 7-13**, blocking ping packets, as seen with the Tony router, can prevent the attacker from learning about the network. Of course, this also prevents the administrator from being able to use this valuable tool for network troubleshooting.

FIGURE 7-14 shows how an attacker can discover the services available on a target host using TCP/SYN scans. The attacker sends packets to common ports and can determine from the response whether the host accepts these services.

Attackers need to know what operating system a potential victim is running. The approach to attacking a system differs based on the target operating system. With **operating system fingerprinting**, an attacker uses port mapping to learn which operating system and version are running on a computer. This can also help an attacker discover computers that might be vulnerable because they don't have patches or may have known exploits. **FIGURE 7-15** shows how operating system fingerprinting can provide attackers with valuable information.

Covert Versus Overt Testers

You can carry out security testing—which can involve both internal and external staff—overtly or covertly. The personnel and methods you use might depend on regulations or on the skill level of internal staff. **FIGURE 7-16** shows the various types of testers.

Lookup

FIGURE 7-11

Whois search results.

7

Auditing, Testing, and Monitoring

Registrar

WHOIS Server: whois.networksolutions.com
URL: http://networksolutions.com
Registrar: NETWORK SOLUTIONS, LLC.
IANA ID: 2
Abuse Contact Email: abuse@web.com
Abuse Contact Phone: +1.8003337680

Status

Domain Status: clientDeleteProhibited
https://www.icann.org/epp#clientDeleteProhibited
Domain Status: clientTransferProhibited
https://www.icann.org/epp#clientTransferProhibited
Domain Status: clientUpdateProhibited
https://www.icann.org/epp#clientUpdateProhibited
Domain Status: serverDeleteProhibited
https://www.icann.org/epp#serverDeleteProhibited
Domain Status: serverTransferProhibited
https://www.icann.org/epp#serverTransferProhibited
Domain Status: serverUpdateProhibited
https://www.icann.org/epp#serverUpdateProhibited

Important Dates

Updated Date: 2015-01-28
Created Date: 1998-04-27
Registration Expiration Date: 2025-04-27

Name Servers

NS1.NETSOL.COM
NS2.NETSOL.COM
NS3.NETSOL.COM

Raw WHOIS Record

Domain Name: NETWORKSOLUTIONS.COM
Registry Domain ID: 4548132_DOMAIN_COM-VRSN
Registrar WHOIS Server: whois.networksolutions.com
Registrar URL: http://networksolutions.com
Updated Date: 2015-01-28T23:20:59Z
Creation Date: 1998-04-27T04:00:00Z
Registrar Registration Expiration Date: 2025-04-27T04.00.007

FIGURE 7-12

Network mapping.

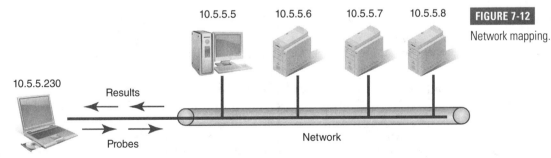

Host Name	IP	Services	OS
user-5	10.5.5.5	http, netbios, ftp	Windows Server 2008
server-6	10.5.5.6	http, netbios	Windows Server 2012
server-7	10.5.5.7	telnet, smtp	Linux
server-8	10.5.5.8	dns, finger, telnet	Solaris

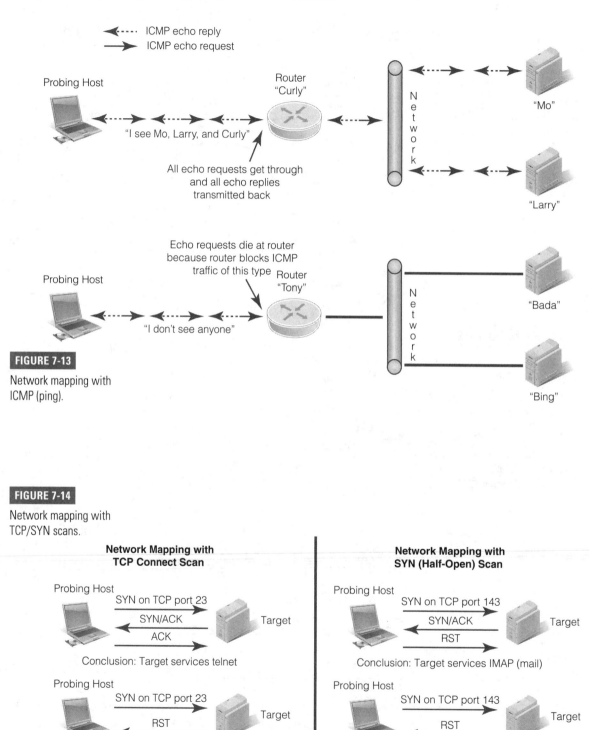

FIGURE 7-13

Network mapping with
ICMP (ping).

FIGURE 7-14

Network mapping with
TCP/SYN scans.

Regardless of who does the testing, you must consider the potential impact of testing activities:

- **Be aware of the potential for harm**—Some tests might crash a system. Other tests will have little effect. Ensure that all potentially affected parties are aware of which tests you will conduct. Make sure you have agreement from all parties if any tests might cause services interruptions or difficulties. Always make plans to recover if the tests—even the safe tests—crash a system.
- **Be aware of the time of day and the day of week**—Although it is tempting to test during low-volume times because it won't affect as many users, it might not be a realistic scenario. An alternative is to do more dangerous tests during off times and safer tests during high-volume hours.

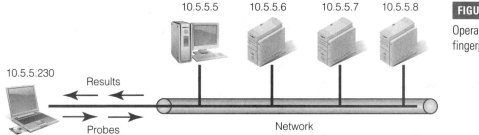

What port mappers "think":

- 10.5.5.5 looks like Windows Server 2003 based on the way its TCP/IP communications are structured....

- 10.5.5.6 looks like Windows Server 2008 because it did not respond with an RST when I sent a FIN and it runs IIS 5 according to the http banner....

- 10.5.5.7 looks like Linux because it did send back an RST in response to my FIN and its TCP/IP communications behave like Linux....

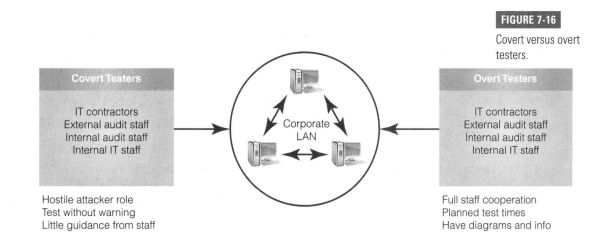

Covert Testers	Overt Testers
IT contractors External audit staff Internal audit staff Internal IT staff	IT contractors External audit staff Internal audit staff Internal IT staff

Hostile attacker role
Test without warning
Little guidance from staff

Full staff cooperation
Planned test times
Have diagrams and info

Testing Methods

Black-box testing uses test methods that aren't based directly on knowledge of a program's architecture or design. The term implies that either the tester does not have the source code or the details of the source code are not relevant to what is being tested. Put another way, black-box testing focuses on the externally visible behavior of the software. For example, it may be based on requirements, protocol specifications, APIs, or even attempted attacks.

In contrast, **white-box testing** is based on knowledge of the application's design and source code. In fact, white-box tests are generally derived from source code. For example, these tests might target specific constructs found in the source code or try to achieve a certain level of code coverage.

Gray-box testing lies somewhere between black-box testing and white-box testing. It uses limited knowledge of the program's internals. In principle, this might mean the tester knows about some parts of the source code and not others. In practice, it usually just means that the tester has access to design documents that are more detailed than specifications or requirements. For example, the tests might be based on an architecture diagram or a state-based model of the program's behavior.

Security Testing Tips and Techniques

Before you start the testing process, consider these points:

- **Choose the right tool**—Choosing tools that are best for testing your software depends on what is to be tested and how the test plan indicates the tests should be carried out. Keep in mind that tool functions often overlap.
- **Tools make mistakes**—You should view preliminary results with skepticism. Watch for false positives or false negatives. Tool results can vary because detection methods often are not consistent.
- **Protect your systems**—Carrying out tests at the wrong time or in the wrong way can damage systems. Take care to protect your systems.
- **Tests should be as real as possible**—Tests should run against production networks and systems to the degree that is possible without impairing system operations. Consider these points when attempting to make your tests as real as possible:
  - You should first run a series of tests that are not likely to crash or have a major impact on a system. Then fix the vulnerabilities those tests detect. After that, you can run tests that might interrupt normal operation during times when an interruption would have the least impact.
  - On the most critical systems, you may be able to run these tests at the same time as business continuity plan testing. For example, test at the alternate site or test at the primary site after successfully running the full interruption test but while still operating at the alternate site.
  - Decide whether to include social engineering as part of the penetration test. The tester and management will decide whether the test should be limited to technical (remote) means or if the tester should try to take advantage of human behavior to get access. Social engineering tests can be difficult to carry out but can reveal additional vulnerabilities if done well.

CHAPTER SUMMARY

In this chapter, you learned about security auditing. You learned how auditing is used to help you create safer systems. You explored why you need these audits and how they create a culture of responsibility and accountability. You discovered how to define your auditing plan, including its scope, and how it works to develop secure systems. You learned about auditing benchmarks, and how they help to create the basis for your auditing plan. You also learned about data collection methods, including how they help you gather information you need to perform a quality audit. You also studied post-audit activities and how they help you complete the process. You explored log collection and analysis, including how they help you monitor your systems. You also learned about log management. You developed an understanding of the types of log information you should capture and the tools that can help you capture it effectively. Finally, you explored monitoring and testing security systems.

KEY CONCEPTS AND TERMS

Anomaly-based IDS
Benchmark
Black-box testing
Clipping level
Covert act
False negative
False positive
Gray-box testing

Hardened configuration
Hardening
Mitigation activities
Network mapping
Operating system fingerprinting
Overt act
Pattern- or signature-based IDS
Penetration testing

Real-time monitoring
Reconnaissance
Security Information and Event
　　Management (SIEM) system
Stateful matching
Vulnerability testing
White-box testing
Zone transfer

CHAPTER 7 ASSESSMENT

1. When you use a control that costs more than the risk involved, you're making a poor management decision.

   A. True
   B. False

2. Which of the following is an example of a level of permissiveness?

   A. Prudent
   B. Permissive
   C. Promiscuous
   D. Paranoid
   E. All of the above

3. An audit examines whether security controls are appropriate, installed correctly, and _____.

   A. Current
   B. Addressing their purpose
   C. Authorized
   D. Cost effective

4. A _____ is a standard used to measure how effective your system is as it relates to industry expectations.

   A. Control objective
   B. Configuration
   C. Benchmark
   D. Policy

5. Post-audit activities include which of the following?

A. Presenting findings to management
B. Data analysis
C. Exit interviews
D. Reviewing of auditor's findings
E. All of the above

6. Some of the tools and techniques used in security monitoring include baselines, alarms, closed-circuit TV, and honeypots.

A. True
B. False

7. _____ is used when it's not as critical to detect and respond to incidents immediately.

A. Non-real-time monitoring
B. A logical access control
C. Real-time monitoring
D. None of the above

8. A common platform for capturing and analyzing log entries is _____.

A. Intrusion detection system (IDS)
B. Honeypot
C. Security Information and Event Management (SIEM)
D. HIPAA
E. All of the above

9. In _____ methods, the IDS compares current traffic with activity patterns consistent with those of a known network intrusion via pattern matching and stateful matching.

A. Signature-based
B. Anomaly-based
C. Heuristic scanning
D. All of the above

10. Host isolation is the isolation of internal networks and the establishment of a(n) _____.

A. HIDS
B. DMZ
C. IDS
D. IPS

11. A hardened configuration is a system that has had unnecessary services enabled.

A. True
B. False

12. The review of the system to learn as much as possible about the organization, its systems, and networks is known as _____.

A. Penetration testing
B. Vulnerability testing
C. Network mapping
D. Reconnaissance

Risk, Response, and Recovery

O RGANIZATIONS MUST CONSTANTLY COPE with change. Shareholders exert new pressures. Governing bodies pass new legislation and set new standards. Organizations must maintain supply chains connecting their suppliers and their customers. Staying competitive means developing strategies to meet business goals. Responding to these changes might require that the organization shift personnel, alter the IT organization, and rearrange logistics. Any of these changes increases risk. The structure of your organization reflects its culture. Likewise, the culture affects your organization's commitment to protecting information and the people and infrastructure that support it.

The way your organization manages risk reflects the value the organization puts on its assets. If the risk isn't considered serious, your organization isn't likely to invest much effort in addressing it. The amount of resources your organization is willing to expend to protect sensitive data affects the risk. Perhaps your organization understands that a specific risk is important, but it simply doesn't have enough budget to address the risk. Or perhaps your organization has a disposable culture, seeking only short-term gains. It may choose to cease operation under adversity. If so, it will likely take only the bare minimum steps to meet required standards. If, however, your organization is committed to long-term success, it will invest in cost-effective plans to reduce risk. Either strategy might be a good fit for a particular organization. The only mistake is not matching risk management spending to the company's culture. For example, a disposable organization should not invest in a sustainable plan, and vice versa.

Chapter 8 Topics

This chapter covers the following topics and concepts:

- How risk management relates to data security
- What the process of risk management is
- What a risk assessment is
- What the differences are between the quantitative and qualitative approaches to risk assessment
- How to develop a strategy for managing risk
- What countermeasures are and what factors you must consider when evaluating them

- What the three types of activity controls are and how they correspond to the security life cycle
- What a business continuity plan (BCP) is and how organizations use it to make sure a disruption doesn't put them out of business
- What role backups play in disaster recovery
- What steps you should take to respond to security incidents
- What a disaster recovery plan (DRP) does
- What the primary steps to disaster recovery are

Chapter 8 Goals

When you complete this chapter, you will be able to:

- Understand the principles of risk management
- Understand how to respond to and analyze incidents
- Understand how to prevent and recover from disruptions using a business continuity plan

Risk Management and Information Security

Risk management is a central concern of information security. Every action an organization takes—or fails to take—involves some degree of risk. Attention to risk management can mean the difference between a successful business and a failing business. That doesn't mean you eliminate every risk. Instead, organizations should seek a balance between the utility and cost of various risk management options. Different organizations have different risk tolerances. For example, an established hospital seeks to limit risk to the highest degree possible. On the other hand, a new startup business with only a handful of employees may be more willing to take on risks that may result in attractive financial returns.

As a security professional, you will work with others to identify risks and to apply risk management solutions. You must remember two key risk management principles:

- Don't spend more to protect an asset than it is worth. This can be more difficult than it first appears. You must understand the true impact of each risk. Security breaches can degrade customer confidence. A successful attack may result in immediate costs but also cause customers to go to a competitor. The true cost can be far higher than immediate cleanup costs.
- A countermeasure without a corresponding risk is a solution seeking a problem; it is difficult to justify the cost.

You play an important role in the risk, response, and recovery aspects of information security. You must help identify risks. Some of them are serious and could put your company out of business. For example, a data breach could hurt your company's reputation and result in lost sales and may even end up costing a lot of money due to fines or settlements. You also must help create and/or maintain a plan that makes sure your company continues to operate in the face of disruption. This type of a plan is a *business continuity plan* (BCP). It is an important concept you will learn about in this chapter. Disruptions do happen, so you must expect they will happen to your organization. Planning for disruption is part of your role as a security professional. You must help develop and maintain a *disaster recovery plan* (DRP) to help address situations that damage or destroy necessary parts of your infrastructure.

As a security professional, your goal is to make sure your systems quickly become available to users after an outage and that you recover any lost or damaged data. However, you also play a role in making sure you handle the recovery process correctly.

> **NOTE**
>
> You should become familiar with the NIST SP 800 series of security practices. You can find the series at *http://csrc.nist.gov /publications/PubsSPs.html*. This basic information is the foundation for your understanding of information security. Advanced security professionals will use some of the more detailed items.

Risk Terminology

Managing risk is the process of identifying risks and deciding what to do about them. The first step in managing risk is identifying and assessing risk. But what is risk? And how are risks assessed? Before you learn about managing risks, it is important to understand a few terms. The following terms describe risk assessment types, or ways to define and discuss risks:

- **Threat**—A **threat** is something (generally bad) that might happen. A threat could be a tornado hitting your data center or an attacker stealing your database of customer data.

- **Vulnerability**—A **vulnerability** is any exposure that could allow a threat to be realized. Some vulnerabilities are weaknesses, and some are just side effects of other actions (such as allowing employees to use their smartphones to connect to the corporate network.)

- **Risk**—**Risk** is the likelihood that a particular threat will be realized against a specific vulnerability. Most risks leads to possible damage or negative results that could damage your organization. Not all risks are inherently bad; some risks can lead to positive results. The extent of damage (or even positive effect) from a threat determines the level of risk.

- **Impact**—**Impact** refers to the amount of harm a threat exploiting a vulnerability can cause. For example, if a virus infects a system, the virus could affect all the data on the system.

> **NOTE**
>
> Many people have never thought of risk as a positive thing. However, uncertainty can result in events that have negative *or* positive effects. For example, suppose your organization plans to deploy new software to your end users based on projected availability from your software vendor. Your risk management plan should address the responses to both an early and a late software delivery. If you receive the software early, you can either perform more exhaustive testing or begin deployment early. If your software vendor is late delivering software, you may miss your projected deployment date. You should have plans in place to address both the positive and negative effects of a delivery date that does not match your schedule.

When a threat is realized, an organization experiences either an event or an incident. An **event** is a measurable occurrence that has an impact on the business. Some events have little effect; others might escalate into incidents. An **incident** is any event that either violates or threatens to violate your security policy. For example, employee warehouse theft is an incident. Incidents are events that justify a countermeasure.

You will learn more about *controls, countermeasures*, and *safeguards* later in this chapter. Many people use these terms interchangeably, although there are subtle differences. They all reduce risk by reducing either a vulnerability or the impact of a threat. **Controls** include both safeguards and countermeasures. Suffice it to say here that controls are actions taken to limit or constrain behavior. **Safeguards** address gaps or weaknesses in the controls that could otherwise lead to a realized threat. **Countermeasures** counter or address a specific threat. A fire sprinkler system is an example of a countermeasure.

Elements of Risk

Assets, vulnerabilities, and threats are all elements of risk. These are component parts rather than a formula. Assets increase or decline in value. Your proactive procedures should discover and address vulnerabilities. New threats emerge to add to existing ones. As these factors change over time, risk changes as well. You should periodically perform risk reassessments to identify new or changed risks.

> **NOTE**
>
> You can find the Cybersecurity Watch Survey at *www.cert.org/insider-threat/research /cybersecurity-watch-survey.cfm?* The CERT Division is part of the Software Engineering Institute, based at Carnegie Mellon University. It has a comprehensive online resource, the CERT Insider Threat Center, at *www.cert.org /insider-threat/cert-insider-threat-center.cfm*. You can find the Verizon *2015 Data Breach Investigations Report* at *www.verizonenterprise .com/DBIR/2015/*.

Don't assume that all threats come from the outside. In 2014, *CSO Magazine*, The CERT Program, Price Waterhouse Cooper, Deloitte, Microsoft, and the U.S. Secret Service released the latest *Cybersecurity Watch Survey*. This report explains that insider attacks make up a little more than a quarter (28 percent) of all reported attacks. Other sources, including the FBI and Verizon's *2015 Data Breach Investigations Report*, state that insider attacks made up just over 20 percent of overall attacks. However, their impact is proportionately worse. Insider attacks are also becoming more sophisticated. In 2013, the National Aeronautics and Space Administration (NASA) shut down its internal database and tightened its remote access policies. These actions were a direct result of suspected intellectual property theft carried out by a foreign national contractor.

New threats appear all the time. The United States Computer Emergency Readiness Team (US-CERT) regularly releases information on new threats via email. You can subscribe to its Technical Cyber Security Alerts, Cyber Security Bulletins, or Cyber Security Alerts through this website: *www.us-cert.gov/ ncas/alerts*. Once you sign up, you'll receive regular email alerts. You can also subscribe to its newsfeeds or follow it on Twitter.

Purpose of Risk Management

The purpose of risk management is to identify possible problems before something bad happens. Early identification is important because it gives you the opportunity to manage those risks instead of just reacting to them. It is important to identify risks:

- Before they lead to an incident
- In time to enable you to plan and begin risk-handling activities (controls and countermeasures)
- On a continuous basis across the life of the product, system, or project

You can never reduce risk to zero. After identifying the risk culture of an organization, you need to evaluate risks and then handle the ones that could have a major effect on the organization first. You must be able to justify the costs of risk-handling methods. In many cases, small risk reductions have significantly high costs. Part of your job is to identify the tolerable risk level and apply controls to reduce risks to that level. You must focus some risk management efforts on identifying new risks so you can manage them before a negative event occurs. Part of this process will include continually reevaluating risks to make sure you have put the right countermeasures in place.

The Risk Management Process

FIGURE 8-1 shows the risk management process. Risk management is a process that never really ends. It is important to periodically move through the complete cycle to be ready for current threats. The process defines how you will carry out the steps of managing risk for your organization. For example, the approach could state that risk analysis will be conducted at specified intervals. The tools for conducting this analysis can include the documents that define, categorize, and rank risks. This approach is consistent with the Project Management Institute's (PMI) Project Management Body of Knowledge (PMBOK). Though the PMI approach isn't the only way to do things, it does provide a prescriptive approach to project management in general, including risk management.

The steps in the risk management process are as follows:

- **Identify risks**—The first step to managing risk is identifying risks. What could go wrong? Answers can include fire, flood, earthquake, lightning strike, loss of electricity or other utility, labor strikes, and transportation unavailability. You must develop scenarios for each threat to assess the threats.

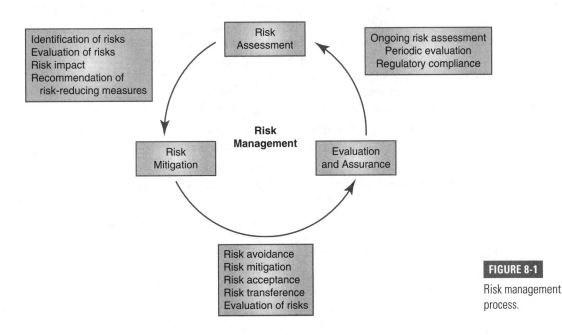

FIGURE 8-1

Risk management process.

- **Assess risks**—Some risks pose a greater possibility of loss than others. Furthermore, not all risks apply to all businesses in all locations. For example, businesses in Montana or Moscow don't need to worry about hurricanes. Of the risks that are possible, impact will be more or less severe depending on the scenario and location. Assessing risk is about determining which risks are the most serious ones.

- **Plan risk response**—Starting with the highest priority risks, explore potential responses to each one. With direction from your organization's upper management, determine the responses to each risk that provide the best value.

- **Implement risk responses**—Take action to implement the chosen responses to each risk from the previous step.

- **Monitor and control risk responses**—Monitor and measure each risk response to ensure that it is performing as expected. This step can include passive monitoring and logging as well as active testing to see how a control behaves.

> **NOTE**
>
> It is important to avoid spending time and money on "movie plot" risks. Scriptwriters can create impossible scenarios and make them look possible or even likely. Spending money to protect against these false threats is almost always a waste. Instead, focus on realistic probabilities.

Identify Risks

The first step in the risk management process is to identify risks. Organizations use many different methods to identify risks. Each method uses a different approach to solve the same problem—identifying as many risks as possible. In each, the basic strategy is to use input from multiple sources to build a comprehensive list of risks. Some of the more popular risk identification methods include these:

- **Brainstorming**—This technique involves getting unstructured input from members in a group meeting. The facilitator should encourage all members to offer suggestions without fear of criticism or ridicule.

- **Surveys**—Organizations that use this technique send lists of prepared questions to participants for input. A variety of people from different areas of the organization should be chosen to get the best input. The Delphi method is a specific type of survey in which responses are anonymized, shuffled, and sent back out to participants for comment. Keeping input anonymous fosters more open dialogue.

- **Interviews**—Interviews, held in either group settings or one on one, can be an effective approach to gather details on risks from the interviewee's perspective.

- **Working groups**—This technique focuses on soliciting feedback from a group of individuals selected from a specific work area. The feedback working groups provide generally helps identify risks in specific areas.

- **Checklists**—Many organizations develop checklists of risks for either their own use or for general distribution. Checklists developed for similar organizations or purposes can be helpful to ensure that you cover the breadth of risks.

- **Historical information**—Unless an organization is brand new, it will have some historical information at its disposal. This information may be a previously encountered risk identification process, or it may be documentation of things that went wrong in the past. Either way, historical information can be valuable to identify current risks.

Most organizations use multiple methods to identify risks. Use the methods that work best for your organizational culture. The most important factor is to engage as many people from different functional areas as possible. The best outcome is to identify far more reasonable risks than your organization can handle. Although that sounds like you're asking for trouble, it is much better than completely missing important risks. Try using as many risk identification methods as possible to find the best mix of methods for your organization.

The result of the risk identification process is a list of identified risks. The PMI calls this list the **risk register**. The risk register can contain many different types of information but should contain at least the following:

- A description of the risk
- The expected impact if the associated event occurs
- The probability of the event occurring
- Steps to mitigate the risk
- Steps to take should the event occur
- Rank of the risk

Emerging Threats

Part of your risk identification activities should address new and emerging threats. These types of threats can come from many different areas and from both internal and external sources. Some examples of emerging threats include the following:

- New technology
- Changes in the culture of the organization or environment
- Unauthorized use of technology (e.g., wireless technologies, rogue modems, smartphones, tablets, unlicensed software)
- Changes in regulations and laws
- Changes in business practices (e.g., outsourcing, globalization)

A proactive security professional watches for new threats that might trigger the need for a new risk review. Two of the most common areas of emerging threats are cloud and virtualization. As organizations move toward outsourcing data and processing to cloud service providers, they encounter new threats. Some threats apply to cloud service providers; others are generally related to internal or external users of virtualization. These threats can include the following:

- Violation of virtualization barriers
- Lack of access controls for outsource resources
- Reliability of cloud or virtualization services
- Cloud service provider (CSP) lock-in
- Insecure application program interfaces (APIs)

- Malicious insiders
- Account hijacking

Although any of these threats may occur in all environments, the risk in a cloud or virtualized environments is of greater concern due to the common practice of delegating responsibilities of these environments to external parties. Always consider new and novel threats when considering cloud or virtualized services.

Static Environments

Another class of threats bearing closer examination relates to static environments. **Static environments** are types of systems that don't change very much or at all after deployment. While "normal," or dynamic, systems do change often, static systems tend to remain much like they were when first installed. Some examples of static systems include:

- **Supervisory Control and Data Acquisition (SCADA)**—SCADA systems are common in industrial settings. SCADA systems control and monitor physical devices, such as manufacturing; power generation; oil, water, and gas distribution; and facility environmental controls. These systems are often built by the manufacturer with static versions of an operating system and other software to produce a fixed software stack. SCADA systems are not easy to patch when security vulnerabilities are discovered in one of its embedded software layers.

- **Embedded systems**—These are generally small computers that are contained in a larger device. The computer components are often enclosed in a chassis that houses the rest of the device. Such devices can include other hardware and mechanical parts. For example, a robotic vacuum device contains an embedded system that controls its movement. The embedded computer is not easily accessible and is difficult to update with security patches.

- **Mobile devices (Android, iOS, Windows)**—Mobile operating system patches and upgrades are available and easy to apply, but not all users update their devices. Bad prior upgrade experiences may prevent users from applying needed patches. This can lead to threats to unpatched mobile endpoints. In addition, many mobile devices are beyond the control of the organizations to which they connect.

- **Mainframes**—These large computers exist primarily in large organization data centers. They handle large-scale data processing and are expensive to maintain. Downtime is expensive and discouraged. For that reason, there isn't much opportunity to apply security patches until a downtime window approaches. Mainframes may operate as vulnerable to emerging threats for some time.

- **Gaming consoles**—These are really just computers that are optimized to handle graphics applications efficiently. Today's gaming consoles are commonly connected to the Internet and are routinely exposed to new threats. Manufacturers do provide security patches, but not all users are diligent about keeping their systems updated. Most users just want to plug in their consoles and play.

- **Vehicle systems**—This final category of static systems is a type of embedded system. Increasing numbers of vehicles contain computing systems that monitor conditions, provide connectivity to the Internet, provide real-time routing, and even control the vehicle's operation (for example, automatic parking and self-driving cars). Intervention systems to enhance safety are included in more and more new vehicles. For example, antilock braking and anticollision systems are available on many models. These systems tend to be very difficult to upgrade or patch due to the effort required to take the vehicle to a service agent who can perform maintenance. If manufacturers make the update process too easy, attackers could easily inject malicious code.

Part of your risk identification process should include these static systems. These systems encounter threats just like other systems. Addressing threats to these types of systems may be more difficult. But a secure system depends on the security of all its components.

Assess Risks

A good risk assessment explains the company's risk environment to managers in terms they understand. It explains what risks could stop a company from operating. Sometimes IT professionals get so emotional about protecting their IT structure, they forget that their systems are there to support the organization's primary objectives. During the risk assessment process, remain focused on "What does this mean to the company?" and "What is the value of this to the company?" rather than "What does this mean for my systems and infrastructure?"

> **NOTE**
>
> Incidents will occur! Risk management (identification, assessment, and response) coupled with disaster planning (covered later in this chapter) often mean the difference between a company surviving or failing after a disruption.

Although you have many choices to respond to risks, a key reason for risk assessment is to provide the data necessary to identify the best response choices. That depends on such things as cost, effectiveness, impact on productivity, and user acceptance.

Two Approaches to Risk Assessment: Quantitative and Qualitative

You can approach risk assessment in two ways:

- **Qualitative risk assessment**—**Qualitative risk assessment** ranks risks based on their probability of occurrence and impact on business operations. Impact is the degree of effect a realized threat would pose. Impact is often expressed from low (insignificant) to high (catastrophic) values. Qualitative risk assessments can be fairly subjective, but they do help determine the most critical risks. This type of assessment requires diverse input from people who work in different departments and encourages the use of relative terms. For example, a qualitative assessment asks which risks are worse than others. This allows the business units and technical experts to understand the ripple effects of an event on other departments or operations.

- **Quantitative risk assessment**—This type of risk assessment attempts to describe risk in financial terms and put a dollar value on each risk. It is more objective than a qualitative analysis. One drawback to this approach is that many risks have values that are difficult to measure. These include reputation and the availability of countermeasures. Exact numbers can be difficult to determine, especially the cost of the impact of future events. On the other hand, quantitative risk assessments are easier to automate than qualitative assessments.

FIGURE 8-2

Quantitative versus
qualitative risk analysis.

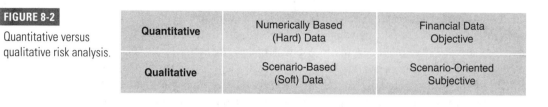

Quantitative	Numerically Based (Hard) Data	Financial Data Objective
Qualitative	Scenario-Based (Soft) Data	Scenario-Oriented Subjective

Quantitative analysis puts a dollar figure on risk. Qualitative analysis defines risks based on the severity of their impact and/or probability. **FIGURE 8-2** compares quantitative and qualitative risk analysis. Neither approach is perfect in itself. A solid risk assessment will often combine both techniques.

In most situations, you can combine the two methodologies. Qualitative risk analysis gives you a better understanding of the overall impact a disruption will have as the effects ripple through an organization. It often leads to better communication between departments in terms of how they must work together to reduce damage. However, it lacks some of the solid financial data of a quantitative risk analysis. You often need this cost information to justify the cost of countermeasures. Therefore, you need to consider both techniques.

Calculating Quantified Risk. To calculate quantified risk, you must figure out how much an asset is worth and the probability that you will encounter a loss. This is the event's **loss expectancy**. Calculating it is a multistep process:

1. **Calculate the asset value (AV)**—An asset is anything of value to an organization. Assets can be tangible (buildings) or intangible (reputation). A first step in risk assessment is to determine all the organization's assets and their value—that is, the importance of each asset to the organization's ability to meet its mission. Asset value should consider the replacement value of equipment or systems. It should also include factors such as lost productivity and loss of reputation or customer confidence.

2. **Calculate the exposure factor (EF)**—This represents the percentage of the asset value that will be lost if an incident were to occur. For example, not every car accident is a total loss. Insurance companies have actuaries who calculate the likely percentage loss for every claim. They know the cost of repairs for every make and model and can predict the exposure factor per claim. Their prediction won't be right for any single claim (except by chance), but it will be right when grouped by the hundreds or thousands.

3. **Calculate the single loss expectancy (SLE)**—You can calculate the value of a single loss using the two preceding factors. If an actuary calculates that the EF of a late-model SUV is 20 percent, then every time he receives a claim, all he needs to do is look up the asset value, multiply by the EF, and he'll have a very good prediction of the payout. This allows the actuary to calculate insurance premiums accurately and reduce the risk of the insurance company losing money.

4. **Determine how often a loss is likely to occur every year**—This is the **annualized rate of occurrence** (ARO), also called the risk **likelihood**. Some AROs are greater than

one. For example, a snowstorm in Buffalo or Berlin will happen many times per year. Others are likely to happen far less often. For example, a warehouse fire might happen once every 20 years. It is often difficult to estimate how often an incident will happen. Sometimes internal or external factors can affect that assessment. Historical data do not always predict the future. An incident such as one stemming from an internal threat is far more likely during times of employee unrest or contract negotiations than at other times.

5. **Determine annualized loss expectancy (ALE)**—The ALE is the SLE (the loss when an incident happens) times the ARO. The ALE helps an organization identify the overall impact of a risk. For infrequent events, the ALE will be much less than the SLE. For example, if you expect an event to occur only once every 10 years, the ARO is 0.10, or 10 percent. If the SLE is $1,000, the ALE is only $100 ($1,000 × 0.10). On the other hand, if the ARO is 20, indicating that it is likely to occur 20 times every year, the ALE is $20,000 ($1,000 × 20).

TABLE 8-1 shows the calculations you can use to determine quantified risk. The purpose of calculating quantified risk is to find the highest amount that you should spend on a countermeasure. The cost of the countermeasure should be less than the ALE.

Consider this example. About 100 users in your organization use laptop computers. The value of each mobile computer is $1,500, which includes the cost of the computer, the software, and the data. In the past two years, the organization has lost an average of six computers a year. This information enables you to calculate the SLE, the ARO, and the ALE.

- The SLE is $1,500.
- The ARO is 6.
- The ALE is $9,000.

Someone has suggested purchasing hardware locks as a countermeasure to protect against the loss of these systems. Users can use these locks to lock unattended computers to furniture, the way bicycle riders lock their bikes to a bike rack. If you purchase the locks in bulk, they cost $10 each. Additionally, if you purchase and use the locks, you estimate that you can reduce the losses from six a year to only one. Is this a cost-effective countermeasure?

- Cost of countermeasure is $1,000 ($10 × 100 computers).
- New ARO is 1.
- New ALE is $1,500.

TABLE 8-1 Determining quantified risk.

CALCULATION	FORMULA
Single loss expectancy (SLE)	AV × EF = SLE
Annualized rate of occurrence (ARO)	ARO = Number of incidents per year
Annualized loss expectancy (ALE)	SLE × ARO = ALE

Clearly, this is a cost-effective control. Instead of losing $9,000 a year, the organization spends $1,000 and only loses $1,500. The total outgoing funds is $2,500. This is much better than the loss of $9,000 you experienced before implementing the new control. On the other hand, if the cost of the countermeasure were $20,000, it wouldn't make sense. You'd be spending $20,000 to potentially save $9,000, which would cost the organization an additional $11,000.

Qualitative Risk Analysis. You can judge every risk on two scales:

- **Probability or likelihood**—Some things—for example, the malfunction of a badge reader on the employee entrance—will seldom happen. Other things, such as employees calling in sick, will almost certainly happen.

- **Impact**—Some things—for example, a workstation that fails to boot up—will have a minor impact on productivity. Other things, such as a production system breaking down, will have a major impact.

You should evaluate events with respect to both scales and then place them on the chart shown in **FIGURE 8-3**.

Notice the quadrant labeled "Focus area for risk management." These are risks with both a high probability and a high impact. You should evaluate these risks first. You can reduce

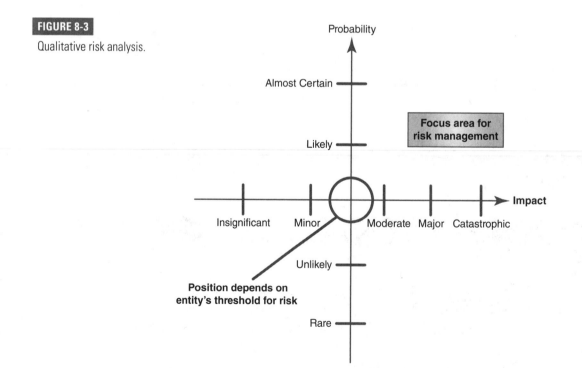

FIGURE 8-3

Qualitative risk analysis.

the probability of the risk or its impact if you apply countermeasures to these risks first. You should not confine your risk management activities solely to the upper-right quadrant, but this is where your risk response efforts should focus. Risk mitigation, transference, acceptance, or avoidance—covered in the next section—reduce the risks in the upper-right quadrant. As a reminder, the goal isn't to eliminate risk but instead to reduce risk to an acceptable level.

Plan a Risk Response

The next two steps in the risk management process are to develop a plan to handle risks and then implement that plan. As you develop risk management strategies, you should understand the most common responses. You can reduce, transfer, accept, and avoid each negative risk:

- **Reduce (reduction/mitigation)**—This approach uses various controls to mitigate or reduce identified risks. These controls might be administrative, technical, or physical. For example, adding antivirus software reduces the risk of computer infection.

- **Transfer (transference/assignment)**—This approach allows the organization to transfer the risk to another entity. Insurance is a common way to reduce risk. An organization "sells" the risk to an insurance company in return for a premium. Other times, you can transfer risk to insulate an organization from excessive liability. A hotel, for example, engages a separate car-parking corporation to manage its parking lot. Losses are the primarily responsibility of the car-parking corporation, not the hotel. An incident in the parking lot is less likely to put the hotel in jeopardy of a lawsuit.

- **Accept (acceptance)**—This allows an organization to accept risk. The organization knows the risk exists and has decided that the cost of reducing it is higher than the loss would be. This can include self-insuring or using a deductible. The level of risk an organization is willing to accept depends on the risk appetite of senior management. For example, a physician buys malpractice insurance and accepts the residual risk of loss equal to the deductible. He can decide to pay an even higher premium to reduce his deductible. But he might decide that the higher premium would not be worth the cost, because he expects to rarely make a claim.

- **Avoid (avoidance)**—Risk avoidance is just that: deciding not to take a risk. A company can discontinue or decide not to enter a line of business if the risk level is too high. With avoidance, management decides that the potential loss to the company exceeds the potential value gained by continuing the risky activity. For example, a company may decide not to open a branch in a country mired in political turmoil.

For positive risks, you can exploit, share, enhance, or accept each risk:

- **Exploit (exploitation)**—When you exploit a positive risk, you take advantage of an opportunity that arises when you respond to that risk. For example, suppose your organization developed training materials for use within your organization to help you address a specific risk. You might exploit the risk by packaging and marketing those training materials to other organizations.

- **Share (sharing)**—When you share a positive risk, you use a third party to help capture the opportunity associated with that risk. For example, banding with another organization to purchase a group of workstation licenses enables both organizations to realize a substantial discount due to the size of the combined order. (In this case, the risk is that the license cost may change.)

- **Enhance (enhancement)**—When you enhance a positive risk, you increase the probability or positive impact of the event associated with the risk. For example, suppose you have a contract to deliver software that includes a $20,000 bonus for early completion. To enhance the positive risk—a delivery date that does not match your schedule—you might offer a subcontractor you've hired a $5,000 bonus for finishing ahead of the deadline.

- **Accept (acceptance)**—When you accept a positive risk, you take no steps to address it because the potential effects of the risk are positive and add value. For example, suppose you have purchased a new automated backup and configuration utility that can help your organization deploy new workstations in half the allotted time. Because the utility is new, it may take some time to learn—meaning it may *not* help your organization save any time deploying new workstations. It's determined that at worst, learning the new utility and using it to manage deployments will take the same amount of time as doing it manually. However, if you realize the positive risk, you will finish the deployments sooner than planned.

Acceptable Range of Risk/Residual Risk

The acceptable range of risk determines how you define activities and countermeasures. The upper bound is the risk impact where the cost would be too great for the organization to bear. The lower bound shows the increased cost of the countermeasures to handle the residual risk. **FIGURE 8-4** illustrates that the goal of risk management is to stay inside the acceptable range.

The top graph represents the total exposure to an organization for a specific risk. The in-place countermeasures are not adequate to reduce the risk from the maximum acceptable residual risk level into the acceptable range. The lower graph shows the proposed countermeasures that will reduce the maximum residual risk level to the acceptable range.

Total risk is the combined risk to all business assets. **Residual risk** is the risk that remains after you have deployed countermeasures and controls:

$$\text{Risk} - \text{Mitigating controls} = \text{Residual risk}$$

Applying countermeasures and controls reduces risk but does not eliminate it. Look at the example of car insurance. When you purchase a brand-new car, it loses value as soon as you drive it off the dealer's lot, because it is now used. If an accident totals the car, insurance may not reimburse you the price you paid for the car originally. The difference between what the insurance company pays and what you actually paid for the car is the residual risk. Other examples include the deductible on insurance or the remaining (but decreased) chance of fire after you implement alarms, sprinkler systems, and training sessions. The difference between total risk and residual risk is shown in **FIGURE 8-5**.

> ### ▌ NOTE
>
> You usually can't eliminate risk entirely. Your organization must select a level of risk it is willing to accept. This is the acceptable range.

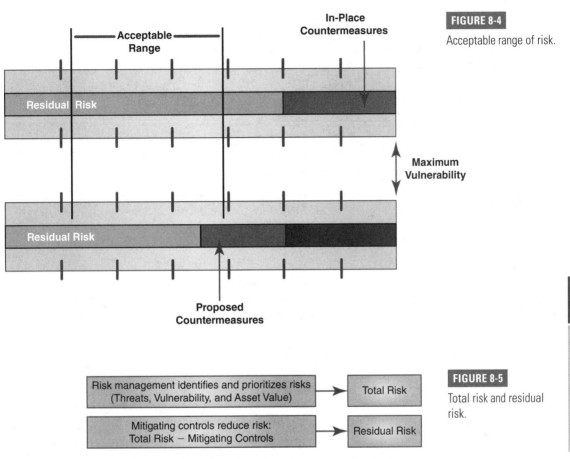

FIGURE 8-4

Acceptable range of risk.

FIGURE 8-5

Total risk and residual risk.

Residual risk should be set to an acceptable level.

You should prepare your organization to accept the cost of residual risk. You may choose not to eliminate risk entirely because doing so is impossible or too expensive. If its cost is too great, you must either eliminate the risky behavior or use a different countermeasure.

Implement the Risk Response Plan

Security controls are the safeguards or countermeasures that an organization uses to avoid, counteract, or minimize loss or system unavailability. As defined by the Institute of Internal Auditors:

The control environment sets the tone of an organization, influencing the control consciousness of its people. It is the foundation for all other components of internal control, providing discipline and structure. Control environment factors include the integrity, ethical values, and competence of the entity's people; management's philosophy and operating style; and the way management assigns authority and organizes and develops its people.

8

Risk, Response, and Recovery

NOTE

NIST also suggests three control categories in NIST SP 800-53a. The three NIST control categories are:

- **Management controls**. These are controls used to manage the entire risk process. For example, reviews of security controls and developing and maintaining the overall security plan are management controls.
- **Operational controls**. These are controls that operational personnel may implement and manage, such as physical security and incident response.
- **Technical controls**. These controls are made up of computer programs, such as identification systems, or the output of computer programs, such as log files for audit trails.

Some controls manage the activity phase of security—the things people do. These are **administrative controls**. Administrative controls develop and ensure compliance with policy and procedures. They tend to be things that employees might do, things employees are supposed to do, or things employees are not supposed to do. A control carried out or managed by a computer system is a **technical control**.

Activity phase controls can be either administrative or technical. They correspond to the life cycle of a security program as follows:

- **Detective controls**—These controls identify that a threat has landed in your system. An intrusion detection system (IDS) is an example of a **detective control**. An IDS can detect attacks on systems such as port scans that try to gain information about a system. The IDS then logs the activity.

- **Preventive controls**—These stop threats from coming in contact with a vulnerability. An example of a **preventive control** is an intrusion prevention system (IPS). An IPS is an IDS that you configure to actively block an attack. Instead of simply logging the activity, it can change the configuration so that the malicious activity is blocked.

- **Corrective controls**—These reduce the effects of a threat. When you reload an operating system after it is infected with malware, you are using a **corrective control**. Forensics and incident response are other examples of corrective controls.

- **Deterrent controls**—These are controls that deter an action that could result in a violation. There is a fine line between **deterrent controls** and preventative controls. Deterrent controls merely attempt to suggest that a subject not take some action, whereas preventative controls do not allow the action to occur. Deterrent controls are valuable when a knowledgeable user needs the ability to perform some action that involves risk. A deterrent control would allow the action after a warning, whereas a preventative control would not allow the action. In short, the decision to choose between a preventative and deterrent control is often a balance between utility and security.

- **Compensating controls**—These controls are designed to address a threat in place of a preferred control that is too expensive or difficult to implement.

Selecting Countermeasures: As discussed earlier in the chapter, *control, safeguard*, and *countermeasure* are not interchangeable terms. A *control* limits or constrains behavior. *Safeguards* and *countermeasures* are controls that exercise restraint on or management of some activity. For example, a safe for storage of valuables is a control. A human guard who watches the safe is a safeguard. Insurance against loss of the valuables, if stolen, is a countermeasure. The countermeasure counters or addresses the loss from a specific incident.

Protecting Physical Security

One special class of risks to the organization is physical security. In fact, good physical security is necessary for a solid overall security plan. Too many IT security professionals dismiss physical security and focus only on technical security controls. Always assess the best security controls as part of your risk management program. You have to ensure that all critical IT assets are physically secured at all times. There are many controls you can implement to ensure physical security. Here is a partial list of the most common environmental and physical controls you'll need to maintain a secure IT environment:

- **Heating, ventilating, and air conditioning (HVAC)**—These are systems that provide proper air flow, temperature, and humidity for IT components to operate. Although this might seem straightforward, these systems must be designed well and operate efficiently to support your IT infrastructure. Data center design should include hot aisles (for IT component heat venting) and cold aisles (for drawing cold air into IT components). They must also be designed to provide necessary services at all times while using as little energy as possible to keep costs down. All environmental controls must be monitored for proper operation to ensure that your data center maintains the required temperature and humidity.
- **Fire suppression**—This includes devices and systems designed to extinguish fires of different types to minimize damage and stop fires from spreading.
- **EMI shielding**—This includes physical barriers placed around wiring or into building materials to limit electromagnetic interference (EMI) emanations from traveling outside protected areas.
- **Lighting**—Lights are placed to ensure all areas are well lit, with few dark spots.
- **Signs**—Clear signage indicates which areas are designated for specific purposes and which areas are off-limits.
- **Fencing**—Physical barriers deter casual intruders or mark boundaries.
- **Barricades**—Physical barriers deter more aggressive intruders or limit vehicle access.
- **Guards**—A physical presence can deter intrusion and humans can react quickly to changing conditions.
- **Motion detectors**—Devices generate an alert when motion is observed in a small defined area.
- **Video surveillance**—Devices monitor many areas of a facility from a central location and record actions for later analysis.
- **Locks**—Physical devices limit physical access from unauthorized personnel. Lock controls can include door locks, cable locks, safes, and locking cabinets.
- **Mantraps**—These are two sets of doors with a small alcove between them. A person must pass through the first set of doors and allow them to close and lock before the second set of doors will open. A mantrap provides a convenient way to control physical access to a secure space.

- **Access lists**—These are lists of personnel authorized to access a physical resource.
- **Proximity readers**—Sensors can read smartcards or devices that are close to the reader to grant access to secure areas or resources to any individual carrying the proper device or smart card.
- **Biometrics**—This is a form of access control based on some physical characteristic or action.
- **Protected access (cabling)**—This involves limiting connectivity to secure IT components by restricting access to connecting cabling.
- **Alarms**—This refers to any signal generated by a control that matches a list of events that warrant immediate action.

Environmental and physical controls are not solely dedicated to security. One important part that most of these controls play is that of personnel safety. The controls listed previously all contribute to a safe environment for your personnel. Additionally, a robust personnel safety plan should include the following:

- **Escape plans**—A primary personnel safety plan that tells each person how to escape in the face of a disruption, including where to go once outside the immediate danger area.
- **Escape routes**—In addition to an escape plan, personnel need to know the best routes to use to escape a disruption. Ideally, each escape route should end up at a defined rally point to allow management to determine whether anyone is missing.
- **Drills**—Crucial walkthrough tests of personnel safety plans. Drills are essential for all personnel to know how to react in the face of a disruption.
- **Control testing**—All controls, regardless of type, should be periodically tested to ensure that they are performing as designed.

There is an unlimited number of possible countermeasures. A countermeasure must have a clearly defined purpose. It must address a risk and reduce a vulnerability. A countermeasure (or control) without an exposure (risk) is a solution seeking a problem. Some specific purposes of countermeasures include the following:

- Fix known exploitable software flaws
- Develop and enforce operational procedures and access controls (data and system)
- Provide encryption capability
- Improve physical security
- Disconnect unreliable networks

Everyone needs to be aware of his or her security responsibilities. Security will be a full-time job for some people. Others will have only infrequent responsibilities, such as locking the door on the way out. Some specific security responsibilities that you may hold include the following:

- Delete redundant/guest accounts
- Train system administrators (specific training)
- Train everybody (general training)
- Install virus-scanning software
- Install IDS/IPS and network-scanning tools

Pricing/Costing a Countermeasure: You must consider many factors in evaluating countermeasures:

- **Product cost**—The price of the product will include its base price, the price of additional features, and costs associated with the service-level agreement or annual maintenance.
- **Implementation cost**—This refers to costs associated with changes to the infrastructure, construction, design, and training. An example is the cost of reinforcing a floor to install new equipment.
- **Compatibility cost**—The countermeasure must fit within (be compatible with) the overall structure. For example, a Windows-only organization would have to carefully consider the additional costs associated with training and interoperability when installing a Linux-based countermeasure.
- **Environmental cost**—If, for example, a countermeasure uses a lot of energy, you would need to consider whether your electric system would be able to provide that energy and to offset the excess heat it will generate.
- **Testing costs**—Testing does take time and money, but it is essential. Note, however, that testing also causes disruptions. You must consider all these as costs.
- **Productivity impact**—Many controls affect productivity. They might generate more calls to the help desk, slower response times for users, and so on.

> ▶ **TIP**
>
> Remember: The cost of a countermeasure is more than just the purchase price of a piece of technology.

Monitor and Control Risk Response

The most important part of putting any control or countermeasure in place is making sure it meets its objectives. The last step in the risk management process is to monitor and control deployed countermeasures. A countermeasure is of no value if it does not actually provide its intended benefit.

When evaluating a countermeasure, first ask, "What problem is this countermeasure designed to solve?" (Your risk management plan should make this clear.) Then ask, "Does this countermeasure solve this problem?" Here are some other points to consider:

- **Countermeasures might pose a new risk to the organization**—For example, implementing a countermeasure might create a false sense of security. Or the countermeasure itself might become a new point of failure on a critical system. Make sure you continuously monitor the countermeasure. Check it for compliance and good design, and perform regular maintenance.
- **You must perform certification and accreditation of countermeasure programs**—No system, control, or application should go into production without first going

through a change control process. This also applies to changes to existing production systems. You must review all controls and countermeasures before performing an installation or making changes. Otherwise, administrators might misconfigure the system or make other errors.

- **You must follow best practices and exercise due diligence**—A good risk management program tells auditors that the company is taking a prudent and diligent approach to security risks. Due diligence is exercised by frequently evaluating whether countermeasures are performing as expected.

Business Continuity Management

The way an organization responds to a disruption might well determine its survival. Poor planning greatly increases risk. With poor planning, an organization will not be able to respond appropriately and may be unable to return to normal operations. Planning for disruptions is part of business continuity management (BCM), which includes both of the following:

- **Business continuity plan (BCP)**—This plan contains the actions needed to keep critical business processes running after a disruption. Disruptions can be minor, such as a power outage, or major, such as weather damage that makes an organization's building unusable.

- **Disaster recovery plan (DRP)**—This plan details the steps to recover from a disruption and restore the infrastructure necessary for normal business operations.

BCM includes not only BCP and DRP but also crisis management, incident response management, and risk management.

A **disruption** is a sudden unplanned event. It upsets an organization's ability to provide critical business functions and causes great damage or loss. Examples of major disruptions include the following:

- **Extreme weather**—Superstorm Sandy in 2012 is one example.
- **Criminal activity**—This might include the theft of credit card numbers or other customer data.
- **Civil unrest/terrorist acts**—One example is the wave of violent protests in Missouri in 2014.
- **Operational**—An example is the electrical blackout in northern India in 2012, which affected nearly 9 percent of the world's population.
- **Application failure**—Two examples are Amazon's E2 cloud services crash in 2011 and Microsoft's cloud services crash in 2014. Businesses that depended on these cloud services had to find other ways to perform business operations until service was restored.

The purpose of BCM is to mitigate incidents and ensure continuity of operations. When an incident does occur, however, the first priority must always be to ensure the safety of people. Containing the damage is secondary.

Terminology

As a security professional, you must understand the following terms:

- **Business impact analysis (BIA)**—This is an analysis of the business to determine what kinds of events will have an impact on what systems. You should not limit the focus of the BIA to the information systems department and infrastructure; a business with a supply-chain disruption (warehouse fire, trucking strike, etc.) could easily suffer a major impact that has nothing to do with technology at all. Some scenarios will affect some departments, some will affect others, and a critical few will affect the entire business. You will learn more about BIA later in this chapter.

- **Critical business function (CBF)**—Once the BIA has identified the business systems that an incident will affect, you must rank the systems from most to least critical. That ranking determines whether the business can survive—and for how long—in the absence of a critical function.

- **Maximum tolerable downtime (MTD)**—MTD is the most time a business can survive without a particular critical system. A major disruption is any event that makes a CBF unavailable for longer than its MTD. Each of the disaster-planning and mitigation solutions must be able to recover CBFs within their MTDs. Systems and functions with the shortest MTDs are often the most critical. The next section covers this topic in more detail.

- **Recovery time objective (RTO)**—RTO is the timeframe for restoring a CBF. RTO must be shorter than or equal to the MTD.

- **Recovery point objective (RPO)**—Incidents can cause loss of data. You must calculate the amount of tolerable data loss for each business function. Recovery procedures must be able to meet the minimums defined here. If the business can afford to lose up to one day's data, then nightly backups might be an acceptable solution. However, if the business must prevent all data loss, a redundant server or storage solution will be required.

- **Emergency operations center (EOC)**—The EOC is the place where the recovery team will meet and work during a disruption. Many businesses have more than one **emergency operations center**. One might be nearby—for use in the event of a building fire, for example. Another might be a significant distance away—for example, for use in the event of an earthquake or regional power outage.

Here is how MTD and RTO work together. Suppose power goes out in the data center. It takes six hours to move to the alternate site (RTO). The business can survive for nine hours without a functioning data center. At this point, there is an event but not yet an incident that you can define as a major disruption or disaster. If you expect power to return within three hours (MTD − RTO), the business might not declare a disaster in anticipation that activity will resume normally. However, if power is still out at the three-hour mark, it is time to declare a major disruption.

> ▶ **TIP**
>
> When considering how often devices may fail, there are a few other terms that you should know. Be familiar with these terms:
>
> - **Mean time to failure (MTTF)**—Average time a device will function before it fails.
> - **Mean time between failures (MTBF)**—Average time between failures (assuming that failures are repaired).
> - **Mean time to repair (MTTR)**—Average time it takes to repair a device and return it to service.

In this example, the three-hour mark is a critical milestone. Imagine that the organization chose not to switch operations to the alternate site at the three-hour mark. Instead, it waited four hours. Because it takes six hours to switch over to the alternate site, the organization will suffer a total loss of 10 hours. This is beyond the MTD of nine hours. While a single hour may not seem like much, it is based on the established MTD. It may be that the data center provides services to other organizations. Service-level agreements dictate outages no longer than nine hours, with monetary penalties for longer outages. That extra hour could cost the organization tens of thousands of dollars (or even more).

Of course, the best way to avoid ever being down longer than your MTD is to never be down in the first place. One important aspect of BCM is providing controls to avoid downtime whenever possible. IT contingency planning addresses how to handle components being out of service, but high-availability planning addresses how to keep critical components operational at all times. High-availability planning involves identifying any critical components and ensuring that their failure doesn't take the whole business process down. Any component that, if it fails, could interrupt business processing is called a **single point of failure (SPOF)**. One goal of BCM is to eliminate all critical SPOFs. For example, suppose your organization uses a single ISP. If the link to your ISP fails, you have no Internet connectivity. One way to address this SPOF is by purchasing Internet service from another ISP as well as your primary ISP. Deploying two or more components that are capable of providing the same service, called **redundancy**, helps increase an organization's ability to avoid downtime (which also called **fault tolerance**).

NOTE

Organizations often provide fault tolerance by deploying redundant components. Some common ways to provide fault tolerance include these:

- **Redundant Array of Inexpensive Disks (RAID)**—These are multiple disk drives that appear as a single disk driver but actually store multiple copies of data in case a disk drive in the array fails. RAID can be deployed with different levels of redundancy.
- **Clustering**—Clustering involves connecting two or more computers to act like a single computer. If one component of a cluster fails, the other component(s) continue operating without crashing.
- **Load balancing**—This is using two or more servers to respond to service requests. When one server is busy, the other servers will respond to requests. This differs from clustering in that load-balancing servers are separate servers and do not coordinate beyond network messaging.
- **Multiple servers or devices**—A more generalized implementation of load balancing simply makes multiple servers or network devices that can respond to the same requests for service available. A failure of one device does not stop all processing. The redundant servers or devices can continue operating.

Assessing Maximum Tolerable Downtime

You determine **maximum tolerable downtime (MTD)** by business requirements. This is closely associated with the RTOs of several integrated functions. For example, consider a website hosted by an organization for purposes of e-commerce. The web servers depend on network services, ISP availability, and electricity. Each of these will have its own incident-dependent RTO, but it will be associated with the MTD.

For example, if you determine that the website has an MTD of four hours, the RTO of the failed network services, ISP availability, and electricity all must be less than four hours. Parts of the recovery will be able to take place in parallel, but some might have to be sequential. In this example, you can't recover network services until you've restored the power. However, once you get power back on, you can work on restoring network services and ISP availability at the same time.

The RPO defines the amount of tolerable data loss. The RPO can come from the business impact analysis or sometimes from a government mandate—for example, banking laws or regulations

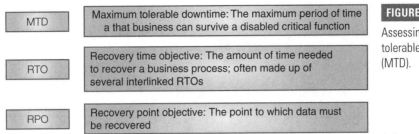

FIGURE 8-6

Assessing maximum tolerable downtime (MTD).

pertaining to pharmaceutical research data retention. **FIGURE 8-6** shows how to assess the MTD, RTO, and RPO.

Business Impact Analysis

A BIA determines the extent of the impact that a particular incident would have on business operations over time. The BIA drives the choice of the recovery strategy and the CBFs.

As a security professional, your job is to ask two questions:

- What can affect the business?
- How will it affect the business?

A successful BIA maps the context, the critical business functions, and the processes on which they rely. You should consider all impacts, including those that are hard to address or are less obvious. Different incidents require different recovery strategies. A fire in the accounting department might call for outsourcing and temporary quarters. A flood in the basement might activate a service bureau plan. An earthquake or hurricane might cause a permanent move to a new facility.

You conduct a business impact analysis for three key reasons:

- To set the value of each business unit or resource as it relates to how the entire organization operates
- To identify the critical needs to develop a business recovery plan
- To set the order or priority for restoring the organization's functions after a disruption

Speed of Impact

Some incidents might become more significant over time. The slow deterioration of a critical processing facility might generate a disaster. Continuous installation of new devices in a computer room might overtax the electrical supply capacity and eventually cause a blackout or a fire.

Some systems are more important during certain times of the year. A company that supplies heating oil is busier in the winter. Even the smallest outage in the winter can jeopardize that company's service agreements. That same company might easily withstand far more severe incidents (longer MTDs) in the summer, when load is minimal.

Critical Dependencies

The BIA must identify what your organization needs to support a company's critical operations:

- Information processing
- Personnel

- Communications
- Equipment
- Facilities
- Other organizational functions
- Vendors
- Suppliers

Assessing the Impact of Downtime

The BIA will identify critical data and systems. Note that the importance of systems and the importance of data are not always the same. A system might be more critical than the data it contains, and vice versa. What is truly important is those systems and data on which the business relies.

Issues you should consider during the BIA fall under the following categories:

- **People**—How will you notify them of the incident and its impact? How will you evacuate, transport, and care for employees (including, for example, paying them)? Who will step in if key personnel are incapacitated or unavailable? (This is called **succession planning**.)
- **Systems**—What portions of your computing and telecommunications infrastructure must you duplicate immediately? How long do you have—a minute, an hour, a day?
- **Data**—What data are critical to running your business? How will you recover critical data that are lost?
- **Property**—What items are essential to your business? Things like tools, supplies, and special forms all must be recoverable or easily replaced.

Assessing the impact of downtime is a planning step in the BIA. You are helping to determine what must be done and in what order to accomplish the goals described in these four categories. Figuring out how to do this is the main thrust of BCM.

Plan Review

You must update and regularly maintain the BCP and the inventory and configuration lists for the systems and applications. Some firms do this annually. Others choose different periods. In addition to the scheduled reviews, any major changes to the company should trigger a review. Besides the obvious benefit of having an up-to-date plan, testing and planning revisions are excellent ways to train new employees. Taking new employees through a hands-on process teaches them your procedures and more about your environment.

Testing the Plan

You should not accept any BCP or DRP without thorough testing. This helps ensure that the plan will work and that you will meet the CBF, MTD, RPO, and RTO objectives. Each stage of the test must consider the continued need for security and the technical resources required both to perform the test and to handle an actual disaster.

Checklist Test

A **checklist test** is a simple review of the plan by managers and the business continuity team to make sure that contact numbers are current and that the plan reflects the company's priorities and structure. This kind of check is a desk check. Each team member checks his or her portion of the plan while sitting at his or her desk. As well as checking their contact lists, team members review whether changes in their departments affect the plan. They also look at expected changes in their departments to see if they will trigger a need to update the plan.

Structured Walk-Through Test

A structured walk-through test is a tabletop exercise. During this test, a team of representatives from each department should do the following:

- Present their portion of the plan to the other teams.
- Review the goals of the plan for completeness and correctness.
- Affirm the scope of the plan as well as any assumptions made.
- Look for overlaps and gaps.
- Review the structure of the organization as well as the reporting/communications structure.
- Evaluate the testing, maintenance, and training requirements.
- Conduct a number of scenario-based exercises to evaluate the plan's effectiveness.
- Meet to step through the plan together in a structured manner.

In the case of the final step, team members should act as though they are executing the plan for a certain type of incident. The goal of the structured walk-through is to find errors in each department's plans, such as gaps or overlaps. Gaps are where one department is under the impression a critical task was to be handled by a different department. Overlaps are situations where two departments think they'll have exclusive (or majority) use of the same resource—for example, two departments think they'll have two-thirds of the replacement desktops.

Simulation Test

A **simulation test** is more than a paper exercise. It requires more planning than a walk-through. All the members of the staff involved in the operations/procedures participate in the test. The test identifies the following:

- Staff reaction and response times
- Inefficiencies or previously unidentified vulnerabilities

You should conduct the simulation on site using only countermeasures defined in the plan. The simulation test involves many of the employees who have not yet participated in plan development. It is common to conduct simulations on an off day, such as a weekend.

The purpose of the simulation test is to identify shortcomings. You should carry out the test as far as possible. If, for example, a critical file is missing, the file should be generated or obtained from the main site and the test should then continue. Ensure that you log any on-the-spot corrections for evaluation and plan to update later. The test should end only when it is completed or if it becomes impossible to continue.

Parallel Test

Most organizations conduct **parallel tests** at the alternate site. A parallel test is the same as a full-interruption test (covered in the next section) except that processing does not stop at the primary site. Here are a few key points with respect to parallel tests:

- A parallel test is an operational test, so it will not include representatives from HR, PR, purchasing, facilities, etc.
- Because a parallel test means activating the alternate site, it will cost a significant amount of money. The test must have senior management approval.
- Compare the results of the test with the processing at the original site.
- A gap analysis exposes any weaknesses or underperformance that requires attention.
- Usually auditors are involved at every step to monitor the success and to make sure the parallel-run data are not mixed into the normal operational data.

Full-Interruption Test

The most common way to conduct this type of test is at the alternate site. This type of test is so disruptive that few organizations conduct it. During the test, you must shut down the original system for the duration. You can use only those processes that exist at the alternate site to continue the business operations.

> ⚠ **WARNING**
>
> This test is high risk! Running a full-interruption test can actually create a disaster. You should run a full-interruption test only after you have successfully run all other types of tests. You must obtain senior management approval prior to the test.

Backing Up Data and Applications

Recovery is possible only if the company has access to backups of its data and applications. Plans must include dealing with backup storage media, location, and access. Tape backup is the traditional choice for backup and still the most common. However, restoration from tape is slow, and many systems have RTOs that are shorter than the tape-restore time. These kinds of sites often use disk-based solutions such as a storage area network (SAN), network attached server (NAS), or even an offsite network-based storage such as **remote journaling**. In remote journaling, the system writes a log of online transactions to an offsite location. The log updates a copy of the database. Should the primary site go down, the offsite copy would be current.

Backups provide extra copies of needed resources, such as data, documentation, and equipment. You can activate a backup site if a primary site goes down. Similarly, you can restore a backup tape, possibly at an alternate site. Then processing can resume.

Types of Backups

Backups and restores are slow. Businesses have three alternatives for processing them:

- **Full backup**. As its name implies, this backup copies everything to a backup media. It is usually tape, but is sometimes CD, DVD, or disk.

Backups Versus Redundancy

Redundancy, or fault-tolerance options, provides for alternate resources if a primary resource fails. In other words, a system can experience a fault but tolerate it and keep operating. However, you must know that redundancies are not replacements for backups.

For example, RAID 1 mirroring writes data to two disks instead of one. Should one disk fail, the system can continue to operate. The data are still available on the second disk. However, imagine that you have a server protected with RAID. If a catastrophic failure in the server destroys all the drives, the data are gone. If you don't have a backup, the data are gone forever.

Similarly, you can set up clustered servers so that standby servers take over if the primary server fails. Again, though, just because a service is using a cluster for fault tolerance, you still need backups.

- **Differential backup**—With this type of backup, you start by making a full backup, perhaps on Sunday, when network traffic is lightest. On Monday through Saturday, you back up changes made since Sunday's full backup on a daily basis. As the week progresses, each night's backup (the differential) takes a little longer.
- **Incremental backup**—Again, you start with a full backup when network traffic is light. Then, each night, you back up only that day's changes. As the week progresses, the nightly (incremental) backup takes about the same amount of time.

It is faster to create the incremental weekday backups than the differential backups. This comes at a price, however. If you need to use the backup images to restore data, systems using differential backups would need to restore only the full backup and then the latest differential. Those using incremental backups would need to restore the full backup and then each day's incremental backups to complete the restore.

You should back up items other than just data. These include router, switch, and other network device configurations, user access permissions and configurations (e.g., Active Directory), and server/workstation operating systems and configurations. To make this more manageable, most large companies have a standard base configuration for workstations that can be reloaded on demand. As long as you keep these up to date (patched and fixed), this is an attractive solution.

Incident Handling

As a reminder, an incident is an event that results in an actual or threatened violation of security policy. When an incident occurs, an organization needs to respond. The incident-handling process includes the following steps:

- Preparation
- Identification
- Notification

> ▶ **TIP**
>
> Remember that minimizing downtime is often about avoiding downtime. Often the simplest way to avoid downtime is to ensure that all computers and devices are patched with the latest security fixes. Patching makes your systems more resistant to many types of attacks and less reliant on redundancy and other fault-tolerance techniques.

- Response
- Recovery and followup
- Documentation

You will learn about each of these steps in the following sections.

Preparation

The first step in an incident response program is to plan how to best respond to a variety of incidents and to build the **incident response team (IRT)**. The IRT will have the training and documentation to respond to incidents as they occur. Members of the IRT should be comfortable enough with one another to communicate freely and handle each incident in a professional manner. The quality of the planning phase determines how well the IRT can handle incidents.

Identification

The first step in actually handling an incident is to determine whether an incident has in fact taken place. Not all events are incidents. You must find out if the incident is serious or whether it is a common, benign occurrence. This is triage—prioritizing the incident. You may receive initial notification of an incident from an alarm, a complaint from a user, an alert from a security vendor, or a log analysis. Make sure you have the procedures in place to react to any type of incident.

Notification

You or another IRT member often will be one of the first people aware of an incident and must know how to react. As a first responder, it is important that you handle the incident properly from the beginning. The goal is to contain the incident and, if possible, to improve the situation. Take care not to make the situation worse. You must find out whether the event is a false positive. Be careful to make sure several false positives do not cause you to become desensitized to real events. A series of seemingly individual events taken independently might not justify a response. However, when taken collectively, they might be important.

You must know how and when to escalate and whom to notify. This works well when you plan response scenarios and train incident-response team members.

Courts and Evidence: The Forensics Process

From time to time, an incident will be the grounds for a civil or even a criminal case. Therefore, you should handle all investigations with care to make sure evidence is not tainted or made inadmissible. Always collect the most volatile data first. Volatile data are data that may change in the near future. The order of volatility (and the order in which you should collect data) is:

1. RAM
2. Swap and paging files

3. Files on disk

4. Logs

5. Archived data

Even if an incident does not end up in court, the threat of court action might be enough to meet the company's needs. For example, rather than prosecuting someone, the company might choose to force a resignation.

The laws of individual countries vary, but the following is true nearly everywhere: Once something makes evidence inadmissible, you can't fix it.

In all common-law countries (and many countries that follow civil law), evidence must be shown to be authentic. In other words, you must prove the evidence was not altered after the incident. That means you have to capture a system image as early as possible and then conduct all analysis on the copy of the image. Doing this ensures that you won't accidentally modify the original evidence. Then you can capture any network traffic and logs, along with video or other media, with appropriate time-stamps. A chain of custody shows how the evidence was gathered and documented. The document lists everyone who had contact with the evidence since its discovery. It shows how it was handled, what was done to it, and how it was protected from alteration.

To demonstrate that all evidence is valid and in the same condition as it was when collected, you can create hashes, take screenshots, and even use witnesses to the event and the collection activities. Make sure that you keep detailed records of all time and expenses used in the forensics processes. You may need to quantify the work needed to collect the evidence. And finally, once you have all of the collected data, you can use analysis techniques, especially emerging big data techniques, to extract useful information from all of the collected data.

Response

Once you identify an incident, the next phase is to limit the damage. An important aspect of this step is containment. Many incidents grow and expand rapidly, possibly affecting other systems, departments, and even business partners. The incident response plan must outline the steps that must be taken to stop the spread of the incident without causing unnecessary outage. For example, if a virus infects a system, a simple way to contain the threat is to unplug the system from the network.

It is essential to have a plan. The odds are slim of correctly guessing the best course of action in the middle of an incident. Remember, people who have the benefit of time and hindsight will evaluate your response after the incident. A preapproved response plan will lead to a better, more effective response while also providing you with blame reduction.

It is essential to identify the source and type of incident so that you can enact proper recovery procedures. Fixing symptoms doesn't solve problems. The responders must find out the extent of the damage and possibly recommend the initiation of the disaster recovery plan if the damage is too severe. A key component of incident management is preventing future incidents. The logs and documentation gathered during the incident must be protected and available for future analysis.

Recovery

After you have contained the incident and eliminated or blocked its source, it is time to recover. Before turning the system over to its normal use, you must deal with the exploited vulnerability so that it doesn't happen again right away. You might need to rebuild systems using uninfected application and data backups. You might also have to clean malicious content from the system to prevent reinfection.

Followup

Learning from the incident will let management establish new procedures and controls to prevent or react to an incident more effectively in the future. It is important to conduct a lessons-learned review of each incident to capture valuable information the IRT can use for future incidents.

Documentation and Reporting

Don't ignore the importance of documenting every step in the incident response process. The documentation you create can be very valuable to the quality of future incidents. You can improve your incident response plan any time you document what actions worked well and those that did not. As you accumulate incident response documentation, you build a valuable resource. You can use this resource to make changes to your incident response plan and your normal security policies and procedures. For example, documenting multiple incidents related to unauthorized personnel in the data center may indicate a need for better controls. Use the information you gain from documenting incident response. It can make your organization more secure.

Recovery from a Disaster

The disaster recovery plan (DRP) does three things:

- It establishes an emergency operations center (EOC) as an alternate location from which the BCP/DRP will be coordinated and implemented.
- It names an EOC manager.
- It determines when that manager should declare an incident a disaster.

A DRP enables you to make critical decisions ahead of time. That way, you can manage and review decisions without the urgency of an actual disaster. If you do not create these plans in advance, you and your managers will have to make best-guess decisions under huge pressure.

DRPs are long-term, time-consuming, expensive projects. The DRP for a large company can cost tens of millions of dollars. It is essential that senior management not only support but also insist upon an effective, well-tested DRP.

The process starts with a business analysis. It identifies critical functions and their maximum tolerable downtimes. Then it identifies strategies for dealing with a wide variety of scenarios that might trigger the plan. As a security professional, you most likely will participate as a member of the disaster-planning and disaster-recovery teams.

Activating the Disaster Recovery Plan

As a security professional, you will play a key role in reestablishing business operations in a crisis by rebuilding the networks and systems that the business requires. The recovery process involves two main phases. The first phase is to restore business operations. In many cases, the recovery might be at an alternate site. You may be required to build a network rapidly from available backup data, backup equipment, and any equipment that might be available from vendors.

The second phase is to return operations to their original state before the disaster. To return to normal operations, you must rebuild the primary site. The transition back to the normal site and the closure of the alternate site should be part of the "Return to Home Site" portion of the BCP/DRP.

Activate salvage and repair teams. They will do their work before people and data can return to the primary site. Security professionals are often on the repair team to rebuild the damaged parts of the network infrastructure. They will match—or increase—previous security levels. If you need new equipment, use this opportunity to improve security.

> **NOTE**
> Remember: A disaster is an event that prevents a critical business function (CBF) from operating for a period greater than the maximum tolerable downtime (MTD).

Operating in a Reduced/Modified Environment

During a crisis, many of the normal conditions, such as controls, support, and processes, might not be available. You must adapt quickly to ensure the secure operation of systems, including backups and reconciliation of errors. Here are a few points to keep in mind:

- You may want to suspend normal processes, such as separation of duties or spending limits. You should compensate with additional controls or by additional auditing. The DRP should give added privileges or spending authority to certain people or for certain tasks.
- If a number of systems are down, users might need more technical support or guidance on how to use alternate systems or access. The BIAs should have identified minimum recovery resources as part of the recovery needs.
- During a disaster and recovery, it might be good to combine services that were on different hardware platforms onto common servers. This might speed up recovery. However, you must manage this process carefully to make sure that the movement and recovery goes smoothly.
- While running at the alternate site, you must continue to make backups of data and systems. This might prevent new disasters if the recovery site fails.

> **NOTE**
> DRPs can lower insurance rates, and the preparation of a DRP can assist in risk management efforts.

> **Primary Steps to Disaster Recovery**
>
> The primary steps to disaster recovery (in order of importance) are:
>
> 1. Ensure the safety of individuals.
> 2. Contain the damage.
> 3. Assess the damage and begin recovery operations according to the DCP and BCP.

8

Risk, Response, and Recovery

Restoring Damaged Systems

You must plan for rebuilding damaged systems. You need to know where to get configuration charts, inventory lists, and backup applications and data. You must have access control lists to make sure that the system allows only legitimate users on it. Keep the following points in mind:

- Once the rebuilding starts, the administrator must make sure to update the operating systems and applications with the most current patches. Backups or installation disks often contain older versions that are not current.
- After you rebuild the system, you must restore the data to the RPO. This includes reconciling books and records. You must make sure the operating systems and applications are current and secure.
- Some organizations overlook access control permissions in recovery plans. You must activate the access control rules, directories, and remote access systems to permit users to get on the new systems. When you are making the plan, be sure that any vendor software will run on alternate processors. Some vendors license their products to operate only on a certain CPU.

Disaster Recovery Issues

Here is a short list of disaster recovery issues that are often overlooked in the maintenance and execution of a DRP.

- **Generators**—Ensure all fuel is fresh and contracts are in place to guarantee a supply of fuel in a crisis. Generators must receive routine maintenance and should be run periodically to make sure they are ready to operate and capable of carrying the expected system load.
- **Safety of damaged site**—You must protect the primary (damaged) site from further damage or looting.
- **Reentry**—You must examine the damaged site using people who are qualified to determine whether it is safe for humans to reenter.
- **Transportation of equipment and backups**—The plan must provide safe transportation of people, equipment, and backup data to and from the alternate site.
- **Communications and networks**—Regular telephone service often fails in a crisis. You might need an alternate method of communication, especially among key team members.

Recovery Alternatives

A business continuity coordinator considers each alternative's ability to support critical business functions, its operational readiness compared with RTO, and the associated cost. He or she examines specifications for workspace, security requirements, IT, and telecommunications.

Three choices usually are considered if a business (or some part of it) has to be moved for recovery:

- A dedicated site operated by the business, such as a secondary processing center
- A commercially leased facility, such as a hot site or mobile facility
- An agreement with an internal or external facility

External commercial providers offer services to many organizations. That means if there is a disaster, it could affect many customers of a commercial provider. What priority will you have if this happens? Know your options (along with prices) for things such as test time, declaration, fees, and minimum/maximum recovery days. Make sure that the specifications for workspace, security requirements, IT, and telecommunications are suitable for your critical business functions. Ensure that suitable accommodations are available for staff, including facilities for resting and showering, as well as catering.

No matter what choice your business makes, the IT department's job is to make sure all necessary equipment is available at the alternate site. This includes the critical files, documentation, and other items identified in the recovery categories. Other items can include additional patch cables, USB drives, or other common items IT personnel may use on a daily basis.

Interim or Alternate Processing Strategies

Regardless where you choose to continue operations, you'll need a location to support your IT infrastructure. There are several options available, depending on cost and the time it takes to become operational. Here are the most common recovery location options:

- An alternate processing center or mirrored site is always ready and under the organization's control. It is the most expensive option because it requires fully redundant or duplicate operations and synchronized data. The organization operates it continuously. Its additional costs might be justified by business needs (such as having a duplicate support staff) other than recovery planning. However, making cost allocations is complex.
- A hot site is one that can take over operations quickly. It has all the equipment and data already staged at the location, though you may need to refresh or update the data. There are two kinds of hot sites. One is company owned and dedicated. The other is a commercial hot site. The hot site's advantage is that it can provide alternative computing facilities quickly, allowing rapid recovery. An internally owned hot site will be more expensive than some other alternatives, but no one else will compete for it during a regional disaster.
- A warm site has some common IT, communications, power, and HVAC, but you will have to purchase and deliver IT equipment such as servers and communications. You will have to retrieve and load data as well. Many organizations own warm sites and often use them for offsite data storage.
- A cold site is an empty data center with HVAC and power. It is the least expensive option. It requires a lot of time to get up and running because you must purchase, deliver, and configure all equipment and telecommunications. Some organizations begin recovery in a hot site and transfer over to a warm site or cold site if the interruption lasts a long time.

TABLE 8-2 Comparing common recovery site options.

FEATURE	HOT SITE	WARM SITE	COLD SITE	MULTIPLE SITES
Cost	High	Medium	Low	No direct costs
Computer equipped	Yes	Yes	No	Yes
Connectivity equipped	Yes	Yes	No	Yes
Data equipped	Yes	No	No	Yes
Staffed	Yes	No	No	Yes
Typical lead time to readiness	Minutes to hours	Hours to days	Days to weeks	Moments to minutes

TABLE 8-2 compares the most common recovery site options.

Processing Agreements

One way to solve recovery problems is to find organizations with similar IT configurations and backup technologies. This could be another company, a contingent carrier, or a service bureau. You then forge an agreement with the other organization to provide support if your company encounters a disaster. IT, security, and legal departments should carefully review draft agreements.

Reciprocal or Mutual Aid

Your company might enter into a reciprocal agreement, also known as **mutual aid** or a **consortium agreement**, with a company that has similar technology. In a consortium agreement, a number of companies agree to support each other. You must carefully consider this approach. For example, can each organization continue its primary business while supporting another? Can the equipment and infrastructure support both organizations? You must do tests to confirm that all systems can handle the extra load and that they are compatible. You also must consider the sensitivity of the data and any regulations that apply to it. The partners' administrators or users might be able to access it. Both parties must warn each other if they upgrade or retire technology that could make their systems incompatible.

Reciprocal Centers

Reciprocal centers often involve businesses that do the same type of work but are not direct competitors. These might include cross-town hospitals or a paperback book publisher paired with a hardcover publisher. Familiarity and commonality have advantages. They may share special codes, industry jargon, and special forms needed in the industry. For example, hospitals use the term "DRG code." It refers to a number that corresponds, in a common database, to a diagnosis, procedure, or disease.

Contingency

An organization might contract for contingency carriers or contingent suppliers if its primary supply method fails. You need to consider maintenance fees and activation time. You also need to check whether the carriers, especially communications carriers, share the same cable or routing paths. It is prudent to ask them.

Service Bureau

A **service bureau** is a service provider that has extra capacity. An example is a call center to handle incoming calls. Your organization can contract for emergency use of it. This can raise the same concerns as those with a reciprocal agreement arrangement. The vendor might increase its business and consume its extra capacity, or the vendor might modify its hardware or configurations.

Using the Cloud

Cloud computing has become very popular in recent years. It is expected that more organizations will incorporate the cloud into at least some of their IT environment. Since cloud computing is based on virtualization, it is easy to copy entire server images from place to place. This technique makes maintaining disaster recovery sites much more affordable. Nearly any organization can maintain a cloud-based disaster recovery site for a fraction of the cost of a physical site.

All of the options you learned about in this chapter are available in the cloud. Cloud-based disaster recovery sites can exist as cold, warm, or hot sites. An even less expensive option is to just back up critical files to cloud-based storage. Of course, you must consider the time required to recover if the primary site fails.

The common virtualization snapshot feature is useful in disaster recovery. You can create a virtual machine (VM) image with all desired patches applied. A snapshot of the desired VM makes a great starting point for a recovery image. Virtualization makes it possible to launch as many virtual alternate sites as necessary to support your operations until you can restore your primary data center. Cloud computing opens more recovery options by potentially lowering the cost of setting up and maintaining alternate environments. As you should do whenever you consider any change to your IT environment, evaluate how using the cloud affects security. You will still have to test all your security controls, even when using virtualization, but this new technology provides many benefits to responding to interruptions or incidents. You don't just have to use virtualization for disaster recovery. You can spin up VM images as isolated servers, or **sandboxes**, if you need to conduct testing that shouldn't affect operations. The options are plentiful. However, as always, you must ensure that you are meeting or exceeding your security policy, regardless of where you choose to store your data or conduct your processing.

CHAPTER SUMMARY

In this chapter, you learned three core principles of information security:

- Identify the risks to the organization.
- Prevent damage as much as possible by using controls.

- Have plans and procedures ready to react to incidents that you cannot prevent. You can express these principles and controls in terms of people, processes, technology, and data.

In this chapter, you learned about the reasons and processes of risk management. You learned how a business continuity plan (BCP) helps you make sure a disruption doesn't put your organization out of business. You learned about risk assessment, including the difference between a quantitative risk assessment and a qualitative risk assessment. You learned the most common responses to risk and how they help you develop a risk reduction strategy. You learned about countermeasures and how to evaluate them.

You learned the three types of activity controls and how they correspond to the security life cycle. You learned how response determines your organization's ability to deal with disruptions and disasters. You learned the three types of backups and what backup models you can use to recover from a disruption. Additionally, you learned the steps you must take for incident response and the role incident response plays in the risk, response, and recovery processes. Finally, you learned the main steps to disaster recovery and the roles you play throughout the disaster recovery plan.

KEY CONCEPTS AND TERMS

Activity phase controls
Administrative control
Annualized rate of occurrence (ARO)
Barricades
Checklist test
Clustering
Compensating controls
Consortium agreement
Control
Corrective control
Countermeasure
Detective control
Deterrent control
Disruption
Emergency operations center (EOC)
EMI shielding
Event
Fault tolerance

Impact
Incident
Incident response team
Likelihood
Load balancing
Loss expectancy
Management control
Mantrap
Maximum tolerable downtime (MTD)
Mean time between failures (MTBF)
Mutual aid
Operational control
Parallel tests
Preventive control
Proximity reader
Qualitative risk assessment
Quantitative risk assessment
Reciprocal centers

Redundancy
Redundant Array of Inexpensive Disks (RAID)
Remote journaling
Residual risk
Risk
Risk register
Safeguard
Sandbox
Service bureau
Simulation test
Single point of failure (SPOF)
Static environments
Succession planning
Technical control
Threat
Total risk
Vulnerability

CHAPTER 8 ASSESSMENT

1. A plan that contains the actions needed to keep critical business processes running after a disruption is called a _____.

   A. Disaster recovery plan (DRP)
   B. Business impact analysis (BIA)
   C. Business continuity plan (BCP)
   D. None of the above

2. A plan that details the steps to recover from a major disruption and restore the infrastructure necessary for normal business operations is a _____.

   A. Disaster recovery plan (DRP)
   B. Business impact analysis (BIA)
   C. Business continuity plan (BCP)
   D. None of the above

3. A vulnerability is any exposure that could allow a threat to be realized.

   A. True
   B. False

4. An IDS is what type of control?

   A. Detective control
   B. Preventive control
   C. Corrective control
   D. Compensating control
   E. All of the above

5. _____ is the limit of time that a business can survive without a particular critical system.

   A. Recovery time objective (RTO)
   B. Critical business function (CBF)
   C. Maximum tolerable downtime (MTD)
   D. None of the above

6. The incident-handling process includes which of the following?

   A. Documentation
   B. Response
   C. Notification
   D. Recovery and followup
   E. All of the above

7. The primary steps to disaster recovery include the safety of individuals, containing the damage, and assessing the damage and beginning the recovery operations.

   A. True
   B. False

8. Any event that either violates or threatens to violate your security policy is known as a(n) _____.

   A. Countermeasure
   B. Impact
   C. Risk
   D. Incident

9. The process of describing a risk scenario and then determining the degree of impact that event would have on business operations is quantitative risk analysis.

   A. True
   B. False

10. Risk that remains even after risk mitigation efforts have been implemented is known as _____ risk.

    A. Qualitative
    B. Quantitative
    C. Residual
    D. None of the above

8

Risk, Response, and Recovery

Cryptography

ACCORDING TO *Webster's Revised Unabridged Dictionary*, cryptography is "the act or art of writing in secret characters." The Free Online Dictionary of Computing says cryptography is "encoding data so that it can only be decoded by specific individuals." The algorithms, or ciphers, used to encrypt and decrypt data are collectively called a **cryptosystem**. Most ciphers take unencrypted data, called **plaintext**, and use one or more keys to transform the plaintext into a secret message. A **key** is a string of numbers or characters known only to the sender and/or recipient. The resulting secret message is **ciphertext**.

The security of a cryptosystem usually depends on the secrecy of the keys rather than the secrecy of the cipher. A strong cryptosystem has a large range of possible keys, making it impossible to try them all in a brute-force attack. A strong system should also produce ciphertext that appears random to all standard statistical tests and resists all known previous methods for breaking codes. The process of breaking codes is **cryptanalysis**.

Essentially, **cryptography** is the art of concealing information from others. You can find cryptography practiced in business and government as well as in personal transactions. Cryptography is not the only way to make information secure. Rather, it is a set of tools for IT security.

Cryptography accomplishes four security goals:

- Confidentiality
- Integrity
- Authentication
- Nonrepudiation

The IT security professional creatively uses these cryptographic tools to meet businesses' security goals.

Chapter 9 Topics

This chapter covers the following topics and concepts:

- What cryptography is
- How cryptography can address business and security requirements
- What cryptographic applications are used in information system security
- What cryptographic principles, concepts, and terminology are

- What cryptographic applications, tools, and resources are
- What the principles of certificates and key management are

Chapter 9 Goals

When you complete this chapter, you will be able to:

- Define the basic concepts of cryptography
- Describe symmetric, asymmetric, and hashing algorithms
- Examine the various uses of cryptography
- Understand the challenges of cryptographic uses
- Define certificate management

What Is Cryptography?

Cryptography is the art of transforming a readable message into a form that is only readable by authorized users:

- **Unencrypted information**—Information in understandable form. Unencrypted information is **plaintext**, also called **cleartext**.
- **Encrypted information**—Information in scrambled form. Encrypted information is **ciphertext**.

Encryption is the process of scrambling plaintext into ciphertext. **Decryption** is the process of unscrambling ciphertext into plaintext.

Encryption uses known mathematical processes for performing its functions. Such a process is known as an **algorithm**. An algorithm is a repeatable process that produces the same result when it receives the same input. A **cipher** is an algorithm to encrypt or decrypt information. This repeatability is important to make sure that information, once encrypted, can be decrypted. **FIGURE 9-1** shows a cryptosystem at work.

Note that the algorithm you use to encrypt information may or may not be the same one you use to decrypt that information. For example, a simple algorithm that adds X to each value to encrypt would have to subtract X from each value to decrypt. In addition, some encryption algorithms have no decryption algorithms. These are **one-way algorithms**, or **hashing functions**. The output of a one-way algorithm is a **hash**. Hashing functions are useful to protect data from unauthorized changes. You will learn about how cryptography is used in various ways later in this chapter.

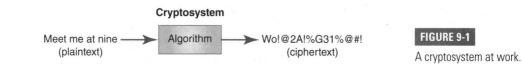

FIGURE 9-1

A cryptosystem at work.

Technical TIP

Not all cryptographic ciphers require keys. Some newer types of cryptographic algorithms derive their keys from other information. This approach is similar to access controls that use inputs other than passwords. For example, **identity-based encryption (IBE)** uses the encryptor's identity to derive a key. **Attribute-based encryption (ABE)** uses descriptive attributes to encrypt and decrypt data.

Most common encryption ciphers require plaintext and at least one key as input. The encryption cipher uses the cryptographic key to vary its output so that the intended correspondents can protect their information from anyone else who has the same cipher. By changing the key, you change the output of the cryptographic function, even if the plaintext remains the same.

Encryption ciphers fall into two general categories:

- Those that use the same key to encrypt and decrypt are **private (symmetric) key** ciphers.
- Those that use different keys to encrypt and decrypt are **public (asymmetric) key** ciphers.

Sometimes, the terms *public key* and *private key* refer to the two different keys in asymmetric ciphers. Together they are a key pair. To avoid confusion, the *symmetric* and *asymmetric* naming convention for ciphers is used here. Note, however, that many sources interchange these terms freely.

> **▶ TIP**
>
> **Key-stretching** techniques can make a weak key more resistant to brute-force attacks. A key-stretching function takes a key (generally a weak key) as input and generates an enhanced key that can withstand a more determined attack.

Basic Cryptographic Principles

A perfect cipher does not exist. Given sufficient time and resources, an attacker can eventually decrypt any ciphertext. The goal of cryptography is to make the cost or the time required to decrypt ciphertext without the key exceed the value of the protected information. Thus, you could effectively protect information that is worth no more than $100 with a cipher that costs $1,000 to break. This is an important concept. It provides one of the basic rationales for selecting cryptographic tools and ciphers.

The number of possible keys to a cipher is a **keyspace**. Without any knowledge of the key, an attacker with access to an encrypted message and the decryption cipher could try every possible key to decode the message. This is a brute-force attack. By making the keyspace large enough, you make the cost of a brute-force attack too high. Assuming that the cipher has no mathematical weaknesses, a larger keyspace usually means more security.

There are public (open-source) ciphers and hidden (closed-source or proprietary) ciphers. **Open ciphers** make it possible for experts around the world to examine the ciphers for weaknesses. Experts subject open-source ciphers to extensive analysis. They find flaws and weaknesses that could diminish the cipher's strength. Any cipher is far more secure if it withstands public scrutiny without anyone identifying major flaws. The most scrutinized cipher in history is the **Data Encryption Standard (DES)**, published in 1977 as Federal Information Processing Standard (FIPS) 46. Modern computing has searched its keyspace of 72 quadrillion keys without finding a single mathematical weakness.

A Brief History of Cryptography

People have used cryptography to protect information for at least 4,000 years. As soon as people learned to write, they sought to protect their words from prying eyes. Early information security was as simple as hiding it. This method is called **steganography**. For example, legend says that Histiaeus, tyrant of Miletus in the 5th century BCE, sent a message tattooed on the scalp of his slave. Any enemy intercepting the messenger would not likely find the information. However, this was not speedy. Miletus had to wait for the messenger's hair to grow back before sending him with the hidden message. In addition, reusability was something of a problem.

> ### ⚠ WARNING
> Always use proven cryptographic algorithms. Do not try to write your own algorithms. History shows that privately developed cryptographic algorithms are weaker than open algorithms. There is no substitute for allowing experts around the world to rigorously validate an algorithm's strength.

Steganography is still used today. A common way to use steganography is to embed a message into a large media file, such as a digital picture. Steganography software can alter a single bit for a range of addresses in a media file. For example, altering a single bit in a series of bytes doesn't alter the way the image appears to humans. To us, the image file, the carrier, appears unmodified. However, the steganography software has loaded the carrier with a secret payload. This method of hiding data makes it very difficult to identify, much less extract, the data. With most encryption algorithms, it is easy to identify ciphertext. It just looks like gibberish. Steganography is a growing concern since criminals are using it more frequently to hide communications from law enforcement authorities.

The science of cryptanalysis, or breaking codes, has been important for many years. Queen Elizabeth I had her cousin, Mary Queen of Scots, executed for treason. Why? Because Sir Francis Willingham cracked the secret code that Mary used to communicate with her co-conspirators. Thus, cryptanalysis altered the course of English history.

20th-Century Cryptography

In World Wars I and II, cryptography played an important role in communications. These were the first major wars in which combatants used radios. All countries used codes to protect communications. Many combatants successfully broke their opponents' codes, sometimes more than once. By decrypting the Japanese Purple cipher and the German Enigma, U.S. and British codebreakers gave military decision makers insight into enemy plans. These codebreakers helped the Allies win decisive military battles, including the Battle of Midway and the Battle of Britain.

The birth of the digital computer made complex ciphers feasible. Digital computers could perform operations in seconds that would normally take hours or days by hand. As a result, modern cryptography moved quickly into the digital realm. The Munitions Control Act of 1950 specifically classified cryptographic ciphers and equipment as Class 13B munitions. That made them tools of warfare subject to export control and government oversight.

In 1976, Whitman Diffie and Martin Hellman at Stanford University published a paper that revolutionized cryptography. They introduced the concept of asymmetric key cryptography. **Symmetric key cryptography** cannot secure correspondence until after the two parties exchange keys. **Asymmetric key cryptography** uses a cipher with two separate keys. One is for encryption and one is for decryption. Correspondents do not first have to exchange secret information in order to communicate securely. With asymmetric key cryptography, an opponent can intercept everything and still not be able decipher the message. Diffie and Hellman introduced a secure method of exchanging symmetric keys using their asymmetric techniques. The most common use for this algorithm is to secure communications between two parties. Today's network applications commonly establish sessions to exchange messages. A secure way to protect the messages exchanged is to create unique keys, called **session keys**, for each session. Using the **Diffie-Hellman algorithm**, a sender and receiver use asymmetric encryption to securely exchange symmetric keys. After the initial key exchange, each party can then use symmetric encryption to encrypt and decrypt data. Why is this important? Because symmetric encryption algorithms are almost always far faster than asymmetric algorithms with similar security guarantees.

The Diffie-Hellman algorithm was an enormous step forward in cryptography. It is the basis for several common key exchange protocols, including **Diffie-Hellman in Ephemeral mode (DHE)**, which uses modular arithmetic to generate keys, and **Elliptic Curve DHE (ECDHE)**, which uses algebraic curves to generate keys. A cryptographic key is called *ephemeral* if it is created as a new key for each new session. DHE and ECDHE both use ephemeral keys for the Diffie-Hellman exchange. This helps make communications sessions more secure. Since each new key exchange uses new asymmetric keys, each communications session setup process is unique. If an attacker compromises a current session's keys, it doesn't put any previous session keys at risk. The property is called **perfect forward secrecy**. Perfect forward secrecy protects past sessions from future session compromises.

Consider the four basic goals of encryption: confidentiality, integrity, authentication, and nonrepudiation. Classic computing, before the digital computer, addressed each of these. By encrypting a message, the sender made sure it was secure as long as an opponent did not have the key and could not find a shortcut to solve it. Integrity often was incidental. If decryption produced gibberish, you knew the message had changed in transit. However, if a forger obtained encryption equipment, a fake message could appear legitimate. Authentication—proving the identity of the sender—was possible if both sender and receiver had the same codebook and exchanged elements of it. However, exchanging this information slowly compromised its contents unless you refreshed the codebook. Finally, nonrepudiation—proving that a party did indeed originate a message—was not possible with symmetric key cryptography. Anyone with access to the shared key could originate a message. Before asymmetric key cryptography, you couldn't "prove" who wrote it.

Cryptography's Role in Information Security

In today's information systems, you will encounter two primary uses of cryptography: to protect data in transit and to protect data at rest. *Data in transit* refers to any data as they are exchanged, most commonly via a network connection. *Data at rest* are any data that are stored on some storage media. Data at rest also include data in memory. Different cryptographic approaches can help solve the problem of securing data in transit and data at rest. Data in transit security is often called communication security.

There are two main approaches to securing communications. One way is to encrypt each message before it is sent. This approach requires some software to encrypt and decrypt messages separate from the communications functions. The other approach is to let the communication functions handle the encryption and decryption. The communications software actually encrypts and decrypts messages as they are transmitted or received. The second approach is often called **connection encryption** or **transport encryption**, since the encryption (and decryption) occurs at the transport layer in the network stack. Common examples of transport encryption protocols include Secure Sockets Layer (SSL) or Transport Layer Security (TLS), which are commonly used to create secure connections between web servers and browsers, and **Secure Shell (SSH)** , which is used to set up secure logon sessions to remote servers.

When it comes to information security, cryptography can satisfy these requirements:

- Confidentiality
- Integrity
- Authentication
- Nonrepudiation

Confidentiality

Confidentiality keeps information secret from unauthorized users. You can lock safes, post armed guards, or whisper in someone's ear in a remote field to ensure confidentiality. These tactics often are not enough, however. Cryptography makes information unintelligible to anyone who doesn't know the encryption cipher and the proper key. Authorized users can get this knowledge. An effective cryptanalysis also can produce it. The value of confidentiality is straightforward. Disclosing certain communications that contain confidential information could either harm the correspondents or help an opponent.

Integrity

Integrity ensures that no one, even the sender, changes information after transmitting it. If a message doesn't decrypt properly, someone or something probably changed the ciphertext in transit.

In addition, cryptography can enforce integrity with hashes or checksums. A **checksum** is a one-way calculation of information that yields a result that is usually much smaller than the original message. It is difficult to duplicate. For example, a simple checksum of the phone number 1-800-555-1212 could be the sum of each digit, 30. You can't recreate the phone number knowing the checksum. Nevertheless, you can tell if the phone number matches the checksum. If you changed one digit—for example, you changed 1-800-555-1212 to 1-900-555-1212—the checksum no longer matches the expected value. Therefore you would question the data's integrity. Note, however, that this is not a practical security method. You could easily modify the data to produce the correct checksum with the wrong phone number. Integrity verification tends to use robust mathematical processes that are hard to reverse-engineer. These are hashes. You'll learn more about hashes later in this chapter.

Authentication

Authentication confirms the identity of an entity. It can be the sender, the sender's computer, some device, or some information. Humans instinctively authenticate each other based on characteristics such as facial appearance, voice, or skin texture. A traditional military authentication method is a password. If you know it, the sentry lets you pass. If you don't, you're in trouble. In the digital realm, cryptography provides a way to authenticate entities.

The most straightforward form is a user ID and password. Note that this is not strong authentication. Anyone else who obtains this fixed information can provide the same information to the recipient, who will think the user is legitimate.

In general, symmetric key cryptography has this problem. If an attacker can listen in on the conversation where the sender and receiver agree on a cipher and key, the attacker can pose as a legitimate user. This approach to exchanging keys uses the same communications channel as the data and is called an **in-band key exchange**. To be able to authenticate in a symmetric key cryptography world, parties must first securely distribute keys among themselves. For example, they could use asymmetric key cryptography to distribute the symmetric keys. Then they would use the symmetric keys for subsequent correspondence. Another less sophisticated way to distribute keys is to use an unrelated communications method. A different communication channel through which you can exchange keys from the one you use for data is called an **out-of-band key exchange**. A physical courier could deliver the key. This is expensive and time-consuming for large numbers of users; however, the value of authenticating all parties is great enough in environments such as the military that it is worth the cost.

Asymmetric key cryptography offers an approach to simpler means of authentication. Along with confidentiality, asymmetric key cryptography is the cornerstone of Internet commerce. But cryptography alone can't solve the authentication problem. One solution is to use a set of authentication and security protocols with cryptography at their core. Microsoft produced the NT LAN Manager (NTLM) protocol suite to prove authentication and provide integrity to users. NTLM provides the structure to establish and manage secure communications among distributed network resources. A newer version of NTLM, NTLMv2, increases security beyond the original version's limitations.

Nonrepudiation

Nonrepudiation enables you to prevent a party from denying a previous statement or action. For example, suppose an investor sends an email to a broker that states, "Buy 1,000 shares of XYZ at 50." Shortly after the exchange executes the order, XYZ stock drops to 20. The investor then denies the buy order and says it was really an order to sell. How does one resolve this type of "he said/she said" dilemma?

Using asymmetric key cryptography, you can prove mathematically—usually to the satisfaction of a judge or jury—that a particular party did indeed originate a specific message at a specific time. The fundamental principle of asymmetric key cryptography is that it uses a

---

FYI

It's easy to confuse public and private keys. If you were encrypting a message to protect its confidentiality and integrity, you would use the recipient's public key. Only the recipient would be able to decrypt the message using the corresponding private key. On the other hand, if you, as the message sender, want to use encryption to enforce nonrepudiation, you would encrypt the message with your private key. Anyone who has access to your public key can decrypt the message, but successful decryption proves that you originated the message.

key pair to encrypt and decrypt. The originator is the only one who knows one of the keys. It has an irrefutable timestamp. The argument in court would go something like this:

"Encryption does more than just keep messages secret. It can validate the identity of the sender. This encrypted message decrypts with this public key. Only the holder of the associated private key could have created this message. The message contains a time-based hash produced by a trusted third-party **timestamping** device. Neither party could have tampered with it. Thus, we know with effective certainty that this message as decrypted is genuine and originated with this known party. This is nonrepudiation."

Business and Security Requirements for Cryptography

In this section, you will learn about information security principles and how cryptography can address them.

Internal Security

A number of security objectives add value to a business. These include the following:

- **Confidentiality**—Confidentiality keeps information readable only by authorized people. It keeps that data away from people who are unauthorized. For example, most companies keep salary information confidential.
- **Privacy**—Privacy is often confused with confidentiality. Privacy differs in that it protects the release of information that could identify an individual. For example, information that discloses that a person who lives in a certain postal code was treated for a broken arm and a facial laceration on a specific day at a certain hospital may reveal a person's identity. Privacy assures that an attacker cannot assemble available information to identify an individual.
- **Integrity**—Integrity ensures that no one has changed or deleted data. For example, payroll data need integrity to make sure no one changes a payment after sending it to the check printer.
- **Authorization**—Authorization means approving someone to do a specific task or access certain data. For example, changing salary plans requires proper authorization from management.
- **Access control**—Access control involves restricting information to the right people. For example, you can store salary plans in a locked file cabinet to which only HR employees have the key.

Security in Business Relationships

A number of security objectives add value to relationships between businesses or between businesses and their customers. In addition to those listed before, they include the following:

- **Message authentication**—Message authentication confirms the identity of the person who started a correspondence. For example, a broker would like to know that a message to "Buy 1,000 shares of XYZ for account ABC" came from ABC.

> **NOTE**
>
> As privacy issues become more and more important, an interesting source of tension in security circles becomes more obvious. Nonrepudiation means that an action can be positively associated with an individual. Privacy means being able to carry out actions without disclosing personal information. Which one is more important? We don't know yet. These two concepts are fundamentally at odds, and the debate continues.

- **Signature**—A **digital signature** binds a message or data to a specific entity. Note that this is not a **digitized signature**, which is an image of an electronically reproduced signature.
- **Receipt and confirmation**—Email messages often use receipt and confirmation. Receipt verifies that an entity acknowledges information has arrived. Confirmation acknowledges that the provider has provided a service.
- **Nonrepudiation**—Nonrepudiation means that the person who sends a message cannot later deny it. For example, if the person who made the buy order were to dispute it after XYZ dropped 50 percent, nonrepudiation would prove the original message was valid.

Security Measures That Benefit Everyone

Beyond business and customer relationships, certain security objectives add value to information systems. In addition to those items already listed, these objectives include the following:

- **Anonymity**—This disguises a user's identity. For example, a dissident in a repressive country might want to post information to a web discussion site without the authorities knowing who he or she is. Unfortunately, criminals and terrorists can use anonymity as well to avoid detection.
- **Timestamping**—This provides an exact time when a producer creates or sends information. For example, people submitting tax returns at the last minute may want to prove they met the deadline.
- **Revocation**—This stops authorization for access to data. For example, a person who loses a credit card calls the issuer to stop use of the card.
- **Ownership**—This associates a person with information to claim legal rights. For example, most documents have copyright notices that tell who wrote them.

Cryptographic Principles, Concepts, and Terminology

There are many different information security objectives. It is important to understand them, how they work together, and how they sometimes oppose one another. They represent most of the goals of security initiatives, including cryptography. One of the best summaries of security objectives is in the *Handbook of Applied Cryptography*. **TABLE 9-1** contains the security objectives summary. When you try to solve a business security problem, you need to understand these terms. Then you can tell if you could use a cryptographic solution.

Cryptographic Functions and Ciphers

A basic understanding of cryptographic ciphers can tell you how cryptography can satisfy your business needs. Each cipher has specific characteristics that may make it desirable or undesirable for any situation. The first issue to consider when evaluating a cipher is its intended use. Are you trying to secure data in transit or data at rest? Different ciphers solve different problems better than others. Once you select a cipher, you still have to make additional decisions about things such as key size and operational mode. Many symmetric ciphers operate as either a stream cipher or a block cipher, depending on the mode you

TABLE 9-1 Information security objectives.

OBJECTIVE	STEPS TO TAKE
Privacy or confidentiality	Keep information secret from all unauthorized users.
Integrity	Ensure that unauthorized users or unknown processes have not altered information.
Entity authentication or identification	Corroborate the identity of an entity (that is, a person, a computer terminal, a credit card, etc.).
Message authentication	Corroborate the source of information; authenticate the data's origin.
Signature	Bind information to an entity.
Authorization	Convey an official sanction to do or be something to another entity.
Validation	Provide timely authorization to use or manipulate information or resources.
Access control	Restrict access to resources to privileged entities.
Certification	Endorse information by a trusted entity.
Timestamping	Record the time a user created or accessed information.
Witnessing	Verify the action to create an object or verify an object's existence by an entity other than the creator.
Receipt	Acknowledge that the recipient received information.
Confirmation	Acknowledge that the provider has provided services.
Ownership	Grant an entity the legal right to use or transfer a resource to others.
Anonymity	Conceal the identity of an entity involved in some process.
Nonrepudiation	Prevent an entity from denying previous commitments or actions.
Revocation	Retract certification or authorization.

9

Cryptography

choose. A **stream cipher** encrypts one byte (or bit) at a time, whereas a **block cipher** encrypts an entire block of data at a time. Deciding on the "best" type of cipher is a complex task. There are many subtleties and very few standard answers. As ciphers become more complex, they rely on new techniques to generate keys and transform plaintext into ciphertext.

Two fertile areas of research are **elliptic curve cryptography (ECC)** and **quantum cryptography**. ECC ciphers depend on the algebraic structures of elliptic curves over finite fields. These ciphers can result in very secure ciphertext using smaller keys than more traditional ciphers. However, ECC imposes a high computational overhead cost. Quantum cryptography bases its algorithms on the properties of quantum mechanics. The basic difference between classic cryptography and quantum cryptography is in the difficulty in breaking the cipher. Breaking classic ciphers is extremely difficult; breaking quantum cryptography ciphers is theoretically impossible. Of course, quantum cryptography implementations are computationally expensive and more difficult to get "right." For those reasons, classic cryptography still dominates in today's implementations.

Business-Security Implementations

Here is a review of the general classifications of security products and services:

- Authentication (non-PKI)
- Access control/authorization
- Assessment and audit
- Security management products
- Perimeter/network security/availability
- Content filtering
- Encryption
- Administration/education
- Outsource services/consultants

By cross-referencing these products and services to the information security objectives mentioned before, you can see which business tools and services satisfy which security objectives. Then you can tell which of these objectives cryptography can address. **TABLE 9-2** shows how security products and security objectives relate to one another.

As you can see, you can use cryptography to reach many security objectives. Specifically, cryptography offers the following capabilities:

- **Privacy or confidentiality**—Cryptography scrambles information so that only someone with the right cipher and key can read it. Note that this person could include a clever cryptanalyst.
- **Integrity**—Cryptography protects integrity by providing checksums or hashes. You can compare these with a known table of good values to prove that the data have not changed.
- **Entity authentication or identification**—Someone's ability to encode or decode a message means that person has the cryptographic key or has the ability to calculate the key. If a business relationship requires that this key remain secret, possession is proof of valid identity.
- **Message authentication**—Similar to entity authentication, a coded message with a private key proves who the message's writer is. Again, this stipulation should be part of any business contract or formal relationship.
- **Signature**—Cryptography can provide a way to make a digital signature. This can prove that a given person sent a specific message.
- **Access control**—This involves encrypting privileged resources or data so that only authorized people can decrypt them and enforce access to them.
- **Certification**—A trusted entity can certify a message or data by adding a cryptographic checksum and a digital signature.
- **Timestamping**—Using asymmetric key cryptography, a trusted device can issue timestamps that attackers cannot forge. Timestamping binds a hash of the timestamped information with the output of a secure, reliable clock.
- **Witnessing**—A third party can add a cryptographic checksum to data to prove that those data exist in a given format at a particular time.
- **Ownership**—This refers to a cryptographic hash created by an owner and added to the data, then submitted to a trusted third party for corroboration. This identifies an entity as the data's owner.

TABLE 9-2 Security objectives and security products.

OBJECTIVE	AUTHENTICATION	ACCESS CONTROL	ASSESSMENT AND AUDIT	SECURITY MANAGEMENT	NETWORK SECURITY	CONTENT FILTERING	ENCRYPTION	ADMINISTRATION	CONSULTANTS
Privacy or confidentiality		X			X		X	X	X
Integrity				X	X		X	X	X
Entity authentication or identification	X	X			X		X	X	X
Message authentication	X				X		X		
Signature	X				X		X	X	
Authorization	X	X			X				
Validation		X	X	X				X	
Access control	X	X			X	X	X	X	
Certification			X	X			X		X
Timestamping		X			X		X		
Witnessing			X				X		X
Receipt					X			X	
Confirmation					X		X		
Ownership			X				X	X	X
Anonymity							X	X	
Nonrepudiation					X		X	X	X
Revocation	X				X		X		

- **Anonymity**—Using cryptography, you can conceal the identity of an entity by passing information in an encrypted format that monitors cannot interpret. In addition, using a series of encrypted hops and getting rid of logs can provide an entity with anonymous presence on the Internet.
- **Nonrepudiation**—An asymmetric key signature of data, agreed to as part of a business relationship, can prove the sender's identity to the receiver.

Types of Ciphers

Ciphers come in two basic forms:

- **Transposition ciphers**—A **transposition cipher** rearranges characters or bits of data.
- **Substitution ciphers**—A **substitution cipher** replaces bits, characters, or blocks of information with other bits, characters, or blocks.

Transposition Ciphers

A simple transposition cipher writes characters into rows in a matrix. It then reads the columns as output. For example, write the message "ATTACK AT DAWN" into a four-column matrix, as shown in **FIGURE 9-2**.

Then, read the information in columns: ACDTKATAWATN. This would be the ciphertext. The key would be {1,2,3,4}, which is the order in which the columns are read. Encrypting with a different key, say, {2,4,3,1}, would result in a different ciphertext—in this case, TKAATNTAWACD.

Note that in this example, the ciphertext contains the frequency of letters. That is, the most common letters in the English language—E, T, A, O, and N—appear a disproportionate number of times in the transposition ciphertext. This is a clue to the cryptanalyst that this is a transposition cipher.

Transposition ciphers keep all the elements of the original message. They simply scramble the information in a way that they can reassemble later. Some basic digital transposition ciphers will swap bits within bytes to make the data appear unintelligible to the casual reader. An example of a spoken transposition cipher is pig Latin.

Substitution Ciphers

One of the simplest substitution ciphers is the **Caesar cipher**. It shifts each letter in the English alphabet a fixed number of positions, with Z wrapping back to A. Julius Caesar used this cipher with a shift of 3. The following illustrates an encryption using a Caesar cipher:

ATTACK AT DAWN

↓

DWWDFN DW GDZQ

Note that there are 25 possible keys for a Caesar cipher. (The 26th key maps characters back onto themselves.) Note also that this is not a transposition cipher, because the letters in the ciphertext were not present in the plaintext.

A popular substitution cipher for children in the 1960s was the Cap'n Crunch© decoder ring. The ring was included in specially marked boxes of Cap'n Crunch cereal. This ring

1	2	3	4
A	T	T	A
C	K	A	T
D	A	W	N

consisted of two alphabets (A to Z) written in a circle. The inner circle didn't move, but you could rotate the outer circle. By rotating the outer circle to a set value, you created a one-to-one mapping from one alphabet to the other. To encrypt, you looked up the desired character in the inner circle and read off the character on the outer circle. To decrypt, you reversed the process. (Yes, this is a Caesar cipher!)

A **keyword mixed alphabet cipher** uses a cipher alphabet that consists of a keyword, minus duplicates, followed by the remaining letters of the alphabet. For example, using the key word CRYPTOGRAPHY, this type of cipher would yield the following:

ABCDEFGHIJKLMNOPQRSTUVWXYZ

↓

CRYPTOGAHBDEFIJKLMNQSUVWXZ

Thus, the plaintext word ALPHABET would encrypt to CEKACRTQ.

Any substitution cipher will use these same basic principles, regardless of complexity. To make it harder to break these codes, you can use multiple encryption schemes in succession. For example, you could encrypt every letter with its own substitution scheme. This is a **Vigenère** (*vee-zhen-AIR*) **cipher**. It works like multiple Caesar ciphers, each with its own shift characters. For example, you could use the word PARTY as the key, which would use five Caesar ciphers. Knowing that each character in the alphabet has a value from 1 to 26, you can calculate the encrypted character by adding the value of the plaintext character to the value of the corresponding character in the key. If the sum is greater than 26, just subtract 26 to find the final value. To encrypt the message ATTACK AT DAWN TOMORROW, you would obtain the following:

Plaintext:	ATTACKATDAWNTOMORROW
Key (repeated to match plaintext length):	PARTYPARTYPARTYPARTYPA
Ciphertext (shift characters using the key):	PTKTAZAKWYLNKHKDRIHU

This gives more security. The output appears much more random. Increasing the key length generally increases the security of a substitution cipher.

Instead of transforming each letter a fixed number of positions, you can increase the complexity of a substitution cipher by allowing any letter to uniquely map to any other letter. You can find this type of cipher, called a **simple substitution cipher**, in many newspapers as a puzzle called a **cryptogram**. In this case, A could map to any of 26 letters, B could map to any of 25 remaining letters, C could map to 24 letters, and so on. Thus, there are (26 factorial), or 403,291,461,126,606,000,000,000,000, possible keys that you can use. Even so, breaking these puzzles is straightforward work. This illustrates an important point: You must never confuse complexity with security.

You must do three things to make sure a substitution cipher stays secure. First, make sure that the key is a random sequence without repetition. Second, make sure it is as long as the encrypted information. Third, use it only once. Such a cipher is a one-time pad. The first use of this strategy was in computer systems based on a design by an AT&T employee named Gilbert Vernam. A Vernam cipher creates a bit stream of zeros and ones that is combined with the plaintext using the exclusive OR function. The exclusive OR operation is true when one and only one of the inputs is true. The exclusive OR function, represented as $\oplus$, has the following properties:

$0 \oplus 0 = 0$

$0 \oplus 1 = 1$

$1 \oplus 0 = 1$

$1 \oplus 1 = 0$

Note that this is equivalent to the $\neq$ (not-equal) function. Using this approach, you can combine a binary stream of data with a binary keystream (stream of characters from a key) to produce ciphertext. This is how hardware or software uses modern substitution ciphers.

Product and Exponentiation Ciphers

A **product cipher** is a combination of multiple ciphers. Each could be a transposition or substitution cipher. The Data Encryption Standard (DES) is a product cipher with a 56-bit key consisting of 16 iterations of substitution and transformation. First published as a Federal Information Processing Standard (FIPS) in 1977, DES is still in use. Its developers thought it was highly secure because the computers available in 1977 would take more than 90 years to break an encrypted message. Many civil libertarians and conspiracy theorists as well as professional cryptographers think designers built certain weaknesses into DES to let the National Security Agency (NSA) open a backdoor in the algorithm to decrypt messages easily. However, after more than 25 years, no one has found such a weakness. Advances in cryptography—including **differential cryptanalysis**, which involves looking for patterns in vast amounts of ciphertext—actually imply that the DES design was even more secure than first suspected. Nonetheless, advances in computing power have made the 56-bit keyspace (72,057,594,037,927,900 keys) less daunting to search. Finally, in 1998, the Electronic Frontier Foundation built a special-purpose computer called Deep Crack, which can search the keyspace in less than three days. You'll read about DES in more detail later in this chapter.

Some ciphers rely on the difficulty of solving certain mathematical problems. This is the basis for asymmetric key cryptography. These ciphers use a branch of mathematics known as **field theory**. Without getting into too much mathematics, a **field** is any domain of numbers in which every element other than 0 has a multiplicative inverse. For example, all rational numbers form a field. Given $x \neq 0$, you can always compute $1/x$. Fields do not have to be infinite. Instead of counting to infinity, you can restart counting after reaching a particular value. For example, in the United States, people tell time with a 12-hour clock. One hour past 10:00 is 11:00, but one hour past 12:00 is 1:00, not 13:00. Many countries use a 24-hour clock, but the wraparound effect is the same. Things get interesting mathematically when the number of integers in a set is prime. The set of integers from 1 to a prime number represents a finite field.

An exponentiation cipher involves computing exponentials over a finite mathematical field. The **Rivest-Shamir-Adelman (RSA)** encryption scheme relies on the difficulty of factoring large numbers. It's straightforward to multiply two numbers together, but it's very difficult to factor one large number. You'll learn the details of this process later in this chapter.

Symmetric and Asymmetric Key Cryptography

In this section, you'll learn more about the differences between symmetric and asymmetric key cryptography and the relative advantages and disadvantages of both.

Symmetric Key Ciphers

Symmetric key ciphers use the same key to encrypt and decrypt. As a result, they require that both parties first exchange keys to communicate. This represents a basic limitation for these cryptosystems. Before you can send a message to another party, you must first talk securely to exchange keys. This chicken-and-egg problem is what made cryptography difficult in the past for any large, dispersed organization, with the exception of governments, the military, and well-funded people.

To illustrate this problem, imagine that two correspondents, Alice and Bob, want to exchange information securely. In this scenario, Alice and Bob work for the ABC Company. They want to exchange pricing information for a proposal to a new client, MNO Plastics. Bob is in the field at the client site and cannot get to the company's internal network. All information must go back and forth across the Internet.

Eva works for an overseas competitor of ABC. Her job is to gather as much intelligence as she can about ABC's proposal and bid. She has authorization to monitor, disrupt, or masquerade any communications to achieve her mission. The obvious legal issues here can be set aside for the sake of discussion. Assume that Eva can monitor all communications to and from Bob. Any messages he sends or receives pass through a node Eva controls.

Here's the problem: How do Alice and Bob create a secure communications session if they have not agreed to anything in advance? Let's say that Alice and Bob agree to use DES to encrypt their information. Because DES is a publicly available algorithm, Eva can download a copy of DES software. Alice sends a message to Bob to use BIGBUCKS as the key. Bob acknowledges this convention and sends his encrypted message to Alice using this key. Eva, listening in on the communications, uses the same key to decrypt Bob's message and sends his information to her company.

Alice and Bob can agree to change keys any number of times, but each time they do, Eva learns of this key change and adjusts accordingly. Using symmetric key cryptography, there is no way around this problem. Each party must exchange keys with the other party to know what key the other is using. Even if you encrypt a key with a special-purpose key or a **key-encrypting key**, you must exchange the key-encrypting key at some point. Key-encrypting keys are keys that you use only to encrypt other keys. Exchanging key-encrypting keys means that an attacker can intercept the key-encrypting key when you exchange it.

The solution to this dilemma requires a message that travels on a different path that Eva can't monitor. This is out-of-band communication using a secure channel. Let's say in this case that Alice and Bob agree to use DES, and Alice tells Bob to call her on his cell phone and tell her what key to he wants to use. Eva, who can read all Internet traffic, can't monitor cell phones. Alice and Bob agree on a 56-bit key and begin exchanging information. Eva is out of the loop. Of course, before Bob left on the business trip, Alice and Bob could have agreed to use a particular key. This, too, is out-of-band communication. It takes place outside the communications channel used for sending and receiving messages.

Now ABC Company has a choice to make. It can issue the same key to all employees, which makes correspondence easy. Any employee can correspond securely with any other employee around the world. This model works well until a disgruntled employee quits and joins a competitor, taking the key with him. Now what? ABC has to create a new key and re-issue the new key to everyone worldwide. This could be time-consuming and expensive.

Alternatively, ABC could decide that a single point of failure is unacceptable and issue separate keys to each employee. However, because both parties have to use the same key with symmetric key ciphers, each employee-employee pair must have its own unique key. Thus, if there were 10 employees, ABC would need 45 key pairs ($9 + 8 + 7 + 6 + 5 + 4 + 3 + 2 + 1$) to begin this scheme. If ABC had 100 employees, it would need 4,950 key pairs. If ABC had 10,000 employees, it would need 49,995,000 key pairs! The number of key pairs required for n correspondents is $(n (n - 1)) / 2$. Moreover, each time an employee joined or left the company, you would have to add or delete a key pair for each of the other employees. Clearly, symmetric key systems do not scale well.

This remained an intractable problem for cryptologists (and governments, militaries, and businesses) until 1976, when Whitfield Diffie and Martin Hellman published their paper, "New Directions in Cryptography," in the *IEEE Transactions on Information Theory* journal. In this paper, they proposed a radical new approach that offered a potential solution to the scalability problem.

Asymmetric Key Ciphers

In their introduction, Diffie and Hellman pointed out, "The cost and delay imposed by this key distribution problem is a major barrier to the transfer of business communications to large teleprocessing networks." They introduced the concept of **public key cryptography**. (Note that this text refers to this concept as *asymmetric key cryptography*.) Public key cryptography is a system that allows correspondents to communicate only over a public channel using publicly known techniques. They can create a secure connection. They do not need to wait until an out-of-band letter arrives with a key in the envelope. Nor do they need to issue and manage millions of key pairs just in case someone wants to communicate securely with a new correspondent. The impact of this discovery is profound and has far-reaching effects on cryptography.

Asymmetric key ciphers have four key properties:

- **Two associated algorithms that are inverses of each other exist**—This solution involves two components associated with each other. That means you use one algorithm to encrypt and another to decrypt.
- **Each of these two algorithms is easy to compute**—You can use this approach in computer software without much difficulty. As a result, it becomes a practical approach for secure digital communications.
- **It is computationally infeasible to derive the second algorithm if you know the first algorithm**—You can post one key widely for anyone to use without compromising the contents of its associated key. These are pairs of a public key and its associated private key, or a public-private key pair. Since public key cryptosystems have private keys, you can see why this chapter has stuck to the asymmetric key-naming convention!

- **Given some random input, you can generate associated key pairs that are inverses of each other**—Any party can create public-private key pairs, keep one private, and post the other in a directory for any correspondent to use. Because the private key is secret and never transmitted, an eavesdropper cannot learn this value.

Here's how public key cryptography works. Suppose Bob wants to send Alice a message. Alice has already created her private key, which she keeps safe, and her public key, which she puts on her website. Bob uses Alice's public key to encrypt the message, "Hi Alice!" Bob then sends the encrypted message to Alice. Because Bob used Alice's public key to encrypt the message, Alice can decrypt it only with her private key. Because she has access to her private key, she uses it to decrypt and read the message, "Hi Alice!" If Alice wanted to respond to Bob's message, she could encrypt her response with Bob's public key and send the message back to Bob.

One of the closest equivalents in the everyday business world to asymmetric key ciphers is the night deposit box at a bank. A merchant takes his receipts to the bank, opens the slot with his key, and drops the money down the chute. The envelope slides down and into the safe. If he turned around and a robber held him up at gunpoint and demanded his key, the merchant can safely surrender the key and run away. The robber can attempt to recover the money, but because the envelope has dropped out of reach, the robber will be unable to access it. The next morning, the bank officer can use her key to open the safe, remove the money, and deposit it into the merchant's account. Each party has a different key, but they are associated with each other. Make this process reversible, where the bank officer could leave messages for the merchant, and you have the equivalent of an asymmetric or public key cryptosystem.

Cryptanalysis and Public Versus Private Keys

Encryption makes plaintext unreadable to anyone except an authorized person with the right software and key. If the data are valuable, however, cybercriminals may try to break the encryption.

You can break a cipher in two ways:

- Analyzing the ciphertext to find the plaintext or key
- Analyzing the ciphertext and its associated plaintext to find the key

A cipher is unconditionally secure if no amount of ciphertext will give enough information to yield a unique plaintext. You can break almost any cipher, given enough time and resources. However, a cipher's main purpose is to make it so difficult to break that it is computationally infeasible to crack. For example, assume that an organization generates new keys every

---

Technical TIP

The only unbreakable cryptographic cipher is the **Vernam cipher**. Another name for it is a **one-time pad cipher**. You'll read more about that later in this chapter. You can also find out more about the Vernam cipher at *www.pro-technix.com/information/crypto/pages/vernam_base.html*.

week. If an attacker can crack any key in 13 days, the cracked keys would be useless by the time the attacker tried to use it; it would already have been superseded by a new key. Thus, a cipher that an attacker cannot break economically (relative to the value of the protected data) is strong or computationally secure.

There are four basic forms of cryptographic attack:

- **Ciphertext-only attack (COA)**—In a ciphertext-only attack, the cryptanalyst has access only to a segment of encrypted data and has no choice as to what those data may be. An example is the cryptogram in some daily newspapers. Note, however, that by understanding the context of the information, one can infer that certain words or formatting may be present. **FIGURE 9-3** shows a ciphertext-only attack. The sample of ciphertext is available, but the plaintext associated with it is not.
- **Known-plaintext attack (KPA)**—In a known-plaintext attack, the cryptanalyst possesses certain pieces of information before and after encryption. For example, all secure logon sessions may begin with the characters LOGON, and the next transmission may be PASS-WORD. A secure encryption cipher should resist an attack by an analyst who has access to numerous plaintext-ciphertext pairs. **FIGURE 9-4** shows a known-plaintext attack.
- **Chosen-plaintext attack**—In a chosen-plaintext attack, the cryptanalyst can encrypt any information and observe the output. This is the best case for the cryptanalyst. It offers the most flexibility (and insight) into the encryption mechanism. An example is the encryption offered by older versions of Microsoft Office software applications. You could encrypt only the letter A, then B, and so on, to try to discern what the cipher is doing.

FIGURE 9-3

A ciphertext-only attack (COA).

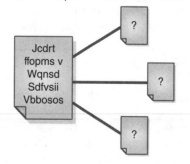

The sample of ciphertext is available, but not the plaintext associated with it.

FIGURE 9-4

A known-plaintext attack (KPA).

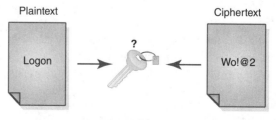

The ciphertext and the corresponding plaintext are both available.

- **Chosen-ciphertext attack**—A chosen-ciphertext attack is a special case. It is relevant in asymmetric key systems and hash functions. In a chosen-ciphertext attack, cryptanalysts submit data coded with the same cipher and key they are trying to break to the decryption device to see either the plaintext output or the effect the decrypted message has on some system. As a simple example, consider an owner who trains a guard dog to respond only to commands spoken in Navajo. A burglar doesn't know Navajo, but he can make a series of noises and sounds. The dog ignores nonsense (from its perspective) but obeys valid commands. Speaking enough gibberish, the burglar might prompt a response from the dog (even if not the response he seeks). By observing the dog's reaction to various apparently nonsensical commands, the burglar might be able to make the dog lie down and play dead. Chosen-ciphertext attacks have particular uses in attacking encrypted email. The complexity of the mathematics involved is too great to allow a discussion of them here.

Symmetric and Asymmetric Key Cipher Resistance to Attack

Cryptanalysis has several objectives, including the following:

- Derive the plaintext of a target message.
- Determine the key used to encrypt a target message.
- Derive the algorithm used by a particular cipher.
- Solve the general mathematical problem underlying the cryptography.

Cryptographers use many tools in cryptanalysis. They have such names as linear cryptanalysis, differential cryptanalysis, brute force, exhaustive search, and information theory. In the most direct case, the analyst must use an encrypted message to derive its associated plaintext. Many ciphers used today are open source. That means that the analyst has access to the logic for the encryption and decryption functions. The security of closed-source or proprietary ciphers stems in part from the fact that the analyst does not necessarily know how the cipher works.

For example, the United States did not have access to a Japanese Purple cipher device in World War II. Codebreakers had to determine how the machine worked by analyzing faint patterns in the ciphertext. Once they figured that out, analysts could then change the order of different keys to decrypt message traffic. Once they identified the key, anyone could read all traffic coded for that time period with the same key.

In some cases, analysts found a solution by attacking the underlying mathematics of a cryptosystem. In the late 1970s, some vendors made security products that used asymmetric key cryptography based on a simplified version of the knapsack problem called the *subset sum problem*. Unfortunately for the vendors, Len Adelman developed a general solution to the subset sum problem in 1982 that could run on an Apple II computer. Overnight, an entire class of security products became obsolete.

Today, the basis of most commercial asymmetric key cryptography is the difficulty of factoring large numbers. For example, it is relatively easy with pen and paper to calculate $757 \times 769 = 582{,}133$. Yet given the result 582,133, deriving its two factors is not as easy. The classic approach would involve trying 2, 3, 5, 7, 11, 13, etc., until a prime factor is found. That would take 134 guesses. Although this becomes much easier with a computer, imagine that the two prime factors are 100 digits each! Just to put this into perspective, here is a 100-digit prime number:

6,513,516,734,600,035,718,300,327,211,250,928,237,178,281,758,494,417, 357,560,
086,828,416,863,929,270,451,437,126,021,949,850,746,381

Moreover, the preceding number would be only one of two factors.

Keys, Keyspace, and Key Management

In this section, you'll learn how to describe the function of keys, the importance of keyspace size, and the requirements for adequate key management.

Cryptographic Keys and Keyspace

You have been reading about keys for some time now. But what are they? A key is a value that is an input to a cryptosystem. The key participates in transforming the message in a particular manner. A well-designed cryptosystem produces different outputs of the same message for each key used. You can think about keys this way: A cipher performs a particular task, and a key gives the specific directions for how to do it.

Physical keys are similar to cryptographic keys, but they're not the same. Many popular door locks have five tumblers, each with 10 possible positions. Thus there are 10^5, or 100,000, possible cuts for house keys. This gives a reasonable assurance that a person trying a random key in your front door won't get in.

The set of all possible keys is a **keyspace**. Usually, although not always, the larger the keyspace, the more secure the algorithm. Let's look at an example.

How large is the keyspace for a briefcase with two three-digit locks? Combinations run from 000–000 to 999–999, so there are 1,000,000 keys in the keyspace. Does this mean a thief would have to try 1 million combinations before guessing the correct combination? Not necessarily. A thief could be incredibly lucky and guess the correct combination on the first try. Alternatively, a thief could be incredibly unlucky and try every possible combination before finding the correct combination on the last try. On average, an attacker will guess the correct combination halfway through searching the keyspace. Does this mean that an attacker would need to try, on average, 500,000 combinations? If each attempt took two seconds, and the attacker worked nonstop day and night, he or she should need more than 11 days to open the briefcase. However, the actual resistance of a briefcase to brute-force attack is closer to 17 minutes! Why is this so?

It has to do with a weakness in the briefcase algorithm. Because there are two separate locks with 1,000 combinations each, on average it takes 500 attempts to guess each subcombination. After finding the left combination, the attacker proceeds to the right combination. At most, the attacker will need to try 1,000 + 1,000, or 2,000, combinations. On average, however, the attacker will need to try only 1,000. At two seconds each, this would take 16 minutes and 40 seconds.

This illustrates nicely that increased keyspace, or even an increase in the number of bits in a key, does not necessarily provide much more security. If a briefcase maker wanted to sell you a product with six three-digit locks, would you want to buy it? The company would be correct in claiming that the briefcase had more possible combinations (that is, keys) than DES. However, knowing what you know now, you can calculate that it would take less than an hour to open this secure briefcase.

Key Management

One of the most difficult and critical parts of a cryptosystem is **key management**. Although the mathematics of a cipher might be difficult for an attacker to solve, weaknesses or errors in key management often offer a means of compromising a system. As you have seen, key management of a symmetric cryptosystem can be difficult and complex. As a result, it sometimes leads to shortcuts that can be fatal to the otherwise secure cipher.

World War II history gives an example of how poor key management can wreck a cryptosystem. From 1940 to 1948, the Soviet Union used one-time pads to encode messages sent over commercial telegraph lines. Theoretically, one-time pads are unbreakable. The key is very close to random. It is as long as the information it protects, and it does not repeat. It is not possible to detect a pattern in the ciphertext. However, as you have read, the difficulty of distributing and managing long keys in a worldwide wartime environment led to some places running out of cipher keys. Each location knew better than to reuse its own keys, but what harm could there be in using another station's one-time pad? Plenty, it turns out.

If you use the exclusive OR function to encrypt, then encrypting message A with key-stream X becomes:

$$A \oplus X = E(A)$$

where $E(A)$ represents the encrypted message containing A. Remember that the exclusive OR function has the interesting property that anything exclusive OR'd with itself is 0, and anything exclusive OR'd with 0 is itself. To decrypt this message, you recombine it with key X to recover the message:

$$E(A) \oplus X = A \oplus X \oplus X = A$$

The problem with reusing keying material from another station is that the United States was trying to capture all encrypted traffic from all locations. It then tried to correlate the messages. For example, a message from New York to Moscow in 1943 might have used the same one-time pad as a message from the embassy in Sydney to the embassy in Cairo in 1944. An interesting thing happens when you combine two messages encrypted with the same key:

$$A \oplus X = E(A) \quad B \oplus X = E(B)$$
$$E(A) \oplus E(B) = A \oplus X \oplus B \oplus X$$
$$= A \oplus B \oplus \cancel{X \oplus X}$$
$$= A \oplus B$$

Now you can use message A to encrypt message B. If you recall from the discussion on transposition ciphers, the ciphertext stores patterns in plaintext. Using one message to encrypt another also keeps much of the statistical properties of the plaintext. It turns out that breaking these messages is rather straightforward. Note that you are solving for the plaintext, not the encryption key! Once the message is decrypted, you could calculate the key by combining the ciphertext with the plaintext.

The United States code-named this project Venona. It continued trying to break these messages from the 1940s all the way until 1980! There are entire books about this project; the U.S. government declassified the intercepted messages between 1995 and 1997. Just in case you didn't think Julius and Ethel Rosenberg spied for the Soviet Union, you can read the decrypted incriminating messages today.

Key Distribution

Key distribution techniques typically take one of three forms:

- **Paper**—Paper distribution requires no technology to use. However, it does require a person to do something to install the key. This human role can introduce errors or give a disgruntled person a chance to compromise a system.
- **Digital media**—Digital distribution can be in the form of CDs or email. Note that you must protect the keys in transit. Some form of secure transmission must be used. For physical media, tamperproof cases and registered mail give some level of assurance. For electronic distribution, a higher-level key, known as a **key-encrypting key**, must protect the keys in transit and storage. This, of course, requires that you first distribute the key-encrypting key by some alternate secure mechanism. You should use key-encrypting keys only to encrypt other keys, not data. Excessive use of any key could lead to it being compromised.
- **Hardware**—You can distribute a key via hardware with a USB flash drive, a smart card, or any other removable storage device. The advantage is that you transfer the keys directly from the key-transport mechanism into the crypto device without anyone viewing them. No copies exist outside of these components.

To protect against key interception in transit, you can split keys. Splitting a key into two equal-sized pieces isn't a good idea. If an attacker intercepts one piece, brute-forcing the other half of the key is much easier (remember the briefcase example). Therefore, one strategy to split a key K is to generate another random key J, which becomes the key-encrypting key. You combine K and J to produce an encrypted key. You would then send this encrypted key on one channel. You would send the key-encrypting key by another channel. If an attacker intercepts one of the two messages, the attacker does not learn the underlying key.

Channel 1: J

Channel 2: $K \oplus J$

Recombine: $J \oplus K \oplus J = K$

Note that this scheme requires a new key-encrypting key for every key.

Key Distribution Centers

Rather than each organization creating the infrastructure to manage its own keys, a number of hosts could agree to trust a common **key-distribution center (KDC)**. All parties must trust the KDC. With a KDC, each entity requires only one secret key pair—between itself and the KDC. Kerberos and ANSI X9.17 use the concept of a KDC.

For example, if Alice wants to initiate a secure communications session with Bob, she sends an encrypted message to the KDC. The KDC picks a random session key, encrypts copies in both Alice's key and Bob's key, and returns both to Alice. Alice decrypts her session key and uses it to encrypt a message to Bob. She sends it, along with the session key encrypted in Bob's key—which Alice can't read—to Bob. Bob gets both messages, decrypts the session key using his secret key, and uses the session key to decrypt Alice's message.

Digital Signatures and Hash Functions

For many business requirements, you should understand the use of digital signatures and hash functions and what types of ciphers to use.

Hash Functions

To ensure that the values of a message have not changed—either deliberately or through transmission error—you can append some summary of the information that you can verify through a repeatable process. This summary is a checksum. For example, to make sure a string of digits has not changed in transmission, you could append the sum of all the digits to the end of the message. If the recipient adds up the digits and reaches a different value, you can assume there was an error in transmission and request a resend.

Credit cards have a hash digit that validates the card number. The algorithm for calculating this digit is the LUHN formula, based on ANSI X4.13. To calculate whether a credit card number is valid, follow these four steps:

1. Starting with the second digit on the right, multiply every other digit by two.
2. If the result of any doubling is greater than 10 (that is, $8 + 8 = 16$), add the digits of this result. Add all the doubled digits.
3. Add all other digits, with the exception of the last digit (the checksum), to this total.
4. The difference between the sum and the next multiple of 10 is the check digit. For example, the correct hash digit for credit card number 5012 3456 7890 123X is 6.

A hash is like a checksum but operates so that a forged message will not result in the same hash as a legitimate message. Hashes are usually a fixed size. The result is a hash value. Hashes act as a fingerprint for the data. Message creators can publish a hash as a reference so that recipients can see whether the information has changed. Software publishers often provide hash values so that customers can check the integrity of the software they receive. To be effective, hashes usually have to be long enough so that creating an alternative message that matched the hash value would take far too much time.

Digital Signatures

Digital signatures are not digitized signatures (electronic images of handwritten signatures). Rather, digital signatures bind the identity of an entity to a particular message or piece of information. They do not provide privacy or secrecy. They ensure the integrity of a message and verify who wrote it. Digital signatures require asymmetric key cryptography. **FIGURE 9-5** shows a digital signature.

You can construct a digital signature with a private key from an asymmetric key pair. It includes signing a hash of the message. This combination provides dual assurance—that a message originated from a particular entity and that no one has changed the contents. Anyone with access to a signer's public key can verify the digital signature. However, only

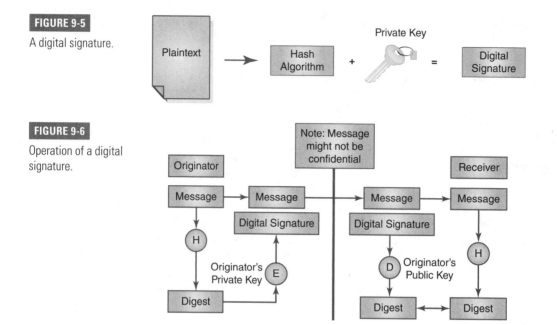

FIGURE 9-5

A digital signature.

FIGURE 9-6

Operation of a digital signature.

the holder of the private key can create the digital signature. **FIGURE 9-6** shows how a digital signature operates.

Rivest-Shamir-Adelman (RSA) and the **Digital Signature Algorithm (DSA)** are the most common digital signature algorithms used. The patent on RSA expired in September 2000. It is now in the public domain. The DSA signs the **Secure Hash Algorithm (SHA)** hash of the message. Although most commercial systems use RSA, the Digital Signature Standard (DSS), DSA, and SHA are U.S. government standards. They are more likely to appear in government products.

Cryptographic Applications and Uses in Information System Security

Many vendors offer security products and services today. In fact, several thousand different offerings are available. These products and services are generally organized into common categories that include:

- Anti-malware
- Compliance/auditing
- Forensics
- ID management
- Intellectual property
- Managed security service providers (MSSPs)
- Messaging safeguards
- Patch management

- Perimeter defenses
- Security information and event management (SIEM) and incident response
- Transaction security (digital certificates, secure file transfer)
- Wireless security

You can find cryptography uses in many of these categories.

Authentication tools include tokens, smart cards, biometrics, passwords, and password recovery. Some tools rely on proximity cards and fingerprint readers. Others use cryptographic techniques such as **public key infrastructure (PKI)** user authentication and tools that securely send passwords across the Internet. PKI is a set of hardware, software, people, policies, and procedures needed to create, manage, distribute, use, store, and revoke digital certificates.

Access control and authorization includes firewalls, timestamping, single sign-on, identity management, and mobile device security. These encryption tools have virtual private networks that may be included with firewalls, but not necessarily the firewalls themselves. They also may secure connectivity across the Internet and provide tools that encrypt contents of hard drives.

Assessment and auditing tools include vulnerability-assessment scanners, penetration-testing tools, forensic software, and log analyzers. Assessment scanners and penetration-testing tools that involve password-cracking modules use cryptographic techniques to try to guess passwords.

Security management products include tools for enterprise security management, configuration and patch management, and security policy development. Integrity-checking tools use cryptographic methods to make sure nothing and no one has modified the software.

Wireless security tools encrypt data to protect them in transit and to limit access to authorized people. Email security tools often involve encrypting data in transit and sometimes at rest. Content filtering includes antivirus products, mobile code scanners, web filters, and spam blockers. They typically do not use encryption, although you may encrypt databases of threat signatures.

Encryption tools include line encryption, database security products, virtual private networks (VPNs), public key infrastructure (PKI), and crypto accelerators. These products use cryptography extensively to do their tasks. A crypto accelerator offloads cryptographic routines from the main processor to cards that have chipsets designed for fast encryption.

Other Cryptographic Tools and Resources

As a security professional, you should understand how to match business needs with cryptographic solutions and select proper tool sets. In this section, you'll learn how to identify tool sets that use symmetric keys and match them to their most common business use. You'll learn how to identify tool sets that can use asymmetric key cryptography and identify the infrastructure required to make a solution. You'll learn how hash functions work, how to identify the ciphers used for hash functions, and how to use them to ensure integrity. You'll learn how to use cryptography to address each issue as well as the differences between each requirement. You'll also learn the differences between digital and digitized signatures and the infrastructure and legal requirements for maintaining digital signatures used for nonrepudiation. Finally, you'll learn how to design a key management model that supports your business requirements.

Symmetric Key Standards

Symmetric key algorithms (or standards) are the most common form of encryption. The same key encrypts and decrypts information. Because symmetric keys can be created easily and changed rapidly, they often are used just once to exchange information between two parties, and then they are discarded. In this situation, they are session keys. Unlike asymmetric key algorithms, symmetric algorithms can be fast and are well suited to encrypting lots of data. The following list of cryptographic algorithms is sorted generally from weakest to strongest. Stronger algorithms are always more secure than weak algorithms but often have a higher computational cost. If a weaker algorithm provides sufficient security, it may be a good choice. Of course, you must periodically review your algorithm choices to ensure that each one provides enough security if needs change. Organizations currently use several symmetric algorithms, including the following:

- **Data Encryption Standard (DES)**—IBM originally developed DES as the Lucifer algorithm. The NSA modified it and issued it as a national standard in 1977. FIPS PUB 46-3 updated its definition. It uses a 56-bit key and operates on 64-bit blocks of data. The algorithm is better for hardware use than for software, and it can rapidly encrypt lots of data. The DES algorithm is in the public domain. DES was once a state-of-the-art algorithm, but with rapid advances in hardware capabilities and attack methods, attackers can now crack it in as little as a few days. It is no longer a secure algorithm.
- **Triple DES (3DES)**—Triple DES is a protocol that consists of three passes of DES (encrypt, decrypt, encrypt) using multiple keys. It increases the keyspace from 56 to 112 or 168 bits, depending on whether two or three keys are used. Triple DES is computationally secure because of the underlying security of the DES algorithm and the vastly increased keyspace. Note that using the same key three times produces the same result as single DES. It, too, is contained in FIPS PUB 46-3 and is in the public domain.
- **International Data Encryption Algorithm (IDEA)**—Like DES, this block cipher operates on 64-bit blocks. It uses a 128-bit key and runs somewhat faster than DES on hardware and software. Ascom-Tech AG holds a patent for IDEA (U.S. patent 5,214,703), but it is free for noncommercial use.
- **CAST**—The CAST algorithm is a substitution-permutation algorithm similar to DES. Unlike DES, its authors made its design criteria public. This 64-bit symmetric block cipher can use keys from 40 to 256 bits. RFC 2144 describes CAST-128; RFC-2612 describes CAST-256. Although it is patented (U.S. patent 5,511,123), its inventors, C. M. Adams and S. E. Tavares, made it available for free use.
- **Blowfish**—Blowfish is a 64-bit block cipher that has a variable key length from 32 to 448 bits. It is much faster than DES or IDEA. Blowfish is a strong algorithm that has been included in more than 150 products as well as v2.5.47 of the Linux kernel. Its author, Bruce Schneier, placed it in the public domain. Schneier's Twofish was a candidate for the Advanced Encryption Standard.

To help defend against dictionary attacks, in which attackers try common key values, some algorithms use an additional value called a **salt value**. A salt value is a set of random characters that you can combine with an actual input key to create the encryption key. The combination of the salt value and the input key makes it far more difficult to compromise an encryption key using common key values.

- **Advanced Encryption Standard (AES)**—Also known as Rijndael (RAIN-doll), AES is a block cipher. Vincent Rijmen and Joan Daemen designed AES, and FIPS PUB 197 published it as a standard. The AES algorithm can use cryptographic keys of 128, 192, and 256 bits to encrypt and decrypt data in blocks of 128 bits. The cipher also can operate on variable block lengths. It is both strong and fast.
- **RC2**—RC2 is a variable key-size block cipher designed by Ronald Rivest (RC stands for Ron's Code). RC2 operates as a drop-in replacement for DES and operates on 64-bit blocks. It uses a salt value as part of its encryption routine to make cryptanalysis more difficult. RSA Security owns it.
- **RC4**—Produced by RSA Security, RC4 is a variable key-size stream cipher with byte-oriented operations. Internet browsers often use RC4 to provide an SSL connection.

Wireless Security

With inexpensive high-bandwidth communications technology, wireless local area networks (WLANs) now are a viable strategy for homes and offices that do not want to link cable to all computers. WLANs are also becoming common in coffee shops and many other public areas. However, this convenience reduces security.

Many wireless access point providers and users install their new technology in a plug-and-play fashion. That is, they open the box, connect the pieces, and turn it on and run the installation wizards. If it works, they never touch the manual. Although wireless products have built-in security, the default configuration generally doesn't enable it. Why? Because most consumers expect a product to work when they plug it in. As a result, most vendors that offer security require the customer to turn it on. Many customers never bother. This can create major security problems.

802.11 Wireless Security. The 802.11, or Wi-Fi, wireless standards emerged in 1999. Wi-Fi provides wireless communications at transmission speeds from 11 Mbps for 802.11b to over 780 Mbps for 802.11ac. New and proposed standards push the maximum transfer rate even further. The 802.11ay standard supports data transmission rates up to 100 Gbps. The most popular standards within the 802.11 specification transmit data using either the 2.4GHz or 5GHz band. Newer standards expand the bandwidth to wider ranges. The ranges of data communications at the most popular standards bandwidths are advertised to be about 100 meters (over 200 meters for 802.11n). Nevertheless, hackers have used high-gain antennas—including one made from a Pringles® potato chip can!—to boost reception to several miles. A sort of informal competition is under way worldwide to see who can create the longest 802.11 wireless connection. At last count, the Swedish Space Corp. posted the

9

Cryptography

record with a stratospheric balloon floating at a height of 29.7 km. It achieved a connection with a base station 310 km away.

The 802.11 wireless protocols allow encryption through Wired Equivalent Privacy (WEP) or the newer Wi-Fi Protected Access (WPA). Users need to have a shared secret that serves as the key to begin secure wireless connections. Since most wireless access points (WAPs) generally do not enable wireless encryption by default, most wireless networks operate with no encryption at all. Any attacker can monitor and access these open networks. In 2000,

> ⚠ **WARNING**
>
> The important lesson to remember is that wireless signals do not stop at a building's perimeter. Therefore, cryptographic protection becomes important to secure your organization's wireless communications.

Peter Shipley drove around the San Francisco Bay area with a portable wireless rig. He found that about 85 percent of wireless networks were unencrypted. Of those that were encrypted, more than half used the default password. Although each WAP has its own service set identifier (SSID), which a client needs to know for access, hackers have tools such as NetStumbler that display the names of all SSIDs within range. Windows simply connects to the first available network signal. As a result, wireless encryption is a minimum requirement to ensure security on a wireless network.

WEP was the first wireless encryption protocol in widespread use. It has some severe limitations, however. Design flaws exist in the protocol, including some key scheduling weaknesses in the RC4 encryption. A hacker using tools such as AirSnort or WEPcrack can guess the encryption key after collecting approximately 5 million to 10 million encrypted packets. To address these weaknesses, current standards and supported hardware also offer WPA. To provide the best protection for wireless network traffic, always use WPA or its newest version, WPA2. Never use WEP. Enable MAC address filtering, which screens out PCs that it doesn't recognize. Place a firewall between the wireless LAN and the rest of the network so that would-be attackers can't get far.

Asymmetric Key Solutions

Recall that key distribution issues keys to valid users of a cryptosystem so they can communicate. The first step in managing keys actually occurs before distributing the keys. Users must be authenticated and authorized for key creation and management through a registration process. This ensures that only authorized users can create keys in the first place. The classic solution to key distribution is to use out-of-band communications through a trusted channel to distribute keys in advance. This could be by registered mail, by courier, or even by telephone, if you are certain no one is tapping the phone lines. However, this strategy is expensive and slow.

Organizations with the resources and the ability to plan develop ways to do this. For example, the U.S. Navy uses a unique distribution system to make sure its cryptosystems remain secure. It includes strict accountability and control procedures to ensure proper use of cryptosystems. This program is the Communications Security Material System, or CMS. Each command appoints a CMS custodian and an alternate. They are responsible for getting, storing, controlling, installing, removing, and destroying keys for Navy cryptosystems. This involves a lot of overhead and expense. However, the high value of the information justifies it.

An asymmetric key distribution system has no need for couriers, back channels, or expensive storage or inventory plans. That's because it doesn't require each party to first share a secret key. This solves the chicken-and-egg problem of first needing a secure channel before creating a secure channel.

Key revocation occurs when someone is no longer trusted or allowed to use a cryptosystem. In a symmetric key system where everyone shares the same secret, compromising one copy of the key compromises all copies. This is similar to all employees having the same office key. If a terminated employee refuses to return the key, the organization must change every lock and issue new keys. After a few dismissals, this process becomes expensive and cumbersome.

In an asymmetric key environment, the **key directory** is a trusted repository of all public keys. If one person no longer is trusted, the directory's manager removes that public key. No one attempting to initiate communications with that person would be able to find that key. That person still could initiate encrypted communications by using other posted public keys. However, if the protocol requires digital signatures for all messages, the recipient would reject the message because it wouldn't be able to find a valid key to check the signature. For example, you can query the MIT PGP Public Key Server at *http://pgp.mit.edu/*. But what happens if the entity that stores the keys ceases to exist? In the current era of outsourcing data and processing to cloud service providers, this is always a real possibility. A **key escrow** is a key storage method that allows some authorized third party access to a key under certain circumstances. Such circumstances could include emergency situations when the key owner cannot access a key.

Ad hoc secure communications are the basis of Internet e-commerce. This is one of the most frequently used forms of cryptography today. Using a symmetric key would be difficult. It would require each party to make contact some other way and agree on a secret key. If such a channel existed, why not just use that? Practically speaking, such a channel doesn't exist.

With an asymmetric key, ad hoc communications are straightforward. The most common form of Internet cryptography is Secure Sockets Layer (SSL) or Hypertext Transport Protocol Secure (HTTPS) encryption. The SSL handshake created the first secure communications session between a client and a server. The Symantec website describes this process nicely (*www.symantec.com/connect/blogs/how-does-ssl-work-what-ssl-handshake*).

The **SSL Handshake Protocol** consists of two phases: server authentication and an optional client authentication. In the first phase, the server, in response to a client's request, sends its certificate—containing the server's public key—and its cipher preferences. The client then creates a master key, which it encrypts with the server's public key. The client then sends the encrypted master key to the server. The server recovers the master key and authenticates itself to the client by returning a message with the master key. The client and server encrypt and authenticate subsequent data with keys derived from this master key. In the optional second phase, the server sends a challenge to the client. The client authenticates itself to the server by returning the client's digital signature on the challenge as well as its public key certificate.

Digital signatures verify a person's identity or that person's association with a message. They require the use of a **certificate authority (CA)** that can vouch for the validity of a credential. Nonrepudiation verifies the digital signature on a document. It proves who sent a message. In some cases, you can combine this with a tamperproof time source to prove when you sent the message. But CAs do more than just provide certificates. They also provide a full suite of important certificate management functions. Two critical services include users requesting certificates and the CA revoking certificates. A user can request a certificate

9

Cryptography

by sending a standard certification signing request (CSR). A CSR standard allows many different types of programs to request certificates from a CA. At some point, most certificates either expire or become invalid. A CA maintains a list of invalid, or revoked, certificates in either a certificate revocation list (CRL) or by maintaining the data to support the newer Online Certificate Status Protocol (OCSP).

Hash Function and Integrity

You should be able to explain in layman's terms how hash functions work, identify the ciphers used for hash functions, and explain their use in ensuring integrity.

Hash Functions

Hash functions help detect forgeries. They compute a checksum of a message and then combine it with a cryptographic function so that the result is tamperproof. Hashes are usually of a known fixed size based on the algorithm used.

Recall that a checksum is a one-way calculation that yields a result that you can check easily by rerunning the data through the checksum function. For example, given a series of decimal numbers such as the following, a simple checksum could be the two rightmost digits of the sum of these numbers:

71 77 61 114 107 75 61 114 100 121

Therefore, in this case, you can add them together to get 901, drop the 9, and your checksum is 01. Now, if you were to send this sequence of 10 numbers to someone over a noisy communications channel, the noise could garble some of the information. By also sending the checksum, the recipient can recalculate to see if the numbers add up. If not, he knows to request a retransmission.

Because checksums are very simple functions, it is possible to have the checksum come out correctly on a garbled message. Of course, it's also possible for someone to deliberately modify the numbers in such a way that the checksum still matches. This illustrates the point that checksums do not ensure security; they ensure reliability.

A hash is a checksum designed so that no one can forge a message in a way that will result in the same hash as a legitimate message. Hashes are usually a fixed size. The result is a **hash value**. In general, hash values are larger than checksum values. Hashes act as a fingerprint of the data. You can make hashes available as a reference so that recipients can see if the information has changed. Software publishers often provide hash values so that customers can verify the integrity of the software they receive. To be effective, hashes usually have to be long enough that a hacker would need a long time to create an alternate message that matched the hash value.

Professor Ronald Rivest of MIT—he's the R in RSA—developed the MD5 **message digest algorithm**. RFC 1321 contains the specifications for the algorithm. It takes an input of any arbitrary length and generates a 128-bit message digest that is computationally infeasible to match by finding another input. This message digest is uniquely associated with its source. You can publish an MD5 hash with information such as compiled source code and then compare the information with the hash. This verifies that no person or process, such as a virus, has modified the information.

Note, however, that the MD5 message digest is not yet a signed hash. Nothing uniquely associates the hash with the originator. That is, if an attacker wanted to modify a program, the attacker could easily recalculate a new MD5 hash and post both together on the website. The presence of an MD5 hash does not prove authenticity of a file; it only proves that the file hasn't changed since you computed the hash.

The Federal Information Processing Standard Publication 180-1 (FIPS 180-1) defines the Secure Hash Algorithm (SHA-1). SHA-1 produces a 160-bit hash from a message of any arbitrary length. Like MD5, it creates a unique fingerprint of a file that is computationally infeasible to reproduce. SHA-1 was so popular that it resulted in developments that produced two additional standards, SHA-2 and SHA-3. Each successive version increases the options for input size and output length. MD5 and SHA aren't the only hashing algorithms. The hash message authentication code (HMAC) is a hash function that uses a key to create the hash, or message digest. RACE Integrity Primitives Evaluation Message Digest (RIPEMD) is a collection of functions that provide hash values for a wide range of applications.

How do you create a digital signature from a hash? The output from the MD5 or the SHA hash provides input for an asymmetric key algorithm that uses a private key as input. The result of this encryption is a value that is uniquely associated with the file. It is computationally infeasible to forge and provably related to the identity of the entity that signs the file. FIPS 180-1 includes the diagram in **FIGURE 9-7** that shows this relationship.

Someone can digitally sign a message, software, or any other digital representation in a way that anyone can easily verify. Note that this presumes the integrity of the public key directory that the recipient uses to look up the key to verify the signature. If an attacker

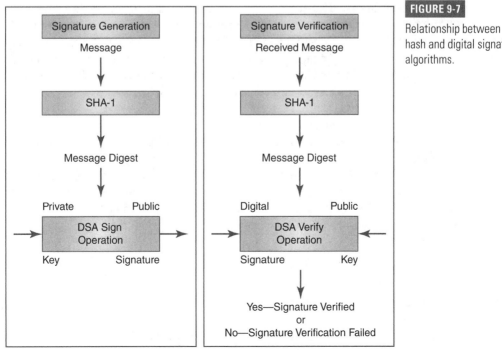

FIGURE 9-7

Relationship between hash and digital signature algorithms.

successfully penetrates the directory, all bets are off. At that point, the fox is vouching for the safety of the henhouse.

There are several software packages to make implementing encryption a little easier. Two of the most popular options are PGP/GPG and Bcrypt. Pretty Good Privacy (PGP) is a program originally written by Phil Zimmerman that provides encryption for data communications. PGP is most often used for protecting email messages. GNU Privacy Guard (GPG) is a freely available alternative to PGP. GPG is commonly used in applications that cannot justify PGP licenses. Another common software application that provides cryptography services is bcrypt. Bcrypt is an application that derives keys from user passwords. It is used in many applications that require passwords that change based on a user's identity. Password-Based Key Derivation Function 2 (PBKDF2) is another software application that helps to derive cryptographic keys. BPKDF2 is part of RSA Laboratory's Public-Key Cryptography Standards (PKCS).

Digital Signatures and Nonrepudiation

Given a sample business case, you should understand how to state, in layman's terms, the differences between digital and digitized signatures. You should be able to explain the infrastructure and legal needs for keeping digital signatures for nonrepudiation.

Digital Signatures Versus Digitized Signatures

Earlier in this chapter, you learned about digital signatures and digitized signatures. Although the difference between the two is straightforward, many people often confuse them. To review, a digitized signature is an image of a physical signature stored in digital format. This file could be in JPG, GIF, or BMP format. Theoretically, it could be stored in a digital camera. The chief value of a digitized signature is printing it onto form letters, sometimes in a different color to make it look more like a handwritten ink signature on the printed page.

A digital signature is something quite different. Recall that a digital signature is a combination of a strong hash of a message, which acts as a fingerprint. You can combine this with a secret key from either a symmetric or an asymmetric cryptosystem. This combination gives dual assurance that a message originated from a particular entity and that no one has altered the contents.

In an asymmetric cryptosystem, anyone with access to a signer's public key can verify the digital signature. However, only the holder of the private key can create it. In a symmetric cryptosystem, both sender and recipient need the same secret key.

Think about this: Which security principle can you satisfy with an asymmetric digital signature but not a symmetric one? The answer is nonrepudiation. If both sender and recipient have the same secret key, you can't prove to someone else that a message exchange started with one party rather than the other. Therefore, the conditions for proving nonrepudiation are as follows:

- An effective asymmetric key algorithm
- A strong hash function
- A means to apply the private encryption key to the hash value to produce a digital signature
- A tamperproof or trusted third-party timing device, if desired

- An agreed-upon protocol for validating digital signatures
- A secure key management and distribution system
- A public key repository that has an assured level of integrity
- Key escrow to be able to produce public keys from reluctant parties
- Procedures to handle disputes

Organizations must spell out all these steps in writing as part of a business agreement. Then, and only then, are you ready to implement nonrepudiation.

Principles of Certificates and Key Management

You learned about key management earlier in this chapter. It includes creating, distributing, storing, validating, updating, replacing, and revoking keys and keying material.

　　Here is a sample classic key management scheme. The Enigma was one of the most famous cryptographic devices of the 20th century. Invented by Arthur Scherbius, it was Germany's chief encryption tool before and during World War II. The machine had more possible keying configurations than the number of atoms in the known universe! In practice, a subset of keys was used to make key changing practical. Nonetheless, the three-rotor Enigma offered a dizzying 158,962,555,217,826,360,000 possible keys at the beginning of World War II.

　　German Enigma operators got a new codebook monthly. This book told which key to use each day. Now, if all messages were encrypted with that same key, Allied cryptanalysts would have a lot of ciphertext, all encrypted with the same key, to attempt to decrypt. This could be a problem. Therefore, the keying protocol required that you use only the key in the codebook as a key-encrypting key. The wartime Enigma had five scramblers. Enigma users employed only three scramblers at any time. Users could place each of those scrambler wheels in one of 26 starting positions—one for each letter of the alphabet. Therefore, every message began with the setting of the scramblers. Senders repeated each message to make sure the key got through any radio interference. With 60 different possible scrambler selections and $26 \times 26 \times 26$, or 17,576, possible starting positions, users could encrypt each day's messages with one of 1,054,560 possible keys. Note that without knowing the initial settings, the cryptanalyst still didn't know which of the 159 quintillion keys to use. The Enigma encryption was totally unbreakable, right? The Germans thought so. They were wrong.

　　Polish cryptographer Marian Rejewski figured it out. There's not enough space to go into detail here about how he did it. You can look up his exploits in a number of books. It's enough to say here that his solution involved a brilliant use of pure mathematics to exploit a weakness in the cipher. The moral of the story is that a key distribution system may appear secure and the number of keys nearly infinite. However, the best key management system in the world does not protect against a brilliant cryptanalyst if the encryption algorithm itself has any weaknesses.

Modern Key Management Techniques

Today, computers handle all business cryptography. Some of the best minds in the field have scrutinized the algorithms of choice, sometimes for decades. Therefore, an attacker most likely will not defeat your cryptography by breaking the mathematics behind it. Human behavior—and, most important, human error—is much more likely to lead to the compromise. Poor key management is often the cause.

This is not the place to examine the technical complexities of each key management technique. Instead, you will look at which techniques are right for different business applications. For example, PKI is a technology that absolutely requires effective key management. PKI vendors have promised tremendous growth for years. However, the practicality of using all the key management components has throttled growth. The rest of this section contains a brief overview of several modern key management techniques. Use this discussion as a starting point to decide which technique works best for your organization.

One of the most important aspects of implementing any key management strategy is trust. You have to trust someone. Otherwise, you wouldn't accept any credentials as valid. The most common trust model is often called the "web of trust." This term refers to a model in which any entity determines who it will trust initially. This is often decided through direct interrogation and authorization. Once an entity is trusted, the organization trusts other organizations that the trusted entity trusts. In other words, "I trust whoever you trust." This model works well when all trusted entities are actually trustworthy. The other model is to require that every entity provide proof of trustworthiness before trust is extended. The web-of-trust model is far easier to implement, but it does allow for abuse. Any untrustworthy entity can trick any other node in the web into trusting it.

AES

The U.S. government currently has no standard for creating cryptographic keys for unclassified applications. However, working groups have been defining an AES key wrap specification that would securely encrypt a plaintext key along with integrity information. This capability would provide a mechanism for key management in unclassified government environments.

IPSec

IPSec protects Internet Protocol (IP) packets from disclosure or change. The protocol provides privacy and/or integrity. Each header contains a security parameter index (SPI) that refers to a particular encryption key. Additionally, the header may contain up to two security headers. The Authentication Header (AH) provides integrity checking. The encapsulating security payload (ESP) encrypts the packet for confidentiality. Hosts using IPSec establish a security association with each other. This involves agreeing which crypto methods and keys to use as well as the SPI host. The Internet Security Association and Key Management Protocol (ISAKMP, pronounced *ICE-a-camp*) provides key management services, which you'll learn about next.

ISAKMP

ISAKMP is a key management strategy growing in popularity. RFC 2408 defines ISAKMP as a set of procedures for authenticating a communicating peer, creating and managing security associations, key generation techniques, and threat mitigation, that is, denial of service and replay attacks. All these are necessary to establish and maintain secure communications via IP Security Service or any other security protocol in an Internet environment.

The **security association (SA)** is the basic element of ISAKMP key management. An SA contains all the information needed to perform a variety of network security services. ISAKMP acts as a common framework for agreeing to the format of SA attributes and for negotiating, modifying, and deleting SAs. It uses a Diffie-Hellman key exchange signed with RSA.

XKMS

The Extensible Markup Language (XML) key management specification (XKMS) gives protocols for distributing and registering public keys for use with XML. XML is a markup language for documents containing structured information. It provides syntax that supports sharing complex structured documents over the Web.

Managed PKI

Some vendors offer a managed service to handle issues associated with public key management. Services include centralized key generation, distribution, backup, and recovery. Rather than create a key management infrastructure, customers can choose to outsource these details.

ANSI X9.17

The financial industry created this standard to define key management procedures. It defines a symmetric key exchange protocol that many manufacturers use in hardware encryption devices. Although asymmetric key exchange offers some advantages, the fact that organizations have invested significant amounts of money in X9.17-compliant equipment means they will continue to use it for some time. According to FIPS Pub 171, X9.17 specifies the minimum standards for the following:

* Control of the keying material during its lifetime to prevent unauthorized disclosure, modification, or substitution
* Distribution of the keying material in order to permit interoperability between cryptographic equipment or facilities
* Ensuring the integrity of keying material during all phases of its life, including its generation, distribution, storage, entry, use, and destruction
* Recovery in the event of a failure of the key management process or when the integrity of the keying material is questioned

When you select a key management product or technique for your organization, do your homework first. Each method has its advantages and disadvantages. Make sure you understand the up-front cost as well as the ongoing maintenance and administration costs.

9

Cryptography

CHAPTER SUMMARY

In this chapter, you learned how cryptography works and how it applies to solving business issues. You learned key cryptographic terms and business principles, how to apply cryptography to these principles, and how to identify security tools that rely on cryptography. You also learned the advantages and disadvantages of symmetric and asymmetric ciphers as they pertain to cryptanalysis.

KEY CONCEPTS AND TERMS

Algorithm	Elliptic curve cryptography (ECC)	Plaintext
Asymmetric key cryptography	Elliptic Curve DHE (ECDHE)	Private (symmetric) key
Attribute-based encryption (ABE)	Encryption	Product cipher
Authentication	Hash	Public (asymmetric) key
Block cipher	Hashing function	Public key cryptography
Caesar cipher	Identity-based encryption (IBE)	Public key infrastructure (PKI)
Certificate authority (CA)	In-band key exchange	Quantum cryptography
Checksum	Integrity	Revocation
Cipher	Key	Rivest-Shamir-Adelman (RSA)
Ciphertext	Key directory	Salt value
Cleartext	Key distribution	Secure Hash Algorithm (SHA)
Confidentiality	Key escrow	Secure Shell (SSH)
Connection encryption	Key management	Security association (SA)
Cryptanalysis	Key revocation	Session key
Cryptography	Key-encrypting key	Simple substitution cipher
Cryptogram	Key stretching	SSL handshake protocol
Cryptosystem	Keyspace	Steganography
Data Encryption Standard (DES)	Keyword mixed alphabet cipher	Stream cipher
Decryption	Message digest algorithm (MD5)	Substitution cipher
Differential cryptanalysis	Nonrepudiation	Symmetric key cryptography
Diffie-Hellman algorithm	One-time pad cipher	Timestamping
Diffie-Hellman in ephemeral mode (DHE)	One-way algorithm	Transport encryption
	Open cipher	Transposition cipher
Digital signature	Out-of-band key exchange	Vernam cipher
Digital signature algorithm (DSA)	Perfect forward secrecy	Vigenère cipher
Digitized signature		

CHAPTER 9 ASSESSMENT

1. _____ offers a mechanism to accomplish four security goals: confidentiality, integrity, authentication, and nonrepudiation.

A. Security association (SA)
B. Secure Sockets Layer (SSL)
C. Cryptography
D. None of the above

2. A strong hash function is designed so that a forged message cannot result in the same hash as a legitimate message.

A. True
B. False

3. The act of scrambling plaintext into ciphertext is known as _____.

A. Decryption
B. Encryption
C. Plaintext
D. Cleartext

4. An algorithm used for cryptographic purposes is known as a _____.

A. Hash
B. Private key
C. Public key
D. Cipher

5. Encryption ciphers fall into two general categories: symmetric (private) key and asymmetric (public) key.

- A. True
- B. False

6. An encryption cipher that uses the same key to encrypt and decrypt is called a(n) _____ key.

- A. Symmetric (private)
- B. Asymmetric (public)
- C. Encrypting
- D. Hash
- E. None of the above

7. _____ corroborates the identity of an entity, whether the sender, the sender's computer, some device, or some information.

- A. Nonrepudiation
- B. Confidentiality
- C. Integrity
- D. Authentication

8. Which of the following is one of the four basic forms of a cryptographic attack?

- A. Ciphertext-only attack
- B. Known-plaintext attack
- C. Chosen-plaintext attack
- D. Chosen-ciphertext attack
- E. All the above

9. The two basic types of ciphers are transposition and substitution.

- A. True
- B. False

10. A _____ is used to detect forgeries.

- A. Hash function
- B. Checksum
- C. Hash value
- D. KDC

11. DES, IDEA, RC4, and WEP are examples of

_____.

- A. Key revocation
- B. 802.11b wireless security
- C. Asymmetric key algorithms (or standards)
- D. Symmetric algorithms (or standards)

12. A _____ signature is a representation of a physical signature stored in a digital format.

- A. Digital
- B. Digitized
- C. Private key
- D. Public key

CHAPTER 10

Networks and Telecommunications

FOR MOST BUSINESSES AND ORGANIZATIONS today, networks and telecommunications are critical parts of business infrastructure. **Telephony** is the field of technology that includes the development and deployment of services to support all electronic communications. Many organizations could not operate if their networks were unavailable *or prone to error.* Network security involves meeting an organization's essential need for network availability, integrity, and confidentiality. The data transmitted through the network is protected from modification (either accidental or intentional), it cannot be read by unauthorized parties, and its source and destination can be verified (nonrepudiation). Business and security requirements are as follows:

- Access control
- Network stability and reliability
- Integrity
- Availability
- Confidentiality or nonrepudiation

This chapter examines how you can secure networks and telecommunications. It introduces the basic elements of a network and explains the security issues surrounding networks. It presents some of the building blocks for securing data as they travel throughout your network.

As a security professional, you need to understand these elements of the networks and telecommunications world:

- The Open Systems Interconnection (OSI) Reference Model
- Network topology
- Transmission Control Protocol/Internet Protocol (TCP/IP) networking
- Wireless networking
- Network security

The Open Systems Interconnection Reference Model

The **Open Systems Interconnection (OSI) Reference Model** is a template for building and using a network and its resources. The OSI Reference Model is a theoretical model of networking with interchangeable layers. The beauty of it is that you can design technology for any one of the layers without worrying about how the other layers work. You merely need to make sure that each layer knows how to talk to the layers above and below it. **FIGURE 10-1** shows each layer of the OSI Reference Model.

The OSI Reference Model layers are as follows:

- **Application Layer**—This layer is responsible for interacting with end users. The Application Layer includes all programs on a computer that interact with the network. For example, your email software is included, since it must transmit and receive messages over the network. A simple game like Solitaire doesn't fit here because it does not require the network in order to operate.

- **Presentation Layer**—This layer is responsible for the coding of data. The Presentation Layer includes file formats and character representations. From a security perspective, encryption generally takes place at the Presentation Layer.

- **Session Layer**—This layer is responsible for maintaining communication sessions between computers. The Session Layer creates, maintains, and disconnects communications that take place between processes over the network.

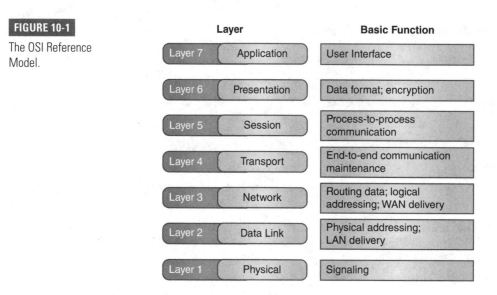

FIGURE 10-1

The OSI Reference Model.

Layer	Basic Function
Layer 7 — Application	User Interface
Layer 6 — Presentation	Data format; encryption
Layer 5 — Session	Process-to-process communication
Layer 4 — Transport	End-to-end communication maintenance
Layer 3 — Network	Routing data; logical addressing; WAN delivery
Layer 2 — Data Link	Physical addressing; LAN delivery
Layer 1 — Physical	Signaling

> ▶ **TIP**
>
> An easy way to remember the layers of the OSI Reference Model is with a mnemonic—for example, "All People Seem To Need Data Processing."

- **Transport Layer**—This layer is responsible for breaking data into packets and properly transmitting it over the network. Flow control and error checking take place at the Transport Layer.

- **Network Layer**—This layer is responsible for the logical implementation of the network. One very important feature of the Network Layer, covered later in this chapter, is logical addressing. In TCP/IP networking, logical addressing takes the familiar form of IP addresses.

- **Data Link Layer**—This layer is responsible for transmitting information on computers connected to the same local area network (LAN). The Data Link Layer uses Media Access Control (MAC) addresses. Device manufacturers assign each hardware device a unique MAC address.

- **Physical Layer**—This layer is responsible for the physical operation of the network. The Physical Layer must translate the binary ones and zeros of computer language into the language of the transport medium. In the case of copper network cables, it must translate computer data into electrical pulses. In the case of fiber optics, it must translate the data into bursts of light.

The OSI Reference Model enables developers to produce each layer independently. If you write an email program that operates at the Application Layer, you only need to worry about getting information down to the Presentation Layer. The details of the network you're using are irrelevant to your program. Other software takes care of that for you. Similarly, if you're making cables at the Physical Layer, you don't need to worry about what Network Layer protocols will travel on that cable. You just need to build a cable that satisfies the requirements of the Data Link Layer.

The Main Types of Networks

As a security professional, you'll learn a lot about networking. In fact, a good working knowledge about networks and how to secure them is crucial to protect your organization from network failure or data breach. Many of the devices used in the security field protect networks. Those that don't protect networks often rely on them to function. In this section, you will examine the two main types of networks—wide area networks (WANs) and local area networks (LANs)—and explore their function. You will also examine some of the ways to connect your LAN to a WAN. Finally, you will take a brief look at the most important network devices.

Wide Area Networks

As the name implies, WANs connect systems over a large geographic area. The most common example of a WAN is the Internet. As shown in **FIGURE 10-2**, the Internet connects many independent networks together. This allows people at different locations to communicate easily with each other. The Internet hides the details of this process from the end user. When you send an email message, you don't have to worry about how the data move. You just click Send and let the network deal with all the complexity.

From a security perspective, it's important to remember that the Internet is an open network. You cannot guarantee data privacy once data leave your network. The data might travel

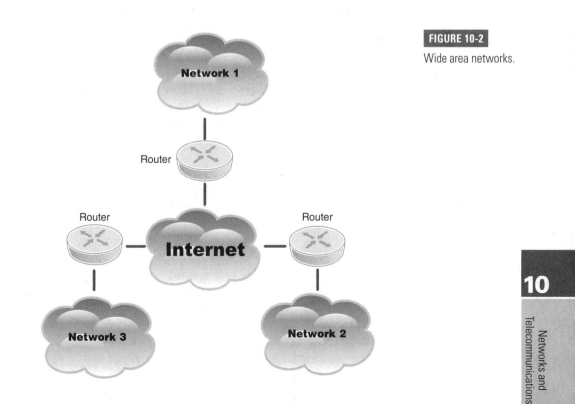

FIGURE 10-2

Wide area networks.

any path to get to their destination. Anyone might be able to read those data along the way. Think of data on the Internet as more like a postcard than a letter in a sealed envelope. Fortunately, security technology such as encryption enables you to hide the meaning of your data when you're sending it across the Internet. This is similar to sending a postcard but writing the message in a secret code. You'll learn more about network encryption later in this chapter.

Most of today's organizations use the Internet to connect different locations to each other and to connect with their customers. This is a low-cost way to connect sites, since it is usually easy and inexpensive to connect a network to the Internet. However, you must make sure that you consider the security issues surrounding the use of an open network such as the Internet. Again, encryption technology can help you reduce the risk of using the Internet.

Some organizations prefer to use their own private networks for connecting remote sites. Some choose to do so for security reasons; others simply want the guaranteed reliability of private networks. Although this is a very good option for security and reliability reasons, it is also very expensive. However, there's no reason you can't work with a communications provider to develop your own private WAN.

Connectivity Options

There are multiple methods you can use to connect to the Internet. Most home users choose either a cable modem or a digital subscriber line (DSL) from the telephone company. But these aren't the only options. Internet service providers (ISPs) are increasingly providing high-bandwidth Internet service using fiber optics. This type of service provides much faster Internet connections than previous service options. Users with no access to cable, DSL, or fiber optic service can still connect to the Internet using satellite or old-fashioned dialup services. As Internet use increases, ISPs add more choices to the ways to connect. In many cases, the number of available options for connecting to the Internet depends on where you live. More densely populated areas tend to offer more options. You can also connect to the Internet through a wireless carrier. Advances in wireless technology make cellular connections affordable in many areas, and service area coverage increases daily.

Smartphones generally connect to third-generation (3G) or fourth-generation (4G) networks. Many of these devices also have the ability to connect to Wi-Fi networks using 802.11 standards. Cellular 3G and 4G networks provide stable Internet and voice communication over a wide area. The connections to the Internet seem to be continuous. However, the devices are actually moving from cell to cell. This handoff from one cell to another is invisible to the user and makes it appear as though connections are continuous. However, most cellular network carriers impose data transfer limits and charge fees for access when users exceed these limits. Mobile device users prefer Wi-Fi network connections due to the higher network speed and lower usage costs. It isn't difficult to find free Wi-Fi access at many coffee shops, hotels, and a wide variety of other locations. This ease of Internet connectivity makes mobile computing a real option for the average user.

These cellular networks are very popular with individual users and businesses. Today's carriers currently offer devices for laptops and mobile access points. In fact, many smartphones and tablets can act as wireless access points for other devices. These mobile access point devices connect to the Internet using a cellular network connection and convert the connection to a Wi-Fi connection for capable devices. That means that you can connect a laptop, smartphone, and even several other devices to the Internet anywhere you are located in your carrier's coverage area. This ability can be a huge advantage over using free Wi-Fi. The Internet connection speeds are generally slower using 3G or 4G wireless access devices. However, such connections are far more secure. You don't have to worry about sharing your Internet connection at a coffee shop with an attacker on the same network. Most public Wi-Fi networks are very insecure. You never know who else is on the same network just listening to all your traffic. Sacrificing a little speed to get a secure connection may be worth it.

Businesses also have many choices for Internet service. Surprisingly, many of them are the same choices available to home users. For example, most ISPs offer business service in addition to their consumer offerings. This is often at a much higher speed than home connections to support the needs of business users. Of course, ISPs generally charge a premium fee for this increased speed.

Think back to the OSI Reference Model for a moment. The important thing to remember is that the connectivity option you choose will not affect what you can do with your network. The differences relate to the way the signal gets into your building (telephone lines, cable lines, or dedicated wires) and the speed and reliability of your service.

Routers

A **router** is a device that connects two or more networks and selectively interchanges packets of data between them. A router connects a LAN to a WAN by examining network addresses to decide where to send each packet.

The placement of a router within the network architecture affects configuration choices. You can place routers in two basic locations (see **FIGURE 10-3**):

- **Border routers**—A border router is subject to direct attack from an outside source. When you configure any router, you should determine whether it is the only point of defense or if it is one part of a multilayered defense. Of course, a multilayered defense is far better and more secure. The lone defense router can protect internal resources but is subject to attack itself.

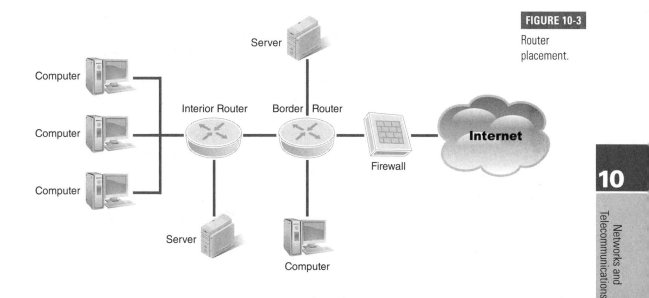

FIGURE 10-3

Router placement.

- **Internal routers**—An internal router can also provide enhanced features to your internal networks. Internal routers can help keep subnet traffic separate. They can keep traffic out of a subnet and keep traffic in a subnet. For example, an internal router that sits between the network of an organization's research department network and the network for the rest of the organization can keep the two networks separate. These routers can keep confidential traffic inside the research department. They can also keep nonresearch traffic from crossing over into the research network from the organization's other networks.

> ▶ **TIP**
>
> Regardless of where you place routers, you must ensure they are secure.
> A **secure router configuration** is a collection of settings that ensure that your router is only allowing valid network traffic to flow to and from valid nodes. You must take the time to configure each router properly, then monitor each one to ensure that no unauthorized configuration changes occur. Attackers like to reconfigure network devices to allow their attacks to be more successful.

You can configure routers to allow all traffic to pass or to protect some internal resources. Routers can use **network address translation (NAT)** and packet filtering to improve security. NAT uses an alternate public IP address to hide a system's real **IP address**. One of the original purposes of NAT was to compensate for a shortage of IP addresses. Today it helps with security by hiding the true IP address of a device. An attacker will have more difficulty identifying the layout of networks behind a firewall that uses NAT.

Packet filtering is a function of a router or firewall. It happens each time the router or firewall receives a data packet. The device compares the packet to a list of rules configured by the network administrator. The rules tell the device whether to allow the packet into the network or to deny it. If no rule specifically allows the packet, the firewall blocks the packet.

NAT and packet filtering are two good ways to use your routers to help defend your network. They provide some defense against basic attacks. It is important to remember, however, that no single technology is a "silver bullet." You should still use firewalls to protect your network and other technologies described in this book to secure your data.

Local Area Networks

LANs provide network connectivity for computers located in the same geographic area. These computers typically connect to each other with devices such as hubs and switches. This switching infrastructure is located behind the organization's router, as shown in **FIGURE 10-4**.

In many cases, systems on the same LAN do not protect themselves from each other. This is intentional, since collaboration often requires connections between LAN systems that you would not normally allow from the Internet. This is why it is extremely important to have good security on systems located on your LAN. If a virus infects a system on the LAN and the other systems do not protect themselves, the virus can spread quickly to all systems on the LAN.

Ethernet Networks

Until about a decade ago, many different types of LANs existed. Now almost every network has switched to a single technology called Ethernet. In early Ethernet networks, all computers connected to a single wire and had to fight with each other for turns to use the network. This was inefficient. Fortunately, technology evolved. Modern Ethernet networks use a

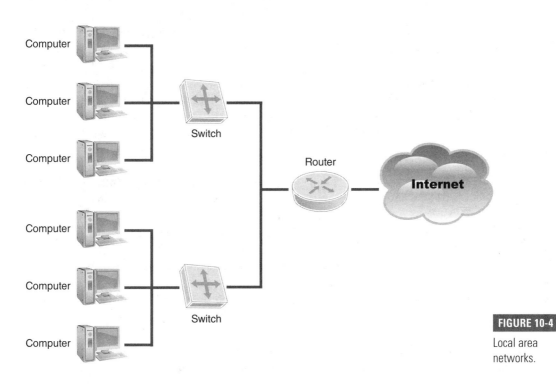

FIGURE 10-4

Local area networks.

dedicated connection for each system. This wire connects each system back to a switch, which controls the LAN.

The Ethernet standard defines the way that computers communicate on the network. It governs both the Physical and Data Link layers of the OSI Reference Model. Ethernet defines how computers use MAC addresses to communicate with each other on the network. Ethernet has become the most common LAN technology in use. Even many competing technologies now have variants that run on top of Ethernet. For example, **Internet Small Computer System Interface (iSCSI)** is a storage networking standard used to link data storage devices to networks using IP for its transport layer. An alternative to iSCSI for both optical and electrical networks is **fibre channel**. Fibre channel was originally used in supercomputers to connect storage devices but has since spread into common use across many types of computers. The **Fibre Channel over Ethernet (FCoE)** protocol makes it even easier to connect fibre channel-capable devices to an Ethernet network. This is yet another example of the way layered network protocols make it easy to implement many different types of network devices.

LAN Devices: Hubs and Switches

Two main devices connect computers on a LAN: hubs and switches. **Hubs** are simple network devices. They contain a number of plugs (or ports) where you can connect Ethernet cables for different network systems. When the hub receives a packet on any port, it automatically retransmits that packet to all the other ports. In this way, every system connected to the hub can hear everything that every other system communicates on the network. This makes the job of the hub quite simple.

The simple nature of a hub is also its major disadvantage. A hub creates a lot of network congestion by retransmitting everything it hears. In the last section, you learned how old-fashioned Ethernet networks had every system connected to the same wire. When you use a hub to connect systems, you get the same result. Every system communicates with every other system on the network, making it difficult for a single system to get a packet in edgewise. This causes network congestion and reduces the speed of the network for everyone using it.

> ⚠ **WARNING**
>
> Hubs also create a security risk. If every computer can see what every other computer transmits on the network, eavesdroppers have an easy time grabbing all the packets they want.

Switches are a much better alternative to hubs. A switch performs the same basic function as a hub: connecting multiple systems to the network. However, switches have one major added feature: They can perform intelligent filtering. Switches "know" the MAC address of the system connected to each port. When they receive a packet on the network, they look at the destination MAC address and send the packet *only* to the port where the destination system resides. This simple feature provides a huge performance benefit.

Switches are now inexpensive and have greatly improved performance. That's why almost every modern network uses switches to connect systems. Generally speaking, only small networks still use hubs.

Virtual LANs

A virtual LAN (VLAN) is any broadcast domain that is isolated from other domains. You create VLANs in the routers and switches configuration setup. A VLAN is a collection of logically related network devices that are viewed as a partitioned network segment. This gives administrators the ability to separate network segments without having to physically separate the network cabling. VLANs can be used to isolate logical groups of devices to reduce network traffic and increase security. For example, if you create a VLAN for your Human Resources (HR) department, all sensitive information traveling from one HR computer to another HR computer is hidden from all non-HR computers.

TCP/IP and How It Works

Imagine a lunch table with a Chinese speaker, a French speaker, and an English speaker. That would be a confusing conversation! The lunch guests must have one language in common if they want to communicate. The same thing is true with computers. Fortunately, almost every computer now speaks a standard language (or protocol) called the Transmission Control Protocol/Internet Protocol (TCP/IP).

A **protocol** is a set of rules that govern the format of messages that computers exchange. A network protocol governs how networking equipment interacts to deliver data across the network. These protocols manage the transfer of data from a server to an endpoint device from the beginning of the data transfer to the end. In this section, you will learn about the protocols that make up TCP/IP and the basics of TCP/IP networking.

TCP/IP Overview

TCP/IP is actually a suite of protocols that operate at both the Network and Transport layers of the OSI Reference Model. It governs all activity across the Internet and through most corporate

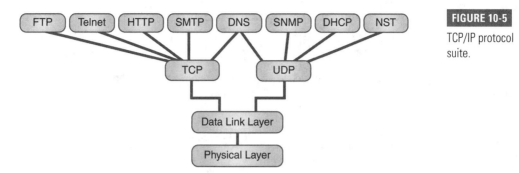

FIGURE 10-5

TCP/IP protocol suite.

and home networks. The U.S. Department of Defense developed TCP/IP to provide a highly reliable and fault-tolerant network infrastructure. Reliability, not security, was the focus.

This suite of protocols has many different responsibilities. **FIGURE 10-5** shows a portion of the TCP/IP suite.

IP Addressing

One of the primary functions of Network Layer protocols is to provide an addressing scheme. This layer contains the addressing scheme in TCP/IP. **IPv4 addresses** are four-byte (32-bit) addresses that uniquely identify every device on the network. With an explosion in the number of network devices during the end of the last century, it was clear that IPv4 did not allow for unique addresses for each device. That's one of the reasons IPv6 was developed. IPv6 addresses are 128 bits long and can provide far more unique device addresses than the older standard. In addition, IPv6 contains many additional features and is more secure. Adopting it is slow, however, and IPv4 is still the most common IP addressing technique in use today.

FIGURE 10-6 shows the difference between the notation for an IPv4 and IPv6 address. As you can see, IPv4 addresses use the dotted-quad notation. This represents each of the 4 bytes as an integer between 0 and 255. Each IPv4 address consists of a network address and a host address. For example, the IPv4 address 192.168.10.1 shown in the figure is for the network address 192.168 and the host address 10.1. The dividing line between the network and host addresses can change based on the way an administrator configures the network. A network configuration parameter known as the **subnet mask** defines this dividing line for a particular network. All hosts that share the same network address are part of a **subnet**. A subnet is a partition of a network based on IP addresses. Since IPv6 addresses are so much larger than IPv4, IPv6 uses a completely different notation. As shown in the figure, IPv6 addresses are expressed as hexadecimal values, separated into eight groups of 16 bits.

Because every computer needs its own IP address, keeping track of address assignments can be time-consuming. Many organizations that use IPv4 use **Dynamic Host Configuration Protocol (DHCP)** within a network to simplify the configuration of each user's computer. This allows each computer to get its configuration information dynamically from the network instead of the network administrator providing the

> **NOTE**
>
> The Internet Assigned Numbers Authority (IANA) has only released about 20 percent of the available IPv6 addresses for use. That means there are still about 4,000 IPv6 addresses available now for every person on Earth.

IPv4

192 . 168 . 10 . 1

11000000 10101000 00001010 00000001

IPv6

DHCP Request

DHCP Reply
IP, DNS, Gateway

Computer

Router

configuration information to the computer. DHCP provides a computer with an IPv4 address, subnet mask, and other essential communication information. It simplifies the network administrator's job. An example of DHCP communication appears in **FIGURE 10-7**. Technically, DHCP works only with IPv4 networks. DHCPv6 provides IPv6 addresses.

Common Ports

Network application software needs to know the address of a remote device in order to establish communication with that device. The networking software stack handles all the details of getting the message from one device to another. Application software also needs to identify more than just the target address. The software needs to tell the receiving (target) device where to send messages once they get there. This destination address is called a **network port**. A network port is just a number that tells a receiving device where to send messages it receives. Client software sends network messages to specific ports, and server software listens to ports for incoming messages. For example, almost all unencrypted traffic between web browsers and web servers uses port 80. Port 80 is commonly used for HTTP traffic. **TABLE 10-1** lists ports that common services use. No one forces software to use the common ports, but most software uses standard ports to make it easy for clients and servers to communicate.

Common Protocols

You have already seen some of the most common network protocols. There are many more protocols that define communication rules for many uses. Although this list is not comprehensive, **TABLE 10-2** contains a list of some of the more common network protocols you should recognize.

Internet Control Message Protocol

Once you have configured all the network components, you need to monitor your network for health and performance. **Internet Control Message Protocol (ICMP)** is a management and control protocol for IP. ICMP delivers messages between hosts about the health of the network. ICMP messages carry information on hosts it can reach as well as information on routing and updates.

TABLE 10-1 Common port numbers.

PORT	SERVICE/USE
20	FTP data transfer
21	FTP control
22	Secure Shell (SSH)
25	Simple Mail Transfer Protocol (SMTP)
53	Domain Name System (DNS)
80	Hypertext Transport Protocol (HTTP)
110	Post Office Protocol v3 (POP3)
139	NetBIOS Session Service
143	Internet Message Access Protocol (IMAP)
443	HTTP over Secure Sockets Layer (SSL)
3389	Terminal Server

TABLE 10-2 Common network protocols.

PROTOCOL	COMMON PORT(S)
DNS (Domain Name Service)	53
FTP (File Transfer Protocol)	20 (data), 21 (control)
FTPS (FTP over TLS/SSL)	989 (data), 990 (control)
HTTP (Hypertext Transport Protocol)	80
HTTPS (Hypertext Transport Protocol over TLS/SSL)	443
iSCSI (Internet Small Computer System Interface)	860, 3260 (target)
NetBIOS (Network Basic Input/Output System)	137, (Name Service) 138, (Datagram service) 139 (Session service)
SCP (Secure Copy—part of SSH)	22
SFTP (Secure File Transfer Protocol—part of SSH)	22
SNMP (Simple Network Management Protocol)	161
SSH (Secure Shell)	22
Telnet	23
TFTP (Trivial File Transfer Protocol)	69

10

Networks and
Telecommunications

> **Technical TIP**
>
> Notice that there isn't a port number listed for SSL or TLS (Transport Layer Security). That's because these two protocols are used to provide encryption for higher-level protocols. For example, HTTPS is just HTTP running over SSL or TLS. That means in this case that SSL or TLS will just use the HTTP port (80). Conventionally, HTTPS from a client browser to the server uses port 443. However, the port itself means nothing with regard to security. The SSL protocol is what encrypts the HTTP data. SSL has been around longer than TLS but is slowly being replaced by the more secure TLS.

Two ICMP tools are ping and traceroute. The ping command sends a single packet to a target IP address called an **ICMP echo request**. This packet is equivalent to asking the question "Are you there?" The computer on the other end can either answer the request "Yes" with an ICMP echo reply packet or ignore the request. Attackers sometimes use the ping command to identify targets for a future attack. Because of this potential vulnerability, many system administrators configure their computers to ignore all ping requests.

The traceroute command uses ICMP echo request packets for another purpose: to identify the path that packets travel through a network. Packets may travel many different routes to get from one point on a network to another. The traceroute command displays the path that a particular packet follows so you can identify the source of potential network problems.

Attackers can use ICMP to create a denial of service attack against a network. This type of attack is known as a **Smurf attack**, named after one of the first programs to implement it. It works by sending spoofed ICMP echo request packets to a broadcast address on a network, hoping that the hosts on that network will all respond. If the attacker sends enough replies, it is possible to bring down a T1 from a dialup connection attack. Fortunately, it is very easy to defend against Smurf attacks by configuring your network to ignore ICMP echo requests sent to broadcast addresses.

Network Security Risks

Any data in transit are a potential attack target. This makes network security important. So far in this chapter you've learned about how networks carry data. You've also learned about a few risks facing networks, such as Smurf attacks and eavesdropping. In this section, you will take an in-depth look at some network security risks. You also will cover some of the network security controls that you can put in place to protect your network.

> ■ **NOTE**
>
> Attackers also want to be able to gain control of systems on your network. They will exploit network security holes. This discussion is beyond the scope of this chapter.

Categories of Risk

The three main categories of network security risk are reconnaissance, eavesdropping, and denial of service. Each of these has different impacts on the availability, integrity, and confidentiality of data carried across a network. They also may affect the security of the network itself. In this section you will examine some of the most common network security risks.

Reconnaissance

Network reconnaissance is gathering information about a network for use in a future attack. Consider an army that wants to attack a country. The attacking army needs a lot of advance information to succeed. Some of the things a commander might want to know are as follows:

* Terrain
* Location of roads, trails, and waterways
* Locations and types of enemy defenses
* Weaknesses in the enemy's perimeter
* Procedures for allowing access through the perimeter
* Types of weapons used by the enemy

Similarly, a network attacker would want to know many things before attacking:

* IP addresses used on the network
* Types of firewalls and other security systems
* Remote access procedures
* Operating system(s) of computers on the network
* Weaknesses in network systems

Normally you wouldn't simply make this information available to an attacker. Unfortunately, however, attackers have many tools to obtain it. You have already learned why it is important to block ICMP echo requests from outside your network. This block stops attackers from using the ping and traceroute tools to gather information. You also want to be sure to configure systems to provide as little information as possible to outsiders. This will limit the effectiveness of network reconnaissance attacks.

Eavesdropping

Attackers also might want to violate the confidentiality of data sent on your network. Before you learn about network eavesdropping, consider a less complex technology: the telephone. If you've seen a spy movie, you know that it's easy to tap a telephone if you can get to the telephone wires. You simply need to hook up a cable to the telephone switch box on the house and connect a handset to listen in on calls.

Network eavesdropping is just as simple. If an attacker has physical access to a cable, he or she can simply tap that cable and see all the data passing through it. You have a few options to protect against this type of attack:

* Limit physical access to network cables.
* Use switched networks. The attacker will then see only information sent to or from the computer attached to the tapped cable.
* Encrypt sensitive data. The attacker still might be able to see the transmission but won't be able to make sense of it.

Network eavesdropping is easier than telephone eavesdropping. Physical access to the network makes it easier but is not required. If an attacker compromises a computer on the network, the attacker can use that computer for eavesdropping. Using switched networks and encryption will help limit the effectiveness of this type of attack. You should also secure systems on your network from malicious code.

■ NOTE

Wireless networking presents a completely new world of eavesdropping challenges. You will learn more about that topic later in the chapter.

Denial of Service

Often an attacker is not interested in gaining access to your network. Rather, he or she simply wants to deny you the use of it. This can be an extremely effective attack tactic. Many businesses can't operate if they lose their networks. An attacker has two primary methods to conduct a denial of service (DoS) attack: flooding a network with traffic and shutting down a single point of failure.

Flooding a network with traffic is the simpler method. You can think of a network as a pipe: It can carry only so much data before it gets full. If you send it more data than can fit in the pipe, the network becomes clogged and useless. Attackers can create a DoS attack by simply sending more data through a network than it can handle. One variation on this theme is a distributed denial of service (DDoS) attack. In this attack, the black-hat hacker uses many systems around the world that he or she has compromised to flood the network from many different directions. It becomes difficult to distinguish legitimate traffic from attack traffic, and the network grinds to a halt.

DDoS attacks have been around for years. However, they are not considered old types of attacks. Attackers still use DDoS attacks to slow down or disable their victims. In September and October 2012, a group of activists with hacking abilities, called **hacktivists**, launched a series of DoS attacks against several major U.S. banks. Hacktivists are behind more and more large-scale attacks to attract attention, generally to some political issue. These attacks continued through the end of 2012 and into 2013. The targets of these attacks included U.S. Bancorp, JPMorgan Chase, Bank of America, PNC Financial Services, and SunTrust Banks. As the attacks have continued, they have affected more organizations. Some customers have been frustrated due to slow bank websites; others were unable to reach their banks online at all. The ongoing attacks continue to disrupt online access to the bank websites but often are not as successful as the earlier attacks. The banks are learning from the earlier attacks and have added new controls to protect their websites.

Previous attacks often focused on large retailers. Several major Internet retailers, including Amazon.com, Walmart, and Expedia, were the victims of DoS attacks since 2009. These attacks shut down all three websites for about an hour in the middle of the winter holiday shopping season. The companies lost revenue as customers turned to other retail websites. And things are getting worse. In December 2014 an unnamed ISP reported an NTP reflection DDoS attack that generated a peak of 400GBs of network traffic—a volume of traffic beyond what any ISP could have handled. Needless to say, the ISP's customers were unable to connect to the Internet during this attack.

Technology advances provide more opportunities for attackers to cause problems with DoS attacks. A fairly new type of attack, the **telephony denial of service (TDoS)** attack, is starting to become more common. A TDoS attack attempts to prevent telephone calls from being successfully initiated or received by some person or organization. These attacks became more prevalent in early 2013. Attackers are targeting an increasing number of organizations that depend on telephone calls as a primary mode of communication. The result is similar to standard DoS attacks. These network attacks that can disrupt or totally disable telephone communication can cause enormous impact. Damage can include revenue loss, potential fines, the inability to conduct operations, and a loss of customer confidence.

Protecting yourself against a DoS attack can be difficult. The most obvious approach is to ensure you have adequate Internet bandwidth to withstand the load. Some new technologies on the market seek to defend against DDoS attacks, but they are unproven and limited in their effectiveness. The best defense is to detect attacks as early as possible and take action to block the incoming traffic before it renders your network unusable.

Basic Network Security Defense Tools

Defense against these kinds of risks begins with some basic hardware and software tools: firewalls, virtual private networks, and network admission control.

Firewalls

A **firewall** controls the flow of traffic by preventing unauthorized network traffic from entering or leaving a particular portion of the network. You can place a firewall between an internal network and the outside world or within the internal network to control access to particular corporate assets by only authorized users. Firewalls are critical elements of networking security, but they are just that: elements. Firewalls will not solve all security problems, but they do add a much-needed deterrent.

FIGURE 10-8 shows the role of a firewall in a network. It separates private networks from the Internet. It also separates different private networks from each other. In this section, you will look at the different types of firewalls and the roles they play in the network topology.

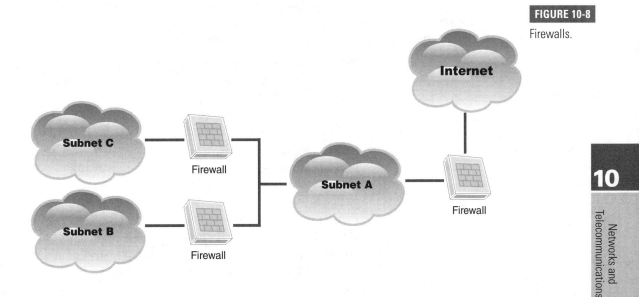

FIGURE 10-8

Firewalls.

Firewalls are powerful tools in securing networks. Since each firewall is configured using rules, they provide the most common way to implement **rule-based management**. Rule-based management is simply managing the security of a network by defining rules of what is acceptable and what is not. **Firewall rules** are filters defined in a firewall's configuration that make it easy to implement many of these security requirements. Different types of firewalls use different types of rules. Even the simplest firewalls support **access control lists**. An access control list simply defines a rule to handle traffic from one or more hosts using a specific protocol and one or more ports. In addition to just securing a host, firewalls can filter traffic based on ports, often simply called **port security**. Access control lists can contain very specific rules or may contain ranges of hosts and ports. Each rule tells the firewall how to handle certain types of messages. The most common actions are allow and deny. If you want to create the most secure network, you could configure your firewall to deny all messages except the ones that you explicitly allow. This approach is called **implicit deny**. It can be very secure, but it requires more effort on the part of network administrators to open ports as needed.

Firewalls can help secure networks in multiple ways. In addition to the filtering features you have already seen, firewalls can provide these security features:

- **Flood guard**—Rules can limit traffic bandwidth from hosts, reducing the ability for any one host to flood a network.

- **Loop protection**—Firewalls can look at message addresses to determine whether a message is being sent around an unending loop. This can be another form of flooding.

- **Network separation**—Filtering rules enforce divisions between networks, keeping traffic from moving from one network to another.

Firewall Types

The basic function of a firewall is quite simple: It must block any traffic that you don't explicitly allow. Firewalls contain rules that define the types of traffic that can come and go through a network. Each time the firewall receives a network message, it checks the message against its rules. If the message matches a rule, the firewall allows the message to pass. If the message does not match a rule, the firewall blocks the message.

Going beyond this basic functionality, firewall technology includes three main types:

- **Packet filtering**—A **packet-filtering firewall** is very basic. It compares received traffic with a set of rules that define which traffic it will permit to pass through the firewall. It makes this decision for each packet that reaches the firewall and has no memory of packets it has encountered in the past.

- **Stateful inspection**—A **stateful inspection firewall** remembers information about the status of a network communication. Once the firewall receives the first packet in a communication, the firewall remembers that communication session until it is closed. This type of firewall does not have to check its rules each time it receives a packet. It only needs to check rules when a new communication session starts.

NOTE

Firewalls aren't simply preventative controls. They also operate as detective controls. Firewalls can log as much information as you can analyze. A structured **log analysis** process can help identify reconnaissance activity or even attacks that have already occurred. You should regularly monitor all firewall logs to identify potential problems.

- **Application proxy**—An **application proxy firewall** goes further than a stateful inspection firewall. It doesn't actually allow packets to travel directly between systems on opposite sides of the firewall. The firewall opens separate connections with each of the two communicating systems and then acts as a broker (or proxy) between the two. This allows for an added degree of protection, because the firewall can analyze information about the application in use when making the decision to allow or deny traffic.

The type of firewall you choose for your network will depend on many different factors. If you're placing a simple firewall at the border of a large network, you may want to use a basic packet filter. On the other hand, if you're protecting a highly secure data center that hosts web applications, an application proxy might be more appropriate.

Firewall-Deployment Techniques

You can deploy firewalls in many different ways on your network. In this section, you will look at a few of the most common firewall deployment techniques: border firewalls, screened subnet (or DMZ) firewalls, and multilayered firewalls. Depending on your organization's security needs, one or more of these approaches may be a good fit.

Border Firewall. The **border firewall** is the most basic approach. Border firewalls simply separate the protected network from the Internet, as shown in **FIGURE 10-9**. A border firewall normally sits behind the router and receives all communications passing from the router into the private network. It also receives all communications passing from the private network to the Internet. Border firewalls normally use either packet filtering or stateful inspection.

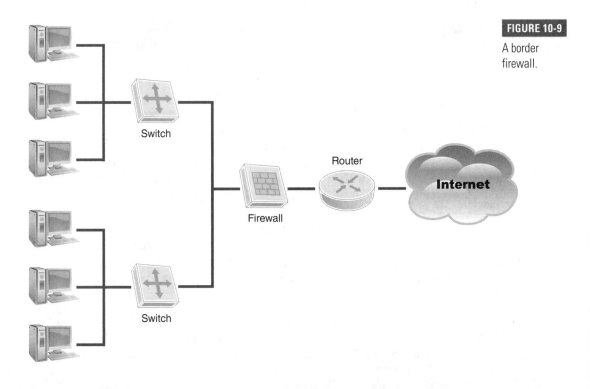

FIGURE 10-9

A border firewall.

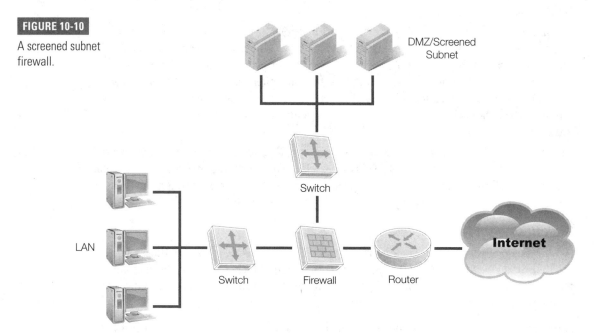

FIGURE 10-10

A screened subnet firewall.

Border firewalls are most common for organizations that do not host public services. If you outsource your website and email, you might not need to allow the public to get into your network at all. In this case, you may simply block most (or sometimes all) inbound traffic. A border firewall excels in this scenario.

Screened Subnet. Often it's not possible to block all traffic into your network. If you host a public website or your own email server, you need to allow inbound connections on a limited basis. The **screened subnet** firewall topology, shown in **FIGURE 10-10**, is the best approach for this type of requirement. The firewall has three network cards. Two are set up identically to a border firewall, with one connected to the Internet and another connected to the private network. The third card connects to a special network known as the screened subnet or **demilitarized zone (DMZ)**.

The DMZ is a semiprivate network used to host services that the public can access. Users have limited access from the Internet to systems in the DMZ to access these services. A secure network does not allow direct access from the Internet to the private network.

> **NOTE**
>
> The screened subnet is the most common firewall topology in use today.

This approach recognizes that systems accessed from the Internet pose a special risk. They are more likely targets of attacks and, therefore, are more likely to suffer successful attacks. If you confine these machines to the DMZ, they can jeopardize only other systems in the DMZ. An attacker who gains access to a DMZ system will not be able to use that system to directly access systems on the private network.

Multilayered Firewalls. In large and/or highly secure environments, organizations often use multiple firewalls to segment their network into pieces. This is the case illustrated in Figure 10-8. In that figure, one firewall acts as the border firewall, protecting subnets A, B, and C from the Internet. However, two other firewalls separate subnets B and C from each other and from subnet A.

Multilayered firewalls are useful when you have networks with different security levels. For example, in Figure 10-8, general users may connect to subnet A. Users working on a secret research project might connect to subnet B. Executives might connect to subnet C. This structure provides the secret project and the executives with protection from the general user community.

Unified Threat Management. Firewalls are so important to network security that they have matured into devices that do far more than just packet inspection. In fact, multipurpose firewalls are more commonly referred to as **unified threat management (UTM)** devices. UTM devices do provide filtering as well as many other security services. Some of the services UTM devices provide include these:

- **URL filter**—This feature filters web traffic by examining the URL as opposed to the IP address.
- **Content inspection**—The device looks at some or all network packet content to determine if the packet should be allowed to pass. This type of inspection can help identify malicious content from trusted sources. This could happen if a trusted source is compromised.
- **Malware inspection**—A specialized form of content inspection, the device looks at packet content for signs of malware.

These unified services make it possible to reduce the number of devices that must analyze network packets. Fewer UTM devices can provide the same level of security as many more older devices. However, even with fewer devices inspecting packets, introducing UTM devices often slows down a network due to the sheer amount of work the devices must accomplish. It takes time to inspect and analyze each network packet at multiple layers of the network stack. For this reason, some organizations have elected a "middle-of-the-road" approach. A **web security gateway** accomplishes some of what a UTM device does, but without all the overhead. In short, a web security gateway performs URL filtering but does not examine the content of the packets.

> **NOTE**
>
> One more useful feature of firewalls is that they can be configured as **load balancers**. A load balancer can dynamically route network traffic to different network segments to avoid congestion. The firewall monitors known network segments and directs traffic on a segment that is appropriate for the destination host and has available bandwidth. This can keep networks from slowing down when the demand is high.

Virtual Private Networks and Remote Access

With the advent of telecommuting, remote access has become a common part of many corporate networks. Today many companies have employees who rarely if ever come into the corporate office. These users work at home or on the road. Even so, they still need access to corporate resources. This means opening access to more corporate resources from the Internet than IT professionals want. The trick is to allow corporate employees the access they need but to keep attackers out of these potentially open doors.

Virtual private networks (VPNs) are a good way to increase the security level of data you transmit across the public data network. They normally use encryption to protect all

VPN access.

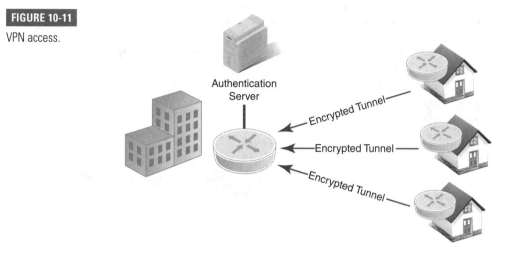

the data they send between a user and the organization's network. Using a VPN for remote access provides security and is cost-effective. The cost difference of using a VPN versus paying for a dedicated connection between two sites is significant. **FIGURE 10-11** shows an example of VPN access to a network.

VPNs require your gateway equipment to have a lot of processing power to handle the encryption algorithms. You can offload this processing power to another device by using a dedicated **VPN concentrator** rather than having your router or firewall terminate the VPN.

In deploying a VPN, you must consider the security of the end users' computers. Once users connect to the corporate network, their PCs could be an open portal into those resources for an attacker who gains access to the PC. For this reason, many organizations require that employees install security software on their home computers. You can also limit VPN access to laptop computers your organization owns and manages.

The three major VPN technologies in use today are as follows:

- **Point-to-Point Tunneling Protocol (PPTP)**—The **Point-to-Point Tunneling Protocol (PPTP)** was once the predominant VPN protocol. For many years, almost all VPNs used PPTP. It is easy to set up on client computers because most operating systems include PPTP support.

- **Secure Sockets Layer (SSL)**—The Secure Sockets Layer encrypts web communications, and many VPNs use SSL to provide encrypted communication. Users connect to an SSL-protected webpage and log on. Their web browser then downloads software that connects them to the VPN. This requires no advance configuration of the system. For this reason, SSL VPNs are quickly growing in popularity.

- **IPSec—Internet Protocol Security (IPSec)** is a suite of protocols designed to connect sites securely. Although some IPSec VPNs are available for end users, they often require the installation of third-party software on the user's system and are not popular. Many organizations use IPSec to connect one site to another securely over the Internet. The required IPSec VPN functionality is built into many routers and firewalls, allowing for easy configuration.

VPNs provide clear benefit to an organization. They offer an inexpensive, secure replacement for dedicated connections between sites. They also enable users to connect securely to the organization network from remote locations. This promises increased productivity because workers can easily get to resources they need while on the road.

Network Access Control

Network access control (NAC) systems enable you to add more security requirements before allowing a device to connect to your network. They perform two major tasks: authentication and posture checking. Although NAC is a new technology, it is growing in popularity. Many organizations now deploy NAC for both internal users and guests using their network. NAC works on wired and wireless networks.

The IEEE 802.1x standard describes the most common NAC technology. Commonly referred to as simply 802.1x or 1x, this standard tells how clients may interact with a NAC device to gain entry to the network. Software on users' computers prompts them to log on to the network. After verifying the user's credentials, the NAC device instructs the switch (for a wired network) or access point (for a wireless network) to grant the user access to the network. This is the authentication component of NAC.

Posture checking is an optional second use of NAC technology. When posture checking is used, the NAC device checks the configuration of the user's computer to ensure that it meets security standards before allowing it access to the network. Some things commonly checked include the following:

- Up-to-date antivirus software
- Host firewall enabled
- Operating system supported
- Operating system patched

If users attempt to connect a noncompliant system to a network, the NAC device offers two options. The administrator can decide to block such systems from the network until they are fixed. Alternatively, the system may connect to a special quarantine network where you may fix the system before gaining access to the main network. The **Extensible Authentication Protocol (EAP)** is an authentication framework that defines the transport of keys and authentication credentials. EAP is commonly used in wireless network authentication. The **Protected Extensible Authentication Protocol (PEAP)** is basically EAP running in a TLS tunnel. PEAP provides more security than EAP for authentication exchanges.

Wireless Networks

Wireless networks have become very popular for connecting devices within the home and office. Wireless networks can connect laptops, desktops, smartphones, and many other devices. Wireless networking allows users to work from any location in the building without worrying about finding a place to plug in a network cable.

Configuring a wireless network is quite easy and inexpensive. The question becomes, what does wireless technology do to the security of your network? If it is so easy for an employee to connect to the network, does that mean that others can connect as well?

Setting up a secure wireless network—at least one as secure as any wired network—is possible. However, it takes careful planning, execution, and testing. Properly configured strong encryption is critical to operating a secure wireless network. In this section, you will examine wireless networking technology and learn how to configure and secure wireless networks.

Wireless Access Points

A **wireless access point (WAP)** is the connection between a wired and wireless network. WAPs are radios, sending and receiving networking information over the air between wireless devices and the wired network. Anyone within radio range of a wireless access point can communicate with it and attempt to connect to the network.

Attackers who want to undermine your security can do several things with a wireless network. First, they understand that wireless networks extend the range of your organization's network beyond your walls. While you can easily control physical access to a wired network, walls and fences don't stop wireless signals. Therefore, wireless networks without proper security present an easy target for attackers who want to connect to your network. Second, they know that it is much easier to eavesdrop on a wireless network than a wired one. It's very simple for anyone within radio range of your network to capture all the data sent on that network. If those data are unencrypted, they are fair game for an attack.

Wireless Network Security Controls

Fortunately, you can do quite a bit to secure your wireless network. In this section, you will look at several examples of wireless network security controls. The most important is the use of wireless encryption to prevent eavesdropping. Other techniques that provide added security include disabling service set identifier (SSID) broadcasting, implementing **MAC address filtering**, and adding strong authentication to your wireless network.

VPN over Wireless

One of the most secure ways to implement secure wireless networks is to use VPNs for all wireless connections. This is easy to manage for internal users, but guest access to a VPN is more difficult. One common solution is to create at least two separate wireless networks—one network for internal users who require VPN access and greater connectivity into your internal network, and one network for guests that does not allow VPN access. The guest network also should have very limited connectivity to your internal network.

Wireless Encryption

Encryption is the single most important thing you can do to secure your wireless network. Encryption makes it impossible for an outsider to view information traveling over the network. Without encryption, all wireless users' activities are visible to anyone who comes within radio range of your network. It would be possible for an attacker to sit in the parking lot of your building with an inexpensive antenna attached to a standard laptop and monitor everything happening on your wireless network.

You must use strong encryption. In the early days of wireless networking, the industry developed a standard called **Wired Equivalent Privacy (WEP)**, which provided basic encryption. WEP relies on the RC4 encryption algorithm created by Ron Rivest for RSA

LEAP and PEAP

Cisco systems developed its own **Lightweight Extensible Authentication Protocol (LEAP)** to help manage wireless keys and authentication. LEAP could use either WEP or **Temporal Key Integrity Protocol (TKIP)** for setting up secure connections. WEP weaknesses were well known, so TKIP emerged as a stopgap substitution for WEP that would operate on existing hardware that supported only WEP.

Later, Cisco, Microsoft, and RSA joined together to address LEAP's weaknesses and created Protected Extensible Authentication Protocol (PEAP), as mentioned earlier in the chapter. PEAP differs from Lightweight EAP in that PEAP does require a certificate on the server.

in the late 1980s. Since its release, security analysts have discovered significant flaws in WEP that make it insecure. With software freely available on the Internet, it is simple to break the encryption on a WEP network in a matter of seconds. In fact, using WEP on a wireless network is probably worse than using no encryption at all because it provides a false sense of security. People feel they are safe because their wireless network encrypts traffic. They don't realize they're using the equivalent of a Cap'n Crunch® decoder ring to protect their data.

Fortunately, there is an alternative to WEP. Actually, several alternatives were developed to address WEP's weaknesses. The **Counter Mode Cipher Block Chaining Message Authentication Code Protocol (CCMP)** is an encryption protocol that implements the 802.11i standard. CCMP provides enhanced security through the use of the Counter Mode of the AES standard. In addition to CCMP, the **Wi-Fi Protected Access (WPA)** standard uses strong AES encryption to protect data on networks and does not share the same vulnerabilities discovered in WEP. WPA refers to the draft of the IEEE 802.11i security standard. This standard was intended to be an intermediate solution to the WEP vulnerabilities. WPA became available in 2003. The more secure standard, WPA2, was made available in 2004. This standard's official name is 802.11i-2004. WPA, and WPA2, too, is quite easy to configure. In their basic form, WPA and WPA2 require entering a shared secret key into the network configuration of every computer on the network. In more advanced forms, you can replace the shared secret key by giving each user a unique username and password. These passwords can be identical to the user's normal credentials by using a central authentication server, such as a Remote Authentication Dial-In User Service (RADIUS) server. RADIUS was introduced in 1991 and quickly became a popular protocol to manage remote user connections. The protocol provides a central method to manage authorization, authentication, and accounting (AAA) services. Its successor, Diameter, was introduced in 1998. Recently, Diameter has become more popular for handling wireless remote connections since it has the ability to address more mobility issues than RADIUS. For example, Diameter includes better roaming support and can use TCP or SCTP protocols.

> ▶ **TIP**
>
> Disabling SSID broadcast provides a small degree of protection, but it is not foolproof. In fact, a skilled attacker can easily discover the presence of your network by using freely available software tools. Using this technique simply means you don't advertise the presence of your network, hoping to avoid the casual attacker's interest.

10

Networks and Telecommunications

SSID Broadcast

By default, wireless networks broadcast their presence to the public. They send out announcements containing the network's SSID. This is the public name of the network. You've seen these before when you boot up in a coffee shop, for instance, and your computer tells you that wireless networks are available. This notice includes the SSIDs of all available networks.

You can stop your network from announcing itself by disabling SSID broadcast on your wireless access points. If you disable SSID broadcast, users connecting to your network will need to know it is there and provide the network name themselves. This is fine if you have regular users, such as in a corporate environment. It will not work well if you allow guests access to your network.

MAC Address Filtering

WAPs also enable you to apply MAC address filters to control which computers can connect to your network. With this technology, you provide a list of acceptable MAC addresses to your WAP. You should allow only approved computers to connect to your network. Deny all other computers access to your network.

The major disadvantage of MAC address filtering is that it is very complicated to maintain. If you have more than a handful of computers on your network, it quickly becomes a major challenge to update the list of acceptable MAC addresses. Imagine if you worked for an organization with 20,000 users. It wouldn't be unusual to see 100 new computers on the network every week. That's in addition to 100 dropping off the network as you replace them. Can you imagine trying to update 200 MAC addresses every week? Use MAC address filtering in cases where it makes sense.

Additional Wireless Security Techniques

In addition to the preceding suggestions, consider the hardware selection and placement of your wireless network devices. Selecting the right hardware and placing that hardware in the right position can have a noticeable impact on your network's security. In particular, pay attention to these aspects of wireless hardware management:

- **Antenna types**—Wireless device antennas can have a large impact on the device's area of coverage. Generally, external antennas can reach farther than internal antennas. Also, antennas can transmit and receive in different ways. They can be omnidirectional (all directions), semidirectional (limited direction), or highly directional (focused direction). Choose the right antenna for your organization's use.

- **Antenna placement**—Once you select the best antennas for your devices, carefully place the antennas to provide coverage that you want, and not for anyone else. Placing an omnidirectional antenna near an external wall will likely make your wireless network available to people outside your building.

- **Power-level controls**—You can change the power a wireless device uses from the configuration settings. Lowering the power settings from the default will reduce the area the device covers. This setting can be helpful when attempting to limit the visibility of your wireless networks.

- **Captive portals**—A captive portal is a webpage that is displayed for all new connections. Your wireless device can redirect all traffic to the captive portal until the connection is authenticated. The most common use of a captive portal is to provide a logon page for your wireless network.

- **Site surveys**—One of the most important nontechnical aspects to securing wireless networks is the site survey. Examine the physical area you want to serve with a wireless network. Facility floor plans can help determine the best placement for wireless devices. Use diagrams to plan your wireless network before you physically place devices.

Although no network is totally secure, putting the right security controls in place can make your networks safer. The main point is, never rely on a single control. Always use layered controls. You should always assume that a savvy attacker will be able to compromise one or more of the controls you have in place. Ensuring that an attacker must compromise multiple controls to get to your data is the best way to make your IT infrastructure as secure as possible.

> ⚠️ **WARNING**
>
> MAC address filtering is another weak security mechanism. Using free tools, attackers can easily discover an active MAC address on your network and then change their NIC to use a valid MAC address. This is one type of address spoofing.

CHAPTER SUMMARY

In this chapter, you learned about the Open Systems Interconnection (OSI) Reference Model and how it serves as an example of how you can build and use a network and its resources. You learned about Network Layer protocols, including an overview of TCP/IP. You learned some basic tools for network security. You also learned how wireless networks work and what threats they pose to the security of your organization. Finally, you gained a better understanding of the need for security policies, standards, and procedures as well as how your IT infrastructure is only as secure as its weakest link.

KEY CONCEPTS AND TERMS

Access control lists
Application proxy firewall
Border firewall
Content inspection
Counter Mode Cipher Block Chaining Message Authentication Code Protocol (CCMP)
Demilitarized zone (DMZ)
Dynamic Host Configuration Protocol (DHCP)
Extensible Authentication Protocol (EAP)

Fibre channel
Fibre Channel over Ethernet (FCoE)
Firewall
Firewall rules
Flood guard
Hacktivist
Hub
ICMP echo request
Implicit deny
Internet Control Message Protocol (ICMP)

Internet Protocol Security (IPSec)
IP address
IPv4 addresses
Internet Small Computer System Interface (iSCSI)
Lightweight Extensible Authentication Protocol (LEAP)
Load balancer
Log analysis
Loop protection
MAC address filter
Malware inspection

10

KEY CONCEPTS AND TERMS, *continued*

Network access control (NAC)

Network address translation (NAT)

Network port

Network reconnaissance

Network separation

Open Systems Interconnection (OSI) Reference Model

Packet-filtering firewall

Point-to-Point Tunneling Protocol (PPTP)

Port security

Protected Extensible Authentication Protocol (PEAP)

Protocol

Router

Rule-based management

Screened subnet

Secure router configuration

Smurf attack

Stateful inspection firewall

Subnet

Subnet mask

Switch

Telephony

Telephony denial of service (TDoS)

Temporal Key Integrity Protocol (TKIP)

Unified threat management (UTM)

URL filter

VPN concentrator

Web security gateway

Wi-Fi Protected Access (WPA)

Wireless access point (WAP)

Wired Equivalent Privacy (WEP)

CHAPTER 10 ASSESSMENT

1. The basic model for how you can build and use a network and its resources is known as the _____.

    A. Dynamic Host Configuration Protocol (DHCP) model
    B. International Organization for Standardization (ISO) model
    C. Open Systems Interconnection (OSI) Reference Model
    D. None of the above

2. The basic job of a _____ is to enforce an access control policy at the border of a network.

    A. Firewall
    B. Router
    C. Switch
    D. Access point

3. A(n) _____ is a critical element in every corporate network today, allowing access to an organization's resources from almost anywhere in the world.

    A. Local area network (LAN)
    B. Wide area network (WAN)
    C. Dynamic Host Configuration Protocol (DHCP)
    D. None of the above

4. A secure virtual private network (VPN) creates an authenticated and encrypted channel across some form of public network.

    A. True
    B. False

5. _____ is a suite of protocols that was developed by the Department of Defense to provide a highly reliable and fault-tolerant network infrastructure.

    A. DHCP
    B. VPN
    C. PPPoE
    D. TCP/IP

6. A _____ is a device that interconnects two or more networks and selectively interchanges packets of data between them.

7. Which simple network device helps to increase network performance by using the MAC address to send network traffic only to its intended destination?

    A. Hub
    B. Switch
    C. Router
    D. Gateway

8. The three basic types of firewalls are packet filtering, application proxy, and stateful inspection.

   A. True
   B. False

9. What technology is the most secure way to encrypt wireless communications?

   A. TCP
   B. WEP
   C. WPA
   D. UDP

10. IP addresses are assigned to computers by the manufacturer.

    A. True
    B. False

11. Which VPN technology allows users to initiate connections over the Web?

    A. SSL
    B. PPTP
    C. IPSec
    D. ICMP

12. What layer of the OSI Reference Model is most commonly responsible for encryption?

    A. Application
    B. Presentation
    C. Session
    D. Transport

13. DHCP provides systems with their MAC addresses.

    A. True
    B. False

14. What firewall topology supports the implementation of a DMZ?

    A. Bastion host
    B. Multilayered firewall
    C. Border firewall
    D. Screened subnet

15. What technology allows you to hide the private IPv4 address of a system from the Internet?

    A. SSL
    B. RADIUS
    C. PPTP
    D. NAT

Malicious Code and Activity

MALICIOUS CODE OR SOFTWARE IS a threat to any Internet-connected device. In this chapter, you'll learn how malicious code operates and how you can combat it. Simply put, malicious software is any program that carries out actions that you, as the computer user, do not intend. Often the goal of malicious software is to cause harm to your system. Malicious software moves through the Internet much as a snake slithers through grass. Attackers use malicious software, or **malware**, to steal passwords, steal confidential information, delete information from your system (or encrypt it), or even reformat hard drives. Unfortunately, you cannot control malicious code with antivirus software alone. That's because malicious code includes more than just viruses, and some malware evades detection.

Malicious code attacks all three information security properties:

- **Confidentiality**—Malware can disclose your organization's private information. In this chapter, you will learn how spyware and Trojans, which are other forms of malware, can capture your organization's proprietary information and send it to unauthorized destinations.

- **Integrity**—Malware can modify database records, either immediately or over a period of time. By the time you discover the changed data, you may find that the malware has corrupted your backups as well. It is important that you verify all your data's integrity any time you suspect a security breach. The process can be expensive and is likely to be an expense you haven't budgeted for.

- **Availability**—Malware can erase or overwrite files or inflict considerable damage to storage media. Some types of malware even render your information unusable without deleting or destroying it.

As a security professional, you'll find it a challenge to convince your organization's personnel that data security is everyone's responsibility. They tend to think it's the responsibility only of the IT department. Not only that, but they also tend to think your security efforts get in the way of their work. These security efforts include the policies, procedures, and technologies you'll need to use to prevent malware attacks. Many data breaches involve some type of malware. Protecting your organization from all types of malware makes your systems more resistant to large-scale data breaches.

Chapter 11 Topics

This chapter covers the following topics and concepts:

* What malware is and how it inflicts harm on your systems
* What the main types of malware are
* What the history of malicious code is
* How malware is a threat to business organizations
* What motivates attackers and what assets they are targeting
* What tools and techniques prevent attacks
* What tools and techniques detect attacks

Chapter 11 Goals

When you complete this chapter, you will be able to:

* Define malicious software and activity
* Define a Trojan, a virus, a worm, spyware, adware, ransomware, and spam
* Understand malicious software risks and threats to individuals
* Understand malicious software risks and threats to businesses
* Understand the phases of a malicious software attack
* Understand who hackers, crackers, and perpetrators are
* Define social engineering
* Understand incident-detection tools and techniques
* Understand attack-prevention tools and techniques

Characteristics, Architecture, and Operations of Malicious Software

Security professionals know about malicious software. Malicious software, or malware, is instructions that run on a computer system and perform operations that you, the user, do not intend. This activity can take several forms:

* An attacker gains administrative control of your system and uses commands to inflict harm.
* An attacker sends commands directly to your system. Your system interprets these commands and then executes them.
* An attacker uses software programs that harm your system or that make the data unusable. These programs can come from physical media (such as a USB drive) or a

communications process (such as the Internet). Viruses, Trojan programs, and worms are all examples of these types of malicious software programs.

* Attackers use legitimate remote administration tools and security probes to identify and exploit security vulnerabilities in your network.

You must make yourself aware of the kinds of malicious code threats you may encounter. This understanding will help you develop reasonable countermeasures to protect your organization.

The Main Types of Malware

From a nontechnical perspective, most computer users think all malicious code is a virus. In fact, there are several different types of viruses, as well as many other forms of malicious code. Each type has unique characteristics and architecture. You must design and implement effective countermeasures to detect, mitigate, and prevent malicious code attacks. To do this, you must develop an understanding of various types of malicious code and how each type is used.

In this section, you will learn how to recognize and describe the characteristics and operation of common types of hostile code. You'll learn how attackers use each type, which helps you understand how to implement appropriate countermeasures.

Virus

A computer **virus** is an executable program that attaches to, or infects, other executable programs. It then replicates to infect yet more programs. Some viruses also perform destructive activities after they replicate. Good anti-malware controls notice and eliminate most viruses with an obvious or damaging payload. The primary characteristic of a virus is that it replicates and generally involves user action of some type. Not all viruses inflict harm; some are

Evidence of Virus Code Activities

Although you may not always identify every virus, viruses have many telltale signs. Any of the following may indicate an infected computer:

* Deteriorating workstation or server responsiveness
* Unexpected and sustained disk activity levels on workstations (churning)
* Sudden sluggishness of user applications, particularly at startup
* Unexplained freezing of applications or unexpected error messages
* Unscheduled hardware resets and crashes, including program aborts
* Sudden antivirus alarm activity
* Disk error messages, including increased "lost cluster" results from disk scanning
* Unexplained decrease in available space on disk or available memory
* In the case of macro viruses, saved documents that open as DOT files
* Applications (or their icons) that disappear or will not execute

merely annoying or focus on replicating. Other viruses hide their payload and install a backdoor. A **backdoor** is a hidden way to bypass access controls. It allows unauthorized access to resources or data. The victim may not notice the virus or may not immediately notice its damage.

There are three primary types of viruses. **System infectors** are viruses that target computer hardware and software startup functions. **File infectors** are viruses that attack and modify executable programs (such as COM, EXE, SYS, and DLL files in Microsoft Windows). **Data infectors** are viruses that attack document files containing embedded macro programming capabilities.

Malicious software activities may occur interactively in real-time sessions between an attacker and the target. Alternatively, they may lie dormant and trigger at some predetermined time or upon some predictable event. They may initiate a destructive action or may simply observe and collect information. **FIGURE 11-1** shows the typical life cycle of a computer virus.

Boot Record Infectors

System infectors are viruses that target key hardware and system software components in a computer. The infected components are usually system startup processes. This type of infection enables the virus to take control and execute before the computer can load most protective controls. The most prevalent types of system infectors are boot device Master Boot Record infectors. These viruses travel primarily through media exchange.

Master Boot Record and System Infectors

A Master Boot Record infector moves or destroys the original Master Boot Record of a boot device, replacing it with viral code. It can then gain control from the bootstrap program and perform its hostile mission. Typically, Master Boot Record infectors perform their tasks and then return control to the legitimate Master Boot Record or the active partition boot record to mask their existence.

Both types of boot record infectors commonly load instructions that can bypass the ROM-based system services. Loading at this level allows the virus to intercept all normal application and operating system hardware requests. These requests include functions such as

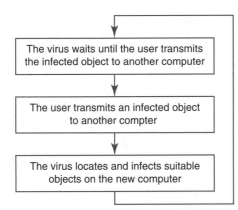

Typical life cycle of a
computer virus.

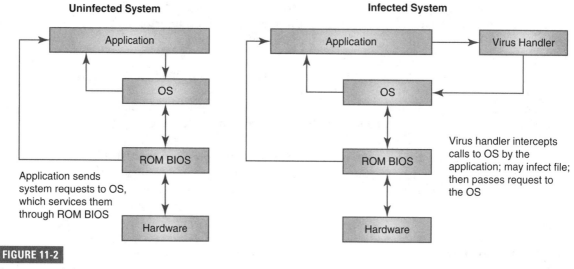

Uninfected System

Infected System

Application sends system requests to OS, which services them through ROM BIOS

Virus handler intercepts calls to OS by the application; may infect file; then passes request to the OS

FIGURE 11-2

How a system infector virus works.

opening and closing files and file directory services. This type of virus can also execute other types of malicious code routines and cover its own tracks.

A virus with this dual-action capability is called a **multipartite virus**. It can subsequently execute file-infection code as well. **FIGURE 11-2** shows how a system infector virus affects a computer.

File (Program) Infectors

File infector viruses exhibit the classic "replicate and attach" behavior. Because of the wide acceptance and popularity of Microsoft Windows–based operating systems, most well-known file infectors target those systems. They typically attack program files with .com or .exe file extensions. Newer virus strains work well with SYS, DLL, and many other Windows file types.

Although Windows computers are common targets, no operating system is immune to malware attacks. The number of attacks on other platforms is increasing. Computers that run Linux and OS X (Apple's operating system) are encountering a growing number of attacks. The number of attacks on mobile devices, such as smartphones and tablets, is also growing rapidly. These mobile devices are attractive to hackers because so few users take the time to secure them. Symantec publishes an annual *Internet Security Threat Report* that contains a wealth of information and statistics on malware activities and recommended countermeasures.

FYI

You can find the latest Symantec *Internet Security Threat Report* at *https://www.symantec.com/content/dam/symantec/docs/reports/istr-21-2016-en.pdf.*

Malware developers write and compile many of these viruses using high-level languages. The C and C++ languages are common choices because of their ability to provide the power and flexibility viruses need to be successful. In contrast, they often use assembly language to write boot record infectors. Although the coding of file infector viruses can be quite complex, the architecture of most executable programs is relatively straightforward.

Viruses of this type attach themselves to the original program file. They control the execution of that file until it can replicate and infect other files and possibly deliver a payload.

One type of file infector, a companion virus, is really a separate program file that does not attach itself to the original host program. Instead it creates a new program with a matching filename but with an extension that executes earlier than the original. For example, Windows executes .com files before it executes.exe files. It creates this file in the same directory path as the real program. When the user runs the program, the operating system calls the malware instead of the legitimate program. After the virus finishes its work, it simply executes the command to start the original program. **FIGURE 11-3** shows how a file infector virus works.

Macro (Data File) Infectors

Macro viruses became a problem when software vendors added recording capabilities to popular office applications. Users use macro-recording capabilities to record their actions in a program. The application in which the actions are recorded stores these instructions with the data file. The user can then execute the actions automatically when he or she opens the file or presses a predefined keystroke sequence. The original purpose of macros was to automate repetitive processes. Users liked the feature because it made applications more convenient and efficient. However, these macros opened the door for malicious code to carry out its own instructions.

Macro viruses infect these document files and insert their own commands. When users share the infected document with other users, the malware spreads and replicates. The connected nature of most office applications makes it easy for infected documents to spread to other computers and users. Macros can move easily between platforms, and they are quite simple to construct. For this reason, macro viruses are extremely popular among hackers.

The electronic mail bomb is a form of malicious macro attack. This type of attack typically involves an email attachment that contains macros designed to inflict maximum damage.

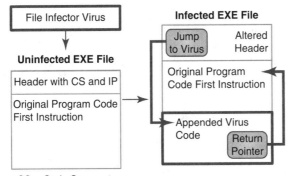

FIGURE 11-3

How a file infector virus works.

FIGURE 11-4

How a macro
virus works.

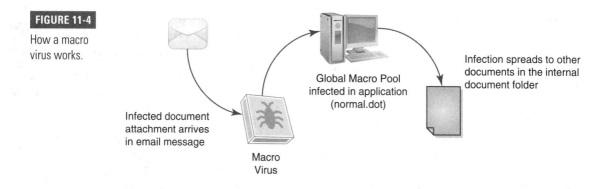

Attackers can send the document attachment through an anonymous remailer to reach its
targets with great precision. Someone who receives the email bomb need only open the attachment to launch the macro virus. In some cases, simply previewing the email message
activates the email bomb. **FIGURE 11-4** shows how a macro virus works.

Other Virus Classifications

Viruses can use any of a number of techniques to propagate and avoid detection by antivirus
software. Most single computer viruses work by copying exact replicas of themselves to each
file, boot sector, or document they infect. The virus accomplishes subsequent infections in
the same manner, making exact duplicates byte for byte. This predictable action produces a
signature pattern. Many antivirus and anti-malware programs look for this signature to detect malware. Some viruses, such as the following, behave differently:

- **Polymorphic viruses**—**Polymorphic viruses** include a separate encryption engine that
  stores the virus body in encrypted format while duplicating the main body of the virus.
  The virus exposes only the decryption routine for possible detection. It embeds the
  control portion of the virus in the decryption routine, which seizes control of the target
  system and decrypts the main body of the virus so that it can execute. True polymorphic
  viruses use an additional mutation engine to vary the decryption process for each itera-
  tion. This makes even this portion of the code more difficult to identify. **FIGURE 11-5** shows
  how a polymorphic virus infects a computer.

- **Stealth viruses**—**Stealth viruses**, also called **armored viruses**, use a number of techniques to conceal themselves from users and from detection software. By installing
  a low-level system service function, they can intercept any system request and alter
  the service output to conceal their presence. Stealth viruses can have size stealth,
  read stealth, or both. **FIGURE 11-6** shows how a stealth/armored virus works.

FIGURE 11-5

How a polymorphic
virus works.

Cleartext Decryption Routine (may change for each replication)
Encrypted Payload Body of Code

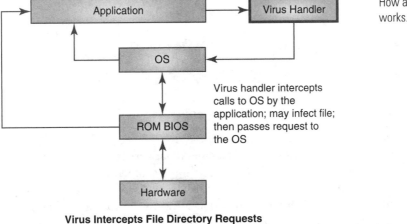

Infected System

Virus handler intercepts
calls to OS by the
application; may infect file;
then passes request to
the OS

Virus Intercepts File Directory Requests

FIGURE 11-6

How a stealth virus
works.

FYI

Size stealth hides the fact that an infected file is bigger than it used to be. The virus intercepts system requests
for file information and subtracts its own size from the reply before passing it back to the requesting process.
Read stealth hides the fact that the virus moved the boot sector code. The virus intercepts read/write requests
for the normal boot sector, which the virus has relocated and replaced with the viral code. The virus redirects the
request to the new hidden location of the original boot sector code.

- **Slow viruses**—**Slow viruses** counter the ability of antivirus programs to detect
  changes in infected files. This class of virus resides in the computer's memory, where
  antivirus software cannot detect it. It waits for certain tasks, like copying or moving
  files, to execute. As the operating system reads the file into memory, the virus alters
  data read from the input file before writing to the output file, making it much harder
  to detect. **FIGURE 11-7** shows how a slow virus works.

- **Retro viruses**—**Retro viruses** attack countermeasures such as antivirus signature
  files or integrity databases. A retro virus searches for these data files and deletes
  or alters them, thereby crippling the antivirus software's ability to function. Other
  viruses, especially boot viruses (which gain control of the target system at startup),
  modify Windows Registry keys and other operating system key startup files to disable AV, firewall, and intrusion detection system (IDS) software if found. **FIGURE 11-8**
  shows how a retro virus works.

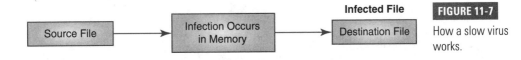

Infected File

FIGURE 11-7

How a slow virus
works.

FIGURE 11-8

How a retro virus
works.

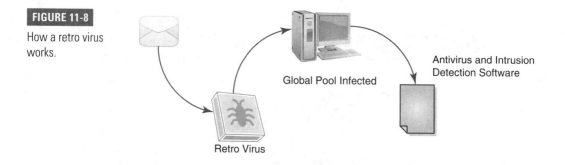

Global Pool Infected

Antivirus and Intrusion
Detection Software

Retro Virus

- **Cross-platform viruses**—**Cross-platform viruses** are less prevalent but can still be potent threats. There have been a number of documented viruses that target multiple operating systems (Apple Macintosh HyperCard viruses, for instance). If those platforms also run Windows emulation software, they become as susceptible to Windows viruses as a native Windows computer.

- **Multipartite viruses**—As previously mentioned, multipartite viruses are hybrid viruses that exhibit multiple behaviors. There are two main types of multipartite virus: Master Boot Record/boot sector viruses and file infecting viruses. Such viruses may exist as file infectors within an application. Upon execution of the infected application, the virus might spawn a Master Boot Record infection, which then infects other files when you restart the system. **FIGURE 11-9** shows how a multipartite virus works.

Some multipartite viruses, such as the One Half virus, isolated in 1994, may also exhibit both stealth and polymorphic characteristics.

Rootkits

A **rootkit** is a type of malware that modifies or replaces one or more existing programs to hide the fact that a computer has been compromised. It is common for rootkits to modify parts of the operating system to conceal traces of their presence. Rootkits can exist at any level, from the boot instructions of a computer up to the applications that run in the

FIGURE 11-9

How a multipartite
virus works.

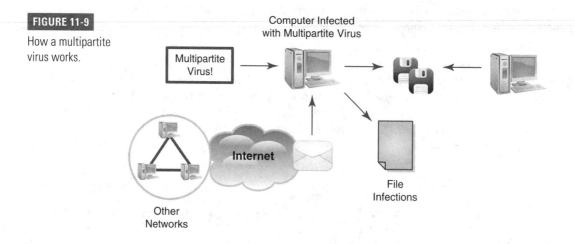

Computer Infected
with Multipartite Virus

Multipartite
Virus!

Internet

Other
Networks

File
Infections

operating system. Once installed, rootkits provide attackers with access to compromised computers and easy access to launching additional attacks. Rootkits are newer than other types of malware and did not appear until around 1990. They can be very difficult to detect and remove since their main purpose is to hide their own existence. But identifying and removing rootkits is crucial to maintaining a secure system.

In 2015, reports began to emerge that described very serious types of rootkits. It was discovered that rootkits could be burned into the firmware of hard disk drives or even into a computer's Basic Input/Output System (BIOS). These rootkits would survive complete operating system reinstallation and hard drive reformatting. In the case of the BIOS rootkit, even replacing a disk drive with a completely new disk drive would not remove the rootkit. These newer types of rootkits are extremely pervasive and difficult to remove without substantial technical skill. In 2016, several sources reported that the U.S. National Security Agency (NSA) has used hard drive firmware rootkits to enable surveillance on specific targets.

Ransomware

Another type of malware attempts to generate funds directly from a computer user. This type of malware is also one of the fastest-growing menaces. **Ransomware** attacks a computer and limits the user's ability to access the computer's data. It can limit access by slowing the computer down, denying access for authorized users, or blocking access to specific programs or resources. Many current ransomware programs operate by encrypting important files or even the entire disk and making them inaccessible.

One of the first ransomware programs was CryptOLOcker, which was released in 2013. Ransomware programs have become even more sophisticated and dangerous since then. The attacker generally alerts the users to the restrictions and demands a payment to restore full access. The demand for a payment, or *ransom*, gives this type of malware its name. The attacker promises to decrypt the user's data or remove any mechanisms that block access once the ransom is paid. Most computer users rely on their computers and the data they store. Few computer users can lose access to their data and other resources without encountering ongoing frustration.

Business users may find ransomware to be far more than a simple annoyance. The inability to access key parts of a business computing system can have the same effect as a DoS attack. A ransomware attack can cost an organization large sums of lost profits in a very short period of time. Attackers that launch ransomware attacks expose themselves to huge risks but also can realize large profits. Ransomware is a growing trend in malware. User reliance on mobile devices makes such devices attractive targets. As computers and other devices become more mobile, they become even more vulnerable to potential ransomware attacks.

> **■ NOTE**
>
> So, how can malware simply take control of a computer? Malware can use many different techniques, but two common ones depend on lazy programmers. A *buffer overflow* is a condition when a program allows more data to be loaded into a variable than it expected. When this happens, the "extra" data can change protected data in memory or even change a program's instructions. A similar weakness is an *integer overflow,* an arithmetic operation that results in a number that is too large to be stored in a simple integer variable. In both cases, programmers should handle the errors and alert the user, but many programs behave in unusual ways when overflows occur.

Spam

Spam is one of the most bothersome challenges faced by network administrators. Not only does spam often contain viruses or other malicious code, it congests networks and mail servers and can waste a lot of user time and productivity. Many viruses now carry software to make an infected computer part of a spam botnet. These spam botnets send out new versions of viruses.

Most anti-spam vendors estimate that 70 to 90 percent of all messaging traffic is spam. Simply put, spam is any unwanted message. However, many users still open unwanted emails or receive unwanted instant messages. They see the promise of jobs, lottery winnings, or reduced prices on products. This makes it hard to classify the message as strictly "unwanted."

Spam is becoming a major problem for organizations of all sizes. Spam uses bandwidth that organizations need to operate, and it wastes employees' time. Spam is also a breeding ground for viruses and worms. If offensive in content, spam can expose the organization to financial liability. Fortunately, automated tools are available to assist the security administrator to help eliminate these messages. Unfortunately, spam generators are very dynamic and quickly change to avoid spam detection filters. Completely eliminating spam turns out to be very difficult.

Despite the increasing deployment of anti-spam services and technology, the number and size of spam messages continue to increase. Although not specifically malicious code, spam represents at least the following threats to organizations:

- Spam consumes computing resources (bandwidth and CPU time).
- Spam diverts IT personnel from activities more critical to network security.
- Spam email is a potential carrier of malicious code (viruses, hostile active content, etc.).
- Spammers have developed techniques to compromise intermediate systems to facilitate remailing services, masking the real source addresses and constituting a DoS attack for victimized systems.
- Opt-out (unsubscribe) features in spam messages can represent a new form of reconnaissance attack to acquire legitimate target addresses.

Worms

Worms are self-contained programs designed to propagate from one host machine to another using the host's own network communications protocols. Unlike viruses, worms do not require a host program in order to survive and replicate. Originally, the distinction

What Is Spam?

SPAM, in all uppercase letters, is a trademark of Hormel Foods. In mixed or lowercase letters, the term refers to unsolicited commercial email. The current use of the term *spam* originated in a Monty Python comedy skit first televised in 1970. The skit portrayed a waiter in a diner where every dish included the product SPAM. Any time one of the characters uttered the word "SPAM," several Vikings in the diner repeatedly chanted "SPAM, SPAM, SPAM, SPAM!" The Vikings' chanting overwhelmed the main dialogue, making it difficult to understand the other characters. As a result, the term *spam* came to mean any noise or other excessive communication that overwhelms the main message.

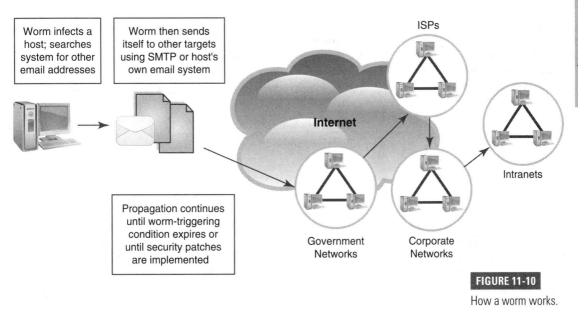

FIGURE 11-10

How a worm works.

between worms and viruses was that worms used networks and communications links to spread and did not directly attach to an executable file. The use of the term *worm* stems from the fact that worms are programs with segments, working on different computers, all communicating over a network.

A worm usually probes network-attached computers to exploit a specific vulnerability. Generally, worms look for a specific piece of server or utility software that will respond to network queries or activity. Examples of worms include the Internet/Morris Worm of 1988. More recent worms include the Conficker and Stuxnet worms, along with a number of Linux worms, such as the Lion worm. **FIGURE 11-10** shows how a worm works. Blaster

---

Evidence of Worm Attacks

Worms leave many telltale signs of their presence. Any of the following may indicate an infected computer:

- Unexplained increases in bandwidth consumption
- High volumes of inbound and outbound email during normal activity periods
- Sudden increase in email server storage utilization (this may trigger alarm thresholds set to monitor and manage disk/user partition space)
- Unexplained decrease in available disk space
- Unusual increase in average message size or increase in volume of attachments
- Unexpected SMTP or POP3 daemon responses for nondelivery of message traffic that was not sent by users
- Sudden increase in user response times across the network or sudden congestion at choke-points near server farms
- Sudden increase in IDS and firewall threshold alarm activity

NOTE

Nimda is another example of a worm. However, it also spreads in a number of other ways, so you could consider it an email virus and a multipartite virus as well.

was possibly one of the most successful early worms, because the function it used, DCOM, was available on all versions of Windows—desktop as well as server.

A worm may spread rapidly without any user action. A worm often attacks server software. This is because many people who write worms know that servers are on all the time. This allows the worm to spread at a faster rate.

Trojan Horses

Trojans, or Trojan horse programs, are the largest class of malware. A Trojan is any program that masquerades as a useful program while hiding its malicious intent. The masquerading nature of a Trojan encourages users to download and run the program. From the cracker's perspective, the advantage to this approach is that the Trojan runs as an authorized process because an authorized user ran it. The success of Trojans is due to their reliance on social engineering to spread and operate. The Trojan has to trick users into running it. If the Trojan appears to be a useful program, it has a better chance of being run and thus spreading. In fact, the most successful Trojans actually do provide useful services, and unwitting users may run the Trojan many times. However, each time the Trojan runs, it also carries out some unwanted action, just like any other type of malware.

Many Trojans spread through email messages or website downloads. In years past, Trojan developers posted the programs on electronic bulletin board systems and file archive sites. Moderators and anti-malware software would soon identify and eliminate malicious programs. More recently, Trojan programs spread by mass email, websites, social networking sites, and automated distribution agents (bots). Trojan programs can spread in a number of disguises. Identifying their malicious payload has become much more difficult.

Some experts consider viruses to be just a type of Trojan horse program. There is some validity to this view. A virus is an unknown quantity that hides and spreads along with a

Evidence of Trojans

Trojans leave many telltale signs. Any of the following may indicate an infected computer:

- Unrecognized new processes running
- Startup messages indicating that new software has been (or is being) installed (Registry updating)
- Unresponsiveness of applications to normal commands
- Unusual redirection of normal web requests to unknown sites
- Unexpected or unscheduled modem connection activity
- Unexpected remote logon prompts at unusual times or unfamiliar logon prompt panels (this may result from routine software upgrades or session resets but can also indicate Trojan key-logging or password-capturing software)
- Sudden or unexpected termination of antivirus scanning software or personal firewall software (either at startup or when user attempts to load)

legitimate program. In addition, you can turn any program into a Trojan by infecting it with a virus. However, the term *virus* specifically refers to the infectious code rather than the infected host. The term *Trojan* refers to a deliberately misleading or modified program that does not reproduce itself.

Logic Bombs

A **logic bomb** is a program that executes a malicious function of some kind when it detects certain conditions. Once in place, the logic bomb waits for a specified condition or time. When the specified condition or time occurs, the logic bomb activates and carries out its tasks. The malicious tasks can cause immediate damage or can initiate a sequence of events that cause damage over a longer period.

Many logic bombs originate with organization insiders. Because people inside an organization generally have more detailed knowledge of the IT infrastructure than outsiders do, they can place logic bombs more easily. In addition, internal personnel generally know more about an organization's weak points and can identify more effective ways to cause damage. For example, a programmer might hide a program within other software that lies dormant. If the company terminates that programmer's employment, he might activate the program. This causes the logic bomb to carry out malicious activities such as deleting valuable files or otherwise causing harm.

Logic bombs can be very difficult to identify because the designer creates them to avoid detection. In addition, the designer generally possesses knowledge of the organization's capabilities and security controls and can place logic bombs where they are less likely to attract attention.

Active Content Vulnerabilities

The term **active content** refers to components, primarily on websites, that provide functionality to interact with users. This includes any dynamic objects that do something when the user opens the webpage. Developers can use many technologies to create active content, including ActiveX, Cascading Style Sheets (CSS), React, Java, JavaScript, VBScript, macros, browser plugins, PDF files, and other scripting languages. This code runs in the context of the user's browser and uses the user's logon credentials. These active content threats are considered mobile code because these programs run on a wide variety of computer platforms.

Many Internet websites now rely on active content to create their look and feel. For these schemes to operate properly, the user must download these bits of mobile code, which can gain access to the hard disk. Once they activate, they can potentially do things such as fill up your desktop with infected file icons. These icons will spawn additional copies of the malicious code.

Active content comes in many types, from application macros to applets to background scripts. Java, JavaScript, Visual Basic Script, ActiveX, CSS, React, macros, Adobe Acrobat files, and browser plugins can all contain malicious software through well-defined and documented active content features. All these have potential weaknesses that malware can exploit.

Malicious Add-Ons

As web browsers become more and more powerful, software developers provide more and more companion programs that work with your web browser. These companion programs are called **browser add-ons**. Browser add-ons can extend the web browser in many ways. For example, they can integrate news and weather alerts into your browser. A browser add-on can add to a web browser's functionality in many ways. Unfortunately, add-ons can also decrease security. Not all add-ons are trustworthy. Malicious add-ons are browser add-ons that contain some type of malware. Once installed, they can perform many malicious actions. The best way to protect yourself from malicious add-ons is to be very careful about the add-ons you do install. Only install browser add-ons from sources you trust. Furthermore, you should periodically check the add-ons that are installed to ensure that you know which ones you are using. If you find any add-ons that you don't recognize, remove them.

> **TIP**
>
> For more information on removing malicious add-ons from any browser, take a look at *https://malwaretips.com/blogs/browser-toolbar-removal/*. This article specifically covers removing toolbars, but the website contains many other helpful articles about battling malware.

Injection

Malicious software uses many different techniques to carry out attacks. You have already learned about overflow techniques. **Injection techniques** are also very popular in malware development. An injection action is when malicious software provides deliberately invalid input to some other software. The purpose of providing invalid input is to cause an error condition and, hopefully, some state that allows an attack to occur. Injection weaknesses are always caused by software that does not properly validate input data. The most popular types of injection techniques include:

- **Cross-site scripting (XSS)**—This technique allows attackers to embed client-side scripts into webpages that users view. When a user views a webpage with a script, the web browser runs the attacking script. These scripts can be used to bypass access controls. XSS effects can pose substantial security risks, depending on how sensitive the data are on the vulnerable site.

- **SQL injection**—A code injection is used to attack applications that depend on data stored in databases. SQL statements are inserted into an input field and are executed by the application. SQL injection attacks allow attackers to disclose and modify data, violate data integrity, or even destroy data and manipulate the database server.

- **LDAP injection**—Another injection attack, the LDAP injection exploits websites that construct LDAP based on user input. Web applications that don't sanitize input enable attackers to alter the way that LDAP statements are constructed. LDAP statements that are modified by an attacker run with the same permissions as the component that executed the command.

- **XML injection**—XML injection is a technique to manipulate the logic of an XML application or service. Injecting XML content into an XML message can alter the logic of an application or even insert malicious content into an XML document.

- **Command injection**—The goal of this type of attack is to execute commands on a host operating system. A vulnerable application provides the ability for this attack to succeed. These attacks are possible only when an application accepts unvalidated user input and passes the input to a system shell.

The primary goal of any injection attack is to allow the attacker to perform unauthorized actions. These actions could be to access or modify data or even to execute code that shouldn't be executed without authorization. The ability to successfully attack a computer or device and run unauthorized code is called an **arbitrary code execution** attack or a **remote code execution** attack.

Botnets

Hacking groups create **botnets** (short for *robotically controlled networks*) to launch attacks. The attackers infect vulnerable machines with agents that perform various functions at the command of the bot-herder or controller. (A **bot-herder** is a hacker who operates a botnet.) Typically, controllers communicate with other members of the botnet using Internet Relay Chat (IRC) channels. IRC is a protocol that enables text conversations over the Internet. Attackers can use botnets to distribute malware and spam and to launch DoS attacks against organizations or even countries. Attackers have established thousands of botnets, and they are a real threat to systems. During 2007, the Storm botnet was the second most powerful supercomputer in the world. Botnets are so powerful that they play a crucial role in today's attacks. The recurring attacks on U.S. banks and infrastructure in late 2012 and 2013 used botnets to launch the attacks. The risk of botnets points out the need to secure every computing device. Attackers can use devices of all types to launch attacks.

Denial of Service Attacks

The purpose of a denial of service (DoS) attack is to overwhelm a server or network segment to the point that the server or network becomes unusable. A successful DoS attack crashes a server or network device or creates so much network congestion that authorized users cannot access network resources.

Standard DoS attacks use a single computer to launch the attack. A distributed denial-of-service (DDoS) attack uses intermediary hosts to conduct the attack. These intermediaries are compromised systems that contain Trojan-handler programs. These Trojan programs then act as agents to execute a coordinated attack on a target system or network. The attacker(s) control one or more master handler servers, each of which can control many agents or daemons. The agents receive instructions to coordinate a packet-based attack against one or more victim systems.

FYI

Botnets are the main source of distributed denial of service (DDoS) attacks and of spam. They are programs that hide on compromised computers and wait for a command to "wake up" and carry out some instructions. Botnets are extremely resistant to takedown and can be hard to detect, since they exist on many different computers. Botnet DoS attacks are growing and spreading so rapidly that authors trying to describe them cannot keep up. F-Secure, a vendor of antivirus software, personal firewalls, and personal IDSs, maintains a series of videos and updates on YouTube at *www.youtube.com/fslabs*.

In September and October 2012 and again starting in February 2013, a group of activists with hacking abilities, called **hactivists**, launched a series of DDoS attacks against several major U.S. bank computer systems. Typically, some customers of attacked sites will likely become frustrated due to slow websites; others may be unable to reach the sites at all. The same hacktivists that launched the attacks against U.S. banks in October 2012 launched a new round of attacks in December 2012 and into 2013 against many of the same banks. The attacks again disrupted online access to the bank websites but were not as successful as the earlier attacks. The banks had learned from the earlier attacks and added new controls to protect their websites.

In 2015 and early 2016, hacktivists launched large-scale successful attacks against the Islamic State of Iraq and Syria (ISIS) and even a U.S. presidential candidate. Hacktivists are behind more and more large-scale attacks, the general intent of which is to attract attention to some political or social issue.

There are three parties in these attacks: the attacker, the intermediaries (handlers and agents), and the victim(s). Even though the intermediary is not the intended victim, the intermediary can also suffer the same types of problems that the victim does in these attacks. You can find additional information on DDoS attacks on the CERT website at *www.cert.org*.

SYN Flood Attacks

One popular technique for DoS attacks is called a **SYN flood**. In a SYN flood, the attacker uses IP spoofing to send a large number of packets requesting connections to the victim computer. These requests appear to be legitimate but in fact reference a client system that is unable to respond to a specific network message during the connection establishment process. The victim computer records each connection request and reserves a place for the connection in a local table in memory. The victim computer then sends an acknowledgment called a **SYN-ACK** message back to the attacker. Normally the client would finish establishing the connection by responding to the SYN-ACK message with an ACK message. However, because the attacker used IP spoofing, the SYN-ACK message goes to the spoofed system. The result is that the client never sends the ACK message. The victim computer then fills up its connections table waiting for ACK messages for all the requests. In the meantime, no legitimate users can connect to the victim computer because the SYN flood has filled the connection table. The victim computer will remain unavailable until the connection requests time out. Even then, the attacking system can simply continue requesting new connections faster than the victim system can terminate the expired pending connections. **FIGURE 11-11** shows how a SYN flood attack works.

Smurf Attacks

In a **smurf attack**, attackers direct forged Internet Control Message Protocol (ICMP) echo request packets to IP broadcast addresses from remote locations to generate DoS attacks. There are three parties in these attacks: the attacker, the intermediary, and the victim. (Note that the intermediary can also be a victim.) The intermediary receives an ICMP echo request packet directed to the IP broadcast address of his or her network. If the intermediary does not filter ICMP traffic directed to IP broadcast addresses, many of the machines on the network will receive this ICMP echo request packet and send an ICMP echo reply packet back. When (potentially) all the machines on a network respond to this ICMP echo request, the result can be severe network congestion or outages. **FIGURE 11-12** shows how a smurf attack works.

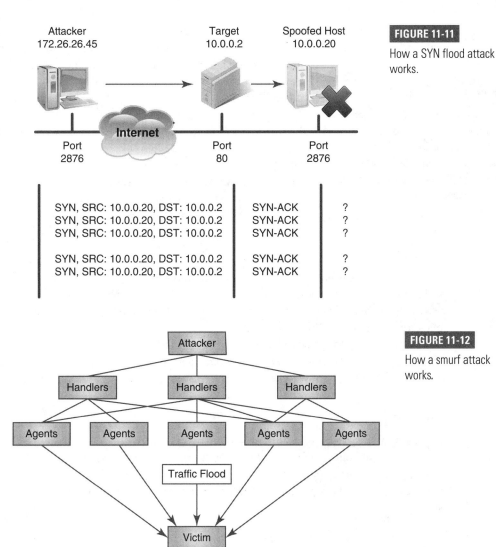

FIGURE 11-11

How a SYN flood attack works.

FIGURE 11-12

How a smurf attack works.

Spyware

Spyware is any unsolicited background process that installs itself on a user's computer and collects information about the user's browsing habits and website activities. These programs usually affect privacy and confidentiality. They typically install when users download freeware programs.

A **cookie** is a small text file that stores information about a browser session. The server side of a user connection to a web server can place certain information in the cookie and then transfer that cookie to the user's browser. Later the same server can ask the browser for the cookie and retrieve the information the browser previously stored. This becomes useful in any intelligent interaction between browser and website, because the browser does not maintain a connection with the server between requests.

Spyware cookies are cookies that share information across sites. Some cookies are persistent and are stored on your hard drive indefinitely without your permission. They can reveal and share private information collected among multiple sites. Spyware cookies include those containing text such as *247media, admonitor, adforce, doubleclick, engage, flycast, sexhound, sextracker, sexlist,* and *valueclick* in their names. Adobe Flash uses Locally Shared Objects (LSOs) in the same way that websites use cookies. In fact, LSOs are often called *Flash cookies*. LSOs store small amounts of data for websites that use Flash applications. These LSOs can be used by attackers to store and disclose sensitive user data. In recent years, Flash has been used in many attacks due to its numerous vulnerabilities.

> **● NOTE**
>
> Cookies and email attachments are the two most common techniques attackers use to spread malware. Unsuspecting users who accept cookies or open attachments provide the easiest way for attackers to place malware on computers or mobile devices.

Adware

Adware programs trigger such nuisances as popup ads and banners when you visit certain websites. They affect productivity and may combine with active background activities such as homepage hijacking code. In addition, adware collects and tracks information about application, website, and Internet activity.

The problem with spyware and adware lies in distinguishing between legitimate and illicit activities. Spyware and adware companies have taken full advantage of this nebulousness, often suing anti-spyware companies for labeling their programs as spyware.

Phishing

A **phishing** attack tricks users into providing logon information on what appears to be a legitimate website but is in fact a website set up by an attacker to obtain this information. If the attacker can obtain logon information for financial institutions, for example, the attacker may be able to steal from the victim. Attackers use very sophisticated technologies to make such sites appear legitimate.

Spear-Phishing

To increase the success rate of a phishing attack, some attackers supply information about the victim that appears to come from the legitimate company. This information can be obtained in many ways, including guessing, sifting through trash ("Dumpster diving"), or sending bogus surveys.

Pharming

The term **pharming** originates from the term *phishing*, which refers to the use of social engineering to obtain access credentials such as usernames and passwords. Pharming is possible through the exploitation of a vulnerability in Domain Name System (DNS) server software. DNS servers are the machines responsible for resolving Internet domain names into their real IP addresses. The vulnerability that exists in DNS server software enables an attacker to acquire the domain name for a site and (for example) redirect that website's traffic to another website. If the website receiving the traffic is a fake website, such as a copy of a bank's website, it can be used to phish or steal a computer user's password, PIN, or account number. For example, in January 2005 an attacker hijacked the domain name for a large New York ISP, Panix, to a site in Australia. Other well-known companies also became victims of this attack. (Note that this is possible only when the original site is not SSL protected or when the user ignores warnings about invalid server certificates.)

Keystroke Loggers

Keystroke loggers are insidious and dangerous tools in the hands of an attacker. Whether software- or hardware-based, a keystroke logger captures keystrokes, or user entries. The keystroke logger then forwards that information to the attacker. This enables the attacker to capture logon information, banking information, and other sensitive data.

To combat keystroke loggers some people have turned to onscreen virtual keyboards. In response, black-hat hackers started distributing malware that would take snapshots of the screen around the area clicked by the mouse. So the battle between security and hackers wages on as each side continues to develop new threats and new solutions.

Hoaxes and Myths

Although virus hoaxes are not always malicious, spreading unverified warnings and bogus patches can lead to new vulnerabilities. Often the objective of the creator of the hoax or myth is merely to observe how widely the ruse can be propagated. This is a new version of the old chain-letter attack, where an attacker sent a person a letter promising good luck or happiness if the person forwarded the message to a dozen people.

Here are some guidelines for recognizing hoaxes, especially virus hoaxes:

- **Did a legitimate entity (computer security expert, vendor, etc.) send the alert?**— Inspect any validation certificates or at least the source uniform resource locator (URL) of the advisory.
- **Is there a request to forward the alert to others?**—No legitimate security alert will suggest that the recipient forward the advisory.
- **Are there detailed explanations or technical terminology in the alert?**—Hoaxes often use technobabble to intimidate the recipient into believing the alert is legitimate. A legitimate advisory typically omits any details, however. It simply refers the recipient to a legitimate website for details. The website also typically provides a suggestion for protection activities.
- **Does the alert follow the generic format of a chain letter?**—In this format, there is a hook, a threat, and a request. The hook is a catchy or dramatic opening or subject line to catch the recipient's attention. The threat is a technical-sounding warning of serious vulnerabilities or damage. The request is a plea to distribute the alert or a suggestion to take some immediate action—for example, to download a patch from a linked website.

Homepage Hijacking

The function of these attacks is to change your browser's homepage to point to the attacker's site. There are two forms of hijacking:

- **Exploiting a browser vulnerability to reset the homepage**—Many types of active content can change the browser's homepage, often without the user's permission. Even without resorting to covert means, it is easy to convince a user to select an action that does more than he or she expects. Just because you click a button that says "Remove Infected Programs from My Computer" doesn't mean that's the action that will occur.

- **Covertly installing a browser helper object (BHO) Trojan program**—This Trojan contains the hijacking code. Once a BHO executes, it can change the browser's homepage back to the hijacker's desired site. Typically, hijacker programs put a reference to themselves into the operating system's startup procedures. That way the hijacker runs every time the computer reboots. If you try to change any of these settings, the hijacker repeatedly changes them back until you find and remove the hijacking software.

Webpage Defacements

The term **web defacement** or **web graffiti** refers to someone gaining unauthorized access to a web server and altering the index page of a site on the server. Usually the attacker exploits known vulnerabilities in the target server and gains administrative access. Once in control, the attacker replaces the original pages on the site with altered versions. For example, **FIGURE 11-13** shows a defaced *New York Times* webpage.

Typically, the defacement represents graffiti. Most security practitioners consider this form of attack to be merely a nuisance. The potential for embedding malicious active content code such as viruses or Trojans into the website does exist, however. Code Red, for instance,

How Can Attackers Attack Web Applications?

Applications that users access using a web browser are called **web applications**. Most people just think of web applications as websites, but they really are far more powerful. A web application generally provides access to data in a database and uses those data to provide some service to the user. For example, online shopping sites are really web applications. Attackers often target web applications since the application provides access to vast amounts of data. One method attackers use is called **session hijacking**. Session hijacking is an attack in which the attacker intercepts network messages between a web server and a web browser. It extracts one or more pieces of data, most commonly a session ID, and uses that to communicate with the web server. The attacker pretends to be an authorized user by taking over the authorized user's session. The technique used when the attacker masquerades as an authorized user is called **header manipulation**. The attacker creates an HTTP message for the web server but changes (manipulates) the HTTP header to include the intercepted session ID. When the web server receives the altered HTTP message, it thinks the attacker is an authorized user. This is an effective attack for web applications that fail to authenticate each request.

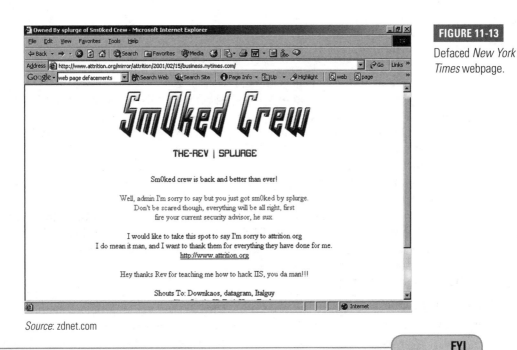

FIGURE 11-13

Defaced *New York Times* webpage.

Source: zdnet.com

FYI

Backdoor programs are typically more dangerous than computer viruses. This is because intruders can use them to take control of a computer and potentially gain network access. These programs are also commonly referred to as *Trojan horses* because they pretend to do something other than what they actually do. Backdoor programs typically arrive as attachments to emails with innocent-looking filenames.

included a payload that installed a backdoor Trojan. This Trojan allowed remote access to an infected IIS server, which attackers could use to deface the front page of the web server. You can minimize the risk of this type of attack by ensuring that you install current software versions and security patches.

A Brief History of Malicious Code Threats

In the early days of computing, malware spread from computer to computer via diskettes that were handed off from person to person. This manual transmission method was called *sneakernet*. With sneakernet, a virus could take months to spread across the globe. In contrast, today's viral infections spread via networks and can cross the globe in a matter of seconds. As the virus-writing community evolved, more and more sophisticated viruses began to emerge. Some could spread via email, mobile code, or macros, and others could spread in multiple ways.

1970s and Early 1980s: Academic Research and UNIX

The idea of self-replicating computer programs has been around for decades. This idea has appeared in literature, scientific papers, and even experiments since the early 1970s.

Researchers made early attempts to perform routine maintenance tasks on large networks using self-distributing code (worms), but the technology did not become widespread or well known.

A key event in hostile code development was the research performed by Dr. Fred Cohen in 1983. Cohen's paper, "Computer Viruses—Theory and Experiments," published in 1984, defined the computer virus and described experiments he and others performed to prove the viability of viral code. Cohen published this work before anyone observed the first computer viruses.

The Internet during this period was a network that primarily connected university computers to one another. This network was vulnerable to programs that could propagate using existing communications protocols. A university student named Robert Morris—who unleashed the first major malware incident, the Morris Worm, in November 1988—demonstrated this idea. This UNIX-based worm overwhelmed almost all computers on the Internet, causing a great deal of media interest and many headlines.

1980s: Early PC Viruses

The first personal computers (PCs) hit the market in the early 1980s. Their popularity grew fast. By the late 1980s, the PC was an indispensable and affordable business technology for many companies. This rapid growth also brought computer technology closer to a larger number of individuals.

The PC operating system was disk-based (DOS), and most software and data files migrated between PCs via floppy diskettes. Two primary types of malicious virus code emerged to exploit this fact: boot sector viruses, which attacked the operating system components located on disks and in memory, and file infector viruses, which attacked the executable files themselves.

Brain (a boot sector virus), Lehigh, and Jerusalem (a file infector) are examples of the earliest viruses. They propagated primarily via floppy disks and downloads from popular computer bulletin board (BBS) archives. Another early virus, Elk Cloner, which targeted the Apple II computer, also spread by floppy disks.

1990s: Early LAN Viruses

Local area networks (LANs) began to appear in business environments by the early 1990s. This development gave the traditional file viruses a fertile environment to propagate. Very few people understood the virus problem at this time, and finding a virus was a rare event. Interested users collected the samples they found and freely distributed those, giving rise to notorious virus exchange bulletin boards. Some viruses did cause damage, and business users started to become aware of the problem. The boot sector virus Form5 became the most widespread virus during this period. Another well-known virus of this era was Dark Avenger, also known as Eddie6. It was a very destructive virus.

By the end of the decade, local area networks had become a key infrastructure in most companies. At the same time, the use of the Internet for communications—particularly email and data file transfer—became widespread. Traditional boot sector and file infector viruses began to diminish in frequency as storage technology advanced with the introduction of CD-ROMs.

Mid-1990s: Smart Applications and the Internet

The popularity of email, combined with the ease of attaching files, gave rise to the extremely widespread distribution of malicious code using the same techniques demonstrated years earlier by Morris: email worms. These programs locate email address files within a user's system and then generate multiple copies of themselves, often disguised as innocent-looking file attachments. The well-known email worms named Melissa and Loveletter are examples. Although many of these earlier programs relied on users to activate the code by opening attachments, newer forms of worms have exploited various security weaknesses in the increasing numbers of always-on computers and servers. For example, Code Red exploited vulnerabilities in Microsoft web servers (IIS) and had exceptional replication speed.

The Internet provides an environment from which individuals and groups can extend their activities beyond functional and geographic boundaries. During the mid-1990s, hacking (or cracking) became a growing business security concern. Using automated tools and more structured approaches, these individuals and groups have continued to evolve. The inherent resiliency of Internet communications protocols became a way to disrupt normal operations and gave rise to DoS attacks against popular websites.

New forms of malicious code evolved in the 1990s, including Trojan programs like Back Orifice and AIDS. More resilient and stealthy variants of virus code also evolved, including polymorphic versions like Tequila. In addition, new programming languages designed for portability and functionality presented new opportunities to develop additional forms of malicious code. StrangeBrew was the first virus to infect Java files. Though harmless, the virus modified CLASS files to contain a copy of itself.

With the introduction of advanced programming features into popular application software, the rise of other forms of malicious code appeared to infect document files. The first macro virus, WM/Concept7, was discovered in August 1995. It spread through the transmission of a simple document file.

2000 to Present

As personal and corporate Internet connectivity has continued to increase in this new century, authors of popular browser technologies have added numerous companion tools or plugins. These tools use specialized scripting codes that can automate common functions. They comprise a generation of active content code that exposes additional opportunities to attackers.

The number of computers and devices now connected to the Internet, especially popular server platforms running Windows and other widely distributed software, has created new vulnerabilities. The replication speed of Internet worms coupled with today's high-speed computers, as well as increasing interactive probing for vulnerabilities by hostile groups, mandate continuous improvement, monitoring, and testing of IT security by organizations and user communities.

The W32/Nimda worm, taking advantage of backdoors left behind by the Code Red II worm, is the first to propagate itself via several methods, including email, network shares, and an infected website. The worm spreads from client to web server by scanning for backdoors. The Klezworm infects executables by creating a hidden copy of the original host file and then overwriting the original file with itself.

The latest communications revolution started with the introduction of the iPhone in 2007 and the Android Smartphone in 2008. The availability of these products started a shift in consumer perception of mobile communication. Mobile devices became more powerful and more prevalent. Today more people use mobile devices than use desktop computers. These devices have become plentiful and nearly essential to everyday life. Attackers know how much users rely on information mobile devices store and process. They also know that the majority of users neglect to secure their mobile devices. Because of the increasing number of vulnerable targets, many new malware attacks target mobile devices instead of traditional computers. And as more and more appliances and other types of devices are Internet-connected, the problem with malware is only growing worse. As watches, refrigerators, cars, and thousands of other types of devices connect to the Internet, attackers see many more opportunities to attack.

Threats to Business Organizations

Security threats from malware originate from a variety of sources. These range from isolated incidents involving a single, unsophisticated perpetrator to complex, structured attacks against multiple targets by organized groups. These threats generally originate outside an organization's IT infrastructure and user community. For this reason, organizations make a significant effort to detect, respond, mitigate, and recover from these attacks.

Less publicized yet equally troublesome are threats that originate from within an organization. These threats are due to improper or deficient security policies and unsafe user practices. It is the IT security practitioner's responsibility to understand the nature and significance of any such internal threat and to implement effective countermeasures and practices.

Types of Threats

Malicious code can threaten businesses in the following ways:

- **Attacks against confidentiality and privacy**—These include emerging concerns with respect to identity theft and trade secrets at both the individual and corporate levels.

- **Attacks against data integrity**—Economic damage or loss due to the theft, destruction, or unauthorized manipulation of sensitive data can be devastating to an organization. Organizations depend on the accuracy and integrity of information. The legitimacy of the source of communications also affects the integrity of the transmitted data.

- **Attacks against availability of services and resources**—Businesses increasingly depend on the Internet as a means of delivery for key network services. As a result, hostile attacks that deny these services to legitimate users have become an increasing concern among IT security practitioners. Aggressive prevention, early detection, and quick recovery are essential to maintaining an acceptable level of service.

- **Attacks against productivity and performance**—Mass bulk email (spam), spyware, persistence cookies, and the like consume computing resources and reduce user productivity. Ransomware can reduce performance to zero by making important data inaccessible until the ransom is paid. Unnecessary reaction to nonexistent code threats, such as hoaxes, can also affect productivity. Security professionals must make regular efforts to minimize the impact of such threats.

- **Attacks that create legal liability**—Unaddressed vulnerabilities can extend beyond the legal boundaries of an organization, creating a potential liability to customers, trading partners, and others.
- **Attacks that damage reputation**—Malicious code attacks can broadcast sensitive information about a company or its customers or otherwise embarrass a company. Such attacks can damage a company's reputation. This can result in a loss of customers and potential business.

Internal Threats from Employees

Although attackers initiate more notorious security threats from outside a target network, a number of significant vulnerabilities exist inside a trusted network. These require the IT security practitioner's attention.

Perhaps the most common of these vulnerabilities exist because of unsafe computing practices by employees. These practices include the following:

- The exchange of untrusted disks or other media among systems
- The installation of unauthorized, unregistered software (application and OS)
- The unmonitored download of files from the Internet
- The uncontrolled dissemination of email or other messaging application attachments

Security breaches also originate from within the victim organization, perpetrated by current and former employees. These breaches often go undetected due to weak personnel and security policies or ineffective countermeasures. They frequently go unreported by the organization involved. These breaches can include the following:

- Unauthorized access to system and network resources
- Privilege escalation
- Theft, destruction, or unauthorized dissemination of data
- Use of corporate network resources to initiate hostile attacks against outside targets
- The accidental or intentional release of malicious code into internal network segments not protected by perimeter controls and intrusion detection countermeasures

Anatomy of an Attack

To understand threats and to develop practical and effective countermeasures, you must understand the objective of malicious code attacks as well as what the attackers are targeting. In this section, you will learn how to identify key targets of malicious code attacks and describe the key characteristics and hostile objectives of each type of attack. This section covers the following:

- What motivates attackers
- The purpose of an attack

- Types of attacks
- Phases of an attack

What Motivates Attackers?

An attacker is no longer simply a social outcast who writes malicious software from his or her parents' basement, with the simple intent of seeing whether he or she can get away with it. Today's attackers are far more sophisticated. They have four primary motivations:

- They want money.
- They want to be famous.
- They want to impose their political beliefs or systems on others.
- They are angry and they want to exact revenge on those who have angered them.

The Purpose of an Attack

There are four main purposes of an attack:

- **Denial of availability**—The goal of some attacks, such as a DoS, DDoS, or ransomware attack, is to prevent legitimate users from accessing a system or data.
- **Data modification**—The attacker might issue commands to access a file on a local or network drive and modify, delete, or overwrite it with new data. Alternatively, the attacker might modify system settings or browser security settings.
- **Data export**—Attackers might seek to steal information from your computer and forward it over the Internet or via email to an attacker. For instance, many Trojan horses forward usernames and passwords to an anonymous attacker's email address on the Web. The attacker can then use the passwords to access protected resources.
- **Launch point** An attacker might target a computer for use as a launch point to infect and target other computers.

Types of Attacks

There are four primary types of attack:

- Unstructured attacks
- Structured attacks
- Direct attacks
- Indirect attacks

Unstructured Attacks

Moderately skilled attackers generally perpetrate unstructured attacks against network resources. Often the initial intent of the attacker is simply personal gratification—the thrill of the challenge—of gaining illegal access. Any level of success can lead to yet more malicious activity, such as defacement or the inadvertent crashing of systems. Occasionally an unstructured attack exposes an unintended vulnerability; the attacker may then switch to a more methodical approach. All such activity is of concern to IT security practitioners because it represents a compromise of defensive measures.

Structured Attacks

Highly motivated and technically skilled attackers use complex tools and focused efforts to conduct structured attacks. These attackers may act alone or in groups. They understand, develop, and use sophisticated hacking techniques to identify, probe, penetrate, and carry out malicious activities. These attackers' motives may include money, anger, destruction, or political objectives.

Regardless of their motivation, these attackers can and do inflict serious damage to networks. Attackers usually conduct structured attacks in phases after an overall goal is established. An attack might target a specific organization or a specific technology, such as an operating system.

Direct Attacks

Attackers often conduct direct attacks against specific targets, such as specific organizations. They may also conduct direct attacks against target classes—that is, networks using certain hardware, operating system versions, or services. An example is an IIS Unicode attack against specific web servers in an organization.

These exploits might be unstructured—for example, when a script kiddie uses well-known hacker tools to uncover vulnerable sites and then conducts random exploits around the compromised network through trial and error. These exploits might also be structured attacks by individual crackers or by coordinated cyberterrorist groups, and they could advance methodically through phases to achieve their desired goals.

Typically, an attacker conducts a real-time direct attack by accessing a target system through remote logon exploits—for example, password guessing or session hijacking. Alternatively, the attacker might exploit a known vulnerability in the target operating system, such as a Unicode vulnerability or an active content vulnerability. **FIGURE 11-14** shows a direct attack.

FIGURE 11-14

How a direct attack works.

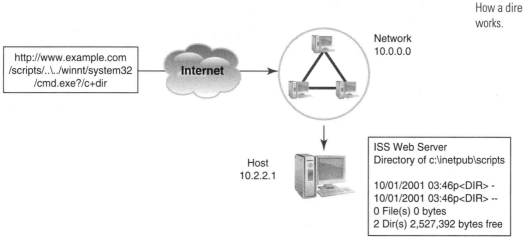

The key characteristic is that the attack occurs in real time. Depending on the sophistication of the attacker, the final objective may simply be to deface a website. Alternatively, it might be a prelude to more malicious structured attacks. For example, the attacker might seek to locate and compromise a weakly protected target system and then implant Trojan programs on it to exploit other resources (files or systems) within the compromised network.

Indirect Attacks

Indirect attacks occur as a natural result of preprogrammed hostile code exploits, such as Internet worms or viruses. These attacks are unleashed indiscriminately. Often they propagate rapidly and widely. Although the worm or virus might exploit a specific system or application vulnerability, its replication and transmission occur indiscriminately.

Most likely, the goal of a direct attack against a specific target might be to establish a starting point for an indirect attack against a more widely dispersed population. For example, the compromise of a single web server to install an email worm as a DoS exploit might be the intended goal.

Phases of an Attack

To develop an attack, attackers need to know the target of the attack. To this end, they develop a strategy. Clever attackers are also concerned about not leaving tracks that allow investigators to identify them. This section details the phases of an attack. **FIGURE 11-15** shows the phases of an attack.

Reconnaissance and Probing

When the overall goal or objective of an attack is clear, the attacker must probe the target network to identify points of possible entry—that is, the vulnerabilities. The reconnaissance and probing phase of an attack is arguably the most important phase. It is in this phase that an attacker collects all the information to conduct the attack. In fact, using the information gathered in this phase is the easy part of an attack. Collecting good information is the best starting point for launching a successful attack. This phase generally involves the use of common tools that are readily available on the Internet. These tools are generally part of the underlying protocol suite or are custom-developed to exploit specific or potential targets.

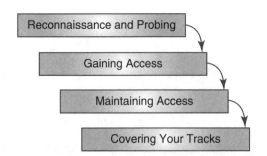

FIGURE 11-15

Phases of an attack.

These tools can include the following:

- DNS and ICMP tools within the TCP/IP protocol suite
- Standard and customized SNMP tools
- Port scanners and port mappers
- Security probes

Attackers might use these tools independently. Alternatively, an attacker might use them as a coordinated suite to gain a complete understanding of a targeted network. This includes the protocols and operating system used, the server platforms employed, the services and ports that are open, the actual or probable network addressing and naming used, and so on.

The Internet and other public sources can provide additional information to profile targets. This information includes the location of facilities, key personnel, and likely business partners. This last piece of information might seem trivial, but an indirect assault committed through a trading partner with serious security breaches is very possible.

DNS, ICMP, and Related Tools: As you learned, domain name servers act like phone books, matching a website's domain name with its IP address. A number of searchable websites enable anyone to find information about registered addresses. In addition, TCP/IP supports discovery tools such as Whois and finger, which you can use to gather preliminary information in profiling a target site. **FIGURE 11-16** shows the output from a Whois lookup.

Reverse DNS lookup and nslookup are additional utility commands that also search DNS information and provide cross-referencing. These services are often free on the Internet. You can locate them by searching on the command name itself.

The Internet Control Management Protocol (ICMP) ping command and several closely related tools are readily available on most computer operating systems. These profiling tools enable attackers to verify that target systems are reachable. For example, attackers can use the ping command with a number of extension flags to test direct reachability between hosts. They can also use the ping command as part of the actual attack plan—for example, to carry out a ping-of-death attack whereby an attacker sends specially constructed ping packets that can crash vulnerable computers. Once a target network has been located, many attackers then perform a ping sweep of all (or a range of) IP addresses within the major network or subnet, to identify other potential hosts that may be accessible. This information alone sometimes exposes the likely network size and topology. In addition, because many networks use a structured numbering scheme, it may also point to likely server and network device locations.

If gaining access is one of the objectives, an attacker can attempt a simple telnet logon to test the softness of perimeter controls. An attacker might also use rpcinfo to determine whether the remote procedure call (RPC) service is active for remote command execution.

SNMP Tools: The Simple Network Management Protocol (SNMP) is an Application Layer protocol that facilitates the exchange of management information between network devices. It is part of the Transmission Control Protocol/Internet Protocol (TCP/IP) suite. SNMP enables network administrators to manage network performance, find and solve network problems, and plan for network growth.

Many popular network management software suites, such as OpenNMS®, Solarwinds® Network Performance Monitor, and Ipswitch WhatsUp® Gold, are SNMP-compliant. They offer full support for managed devices, agents, and network management systems. In addition, there are many utility programs that can be used to gather network device information,

FIGURE 11-16

Results from a
Whois lookup.

FIGURE 11-16

Results from a
Whois lookup.

WHOIS information for **boxtwelve.com**

```
michael@primarchGazelle:~/Downloads$ whois boxtwelve.com

Whois Server Version 2.0

Domain names in the .com and .net domains can now be registered
with many different competing registrars. Go to http://www.internic.net
for detailed information.

    Domain Name: BOXTWELVE.COM
    Registrar: FASTDOMAIN, INC.
    Sponsoring Registrar IANA ID: 1154
    Whois Server: whois.fastdomain.com
    Referral URL: http://www.fastdomain.com
    Name Server: NS1.HOSTMONSTER.COM
    Name Server: NS2.HOSTMONSTER.COM
    Status: clientTransferProhibited https://icann.org/epp#clientTransferProhibited
    Updated Date: 07-mar-2016
    Creation Date: 07-mar-2007
    Expiration Date: 07-mar-2017

>>> Last update of whois database: Wed, 11 May 2016 22:34:15 GMT <<<

For more information on Whois status codes, please visit https://icann.org/epp

NOTICE: The expiration date displayed in this record is the date the
registrar's sponsorship of the domain name registration in the registry is
currently set to expire. This date does not necessarily reflect the expiration
date of the domain name registrant's agreement with the sponsoring
registrar.  Users may consult the sponsoring registrar's Whois database to
view the registrar's reported date of expiration for this registration.

TERMS OF USE: You are not authorized to access or query our Whois
database through the use of electronic processes that are high-volume and
automated except as reasonably necessary to register domain names or
modify existing registrations; the Data in VeriSign Global Registry
Services' ("VeriSign") Whois database is provided by VeriSign for
information purposes only, and to assist persons in obtaining information
about or related to a domain name registration record. VeriSign does not
guarantee its accuracy. By submitting a Whois query, you agree to abide
by the following terms of use: You agree that you may use this Data only
```

including platform, operating system version, and capabilities. Poorly configured network management facilities would allow moderately skilled attackers to gather significant attack profile information. **FIGURE 11-17** shows the Remote SNMP Agent Discovery tool.

Port-Scanning and Port-Mapping Tools: After an attacker identifies a target network, the next step might be to explore what systems and services are accessible. To achieve this goal, an attacker might use several popular port-scanning applications. One of the most popular is Nmap Security Scanner®, available for UNIX, Linux, and Windows. Angry IP Scanner is another network reconnaissance tool, this one for Windows, Linux, and OS X. By design, it's fast and easy to use. **FIGURE 11-18** shows Zenmap®, a Windows GUI front end for the Nmap port-scanning tool.

These tools permit an attacker to discover and identify hosts by performing ping sweeps, probe for open TCP and UDP service ports, and identify operating systems and applications running.

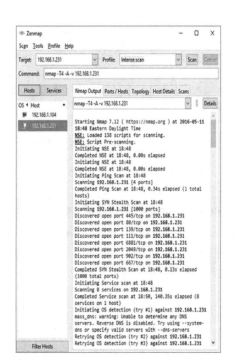

FIGURE 11-17

Remote SNMP
Agent Discovery
enables you
to discover
responsive
SNMP agents on
the network.

FIGURE 11-18

Zenmap, a Windows
GUI front end for the
Nmap port-mapping
tool.

Security Probes: Nessus or its open source variant, OpenVAS, helps security administrators evaluate a large number of vulnerabilities. It recognizes several common networking, operating system, and application-related security problems. It can report the problems without actually exploiting them. Nessus and OpenVAS collect information available to anyone with access to the network. With a properly configured firewall in place, you can properly implement policies to protect information from unauthorized access. These tools are each a double-edged sword, however. As with many tools, attackers can use them as easily as security professionals can. It is a good idea to include scanning for evidence of Nessus® or OpenVAS reconnaissance of your network.

Access and Privilege Escalation

Once an attacker profiles and probes a target network for potential vulnerabilities, he or she must access the target system(s). The primary goal of access is to establish the initial connection to a target host (typically a server platform). To conduct additional reconnaissance activities such as covertly installing hacking toolkits, the attacker must then gain administrative rights to the system.

The method of access depends on the connection technology necessary to reach the target network. As many organizations evolve to web-centric business models, they often maintain legacy dialup access infrastructures, either as secondary remote gateways or due to oversight. In some instances, organizations may not even be aware of modem facilities

Password Capturing and Cracking

One method of gaining access is to capture or crack passwords. An attacker can install a password logger as a backdoor Trojan on a target machine and monitor specific protocol and program activity associated with remote logon processes. Alternatively, if the attacker captures logon strings remotely, a program such as LophtCrack (*www.l0phtcrack.com*) can quickly decrypt and compromise administrator and user passwords. In fact, compromising passwords is so attractive that many attackers have become quite resourceful at this task. They have identified existing computer hardware that works well at password cracking. Many newer personal computers have powerful graphics processing units (GPUs) on their video cards. These GPUs are designed to handle the advanced math calculations required for rendering graphic images. Attackers have found that GPUs also work well in cracking passwords. Many new password-cracking tools offload much of the math to video card GPUs to speed up the whole process.

Maintaining Access Using a Remote Administration Tool

Remote Access Tool (RAT) is a Trojan that, when executed, enables an attacker to remotely control and maintain access to a compromised computer. This is done via one of the following:

- **A server on the victim's machine**—This server listens for incoming connections to the victim. When it receives a connection, it provides remote access for the client that connects. It runs invisibly, with no user interface.
- **A client on the attacker's machine**—This is a GUI front end that the attacker uses to connect to and manage servers on victim machines.

What happens when a server is installed on the victim's machine depends on the capabilities of the Trojan, the interests of the attacker, and whether another attacker, who might have entirely different interests, manages to gain control of the server.

Across all types of devices, including servers, desktop computers, laptops, and mobile devices, infections by remote administration are becoming as frequent as viruses. One common source is through file and printer sharing. Attackers can use file and printer sharing to gain access to a hard drive. The attacker can then place the Trojan in the startup folder. The Trojan will then run the next time a legitimate user logs on. Another common attack method is to simply email the Trojan to the user. The attacker then uses social engineering to convince the user to run the Trojan.

Authors of these programs often claim that they are not intrusion tools. Rather, they are simply remote-control tools or tools to reveal weaknesses in an operating system. Based on past activity, however, it's clear that their real purpose is to gain access to computers for unauthorized use.

left connected to outside phone lines or private branch exchanges (PBXs). Alternatively, they may not consider the security risks of leaving unattended modem connections, which often compromise existing network perimeter defenses. These connections provide another entry point for malicious code attacks.

Covering Traces of the Attack

One of the most important phases for an attacker avoiding detection is to remove any traces of an attack. Though the specific actions an attacker takes may differ from one attack to another, the basic steps are the same. Experienced attackers first attempt to remove any files they may have created and restore as many files to their preattack condition as possible. Second, the attacker will likely attempt to remove any log file entries that may provide evidence of the attack. The second step is generally much more difficult than the first step. Most systems use auditing methods that protect log files from modification. That means attackers may have to attack the log files or the auditing system to erase their tracks. Regardless of the effort, cleaning any tracks they left behind greatly increases the likelihood that an attack will go unnoticed. Make sure that you protect your detective security controls as well as other valuable assets. That way, even if you don't stop an attack, you can detect that it happened (or is currently happening).

Attack Prevention Tools and Techniques

IT security practitioners must understand how to implement effective countermeasures to defend against malicious code attacks. They must also continuously monitor, test, and improve these countermeasures.

Defense in depth is the practice of layering defenses into zones to increase the overall protection level and provide more reaction time to respond to incidents. Defense in depth combines the capabilities of people, operations, and security technologies to establish multiple layers of protection, eliminating single lines of defense and effectively raising the cost of an attack. By treating individual countermeasures as part of an integrated suite of protective measures, you can ensure that you have addressed all vulnerabilities. Managers must strengthen these defenses at critical locations. They must then monitor attacks and react to them quickly.

With respect to malicious code threats, these layers of protection extend to specific critical defensive zones:

* Application defenses
* Operating system defenses
* Network infrastructure defenses

The goals of defense in depth are as follows:

* There should be layers of security and detection, even on single systems.
* Attackers must break through or bypass each layer undetected.
* Other layers can cover a flaw in one layer.
* Overall system security becomes a set of layers within the overall network security.
* Security improves by requiring the attacker to be perfect while ignorant.

Application Defenses

Software applications provide end users with access to shared data. Some of these data are sensitive or confidential and are not available to all users. Attackers commonly launch attacks on application software to attempt to access or damage sensitive data. You should deploy appropriate controls to secure all application software running on all computers. Some common controls include the following:

* Implementing regular antivirus screening on all host systems
* Ensuring that virus definition files are up to date
* Requiring scanning of all removable media
* Installing firewall and IDS software on hosts as an additional security layer
* Deploying change detection software and integrity checking software and maintaining logs
* Implementing email usage controls and ensuring that email attachments are scanned
* Requiring all users to enable pop-up blockers in their web browsers to stop attackers from displaying pop-up widows and reducing exposure to accidental malware execution
* Establishing a clear policy regarding software installations and upgrades
* Ensuring that only trusted sources are used when obtaining, installing, and upgrading software through digital signatures and other validations

Operating System Defenses

The operating system serves as an interface between application software and hardware resources. Any attack that compromises the operating system can yield nearly unlimited

---

Staying Ahead of the Attackers

Most anti-malware software depends on an up-to-date malware signature database. These most common anti-malware solutions can only detect known exploits. But what happens to attacks based on new exploits that no one knows about? These are called **zero-day** attacks because the attacks are initially undetectable using malware signature databases. Once an attack is reported, anti-malware software vendors have to update their signature databases and release an update. Then users have to download and install the updated software or database. This time lag gives attackers a window of time to conduct attacks with little resistance.

One way to combat malware, including zero-day attacks, is to use blacklisting or whitelisting. **Blacklisting** is maintaining a list of all known dangerous sites. Any messages from a site in the blacklist is dropped. The main problem with blacklisting is keeping the blacklist up to date. Also, any site that gets into a blacklist by mistake will have its access dramatically decreased, with multiple would-be customers ignoring connections and network messages. To make matters worse, attackers are very good at changing host or site addresses frequently, requiring constant blacklist updating.

Whitelisting is maintaining a list of trusted sites. All messages and connection requests from sites not in the whitelist are ignored. Whitelisting is safer than blacklisting, but it is more restrictive. Any site that you wish to use must be added to your whitelist before connections are allowed. Both blacklisting and whitelisting can be used as an additional layer of protection to avoid malware attacks.

access to system resources that store sensitive data. Successful attacks against the operating system can also allow an attacker to own a computer and use it for multiple purposes. Controls to secure the operating system are important. These include the following:

- Deploying change-detection and integrity-checking software and maintaining logs
- Deploying or enabling change-detection and integrity-checking software on all servers
- Ensuring that all operating systems are consistent and have been patched with the latest updates from vendors
- Ensuring that only trusted sources are used when installing and upgrading OS code
- Disabling any unnecessary OS services and processes that may pose a security vulnerability

Network Infrastructure Defenses

Nearly all computers and more and more devices in today's organizations connect to a network at some point. Most attacks on computers and devices are possible because networks make it easier to access targets remotely. Malicious software often uses networks to spread. Because networks are necessary for end-user access, the networks themselves can be targets. You must deploy controls to protect your network, including the following:

- Creating chokepoints in the network
- Using proxy services and bastion hosts to protect critical services
- Using content filtering at chokepoints to screen traffic
- Ensuring that only trusted sources are used when installing and upgrading OS code
- Disabling any unnecessary network services and processes that may pose a security vulnerability
- Maintaining up-to-date IDS signature databases
- Applying security patches to network devices to ensure protection against new threats and to reduce vulnerabilities

One of the simplest prevention techniques is to disable unnecessary network services, especially certain TCP and UDP listening ports. This will defeat any attack that focuses on exploiting those services. This technique may not be efficient if those services are required for legitimate users, however.

You can employ a wide variety of countermeasures and practices to prevent malicious code attacks on network resources. These include the following:

- Employing filtering software that blocks traffic to and from network segments or specific services
- Employing active sensors (intrusion detection, antivirus detection) that react quickly enough to prevent or mitigate damage
- Employing chokepoints in the network to force traffic to flow through zones of protection
- Allowing sensors and filters to inspect traffic before permitting it to pass into the protected network
- Setting security properties within browsers to prohibit or prompt before processing scripts and active code

- Eliminating unnecessary remote connections to the network and employing effective access control measures to protect those required to remain available
- Avoiding the circumvention of existing control systems and countermeasures

Although these suggestions are valid, implementing them for all network devices is becoming more and more difficult. You learned earlier about the increasing number and types of devices that are connected to networks. These new types of devices include appliances, vehicles, environmental sensors and controls, and even wearable accessories. This growing collection of many devices connected to networks is often called the Internet of Things (IoT). Keeping all of these devices (and the network they connect to) secure is becoming more difficult due to the speed at which the number of networked devices is growing.

Safe Recovery Techniques and Practices

Regardless how effective your countermeasures are, it is likely you will eventually encounter some type of data loss due to malware. Your ability to recover from data loss depends on how well you have prepared for that situation. You cannot completely recover unless you can ensure a completely malware-free recovery process. Here are a few guidelines to help you ensure that your recovery media and procedures do not reintroduce any malware:

- Consider storing OS and data file backup images on external media to ease recovering from potential malware infection.
- Scan new and replacement media for malware before reinstalling software.
- Disable network access to systems during restore procedures or upgrades until you have re-enabled or installed protection software or services.

Implementing Effective Software Best Practices

All organizations should adopt an acceptable use policy (AUP) for network services and resources. A good AUP includes prohibitions on certain network activities and computer user habits regarding software licensing and installation as well as procedures for transmitting files and media. Adopt standardized software so that you can control patches and upgrades to ensure that you address vulnerabilities.

Consider implementing an ISO/IEC 27002-compliant security policy. ISO/IEC 27002 is the most widely recognized security standard. Compliance with ISO/IEC 27002, or indeed any detailed security standard, is, therefore, a far from trivial undertaking, even for the most security conscious of organizations. Certification can be even more daunting. You can find out more at *www.iso27001security.com/html/27002.html*.

Intrusion Detection Tools and Techniques

Intrusion detection tools are an integral component of defense in depth. Each organization should deploy a defense-in-depth approach in critical areas of the network as an early warning system. There are various implementations. Each implementation has features that provide unique capabilities to protect networks and hosts from malicious activity.

A layered defense-in-depth approach would suggest deploying both network-based and host-based intrusion detection. It might also involve deploying products that permit both signature-based and anomaly-based detection schemes.

Antivirus Scanning Software

Today most computer users use some form of virus protection to detect and prevent infection. Many mobile device users are not as careful. Several surveys indicate that fewer than half of all users have basic security and antivirus software on their mobile devices. Just as you can layer intrusion detection at the host and network levels, you should deploy antivirus protection on all devices that support it.

The key vulnerabilities to host-based antivirus software are as follows:

> **NOTE**
>
> Anomaly detection involves developing a network baseline profile of normal or acceptable activity, such as services or traffic patterns, and then measuring actual network traffic against this baseline. This technique might be useful for detecting attacks such as denial of service or continuous logon attempts, but it requires a learning or preconfiguration period.

* The continuing requirement to keep every host system updated to the most current virus definition files
* Potential compromise of the protection through unsafe user practices, such as installing unlicensed or unauthorized software or indiscriminately exchanging infected email or document files

Network-based antivirus software is an option that permits screening of files and email traffic on servers and provides remote scanning and inoculation of clients on a consistent basis.

Many organizations employ both network and host-based protection; some deploy multiple products in order to maximize detection capabilities. It is imperative that you keep virus definition files up to date. Most vendors now offer automatic updating of software as soon as they release new definitions.

Network Monitors and Analyzers

To ensure that security practices remain effective, you should regularly monitor network software and appliances as well as periodically analyzing network traffic. Every so often, run a vulnerability scanner such as Nessus, Microsoft Baseline Security Analyzer, or some combination of the two, depending on your operating systems. Keep in mind that attackers use these tools as well. You should scan the network for unnecessary open service ports on a regular basis; upgrades to software often reset systems to their default settings.

Content/Context Filtering and Logging Software

You must balance privacy and security when implementing countermeasures that filter content. When combined with a clear corporate policy on acceptable use, however, this becomes an additional layer of defense against malicious code. Plugins to screen email attachments and content as well as context-based filtering (access control lists) on network routers also permit an additional layer of security protection.

What Is a Honeynet?

A *honeynet* is a group of honeypots made to simulate a real, live network. Honeynets are beneficial because they provide more data and are more attractive to attackers. However, the setup and maintenance requirements of a honeynet are a little more advanced. A honeynet may include many servers, a router, and a firewall. A honeynet may be identical to the production network, or it might be a research lab. Either way, honeynets allow for a more real environment for an attacker to attack.

Content-based filtering includes analyzing network traffic for active code (Java, ActiveX, etc.) components and disabling script processing on web browser software. Context-based filtering involves comparing patterns of activity with baseline standards so that you can evaluate unusual changes in network behavior for possible malicious activity.

Honeypots and Honeynets

Honeypots are sacrificial hosts and services deployed at the edges of a network to act as bait for potential hacking attacks. Typically, you configure these systems to appear real. In fact, they may be part of a suite of servers placed in a separate network called a **honeynet**, isolated from the real network. The purpose of the honeypot is to provide a controlled environment for attacks. This enables you to easily detect and analyze the attack to test the strength of the network. You install host-based intrusion detection and monitoring software to log activity.

All traffic to and from the honeypot is suspicious because the honeypot contains no production applications. You should produce few logs on the honeypot unless the honeypot is under heavy attack. Logs should be easy to read and understand. When an attacker probes a honeypot, an administrator can place preventive controls on his or her real production network.

A honeypot should contain at least the following elements:

- It looks and behaves like a real host.
- At no point should it disclose its existence.
- It has a dedicated firewall that prevents all outbound traffic in case it is compromised.
- It lives in a network demilitarized zone (DMZ), untouched by normal traffic.
- It sounds silent alarms when any traffic goes to or from it.
- It begins logging all intruder activity when it first senses an intrusion.

A low-involvement honeypot provides a number of fake services, such as Hypertext Transfer Protocol (HTTP) or Simple Mail Transfer Protocol (SMTP). Low-involvement honeypots allow attackers to connect to services but do nothing else. With this type of honeypot, an attacker usually cannot gain operating system access. Therefore, the attacker poses no threat.

A high-involvement honeypot produces genuine services and vulnerabilities by providing a real operating system for the attacker. The purpose of this class of honeypot is for attackers to compromise it so you can collect realistic data. The problem with high-involvement honeypots is that you must tightly control the environment. A compromised system can become a host to begin an attack on another system.

CHAPTER SUMMARY

In this chapter, you learned about the different types of malware and how each type operates. You learned about spam, spyware, and ransomware and their effect on today's organizations. You learned about different types of network attacks and methods to protect your networks from attacks. You also learned about the dangers of keystroke loggers hoaxes, and webpage defacements. You learned about the history of malware and how threats have emerged for today's organizations. Finally, you learned about different types of attacks and how attackers use tools to carry them out.

KEY CONCEPTS AND TERMS

Active content	Honeynet	Slow virus
Adware	Honeypot	Smurf attack
Arbitrary code execution	Injection techniques	Spam
Armored Virus	Keystroke logger	Spyware
Backdoor	Logic bomb	Stealth virus
Blacklisting	Macro virus	SYN flood
Bot-herder	Malware	SYN-ACK
Botnet	Multipartite virus	System infector
Browser add-ons	Pharming	Trojan
Cookie	Phishing	Virus
Cross-platform virus	Polymorphic virus	Web applications
Data infector	Ransomware	Web defacement
Defense in depth	Remote code execution	Web graffiti
File infector	Retro virus	Whitelisting
Hactivist	Rootkit	Worm
Header manipulation	Session hijacking	Zero day

CHAPTER 11 ASSESSMENT

1. Which type of malware attaches to, or infects, other programs?

   A. Spyware
   B. Virus
   C. Worm
   D. Rootkit

2. _____ is any unwanted message.

3. Which type of malicious software is a standalone program that propagates from one computer to another?

   A. Spyware
   B. Virus
   C. Worm
   D. Snake

4. In the malware context, which of the following best defines the term *mobile code*?

  A. Website active content
  B. Malware targeted at PDAs and smartphones
  C. Software that runs on multiple operating systems
  D. Malware that uses networks to propagate

5. A(n) _____ is a network of compromised computers that attackers use to launch attacks and spread malware.

  A. Black network
  B. Botnet
  C. Attacknet
  D. Trojan store

6. What does the TCP SYN flood attack do to cause a DDoS?

  A. Causes the network daemon to crash
  B. Crashes the host computer
  C. Saturates the available network bandwidth
  D. Fills up the pending connections table

7. Which type of attack tricks a user into providing personal information by masquerading as a legitimate website?

  A. Phreaking
  B. Phishing
  C. Trolling
  D. Keystroke logging

8. The best defense from keystroke loggers is to carefully inspect the keyboard cable before using a computer because the logger must connect to the keyboard's cable.

  A. True
  B. False

9. How did viruses spread in the early days of malware?

  A. Wired network connections
  B. Punch cards
  C. Diskettes
  D. As program bugs

10. What is the most common first phase of an attack?

  A. Vulnerability identification
  B. Reconnaissance and probing
  C. Target selection
  D. Evidence containment

11. Which software tool provides extensive port-scanning capabilities?

  A. Ping
  B. Whois
  C. Rpcinfo
  D. Nmap

12. The _____ strategy ensures that an attacker must compromise multiple controls to reach any protected resource.

13. A honeypot is a sacrificial host with deliberately insecure services deployed at the edges of a network to act as bait for potential hacking attacks.

  A. True
  B. False

PART III

Information Security Standards, Education, Certifications, and Laws

Information Security Standards

I T IS NEARLY IMPOSSIBLE to purchase all hardware and software from one vendor. Today's organizations get parts for their IT infrastructure from multiple vendors—and expect these products to work together.

How can so many products from different vendors work together? They work together because of **standards**. Standards are necessary to create and maintain a competitive market for hardware and software vendors. Standards also guarantee compatibility between products from different countries. They provide guidelines to ensure that products in today's computing environments work together.

Several organizations develop and maintain standards for computers. In this chapter, you will learn about the most common standards for computer and networking products and services. You will specifically learn about those standards that relate to security.

Chapter 12 Topics

This chapter covers the following topics and concepts:

- What standards organizations apply to information security
- What ISO 17799 is
- What ISO/IEC 27002 is
- What PCI DSS is

Chapter 12 Goals

When you complete this chapter, you will be able to:

- Identify prominent information security standards organizations
- Summarize what ISO 17799 contains
- Explain how ISO/IEC 27002 pertains to information security
- Describe PCI DSS requirements

Standards Organizations

The earliest computers were custom built for specific purposes. Designers decided how to connect components and how they communicated based on the specific computer's needs. Soon, however, designers realized that by implementing communications standards, they could enable different vendors' components to work together. This standardization increased customer confidence in computers. Customers felt more comfortable buying products based on standards. Some proprietary systems, however, did not support standards.

Adhering to standards is necessary to increase market appeal and, in many cases, to comply with regulations. It is important that you know about the most influential organizations that develop and maintain the standards that govern various aspects of computing and network communications.

National Institute of Standards and Technology

The **National Institute of Standards and Technology (NIST)** is a federal agency within the U.S. Department of Commerce. Founded in 1901 as the National Bureau of Standards (NBS), NIST was the United States' first federal physical science research laboratory. NIST's mission is to "promote U.S. innovation and industrial competitiveness by advancing measurement science, standards, and technology in ways that enhance economic security and improve our quality of life." NIST provides standards for measurement and technology on which nearly all computing devices rely. In addition, NIST maintains the atomic clock that keeps the United States' official time. Although NIST is a nonregulatory agency, many organizations respect and adopt its publications.

NIST executes its primary mission through four cooperative programs:

- **NIST Laboratories**—Laboratories that conduct research to advance U.S. technology infrastructure. The nation's industry uses this infrastructure to improve the quality of products and services.

- **Baldrige National Quality Program**—A national program that empowers and encourages excellence among U.S. organizations, including manufacturers, service organizations, educational institutions, healthcare providers, and nonprofit organizations. It also strives to increase quality and recognize organizations that achieve quality goals.

- **Hollings Manufacturing Extension Partnership**—A network of centers around the nation that offer technical and business assistance to small and medium-sized manufacturers.

- **Technology Innovation Program**—Another national program that offers awards to organizations and universities to support potentially revolutionary technologies that apply to critical needs of national interest.

NIST maintains a list of standards and publications of general interest to the computer-security community. NIST established this collection of documents, called the Special Publications 800 series, in 1990 to provide a separate identity for information technology security publications. The publications in this series report on research and guideline efforts related to computer security in government, industry, and academic organizations.

NOTE

You can find more information about NIST on its webpage at *www.nist.gov*. For more information on NIST special publications, see *http://csrc.nist.gov /publications/PubsSPs.html*.

Many in the field refer to publications in the 800 series by the name *NIST SP*. For example, many people refer to the document titled "NIST Special Publication 800-66" as NIST SP 800-66. (NIST SP 800-66 contains introductory guidance for complying with HIPAA.)

The NIST Special Publications 800 series contains many standards that provide guidance for information systems security activities. **TABLE 12-1** lists just a few of the resources you can find in the NIST Special Publications 800 series.

Starting in 2015, NIST initiated a subseries of special publications, SP 1800, *NIST Cybersecurity Practice Guides*. SP 1800 extends SP 800 and targets specific issues related to implementing cybersecurity in the public and private sectors. **TABLE 12-2** lists the publications within SP 1800.

International Organization for Standardization

The **International Organization for Standardization (ISO)** formed in 1946. It is a nongovernmental international organization. Its goal is to develop and publish international standards. ISO, based in Geneva, Switzerland, is a network of 161 national standards institutes. ISO serves as a bridge between the public and private sectors. Some members are governmental

TABLE 12-1 NIST Special Publications 800 series sample documents.

NUMBER	TITLE
800-61 Rev. 2	*Computer Security Incident-Handling Guide*
800-73-4	*Interfaces for Personal Identity Verification (3 Parts)* *Part 1: PIV Card Application Namespace, Data Model & Representation* *Part 2: PIV Card Application Card Command Interface* *Part 3: PIV Client Application Programming Interface*
800-83 Rev. 1	*Guide to Malware Incident Prevention and Handling for Desktops and Laptops*
800-88 Rev. 1	*Guidelines for Media Sanitization*
800-94 Rev. 1	*DRAFT Guide to Intrusion Detection and Prevention Systems (IDPS)*
800-107 Rev. 1	*Recommendation for Applications Using Approved Hash Algorithms*
800-121 Rev. 1	*Guide to Bluetooth Security*
800-124 Rev. 1	*Guidelines for Managing and Securing Mobile Devices in the Enterprise*
800-133	*Recommendation for Cryptographic Key Generation*
800-146	*Cloud Computing Synopsis and Recommendations*
800-153	*Guidelines for Securing Wireless Local Area Networks (WLANs)*
800-162	*Guide to Attribute Based Access Control (ABAC) Definition and Considerations*
800-164	*Guidelines on Hardware-Rooted Security in Mobile Devices*
800-177	*DRAFT Trustworthy Email (Second draft)*

TABLE 12-2 NIST Special Publications 1800 series documents.	
NUMBER	**TITLE**
1800-1	DRAFT *Securing Electronic Health Records on Mobile Devices*
1800-2	DRAFT *Identity and Access Management for Electric Utilities*
1800-3	DRAFT *Attribute-Based Access Control*
1800-4	DRAFT *Mobile Device Security: Cloud and Hybrid Builds*
1800-5	DRAFT *IT Asset Management*

12

Information Security Standards

entities; others are in the private sector. ISO's goals are to develop standards that do not cater to either group exclusively but reach consensus.

Although the organization's short name, ISO, appears to be an acronym, it is not. Because ISO is an international organization, its full name is different depending on the language. ISO members agreed on the short name ISO derived from the Greek word *isos*, which means *equal*. ISO strives for consensus, even in the choice of its name. This focus on consensus is what makes ISO such a successful authority in developing and promoting standards in many areas.

ISO publishes many standards for nearly all industries. For example, the International Standard Book Number (ISBN) is an ISO standard. For those in information technology, perhaps the best-known ISO standard is the Open Systems Interconnection (OSI) Reference Model shown in **FIGURE 12-1**. This internationally accepted framework of standards governs how separate computer systems communicate using networks. The reference model contains seven distinct layers that address seven different issues related to networked communications. The reference model defines the standards that enable computers and devices from different vendors to communicate.

Each layer in the model represents a collection of related functions. Each function provides services to the layer immediately above it and receives services from the layer

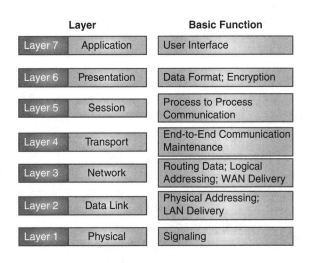

FIGURE 12-1

The OSI Reference Model.

immediately below it. For example, the Transport Layer (Layer 4) provides error-free communications across a network. It also provides the connections needed by software functions in the Session Layer (Layer 5). In addition, it calls functions in the Network Layer (Layer 3), the next layer down, to send and receive packets that make up the contents of the network communication.

Although many newer networking solutions do not strictly correspond to a structure of seven distinct layers, the OSI Reference Model is still the predominant tool used to teach networking concepts. The OSI Reference Model has long been the basis of understanding how networks provide general services in a standard environment.

Even though other models may map more directly to current software, the OSI Reference Model is still a relevant tool to teach networking fundamentals.

ISO organizes its many standards by both the International Classification for Standards (ICS) and the Technical Committee (TC) to which it assigns each standard. You can find standards spread among 40 different Level 1 ICSs, assigned to one of over 200 TCs. This gives you a feel for the breadth of standards.

> **NOTE**
>
> You can browse ISO standards and get more information about the organization at its website: *www.iso.org/iso/home .html*.

International Electrotechnical Commission

The **International Electrotechnical Commission (IEC)** is a standards organization that often works with the ISO. The IEC is the preeminent organization for developing and publishing international standards for technologies related to electrical and electronic devices and processes. People refer to the collective body of knowledge addressed by the IEC as **electrotechnology**.

The IEC formed in 1906 to address issues with the expanding technologies related to electrical devices. Today the IEC's standards address a wide variety of areas, including the following:

* Power generation
* Power transmission and distribution
* Commercial and consumer electrical appliances
* Semiconductors
* Electromagnetics
* Batteries
* Solar energy
* Telecommunications

> **NOTE**
>
> *Gauss* is a measurement of a magnetic field, *hertz* is a representation of cycles per second, and *weber* is a measure of magnetic flux.

The IEC was instrumental in the development of standards for electrical measurements, including gauss, hertz, and weber. The IEC works closely with ISO and the ITU-T (discussed later in this chapter) to synergize efforts. To ensure international acceptance and maximum usage of its standards, the IEC encourages participation from as many countries as possible. At the time of this writing, there are 60 full IEC members, also called National

Committees (NCs), and 23 associate IEC members. In 2001 the IEC expanded its membership to include more developing nations. The Affiliate Country Programme includes 84 smaller countries.

As an IT professional, you will most likely encounter IEC standards relating to physical computer and networking hardware. The focus of the IEC has expanded since its inception as the electrical and electronics industries have changed. Today much of the IEC's focus includes standards that address emerging power needs and how they affect other functional areas. The IEC is active in developing standards that support safety, performance, environmental responsibility, energy efficiency, and renewable energy sources and use.

> **NOTE**
>
> You can get more information about the IEC organization and its standards at its website: *www.iec.ch*.

World Wide Web Consortium

The creation of the World Wide Web in 1990 marked a turning point in the way users accessed resources on the Internet. In the early days of the Internet, competing vendors released their own versions of the primary language of the Web, HyperText Markup Language (HTML). These versions were incompatible with those of other vendors. These incompatibilities caused issues with web browsers and limited the Web's functionality. As interest in the Web grew, the need to standardize its primary language became clear. Sir Tim Berners-Lee, the computer scientist who wrote the original proposal for what eventually became the World Wide Web, founded the **World Wide Web Consortium (W3C)** in 1994 to address the lack of standards.

The W3C immediately became the main international standards organization for the World Wide Web. The stated purpose of the W3C is to develop protocols and guidelines that unify the World Wide Web and ensure its long-term growth. The W3C currently has 419 members, representing businesses, nonprofit organizations, universities, and various government agencies.

The W3C develops many web-related standards that govern and coordinate many aspects of web development and operation. Standards the W3C has developed or endorsed include the following:

- Cascading Style Sheets (CSS)
- Common Gateway Interface (CGI)
- HyperText Markup Language (HTML)
- Simple Object Access Protocol (SOAP)
- Web Services Description Language (WSDL)
- Extensible Markup Language (XML)

Each of these standards and specifications is necessary to ensure that web applications interact with web components from other vendors. If you work with any World Wide Web components, you will likely encounter one or more W3C standards.

Internet Engineering Task Force

The **Internet Engineering Task Force (IETF)** develops and promotes Internet standards. According to the IETF website, the organization's

> **NOTE**
>
> For more information about the W3C, its standards, and its work in providing standards and guidelines for the World Wide Web, see the W3C website at *www.w3.org*.

purpose is to "make the Internet work better." The IETF focuses on the engineering aspects of Internet communication and attempts to avoid policy and business questions. The IETF works closely with the W3C and ISO/IEC, focusing primarily on standards of the TCP/IP or Internet protocol suite. The IETF is an open organization. There are no membership requirements. All participants, including contributors and leaders, are volunteers. Their employers usually fund their work.

NOTE

For more information on the IETF and its activities, visit the IETF webpage at *www.ietf.org.*

The IETF first met in 1986 as a group of 21 researchers who wanted to formalize the main Internet communication protocols. Today the IETF is a collection of working groups (WGs), with each group addressing a specific topic. There are currently more than 100 WGs. Because WGs tend to operate independently, the IETF sets minimum standards for each group. Each WG has an appointed chair or group of cochairs and a charter that documents the group's focus and expected deliverables.

Every WG has a dedicated mailing list to which anyone can subscribe. These WG mailing lists serve as the primary communication medium for participants. Most participants get started by simply subscribing to one or more WG mailing lists of interest. WGs also hold periodic meetings, which are open to all participants. Although it is generally beneficial to attend meetings, it is possible to participate in a WG by just interacting via the mailing list.

Request for Comments

The IETF produces **requests for comments (RFCs)**. An RFC is a document that ranges from a simple memo to several standards documents. Each RFC's introduction indicates its status. The RFC model allows input from many sources and encourages collaboration and peer review. The IETF publishes guidelines for RFCs. Here are a few points about RFCs:

- **Only some RFCs specify standards**—Only RFCs that open with phrases like "This document specifies . . ." or "This memo documents . . ." should be considered standards or normative documents.

- **RFCs never change**—Any change to an RFC gets a new number and becomes a new RFC. Always look for the latest RFC, because previous documents may be out of date.

- **RFCs may originate with other organizations**—The IETF creates only some RFCs. Others may come from independent sources, the IAB, or the Internet Research Task Force (IRTF).

- **RFCs that define formal standards have four stages**—As an RFC moves from one stage to the next, it becomes more formal and more organizations accept it. The stages are as follows:
  - **Proposed Standard (PS)**—The initial official stage of a standard.
  - **Draft Standard (DS)**—The second stage of a standard, after participants have demonstrated that the standard has been deployed in working environments.
  - **Standard (STD)**—The final stage of a standard, after it has been shown to be widely adopted and deployed.
  - **Best Current Practice (BCP)**—The alternative method used to document operational specifications that are not formal standards.

Some examples of IETF standards include RFC 5878 and RFC 5910. RFC 5878, "Transport Layer Security (TLS) Authorization Extensions," contains the specification for extensions to the TLS handshake protocol. RFC 5910, "Domain Name System (DNS) Security Extensions Mapping for the Extensible Provisioning Protocol (EPP)," describes EPP extension mapping for DNSSEC domain names stored in a central repository. Neither of these RFCs makes for lightweight reading. They contain very technical details that define how the Internet operates.

Internet Architecture Board

The Internet Architecture Board (IAB) is a subcommittee of the IETF. It also serves as an advisory body to the Internet Society (ISOC). The IAB is composed of independent researchers and professionals who have a technical interest in the well-being of the Internet.

> **NOTE**
>
> You can find more information about RFCs and access an RFC search engine from IETF's RFC webpage at *www.ietf.org/rfc.html*.

The IAB serves as an oversight committee for many IETF activities. The IAB provides oversight for the following:

- Architecture for Internet protocols and procedures
- Processes used to create standards
- Editorial and publication procedures for RFCs
- Confirmation of IETF chair and technical area directors

The IAB provides much of the high-level management and validation of the processes of conducting IETF business. The IAB is an important committee that has substantial influence over many standards that affect the Internet.

Institute of Electrical and Electronics Engineers

> **NOTE**
>
> According to the ISOC's website, *www.internetsociety.org*, the ISOC is "an independent international nonprofit organisation founded in 1992 to provide leadership in Internet related standards, education, and policy around the world."

According to its website (www.ieee.org/index.html), the Institute of Electrical and Electronics Engineers (IEEE) is "the world's largest professional association for the advancement of technology." The IEEE is an international nonprofit organization that focuses on developing and distributing standards that relate to electricity and electronics. With more than 420,000 members in approximately 160 countries, it has the largest number of members of any technical professional organization in the world. The IEEE formed in 1963 through the merger of two older organizations: the Institute of Radio Engineers, formed in 1912, and the American Institute of Electrical Engineers, formed in 1884.

The IEEE supports 39 societies that focus activities on specific technical areas. These technical areas include magnetics, photonics, and computers. Each society develops publications, holds conferences, and promotes activities and events to further knowledge and interest in a specific area. IEEE also provides many training and educational opportunities covering a large number of engineering topics.

IEEE is also one of the largest standards-producing organizations. The IEEE Standards Association (IEEE-SA) manages these standards. IEEE standards cover many industries, including information technology. IEEE currently publishes or sponsors more than 1,300

TABLE 12-3 Common IEEE 802 standard working groups.

WORKING GROUP	NAME
802.1	Higher Layer LAN Protocols
802.3	Ethernet
802.11	Wireless LAN (802.11a, 802.11b, 802.11g, 802.11n, 802.11ad, etc.)
802.15	Wireless Personal Area Network (WPAN)
802.16	Broadband Wireless Access (WiMAX)
802.18	Radio Regulatory TAG
802.19	Wireless Coexistence
802.20	Mobile Broadband Wireless Access

> **NOTE**
>
> The 802 working group takes its name from the date it first convened, in February (month 2) of 1980.

standards and projects. The best-known standard that relates to information security is the IEEE 802 LAN/MAN standard family. This group of standards defines how various types of local area network (LAN) and metropolitan area network (MAN) protocols work. **TABLE 12-3** lists some of the more recognizable working groups in the IEEE 802 LAN/MAN standard.

IEEE is open to members from the technical community who meet certain professional requirements. Full members can vote in IEEE elections. Students can obtain student memberships to IEEE; they can enjoy all the benefits of full membership except the right to vote. For interested parties who are not students and do not meet the technical requirement, IEEE offers associate memberships with limited privileges.

International Telecommunication Union Telecommunication Sector

The **International Telecommunication Union (ITU)** is a United Nations agency. It is responsible for managing and promoting information and technology issues. The ITU is a global point of focus for both governmental and commercial development of networks and related services. The ITU was formed in 1865 as the International Telegraph Union to develop international standards for the emerging telegraph communications industry. The ITU became a UN agency in 1947. It was renamed the International Telegraph and Telephone Consultative Committee (CCITT) in 1956 and eventually adopted its current name in 1993. ITU headquarters are in Geneva, Switzerland. Memberships include 193 member states and more than 700 sector members and associates.

The oldest and most recognizable activity of the ITU is its work developing standards. The **ITU Telecommunication Sector (ITU-T)** performs all ITU standards work. The ITU-T is responsible for ensuring the efficient and effective production of standards covering all fields of telecommunications for all nations. ITU-T also defines tariff and accounting principles for international telecommunication services. Timeliness has become an important focus of ITU-T standards. In 2001, the organization overhauled its antiquated standards-development procedures to reduce by 95 percent the time required to create standards.

ITU-T calls the international standards it produces **recommendations**. They become mandatory only when adopted as part of a member state's national law. Because the ITU-T is a UN agency, its standards carry significant international weight. Even though ITU-T calls its standards recommendations, they tend to carry substantial authority.

ITU-T divides its recommendations into 26 separate series, each bearing a unique letter of the alphabet. For example, switching and signaling recommendations are in the Q series. Data networks, open systems communications, and security recommendations are in the X series. ITU-T has developed and published many communication recommendations that address technical details of all types of communication. Several of the X series recommendations relate directly to information security. **TABLE 12-4** lists some of the ranges of ITU-T recommendations that relate to information security.

> **NOTE**
> You can find more information about ITU and ITU-T on the ITU webpage at *www.itu.int*.

American National Standards Institute

One of the leading standards agencies in the United States is the **American National Standards Institute (ANSI)**. ANSI's goal is to strengthen the U.S. marketplace within the global economy. At the same time, it strives to ensure the safety and health of consumers and the protection of the environment. It seeks to accomplish this goal by promoting voluntary consensus standards and conformity assessment systems.

TABLE 12-4 ITU-T recommendations that relate to information security.

ITU-T RECOMMENDATION	DESCRIPTION
X.800 – X.849: Security	Recommendations in this series address security issues as they relate to different networking layers
X.1000 – X.1099: Information and network security	General network security
X.1100 – X.1199: Secure applications and services	Ensuring that applications and services are developed and deployed in a secure manner
X.1200 – X.1299: Cyberspace security	Overall cybersecurity, identity management, and countering spam
X.1300 – X.1399: Secure applications and services	Different from X.1100 – X.1199, this series focuses on emergency communications and sensor network security
X.1500 – X.1599: Cybersecurity information exchange	Focused on exchanging information between actors in a secure manner
X.1600 – X.1699: Cloud computing security	Security topics specifically related to cloud environments

ANSI oversees the creation, publication, and management of many standards and guidelines that directly affect businesses in nearly every sector. ANSI standards cover such business sectors as acoustical devices, construction equipment, dairy and livestock production, and energy distribution.

ANSI was formed in 1918 through the merger of five engineering societies and three government agencies. These groups merged to form the American Engineering Standards Committee (AESC). In 1928, the AESC became the American Standards Association (ASA). In 1966, the ASA reorganized and became the United States of America Standards Institute (USASI). Finally, in 1969, the USASI became ANSI. Today, ANSI is composed of government agencies, organizations, educational institutions, and individuals. ANSI represents more than 125,000 companies and 3.5 million professionals.

> **NOTE**
>
> You can find more information about ANSI on the organization's webpage at *www.ansi.org.*

ANSI produces standards that affect nearly all aspects of IT. Unlike other organizations that specifically focus on engineering or technical aspects of computing and communication, ANSI primarily addresses standards that support software development and computer system operation. **TABLE 12-5** lists some ANSI standards you will encounter in the information security and software development realms.

European Telecommunications Standards Institute Cyber Security Technical Committee

ETSI, the European Telecommunications Standards Institute, develops standards for information and communications technologies (ICT) that are commonly adopted by member countries in the European Union (EU). ETSI standards cover both wired and various wireless communication technologies. They have more than 800 member organizations from 66 different countries. ETSI is officially recognized by the EU as a European Standards Organization. In 2014, ETSI organized a Cyber Security Technical Committee, called TC CYBER. TC CYBER centralizes all cybersecurity standards within ETSI committees. The TC CYBER standards are intended to result in international standards that will initially be adopted by member EU states. These standards initially focus on security issues related to the Internet and the business communications it transports. The entire organization proposes standards

TABLE 12-5 Important ANSI standards.

STANDARD	DESCRIPTION
ANSI code	The ANSI code is a standard that defines a set of values used to represent characters in computers. A standard is necessary to enable multiple computers to share data and communicate with each other. The ANSI code set is an extension of the older ASCII seven-bit code set.
American Standard Fortran	American Standard Fortran was the first standard programming language, also called Fortran 66. ANSI published this standard language in March of 1966.
ANSI C	ANSI published ANSI C as a standard version of the programming language C in 1989.

to enforce privacy and security for organizations and citizens across Europe. Although any results published by TC CYBER will be Europe-centric, they will likely have far-reaching effects and impact far beyond European organizations.

ISO 17799 (Withdrawn)

ISO 17799 is a former international security standard that has been withdrawn. It wasn't withdrawn because anything was wrong. In fact, it was so well received and successful that it was completely updated and turned into a new standard with a new name. You will learn about the new standard in the next section. Because ISO 17799's original form was such an important information security standard, it is important to understand it. This standard documents a comprehensive set of controls that represent best practices in information systems. The standard actually consists of two separate parts:

* The ISO 17799 code of practice
* The BS 17799-2 specification for an information security management system

The main purpose of the standard is to identify security controls needed for information systems in business environments. The standard originally appeared as the "DTI Code of Practice" in Britain and was later renamed BS 7799. It did not gain wide international popularity due to its inflexibility and overly simplistic approach to control. Developers released version 2 in 1999 to address the standard's weaknesses. Developers submitted the standard to ISO for accreditation and publishing. ISO published the standard as ISO 17799 in 2000.

Interest in the standard increased quickly. Several companies began providing tools and services to help implement ISO 17799. It quickly became the predominant information security standard. ISO 17799 gave many organizations a framework on which to build their security policy. Full compliance with the standard quickly became a goal. It also became a differentiator among competitors. The standard enabled potential customers to evaluate organizations on their efforts toward securing data.

The ISO divides the standard into 10 major sections:

* **Security Policy**—A statement of management direction.
* **Security Organization**—Governance of information security, or how information security should be enforced.
* **Asset Classification and Control**—Procedures to classify and manage information assets.
* **Personnel Security**—Guidance for security controls that protect and limit personnel.
* **Physical and Environmental Security**—Protection of computer facilities.
* **Communications and Operations Management**—Managing technical security controls in systems and networks.
* **Access Control**—Controls that limit access rights to network resources, applications, functions, and data.
* **System Development and Maintenance**—Guidelines for designing and incorporating security into applications.

- **Business Continuity Management**—Protecting, maintaining, and recovering business-critical processes and systems.
- **Compliance**—Ensuring conformance with information security policies, standards, laws, and regulations.

A newer standard, ISO/IES 27002, has superseded ISO 17799. It provides a generic information security standard accessible by all organizations, regardless of size, industry, or location. Although ISO/IES 27002 replaced the withdrawn ISO 17799, you will still see references to ISO 17799 as a leading information security standard.

ISO/IEC 27002

ISO/IEC 27002 appeared in 2005 as an update to the ISO 17799 standard. Originally named ISO 17799:2005, ISO changed its name to ISO/IEC 27002:2005 in 2007. This was to conform to the naming convention used by other 27000-series ISO/IEC standards. The ISO/IEC 27000 series is a growing family of general information security standards. ISO/IEC 27002 is "Information Technology Security Techniques Code of Practice for Information Security Management."

Like its predecessor, ISO/IEC 27002 provides organizations with best-practice recommendations on information security management. The standard directs its recommendations to management and security personnel responsible for information security management systems. Information security is within the standard in the context of the CIA triad:

- **Confidentiality**—Ensuring only authorized users, and no one else, can access data.
- **Integrity**—Ensuring only authorized users, and no one else, can modify data.
- **Availability**—Ensuring that authorized users have access to information when it is requested.

ISO/IEC 27002 expands on its predecessor by adding two new sections and reorganizing several others. The ISO divides the new standard into 12 major sections:

- **Risk Assessment**—Formal methods of identifying and classifying risks.
- **Security Policy**—A statement of management direction.
- **Organization of Information Security**—Governance of information security or how information security should be enforced.
- **Asset Management**—Procedures to acquire, classify, and manage information assets.
- **Human Resources Security**—Security guidelines for personnel joining, leaving, or moving within an organization.
- **Physical and Environmental Security**—Protection of computer facilities.
- **Communications and Operations Management**—Managing technical security controls in systems and networks.
- **Access Control**—Controls that limit access rights to network resources, applications, functions, and data.

- **Information Systems Acquisition Development and Maintenance**—Guidelines for designing and incorporating security into applications.
- **Information Security Incident Management**—Anticipating and responding appropriately to information security breaches.
- **Business Continuity Management**—Protecting, maintaining, and recovering business-critical processes and systems.
- **Compliance**—Ensuring conformance with information security policies, standards, laws, and regulations.

The standard specifies and outlines the recommended security controls within each section. Most people regard the information security controls as best practices. These best practices provide methods of achieving each objective. ISO/IEC 27002 also provides guidance for implementing each of the recommended controls.

> **NOTE**
>
> You can find more information about ISO/IEC 27002 at the official ISO website, *www.iso.org/iso/catalogue_detail?csnumber=50297*.

Payment Card Industry Data Security Standard

The Payment Card Industry Data Security Standard (PCI DSS) is an international standard for handling transactions involving payment cards. The Payment Card Industry Security Standards Council (PCI SSC) developed, publishes, and maintains the standard. PCI DSS is different from other standards you have seen so far. Some of the largest payment card vendors in the world formed PCI DSS. These vendors include the following:

- Visa
- MasterCard
- Discover
- American Express
- Japan Credit Bureau

Each of these organizations had its own standard for protecting payment card information. These organizations combined their efforts and published the first version of the PCI DSS in December 2004. The latest version, PCI DSS version 3.2, was released in April 2016. They created PCI DSS to protect payment card users from fraud and to preempt legislative requirements on the industry. It requires layers of controls to protect all payment card-related information as it is processed, transmitted, and stored. The standard applies to all organizations that participate in any of the processes surrounding payment card processing.

Compliance with PCI DSS standards is a prerequisite for doing business with any of the member organizations. If any organization violates PCI DSS standards, it could lose its ability to process payment cards. In most cases, noncompliance results in fines and/or audits that are more frequent. Habitual offenders may find their processing privileges revoked. For most organizations that depend on payment cards as a means of receiving payment, compliance is a business requirement.

The rules with which an organization must comply depend on the number of payment card transactions the organization processes. Organizations assess compliance at least

TABLE 12-6 PCI DSS control objectives and requirements.

CONTROL OBJECTIVE	REQUIREMENT
Build and maintain a secure network and systems.	Install and maintain a firewall configuration to protect cardholder data. Do not use vendor-supplied defaults for system passwords and other security parameters.
Protect cardholder data.	Protect stored cardholder data. Encrypt transmission of cardholder data across open, public networks.
Maintain a vulnerability management program.	Use and regularly update antivirus software on all systems commonly affected by malware. Develop and maintain secure systems and applications.
Implement strong access control measures.	Restrict access to cardholder data by business need to know. Assign a unique ID to each person with computer access. Restrict physical access to cardholder data.
Regularly monitor and test networks.	Track and monitor all access to network resources and cardholder data. Regularly test security systems and processes.
Maintain an information security policy.	Maintain a policy that addresses information security.

NOTE

You can find more information about PCI DSS at the official PCI Security Standards Council website, *www.pcisecuritystandards.org*.

annually. Organizations that handle large volumes of transactions must have their compliance assessed by an independent qualified security assessor (QSA). Organizations that handle smaller volumes of transactions can choose to self-certify using a PCI DSS self-assessment questionnaire (SAQ).

PCI DSS version 3.2 defines 12 requirements for compliance, organized into six groups, called **control objectives**. TABLE 12-6 lists the 12 PCI DSS control objectives and requirements.

CHAPTER SUMMARY

A number of organizations define standards that document technical specifications or other specific criteria for use as rules, guidelines, or definitions of characteristics. Organizations and industries also use standards to ensure that products and services are consistent. The ability of different products from different organizations to work well together depends on standards. As the IT industry advances, so does the need for new and updated standards. In this chapter, you learned about some of the standards organizations and a few standards that directly affect information security. Research these standards organizations and familiarize yourself with their work. It is likely you will see them again.

KEY CONCEPTS AND TERMS

American National Standards Institute (ANSI)

Control objectives

Electrotechnology

International Electrotechnical Commission (IEC)

International Organization for Standardization (ISO)

International Telecommunication Union (ITU)

Internet Engineering Task Force (IETF)

ISO 17799

ISO/IEC 27002

ITU Telecommunication Sector (ITU-T)

National Institute of Standards and Technology (NIST)

Recommendations

Request for comments (RFC)

Standards

World Wide Web Consortium (W3C)

CHAPTER 12 ASSESSMENT

1. The earliest digital computers were the result of experimental standards.

A. True
B. False

2. Which standards organization's name derives from the Greek word for *equal*?

A. IEC
B. ISO
C. PCI
D. W3C

3. Which standards organization formed in 1906 and handles standards for batteries?

A. IEC
B. ISO
C. PCI
D. W3C

4. Which standards organization publishes standards such as CGI, HTML, and XML?

A. IEC
B. ISO
C. PCI
D. W3C

5. The IETF primarily focuses on standards of the _____ Internet protocol suite.

6. The IETF produces documents called _____.

7. Which of the following is the most well-known ISO standard?

A. OSI Reference Model
B. TCP/IP protocol
C. TCP/IP Reference Model
D. OSI protocol

8. The _____ is the world's largest professional association for the advancement of technology.

9. Which standards organization publishes the 802.11g standard?

A. ISO
B. IEC
C. ITU-T
D. IEEE

10. Which standards organization publishes American Standard Fortran?

A. IEEE
B. ANSI
C. ITU-T
D. NIST

Information Systems Security Education and Training

YOU WANT TO BE AN INFORMATION SYSTEMS security or cybersecurity professional. Your primary job will be to ensure the availability, confidentiality, and integrity of your organization's IT infrastructure. You will also ensure the security and privacy of your organization's sensitive data. This requires a high level of responsibility, authority, and trust. You must know information technology. You must also know the organization's IT and IT security policies, standards, and procedures. Technology changes every day. So do risks, threats, and vulnerabilities. Education is critical to staying current with these rapid changes. Demand for these skills continues to increase. A steady supply of job candidates is critical. Candidates must possess the proper educational background. More important, they must have the necessary hands-on skill sets to implement security countermeasures and controls. In this chapter, you will learn about information systems security or cybersecurity education and training opportunities. In addition, you will learn where you can obtain the hands-on skill sets needed to perform your job duties as an information systems security professional.

Chapter 13 Topics

This chapter covers the following topics and concepts in information systems security education:

- How to learn information systems security through self-study education programs
- What continuing education programs are available
- What postsecondary degree programs are available
- What information systems security training programs are available
- What security awareness training is and what it should include

Chapter 13 Goals

When you complete this chapter, you will be able to:

- Identify self-study education programs in information systems security
- Locate continuing education programs in information systems security
- Compare postsecondary higher education degree programs in information systems security
- Identify which organizations offer information systems security education programs
- Identify an organization's security awareness programs

Self-Study Programs

The easiest and quickest way to learn about information systems security is to teach yourself. Having a high comfort level with computers, software, and browsing the Internet is a typical prerequisite. Many information systems security and cybersecurity resources exist, both online and in book form, but you must be proficient in finding them. Your local bookstore likely carries many books and magazines that cover information systems security or cybersecurity topics. In fact, you may find it difficult to narrow your choices to just a few.

Before you embark on continuing your education in information systems security or cybersecurity, you need to assess whether self-study is the best approach for you. Self-study can be a very cost-effective and convenient option, but it might not be the best solution in all cases.

First, consider some of the advantages of self-study or self-instruction:

- **Self-motivation**—If you are a self-motivated individual and can work long hours in front of your own computer, then information systems security and cybersecurity may be for you. After all, hackers and perpetrators spend countless hours on their computers planning attacks and conducting reconnaissance and port scanning on selected targets. Equal time should be spent learning to avoid their attacks.

- **Low cost**—Self-study is generally the least expensive training option, given that open source tools and applications are available in the public domain for hands-on labs and skills-set readiness. You need to buy only those materials required to meet your goals. You can choose the materials that best fit your budget. Some self-study materials are available for no cost. Purchasing network equipment, computers, RAM, storage media, and high-speed Internet connectivity may also be required if you build your own information systems security or cybersecurity test lab. Virtualizing your lab systems reduces your costs.

- **Flexible materials**—With self-study, you select the resource materials you like best. Different people learn in different ways. You might prefer a video course, whereas another person might prefer a printed book. Either way, self-study gives you the option to find the resources that best suit your learning style.

- **Flexible schedule**—You can study when it works best for your schedule. Some people study better in the morning; others study better in the evening. The self-study option lets you decide which study schedule works best for you.

- **Personal pace**—When you're doing it yourself, you get to set the pace. The self-study option lets you decide how fast you want to cover the training material. You may need to explore some topics slowly and others more quickly. An additional advantage is that you can go back and cover a topic again if you need to.

- **Supplemental materials**—No one is an expert in every area, and no area is exclusively taught by one expert. Most students in any subject benefit from additional materials at one time or another. When you select your own resources, you can decide when to use supplemental materials. Your initial search for primary materials will likely give you a feel for good additional materials if and when you need them.

There are also some disadvantages to choosing the self-study option. Carefully consider these concerns when deciding if self-study is right for you:

- **Procrastination**—One of the most common pitfalls of self-study is procrastination. There are so many demands on your time, it is often difficult to justify setting aside time to study. Furthermore, you may find that self-study takes more time than you planned. You will need discipline and commitment to stay on schedule. Seriously consider how well you will be able to stick to a study schedule when you're studying on your own time.

- **Resource selection**—Although choosing your own resources can be an advantage, it can also be a disadvantage. It is very difficult to assess the value of a resource without really studying it first. Some resources look great at first glance but don't have the depth or value you need. The large number of options available to you can make the process of identifying the best products difficult.

- **Lack of interaction**—Self-study is a one-way instruction technique. You don't get any feedback from other students or an instructor. If you like learning with others, self-study may not be the best option for you. Although most people do benefit from interaction, the inconvenience and cost of other options may limit you to self-study.

- **Quality**—Most self-study resources specifically target the low-cost student market. In other words, they are low-cost products to meet limited budgets. That doesn't mean these products aren't good; it just means they don't have the same appearance as the high-cost products. In some cases, quality directly relates to cost. However, there are very good inexpensive resources, and there are expensive resources that have limited value. Carefully look over the materials you purchase.

- **Validated outcome**—If you are using self-study just to learn about security topics, validation may not be a concern for you. However, it is good to get validation that you successfully completed an area of study. Most other training methods include some sort of assessment and validation process. Self-study does not have such a process. Your validation is your ability to demonstrate what you have learned. This could be passing a certification exam or just having more knowledge and skills than before you started.

Another important aspect of making a decision to pursue self-study is to decide on the purpose for your study. The specific reasons that you want to study a topic can help you decide the best approach. In most cases, you'll pursue some form of study for at least one reason, including the following:

- **General knowledge**—General security knowledge is necessary to understand the big picture. Security involves all domains of the IT infrastructure and several areas outside the IT infrastructure. As a result, a security professional should have a good understanding of general security topics. Most professionals focus on one or more specific areas of security. These professionals would benefit from a better overall understanding of security works. In addition, many security managers need a more general knowledge set rather than a command of the specific security details.

- **Specific knowledge and skills**—Most security tasks require general knowledge and specific area knowledge. In addition, you may need specific skills to carry out a task. For example, setting up firewall rules can be very complex. You'll need to know the details of firewall configuration and how to maintain rules on your organization's devices. General knowledge is good for a high-level view, but hands-on practitioners need specific knowledge as well. Make sure any self-study materials you use cover the topics you need in sufficient detail.

- **Certification preparation**—One common use for self-study is in preparing for a certification exam. You may meet the requirements to take a certification exam but want to review the material and fill in any knowledge gaps. Self-study may be a good fit for this need.

- **Skill-set readiness hands-on labs**—One of the most important criteria for employment or career advancement is your ability to demonstrate hands-on skill-set readiness as an information systems security professional. Many self-study courses or training programs do not have a capability for you to perform hands-on labs that mimic real-world IT infrastructures. You'll need to know how to apply your knowledge of information systems security into real-world IT infrastructures. By incorporating experiential learning with hands-on labs into the self-study learning process, you will be able to bridge the gap between having book knowledge and sharpening your hands-on skills.

There are many sources for self-study in IT security or information assurance training. This isn't a complete list, but it should help you get started. Remember, everyone's approach to self-study training is different. Not all self-study training programs offer the same materials. To find the best training materials for self-study learning, follow these guidelines:

- **Reputable sources**—Don't buy resources from just any website. Make sure the company has a good reputation. Leading product companies such as IBM and Cisco already have a good product reputation. Smaller companies may not be so well known. Both the large and smaller companies might offer product training. Do some research to find comments and reviews on the company before you buy any products. You should buy materials only from a reputable business that has multiple positive customer reviews.

- **Material reviews**—Even reputable companies can sell training products that don't meet your needs. In addition to checking the reviews for each vendor, look for product reviews, too. You should be able to find positive reviews for the book or course you want to buy. A simple Internet search on the product name should provide reviews or comments on its quality.

- **Multiple products**—Retailers that provide multiple products tend to have better-quality training products. It takes a substantial investment to develop and market a range of related products. The product creators want to ensure that the quality is high, to generate additional sales. Be careful, though. Don't blindly assume that quantity is the same as quality. Some retailers just carry anything they can sell. When in doubt, search for product and vendor reviews.

- **Hands-on skill-set labs**—Many self-study training programs do not offer a hands-on lab or virtual lab capability; thus, these programs are void of a critical learning element. If you are interested in learning and passing a professional certification exam, you may not need hands-on skill sets. If you are trying to learn a new skill set and need hands-on experience performing information systems security or information assurance tasks, make sure your training program incorporates hands-on lab activities. You will need to build your own information systems security or cybersecurity test lab. By having your own cybersecurity

NOTE

Every tool and application that hackers use is a tool and application that an information systems security or cybersecurity professional must learn to use. As an ethical hacker, you must learn what tools and applications hackers use so that you know how to combat the IP packets and IP traffic that is generated by these tools and applications. Open source or free tools and applications that must be part of any hands-on lab typically include Wireshark® (*www.wireshark.org*), Nmap® (*https://nmap.org*), Meta Sploit™ (*www.metasploit.com*), and Kali Linux® penetration testing tools (*https://tools.kali.org*).

lab you will be able to obtain the hands-on skills-set needed to practice combating hackers and perpetrators.

TABLE 13-1 contains only a limited list of self-study resources. An Internet search will produce many additional resources. Try searching for "information security training" or "cybersecurity training." You'll find many options from various training organizations as well as public domain content for self-study materials.

Whether self-study is a good option for you depends on your situation. Consider your budget, schedule, learning style, and experience before making a decision. Self-study isn't the only way to go. In the following sections, you'll learn about other options to pursue security training and education.

Instructor-Led Programs

An alternative to self-study learning is instructor-led training in a classroom. Many colleges and universities promote and market **continuing education** programs as part of local community workforce development. The continuing education group can be part of the school or a closely related educational unit. In some cases, it is actually one of the schools within the university. The purpose of continuing education is to provide formal training courses that lead to a certificate or professional certification and not a degree. In many cases, the students already have degrees and are looking to update their skills and knowledge. The courses can range from very general to highly specific and technical. These courses meet various needs of community members, including the following:

- Preparatory classes for degree programs
- Enrichment classes for adults
- Summertime camp-style classes for children and youth
- Professional training
- Certification preparation

The last category listed covers both security and many other instructional areas. Continuing education courses often try to meet needs of adult students. Because most adult students have jobs, you'll find that many continuing education classes meet in the evenings or on weekends.

Certificate Programs

Continuing education programs are typically offered as part of an evening curriculum that leads to a **certificate of completion**. A certificate of completion is a document that is given to a student upon completion of the program and signed by the instructor. A certificate of completion attests that you have completed the course and made a sufficient score on an

TABLE 13-1 IT security self-study resources.

RESOURCE	COMMENTS
Vendor-specific training	Vendor-specific self-study training programs vary depending on the vendor or manufacturer, such as Cisco Systems or Microsoft. Cisco Systems online e-learning self-study programs are offered through the Cisco Learning Network at *https://learningnetwork.cisco.com/index.jspa*. Microsoft online e-learning self-study programs are available anytime, from any location with Internet access. You can find more information at *https://www.microsoft.com/en-in/learning/default.aspx*. These comprehensive courses and clinics offer interactive features such as hands-on virtual labs and the ability to track your progress.
YouTube training	YouTube has actual training videos uploaded by hackers, perpetrators, security educators, and professionals. If you want to combat what the hacking community shares, search the hundreds of "How to hack. . ." videos uploaded by hackers all over the world, then build an information systems security and cybersecurity countermeasure for each hacking video that you review. This knowledge of "How to hack" and "How to secure" can be obtained by watching training videos with audio narration on YouTube.
SANS Institute self-study	SANS Institute (*www.sans.org/selfstudy/*) offers self-study training programs for students who enjoy working independently. Courses include a textbook and CD-ROM with MP3 audio and video files and/or other courseware supplements. Some courses include the use of virtual machines, such as VMWare®, needed to perform hands-on virtual labs so that students can practice their hands-on skills-set readiness.
Jones & Bartlett e-learning	Jones & Bartlett Learning, the publisher of this text, offers the online e-learning Information Systems Security & Assurance (ISSA) curriculum at *www.issaseries.com*. Each of the 12 ISSA courses can be purchased as a self-study, online, e-learning course. ISSA self-study and live virtual instructor training solutions are also available through Security Evolutions, Inc., at *www.security-evolutions.com*.
Cybrary	Cybrary, which can be found at *www.cybrary.it*, offers self-study, video recorded content with audio narration from a live instructor. There is content for basic, intermediate, and advanced information systems security, cybersecurity, and professional certification readiness. There is no dialogue or interaction with a live virtual instructor. The content provides a good definition and starting point for beginners in the field.
(ISC)²® self-paced e-learning	(ISC)² self-paced e-learning is based on the CBK® Review Seminars for either the CISSP® or SSCP® credential. These e-learning solutions are most effective when coupled with an instructor-led event, but they can be taken as self-study. For example, the (ISC)² self-paced e-learning program is available for self-study by a 30-, 60-, or 90-day subscription. These dynamic e-learning courses include narrated lectures and exercises and are delivered by Certification Partners, Inc. All e-learning offerings qualify for continuing professional education credits (CPEs).
Bookstore	Visit your local bookstore or go online—for example, to *www.amazon.com* or *www.barnesandnoble.com*—and browse through "information systems security" and "cybersecurity" titles. Check each title's publication date to ensure that it contains the latest information and updates.
Library	Your local library may have information systems security or cybersecurity titles or publications but often have out-of-date materials. If you look for resources at your library, make sure you have the latest editions and most recent publications of the material.

assessment. Remember, the difference between a certificate of completion and a professional certification is that the certificate of completion merely states that you have taken the course and completed the tasks and assignments. A professional certification requires a job-task analysis and requires a passing grade on a certification exam that must be defensible in court.

Certificate programs are commonly specific to the educational institution. Similar programs at different schools may have different requirements. Each institution also dictates its own methods of delivery. It is very common to see blended programs that include both traditional classes and online offerings. If a certificate program interests you, start by contacting your local colleges and universities. Many continuing education providers work closely with practitioners in each subject area to ensure that their classes meet the needs of local employers and other organizations. You may find that the classes you take at local institutions provide specific content encouraged by local organizations. That can help you gain the specific knowledge and skills local companies need and want.

Because many continuing education providers have online programs, you don't have to limit your search to local providers. An Internet search will show you many continuing education offerings for nearly any interest area. Try searching for "continuing education in information security." You'll find many institutions that provide certificate programs.

Continuing Education Programs

Continuing education programs also include courses that don't lead to a certificate. Many courses exist just to keep practitioners current and informed. These courses are often called **continuing professional education (CPE)** or **continuing professional development (CPD)** courses. These courses generally target practitioners who are already working in their chosen fields.

Most certifications require certification holders to pursue additional education each year to keep their certifications current. Certifications that require additional education generally specify the number of credits each certificate requires. If a certificate holder fails to earn the minimum number of credits, he or she may lose the certification.

To make easier the process of validating continuing education, most institutions offer credit for courses in a standard unit. Institutions assign each course a CPE value. Each CPE credit represents 50 minutes of classroom instruction. Students can select courses based on the number of CPE credits they can earn. Students who hold certifications can prove they completed a course and then claim the CPEs toward their certification maintenance requirements.

A continuing education program is a great way to pursue new knowledge and keep certifications current. Contact your local colleges and universities to find out what courses they offer. As you look for continuing education course offerings, don't forget to search online. You may find just what you're looking for in an online course. If you're just looking for online courses, you can look beyond your local colleges and universities.

> **NOTE**
>
> Make sure you note the CPE requirements for each certification you hold and keep track of the CPEs you earn. You'll need CPEs each year to maintain most certifications.

> **⚠ WARNING**
>
> Before you select a program of study, investigate whether the program is **accredited**. Most prospective employers value accredited programs more than unaccredited ones. Accreditation is granted by the State Department of Education in the state that the school operates.

Postsecondary Degree Programs

Colleges and universities also provide degree programs related to information systems security, cybersecurity, or information assurance. The number of colleges and universities offering two-year associate's, four-year bachelor's, and two-year master's degree programs is climbing. This includes both not-for-profit schools and for-profit schools offering accredited degree programs. Today you can find classroom-delivered, online-delivered, and blended-delivered curriculums and courseware for degrees ranging from associate level up to PhD. When considering a degree in information systems security, cybersecurity, or information assurance, consider what career opportunities and employment you seek first.

Nearly any college or university can offer an information systems security or cybersecurity-related degree program once it obtains accreditation for the curriculum from that state's board of education. In February 2003, the National Strategy to Secure Cyberspace called for a program to recognize educational and research institutions that provide quality security education and conduct pertinent research. In response to that strategy, the National Security Agency (NSA) and the U.S. Department of Homeland Security (DHS) jointly sponsor two important programs:

- **The National Centers of Academic Excellence in Information Assurance Education (CAE/IAE) program** (*https://www.nsa.gov/resources/educators/centers-academic-excellence/cyber-defense/*)—The CAE/IAE program identifies educational institutions that meet the program's information assurance educational guidelines.

- **The National Centers of Academic Excellence in Research (CAE/R) program**—The CAE/R program, available at the same URL, identifies institutions that meet the research guidelines.

According to the NSA website, "[T]he goal of these programs was to reduce vulnerability in our national information infrastructure by promoting higher education and research in information assurance (IA) and producing a growing number of professionals with IA expertise in various disciplines."

The NSA established the National Centers of Academic Excellence (CAE) for the Cyber Operations Program. Many colleges and universities have certified their information assurance degree programs to various NSA standards. The CAE program is in support of the National Initiative for Cybersecurity Education (NICE): Building a Digital Nation.

Colleges and universities that have obtained the coveted Center of Excellence designation demonstrate their commitment to educating the nation's cybersecurity workforce. Together, these two programs designate the nation's top information assurance degree programs and graduate-level research. Obtaining NSA's coveted CAE/IAE or CAE/R designation means the curriculum and research institutions meet or exceed the standards defined by the NSA. The approval process requires a rigorous mapping of curriculum learning objectives to NSA's various information systems security and information assurance standards for cybersecurity job roles. The list of Centers of Excellence for Academia or Research provides a complete listing of colleges and universities offering degree programs

> **▌ NOTE**
>
> A list of accredited degree programs that have properly mapped their cybersecurity curriculums to the NSA CAE content mapping requirements can be found here: *https://www.iad.gov/nietp/reports/current_cae_designated_institutions.cfm*

mapped to NSA standards. Students interested in information systems security or information assurance degree programs should investigate.

Associate's Degree

One type of degree that many institutions offer is the associate's degree. This degree is the most accessible because it generally represents a two-year program. Some institutions offer accelerated programs that allow students to complete the degree in less than two years. Either way, an associate's degree provides a basic education for people who want to enter the information security field without spending four or more years in school. These programs can prepare you for a wide range of entry-level positions in IT and information security. **TABLE 13-2** lists some associate's degree programs offered by various institutions.

Different institutions offer different types of associate's degrees. Just to name a few, you can pursue an associate of science (AS), associate of technical arts (ATA), or associate of applied sciences (AAS) degree. You can find both traditional and online degree programs at every level.

Bachelor's Degree

The bachelor's degree is the next-higher level of degree many institutions offer. The standard bachelor's degree is a four-year degree program. However, many institutions offer accelerated programs to complete the degree requirements in less than four years. The bachelor's degree is often a requirement for any information security position other than entry-level positions. In fact, some entry-level positions even require a bachelor's degree as a minimum.

There are many types of bachelor's degree programs. Some degree programs focus on knowledge breadth; others focus on knowledge depth. In general, liberal arts institutions and larger universities offer programs that focus on breadth. Technical institutions generally focus more on depth. Consider the various degree programs offered by institutions and compare the courses you'll take to satisfy the degree requirements. Find a program that fits your professional goals.

As with other degree programs, you can find institutions that offer both traditional and online programs of study. The current term for online study is distance learning. If this type of study interests you, try searching for "information security distance learning degree programs" online. You'll find that there are many choices available.

You can pursue several different types of bachelor's degree. Some of the choices include bachelor of science (BS or BSc), bachelor of science in information technology (BScIT), bachelor of applied science (BASc), and bachelor of technology (B.Tech). The degree programs differ in the courses you must take and in the subject matter on which the degree programs focus. For example, a BS degree would likely focus more on a wide breadth of subjects, whereas a B.Tech degree would likely consist of mostly technical courses. Again, select the program of study that best fits your plans. **TABLE 13-3** lists some of the bachelor's degree programs offered by various institutions.

TABLE 13-2 Associate's degree programs with cybersecurity concentrations.

INSTITUTION	DESCRIPTION
ITT Technical Institute	ITT offers online and classroom-delivered two-year associate's degrees in computer network administration. The program covers TCP/IP and computer networking. Students investigate these topics through classroom theory and hands-on labs. For more information, visit *www.itt-tech.edu/programs/*.
Strayer University	Strayer University offers online and classroom-delivered information systems degrees. For more information, visit www.strayer.edu/academic-program-finder/associate.
Herzing University	Herzing University offers online and classroom-delivered associate's degrees in computer science. For more information, visit *www.herzing.edu/career-programs /undergraduate-degrees/technology*.
Northern Virginia Community College (NOVA)	Northern Virginia Community College offers a two-year AAS cybersecurity degree. "This curriculum is designed for those who seek employment in the field of cybersecurity (information assurance), for those who are presently in IT or a security field and who desire to increase their knowledge and update their skills, and for those who must augment their abilities in other fields with knowledge and skills in information security. The curriculum is mapped to the NSA/DHS Knowledge Units necessary for NOVA's designation as a Center of Academic Excellence." For more information, visit *http://www.nvcc.edu/cybersecurity/cae.html*.
Edmonds Community College	Edmonds Community College offers online and classroom-delivered associate's degrees in computer information systems, information security, and digital forensics. For more information, visit *http://catalog.edcc.edu/content.php?catoid=14&navoid=5902*.

Master of Science Degree

The next type of academic degree is the master's degree. A master's degree program goes beyond the level of a bachelor's degree program. It generally consists of two years of study beyond a bachelor's degree. Some institutions offer accelerated programs that enable students to earn a master's degree more quickly than two years. A master's degree shows that the holder possesses a deeper level of knowledge than the general population of information security practitioners.

Master's programs are generally very specific to a field of study. When you enter a master's program, you normally spend most of your time focusing on a specific area of study. Programs at this level focus more on depth of knowledge than on breadth of knowledge.

There are several different master's degrees available. These include master of science (MS or MSc), master of science in information technology (MScIT), and master of business administration (MBA). There is a definite difference in degree programs at this level. The main difference exists between the MS and MBA degrees. Each one has a different focus and targets a different group of students.

The master of science degrees—MS, MSc, and MScIT—focus on the technical aspects of information security. In other words, these degrees are appropriate for security

TABLE 13-3 Bachelor's degree programs with cybersecurity concentrations.

INSTITUTION	DESCRIPTION
ITT Technical Institute	ITT Tech offers online and classroom-delivered BS degrees in information systems security and information systems and cybersecurity. For more information, visit *www.itt-tech.edu/programs/*.
Capella University	Capella University offers online BS degrees in information technology with information assurance and security specialization. Capella University has earned an NSA and Homeland Security designation. For more information, visit *www.capella.edu/business-technology-degrees/undergraduate/programs/*.
George Washington University	George Washington University (GWU) offers a BS degree in cybersecurity for students with associate's or nontechnical bachelor's degrees. For more information, visit *https://cps.gwu.edu/cybersecurity-bachelors*.
Kaplan University	Kaplan University offers online BS degrees in information technology with the opportunity to focus on security and forensics concentrations. For more information, visit *http://www.kaplanuniversity.edu/programs/bachelors-degrees.aspx*.
University of Maryland/University College	The University of Maryland/University College offers a BS degree program in cybersecurity management and policy, computer networks and cybersecurity, and software development and security. Each concentration is designed to help you reach your career goals. For more information, visit *www.umuc.edu/cybersecurity/academics/bachelors-degrees.cfm*.
Southern New Hampshire University	Southern New Hampshire University's online BS degrees can include an IT security, information assurance, or forensics concentration. Learn to defend and protect networks and information systems against cyberattacks with the cyber security concentration in the BS in Information Technologies online degree. For more information, visit *http://www.snhu.edu/online-degrees/bachelors/bs-in-information-technologies/cyber-security*.
University of Phoenix	The University of Phoenix offers online and classroom-delivered IT BS degrees. These IT BS degrees can include IT security, information assurance, or forensics concentrations. For more information, visit *www.phoenix.edu/programs/degree-programs/technology/bachelors/bsit-iss.html*.
Strayer University	Online and classroom-delivered BS degrees in information systems are offered with specific concentrations in forensics, cybersecurity, and homeland security. For more information, visit *www.strayer.edu/degree/bachelors-degree/bachelor-science-information-systems/*.

practitioners. If you want to work in a hands-on environment and perform security-related work, these degrees may be good choices. These types of degree programs detail how the IT infrastructure operates and how to design and implement proper security controls. Master of science degree programs prepare you to enter the field of information security and perform the work of securing systems. **TABLE 13-4** lists some master of science degree programs offered by various institutions.

TABLE 13-4 Master of science degree programs with cybersecurity concentrations.	
INSTITUTION	**DESCRIPTION**
SANS Institute	SANS Institute offers online, self-study, and classroom-based information technology degrees. SANS enables students to master communications, project management, teaching, mentoring, and persuasive skills. For more information, visit *www.sans.edu*. Note: SANS, highly regarded in the field, is authorized by the State of Maryland to grant master's degrees.
Capella University	Capella is one of the select four-year colleges and graduate-level universities designated as a National Center of Academic Excellence in Information Assurance Education (CAE/IAE) by the National Security Agency. In addition, Capella offers unique MS degrees with specific security concentrations. For more information, visit *http://www.capella.edu/online-information-technology-degrees/masters-programs/*.
Kaplan University	Kaplan University offers an online MS degree in cybersecurity management with the opportunity to specialize in information security and assurance. For more information, visit *www.kaplanuniversity.edu/information-technology/cybersecurity-management-master-degree.aspx*.
University of Phoenix	The University of Phoenix offers online and classroom-delivered MS management information system (MIS) degrees. This program can include information assurance or cybersecurity concentrations. For more information, visit *www.phoenix.edu/programs/degree-programs/technology/masters/mis.html*.
Southern New Hampshire University	Southern New Hampshire University offers an online MS degree in information technology with an information security concentration. Students learn how to enforce network-level security policies and how to properly secure an organization's IT infrastructure. For more information, visit *www.snhu.edu/campus-majors/graduate/ms-information-technology/information-security/*.
Strayer University	Strayer University offers online and classroom-delivered MS degrees in information systems with a computer security management or computer forensics management concentration. For more information, visit *www.strayer.edu/degree/masters-degree/information-systems/*.
Liberty University	Liberty University offers an online MS degree in information technology with network and security concentrations. For more information, visit *www.liberty.edu/online/degrees/masters/information-technology-network-design-and-security/*.

13

Information Systems Security
Education and Training

Master of Business Administration

The master of business administration degree (MBA) focuses on managing the process of securing information systems. Whereas MS programs prepare students to perform information security work, MBA programs prepare students to manage and maintain the people and environment of information security. A person who holds an MBA degree in information security fields will be prepared to manage information security or IT groups. The skills necessary to manage any technical environment are different from the skills necessary to perform technical work. A separate degree program prepares students to enter the specific field of their choice. **TABLE 13-5** lists some MBA degree programs offered by various institutions.

TABLE 13-5 Master of business administration degree programs with cybersecurity concentrations.

INSTITUTION	DESCRIPTION
George Washington University	George Washington University offers a global MBA with a cybersecurity specialization. Experts at the top echelons of the field teach the students enrolled in the program to focus on the dimensions of cybersecurity most relevant to them, from liability and legal regimes to information assurance technology and practices. For more information, visit *http://business.gwu.edu/brave-new-world-of-cyber-security/*.
Ferris State University	Ferris State University's Master's in Information Security and Intelligence program prepares students for careers in business intelligence, proactive and reactive incident response, and project management utilizing secure practices. For more information, visit *www.ferris.edu/business/program/misi/*.
James Madison University	James Madison University offers an MBA degree with information security. This MBA degree not only provides students with a sound foundation in all of the business principles, it also ensures they have a strong understanding of the business implications of information security. For more information, visit *www.jmu.edu/academics/graduate/programs/business-administration.shtml*.
DeVry/Keller Graduate School of Management	Keller University offers an online and classroom-delivered MBA, with a concentration in information security. Its MBA in Information Security program was designed to provide students with sought-after skills and knowledge to fill this increasingly important role in today's business world, including coursework in information protection, intrusion detection, security procedures, and legal and ethical considerations within the field. For more information, visit *www.keller.edu/graduate-degree-programs/mba-program/mba-in-information-security.html*.

Doctoral Degree

The highest level of academic degree is the doctoral degree. This degree represents the most respected academic honor and is the most difficult to obtain. A doctoral program goes even further than the level of study required for a master's degree. Depending on the type of degree, requirements normally include rigorous coursework and extensive research that makes a meaningful contribution to the field. Unlike other degrees, doctoral degrees do not involve a set amount of time. Many doctoral programs take from three to five years, but there is no standard timeframe for completing the degree.

A doctoral degree identifies the holder as one who values extensive education in a chosen field of study. This person will possess the ability to function at a level that requires exceptional abilities and insight. In the field of information security, people who hold doctoral degrees often work in research, in large enterprise information security management, or in academic roles.

Several types of doctoral degree are available, depending on whether you want to pursue an academic, technical, or management path. Some of the available doctoral degrees in the areas of information security include doctor of science (DSc), doctor of information technology (DIT), doctor of technology (DTech), and the most widely recognized doctoral degree, the doctor of philosophy (PhD). Even at this level, institutions offer degree programs in both

TABLE 13-6 Doctoral degree programs.

INSTITUTION	DESCRIPTION
Capella University	Capella University offers an online PhD in information assurance. This PhD program is designed to advance your information security expertise in a way that fits your career. It provides opportunities for advanced skill development and doctoral research in such topics as information confidentiality, integrity, governance, compliance, and risk management. For more information, visit *www.capella.edu/online-degrees /phd-information-assurance-security/*.
Colorado Technical University	Colorado Technical University (CTU) offers an online PhD program in computer science with an information assurance concentration. CTU's program is designed to help develop the theoretical, research, and applications capabilities needed to manage and forecast future issues and developments in this field. It will challenge students to demonstrate expertise in a subdiscipline of information assurance by selecting and conducting research on an important problem, then communicating results and preparing them for publication. For more information, visit *www.coloradotech.edu/degrees /doctorates/computer-science/information-assurance/*.
Dakota State University	Dakota State University offers an online PhD in information assurance that specializes in cyber operations activities, including data collection, software exploitation, analysis of malicious code, and reverse engineering. These technologies are critical to intelligence, military, and law enforcement organizations, as well as to employers in other data-driven industries. For more information, visit *http://dsu.edu/graduate-students/dsccs/*.
Northcentral University	Northcentral University offers an online PhD in business administration with a concentration in computer and information security. The specialization focuses on developing best practices for forensic investigations and evidence handling, federal and state privacy, intellectual property, search and seizure process, and cybercrime laws. For more information, visit *www.ncu.edu/school-of-business-and-technology /doctor-of-business-administration/computer-and-information-security/*.
Nova Southeastern University	Nova Southeastern University offers an online and classroom-delivered PhD degree program in information assurance. This graduate program is a comprehensive, multi-disciplinary research program that prepares graduates for key positions in academia; in federal, state, and local government agencies; and in business and industry. The curriculum combines both technically intensive and management-focused security courses in a comprehensive approach to the study of information assurance/information security. For more information, visit *http://cec.nova.edu/doctoral/dia/index.html*.

traditional and online formats. **TABLE 13-6** lists some of the doctoral degree programs offered by various institutions.

Information Security Training Programs

Traditional education programs normally focus on students learning a bulk of information through a quarter or semester. Although some programs do introduce hands-on skills, educational institutions focus on complete coverage of topics. They want students to understand the reasons behind decisions and topics. Sometimes all students want is to learn skills or acquire very specific knowledge. Security training programs fill this need with many different offerings.

In general, security training programs differ from security education programs in their focus on hands-on skills and in their duration. Whereas education classes generally meet for a few hours a week over several months, security training classes often meet for intensive sessions lasting from a few hours to several days. The main purpose of security training courses is to rapidly train students in one or more skills or to cover essential knowledge in one or more specific areas. Full-time employees might find an intense week-long course more possible; others could only attend, for example, evening classes spread over several weeks. Many security training courses specifically prepare students for certification exams.

Security Training Requirements

The National Institute of Standards and Technology (NIST) 800 Series publications cover all NIST-recommended procedures for managing information security. The publications also provide guidelines for enforcing security rules. These publications set forth many procedures that are necessary to keep IT environments secure. It is important that users receive training to ensure they understand the security procedures and can implement them.

The U.S. Office of Personnel Management (OPM) requires that federal agencies provide training suggested by the NIST guidelines. It requires agencies to train all current employees and to train all new employees within 60 days of each employee's hire date. Under the OPM requirements, agencies must also provide training whenever any of the following conditions occur:

- There is a significant change in the agency's IT security environment.
- There is a significant change in the agency's security procedures.
- An employee enters a new position that deals with sensitive information.

Agencies must also provide periodic refresher training at specified intervals. In addition, the regulations require that all employees or other personnel receive specialized security training before they receive access to secure IT applications and systems.

The Health Insurance Portability and Accountability Act (HIPAA) also includes directives that require security awareness and training. Implementation specifications include the following:

- Establishing a security awareness program
- Providing training in malicious software
- Providing training on logon monitoring procedures
- Providing training on password management

The Computer Security Act of 1987 mandated that NIST and OPM create guidelines on computer security awareness and training. It directed these agencies to create training that is specific to an agency's functional organizational roles. NIST Special Publication 800-16, *Information Technology Security Training Requirements: A Role- and Performance-Based Model,* includes these guidelines. The publication also contains a methodology that some organizations use to develop training courses for different audiences that have significant information security responsibilities. Special Publication 800-50, *Building an Information Technology Security Awareness and Training Program*, is another NIST document related to information security awareness and training. The four main areas in NIST SP 800-50 are as follows:

- **Awareness**—A continuous process to help keep all personnel vigilant. This can include acceptable use policy (AUP), reminders, logon banners, posters, email messages, and any other techniques to keep personnel thinking about security.
- **Training**—Teach necessary security skills and competency to the staff as a whole as well as those whose jobs are in IT.
- **Education**—Integrate security skills and competencies into a common body of knowledge.
- **Professional development (organizations and certifications)**—Meet a standard by applying evaluation or measurement criteria.

The PCI DSS v3.2 standard for self-assessment questionnaire (SAQ) Requirement 12.6 states the following: "Implement a formal security awareness program to make all personnel aware of the cardholder data security policy and procedures." This PCI DSS v3.2 requirement must be supported with new hire training and at least annual security awareness training updates. In addition, PCI DSS v3.2 requires that personnel acknowledge at least annually that they have read and understood the security policy and procedures.

These are just a few examples of regulations that require an ongoing security training and awareness program. Many organizations also include security awareness and training in their security policy. Ensuring that your personnel are aware of the security policies and procedures is a primary responsibility of your organization's management. Security and training personnel may develop and deliver the security message, but management is responsible for ensuring that they communicate their policy.

Merely providing security training isn't enough, though. Each organization should provide training that is specific to each job function. Some job functions, such as data owners, need different training from other job functions, such as managers. You should ensure that all personnel receive the training that is specific to their job functions.

Security Training Organizations

Some organizations cannot provide the level and amount of security training their personnel need. In such cases, separate security training organizations play a major part in providing the necessary training and certification for security personnel. Some organizations provide specific security training and others provide certification programs.

Many vendors provide security training. As with educational institutions, you can find vendors that will provide classroom, online, and prepackaged study options. Choose the course-delivery option that works best for your budget, learning style, and schedule. There are many options for you, so take some time to evaluate the available products. **TABLE 13-7** lists some of the larger security training vendors and their offerings.

You can choose from among many quality training organizations. Visit each one's website to look at current course offerings. You'll probably be able to find a class and delivery method that fit your needs.

TABLE 13-7 Security training vendors.

VENDOR	DESCRIPTION
SANS Institute	SANS is one of the largest and most trusted sources for information security training in the world. It offers classes on many security topics that cover development, implementation, management, and auditing roles. SANS classes range from a half day to six days, are available globally, and tend to be very hands-on and focused. For more information, visit the SANS website at *www.sans.org*.
IT Professional Group, Inc. (ITPG)	ITPG has been delivering and fulfilling professional certification programs for the International Information Systems Security Certification Consortium, known as (ISC)^2, globally and throughout North America. Visit the ITPG website at *http://itpg .org* for more information.
InfoSec Institute	InfoSec Institute is a large security training organization that holds regular classes across the United States. Its goal is to provide the best possible hands-on training for students in topics ranging from certification preparation to very specific technical security topics. You can get more information at the InfoSec Institute's website, *www.infosecinstitute.com*.
Information Systems Audit and Control Association (ISACA)	ISACA is a nonprofit global organization that promotes "the development, adoption, and use of globally accepted, industry-leading knowledge and practices for information systems." It holds conferences and training events related to information systems auditing and management around the world. Visit the ISACA website for more information: *www.isaca.org*.
Phoenix TS	Phoenix Technology Solutions (Phoenix TS) provides cost-effective, hands-on computer training, IT certification, and management courses to government and commercial organizations in the Maryland, Virginia, and Washington, DC, area. For more information, visit *www.phoenixts.com/*.
Security Evolutions, Inc. (SEI)	SEI provides online, e-learning, self-study, and live virtual instructor delivery of various professional certification programs in IT security and information assurance. These include Security+$^®$, SSCP$^®$, CISSP$^®$, NSA 4011, and NSA 4013-Advanced. For more information, visit *www.security-evolutions.com/*.

Security Awareness Training

Every organization, regardless of the industry vertical or regulatory compliance law requirement, must have a new-hire and ongoing or annual **security awareness training** program. This security awareness training course must be part of an organization's **security awareness campaign**. A security awareness campaign consists of training, periodic newsletters or memos, "lunch and learn" training sessions, and security incidents that are opened as a result of a security policy violation. Depending on how an organization's employees react to policies and procedures and their compliance, security awareness training may need to increase. Remember, the User Domain contains the weakest link in an entire IT infrastructure: humans.

> **NOTE**
>
> Personally identifiable information (PII) is private data of employees or individual customers of the organization. Protected health care information (PHI) is the unique health data of an individual.

The following elements are typically included in an organization's new-hire security awareness training course. These topics may be reinforced in the acceptable use policy (AUP) and the organization's annual security awareness training, depending on need:

- **Compliance with regulatory requirements and laws**—Security awareness training typically includes topics regarding your organization's regulatory compliance and legal requirements as an employee. This may include regulatory compliance and protection of sensitive data such as personally identifiable information (PII), protected health care information (PHI), or cardholder data (credit card numbers).

- **Password behaviors**—The organization's password management policy and complex password requirements are typically reviewed in annual security awareness training.

- **Information/data classification, handling, and labeling**—This is an important part of security awareness training that reminds employees of proper handling for regulated sensitive data versus nonregulated data.

- **Clean desk policies**—Security awareness training should remind employees to ensure confidentiality by not leaving any sensitive information or documents on their desks.

- **Prevent tailgating**—Employees should be reminded not to let secure doorways or entranceways be compromised by individuals approaching behind them.

- **Personally owned devices**—Organizations that permit the use of personally owned devices such as laptop computers or smartphones must address the bring-your-own-device (BYOD) policy in annual security awareness training.

- **New threats and new security trends/alerts**—Security awareness training is a good tool for educating employees on new attack methods and trends from hackers and perpetrators.

- **New viruses (e.g., ransomware, cryptolocker, etc.)**—Security awareness training is a good tool to educate employees on new attack viruses and malicious software such as ransomware and cryptolocker software.

- **Phishing attacks**—Reminders about phishing emails and targeted phishing emails are typically communicated in annual security awareness training.

- **Zero-day exploits**—Malware and malicious software that may not have an anti-malware solution can cause a zero-day exploit that may force your organization to remove an IT asset from production. Zero-day attacks and exploits are typically communicated in annual security awareness training.

- **Use of social networking and peer-to-peer communications**—Both are typically prohibited in the AUP and in other policy definitions; hence, this topic is commonly shared in annual security awareness training.

Without periodic security awareness training, employees will not be aware of new policies and procedures regarding security and privacy. Some organizations require a policy for ensuring that security awareness training is updated and delivered annually to all employees and contractors. This is an important risk-mitigating requirement to address the risk created from the User Domain and humans. Human resources staff may be required to generate reports confirming that employees have taken and have passed the annual security awareness training program. This may be requested by auditors when they're on site performing regulatory compliance audits.

CHAPTER SUMMARY

Being a qualified security professional requires pertinent knowledge and skills. You have to understand security issues and be able to act on that understanding. Education and training organizations can provide you with the necessary knowledge and help to develop required skills. You explored several different options to learn more about information systems security. You learned that self-study is a viable choice in some cases. It is also the least expensive. Regardless of where or how you acquire additional knowledge and skills, reading and researching the information provided in this chapter should have given you a better understanding of what's out there.

The learning doesn't stop with a certificate or a degree. You learned about continuing education offerings for informal education and degree programs for varying levels of formal education. You also learned about some of the organizations that offer focused training in short courses. On the job, security awareness is the number-one security control an organization can implement to mitigate the risk created by humans. Many organizations require annual security awareness training, and human resources staff may be required to generate reports confirming that employees have taken and have passed the annual security awareness training program. These reports may be required by auditors.

KEY CONCEPTS AND TERMS

Accredited

Certificate of completion

Continuing education

Continuing professional development (CPD)

Continuing professional education (CPE)

National Centers of Academic Excellence in Information Assurance Education (CAE/IAE)

National Centers of Academic Excellence in Research (CAE/R)

Security awareness campaign

Security awareness training

CHAPTER 13 ASSESSMENT

1. One of the disadvantages of self-study is that the materials are generally expensive.

   A. True
   B. False

2. Which of the following would be the least likely resource to have current self-study materials?

   A. Online bookstore
   B. Local bookstore
   C. Local library
   D. Online e-library
   E. None of the above

3. When selecting self-study materials, a vendor that sells many products always has higher quality products.

   A. True
   B. False

4. Which of the following generally holds classes that do not lead to a degree but are associated with a college or university?

   A. Associate program
   B. Extension program
   C. Continuing education
   D. Professional training organization
   E. None of the above

5. Which term refers to the unit of credit many certifications require to keep current?

   A. Credit hour
   B. Quality point
   C. GPA
   D. CPE

6. A _____ classroom is one in which students and at least one instructor are all in the same room.

7. Which two organizations sponsor the National Centers of Academic Excellence?

   A. NSA and DHS
   B. HHS and DOD
   C. DOD and DHS
   D. NSA and HHS
   E. None of the above

8. Which term means that an educational institution has successfully undergone evaluation by an external body to determine whether the institution meets applicable standards?

   A. Certified
   B. Accredited
   C. Audited
   D. Accepted
   E. None of the above

9. Which U.S. agency requires that all federal agencies provide security training to their employees?

   A. DOD
   B. NIST
   C. OPM
   D. NSA
   E. All of the above

10. Which of the following is *not* one of the main areas in NIST Special Publication 800-50?

    A. Responsibility
    B. Awareness
    C. Training
    D. Professional development
    E. None of the above

11. Security awareness training should be conducted:

    A. During initial HR orientation and onboarding
    B. Prior to granting any access control login credentials
    C. At least annually
    D. When a policy violation occurs to reinforce security awareness
    E. All of the above

12. Which of the following is *not* typically included in annual security awareness training?

    A. New policies or procedures
    B. Password behavior do's and don'ts
    C. Phishing email attacks
    D. How to log on to your computer
    E. Risks associated with peer-to-peer communications

13. An acceptable use policy (AUP) with periodic security awareness training is the best security countermeasure to mitigate risk caused within the User Domain.

   A. True
   B. False

14. Which of the following open source tools and applications do you recommend for your cybersecurity hands-on lab?

   A. Wireshark
   B. Nmap
   C. Metasploit
   D. Kali Linux
   E. All of the above

15. What is the primary job of the information systems security or cybersecurity professional?

   A. Conduct security awareness training for all employees
   B. Ensure the availability, confidentiality, and integrity of your organization's IT infrastructure
   C. Be aware of new threats and new security trends/alerts
   D. Develop the organization's IT and IT security policies, standards, and procedures
   E. None of the above

Information Security Professional Certifications

NFORMATION SECURITY IS BECOMING more complex. As new and more capable software and hardware products emerge, attackers find more vulnerabilities. In the process, it becomes more difficult for security professionals to stay current. In addition, it becomes more difficult for employers to identify people who are qualified to keep their organizations' systems secure.

Today one of the most common methods for identifying the skills a security professional possesses is **certification**. A certification proves that the holder has obtained a measurable level of competency. It also may prove that the holder has a certain level of experience and has passed an examination. Each certification attests to a different skill set and has different requirements.

Today there are many certifications that relate to information systems security or cybersecurity. These certifications are for personnel in areas ranging from high-level security management to very detailed hands-on practitioners. Regardless of your interest or experience in the information systems security field, it is likely there is a certification for you. Certifications can help identify you as someone who has pursued training and who complies with the certification's knowledge objectives. In this chapter, you will learn about the most popular information systems security certifications and their requirements.

Chapter 14 Topics

This chapter covers the following topics and concepts:

- What the U.S. DoD/military standards for the cybersecurity workforce are
- What the popular vendor-neutral professional certifications are
- What the popular vendor-specific professional certifications are

Chapter 14 Goals

When you complete this chapter, you will be able to:

- Identify professional certifications in the information systems security and cybersecurity space
- Distinguish between the U.S. DoD/military Directive 8570.01 and the new DoDD 8140.01
- Describe popular vendor-neutral professional certifications
- Identify popular vendor-specific professional certifications

U.S. Department of Defense/Military Directive 8570.01

The U.S. Department of Defense (DoD) has developed many standards and requirements to govern nearly every aspect of daily operation and behavior. Although not all DoD standards apply directly to information security, some do. The DoD Directive 8570.01, "Information Assurance Training, Certification and Workforce Management," defines many requirements for DoD personnel and contractors with respect to information security. DoD Directive 8570.01 requires "all DoD personnel and contractors who conduct information assurance functions in assigned duty positions to achieve very specific levels of certification." Different jobs carry different certification requirements. This directive first came out in December 19, 2005. The most recent update incorporated Change 4 in November 20, 2015.

The Gov IT Wiki, *http://govitwiki.com/wiki/8570.01*, is a great resource for additional information on DoD Directive 8570.01. Here you can find more details about the specific certification requirements for each job type. You can also find explanations of how the requirement may affect your organization or job. In general, DoD Directive 8570.01 affects any DoD facility or contractor organization. It ensures that all personnel who are directly involved with information security possess security certifications. The purpose of this directive is to reduce the possibility that unqualified personnel can gain access to secure information.

DoD Directive 8570.01 has created a new segment of opportunity for training and certification organizations. Many providers of security training and certifications target DoD employees and contractors to offer paths to DoD Directive 8570.01 compliance. This mandatory certification requirement has increased the number of personnel who pursue certifications. It also maintains a steady flow of students through security classes to earn continuing professional education (CPE) credits to keep credentials current. Some have questioned its effectiveness, but DoD Directive 8570.01 has increased the number of security personnel seeking ongoing security training.

> **NOTE**
>
> DoD Directive 8570.01 has since been replaced by DoD Directive (DoDD) 8140. Like its predecessor, DoDD 8140 requires DoD IT personnel and contractors to obtain certifications in their work area specializations. DoDD 8140 addresses knowledge, skills, and abilities (KSA). At the time of this writing, a complementary manual (expected to be denoted as 8140.01-M) is not yet written. Thus DoDD 8140 has adopted the 8570.01-M until the 8140.01-M is approved.

U.S. DoD/Military Directive 8140

The Defense Information Systems Agency (DISA) is the agency arm of the U.S. Department of Defense that provides information technology and communications support to the White House, Secretary of Defense, and all military sectors that contribute to the defense of the United States of America. DISA is developing a new, operationally focused cybersecurity training framework that will replace the previous 8570.01 directive.

The vision of this new cybersecurity training framework is to "establish a robust workforce training and certification program that will better prepare DoD cyberwarriors to operate and defend our networks in an increasingly threat-based environment."

General Keith Alexander, former director of the National Security Agency and head of the United States Cyber Command, has said, "Whether we do our cybertraining at one school or at multiple schools, the training will have to be executed to one standard. I think that's what we need to do so that the combatant commanders and the forces in the field know that whether they get a soldier, marine, airman, or sailor, that person is trained to a standard and can accomplish the mission that is expected of them."

The basic tenets for the new Directive 8140 for the cybersecurity workforce include the following:

- A "Training Strategy Roadmap" for role-based and crew certification will be provided.
- Commercial certifications, which have long been relied on, although they are often just too broad for military use, will be adapted and tightened to better meet Defense Department needs.
- DISA can produce focused, relevant qualifications and certifications for the cyberwarriors of the United States.
- Crew certification is a grouping of qualified role-based operators who obtain the desired effects necessary to defend and operate in cyberspace.
- A "Cyber Defense Academy" will qualify role-based individuals to work effectively as part of crews and teams.
- Joint Cyberspace Training & Certification Standard (JCT&CS) is the current baseline for work-role definition.
- The National Initiative for Cybersecurity Education (NICE) will be the baseline for federal and DoD work-role definitions.

FIGURE 14-1 presents the specific role-based requirements for fulfilling the 8140 cybersecurity workforce development initiative.

The following DoD initiatives will support this new DoDD 8140 cybersecurity workforce development standard:

- DoDD 8140 workforce requirements initiative (this will define the requirements for the cybersecurity roles identified by the JCT&CS)
- Learning Management System selection by Office of the Under Secretary of Defense for Personnel and Readiness (OSD P&R)
- JCT&CS concept of operations (CONOPs) and Implementation Plan
- Department of Homeland Security (DHS) and National Security Agency (NSA) Centers of Academic Excellence
- DISA Cyber Workforce Developments

This shift from the previous 8570.01 directive to the more role-based DoDD 8140 provides a more succinct solution to fulfilling the various cybersecurity roles required for combat support. The roles identified by the 8140 directive include the following:

- Security provision
- Operate and maintain
- Protect and defend
- Analyze
- Operate and collect
- Oversight and development
- Investigate

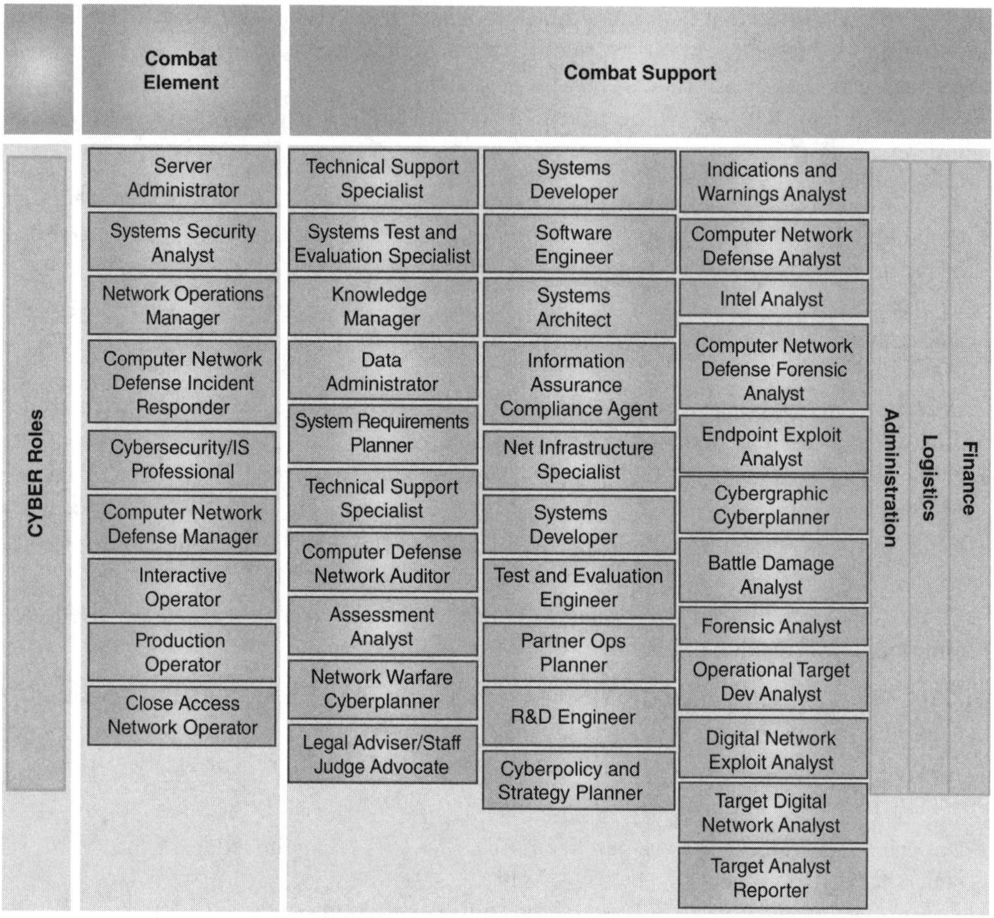

CYBER Roles	Combat Element	Combat Support			Administration	Logistics	Finance
	Server Administrator	Technical Support Specialist	Systems Developer	Indications and Warnings Analyst			
	Systems Security Analyst	Systems Test and Evaluation Specialist	Software Engineer	Computer Network Defense Analyst			
	Network Operations Manager	Knowledge Manager	Systems Architect	Intel Analyst			
	Computer Network Defense Incident Responder	Data Administrator	Information Assurance Compliance Agent	Computer Network Defense Forensic Analyst			
	Cybersecurity/IS Professional	System Requirements Planner	Net Infrastructure Specialist	Endpoint Exploit Analyst			
	Computer Network Defense Manager	Technical Support Specialist	Systems Developer	Cybergraphic Cyberplanner			
	Interactive Operator	Computer Defense Network Auditor	Test and Evaluation Engineer	Battle Damage Analyst			
	Production Operator	Assessment Analyst	Partner Ops Planner	Forensic Analyst			
	Close Access Network Operator	Network Warfare Cyberplanner	R&D Engineer	Operational Target Dev Analyst			
		Legal Adviser/Staff Judge Advocate	Cyberpolicy and Strategy Planner	Digital Network Exploit Analyst			
				Target Digital Network Analyst			
				Target Analyst Reporter			

FIGURE 14-1

Joint cyberspace training and certification standards.
Defense Information Systems Agency (DISA), Deputy Director, Field Security Operations.

U.S. DoD/NSA Training Standards

Information security is a growing discipline that becomes more complex with every passing day. The DoD and the NSA have identified many areas of interest and concern related to information security. The DoD and NSA have adopted several training standards to serve as a pathway to satisfy Directive 8140. Although they are called standards, these training standards are not true information security standards in the usual sense. They are really training requirements for specific job responsibilities. These training standards include long lists of learning objectives for topics related to specific job responsibilities. They were developed by the Committee on National Security Systems (CNSS) and the National Security Telecommunications and Information Systems Security (NSTISS) Committee. They provide guidance for course and professional certification vendors to develop curriculum and materials that meet the DoD/NSA requirements. Some of the standards define different levels of expertise,

TABLE 14-1 DoD/NSA training standards.	
TRAINING STANDARD	**DESCRIPTION**
NSTISS-4011	National Training Standard for Information Systems Security (InfoSec) Professionals
CNSS-4012	National Information Assurance Training Standard for Senior System Managers
CNSS-4013	National Information Assurance Training Standard for System Administrators (SA)
CNSS-4014	Information Assurance Officer (IAO) Training
NSTISSC-4015	National Training Standard for System Certifiers
CNSS-4016	National Information Assurance Training Standard for Risk Analysts

such as entry, intermediate, and advanced. Others address general requirement targets at a single level. **TABLE 14-1** shows the current CNSS/NSTISS training standards that relate to information security.

These training standards provide comprehensive descriptions of job competencies. They provide guidance for potential and existing InfoSec professionals. Anyone who currently works in InfoSec or wants to work in the field can use these standards to ensure they possess the necessary skills. Perhaps more important, they lay the groundwork for equipping the next generation of InfoSec professionals in different job functions.

> **NOTE**
>
> These standards help vendors develop materials that satisfy the DoD/NSA requirements. In fact, the Jones & Bartlett Learning Information Systems Security & Assurance (ISSA) Curriculum satisfies both NSTISS-4011 and CNSS-4013-Advanced and includes both Entry and Intermediate levels. The Jones & Bartlett Learning ISSA curriculum is approved by the NSA and the National Initiative for Cybersecurity Education (NICE).

Vendor-Neutral Professional Certifications

A certification is an official statement that validates the fact that a person has satisfied specific job requirements. These requirements often include the following:

- Possessing a certain level of experience
- Completing a course of study
- Passing an examination

An organization that is empowered to state that an individual has met the certification's requirements issues the certification.

Although certifications are not perfect, obtaining them is a standard way for security professionals to further their security education and training. Certifications show that a security professional has invested time, effort, and money into learning more about security. Many prospective employers consider security certifications as they screen job applicants. True security expertise involves more than merely holding a certification. However, certification preparatory organizations have developed curricula that do a good job of educating certification candidates as well as preparing them for an exam.

NOTE

A certification does not guarantee that a person is good at a specific job. Unfortunately, there are bad security professionals who have certifications. There are also excellent security professionals who hold no certifications. Typically, if the certification is a professional industry certification, it must undergo a **job task analysis**, a study that identifies the skills, knowledge, and experience needed to perform a job. A job task analysis is what makes a professional certification defensible in court given that a thorough and proper job task analysis was conducted.

Certifications target specific areas of knowledge and expertise. There is at least one certification for most security-related job functions and expertise levels. The first type of certification is the **vendor-neutral certification**. This type of certification covers concepts and topics that are general in nature. It does not focus on a specific product or product line. Several organizations provide certifications that the security community recognizes as having high value. The following sections cover some of the many certification organizations and their credentials.

International Information Systems Security Certification Consortium, Inc.

The International Information Systems Security Certification Consortium, Inc. (ISC)^2 is one of the most respected global certification organizations. (ISC)^2 is a not-for-profit organization that focuses on educating and certifying security professionals from all experience levels. (ISC)^2 offers four main credentials, each addressing a different security professional role. The seven main (ISC)^2 credentials are as follows:

- Systems Security Certified Practitioner (SSCP®)
- Certified Information Systems Security Professional (CISSP®)
- Certified Authorization Professional (CAP®)
- Certified Secure Software Lifecycle Professional (CSSLP®)
- Certified Cyber Forensics Professional (CCFP®)
- HealthCare Certified Information Security Privacy Practitioner (HCISPP®)
- Certified Cloud Security Professional (CCSP®)

NOTE

For more information on (ISC)^2 professional certification credentials, visit the (ISC)^2 website at *www.isc2.org*.

SSCP®

The Systems Security Certified Practitioner (SSCP) credential enables security practitioners to demonstrate their level of competence. The SSCP covers the seven domains of best practices for information security. (ISC)^2 publishes the security best practices in the SSCP Common Body of Knowledge (CBK). The SSCP credential is ideal for those who are working toward or already hold positions as senior network security engineers, senior security systems analysts, or senior security administrators.

CISSP®

(ISC)^2's flagship credential is the Certified Information Systems Security Professional (CISSP). The CISSP was the first ANSI/ISO-accredited credential in the field of information security. The CISSP provides information security professionals with an objective measure of competence and a globally recognized standard of achievement. The CISSP credential demonstrates competence in the eight domains of the (ISC)^2 CISSP CBK. The CISSP credential targets middle- and senior-level managers who are working toward or already hold positions as chief information security officers (CISOs), chief security officers (CSOs), or senior security engineers.

CAP®

The Certified Authorization Professional (CAP) credential provides a method to measure the knowledge and skills necessary for professionals involved in the process of authorizing and maintaining information systems. The best fits for the CAP credential are personnel responsible for developing and implementing processes used to assess risk and for establishing security requirements. Professionals seeking the CAP credential could include authorization officials, system owners, information owners, information security officers, and certifiers. This credential is appropriate for both private-sector and U.S. government personnel.

> **NOTE**
>
> The CISSP® CBK was changed from 10 domains to 8 domains. The 8 domains of the CISSP CBK are:
>
> * Security and Risk Management
> * Asset Security
> * Security Engineering
> * Communications and Network Security
> * Identify and Access Management
> * Security Assessment and Testing
> * Security Operations
> * Software Development Security

CSSLP®

The Certified Secure Software Lifecycle Professional (CSSLP) is one of the few credentials that address developing secure software. The CSSLP credential evaluates professionals for the knowledge and skills necessary to develop and deploy secure applications. This credential is appropriate for software developers, software architects, and anyone involved in the software development and deployment process.

CCFP®

The Certified Cyber Forensics Professional (CCFP) credential is not an elementary forensics certification but rather builds on an already existing forensics certification or experience using a commercially available forensics application such as EnCase® Forensic or Forensic Toolkit® (FTK®). The CCFP credential will test and evaluate professionals for the knowledge and skills necessary to perform and conduct a digital forensics investigation. This credential is appropriate for law enforcement officials, cybercrime and cybersecurity professionals, forensic engineers, and forensic consultants.

HCISPP®

The HealthCare Certified Information Security and Privacy Practitioner (HCISPP) was developed to address the health care industry and the protection of protected health care information (PHI) or electronic protected health care information (ePHI). The HCISPP credential will test and evaluate professionals for the knowledge and skills necessary to perform and conduct security and privacy work for health care organizations. This credential is appropriate for individuals seeking an IT or IT security career path within a health care organization.

CCSP®

With the rapid growth in cloud and virtual computing, the Certified Cloud Security Professional (CCSP) certification was built by both (ISC)² and the Cloud Security Alliance (CSA). The CCSP credential will test and evaluate professionals for the knowledge and skills necessary to secure and manage cloud computing environments. This credential is appropriate for IT, IT security, system administrators, and system architects who are designing, implementing, hosting, and managing applications in cloud infrastructures.

Additional (ISC)² Professional Certifications

After the original conception of the CISSP and the continuous evolution of information systems security, (ISC)² discovered a need to develop concentration credentials that address more advanced content, including information systems security architecture, engineering, and management. These CISSP concentrations are in the following functional areas:

- Architecture (CISSP-ISSAP®)
- Engineering (CISSP-ISSEP®)
- Management (CISSP-ISSMP®)

ISSAP®

The ISSAP concentration requires a candidate to demonstrate two years of professional experience in the area of architecture and is an appropriate credential for chief security architects and analysts, who typically work as independent consultants or in similar capacities.

> ■ **NOTE**
> For more information on the CISSP® concentration certifications, visit *https://www.isc2.org/concentrations/default.aspx.*

ISSEP®

The ISSEP concentration was developed in conjunction with the NSA, providing an invaluable tool for any systems security engineering professional. The ISSEP concentration is the road map for incorporating security into projects, applications, business processes, and all information systems.

ISSMP®

The ISSMP concentration requires that a candidate demonstrate two years of professional experience in the area of enterprise-wide security operations and management. This concentration contains deeper managerial elements such as project management, risk management, setting up and delivering a security awareness program, and managing a business continuity planning program.

Global Information Assurance Certification/SANS Institute

The next major certification organization is also a global organization that is ANSI accredited. The Global Information Assurance Certification (GIAC) offers approximately 30 individual credentials. These credentials span several information security job disciplines:

- Audit
- Forensics
- Legal
- Management
- Security administration
- Software security

GIAC, formed by the SANS Institute in 1999, is the governing body which issues the various certifications. SANS Institute provides specific training that prepares students for each of the GIAC credentials. You can pursue individual GIAC credentials or follow a path to earn higher-level credentials.

Anyone who holds a GIAC credential can submit a technical paper that covers an important area of information security. An accepted technical paper adds the Gold credential to the base GIAC credential. The Gold credential enables security professionals to stand out from other credential holders. The GIAC Security Expert (GSE) credential provides another method for security professionals to stand apart from other credential holders. The GSE requirements include holding three GIAC credentials (with two of the credentials being Gold, denoting an assessed writing component), passing a GSE exam, and completing an intensive two-day hands-on lab. The GSE represents the highest-level credential within GIAC.

TABLE 14-2 lists the current GIAC credentials and their respective levels, according to GIAC.

> **NOTE**
>
> For more information on GIAC security certifications, visit the GIAC website at *https://www.giac.org/certifications /categories*.

Certified Internet Webmaster

Certified Internet Webmaster (CIW) offers several credentials that focus on both general and web-related security. Several of CIW's advanced credentials require a combination of passing an exam and holding at least one recognized credential from another vendor. CIW uses this blended approach to encourage a breadth of security knowledge and skills. **TABLE 14-3** lists the CIW security-related credentials and their general requirements.

The CIW-approved credential list contains the credentials from other vendors that satisfy the CIW Web Security Specialist and CIW Web Security Professional credentials. Other credentials that satisfy CIW requirements include the following:

- (ISC)^2 SCCP or CISSP
- Various GIAC credentials, such as GSE, GCFW, GCIH, and so on
- CompTIA Security+
- Several vendor-specific credentials

> **NOTE**
>
> For more information about CIW credentials and current requirements, see the CIW website at *www .ciwcertified.com*.

CompTIA

CompTIA's Security+ certification is a vendor-neutral credential. Security+ is a globally recognized foundational certification for any IT or IT security professional. CompTIA's Security+ certification has become the entry-level information security certification of choice for IT professionals who want to pursue further work and knowledge in this area.

TABLE 14-2 GIAC credentials.

JOB DISCIPLINE	LEVEL	CREDENTIAL
Audit	Intermediate	GIAC Certified ISO-27000 Specialist (G2700)
	Advanced	GIAC Systems and Network Auditor (GSNA)
Forensics	Intermediate	GIAC Certified Forensic Examiner (GCFE)
	Advanced	GIAC Certified Forensic Analyst (GCFA)
	Expert	GIAC Reverse Engineering Malware (GREM)
Legal	Advanced	GIAC Legal Issues (GLEG)
Management	Intermediate	GIAC Information Security Professional (GISP)
	Advanced	GIAC Security Leadership Certification (GSLC)
	Advanced	GIAC Certified Project Manager Certification (GCPM)
Security administration	Introductory	GIAC Information Security Fundamentals (GISF)
	Intermediate	GIAC Security Essentials Certification (GSEC)
	Intermediate	GIAC Continuous Monitoring (GMON)
	Advanced	GIAC Certified Firewall Analyst (GCFW)
	Advanced	GIAC Certified Intrusion Analyst (GCIA)
	Advanced	GIAC Certified Incident Handler (GCIH)
	Advanced	GIAC Certified UNIX Security Administrator (GCUX)
	Advanced	GIAC Certified Windows Security Administrator (GCWN)
	Advanced	GIAC Certified Penetration Tester (GPEN)
	Advanced	GIAC Web Application Penetration Tester (GWAPT)
	Expert	GIAC Assessing Wireless Networks (GAWN)
	Expert	GIAC Exploit Researcher and Advanced Penetration Tester (GXPN)
Software security	Advanced	GIAC Secure Software Programmer—.NET (GSSP-NET)
	Advanced	GIAC Secure Software Programmer—Java (GSSP-JAVA)
GSE	Expert	GIAC Security Expert (GSE)

TABLE 14-3 CIW credentials.

CREDENTIAL	REQUIREMENTS
CIW Web Security Associate	Pass Web Security Associate exam (1D0-571)
CIW Web Security Specialist	Pass Web Security Associate exam (1D0-571), plus earn one credential from the CIW-approved credential list
CIW Web Security Professional	Pass Web Security Associate exam (1D0-571), plus earn two credentials from the CIW-approved credential list

CompTIA's Security+ certification is postured to reach the masses of recent college graduates or entry-level IT professionals who are trying to decide what specific career path to take within IT, security being one of them.

For those professionals seeking an entry-level information systems security or cybersecurity certification credential, the CompTIA Security+ certification has the following benefits:

- Is a globally recognized credential with certified professionals in 147+ countries
- Meets the ISO 17024 standard and is approved by the DoD 8570.01-M requirements
- Is industry–supported, given that Security+ is developed and maintained by leading IT experts
- Provides a career path in information systems security and the pursuit of additional security certifications

For security professionals possessing 5 to 10 years of experience, CompTIA offers the CASP™, or CompTIA Advanced Security Practitioner, credential. According to CompTIA's website on the certification, CASP "meets the ISO 17024 standard and is approved by U.S. Department of Defense to fulfill directive 8570.01-M requirements. It is compliant with government regulations under the Federal Information Security Management Act (FISMA)."

ISACA®

ISACA, formerly known as the Information Systems Audit and Control Association, is a nonprofit global organization that promotes "the development, adoption, and use of globally accepted, industry-leading knowledge and practices for information systems." ISACA provides security training at conferences and training events. The organization offers four certification programs for IT security professionals. **TABLE 14-4** lists the ISACA certifications.

Other Information Systems Security Certifications

The previous vendors and certifications aren't the only ones that have value. There are many other certifications that address niche areas in the discipline. The following table of certifications is not an exhaustive list but rather a starting point for researching some of the many available options. Before deciding on the right certification to pursue, research the most current offerings in your area of interest. Vendors introduce new certifications continually. They also frequently update their existing products. Make sure that you conduct your own search for the latest information on the certifications you most want to pursue. **TABLE 14-5** lists some of the more popular certifications that have not been covered thus far in this chapter.

> **NOTE**
>
> For more information on CompTIA's credentials, visit its website at *www.comptia.org/certifications.aspx*.

> **NOTE**
>
> You can learn more about ISACA's certifications and their requirements at the ISACA website. Visit *www.isaca.org* for more information.

Vendor-Specific Professional Certifications

Several vendors of hardware and software products also offer certification programs. These **vendor-specific certifications** help identify professionals who possess in-depth product

TABLE 14-4 ISACA certifications.

CERTIFICATION	DESCRIPTION
Certified Information Security Manager (CISM)	The CISM certification program is a credential for experienced information security professionals who are involved in security management. It provides a way to measure the knowledge and skills necessary to design, implement, and manage enterprise security programs.
Certified Information Systems Auditor (CISA)	The CISA certification program targets information systems audit, control, and security professionals. It defines and promotes the skills and practices that are the building blocks of success in the IT audit and control field.
Certified in the Governance of Enterprise IT (CGEIT)	The CGEIT is a new ISACA certification program. It targets security professionals who ensure that their organization satisfies IT governance requirements. The CGEIT bases its requirements on the ISACA and the IT Governance Institute's (ITGI's) audit and control guidelines, which come from global subject-matter experts.
Certified in Risk and Information Systems Control (CRISC)	The CRISC certification applies to a wide range of security professionals. This certification focuses on the knowledge and skills required to design, deploy, monitor, and manage security controls to address risk. CRISC addresses all risk management areas, including identification, assessment, response, and monitoring.

knowledge. Many organizations use these certifications, along with vendor-neutral certifications, when evaluating prospective employees and personnel. As with vendor-neutral certifications, holding a certification for a specific vendor does not guarantee competence, but it does imply it. If an applicant meets the requirements for a certification, it means that applicant has a certain level of knowledge and skills.

In this section, you'll learn about some of the vendor-specific certification programs. Certification programs change frequently. You should visit the vendor website for each of the software and hardware products active in your IT infrastructure. You will find that many vendors offer certifications. The following sections introduce a few of the many vendor-specific certifications for security personnel.

Cisco Systems

Cisco Systems is one of the largest manufacturers of network security devices and software. Cisco offers a range of certifications for its networking products. Its training and certification process helps ensure that security professionals who work with Cisco products possess the knowledge and skills they need to secure their environments. Cisco offers several different certification levels along different tracks. These options enable security professionals to focus their efforts on the specific knowledge and skills they need to get the most out of their Cisco equipment.

Cisco offers certifications at five different levels to address the needs of professionals with different experience levels. Entry-level professionals can work their way up the

TABLE 14-5 Additional information systems security certifications.

VENDOR	CERTIFICATIONS	FOR MORE INFORMATION
International Council of E-Commerce Consultants (EC-Council)	Certified Ethical Hacker (CEH) Computer Hacking Forensic Investigator (CHFI) EC-Council Certified Security Analyst (ECSA)/Licensed Penetration Tester (LPT)	http://cert.eccouncil.org/
Software Engineering Institute—Carnegie Mellon University	CERT—Certified Computer Security Incident Handler SEI—Authorized CERT Instructor	https://www.sei.cmu.edu /training/certificates/security /handler.cfm
Mile 2	Multiple security certifications	www.mile2.com/
Certified Wireless Security Professional	Multiple wireless security certifications	www.cwnp.com/certifications /cwsp/
High Tech Crime Network	Certified Computer Crime Investigator (Basic, Advanced) Certified Computer Forensic Technician (Basic, Advanced)	www.htcn.org
The International Society of Forensic Computer Examiners	Certified Computer Examiner (CCE)	www.isfce.com/certification .htm
CyberSecurity Institute	CyberSecurity Forensic Analyst (CSFA)	www.cybersecurityforensican alyst.com/
Offensive Security	Multiple certifications	www.offensive-security.com /information-security-certifications/

sequence with additional training and experience. Those who already possess substantial Cisco equipment experience may choose to start with a higher level. Cisco offers certifications at these levels:

* Entry
* Associate
* Professional
* Expert
* Architect

Cisco challenges applicants differently depending on the level of certification. Entry-level certifications require only a single exam; more advanced certifications require multiple courses and exams. Cisco also offers multiple paths for associates, professionals, and experts. These paths enable Cisco credential holders to specialize in specific areas. You can earn a Cisco certification in the following paths:

* Design
* Security

NOTE

For more information on Cisco's certification programs, visit the Cisco website at *www
.cisco.com/c/en/us/training-events/training
-certifications/certifications.html.*

- Voice
- Wireless
- Routing and switching
- Service provider operations

TABLE 14-6 lists the Cisco certifications.

LEVEL	CERTIFICATION
Entry	Cisco Certified Entry Networking Technician (CCENT)
	Cisco Certified Technician (CCT)
Associate	Cisco Certified Design Associate (CCDA)
	Cisco Certified Network Associate (CCNA) Data Center
	Cisco Certified Network Associate (CCNA) Routing and Switching
	Cisco Certified Network Associate (CCNA) Security
	Cisco Certified Network Associate (CCNA) Service Provider
	Cisco Certified Network Associate (CCNA) Service Provider Operations
	Cisco Certified Network Associate (CCNA) Video
	Cisco Certified Network Associate (CCNA) Voice
	Cisco Certified Network Associate (CCNA) Wireless
Professional	Cisco Certified Design Professional (CCDP)
	Cisco Certified Network Professional (CCNP)
	Cisco Certified Network Professional (CCNP) Data Center
	Cisco Certified Network Professional (CCNP) Security
	Cisco Certified Network Professional (CCNP) Service Provider
	Cisco Certified Network Professional (CCNP) Service Provider Operations
	Cisco Certified Network Professional (CCNP) Voice
	Cisco Certified Network Professional (CCNP) Wireless
Expert	Cisco Certified Design Expert (CCDE)
	Cisco Certified Internetwork Expert (CCIE) Data Center
	Cisco Certified Internetwork Expert (CCIE) Routing and Switching
	Cisco Certified Internetwork Expert (CCIE) Security
	Cisco Certified Internetwork Expert (CCIE) Service Provider
	Cisco Certified Internetwork Expert (CCIE) Service Provider Operations
	Cisco Certified Internetwork Expert (CCIE) Voice
	Cisco Certified Internetwork Expert (CCIE) Wireless
Architect	Cisco Certified Architect (CCAr)

TABLE 14-6 Cisco certifications.

Juniper Networks

Juniper Networks manufactures a variety of network security hardware and software. Juniper also offers a varied range of certifications for its networking product line. Like Cisco, Juniper Networks offers multiple certification levels and different tracks. Its certifications help personnel who work for organizations that use Juniper Networks hardware to get the most from the products.

Certification candidates can take courses and exams to qualify for certifications at 4 levels from 11 different tracks. Juniper Networks does not offer certifications at all levels for every track. **TABLE 14-7** shows the Juniper Networks certification levels and the tracks available at each level.

RSA

RSA is a global provider of security, risk, and compliance solutions for enterprise environments. RSA products include identity assurance, data loss prevention, encryption, and tokenization devices. They also provide specific training and certifications to help security professionals acquire and demonstrate the knowledge and skills to use RSA products effectively. Because organizations commonly use RSA products in various capacities in an enterprise environment, RSA offers several certification options. RSA currently offers certifications for RSA Archer and RSA SecurID. Each certification requires the applicant take one or more required courses and then pass a required exam.

> **NOTE**
>
> For more information on Juniper Networks certifications, visit the Juniper Networks website at *www.juniper.net/us /en/training/certification/.*

> **NOTE**
>
> For more information on RSA certifications, visit its website at *www.emc.com /training/rsa-education-services /certification.htm.*

Symantec

The Symantec Corporation provides a wide range of security software products. Like other vendors we've mentioned, Symantec offers certifications for its product lines. These certifications provide specific product training and validate practitioners' knowledge and skills related to the Symantec product line.

Here is a list of the available certifications in the Symantec Certified Specialist (SCS) program:

> **NOTE**
>
> For more information about Symantec certifications, visit its website at *https:// www.symantec.com/products-solutions /training/certification/.*

- Administration of Veritas Storage Foundation 6.0 for UNIX
- Administration of Veritas Cluster Server 6.0 for UNIX
- Administration of Symantec NetBackup 7.5 for UNIX
- Administration of Symantec Enterprise Vault 10.0 for Exchange
- Administration of Symantec Endpoint Protection 12.1
- Administration of Symantec Backup Exec 2012
- Administration of Veritas Storage Foundation and High Availability Solutions 6.0 for Windows
- Administration of Symantec NetBackup 7.5 for Windows
- Administration of Symantec Client Management Suite 7.1/7.x
- Administration of Symantec Management Platform 7.1

Juniper Networks

TABLE 14-7 Juniper Networks certification levels and tracks.

TRACK	JUNIPER NETWORKS CERTIFIED INTERNET ASSOCIATE (JNCIA)	JUNIPER NETWORKS CERTIFIED INTERNET SPECIALIST (JNCIS)	JUNIPER NETWORKS CERTIFIED INTERNET PROFESSIONAL (JNCIP)	JUNIPER NETWORKS CERTIFIED INTERNET EXPERT (JNCIE)
E Series	JNCIA-E	JNCIS-E	JNCIP-E	
Enterprise Routing and Switching	JNCIA-ENT	JNCIS-ENT	JNCIP-ENT	JNCIE-ENT
Firewall/VPN		JNCIS-FWV		
Intrusion Detection and Prevention (IDP)	JNCIA-IDP			
Junos Pulse Access Control		JNCIS-AC		
Junos Pulse Secure Access		JNCIS-SA		
Junos Security	JNCIA-JUNOS	JNCIS-SEC	JNCIP-SEC	JNCIE-SEC
QFabric		JNCIS-QF		
Service Provider Routing and Switching	JNCIA-JUNOS	JNCIS-SP	JNCIP-SP	JNCIE-SP
Wireless LAN		JNCIS-WLAN		
WX	JNCIA-WX			

TABLE 14-8 Check Point certifications.			
LEVEL	**NETWORK SECURITY**	**MANAGED SECURITY**	**ENDPOINT SECURITY**
Associate	Check Point Certified Security Principles Associate (CCSPA)		
Administrator	Check Point Certified Security Administrator (CCSA)		Checkpoint Endpoint Administrator (CCEPA)
Expert	Check Point Certified Security Expert (CCSE)	Check Point Certified Managed Security Expert (CCMSE)	Check Point Certified Endpoint Expert (CCEPE)
Master	Check Point Certified Master Architect (CCMA)	Check Point Certified Master Architect (CCMA)	

- Administration of Symantec Clearwell eDiscovery Platform 7.x
- Administration of Symantec Data Loss Prevention 11.5
- Administration of Symantec Network Access Control 12.1

Symantec also offers a more advanced certification. The Symantec Certified Professional (SCP) represents more experience and more in-depth knowledge than the SCS certifications. Currently, Symantec offers the SCP certification for Cloud Security.

Check Point

Check Point is another global manufacturer of network and security devices and software. Check Point provides training and certification paths for security professionals to encourage the highest level of knowledge and skills in the use of Check Point products. Security professionals have several certification options and can choose from among three tracks and three levels. Check Point certifications require that applicants pass an exam that involves 80 percent study materials and 20 percent hands-on experience. **TABLE 14-8** shows the Check Point certifications for each level and track.

> **NOTE**
>
> For more information on Check Point certifications, visit their website at *www.checkpoint.com/support-services /training-certification/index.html*.

14

Information Security
Professional Certifications

CHAPTER SUMMARY

In this chapter, you learned about some of the available security certifications. Although security certifications don't guarantee competence, they can provide employers with confidence that the credential holder possesses a standard level of knowledge and skills. Most organizations issue credentials for limited time periods, so you can also determine that a current credential relates to current knowledge and skills. You learned about vendor-neutral and vendor-specific certifications. Professional certifications from organizations such as (ISC)^2 and CompTIA offer vendor-neutral certifications. Vendors such as Cisco, Juniper, and Check Point all have vendor-specific certifications. You also learned about the U.S. DoD/military directive 8570.01 defining a standard for information assurance training, certification, and workforce management. This has been replaced with the newer role-based Standard 8140 for cybersecurity workforce development.

You should use certifications to help you direct your learning and measure your knowledge and experience throughout your information systems security or information assurance career. However, don't measure your value or abilities only by the number of certifications you hold. Employers do use certifications to help assess prospects, but the best assessment is the prospect's actual performance.

KEY CONCEPTS AND TERMS

Certification   Vendor-neutral certification   Vendor-specific certification
Job task analysis

CHAPTER 14 ASSESSMENT

1. A certification is an official statement validating that a person has satisfied specific requirements.

   A. True
   B. False

2. Which (ISC)^2 certification covers seven domains of security for practitioners?

   A. CISM
   B. CCNA
   C. SSCP
   D. GSEC
   E. None of the above

3. Which (ISC)^2 certification specifically addresses developing secure software?

   A. CISSP
   B. CSSLP
   C. GSEC
   D. CISA
   E. None of the above

4. Which certification is the highest level GIAC credential?

   A. CAP
   B. GSEC
   C. GCIH
   D. GSE
   E. None of the above

5. The _____ Specialist and Professional certifications require that you hold one or more certifications from an approved vendor.

6. Which CompTIA certification targets foundational security topics?

   A. Security+
   B. TIA practitioner
   C. TIA+
   D. InfoSec practitioner
   E. None of the above

7. Which ISACA certification applies to security auditors?

A. CISSP
B. SSCP
C. GSEC
D. CCNA
E. None of the above

8. The _____ professional certification is specific to performing an information systems audit.

A. CISSP
B. CISA
C. GSEC
D. CCNA
E. None of the above

9. Which network device manufacturer offers certifications in five levels: entry, associate, professional, expert, and architect?

A. Cisco Systems
B. Check Point
C. Juniper Networks
D. Symantec
E. None of the above

10. Which vendor offers separate certifications for its products in UNIX and Windows environments?

A. Cisco
B. Check Point
C. Juniper Networks
D. Symantec
E. None of the above

11. What is the main purpose of DoD Directive 8570?

A. It requires that the DoD workforce including contractors have a minimum level of training and certifications to perform their job duties.
B. It requires personnel to acquire security training.

C. It requires personnel to acquire security certifications.
D. It requires DoD facilities and contractors to provide security training.
E. It requires DoD facilities and contractors to enforce security policies.

12. Which is the purpose of a job task analysis?

A. Identify pertinent skills
B. Define the required knowledge
C. Determine the amount of experience required
D. To ensure that the job description is defensible in court
E. All of the above

13. A vendor-neutral certification is better than a vendor-specific certification.

A. True
B. False

14. Having a certification does not guarantee your level of competency in performing a job task or job function.

A. True
B. False

15. Which of the following is true about the CompTIA Security+ certification?

A. Globally recognized
B. Entry-level foundational certification
C. Requires a thorough understanding of security terms and definitions
D. Approved by the DoD for foundational, entry-level information systems security training
E. All of the above

14

Information Security
Professional Certifications

U.S. Compliance Laws

EVERY DAY CYBERSPACE BRINGS NEW threats to U.S. citizens and organizations. People are sharing more data than ever before. People share data online to purchase goods and services. They also share data to network with colleagues and connect with friends. Organizations collect and use data to conduct business. Federal and state governments collect and use information to provide for their citizens.

With the increased collection of data comes questions about proper use of data. People demand that the organizations entrusted with their sensitive data take steps to protect data. If the organizations don't voluntarily protect those data, people often say, "There ought to be a law." The United States doesn't have one comprehensive data protection law. Instead, many federal data protection laws focus on specific types of data. These laws require organizations to use security controls to protect the different kinds of data that they collect. Laws aren't optional. If a law applies to an organization, the organization must follow it. Sometimes organizations must follow a number of data protection laws. This chapter presents the U.S. compliance laws enacted in the past 15 years. It focuses on the security and privacy protection requirements required by those laws. This chapter also introduces the international Payment Card Industry Data Security Standard (PCI DSS) that, though not a law, must be followed for any organizations storing, processing, or transmitting cardholder data (CHD).

Chapter 15 Topics

This chapter covers the following topics and concepts:

- What compliance is
- What the Federal Information Security Modernization Act is
- What the Health Insurance Portability and Accountability Act is
- What the Gramm-Leach-Bliley Act is
- What the Sarbanes-Oxley Act is
- What the Family Educational Rights and Privacy Act is
- What the Children's Internet Protection Act is
- What the Payment Card Industry Data Security Standard (PCI DSS) is
- How to make sense of information security compliance laws

Chapter 15 Goals

When you complete this chapter, you will be able to:

- Explain what compliance is and how it's related to information security
- Describe the main features of the Federal Information Security Modernization Act
- Describe the main features of the Health Insurance Portability and Accountability Act
- Describe the main features of the Gramm-Leach-Bliley Act
- Describe the main features of the Sarbanes-Oxley Act
- Describe the main features of the Family Educational Rights and Privacy Act
- Describe the Children's Internet Protection Act
- Describe the requirements of the Payment Card Industry Data Security Standard

Compliance Is the Law

Organizations use and store a lot of data. For many organizations, information is one of their most important assets. They use it to conduct business. They use large and complex databases to keep track of customer product preferences. They use these same information technology (IT) systems to manage the products and services that they offer customers. Organizations also transfer data to other businesses. They often collect data that most people consider sensitive. These are data that you can use to identify a person, called **personally identifiable information (PII)**. PII includes the following:

- First, middle, and last name
- Home mailing address
- Social Security numbers
- Driver's license numbers
- Financial account data, such as account numbers or personal identification numbers (PINs)
- Health data and biometric data
- Authentication credentials, such as logon or usernames and passwords

Unfortunately, organizations sometimes don't do a very good job of protecting PII. They might lose the data. News headlines call this a *data breach*. They also could use it in ways their customers and clients don't approve. When organizations don't voluntarily protect PII, governments create laws that force them to. Once the laws are enacted, these organizations must follow them. This is called **compliance**.

Compliance is an important legal concept. In the legal system, compliance is the act of following laws, rules, and regulations that apply to your organization. For an organization, compliance involves not only following laws and regulations but interpreting them so that policies and procedures can be defined. An organization must document policies, standards, procedures, or guidelines as part of its compliance activities. An organization must be able to prove it is compliant in case of a lawsuit or litigation.

Organizations under a compliance law should do the following:

- Review the compliance law and its requirements.
- Assign a designated compliance officer or individual responsible and accountable for your organization's compliance.
- Create policies, standards, procedures, and guidelines to comply with legal and regulatory requirements.
- Identify your organization's gaps in compliance and prioritize the gap remediation.
- Implement proper security controls and countermeasures throughout your IT infrastructure in support of the compliance law's requirements.
- Create and deliver annual security awareness training that educates employees about the organization's legal requirements for compliance.

> **TIP**
>
> Demonstrating proper forward due diligence is paramount if your organization is not in compliance. An organization must be able to prove that it's complying with laws every day. A starting point for any organization's compliance is to define and document policies, standards, procedures, and guidelines. Once documented, implementing these policies and procedures is required to demonstrate implementation maturity.

> **TIP**
>
> Organizations typically implement role-based access control mechanisms in their applications to ensure the confidentiality of sensitive data. Masking is used to "X out" pertinent characters of sensitive data. For example, a 16-digit primary access number (PAN) would be masked as follows: XXXX-XXXX-XXXX-1234, displaying only the last four numbers of the 16-digit credit card number. Full data encryption would of course make the sensitive data "unreadable" as follows: @#$2 – AAD8 – @#(+ – !@#D.

Compliance not only includes the actual state of being compliant; it also includes the steps and processes taken to become compliant. Compliance usually asks the questions: What are the rules? How must the rules be followed? If an organization fails to meet its obligations, it can be subject to penalties.

The United States doesn't have one comprehensive data protection law. Instead, many laws focus on different types of data found in different vertical industries. These laws contain privacy and information security concepts and requirements. They also focus on how data can be used and how data must be protected. A number of federal agencies regulate compliance with these types of laws. You will learn briefly about these laws in this chapter. Be aware, though, that each one of these laws is long and detailed and will require more scrutiny than can be provided here. In fact, each one could easily be a book topic on its own. Later in this chapter, you will be introduced to the Payment Card Industry Data Security Standard (PCI DSS), which is the governing standard, though not an actual law, for how merchants and service providers are to store, process, or transmit cardholder data (CHD). **TABLE 15-1** lists the relevant laws, the type of data they address, and the federal government authority or certification body that regulates compliance with them.

As an information systems security professional, you must be familiar with the compliance laws that impact your organization. Your job is not to understand the legal implications of the law but rather know how that law impacts your organization and what you must do from an IT security perspective. As an information systems security professional, you will be responsible for working with your organization's legal counsel, executive

TABLE 15-1	Laws that influence information security.

NAME OF LAW	INFORMATION REGULATED	REGULATING AGENCY
Children's Internet Protection Act (CIPA)	Internet access in certain schools and libraries	Federal Trade Commission (FTC)
Family Educational Rights and Privacy Act (FERPA)	Student educational records	U.S. Department of Education (DOE)
Federal Information Security Management Act (FISMA 2002)	Federal information systems	Office of Management and Budget (OMB)
Federal Information Security Modernization Act (FISMA 2014)	Federal information systems	Office of Management and Budget (OMB) and U.S. Department of Homeland Security (DHS)
Gramm-Leach-Bliley Act (GLBA)	Consumer financial information	FTC
Health Insurance Portability and Accountability Act (HIPAA)	Protected health information	Department of Health and Human Services (DHHS)
Payment Card Industry Data Security Standard (PCI DSS)*	Cardholder data: First and last name, 16-digit primary access number (PAN), three-digit authorization code (CVV), expiration date (MM/YY)	Payment card issuers: VISA, MasterCard, Discover, American Express, and JCB
Sarbanes-Oxley Act (SOX)	Corporate financial information	Securities and Exchange Commission (SEC)

* PCI DSS is an international standard, not a law.

How Are Privacy and Information Security Related?

Most federal data protection laws contain both privacy and information security requirements. Information security and privacy are closely related. However, it's important for you to know that they're not the same. *Privacy* is a person's right to control the use and disclosure of his or her own personal information. This means that people have the opportunity to assess a situation and determine how their data are used. *Information security* is the process used to keep data private. Security is the process; privacy is a result.

Privacy is a simple term that describes a number of different but related concepts. At its core, privacy means that a person has control of his or her personal data. *Control* means that a person can decide how his or her data can be collected, used, and shared with third parties. This is accomplished via an organization's privacy policy statement. Individuals are provided with an "opt-in" or "opt-out" option regarding the organization's use of their privacy data.

Most traditional views on privacy also include the belief that the government's power to interfere in the privacy of its citizens is limited. This means that people and their information must be free from unreasonable government intrusion. The government must not investigate people or their personal information without a good reason. Courts spend a lot of time defining the reasons to allow governments to investigate their citizens. This is a core privacy concept for most Americans.

Information systems security is about ensuring the confidentiality, integrity, and availability of IT infrastructures and the systems they comprise. Securing data is one thing; making data private is another. Many organizations prevent their own employees from accessing customer privacy data; for instance, some customer relationship management systems block out the first five digits of an individual's Social Security number, requiring only the last four digits for authentication. Just because information is secure doesn't mean it's private.

Information security is about maintaining the confidentiality of data. Data can be business data or customer privacy data. Data encryption can secure the data. Role-based access controls can ensure that only authorized individuals can access the private data. Systems grant access to data based on the role of that employee. By implementing security controls, privacy of data can be achieved within an organization.

management, and IT organizations. Your key responsibility is to help bridge the gap between the compliance law's requirements and your organization's implementation of security controls to achieve compliance.

Federal Information Security

The federal government is the largest creator and user of information in the United States.[1] Government IT systems hold data that are critical for government operations. These systems contain data that are important for running the business of the federal government. They also hold sensitive military data. These systems also hold personal information about U.S. citizens. All of these personal data are very sensitive, too.

Federal IT systems and the data in them are attractive criminal targets. In 2010, the federal chief information officer (CIO), Vivek Kundra, said that the government's computers are attacked millions of times each day.[2] This isn't very surprising.

The Federal Information Security Management Act of 2002

In 2002, Congress created the Federal Information Security Management Act (FISMA).[3] This act was created partly in response to the September 11, 2001, terrorist attacks. The attacks stressed the need for better information security in the federal government. After the attacks, the government realized that computer security for federal IT systems wasn't what it should be. FISMA changed the government's approach to information security. It superseded most of the federal government's previous computer security laws. It's now the primary law that defines how federal agencies must secure their IT systems.

FISMA applies to federal agencies and their IT systems. Federal agencies fall under the executive branch of the U.S. government. They report to the president. The Office of Management and Budget (OMB) is responsible for FISMA compliance.

Purpose and Main Requirements

FISMA defines *information security* as protecting federal agency IT systems to provide confidentiality, integrity, and availability.[4] Agencies must protect their IT systems (and data in those systems) from unauthorized use, access, disruption, modification, and destruction.

FISMA requires each federal agency to create an agency-wide information security program that includes:

- **Risk assessments**—Agencies must perform risk assessments. They must measure the harm that could result from unauthorized access to or use of their IT systems. Agencies must base their information security programs on the results of these risk assessments.

- **Annual inventory**—Agencies must inventory their IT systems. They must update their inventory each year.

- **Policies and procedures**—Agencies must create policies and procedures to reduce risk to an acceptable level. The policies must protect IT systems throughout their life cycles. Agencies also must create configuration management policies.

- **Subordinate plans**—Agencies must make sure they have plans for securing networks, facilities, and systems or groups of IT systems. These plans are for technologies or system components that are a part of the larger information security program.

- **Security awareness training**—Agencies must give training to employees and any other users of their IT systems, including contractors. This training must make people aware of risks to the agency's IT systems. It also must make them aware of their duties to protect these systems.

- **Testing and evaluation**—Agencies must test their security controls at least once a year. They must test management, operational, and technical controls for each IT system.

- **Remedial actions**—Agencies must have a plan to fix weaknesses in their information security programs.

- **Incident response**—Agencies must have an incident response procedure. They must state how the agency detects and resolves incidents. Agencies also must report incidents to the Department of Homeland Security (DHS).

- **Continuity of operations**—Agencies must have business continuity plans as part of their information security programs.

An agency's information security program applies to any other organization that uses the agency's IT systems or data. An agency must protect the IT systems that support its operations. It must protect them even if another agency or contractor owns the IT systems. This can broaden the scope of FISMA beyond a federal agency. This is important because IT systems and functions are often outsourced. Systems security professionals must know if any of their organization's IT systems use or process information belonging to federal agencies. If they do, then FISMA may apply.

One of the most important parts of a FISMA information security program is that agencies test and evaluate it. FISMA requires agencies to test their IT systems at least yearly. They must test IT systems with greater risk more often. Agencies also must review the information security controls on these systems. FISMA requires agencies to apply some types of controls, such as access control measures. Agencies must make sure their controls work. Yearly testing recognizes that security is an ongoing process. Agencies must always monitor their security risk. They also must monitor the controls put in place to address that risk.

> **NOTE**
>
> Under FISMA, agencies must name a senior official in charge of information security. In most cases, this is the chief information security officer (CISO). These officials must be information security professionals with security experience.[5]

Each agency must report yearly to the OMB on its FISMA compliance work. The report must review the agency's information security program. It also must assess the agency's progress on fixing any weaknesses in the program or security controls. An agency's report is shared widely. An agency must send a copy to certain congressional committees and other federal agencies. The OMB says that agencies shouldn't include too much information about actual IT system operations in their reports. It's possible that criminals could learn about weaknesses in federal IT systems by reading the reports.

The FISMA yearly reporting process is time consuming. Agencies spend a lot of time creating their reports. The OMB spends a lot of time reviewing them. It takes almost three full-time employees over a month to review the reports.[6] The process also is very paper-intensive. For example, in six years the Department of State spent $133 million to produce 95,000 pages of paper to meet its reporting requirements.[7] In 2010, the OMB began requiring all federal agencies to file their reports electronically. The new electronic reporting tool will allow agencies and the OMB to assess quickly the agency's information security posture.[8]

> **NOTE**
>
> You can read the OMB's 2010 FISMA report instructions at *www.whitehouse.gov /sites/default/files/omb/assets/egov_docs /fy12_fisma.pdf.*

The Federal Information Security Modernization Act of 2014

The Federal Information Security Modernization Act of 2014 was enacted in December 2014. The act formally assigned the DHS with the responsibility for developing, implementing, and ensuring federal government-wide compliance as per FISMA information security policies, procedures, and security controls. FISMA 2014 does not introduce additional security requirements, but it does clearly define the roles, responsibilities, accountabilities, requirements, and practices that are needed to fully implement FISMA security controls and requirements.

The following presents a side-by-side comparison of the FISMA 2002 and FISMA 2014 legislation:

* DHS was anointed as the governing organization that is responsible for ensuring FISMA 2014 compliance, along with the OMB.
* Reporting requirements for U.S. federal government agencies were defined.
* New guidance and reporting requirements for security incidents were announced.
* Policies and guidelines were detailed for data breach notification compliance.

OMB has the responsibility for ensuring information security policies and practices and overseeing NIST's development of standards and guidelines. DHS is leading the efforts to ensure that all U.S. federal government agencies conform to these new information security policies, standards, procedures, and guidelines. This separation of duties with FISMA 2014 is consistent with the OMB Memorandum M-10-28, which defines cybersecurity responsibilities between OMB and DHS.

Security incident response reporting and data breach notification are clearly defined in the FISMA 2014 legislation. FISMA 2014 defines a security incident as follows: "An occurrence that actually or imminently jeopardizes, without lawful authority, the integrity, confidentiality, or availability of information or an information system; or constitutes a violation or imminent threat or violation of law, security policies, security procedures, or acceptable use policies." In addition, each U.S. federal government agency is now required to report major incidents, within seven days, to Congress and additional U.S. federal government officials in OMB and/or the DHS.

The Role of the National Institute of Standards and Technology

Both versions of FISMA rely on the U.S. Department of Commerce to create information security standards and guidelines. The Department of Commerce delegated this duty to one of its agencies, the National Institute of Standards and Technology (NIST). It creates guidance that all federal agencies use for their information security programs. NIST creates standards that agencies use to classify their data and IT systems. It also creates guidelines and minimum information security controls for IT systems. Agencies must follow these standards and guidelines.

NIST creates two different types of documents. They are called Federal Information Processing Standards (FIPSs) and Special Publications (SPs). FIPSs are standards. SPs are guidelines. Under FISMA, federal agencies must follow both FIPSs and SPs.

NIST recommends using a risk management framework (RMF) approach for FISMA compliance.[9] Government agencies that organize and prioritize risk can adopt an information systems security program to mitigate that risk. The NIST RMF outlines six steps to protect federal IT systems. These steps are:

> **NOTE**
>
> You can read the updated Federal Information Security Modernization Act of 2014 here: *www.whitehouse .gov/sites/default/files/omb/assets /egov_docs/fy_2013_fisma_report _05.01.2014.pdf.*

> **NOTE**
>
> Generally, a *standard* states mandatory actions that an organization must take to protect its IT systems. A *guideline* states recommended actions that an organization should follow.

United States Computer Emergency Readiness Team

Under FISMA, the government must have a federal incident response (IR) center. The OMB is responsible for this center. In 2003, the DHS was given the responsibility to run a federal IR center. It absorbed its predecessor into a new IR center. The DHS center is called the United States Computer Emergency Readiness Team, or US-CERT.

Under FISMA, all federal agencies must report security incidents to the US-CERT. This includes incidents involving national security systems. An *incident* is a violation of computer security policies or practices. It also includes an imminent threat of violation of these policies or practices. The government has six IR categories. Agencies must report incidents within certain time periods. The reporting period depends on the incident category. Some incidents must be reported as soon as they are discovered.

The *www.us-cert.gov* website, sponsored by the DHS, provides useful cyber-awareness content for users and businesses. Those with more technical backgrounds will find the alerts, current activity, or bulletins useful. Users looking for more general-interest pieces can read the tips. Be sure to visit *www.us-cert.gov/ncas*, the National Cyber Awareness System webpage.

- **Categorize information systems**—An agency must sort its IT systems based on risk.
- **Select the minimum security controls**—An agency must select controls for its IT systems based on their risk category.
- **Implement security controls in IT systems**—An agency must apply controls in certain areas that are specified by NIST. Included in these areas are access control, contingency planning, and incident response.
- **Assess security controls for effectiveness**—An agency must assess its controls on a continuous basis to make sure that they're effective in reducing risk.
- **Authorize the IT system for processing**—An agency must test its IT systems and approve their operation. An agency specifically must accept the risks of operation prior to allowing a system to operate. This process used to be known in FISMA terminology as *certification and accreditation*.
- **Continuously monitor security controls**—An agency must monitor its security controls continuously to make sure they're effective. They also must document any changes to their IT systems. They must assess changes for new risks.

NIST's RMF recommends a continuous process of categorization and assessment. It also requires continuous monitoring. **FIGURE 15-1** shows the RMF process.

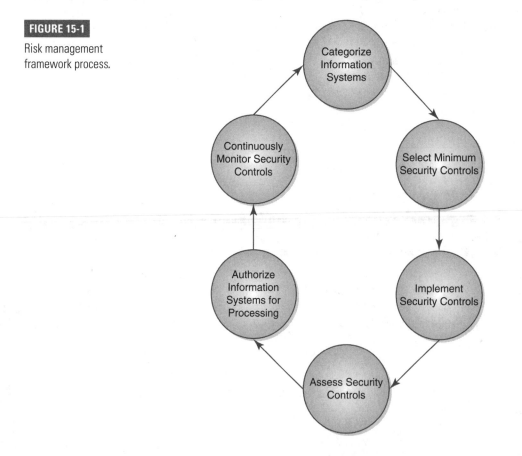

FIGURE 15-1

Risk management
framework process.

National Security Systems

FISMA requires federal agencies to secure national security systems (NSSs) using a risk-based approach. These systems are used for:

- Intelligence activities
- National defense
- Foreign policy
- Military activities

These systems must be specially protected due to their national security significance.

The Committee on National Security Systems (CNSS) oversees FISMA activities. The CNSS reports to the President of the United States. It has 21 voting members. They include officials from the National Security Administration (NSA), Central Intelligence Agency (CIA), and Department of Defense (DoD). You can learn more about the CNSS at *www.cnss.gov*.

Federal agencies with national security systems must follow CNSS policies, which use the same six-step process for protecting these systems as the NIST RMF. NIST and the CNSS worked together to create these policies.

The Health Insurance Portability and Accountability Act

Most people consider their health information to be among the most sensitive types of personal information. It can be full of private details. People share this information with health care providers to receive treatment. Their medical records include details on illness diagnoses, lab results, and treatment options. These records also contain details about lifestyle, chronic conditions, or mental health counseling.

People fear they will be embarrassed if their health data aren't kept secret. Some people may even fear for their lives if particularly intimate facts, such as reasons for health counseling, are disclosed. Other people may fear that insurance companies or employers could reject them because of information in their health records.

People often feel that they have little control over how their health information is shared and protected. Almost every day media reports confirm that these are valid concerns. For example, in November 2009, Health Net of the Northeast, Inc., reported that 1.5 million patient records were affected when it lost an external hard drive. The hard drive also contained the personal information of physicians who participated in its network. The data on the drive weren't encrypted.

The federal government recognizes that health information is highly sensitive. It created the Health Insurance Portability and Accountability Act to protect it.

Purpose and Scope

Congress passed the Health Insurance Portability and Accountability Act (HIPAA) in 1996. It was amended in 2009 by the Health Information Technology for Economic and Clinical Health (HITECH) Act. HIPAA is best known for its data protection rules that address the security and privacy of personally identifiable health information. The Department of Health and Human Services (HHS) makes these rules and oversees their compliance.

HIPAA applies to **protected health information (PHI)**. PHI is any individually identifiable information about a person's health. It includes mental and physical health data as well as past, present, or future information.[10] It also includes information about paying for health care. PHI can be in any form. It's commonly considered to be all information that is put into a person's medical record.

Under HIPAA, covered entities may only use PHI in certain ways. The term **covered entity** is defined by the law. It refers to very specific types of entities that must follow HIPAA. These entities include:

- Health plans
- Health care clearinghouses
- Any health care provider that transmits PHI in an electronic form

Determining which entities are covered under HIPAA can be complicated. Generally speaking, HIPAA covers most health care providers. HHS provides tools to help entities determine whether they're covered by HIPAA. Those tools are available at *www.hhs. gov/ocr/privacy/hipaa/understanding/coveredentities/index.html.*

HIPAA also applies to the **business associates** of covered entities. A business associate is an organization that performs a health care activity for a covered entity. Covered entities may outsource some health care functions, such as claims and billing, to these organizations. They must comply with HIPAA. Under the HITECH Act, HHS may directly require business associates to comply with HIPAA.

The HITECH Act, enacted as part of the American Recovery and Reinvestment Act of 2009, was designed to promote the widespread adoption and standardization of health information technology. Providers that adopted electronic health record (EHR) systems can apply for meaningful use incentives to help pay for transition to EHR platforms. Participation in federally funded programs such as the meaningful use program requires providers to maintain HIPAA security and privacy rule compliance.

Main Requirements of the HIPAA Privacy Rule

The Privacy Rule determines how covered entities must protect the privacy of PHI. HHS published the final Privacy Rule in December 2000. Compliance with the Privacy Rule was required in April 2003. The Privacy Rule represents the first time the U.S. government specified federal privacy protections for PHI.

Under the Privacy Rule, covered entities may not use or disclose a person's PHI without his or her written consent. The term *use* refers to the way a covered entity shares or handles PHI within its organization. *Disclosure* refers to the way a covered entity shares PHI with other organizations that may not be affiliated with it.

There are some exceptions to the Privacy Rule. These exceptions allow a covered entity to share a person's PHI without a person's written consent. The main permitted use and disclosure of PHI under the Privacy Rule is for the entity's own treatment, payment, or health care operations. A covered entity doesn't need a person's written consent to share PHI for this purpose, because it's assumed that most people want their health care providers to use their PHI to provide medical treatment. Treatment, payment, and health care operations are common covered-entity activities. Requiring a person's written consent to complete these functions would be inefficient.

There are other times in which a covered entity may disclose PHI without consent, such as reporting victims of child abuse and neglect. The rules for disclosing PHI without consent are complicated. Covered entities must analyze the rules carefully to make sure that they follow them.

Even if a covered entity is allowed to use or disclose PHI without written consent, it must follow the **minimum necessary rule**.[11] A covered entity may disclose the amount of PHI necessary to satisfy the reason why the information is being used or disclosed, but no more. A covered entity must use its professional judgment and make reasonable efforts to limit its use or disclosure. A health care provider shouldn't disclose a person's entire medical record if only a portion of it is needed to respond to a request.

A covered entity must inform people about how it uses and discloses PHI.[12] It does this in a privacy notice. The covered entity must only use and disclose PHI in the ways described by this notice. The Privacy Rule has many requirements for how these notices must be written. The most important requirement is that a covered entity must use plain language to draft its notice. An average person must be able to understand it.

The Privacy Rule requires covered entities to mitigate an unauthorized use or disclosure of PHI.[13] Prior to the HITECH Act, a covered entity didn't have to notify people if their PHI was used or disclosed in an unauthorized manner. The HITECH Act now requires them to do so. It creates notification requirements that covered entities must follow in the event of a breach of unsecured PHI.[14] PHI must be encrypted through an HHS-approved process to be considered secure.

Both covered entities and business associates must follow the breach notification rules. If a covered entity has a breach of unsecured PHI, it must notify the victims within 60 days of the discovery. A breach is "discovered" on the first day that the covered entity knows about it. Individuals must be notified without "unreasonable delay." A covered entity may delay notification if a law enforcement official requests it. HIPAA has many rules for how notice of a breach must be given.

> **NOTE**
>
> Under HIPAA, a *breach* is any impermissible use or disclosure of unsecured PHI that harms its security or privacy. The use or disclosure must cause a significant risk of harm to the affected person. The harm can be financial or reputational.[15]

Under the breach notification rules, business associates also are required to notify covered entities following their discovery of a breach of unsecured PHI. The business associate must tell the covered entity no later than 60 days after it discovers the breach. It must help the covered entity notify victims.

CMS, the Centers for Medicare & Medicaid Services (www.cms.gov) actually tracks covered entities that have had a data breach or HIPAA violation assessed by DHHS. In addition, CMS released the publication *Risk Management Handbook: Incident Handling*, a manual for covered entities participating in federally funded programs. This document can be found here: *www.cms.gov/Research-Statistics-Data-and-Systems/CMS -Information-Technology/InformationSecurity/Downloads/RMH_VII_7-2_Incident _Handling_Procedure.pdf*.

Main Requirements of the HIPAA Security Rule

Since 2005, the HHS's Security Rule has required covered entities to protect the confidentiality, integrity, and availability of electronic PHI. This rule requires covered entities to use security safeguards to protect **electronic protected health information (EPHI)**. EPHI is PHI that is stored in electronic form.

Like the Privacy Rule, the Security Rule was the first time the federal government addressed security safeguards for electronic PHI. The rule requires covered entities to protect all EPHI they create, receive, or maintain. They also must protect EPHI they transmit.[16]

They must protect EPHI from reasonably anticipated threats. They also must guard it from uses or disclosures that aren't allowed by the Privacy Rule.

The Security Rule requires covered entities to create an information security program.[17] They have flexibility in creating these programs. They don't have to use specific types of security technology. To create its program, the covered entity must consider:

- Its size and complexity
- Its technical infrastructure, hardware, and software security resources
- The costs of security measures
- The potential risks to EPHI[18]

> **NOTE**
>
> An information security safeguard is also called an *information security control*. Different laws use either the term *safeguard* or *control*. Sometimes laws use these terms interchangeably. They mean the same thing.

The Security Rule also requires covered entities to use information security principles to protect EPHI. They must use administrative, physical, and technical safeguards. The rule contains instructions on each type of safeguard. Some safeguards are *required*. Covered entities must implement them. Others are *addressable*. Covered entities have discretion in implementing addressable specifications. For addressable specifications, the entity must assess whether the control is reasonable and appropriate in its environment.[19] If it is, the covered entity must use it. If it isn't, the covered entity doesn't have to use it.

Half of the safeguards required by the Security Rule are administrative controls. They are actions, policies, and procedures that a covered entity must implement to follow the Security Rule. There are nine different administrative safeguards. **TABLE 15-2** summarizes them.

Physical safeguards are controls put in place to protect a covered entity's physical resources. They protect information systems, equipment, and buildings from environmental threats. The Security Rule contains four physical security standards. **TABLE 15-3** summarizes the required and addressable physical safeguards required by the Security Rule.

Technical safeguards are applied in the hardware and software of an information system. The Security Rule contains five technical security standards. **TABLE 15-4** summarizes the required and addressable technical safeguards required by the Security Rule.

Oversight

HHS oversees compliance with the HIPAA Privacy and Security Rules. It delegated this function to its Office for Civil Rights (OCR). The OCR enforces rules against both covered entities and business associates. The OCR investigates and responds to complaints from people who claim that a covered entity has violated HIPAA.

TABLE 15-2 Security Rule administrative safeguards.

SAFEGUARD	REQUIRED SPECIFICATIONS	ADDRESSABLE SPECIFICATIONS
Security Management Process	Risk analysis Risk management Sanction policy Information system activity review	
Name an Official Responsible for Security Rule Compliance	Required	
Workforce Security Measures to Protect EPHI		Authorization and/or supervision Workforce clearance procedure Termination procedures
EPHI Access Management	Isolating health care clearinghouse function	Access authorization Access establishment and modification
Security Awareness and Training		Security reminders Protection from malicious software Logon monitoring Password management
Security Incident Procedures	Response and reporting	
Contingency Plan	Data backup plan Disaster recovery plan Emergency mode operation plan	Testing and revision procedure Applications and data criticality analysis
Evaluation of Security Safeguards Program	Required	
Business Associate Contracts and Other Arrangements	Written contracts or other arrangements	

TABLE 15-3 Security Rule physical safeguards.

SAFEGUARD	REQUIRED SPECIFICATIONS	ADDRESSABLE SPECIFICATIONS
Facility Access Controls		Contingency operations Facility security plan Access control and validation procedures Maintenance records
Workstation Use	Required	
Workstation Security	Required	
Device and Media Controls	Disposal Media reuse	Accountability Data backup and storage

TABLE 15-4 Security Rule technical safeguards.

SAFEGUARD	REQUIRED SPECIFICATIONS	ADDRESSABLE SPECIFICATIONS
Access Control	Unique user identification Emergency access procedure	Automatic logoff Encryption and decryption
Audit Controls	Required	
Integrity		Mechanism to authenticate electronic protected health information
Person or Entity Authentication	Required	
Transmission Security		Integrity controls Encryption

> **NOTE**
>
> Information about the OCR complaint process is available at *www.hhs.gov/ocr /privacy/hipaa/complaints/index.html.*

The OCR acts as the police force enforcing HIPAA compliance. The OCR also can levy fines on a covered entity that is in violation of HIPAA security or privacy rule compliance. The HITECH Act defined a tiered system for assessing the level of each HIPAA privacy violation and, therefore, its penalty:

- **Tier A**—This tier represents violations for which the offender didn't realize that he or she violated the act and would have handled the matter differently if he or she had. This results in a $100 fine for each violation, and the total imposed for such violations cannot exceed $25,000 for the calendar year.

- **Tier B**—For violations due to reasonable cause but not "willful neglect." The result is a $1,000 fine for each violation, and the fines cannot exceed $100,000 for the calendar year.

- **Tier C**—For violations due to willful neglect that the organization ultimately corrected. The result is a $10,000 fine for each violation, and the fines cannot exceed $250,000 for the calendar year.

- **Tier D**—For violations of willful neglect that the organization did not correct. The result is a $50,000 fine for each violation, and the fines cannot exceed $1,500,000 for the calendar year.

Omnibus Regulations

In January 2013, the Omnibus Rule was released, providing a catchall update to HIPAA and the HITECH Act rulings. The Omnibus Rule tightens the requirements of covered entities and business associates in the following capacities:

- Modification to the standard for reporting breaches of unsecured PHI
- Extension of HHS enforcement authority over business associates
- Expansion of the definition of the term *business associate* to include health information organizations, e-prescribing gateways, entities that provide data transmission services for PHI and that require routine access to such PHI, and personal health record vendors

- Modifications to the requirements for business associate agreements
- New obligations for business associates to enter into business associate agreements
- Removal of limitations on the liability of covered entities for the acts and omissions of business associates
- Changes to the requirements for notices of privacy practices
- New limitations on the sale of PHI
- New limitations on and clarifications concerning the use and disclosure of PHI for marketing
- Relaxation of certain limitations on the use of PHI for fundraising
- Improvement to the regulations concerning authorizations for the use or disclosure of PHI for research

Covered entities and business associates must have updated their HIPAA policies and procedures, notice of privacy practices, and business associate agreements in order to be omnibus compliant by September 30, 2013.

The Gramm-Leach-Bliley Act

According to the Verizon *2013 Data Breach Investigations Report*, during the period 2003–2012, more than 2,500 known data breaches occurred, with over 1.1+ billion compromised records.[20] Leading the pack of victims at 37 percent of all breaches in 2012 were financial organizations. According to the study, 92 percent of all breaches were perpetrated by actors outside the organization. State-affiliated perpetrators tied to the People's Republic of China topped the list for efforts to steal intellectual property (IP) assets from U.S. interests. This finding represents about one-fifth of all breaches involving the theft of IP.

> **NOTE**
>
> According to the FTC, CY2012 alone accounted for more than $21 billion in identity theft fraudulent purchases. The total cost to consumers, financial institutions, and merchants is even higher.

Consumer financial information is personally identifiable information. It's information that a person provides to a vendor to get a good or service. Customers can provide it to get services from banks or other financial institutions. These institutions collect and use these data to provide home or car loans, approve credit cards, or open checking accounts. Consumers demand that their financial institutions protect this information.

The Gramm-Leach-Bliley Act (GLBA) addresses the privacy and security of consumer financial information. GLBA, also known as the Financial Services Modernization Act of 1999, made great changes in the banking industry. Its main purpose was to allow banks, securities, and insurance companies to merge. This wasn't allowed before GLBA. The financial industry urged Congress to pass GLBA so that customers could use one company for all their financial service needs.

After GLBA, these new, larger corporations would have access to large amounts of consumer financial information. People feared that their privacy would suffer. To help ease that fear, Congress included privacy and security protections in GLBA. This is similar to the HIPAA rule where both privacy and security requirements are now mandated.

In concert with GLBA is the Federal Financial Institutions Examination Council's (FFIEC) regulatory committee that services the U.S. banking community. The Council is a formal inter-agency body responsible for defining and prescribing uniform principles, standards, and report forms for the federal examination of financial institutions by the Board of Governors of the Federal Reserve Board (FRB), the Federal Deposit Insurance Corporation (FDIC), the National Credit Union Administration (NCUA), the Office of the Comptroller of the Currency (OCC), and the Consumer Financial Protection Bureau (CFPB). In 2006, the State Liaison Committee (SLC) was added to the Council to address state-chartered banks. The Council also included members from the Conference of State Bank Supervisors (CSBS), the American Council of State Savings Supervisors (ACSSS), and the National Association of State Credit Union Supervisors.

The FFIEC Council developed a Cybersecurity Assessment Tool (Assessment) that can be used as a self-assessment tool for identifying your bank or financial institution's cybersecurity maturity. The FFIEC Cybersecurity Assessment Tool consists of two parts:

- Inherent Risk Profile Posture Assessment
- Cybersecurity Maturity Posture Assessment

The FFIEC inherent risk profile posture assessment covers the following categories:

- Technologies and Connection Types
- Delivery Channels
- Online/Mobile Products and Technology Services
- Organizational Characteristics
- External Threats

Your executive management organization must then evaluate your organization's Cybersecurity Maturity level for each of the following domains:

- Cyber Risk Management and Oversight
- Threat Intelligence and Collaboration
- Cybersecurity Controls
- External Dependency Management
- Cyber Incident Management and Resilience

By examining your organization's inherent risk profile and cybersecurity maturity posture level across all the domains, management can assess whether gap remediation and hardening are required to lower the risk impact while increasing the organization's overall cybersecurity posture. FFIEC is used to complement a banking or financial organization's ongoing risk management program and cybersecurity implementations.

In *The Consumer Sentinel Network Data Book*, the Federal Trade Commission (FTC) tracks consumer complaints for identity theft, fraud, and other consumer-related scams like Ponzi schemes. In the period January–December 2012, the FTC recorded over 2 million consumer complaints, of which fraud complaints represented just over half the total (see **FIGURE 15-2**).

Every year the FTC releases a report about fraud and identity theft based on complaints to its Consumer Sentinel Database. You can download the latest annual report at *www.ftc.gov/enforcement/consumer-sentinel-network/reports*.

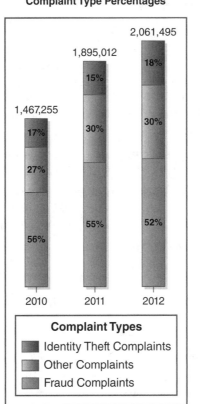

**Consumer Sentinel Network
Complaint Type Percentages**

2,061,495

1,895,012

1,467,255

18%

15%

17%

30%

30%

27%

55%

52%

56%

2010   2011   2012

Complaint Types
- Identity Theft Complaints
- Other Complaints
- Fraud Complaints

FIGURE 15-2

Consumer complaints documented by the FTC. Reproduced from Federal Trade Commission

Purpose and Scope

Because of their vulnerability to fraud, financial institutions must follow GLBA privacy and security rules to help mitigate data breaches and identity theft. Any financial transaction, such as borrowing, lending, credit counseling, debt collection, or similar activities, requires special attention in maintaining privacy of consumer data. These are transactions that have to do with money or investments. This definition is very broad. Any institution that engages in these activities must follow GLBA. GLBA applies to consumer financial activities only. These are transactions made for personal, family, or household services. GLBA doesn't apply to business transactions.

GLBA requires financial institutions to protect consumers' nonpublic financial information. **Nonpublic personal information (NPI)** is personally identifiable financial information that a consumer gives to a financial institution. It's the data that a consumer shares during a financial transaction. NPI also includes PII that an institution gets from sources other than the consumer. NPI can be in paper or electronic form. Under GLBA, NPI includes:

- Social Security number
- Financial account numbers
- Credit card numbers

15

U.S. Compliance Laws

- Date of birth
- Name, address, and phone numbers when collected with financial data
- Details of any transactions or the fact that an individual is a customer of a financial institution

GLBA is a complicated law. Compliance can be tricky. One reason is that different federal agencies have GLBA oversight responsibilities. Their responsibilities are based on the type of financial institution under review. The agencies with GLBA oversight responsibilities are:

- **The Securities and Exchange Commission (SEC)**—Oversees securities brokers and dealers.
- **The Federal Reserve System (the Fed)**—Oversees state-chartered member banks and bank holding companies.
- **The Federal Deposit Insurance Corporation (FDIC)**—Oversees state-chartered banks that aren't members of the Fed.
- **The National Credit Union Administration (NCUA)**—Oversees federally insured credit unions.
- **The Office of the Comptroller of the Currency (OCC)**—Oversees nationally chartered banks.
- **The Office of Thrift Supervision (OTS)**—Oversees all nationally chartered and some state-chartered thrifts.
- **Federal Trade Commission (FTC)**—Oversees GLBA for any financial institution that isn't regulated by one of the other agencies.

Main Requirements of the GLBA Privacy Rule

The GLBA Privacy Rule[21] went into effect July 1, 2001. All the GLBA regulatory agencies worked together to create it. Under this rule, a financial institution may not share a consumer's NPI with nonaffiliated third parties. A financial institution can share this information only when it first provides the consumer with notice of its privacy practices. This notice must tell consumers about the types of data that the institution collects. It also must state how the institution uses the collected information. The notice also must describe how the institution protects a consumer's NPI. The Privacy Rule requires that consumers have a chance to opt out of certain types of data sharing with nonaffiliated third parties.

GLBA distinguishes between customers and consumers for its notice requirements. A *consumer* is any person who gets a consumer financial product or service from a financial institution. A *customer* is a consumer who has a continuing relationship with the institution. An example of a consumer without a customer relationship is a person who withdraws cash from an ATM that doesn't belong to his or her personal bank. The person is a consumer of the bank's ATM service, but he or she is not a customer of that bank. Customers must receive the financial institution's privacy notices. A financial institution doesn't have to give a privacy notice to a consumer if it doesn't share the consumer's NPI with nonaffiliated parties.

An institution must give a customer notice of its privacy practices as soon as the customer relationship begins. Customers also must receive a copy of the privacy notice each year for as long as the relationship continues. The notice must be provided in writing and be understandable.

Financial institutions must give their privacy notice to consumers if they plan to share the consumer's NPI with nonaffiliated parties. The privacy notice must give the consumer a chance to stop the financial institution from sharing the consumer's NPI with nonaffiliated third parties. This is called an *opt-out provision*. The privacy notice must tell consumers how to opt out. If a consumer doesn't opt out, the financial institution can share NPI in ways described by its privacy notice.

GLBA doesn't give consumers the right to opt out of situations where a financial institution shares NPI with its affiliates. In some instances, consumers don't have the ability to opt out at all. For example, consumers can't opt out of a disclosure that is required by law.

> **NOTE**
>
> A *nonaffiliated party* is an entity that isn't legally related to a financial institution. It is not the same as an affiliated party. *Affiliated parties* have a legal relationship. They are members of the same corporate family. An affiliated party is any entity that controls, is controlled by, or is under the common control of another entity. Nonaffiliated parties don't have these legal relationships with one another.

Main Requirements of the GLBA Safeguards Rule

GLBA requires the agencies that regulate financial institutions to issue security standards for those institutions to follow. This requirement is called the Safeguards Rule. The law requires each agency to create security standards that:

* Protect the security and confidentiality of customer data
* Protect against threats to the security or integrity of customer data
* Protect against unauthorized access to or use of customer data that could result in harm to a customer[22]

Unlike the Privacy Rule, the agencies with GLBA oversight responsibilities didn't work together to create one safeguards rule. The SEC issued its rule in June 2000. The Fed, FDIC, NCUA, OCC, and OTS worked together to issue a joint rule in early 2001. The FTC issued its Safeguards Rule in May 2002. These rules are all very similar to one another. For simplicity's sake, this section refers to the FTC Safeguards Rule.

The FTC Safeguards Rule[23] requires a financial institution to create a written *information security program*. The program must state how the institution collects and uses customer data. It also must describe the controls used to protect those data. Financial institutions must use administrative, technical, or physical controls. The program must protect information in paper and electronic forms.

The Safeguards Rule allows financial institutions some flexibility. It doesn't have general security program requirements that all institutions must follow. Instead, it requires financial institutions to have programs that are a good fit for their size and complexity. The programs also must be suitable for the sensitivity of the customer data that the institution uses. Data that are more sensitive require more protection. The rule also requires institutions to:

* Assign an employee to run the program
* Conduct a risk assessment to identify risks to customer information

- Assess current safeguards to make sure they're effective
- Design and implement safeguards to control risks
- Select service providers and make sure that contracts with them include terms to protect customer information
- Review the information security program regularly to account for changes in business

The Safeguards Rule allows financial institutions to pick the controls that best protect customer data. It specifies three areas that institutions must review for their programs:

- Employee management and training
- Information systems design
- Detecting and responding to attacks and system failures

Institutions must be sure to address these areas when conducting their risk assessments. They also must make sure that these areas are addressed in their information security programs.

Oversight

The agencies that oversee GLBA compliance may take action against the financial institution that they regulate. Institutions that violate GLBA can be subject to both criminal and civil penalties. Monetary fines can be substantial.

GLBA requires financial institutions to follow privacy and security rules. If your organization is a financial institution or engages in financial activities, you need to know about these rules. You will want to make sure that your organization's IT systems operate in a way that complies with the law.

The Sarbanes-Oxley Act

Many large corporate scandals rocked the early 2000s. Companies such as Enron, Adelphia, and WorldCom made news for their inaccurate and misleading financial reporting practices. These practices duped investors by making the corporations look more successful than they actually were. Many of these investors, which included corporate employees, lost large amounts of money. By the time everyone knew the truth, it was too late to recover investment losses. When these scandals came to light, they shook investor confidence in the U.S. economy. As a result, the decade from 2000 to 2009 had some of the worst stock market performance ever.[24]

Accurate information is the "investor's best tool."[25] People need accurate financial information so that they can invest wisely and make money. Investors have a hard time detecting fraud. Congress passed the Public Company Accounting Reform and Investor Protection Act in 2002 to help protect investors.[26] This law is more commonly known as the **Sarbanes-Oxley Act of 2002**. It's called SOX or Sarbox in many resources. President George W. Bush signed SOX into law on July 30, 2002. At that time, he called SOX "the most far-reaching reforms of American business practices since the time of Franklin Delano Roosevelt."[27]

Purpose and Scope

The main goal of SOX is to protect investors from financial fraud. SOX supplements other federal securities laws. It applies to **publicly traded companies** that must register with the Securities and Exchange Commission. Investors own a publicly traded company by buying its stock on a stock exchange. SOX doesn't apply to **privately held companies.**

SOX is a very detailed act with many provisions. When it was first enacted, most companies assumed that it didn't have any IT components. Congress didn't mention IT anywhere within the act. This opinion changed as companies began to study SOX more carefully. Many SOX provisions require companies to verify the accuracy of their financial information. Since IT systems hold many types of financial information, companies and auditors quickly realized that these systems were part of SOX compliance. That meant that the way those systems are used and the controls used to safeguard those systems had to be reviewed for SOX compliance.

> **NOTE**
>
> The two most popular U.S. stock exchanges are the New York Stock Exchange (NYSE) and the NASDAQ Stock Market. National securities exchanges are registered with the SEC. You can learn more at *www .sec.gov/divisions/marketreg /mrexchanges.shtml.*

The relationship between IT and SOX compliance continues to evolve. This section focuses on SOX Section 404 certification requirements. Section 404 requires an organization's executive officers to establish, maintain, review, and report on the effectiveness of the company's internal controls over financial reporting (ICFR). An organization's executives must understand how the organization's IT systems work in order to make these certifications. This section has caused compliance headaches for IT professionals.

SOX Control Certification Requirements

SOX Section 404 requires a company's executive management to report on the effectiveness of the company's ICFR. Management makes this certification to help ensure that a company's financial reports are accurate. It helps protect investors from fraudulent financial activities. Management must make this certification on documents that a company files with the SEC.

A company must create, document, and test its ICFR. It must report on its ICFR every year. After a company makes its yearly report, outside auditors must review it. The outside auditors must verify that the ICFR specified in the report actually work.

Under SEC rules, ICFR are processes that provide reasonable assurance that an organization's financial reports are reliable. ICFR provide management with reasonable assurance that:

- Financial reports, records, and data are accurately maintained.
- Transactions are prepared according to accounting rules and are properly recorded.
- Unauthorized acquisition or use of data or assets that could affect financial statements will be prevented or detected in a timely manner.

Companies trying to comply with Section 404 quickly learned that they needed to review their IT systems. Specifically, they needed to review the ICFR on their IT systems. An Ernst & Young survey found that public companies spent 70 percent of their time addressing IT

15

controls in their first year of SOX compliance.[28] Companies spent a lot of time on IT controls because their IT systems contain financial data. An error in these systems could cause financial statements to contain errors or mistakes. To comply with Section 404, companies had to make sure that systems data were accurate. They had to make sure that they had processes in place to detect inaccurate data.

SOX Section 404 compliance isn't easy. Section 404 is very general about the types of ICFR that companies must implement. It doesn't give a good definition for ICFR generally. It doesn't address IT controls at all. In 2007, the SEC issued additional guidance to help companies assess ICFR during their Section 404 review. It did this in response to many complaints about the large scope of a Section 404 review. Many of these complaints focused on how to address IT controls.

The SEC stated two broad principles in its guidance:

- Management should assess how its internal controls prevent or detect significant deficiencies in financial statements.
- Management should perform a risk-based review of the effectiveness of these controls.

 NOTE

SOX doesn't specify the IT controls that companies need to implement. Instead, companies must determine the best controls for their systems.

The SEC also said that management must exercise its professional judgment to limit the scope of a Section 404 review. It reminded companies that SOX applies to internal controls, including IT controls that affect financial reporting only.[29] This means that a Section 404 review certainly applies to IT systems that process financial data. It might not apply to IT systems that process nonfinancial data.

Management must review general IT controls to make sure that IT systems operate properly and consistently. Organizations use many approaches to evaluating their IT controls. The controls must provide management with reasonable assurance that IT systems operate properly to protect financial reporting. **TABLE 15-5** shows how the goals of ICFR match up with information security goals.

A company can't escape SOX Section 404 liability by outsourcing financial functions. SOX requires companies to monitor ICFR for outsourced operations as well. Many companies do this by asking their outsourcing companies to provide them with a special audit report about the outsourced operations. A company must review this report to determine whether the outsourcing company's controls are sufficient.

TABLE 15-5 Internal controls and information security goals.

STEPS TAKEN TO MEET INTERNAL CONTROLS	INFORMATION SECURITY GOALS
Financial reports, records, and data are accurately maintained.	Integrity
Transactions are prepared according to GAAP rules and properly recorded.	Integrity, availability
Unauthorized acquisition or use of data or assets that could affect financial statements will be prevented or detected in a timely manner.	Confidentiality, integrity, availability

SOX Records Retention Requirements

SOX contains some records retention provisions. As a systems security professional, you must know about these requirements. This is because most companies store many of their records electronically. Some studies estimate that 93 percent of all business documents are created and stored electronically.[30] Companies must understand how their IT systems work in order to meet SOX retention requirements. You will be instrumental in helping your organization understand how to manage and secure its electronic records.

SOX requires public companies to maintain their financial audit papers for seven years.[31] Audit papers are most documents used in an audit. They're the materials that support the conclusions made in an audit report. SOX takes a very broad view of the type of records that must be saved. This includes work papers, memoranda, and correspondence. It also includes any other records created, sent, or received in connection with the audit. SOX includes electronic records.

SOX requires that a public company retain the records and documentation that it uses to assess its internal controls over financial reporting.[32] Guidance issued by the SEC recognizes that this documentation takes a number of different forms. It also includes electronic data. Companies must permanently retain this information.

The penalties for failing to retain records for the right amount of time can be severe. SOX makes it a crime for a person or company to knowingly and willfully violate its records retention provisions. A person who violates this provision can face fines and up to 10 years in prison.

Oversight

The Securities and Exchange Commission oversees and enforces most SOX provisions. The SEC was created under the Securities and Exchange Act of 1934. Its mission is to protect investors and maintain the integrity of the securities industry. The SEC has the power to investigate and sanction public companies that don't comply with SOX.

The SEC has five commissioners, appointed by the U.S. president. These commissioners serve for five-year terms. No more than three of the commissioners may belong to the same political party. The SEC has 11 regional offices in the United States.

SOX requires the SEC to review a public company's yearly and quarterly reports at least once every three years.[33] It must do this to try to detect fraud and inaccurate financial statements that could harm the investing public. The SEC has discretion in deciding how often to review companies.

> **FYI**
>
> Many federal and state laws contain records retention requirements. SOX is another law to add to that list. Organizations should develop document retention policies to help them track their various obligations.

The Family Educational Rights and Privacy Act

Educational institutions such as colleges, universities, and grade schools have access to lots of information about their students. They can collect and store the following types of student data:

- Demographic information
- Address and contact information
- Parental demographic information
- Parental address and contact information
- Grade information
- Disciplinary information

These data are useful to educational institutions in educating students. This information also is very sensitive. Privacy concerns are raised if an educational institution improperly discloses this information to third parties. It could be embarrassing for the student and the student's family. The Family Educational Rights and Privacy Act (FERPA) is the main federal law protecting the privacy of student information.

Purpose and Scope

Congress created FERPA in 1974.[34] It applies to any education agency or institution that receives federal funding. Educational institutions include:

- Community colleges
- Colleges and universities
- Primary and secondary schools (kindergarten through 12th grade)
- State and local educational agencies (such as a school board)
- Schools or agencies offering a preschool program
- Any other educational institution that receives federal funding

This section collectively refers to these educational institutions as *schools*. Most educational institutions receive some kind of funding from the U.S. Department of Education. If a school chooses not to comply with FERPA, it can't receive any federal funds. Federal funding is very important to most schools. As a result, almost all of them comply with FERPA. It's possible that some small private schools don't receive federal funds. If they don't receive federal funds, they don't have to comply with FERPA.

FERPA is a very detailed act with many provisions. Its primary goal is to protect the privacy of student records. A *student record* includes any data about a student that a school keeps. These records include written documents, computer media, video, film, and photographs. They also include any records maintained by an outside party acting on a school's behalf. The records can be in paper or electronic form.

FERPA doesn't require that specific information security controls be implemented to protect student records. However, systems security professionals must be aware of FERPA's requirements. If an organization is an educational institution or maintains records for a

FYI

Unlike the generic definition for personally identifiable information that has been used throughout this section, FERPA specifically defines personally identifiable information. When you read any law, you always must be sure to check how that law defines specific terms. Sometimes a word's legal definition can be very different from its generic definition.

school, FERPA may apply to the data it uses. The organization must then implement security controls in IT systems to protect the privacy of electronic student records.

Main Requirements

Under FERPA, students (or their parents, if the student is under 18) have the following rights:

- The right to know what data are in the student's student record and the right to inspect and review that record
- The right to request that a school correct errors in a student record
- The right to consent to have certain kinds of student data released

A school must protect its student records. In particular, it must protect the personally identifiable information that is located in the records. Under FERPA, personally identifiable information includes direct identifiers such as a student's name, Social Security number, and student number. It also can include indirect identifiers when they're matched with a student name. *Indirect identifiers* are personal characteristics that can be used to easily identify a student. Generally a school can't release a student's records to a third party without the student's written consent.

There are some exceptions in which a school can release student records without the student's consent. For example, some school officials can view student records when required by their job duties. In addition, a school can transfer a student's record from the old school to a new school without the student's consent. Schools can transfer student records for some financial aid or accreditation purposes. Schools can disclose some student information in order to comply with a court order or lawful subpoena.

FERPA allows a special category of personally identifiable information to be disclosed without student consent. A school can do this so long as it has given notice to the student that it will disclose this information. This category of information is called **directory information**. Directory information is information that is publicly available about all students. Directory information includes information such as a student's name, address, or telephone number. Many schools give out this information. Colleges and universities often provide this type of information in an online directory.

A school can release directory information without a student's consent. However, a student can choose to forbid the release of this type of information. The student must tell the school not to release this type of information. If a student tells a school not to release directory information, the school must put measures in place to make sure that this information is not released.

FERPA requires schools to give students and parents an annual notice about the school's FERPA practices. This notice informs students and parents about their FERPA rights. It tells students about the school officials who have access to records without student consent. For example, FERPA allows any official who has a legitimate educational interest in the school record to view it without the student's consent. The school must identify these officials. They could be teachers, instructors, or professors. They also could be administrative personnel such as principals or provosts.

IT and information systems security professionals who work for higher-education institutions must also comply with FERPA. Student privacy data includes PII and transcript grades. Typically, schools share student privacy data when students are transferring or applying for graduate school. IT departments within higher-education institutions are responsible and accountable for maintaining the confidentiality of student privacy data.

> **NOTE**
>
> For more information about your FERPA privacy rights as a student or parent, visit *www.ed.gov/policy/gen/guid/fpco/ferpa /index.html.*

Oversight

The Family Policy Compliance Office (FPCO) oversees FERPA compliance. The FPCO has the authority to review and investigate FERPA complaints. Schools that violate FERPA can lose their federal funding. Students who have had their FERPA rights violated aren't allowed to sue a school for that violation. Only the FPCO is allowed to sanction schools that violate FERPA.

The Children's Internet Protection Act

The purpose of the Children's Internet Protection Act (CIPA) is to protect our children from exposure to offensive Internet content. CIPA requires public school systems and public library systems that participate in E-Rate federal funding to be in compliance with CIPA. CIPA provides best practices for parents and providers of free, public Wi-Fi access to protect our children from offensive content.

Purpose and Scope

Congress passed CIPA in 2000.[35] It requires certain schools and libraries to filter offensive Internet content so that children can't access it. CIPA defines a minor as anyone under the age of 17. Offensive content includes any visual depictions that are obscene, child pornography, or harmful to minors (if the computers are accessed by minors). CIPA defines the phrase "harmful to minors" as any visual picture that:

- Appeals to a prurient interest in nudity, sex, or excretion with respect to what is suitable for minors
- Depicts, describes, or represents sexual acts, contact, or genitalia in a patently offensive way with respect to what is suitable for minors
- Taken as a whole, lacks serious literary, artistic, political, or scientific value with respect to what is suitable for minors

Not every school or library has to comply with CIPA. But any school or library receiving federal funding from the E-Rate program must do so. The E-Rate program provides discounts to most primary and secondary schools and libraries for Internet access.

Discounts range from 20 percent to 90 percent of the actual costs. Schools and libraries don't have to accept these funds. They can either pay for the Internet access with private funds or choose not to use the Internet. The Federal Communications Commission (FCC) manages the E-Rate program.

CIPA was quickly challenged. The American Library Association and the American Civil Liberties Union claimed that CIPA violated the free speech rights of adults. They also claimed that the law could prevent minors from getting information about topics such as breast cancer. A federal court agreed that CIPA violated free speech rights. That court temporarily overturned CIPA in 2002.

The government appealed the decision of the federal court to the U.S. Supreme Court. The case is called *United States et al. v. American Library Association, Inc. et al.* In 2003, the Supreme Court overturned the lower court and upheld the law. The Supreme Court held that only schools and libraries that receive E-Rate funding for Internet access must comply with CIPA. A school or library can choose not to accept the funding, if desired. The case also specifically held that CIPA applies to minors only. Schools and libraries must have some way to allow adults unfiltered Internet access. If they don't, they face scrutiny for censorship and violating the First Amendment rights of the adult.

> **NOTE**
>
> The law refers to anyone who is not of legal adult age as a minor. A minor is a child. Different laws may state different ages for determining when a person is a minor and when he or she is not.

> **NOTE**
>
> The First Amendment of the U.S. Constitution sets forth the right to freedom of religion, speech, the press, and assembly. Within these rights is the implicit right of freedom of thought, which has a privacy component. Censorship actions can violate the First Amendment.

Main Requirements

CIPA requires covered schools and libraries to filter offensive Internet content so that children can't get to it. Schools and libraries can use technological tools to meet this requirement. CIPA identifies these tools as a **technology protection measure (TPM)**. A TPM is any

---

Defining Obscene and Objectionable Material

Most people agree that children should be protected from obscene material. However, the definition of the term *obscene material* is complex. *Miller v. California*, a 1973 U.S. Supreme Court case, helps define what is obscene. The Supreme Court said that for material to be identified as *obscene*, it must meet three conditions. The conditions are based on the average person applying contemporary community standards. Under the test, material is obscene if it:

- Appeals predominantly to prurient interests; *prurient* indicates a morbid, degrading, and unhealthy interest in sex
- Depicts or describes sexual conduct in a patently offensive way
- Lacks serious literary, artistic, political, or scientific value

This test is commonly known as the **Miller test**. Courts use it to determine whether material is obscene.

technology that can block or filter the objectionable content. A proxy server used to filter content is an example of a TPM.

The FCC recognizes that a TPM cannot be 100 percent effective. However, neither CIPA nor the FCC defines what level is acceptable. A third-party company may claim that its filter is CIPA compliant. However, no certification process exists to verify that a filter is CIPA compliant. The FCC has stated that local authorities should determine which measures are most effective for their community.

CIPA states what must be filtered but not how to filter it. In addition to the TPM, the school or library must create an Internet safety policy and identify a method for addressing filtering exceptions.

Schools and libraries must adopt and enforce an Internet safety policy to comply with CIPA. Provisions in this policy must be able to monitor children's online activity. The policy also must state how the school or library will restrict access to objectionable online materials. It must address the safety and security of children when they're using email, chat rooms, or other electronic communications. It must address situations in which a child uses the Internet for unlawful activities, and it must address the unauthorized use of a child's personal information.

> **NOTE**
>
> Many companies use proxy servers for various purposes. Their use isn't restricted to CIPA compliance. For example, they can be used to restrict employees' access to particular Internet websites.

Under CIPA, a library or school must be able to disable the TPM for any adult if that adult needs to use a computer. This is an important point. If you can't disable the TPM for an adult, you run the risk of violating the adult's First Amendment rights. Adults should be able to use the system without any filtering.

Libraries can use any method to disable the TPM that works best for their location. For example, library personnel could label some computers as "adult only." Librarians would prevent minors from using these computers. Librarians also could log on to a program designed to disable the TPM. Only personnel with the proper credentials could disable the TPM. Another method is to require an administrator to disable the TPM. Upon request by a patron, the librarian could contact an administrator to disable the TPM for the patron.

Oversight

The FCC has oversight for CIPA. However, little oversight action is required. When a public school or library requests E-Rate funding, they must certify that they comply with CIPA. This certification is usually all that's required.

If a TPM fails, the school or library is expected to take steps to resolve the failure. If the library doesn't resolve them, the patron can file a complaint with the FCC. If the FCC receives complaints that too many objectionable images are getting through, it may investigate.

The FCC presumes that Congress never intended libraries to be fined if they don't comply with CIPA. At most, the FCC may require a library to refund the E-Rate discount for the period of time it wasn't in compliance.

Payment Card Industry Data Security Standard

Credit card data breaches are top of mind in today's news headlines. Someone or some organization is getting breached right now, whether via identity theft or an actual data breach or data compromise. Five major international credit card brands (American Express, Discover,

JCB, MasterCard, and Visa) formed the PCI Council in 2006 to share in defining the governance and execution of the Council's standards for ensuring the confidentiality, integrity, and availability of cardholder data and transaction-processing functions.

Purpose and Scope

The PCI Council has two major priorities. Priority number one is to assist merchants and financial institutions in understanding and implementing standards for security policies, technologies, and ongoing processes that protect their payment systems from breaches and theft of cardholder data. Its second priority is to help vendors understand and implement the PCI standards and requirements for ensuring secure payment solutions are properly implemented.

> **NOTE**
>
> Access the PCI security standards council homepage at https://www.pcisecuritystandards.org. For specific information about the new PCI DSS v3.2 standard definition, review the standard at *https://www.pcisecuritystandards.org/documents/PCI_DSS_v3-2.pdf*. To see a summary of the differences between v3.1 and v3.2, review the document at *https://www.pcisecuritystandards.org/documents/PCI_DSS_v3-2_Summary_of_Changes.pdf*.

The PCI Data Security Standard (PCI DSS) v3.2 standard[36] is the latest version of the PCI standard definition. This standard addresses security matters, PCI compliance requirements, securing your IT infrastructure, and performing ongoing security risk assessments, security testing, and annual verification that specific risk management functions are being performed, such as annual security awareness training for all employees.

TABLE 15-6 presents the PCI Data Security Standard's requirements for compliance. These requirements are organized into groups called **control objectives**.

To validate compliance, all merchants and service providers, regardless of credit card transaction volume and acceptance channel, must fulfill two validation requirements. Some merchants and service providers validate compliance through an annual on-site PCI audit, performed by a **qualified security assessor (QSA)**, a certified professional who passed a certification exam. In addition, quarterly vulnerability assessment scanning must be performed by an **approved scanning vendor (ASV)**. This requires the company to perform patch remediation prior to rescanning to verify a passing grade. Other organizations are required to complete an annual **self-assessment questionnaire (SAQ)** with quarterly vulnerability assessment scanning from an approved ASV scanning company.

TABLE 15-7 depicts the PCI compliance requirements for merchants at the various tier levels. A tier-level designation is determined by aggregating the annual credit card transaction volume total. Once that is determined, the merchant tier level can be identified.

TABLE 15-8 depicts the PCI compliance requirements for service providers at the various tier levels. A tier-level designation is determined by aggregating the annual credit card transaction volume total. Once that figure is determined, the service provider tier level can be identified.

> **NOTE**
>
> The annual on-site security audit requires that a **report of compliance (ROC)** be completed. The ROC is needed such that an **attestation of compliance (AOC)** can be completed and signed by the CEO and the QSA who performed the actual PCI compliance audit (e.g., ROC) and filled in the AOC. The AOC is what holds the CEO accountable for PCI compliance for their organization.

Self-Assessment Questionnaire

The self-assessment questionnaire (SAQ) lists all the security control requirements that are needed for the various SAQ levels. The type of SAQ that your organization must use is based on the methods or types

TABLE 15-6 PCI Data Security Standard requirements.

CONTROL OBJECTIVES	PCI DSS REQUIREMENTS
Build and maintain a secure network	1. Install and maintain a firewall configuration to protect cardholder data 2. Do not use vendor-supplied defaults for system passwords and other security parameters
Protect cardholder data	3. Protect stored cardholder data 4. Encrypt transmission of cardholder data across open, public networks
Maintain a vulnerability management program	5. Use and regularly update antivirus software on all systems commonly affected by malware 6. Develop and maintain secure systems and applications
Implement strong access control measures	7. Restrict access to cardholder data by business need to know 8. Assign a unique ID to each person with computer access 9. Restrict physical access to cardholder data
Regularly monitor and test networks	10. Track and monitor all access to network resources and cardholder data 11. Regularly test security systems and processes
Maintain an information security policy	12. Maintain a policy that addresses information security

of credit card transactions that are performed by your organization. **TABLE 15-9** depicts what each credit card transaction method or type requires from an SAQ compliance perspective.

Main Requirements

The PCI DSS v3.2 standard was released in April 2016. This standard provided clarifications and included some addition requirements that are now included in updated SAQs for compliance validation. These additional requirements were distributed throughout the 12 requirement categories of the SAQ. These new v3.2 security control requirements are as follows[37]:

- **Requirement 3.3**—Updated requirement to clarify that any displays of the primary access number (e.g., a 16-digit credit card number) greater than the first six/last four digits of the PAN requires a legitimate business need. Added guidance on common masking scenarios.

- **Requirement 8.3**—Expanded Requirement 8.3 into subrequirements that require multi-factor authentication for all personnel with nonconsole administrative access and all personnel with remote access to the CDE.

  - **Requirement 8.3.1** (*effective February 1, 2018*)—A new requirement that addresses multifactor authentication for all personnel with nonconsole administrative access to the CDE.

TABLE 15-7 PCI Data Security Standard merchant tier levels.

TIER	CRITERIA	ON-SITE SECURITY AUDIT	SELF-ASSESSMENT QUESTIONNAIRE	NETWORK SCAN	VALIDATED THIRD-PARTY PAYMENT APPLICATION
1	Any merchant, regardless of acceptance channel, processing more than 6 million transactions per year Any merchant that suffered a security breach resulting in an account compromise	Required annually (requires a QSA, ROC, and AOC)		Required quarterly	Required
2	Any merchant processing between 1 and 6 million transactions per year	Required annually (requires an ROC and AOC)		Required quarterly	Required
3	Any merchant processing between 20,000 and 1 million transactions per year		Required annually	Required quarterly	Required
4	All other merchants not in Levels 1, 2, or 3, regardless of acceptance channel		Required annually	Required quarterly	Required

TABLE 15-8 PCI Data Security Standard service provider tier levels.

TIER	CRITERIA	ON-SITE SECURITY AUDIT	SELF-ASSESSMENT QUESTIONNAIRE	NETWORK SCAN	VALIDATED THIRD-PARTY PAYMENT APPLICATION
1	All processors and all payment gateways	Required annually (requires a QSA, ROC, and AOC)		Required quarterly	Required
2	Any service provider that is not in Level 1 and that stores, processes, or transmits more than 1 million accounts/transactions annually	Required annually (requires an ROC and AOC)		Required quarterly	Required
3	Any service provider that is not in Tier 1 and that stores, processes, or transmits less than 1 million accounts/transactions annually		Required annually	Required quarterly	Required

TABLE 15-9 SAQ is determined by the processing type of the credit card transaction.

SAQ	DESCRIPTION
A	Card-not-present merchants (e-commerce or mail/telephone orders) that have fully out-sourced all cardholder data functions to PCI DSS validated third-party service providers, with no electronic storage, processing, or transmission of any cardholder data on the merchant's systems or premises. *Not applicable to face-to-face channels.*
A-EP	E-commerce merchants that outsource all payment processing to PCI DSS validated third parties and that have a website(s) that doesn't directly receive cardholder data but that can impact the security of the payment transaction. No electronic storage, processing, or transmission of any cardholder data on the merchant's systems or premises. *Applicable only to e-commerce channels.*
B	Merchants using only: • Imprint machines with no electronic cardholder data storage; and/or • Standalone, dial-out terminals with no electronic cardholder data storage. Not applicable to e-commerce channels.
B-IP	Merchants using only standalone, PTS-approved payment terminals with an IP connection to the payment processor, with no electronic cardholder data storage. *Not applicable to e-commerce channels.*
C-VT	Merchants who manually enter a single transaction at a time via a keyboard into an Internet-based virtual terminal solution that is provided and hosted by a PCI DSS validated third-party service provider. No electronic cardholder data storage. *Not applicable to e-commerce channels.*
C	Merchants with payment application systems connected to the Internet; no electronic cardholder data storage. *Not applicable to e-commerce channels.*
P2PE-HW	Merchants using only hardware payment terminals that are included in and managed via a validated, PCI SSC-listed P2PE solution, with no electronic cardholder data storage. *Not applicable to e-commerce channels.*
D	*SAQ D for Merchants:* All merchants not included in descriptions for the above SAQ types. *SAQ D for Service Providers:* All service providers defined by a payment brand as eligible to complete a SAQ.

- **Requirement 8.3.2**—A new requirement that incorporates former Requirement 8.3 and addresses multifactor authentication for all personnel with remote access to the CDE.
- **Requirement 10.8.1** (*effective February 1, 2018*)—A new requirement for service providers to detect and report on failures of critical security control systems.
- **Requirement 11.3.4.1** (*effective February 1, 2018*)—A new requirement for service providers to perform penetration testing on segmentation controls at least every six months.
- **Requirement 12.4** (*effective February 1, 2018*)—A new requirement for service providers' executive management to establish responsibilities for the protection of cardholder data and a PCI DSS compliance program.

- **Requirement 12.11.1** (*effective February 1, 2018*)—A new requirement for service providers to perform reviews at least quarterly, to confirm that personnel are following security policies and operational procedures.

Making Sense of Laws for Information Security Compliance

The United States doesn't have one single data protection law. As a result, many laws focus on different types of data. This chapter focused specifically on federal data protection laws. You must remember that states have data protection laws too. A discussion of all the different kinds of state data protection laws could consume a book in itself. It's important to remember that organizations must comply with federal laws *and* laws of the states where they are located. When systems security professionals work on compliance projects, they must be aware of both kinds of laws.

It's not practical to have separate information security programs for each law an organization must follow. IT systems can hold many different types of data. It's possible that an organization will need to make sure that its systems are compliant with a number of laws. As a result, an organization's information security program must be comprehensive. It must be able to accommodate a general response to many laws. To do this, systems security professionals must understand what each law has in common from an information security standpoint.

For example, many of the laws discussed in this chapter require an organization to assess the security of its IT systems. To do this, the organization must perform a risk assessment. This is a stated requirement of many laws. FISMA, GLBA, HIPAA, and SOX all contain this requirement. Systems security professionals often are responsible for performing these risk assessments. They help organizations identify where their IT systems are vulnerable. They allow the organization to take steps to reduce any risks. The process of performing a risk assessment and taking steps to reduce risk is known as **risk management**.

System security professionals are in a unique position. They must appreciate the impact these laws and regulations have on how IT systems operate. They also must appreciate how the basic tenets of information security influence these laws. Almost all the laws discussed here focus on protecting the confidentiality of certain types of data. FISMA, HIPAA, GLBA, and FERPA all have confidentiality requirements. Information security isn't just a good idea; it's the law.

Some of the laws have integrity requirements. Both FERPA and HIPAA require organizations to have a way to identify inaccurate data. They also must be able to correct it. SOX requires that organizations test and certify the internal controls on their IT systems. These controls must protect financial data from being modified without proper authorization.

Other laws have availability requirements. CIPA requires that certain types of online materials be available to one population (adults), but those same materials must be denied to another population (children). This is an availability concept. An organization will need to use access control measures to comply with CIPA. FISMA requires federal agencies to create contingency plans for their IT systems. HIPAA has a similar requirement. These plans ensure that IT systems are available during and after an incident or disaster. Even if a law doesn't specifically address availability, it's an important requirement for almost every organization. Organizations need their data and IT systems to be available in order to conduct business.

TABLE 15-10 Laws and information security concepts.

CONFIDENTIALITY	INTEGRITY	AVAILABILITY
FISMA	FISMA	FISMA
HIPAA	HIPAA	HIPAA
GLBA	SOX	GLBA
FERPA	FERPA	SOX
		CIPA
PCI DSS v3.2*	PCI DSS v3.2*	PCI DSS v3.2*

* PCI DSS is an international standard, not a law.

TABLE 15-10 shows how you can think about the laws discussed in this chapter with respect to information security concepts. This chart shows the laws as they are discussed in this chapter.

As a systems security professional, you will possess the skills needed to make sense of these compliance laws. You will understand how IT systems must be configured in order to meet your organization's compliance requirements. You will be able to explain how these laws affect IT systems. You also will be able to explain the steps that your organization took to be compliant with these laws.

> **NOTE**
>
> Contingency plans include incident response and disaster recovery plans.

CHAPTER SUMMARY

This chapter presented U.S. compliance laws in various vertical industries. These laws have either a security component or a privacy component, or both. Organizations that operate within any of these vertical industries are required to be in compliance. It isn't optional; it's mandatory, since it's a federal law. An organization must document its compliance with these laws and be able to prove they have done so if they're audited.

Because of these compliance laws, information systems security professionals are busy. They must be able to translate the legal requirements into tactical security implementation. They must be able to implement security controls throughout the IT infrastructure. Protecting confidential information such as privacy data requires implementation of proper security controls.

The PCI DSS standard, although not a law, must be followed by PCI merchants and service providers that either store, process, or transmit cardholder data. PCI has specific requirements for ensuring the confidentiality, integrity, and availability of cardholder data used for performing credit card transaction processing. How you process credit card transactions defines which SAQ your organization must abide by. The number of annual credit card transactions will define the organization's merchant or service provider tier level. New requirements were added to the new PCI DSS v3.2 standard and SAQ checklists in April 2016.

15

KEY CONCEPTS AND TERMS

Approved scanning vendor (ASV)
Attestation of compliance (AOC)
Business associates
Compliance
Control objectives
Covered entity
Directory information
Electronic protected health
  information (EPHI)

Miller test
Minimum necessary rule
Nonpublic personal
  information (NPI)
Personally identifiable
  information
Privately held companies
Protected health
  information (PHI)

Publicly traded companies
Qualified security assessor (QSA)
Report of compliance (ROC)
Risk management
Sarbanes-Oxley Act of 2002
Self-assessment
  questionnaire (SAQ)
Technology protection measure
  (TPM)

CHAPTER 15 ASSESSMENT

1. An addressable HIPAA security rule cita-
tion requirement must be implemented if it's
_____ for your environment.

2. What elements must a written GLBA information
security program include?

   A. Technical safeguards
   B. Physical safeguards
   C. Administrative safeguards
   D. A designated employee to run the program
   E. All of the above

3. What types of companies must follow all
Sarbanes-Oxley Act provisions?

   A. Public
   B. Private
   C. Nonprofit
   D. Governmental
   E. None of the above

4. CIPA requires a library to be able to disable the
TPM for some situations.

   A. True
   B. False

5. What law governs the release of student
information?

   A. HIPAA
   B. SOX
   C. FERPA
   D. CIPA
   E. None of the above

6. What is the maximum yearly fine for a violation of
the HIPAA Privacy or Security Rule?

   A. $100   D. $1.5 million
   B. $1,500   E. It is unlimited.
   C. $1 million

7. The United States has one comprehensive data
protection law.

   A. True   B. False

8. What must an educational institution get prior to
releasing student personal information to a third
party?

   A. Verbal consent
   B. Notarized consent
   C. Signed affidavit
   D. Written consent
   E. None of the above

9. Who is considered a "minor" under CIPA?

   A. Anyone under the age of 13
   B. Anyone under the age of 17
   C. Anyone under the age of 20
   D. Anyone under the age of 21
   E. None of the above

10. What is personally identifiable information?

   A. First and last name
   B. Date of birth
   C. Social Security number
   D. Home address
   E. All of the above

11. FISMA requires federal agencies to test their information security controls at least annually.

   A. True

   B. False

12. What is the main goal of the PCI Security Council?

   A. Define a standardized approach for protecting cardholder data

   B. Recommend firewall solutions

   C. Define how to process credit cards

   D. Mandate organizations follow a standard to protect cardholder data

   E. None of the above

13. Which PCI DSS merchant tier level(s) requires an on-site annual audit that must be performed by a certified QSA professional?

   A. 1

   B. 2

   C. 3

   D. 4

   E. Both A and B

14. Regarding PCI DSS, a service provider is required to comply with the security control requirements defined in which SAQ?

   A. A

   B. B-IP

   C. C-VT

   D. D

   E. AB

15. How many requirement sections are in the PCI DSS v3.2 standard and SAQ-D?

   A. 6

   B. 7

   C. 8

   D. 10

   E. 12

ENDNOTES

1. U.S. Office of Management and Budget, Circular No. A-130, "Management of Federal Information Resources," December 2000, www.whitehouse.gov/omb/circulars_a130 _a130trans4/ (accessed April 21, 2010).

2. Committee on Oversight and Government Reform, "Federal Information Security: Current Challenges and Future Policy Considerations," March 24, 2010, https://oversight .house.gov/hearing/federal-information -security-current-challenges-and-future -policy-considerations/ (accessed April 21, 2010). See prepared testimony of Mr. Vivek Kundra.

3. Federal Information Security Management Act, Title III of the E-Government Act of 2002, P.L. 107-347; U.S. Code Vol. 44, sec. 3541 et seq.

4. U.S. Code Vol. 44, sec. 3542(b)(1).

5. U.S. Code Vol. 44, sec. 3544(a)(3)(A)(ii).

6. GovInfoSecurity.com, "Automated FISMA Reporting Tool Unveiled," October 30, 2009, www.govinfosecurity.com/articles.php?art _id=1894 (accessed April 24, 2010).

7. Committee on Oversight and Reform, "Federal Information Security: Current Challenges and Future Policy Considerations," March 24, 2010. See prepared testimony of Mr. Vivek Kundra.

8. The White House Blog, Vivek Kundra, "Faster, Smarter Cybersecurity," April 21, 2010, www.whitehouse.gov/blog/2010/04/21/faster -smarter-cybersecurity (accessed April 23, 2010).

9. National Institute of Standards and Technology, SP 800-37, "Guide for Applying the Risk Management Framework to Federal Information Systems: A Security Life-Cycle Approach," February 2010, http://csrc.nist.gov/publications /nistpubs/800-37-rev1/sp800-37-rev1-final.pdf (accessed May 21, 2010).

10. Code of Federal Regulations, Title 45, sec. 160.103.

11. Code of Federal Regulations, Title 45, sec. 165.502(b).

12. Code of Federal Regulations, Title 45, sec. 164.520.

13. Code of Federal Regulations, Title 45, sec. 164.530(f).

14. Health Information Technology for Economic and Clinical Health Act (2009), Pub. L. No. 111-5, sec. 13402.

15. Ibid.

16. Code of Federal Regulations, Title 45, sec. 164.306.

17. Code of Federal Regulations, Title 45, sec. 164.316.

18. Code of Federal Regulations, Title 45, sec. 164.306.

19. Ibid.

20. Verizon Business, 2009 *Data Breach Investigations Report*, April 15, 2009, www.verizonbusiness.com/resources/security/reports/2009_databreach_rp.pdf (accessed March 1, 2010).

21. U.S. Code Vol. 15, sec. 6801-6803.

22. U.S. Code Vol. 15, sec. 6801(b).

23. Standards for Insuring the Security Confidentiality, Integrity and Protection of Customer Records and Information ("Safeguards Rule"), Code of Federal Regulations, Title 16, sec. 314.

24. *The Wall Street Journal*, "Investors Hope the '10s Beat the '00s," December 20, 2009, http://online.wsj.com/article/SB10001424052748704786204574607993448916718.html (accessed April 16, 2010).

25. U.S. Securities and Exchange Commission, "Information Matters," February 22, 2006, www.sec.gov/answers/infomatters.htm (accessed April 16, 2010).

26. Sarbanes-Oxley Act of 2002, Pub. L. No. 107-204, 116 Stat. 745 (codified as amended in scattered sections of U.S. Code Vol. 15).

27. *The New York Times*, "Bush Signs Bill Aimed at Fraud in Corporations," July 30, 2002, www.nytimes.com/2002/07/31/business/corporate-conduct-the-president-bush-signs-bill-aimed-at-fraud-in-corporations.html?pagewanted=1 (accessed April 16, 2010).

28. Ernst & Young, "Emerging Trends in Internal Controls: Fourth Survey and Industry Insights," September 2005, www.sarbanes-oxley.be/aabs_emerging_trends_survey4.pdf (accessed April 16, 2010).

29. Commission Guidance Regarding Management's Report on Internal Controls Over Financial Reporting, Code of Federal Regulations, Title 17, sec. 241.

30. Marcella, Albert J., "Electronically Stored Information and Cyberforensics," *Information Systems Control Journal*, Vol. 5 (2008).

31. U.S. Code Vol. 15, sec. 7213m.

32. Commission Guidance Regarding Management's Report on Internal Controls Over Financial Reporting, Code of Federal Regulations, Title 17, sec. 241.

33. U.S. Code Vol. 15, sec. 7266.

34. U.S. Code Vol. 20, sec. 1232g.

35. The Children's Internet Protection Act, Pub. L. No. 106-554, 114 Stat. 2763A-335 (codified in scattered sections of U.S. Code).

36. PCISecurityStandards.org, "Summary of Changes from PCI DSS Version 3.1 to 3.2 Payment Card Industry (PCI) Data Security Standard," April 2016, https://www.pcisecuritystandards.org/documents/PCI_DSS_v3-2_Summary_of_Changes.pdf (accessed May 13, 2016).

37. PCISecurityStandards.org, "Payment Card Industry (PCI) Data Security Standard," April 2016, https://www.pcisecuritystandards.org/documents/PCI_DSS_v3-2.pdf (accessed May 13, 2016).

Answer Key

CHAPTER 1	Information Systems Security

1. A   2. A   3. C   4. A   5. B   6. E   7. E   8. D   9. A   10. A   11. A
12. A   13. E   14. D   15. B

CHAPTER 2	The Internet of Things Is Changing How We Live

1. A   2. E   3. D   4. E   5. E   6. E   7. B   8. A   9. B   10. E   11. B   12. C

CHAPTER 3	Malicious Attacks, Threats, and Vulnerabilities

1. A   2. E   3. B   4. packet sniffer   5. A   6. A   7. D   8. E   9. A
10. C   11. C   12. threat   13. vulnerability   14. B   15. D

CHAPTER 4	The Drivers of the Information Security Business

1. A   2. A   3. B   4. E   5. B   6. D   7. E   8. A   9. A   10. D   11. C
12. E   13. HIPAA   14. A   15. E

CHAPTER 5	Access Controls

1. A   2. D   3. B   4. A   5. C   6. A   7. B   8. B   9. D   10. B   11. E
12. B   13. D   14. A   15. D

CHAPTER 6	Security Operations and Administration

1. A   2. D   3. B   4. C   5. B   6. B   7. D   8. E   9. A   10. B   11. B
12. A   13. E   14. A   15. D   16. A   17. E   18. B

CHAPTER 7	Auditing, Testing, and Monitoring

1. A   2. E   3. B   4. C   5. E   6. A   7. A   8. C   9. A   10. B
11. B   12. D

CHAPTER 8	Risk, Response, and Recovery

1. C   2. A   3. A   4. A   5. C   6. E   7. A   8. D   9. B   10. C

CHAPTER 9	Cryptography

1. C   2. A   3. B   4. D   5. A   6. A   7. A   8. E   9. A   10. B   11. D   12. A

| CHAPTER 10 | Networks and Telecommunications |

1. C   2. A   3. B   4. A   5. D   6. Router   7. B   8. A   9. C   10. B
11. A   12. B   13. B   14. D   15. D

| CHAPTER 11 | Malicious Code and Activity |

1. B   2. Spam   3. C   4. A   5. B   6. D   7. B   8. A   9. C   10. B
11. D   12. Defense in depth   13. A

| CHAPTER 12 | Information Security Standards |

1. A   2. B   3. A   4. D   5. TCP/IP   6. Request for Comments (RFC)
7. A   8. IEEE   9. D   10. B

| CHAPTER 13 | Information Systems Security Education and Training |

1. B   2. C   3. B   4. C   5. D   6. Instructor-led   7. A   8. B   9. C
10. D   11. E   12. D   13. A   14. E   15. B

| CHAPTER 14 | Information Security Professional Certifications |

1. A   2. C   3. B   4. D   5. CIW   6. A   7. E   8. B   9. A   10. D
11. A   12. E   13. B   14. A   15. E

| CHAPTER 15 | U.S. Compliance Laws |

1. Reasonable and appropriate   2. E   3. A   4. B   5. C   6. E   7. B
8. D   9. B   10. E   11. A   12. A   13. A   14. D   15. E

Standard Acronyms

3DES	triple Data Encryption standard
ACK	acknowledgment
ACL	access control list
AES	Advanced Encryption Standard
ANSI	American National Standards Institute
AP	access point
API	application program interface
B2B	business-to-business
B2C	business-to-consumer
BBB	Better Business Bureau
BCP	business continuity plan
CA	certificate authority
CCC	CERT Coordination Center
CCNA	Cisco Certified Network Associate
CISA	Certified Information Systems Auditor
CISM	Certified Information Security Manager
CISSP	Certified Information System Security Professional
COPPA	Children's Online Privacy Protection Act
DBMS	database management system
DDoS	distributed denial of service
DES	Data Encryption Standard
DMZ	demilitarized zone
DoS	denial of service
DPI	deep packet inspection
DRP	disaster recovery plan
DSL	digital subscriber line
DSS	Digital Signature Standard
DSU	data service unit
EDI	Electronic Data Interchange
EIDE	Enhanced IDE
FACTA	Fair and Accurate Credit Transactions Act

FAR	false acceptance rate
FBI	Federal Bureau of Investigation
FDIC	Federal Deposit Insurance Corporation
FEP	front-end processor
FRCP	Federal Rules of Civil Procedure
FRR	false rejection rate
FTC	Federal Trade Commission
FTP	file transfer protocol
GIAC	Global Information Assurance Certification
GLBA	Gramm-Leach-Bliley Act
HIDS	host-based intrusion detection system
HIPAA	Health Insurance Portability and Account-ability Act
HIPS	host-based intrusion prevention system
HTML	hypertext markup language
HTTP	hypertext transfer protocol
IAB	Internet Architecture Board
ICMP	Internet Control Message Protocol
IDEA	International Data Encryption Algorithm
IDPS	intrusion detection and prevention system
IDS	intrusion detection system
IEC	International Electrotechnical Commission
IEEE	Institute of Electrical and Electronics Engineers
IETF	Internet Engineering Task Force
InfoSec	information security
IPS	intrusion prevention system
IPSec	IP security
IPv4	Internet protocol version 4
IPv6	Internet protocol version 6

IRS	Internal Revenue Service
(ISC)²	International Information System Security Certification Consortium
ISO	International Organization for Standardization
ISP	Internet service provider
ISS	Internet security systems
ITRC	Identity Theft Resource Center
ITU	International Telecommunication Union
IVR	interactive voice response
LAN	local area network
MAN	metropolitan area network
MD5	Message Digest 5
modem	modulator demodulator
NAT	Network Address Translation
NFIC	National Fraud Information Center
NIDS	network intrusion detection system
NIPS	network intrusion prevention system
NIST	National Institute of Standards and Technology
NMS	network management system
OS	operating system
OSI	open system interconnection
PBX	private branch exchange
PCI	Payment Card Industry
PGP	Pretty Good Privacy
PKI	public key infrastructure
RAID	redundant array of independent disks
RFC	Request for Comments
RSA	Rivest, Shamir, and Adleman (algorithm)
SAN	storage area network
SANCP	Security Analyst Network Connection Profiler
SANS	SysAdmin, Audit, Network, Security
SAP	service access point

SCSI	small computer system interface
SET	secure electronic transaction
SGC	server-gated cryptography
SHA	Secure Hash Algorithm
S-HTTP	secure HTTP
SLA	service level agreement
SMFA	specific management functional area
SNMP	Simple Network Management Protocol
SOX	Sarbanes-Oxley Act of 2002 (also Sarbox)
SSA	Social Security Administration
SSCP	Systems Security Certified Practitioner
SSL	Secure Sockets Layer
SSO	single system sign-on
STP	shielded twisted cable
TCP/IP	Transmission Control Protocol/Internet Protocol
TCSEC	Trusted Computer System Evaluation Criteria
TFTP	Trivial File Transfer Protocol
TNI	trusted network infrastructure
UDP	User Datagram Protocol
UPS	uninterruptible power supply
USB	universal serial bus
UTP	unshielded twisted pair cable
VLAN	virtual local area network
VoIP	Voice over Internet Protocol
VPN	virtual private network
W3C	World Wide Web Consortium
WAN	wide area network
WEP	Wired Equivalent Privacy
Wi-Fi	Wireless Fidelity
WLAN	wireless local area network
WNIC	wireless network interface card
WPA	Wi-Fi Protected Access
WWW	World Wide Web

Earning the CompTIA Security+ Certification

Why Choose InfoSec as a Career

According to the 2016 State of the CIO report, security management has risen to become the third most important area of focus for surveyed CIOs. Improving cybersecurity has often been a management directive that lagged behind most other areas of focus, but that is changing. Improving cybersecurity is becoming more and more important, while it is becoming clear that the pool of trained security personnel is insufficient to meet the need. The 2015 (ISC)^2 Global Information Security Workforce Study projects a shortfall of 1.5 million trained security personnel by the year 2020. Now is a great time to enter the InfoSec domain and be part of the solution.

InfoSec professionals hold positions ranging from security practitioner to chief information officer, and the average salary for an experienced, certified information security professional is about $100,000 per year. And because information security is an international problem, these skills are in demand worldwide. The following sections give you a few tips for getting started.

> **NOTE**
>
> You can download and read the complete 2016 State of the CIO report at: *http://www.cio.com/article/3022833/cio-role/state-of-the-cio-2016-its-complicated.html.*
>
> The 2015 (ISC)^2 Global Information Security Workforce Study is available at: *https://www.isc2cares.org/uploadedFiles/wwwisc2caresorg/Content/GISWS/FrostSullivan-(ISC)%C2%B2-Global-Information-Security-Workforce-Study-2015.pdf.*

Break into the Information Security Field

Get Educated—If you choose a career in information security, specialized education will be necessary to address the evolving threats to information systems. The weaknesses and threats that have been witnessed for many years are still valid today—hacking, worms, viruses, data theft, and corruption—but new threats continue to develop—mobile security, cloud computing, software/application, and social media vulnerabilities.

Pursue a certification—Of course, most students and recent graduates will not have the experience necessary to acquire the most elite certifications. But after gaining some practical experience, more certifications become available. A great place to start is to pursue an entry-level security certification, such as the CompTIA Security+ certification. The Security+ certification is vendor-neutral and often separates the holder from other entry-level candidates being considered for employment opportunities. It shows that you have taken the time to acquire the breadth of knowledge necessary to operate in the information security domain.

Gain Experience—The right education and certification are important, but experience is paramount. Experience deepens your practical knowledge in multiple areas and also qualifies you for more elite certifications. By obtaining one or more globally recognized elite certifications, you will prove your knowledge, skills, and abilities in information systems security, giving you the edge among your competition.

Consider the CompTIA Security+ to Help Start Your Career

The CompTIA Security+ certification is a technical certification that doesn't require any level of experience. However, CompTIA does recommend that candidates have at least 2 years of related IT administration experience, and hold the Network+ certification. The Security+ certification is for the hands-on practitioner who continuously monitors information systems to safeguard against security threats while having the knowledge to apply security concepts, tools, and procedures to react against security incidents. This certification is geared toward individuals who may hold, or are working toward, technical and engineering-related information security positions as well as nonsecurity-specific information technology positions. For example, you could be working as a network security engineer, systems security analyst, or security administrator. This certification could also be a good option for those working in an information technology position that requires an understanding of security concepts and best practices. Such nonsecurity-related positions could include system administrators, application programmers, database administrators, and systems analysts. The certification's focus is on the technical aspects of information security and on the design, implementation, and administration of information systems in compliance with stated policies. To add to the Security+ certification's value, the certification is also approved by the U.S. Department of Defense to meet Directive 8570.1 requirements. If you want to pursue employment in a government position in information security, a certification that satisfies Directive 8570.1 requirements will be a big help.

Due to rapidly emerging technologies, the exam objectives of the Security+ certification will continue to evolve, which is why CompTIA periodically updates its exam. This certification exam addresses today's information security concerns, such as mobile computing, cloud computing, risk management, software security, business continuity planning, and how to recover from a disaster.

The six domains of the CompTIA Security+ exam covered by this textbook are:

- 1.0 Network Security
- 2.0 Compliance and Operational Security
- 3.0 Threats and Vulnerabilities
- 4.0 Application, Data, and Host Security
- 5.0 Access Control and Identity Management
- 6.0 Cryptography

Why Certification Is Important

Over 90 percent of hiring managers globally and in the United States said their biggest hiring challenges were finding candidates with the right skills and level of experience. Employers understand that candidates holding a certification such as the Security+ have proved their knowledge in the field of information security. They don't have to sift through a résumé to uncover knowledge. Of course, they look for the experience that accompanies the certification, but that's sometimes hard to offer when you are applying for your first job. And it is acknowledged that certain certification holders earn around 20 percent more than information security practitioners/professionals who do not hold a certification.

When you are making your decision on which certification(s) to pursue, it is important to plan ahead. Here are some things you should consider:

- Is the certification technology or vendor specific? Can the tested skills apply to any type of environment?
- Is the certification globally recognized? If you want to apply for jobs internationally, how can you be sure that an employer appreciates your skills?
- Many organizations and government agencies require their candidates to be certified; does the certification you are considering meet their needs?
- After you have earned your first certification and you want to progress down your career path, are other certifications available that will help you in your journey?
- Does holding the certification present you with more educational opportunities to help ensure that your skills are always up to date?
- Does the certifying body provide its members with free or low-cost global events and networking opportunities?

About CompTIA

The Computing Technology Industry Association (CompTIA) is a non-profit trade association formed in 1982 to offer education and vendor-neutral professional certifications for the information technology industry. CompTIA offers a wide range of certifications, in addition to the Security+ certification. Other popular CompTIA certifications include: A+ (computer technician), Network+, CompTIA Advanced Security Practitioner (CASP), Server+, Certified Technical Trainer (CTT+), Certified Document Imaging Architect (CDIA+), Linux+, Project+, Convergence Technologies Professional (CTP+), Cloud+, and Network+. For more information on CompTIA, visit *https://www.comptia.org/*.NOTE

You can download and read the complete 2016 State of the CIO report at: *http://www.cio.com/article/3022833/cio-role/state-of-the-cio-2016-its-complicated.html*.

The 2015 (ISC)² Global Information Security Workforce Study is available at: *https://www.isc2cares.org/uploadedFiles/wwwisc2caresorg/Content/GISWS/FrostSullivan-(ISC)%C2%B2-Global-Information-Security-Workforce-Study-2015.pdf*.

C

Earning the CompTIA
Security+ Certification

Glossary of Key Terms

A

Acceptable use policy (AUP) | An organization-wide policy that defines what is allowed and disallowed regarding use of IT assets by employees and authorized contractors.

Access control | The process of protecting a resource so that it is used only by those allowed to use it; a particular method used to restrict or allow access to resources.

Access control list (ACL) | An implementation technique to control access to a resource by maintaining a table of authorized user IDs; also used to permit or deny IP packets to/from router and switch interfaces to managed IP traffic flow.

Access control policy | An organizational policy definition that defines how authorized users gain access to resources based on their role and job functions and duties. This policy defines the rules for how employees and authorized contractors are granted access and how their access is removed.

Accountability | Defining the roles, responsibilities, and what key IT security employees and incident response team members must do.

Accounting | The process of recording audit trails and events in log files when monitoring access controls to information systems and applications.

Accreditation | The formal acceptance by the authorizing official of the risk of implementing the system.

Accredited | Refers to an educational institute that has successfully undergone evaluation by an external body to determine whether the institution meets applicable standards.

Actions | The activities that authorized users can perform using IT assets, systems, applications, and data.

Active content | Refers to components, primarily on websites, that provide functionality to interact with users.

Activity phase controls | Security controls that can be either technical or administrative and are classified as follows:

- Preventative controls exist to prevent the threat from coming in contact with the weakness.
- Detective controls exist to identify that the threat has landed in our systems.
- Corrective controls exist to mitigate or lessen the effects of the threat being manifested.

Address Resolution Protocol (ARP) | ARP is used to map an Internet Protocol (IP) address to a physical or MAC address.

Administrative control | A control involved in the process of developing and ensuring compliance with policy and procedures.

Adware | A software program that collects information about Internet usage and uses it to present targeted advertisements to users.

Agile development | A method of developing software that is based on small project iterations, or sprints, instead of long project schedules.

Algorithm | A mathematical process or formula for performing some kind of math function.

American National Standards Institute (ANSI) | A U.S. standards organization whose goal is to empower its members and constituents to strengthen the U.S. marketplace position in the global economy, while helping to ensure the safety and health of consumers and the protection of the environment.

Annualized rate of occurrence (ARO) | How often a loss is likely to occur every year, also called likelihood. The annualized loss expectancy (ALE) is the product of this rate and the single loss expectancy (SLE). It is mathematically expressed as: $ALE = ARO \times SLE$

Anomaly-based IDS | An intrusion detection system that compares current activity with stored profiles of normal (expected) activity.

Antivirus | Software designed to detect and mitigate some types of malware, including mainly viruses, worms, and Trojan horses.

Anything as a Service (AaaS) | A new technology offering a solution that is hosted by a third-party vendor typically within a cloud infrastructure. By hosting within a cloud infrastructure, a one-to-many delivery solution can be supported. This type of delivery solution allows for a recurring revenue model where the customer pays a monthly fee for the use of the technology, hardware, or software solution.

Application attacks | Attacks, usually in the form of intrusive penetration tests, directed at public-facing web servers, applications, and back-end databases.

Application proxy firewall | An advanced firewall that process all traffic between two systems. Instead of allowing a direct connection between two systems, the proxy connects to each system separately and passes filtered traffic to the destination based on filtering rules.

Application gateway | A network device or computer that serves as a firewall and an intermediary between internal computers and computers on the Internet.

Application service provider (ASP) | A software company that builds applications hosted in the cloud and on the Internet and commercially sells that application in a one-to-many delivery model.

Approved Scanning Vendor (ASV) | A qualified and approved company able to perform Payment Card Industry (PCI) vulnerability assessment scans.

Arbitrary code execution | An exploit that allows a hacker to run unauthorized command line functions on a compromised system. Buffer overflow attacks and SQL injection attacks can often allow arbitrary code execution.

Armored virus | A virus that attempts to conceal itself from discovery, reverse engineering, or removal.

Asset | Any item that has value to an organization or a person.

Asymmetric key cryptography | A cryptographic technique that uses two mathematically related keys—one key to encrypt data and another key to decrypt data.

Asynchronous token | An authentication token used to process challenge-response authentication with a server. The token takes the server's challenge value and calculates a response. The user enters the response to authenticate a connection.

Attack | An attempt to exploit a vulnerability on an IT hardware asset or application.

Attestation of Compliance (AOC) | Defined by the PCI Data Security Standard, this is an annual written statement of an organization's compliance signed by the Chief Executive Officer with any gaps or compensating security controls identified and documented.

Attribute-based encryption (ABE) | A type of public-key encryption in which the secret key of a user and the ciphertext are dependent upon attributes of the sender such as country or state.

Audio conferencing | A software application that uses voice over IP (VoIP) that lets two or more speakers have a conversation over their computers rather than using a telephone.

Audit | An independent third party review of an organization's existing financial situation, IT implementation, and/or IT security implementation.

Authentication | The process of proving you are the person or entity you claim to be.

Authentication, authorization, and accounting (AAA) | Core services provided by one or more central servers to help standardize access control for network resources.

Authority-level policy | An authorization method in which access resources are decided by the user's authority level.

Authorization | The process of deciding who is approved for access to specific resources.

Authorizing official (AO) | A designated senior manager who reviews a certification report and makes the decision to approve the system for implementation.

Availability | A mathematical formula that quantifies the amount of uptime for a system compared to the amount of downtime. Usually displayed as a ratio or percentage in a given calendar month.

B

Backdoor | An undocumented and often unauthorized access method to a computer resource that bypasses normal access controls.

Baseline | A benchmark used to make sure that a system provides a minimum level of security across multiple applications and across different products.

GLOSSARY OF KEY TERMS

Bell-La Padula model | An access control model that provides multilayered security for access to systems, applications, and data based on a hierarchy.

Benchmark | The standard by which your computer or device is compared to determine if it's securely configured.

Biba integrity model | Access control rules designed to ensure data integrity. Data and subjects are grouped into ordered levels of integrity; this prevents users from corrupting data at a higher level than what the user may have access to and helps ensure data integrity.

Biometrics | A physiological or behavioral human-recognition system (e.g., fingerprint reader, a retina scanner, a voice-recognition reader, etc.).

Birthday attacks | A cryptographic attack on hash collisions (different text with same key), so named after the surprisingly high probability of any two classroom students (or any members in a group) sharing a birthday.

BlackBerry | A brand name for a line of smartphones and handheld mobile devices.

Black-box testing | A method of security testing that isn't based directly on knowledge of a program's architecture.

Black-hat hacker | A computer attacker who tries to break IT security for the challenge and to prove technical prowess.

Blacklisting | The act of maintaining a list of all known dangerous websites or destination IP addresses. Any messages from a site or this destination IP address in the blacklist is dropped.

Blanket Purchase Agreement (BPA) | An agreement that defines a streamlined method of purchasing supplies or services.

Block cipher | Cryptographic cipher that encrypts an entire block of input at a time.

Bluejacking | Sending unsolicited messages to another device using Bluetooth to get the recipient to open them and potentially infect the recipient device.

Bluesnarfing | Accessing a Bluetooth-enabled device with the intention of stealing data.

Border firewall | A firewall that separates the closed or secure network from external or public networks such as the Internet.

Bot-herder | A hacker who operates a botnet.

Botnets | Robotically controlled network. A botnet consists of a network of compromised computers that attackers use to launch attacks and spread malware.

Brewer and Nash integrity model | Based on a mathematical theory published in 1989 to ensure fair competition.

Bring Your Own Device (BYOD) | An organizational policy of allowing or even encouraging employees, contractors, and others to connect their own personal equipment to the corporate network; this offers cost savings but requires proper security controls, policies, and procedures.

Browser add-ons | Companion programs that work with your web browser.

Brute-force password attack | A method used to attempt to compromise logon and password access controls by attempting every input combination. Brute-force password attacks usually follow a specific attack plan, including the use of social engineering to obtain user information.

Buffer overflow | A condition in which a memory buffer exceeds its capacity and extends its contents into adjacent memory. Often used as an attack against poor programming techniques or poor software quality control. Hackers can inject more data into a memory buffer than it can hold, which may result in the additional data overflowing into the next area of memory. If the overflow extends to the next memory segment designated for code execution, a skilled attacker can insert arbitrary code that will execute with the same privileges as the current program. Improperly formatted overflow data may also result in a system crash.

Business associates | Under HIPAA, organizations that perform a health care activity on behalf of a covered entity where access to PHI or ePHI is required.

Business continuity plan (BCP) | A plan for how to handle outages to IT systems, applications, and data access in order to maintain business operations.

Business drivers | Include people, information, financials, and performance goals that support business objectives.

Business impact analysis (BIA) | A prerequisite analysis for a business continuity plan that prioritizes business operations and functions and their associated IT systems, applications, and data and the impact of an outage or downtime.

Business-to-business (B2B) | A term used to describe a business that builds online systems with links for conducting business-to-business transactions, usually for integrated supply-chain purchases and deliveries.

Business-to-consumer (B2C) | A term used to describe an online storefront for consumers to purchase goods and services directly. An example of a B2C site is *http://www.amazon.com*.

C

California Database Security Breach Act (SB 1386) | The first law of its kind, it requires any company that stores customer data electronically to notify its customers any time there is a security breach.

Cardholder data | On a credit card, the 16-digit credit card number, name of card owner, expiration date, and the 3-digit security code on the back of the credit card.

Carrier Sense Multiple Access/Collision Detection (CSMA/CD) | The IEEE 802.3 Local Area Network standard for access and collision detection on an Ethernet Local Area Network segment.

Certificate authority (CA) | A trusted entity that stores and distributes verified digital certificates such as Verisign or Computer Associates.

Certificate of completion | A document that verifies a student has completed courses and earned a sufficient score on an exam.

Certification | The technical evaluation of a system to provide assurance that you have implemented the system correctly. Also, an official statement that attests that a person has satisfied specific requirements. Requirements often include possessing a certain level of experience, completing a course of study, and passing an examination.

Certified Information Systems Security Professional (CISSP®) | A globally recognized information systems security professional certification offered by $(ISC)^2$.

Certifier | The individual or team responsible for performing the security test and evaluation (ST +E) for the system. The certifier also prepares the report for the authorizing officer on the risk of operating the system.

Challenge-Handshake Authentication Protocol (CHAP) | Decentralized authentication protocol that hashes passwords with a one-time challenge number to defeat eavesdropping and replay attacks.

Change control | The process of managing changes to computer/device configuration or application software.

Change control committee | A group that oversees all proposed changes to IT systems, applications, and production assets.

Characteristic | In authentication, a unique physical attribute or manner of expression, such as a fingerprint or a signature. Such attributes are often referred to as "something you are."

Checklist test | A simple review of the plan by managers and the business continuity team to make sure that contact numbers are current and that the plan reflects the company's priorities and structure.

Checksum | The output of a one-way algorithm. A mathematically derived numerical representation of some input.

Children's Internet Protection Act (CIPA) | A federal law enacted by Congress to address concerns about access to offensive content over the Internet on school and library computers where children and minors have access.

Children's Online Privacy Protection Act (COPPA) | Made effective in 2000, the COPPA Rule restricts how online information is collected from children under 13 years of age.

Christmas attack | *See Xmas attack.*

Cipher | An algorithm to encrypt or decrypt information.

Ciphertext | Encrypted data, the opposite of cleartext. Data sent as ciphertext is not intelligible or decipherable.

Clark and Wilson integrity model | Published in 1987 by David Clark and David Wilson, this model focuses on what happens when users allowed into a system try to do things they are not permitted to do.

Clean desk/clear screen policy | A policy stating that users must never leave sensitive information in plain view on an unattended desk or workstation.

Cleartext | Unencrypted data, the opposite of ciphertext. Data sent as cleartext is readable and understandable.

Client-side attack | Attacks relying on the user's workstation connecting with a malicious server or application.

Clipping level | A value used in security monitoring that tells the security operations personnel to ignore activity that falls below a stated value.

Cloud computing | The practice of using computing services that are hosted in a virtualized data center with remote access to the application and data (e.g., Software as a Service [SaaS] utilizes cloud computing).

Cloud Security Alliance (CSA) | A nonprofit organization with a mission to promote security best practices for using cloud computing.

Cloud service provider (CSP) | A company that maintains data centers with racks of server computers, each running multiple virtual machines, and is able to provide services to many clients simultaneously. Organizations of all types turn to CSPs to avoid having to maintain their own data centers.

Clustering | A logical division of data composed of one or more sectors on a hard drive. A cluster is the smallest addressable unit of drive storage, usually 512, 1,024, 2,048, or 4,096 bytes, depending on the logical volume size.

Collaboration | A software-based application like WebEx that supports audio conferencing and sharing of documents (text, spreadsheets, presentations, etc.) for real-time discussions with team members or colleagues.

Colluding | The action of multiple attackers planning a cyber attack; others working secretly especially in order to do something illegal or unauthorized.

Collusion | Two or more people working together to violate a security policy.

Command injection | *See directory traversal.*

Common Criteria for Information Technology Security Evaluation | ISO/IEC 15408 standard for computer security.

Compensating control | A control that is designed to address a threat in place of a preferred control that is too expensive or difficult to implement.

Compliance | The act of following laws, rules, and regulations that apply to your organization and its use of IT systems, applications, and data.

Compliance liaison | A person whose responsibility it is to ensure that employees are aware of and comply with an organization's security policies.

Confidentiality | The requirement to keep information private or secret.

Configuration control | The process of managing the baseline settings of a system or device.

Connection encryption | Assurance that communication is secured from end to end, for example between an HTTPS website and secure browser connection with a desktop or mobile device.

Consortium agreement | The legal definition for how members of a group will interact with one another.

Constrained user interface | Software that allows users to enter only specific information and perform only specific actions.

Content filtering | The blocking of specific keywords or phrases in domain-name and URL lookups. Specific URLs and domain names can be prevented from being accessed with web content filtering enabled.

Content inspection | Looking within an IP packet to determine if the packet should be allowed to pass through the IP stateful firewall.

Continuing education | An educational program that is generally associated with a college or university that provides formal courses that do not lead to degree programs but do contribute to continuing education credits.

Continuing professional development (CPD) | A measurement of what one learns, trains, and applies in a professional work environment.

Continuing professional education (CPE) | A standard unit of credit that equals 50 minutes of instruction.

Continuous authentication | An authentication method in which a user is authenticated at multiple times or event intervals.

Control | Any mechanism or action that prevents, detects, or addresses an attack.

Control objectives | The goal or final outcome of what a control or requirement must achieve when implemented correctly.

Cookie | A text file sent from a website to a web browser to store for later use. Cookies contain details gleaned from visits to a website.

Corrective control | A control that mitigates or lessens the effect of the threat.

Counter Mode Cipher Block Chaining Message Authentication Code Protocol (CCMP) | An encryption protocol that implements the 802.11i standard. CCMP provides enhanced security through the use of the Counter Mode of the AES standard.

Countermeasure | A measure installed to counter or address a specific threat.

Covered entity | Health plans, health care clearinghouses, and any health care provider that transmits certain types of health information in electronic form. These entities must follow the HIPAA Security and Privacy Rules.

Covert act | An act carried out in secrecy.

Covert channels | These are hidden ways of passing information against organizational policy.

Cracker | A computer attacker who has hostile intent, possesses sophisticated skills, and may be interested in financial gain.

Credential management | A system for collecting, managing, and using the information associated with access controls such as login IDs and passwords.

Crossover error rate | The point where a biometric device's sensitivity returns false rejections and false acceptance equally.

Cross-platform virus | Viruses that are harmful on more than one platform or operating system, such as a virus effective on both Linux and Windows.

Cross-site Request Forgery (XSRF) | Similar to the XSS attack, an attacker provides script code that causes a trusted user who views the input script to send malicious commands to a web server. The XSRF attack exploits the trust a server has in a user.

Cross-site scripting (XSS) | An attack in which an attacker inputs client-side script code to a web application. The code would then be viewed by other users and their client software would execute the script instructions. The XSS attack exploits the trust users have for a server. The results of an XSS attack can include the corruption of the data on the website or identity theft of the site's visitors.

Cryptanalysis | The process of breaking codes without knowledge of the key.

Cryptogram | A small encrypted message.

Cryptographic hash | An algorithm that converts a large amount of data to a single number.

Cryptography | The study or practice of hiding information.

Cryptolocker | A specific form of ransomware that encrypts critical files or data until the victim pays a ransom to obtain the decryption keys.

Cryptosystem | The algorithms or ciphers used to encrypt and decrypt data.

Cybersecurity | The act of securing and protecting individuals, businesses, organizations, and governments that are connected to the Internet and the Web.

Cyberspace | The global online virtual world created by the Internet where individuals, businesses, organizations, and governments connect to one another.

D

Data breach | An incident in which sensitive data is accessed and stolen.

Data classification standard | A definition of different data types with respect to security sensitivity.

Data Encryption Standard (DES) | Encryption cipher that is a product cipher with a 56-bit key consisting of 16 iterations of substitution and transformation. First published as a Federal Information Processing Standard (FIPS) in 1977.

Datagram | The collective name for the Internet Protocol (IP) packet including the header and the payload or data.

Data infector | A type of virus that attacks document files containing embedded macro programming capabilities.

Decentralized access control | A system that puts access control into the hands of people such as department managers who are closest to system users; there is no one centralized entity to process access requests in this system.

Decryption | The act of unscrambling ciphertext into plaintext.

Defense in depth | Also named the Castle Approach, the implementation of multiple layers of security (defense) throughout the IT infrastructure (depth).

Degausser | A device that creates a magnetic field that erases data from magnetic storage media.

De-identified data | Data about an individual that contains no information that could be linked to a specific individual's identity (e.g., name, address, date of birth, etc.).

Delphi method | An information- and opinion-collection method that employs formal anonymous surveys in multiple rounds.

Demilitarized zone (DMZ) | An exterior network that acts as a buffer zone between the public Internet and an organization's IT infrastructure (i.e., LAN-to-WAN Domain).

Denial of service (DoS) | An attack that uses ping or ICMP echo-request, echo-reply messages to bring down the availability of a server or system. DoS attacks are usually sourced from a single-host device.

Detective control | A control that detects when an action has occurred. Detective controls include smoke detectors, log monitors, and system audits.

Deterrent control | A control that warns the user that completing a requested action could result in a violation or threat.

DIAMETER | A popular centralized access control protocol that succeeded RADIUS and provides access control for stable and static workforces.

Dictionary password attack | An attack method that takes all the words from a dictionary file and attempts to log on by entering each dictionary entry as a password.

Differential cryptanalysis | The act of looking for patterns in vast amounts of ciphertext.

Diffie-Hellman algorithm | An algorithm in which a sender and receiver use asymmetric encryption to securely exchange symmetric keys.

Diffie-Hellman in ephemeral mode (DHE) | Asymmetric cryptographic key exchange algorithm that uses modular arithmetic to generate keys.

Digital media | Any digitally recorded or captured audio, video, or image file.

Digital signature | An object that uses asymmetric encryption to bind a message or data to a specific entity.

Digital Signature Algorithm (DSA) | The NIST standard for digital signatures. First published as a Federal Information Processing Standard (FIPS) in 1993.

Digitized signature | An image of an electronically reproduced signature.

Directory information | Information that is publicly available about users of a computer system, such as all students at a school.

Directory traversal | The act of accessing a file directory outside a web server's root directory, and where possible, including a command to execute from unauthorized directory.

Disaster recovery plan (DRP) | A written plan for how to handle major disasters or outages and recover mission-critical systems, applications, and data.

Disclosure | 1. Any instance of an unauthorized user accessing protected information. 2. A reference, under HIPAA, to how a covered entity shares protected information with other organizations.

Discretionary access control (DAC) | A means of restricting access to objects based on the identity of subjects and/or groups to which they belong.

Disruption | A sudden unplanned event.

Distributed denial of service (DDoS) | An attack that uses ping or ICMP echo-request echo-replay messages to bring down the availability of a server or system. DDoS attacks initiate from more than one host device.

DNS poisoning | A form of exploitation in which the data on a DNS (*see Domain Name System*) server are falsified so subsequent responses to DNS resolution queries are incorrect. DNS poisoning can wage man-in-the-middle attacks.

Domain Name System (DNS) | A network service that resolves fully qualified domain names (FQDNs) into their corresponding IP address. DNS is an essential service of most networks and their directory services.

Downtime | The amount of time that an IT system, application, or data is not available to users.

Dumpster diving | A type of reconnaissance in which an attacker examines an organization's trash or other discarded items to learn internal or private information. The results of Dumpster diving are often used to wage social engineering attacks.

Dynamic Host Configuration Protocol (DHCP) | A protocol used on IP networks to provide configuration details automatically to client computers.

 E

E-commerce | The buying and selling of goods and services online through a secure website, with payment by credit card or direct debit from a checking account.

Electronic protected health information (ePHI) | Patient health information that is computer based. It is PHI stored electronically.

Electrotechnology | The collective body of knowledge addressed by the International Electrotechnical Commission (IEC).

Elliptic curve cryptography (ECC) | A public key cryptographic algorithm based on the structure of elliptic curves.

Elliptic Curve DHE (ECDHE) | An asymmetric cryptographic key exchange algorithm that uses algebraic curves to generate keys.

Emergency operations center (EOC) | The place in which the recovery team will meet and work during a disaster.

Emergency operations group | A group that is responsible for protecting sensitive data in the event of a natural disaster or equipment failure, among other potential emergencies.

EMI shielding | The practice of using magnetic or conductive material to reduce the effect of outside electromagnetic interference (EMI) on sensitive electronic equipment.

Encryption | The act of transforming cleartext data into undecipherable ciphertext.

End of life (EOL) | A term used to describe the date by which the vendor or manufacturer ceases to support and provide software updates and patches for a product or software application.

End-User License Agreement (EULA) | A licensing agreement between the software manufacturer and users, which limits the liability for software errors, bugs, or vulnerabilities.

Ethernet | An IEEE 802.3 CSMA/CD standard for Ethernet networking supporting speeds from 10 Mbps to over 10 Gbps.

Ethical hacker | An information security or network professional who uses various penetration test tools to uncover or fix vulnerabilities. Also called a white-hat hacker.

Event | Any observable occurrence within a computer or network.

Event logs | A software or application-generated record that some action has occurred.

Event-based synchronization system | An authentication method in which a token's value is synchronized with a server based on each access request. The token's counter is increased each time a new value is requested.

Evil twin | A form of wireless network attack in which an attacker creates a bogus open or public wireless network in order to sniff and capture all IP packets when a user connects to it.

Exploit software | An application incorporating known software vulnerabilities, data, and scripted commands to "exploit" a weakness in a computer system or IP host device.

Extensible Authentication Protocol (EAP) | An authentication framework that defines the transport of keys and authentication credentials. EAP is commonly used in wireless network authentication.

F

False negative | Incorrectly identifying abnormal activity as normal.

False positive | Incorrectly identifying normal activity as abnormal.

Familiarity | A type of social engineering attack that relies on constant and frequent interaction with individuals to create a comfort with (or familiarity and liking for) an individual to extract information.

Family Educational Rights and Privacy Act (FERPA) | A U.S. federal law that protects the private data of students, including their transcripts and grades, with which K–12 and higher-education institutions must comply.

Fault tolerance | The ability to encounter a fault, or error, of some type and still support critical operations.

Federal Financial Institutions Examination Council (FFIEC) | An interagency body of five U.S. regulatory agencies that exist to "promote uniformity and consistency in the supervision of financial institutions." *See https://www.ffiec.gov/.*

Federal Information Security Management Act 2002 (FISMA) | A U.S. federal law that requires U.S. government agencies to protect citizens' private data and have proper security controls in place.

Federal Information Security Modernization Act 2014 (FISMA) | A U.S. federal law enacted to bring the requirements of the Federal Information Security Management Act 2002 up to date with modern threats and security practices.

Federation | A collection of servers that share authentication credentials.

Fibre channel | A storage networking protocol originally used in supercomputers to connect storage devices.

Fibre Channel over Ethernet (FCoE) | A protocol used to connect fibre channel capable devices to an Ethernet network.

FICO | A publicly traded company that provides information used by the consumer credit reporting agencies Equifax, Experian, and TransUnion.

File infector | A type of virus that primarily infects executable programs.

File Transfer Protocol (FTP) | A non-secure file-transfer application that uses connection-oriented TCP transmissions with acknowledgments.

Firewall | A program or dedicated hardware device that inspects network traffic passing through it and denies or permits that traffic based on a set of rules you determine at configuration.

Firewall rules | Filters defined in a firewall's configuration that enable the security professional to implement security requirements.

Flash cookies | A type of web application attack that uses Flash to plant cookie-like objects on the user's system even when he thinks he has cleared his computer of such objects. *Less commonly called a local shared object (LSO).*

Flood guard | Firewall rules that can limit traffic bandwidth from hosts, reducing the ability for any one host to flood a network.

Functional policy | A statement of an organization's management direction for security in such specific functional areas as email, remote access, and Internet surfing.

Fuzzing | A software testing method that consists of providing random input to software to see how it handles unexpected data.

G

Gap Analysis | A comparison of security controls in place and the controls that are needed to address all identified threats.

Generation Y | The generation composed of those born between 1980 and 2000 in the United States. Members of Generation Y grew up with technologies that baby boomers did not have (i.e., cell phones, cable TV, Internet, iPods, etc.).

Government Information Security Reform Act (Security Reform Act) | The precursor to the Federal Information Security Management Act (FISMA), the Security Reform Act required U.S. government agencies to have an information security program, perform periodic risk assessments and made security awareness training mandatory for U.S. government employees.

Gramm-Leach-Bliley Act (GLBA) | A U.S. federal law requiring banking and financial institutions to protect customers' private data and have proper security controls in place.

Gray-box testing | Security testing that is based on limited knowledge of an application's design.

Gray-hat hacker | A computer attacker with average abilities who may one day become a black-hat hacker. Also called wannabe.

Group membership policy | An authorization method in which access to resources is decided by what group(s) you are in.

Group Policy | A centralized set of rules that govern the way Windows operates.

Group Policy Object (GPO) | A named object that contains a collection of Group Policy settings.

Guideline | A recommendation for how to use or how to purchase a product or system.

H

Hacker | A computer expert who explores computing environments to gain knowledge.

Hactivist | A hacker who is, or claims to be, motivated by political or social justice concerns and uses hacking skills to reinforce his or her chosen position.

Hardened configuration | The state of a computer or device in which you have turned off or disabled unnecessary services and protected the ones that are still running.

Hardening | A process of changing hardware and software configurations to make computers and devices as secure as possible.

Hash | An algorithm that converts a large amount of data to a single (long) number. Once mathematically hashed, the hash value can be used to verify the integrity of that data.

Hashing function | A one-way function that takes input and produces output that is hard to replicate and extremely difficult to reverse.

Header manipulation | The act of stealing cookies and browser URL information and manipulating the header with invalid or false commands to create an insecure communication or action.

Health Insurance Portability and Accountability Act (HIPAA) | A U.S. federal law requiring health care institutions and insurance providers to protect patients' private data and have proper security controls in place.

Hijacking | A type of attack in which the attacker takes control of a session between two machines and masquerades as one of them.

HMAC-based one-time password (HOTP) | An algorithm that provides a very secure method to authenticate a mobile device user using an authentication server.

Hoax | An act intended to deceive or trick the receiver. In this context, hoaxes normally travel in email messages. Often, these messages contain warnings about devastating new viruses.

Honeynet | A group of honeypots made to simulate a real live network, but isolated from it.

Honeypot | A host or service deployed at the edge of a network to act as bait for potential hacking attacks. The purpose of the honeypot is to provide a controlled environment for attacks. This enables you to easily detect and analyze the attack to test the strength of the network.

Hub | A network device that connects network segments, echoing all received traffic to all other ports.

Hypertext Transfer Protocol (HTTP) | An application layer protocol that allows users to communicate and access content via web pages and browsers.

Hypertext Transfer Protocol Secure (HTTPS) | The combination of HTTP and SSL/TLS encryption to provide security for data entry by users entering information on secure web pages, like those found on online banking websites.

I

ICMP echo request | An Internet Protocol (IP) communication mechanism that sends a ping request expecting a ping reply.

Identification | The process of providing credentials to claim to be a specific person or entity.

Identity-based encryption (IBE) | Uses the sender's identity to derive a key.

Identity theft | The act of stealing personally identifiable information with the intent to open new accounts, make purchases, or commit fraud.

IEEE 802.3 CSMA/CD | An IEEE standard for local area networking that allows multiple computers to communicate using the same cabling. This is also known as Ethernet.

IM chat | *See Instant messaging (IM) chat.*

Impact | The magnitude of harm that could be caused by a threat exercising a vulnerability.

Impersonation | From a website or web application perspective, an attacker's attempt to use the session credentials of a valid user.

Implicit deny | Firewall configuration that will deny all messages, except the ones that you explicitly allow.

In-band key exchange | The use of one's own IP data network to exchange keys.

Incident | An event that results in violating your security policy, or poses an imminent threat to your security policy.

Incident response team | The members of the organization's security incident response team that includes an incident team leader, communications team leader, and IT and IT security personnel.

Information security | The protection of data itself.

Information systems | The servers and application software on which information and data reside.

Information systems security | The protection of information systems, applications, and data.

Initiative for Open Authentication (OATH) | A collaborative organization supporting open standards and use of encryption for authentication.

Injection technique | A technique used to carry out attacks by deliberately inputting invalid data to disrupt or circumvent software controls.

Insider threat | The danger originating from an employee, contractor, or person trusted within the organization.

Instant messaging (IM) chat | A session initiation protocol (SIP) application supporting one-to-one or one-to-many real-time chat. Examples include AOL IM, Yahoo! Messenger, and Google Talk.

Institute of Electrical and Electronics Engineers (IEEE) | A standards body that defines specifications and standards for electronic technology.

Integer overflow | The act of creating a mathematical overflow that exceeds the maximum size allowed. This can cause a financial or mathematical application to freeze or create a vulnerability and attack opening.

Integrity | The validity of information or data. Data with high integrity has not been altered or modified.

Intellectual property | The unique knowledge a business possesses that gives it a competitive advantage over similar companies in similar industries.

Interconnection Security Agreement (ISA) | An interoperability agreement, often an extension of an MOU, that documents technical requirements of interconnected assets.

International Electrotechnical Commission (IEC) | The predominant organization for developing and publishing international standards for technologies related to electrical and electronic devices and processes.

International Information Systems Security Certification Consortium | *See (ISC)².*

International Organization for Standardization (ISO) | An international nongovernmental organization with the goal of developing and publishing international standards.

International Telecommunication Union (ITU) | The main United Nations agency responsible for managing and promoting information and technology issues.

Internet | A global network of computer networks that uses the TCP/IP family of protocols and applications to connect nearly 2 billion users.

Internet Architecture Board (IAB) | A subcommittee of the IETF composed of independent researchers and professionals who have a technical interest in the overall well-being of the Internet.

Internet Control Message Protocol (ICMP) | A management protocol for IP networks.

Internet Engineering Task Force (IETF) | A standards organization that develops and promotes Internet standards.

Internet of Things (IoT) | A term used to refer to the large number of networked devices (e.g., personal items, home appliances, cloud services, vehicles, etc.) that can now connect to the Internet.

Internet Protocol Security (IPsec) | A suite of protocols designed to connect sites securely using IP networks.

Internet Small Computer System Interface (iSCSI) | A storage networking protocol used to link data storage devices to IP networks.

Interoperability | A term used to describe computers, devices, or applications that can be configured to work together.

Intrusion detection system/intrusion prevention system (IDS/IPS) | Network security appliances typically installed within the LAN-to-WAN Domain at the Internet ingress/egress point to monitor and block unwanted IP traffic.

Intrusive penetration testing | The testing that a hacker performs to break into a computer system or IP host device; intrusive testing generates malicious network traffic.

IP address | A 32-bit (IPv4) or 128-bit (IPv6) number that uniquely identifies a device, such as a computer, on a network.

IP default gateway router | The router interface's IP address that acts as your LAN's ingress/egress device.

IP stateful firewall | A device that examines the IP, TCP, and UDP layers within a packet to make blocking or forwarding decisions. Firewalls are placed at the ingress/egress points where networks interconnect.

IPv4 addresses | Four-byte (32-bit) addresses that uniquely identify every device on the network.

(ISC)²© | The International Information Systems Security Certification Consortium. A nonprofit organization dedicated to certifying information systems security professionals.

ISO 17799 | An international security standard that documents a comprehensive set of controls that represent information system best practices.

ISO/IEC 27002 | An update to the ISO 17799 standard.

IT security policy framework | A set of rules for security. The framework is hierarchical and includes policies, standards, procedures, and guidelines.

ITU Telecommunication Sector (ITU-T) | The committee of the ITU responsible for ensuring the efficient and effective production of standards covering all fields of telecommunications for all nations.

IV attack | A wireless network attack that modifies the initialization vector of an encrypted IP packet in transmission in hopes of being able to decrypt a common encryption key over time.

Jamming | The act of sending radio frequencies in the same frequency as wireless network access points to jam and interfere with legitimate wireless communications.

Job rotation | A strategy to minimize risk by rotating employees between various systems or duties.

Job task analysis | The survey of how job tasks and responsibilities align with a particular role.

K

Key | A secret value a cipher uses to encrypt or decrypt information.

Key directory | A trusted repository of all public keys.

Key distribution | The process of securely transporting an encryption key from the key generator to the key user, without disclosing the key to any unauthorized user.

Key distribution center | The process of issuing keys to valid users of a cryptosystem so they can communicate.

Key escrow | An external key storage method that allows some authorized third party access to a key under certain circumstances.

Key management | The process of managing and maintaining encryption keys.

Key revocation | A situation in which someone is no longer trusted or allowed to use a cryptosystem. In a symmetric key system, where everyone shares the same key, compromising one copy of the key comprises all copies.

Key stretching | A function that takes a key (generally a weak key) as input and generates an enhanced key that can withstand a more determined attack.

Key-encrypting key | An encryption key used to encrypt other keys before transmitting them.

Keyspace | The set of all possible encryption keys.

Keystroke logger | Surveillance software or hardware that records to a log file every keystroke a user logs; also known as a keylogger.

Keyword mixed alphabet cipher | An encryption cipher that uses a cipher alphabet that consists of a keyword, less duplicates, followed by the remaining letters of the alphabet.

Knowledge | In authentication, this is something you know, such as a password, a passphrase, or a PIN.

L

Layer 2 switch | A network switch that examines the MAC layer address of an IP packet to determine where to send it. A Layer 2 switch supports LAN connectivity, typically via unshielded twisted-pair cabling at 10/100/1000 or 10 Gbps Ethernet speeds.

Layer 3 switch | A network switch that examines the network layer address of an Ethernet frame to determine where to route it. A Layer 3 switch supports LAN connectivity, typically via unshielded twisted-pair cabling at 10/100/1000 or 10 Gbps Ethernet speeds and is the same thing as a router.

LDAP injection | An attack that exploits websites that constructs LDAP based on user input. Web applications that don't sanitize input enable attackers to alter how LDAP statements are constructed. LDAP statements that are modified by an attacker run

with the same permissions as the component that executed the command so a fake or bogus ID and authentication LDAP commands and packets can be sent to a web application to authenticate.

Least privilege | The principle in which a subject—whether a user, application, or other entity—should be given the minimum level of rights necessary to perform legitimate functions.

Lightweight Directory Access Protocol (LDAP) | A directory service for network-based authentication. LDAP communication can be encrypted.

Lightweight Extensible Authentication Protocol (LEAP) | Wireless authentication framework developed by Cisco systems to help manage wireless keys and authentication. LEAP could use either WEP or TKIP for setting up secure connections.

Likelihood | The probability that a potential vulnerability might be exercised within the construct of an associated threat environment.

Load balancer | A network device (often a firewall) that can dynamically route network traffic to different network segments to avoid congestion.

Load balancing | Routing protocols that divide message traffic over two or more links.

Local area network (LAN) | A collection of computers that are connected to one another or to a common medium. Computers on a LAN are generally within an area no larger than a building.

Local shared objects (LSO) | *See Flash cookies.*

Log analysis | The process of reviewing firewall and other network device log files to identify reconnaissance activity or even attacks that have already occurred.

Log files | Journaled entries that provide details such as who logged on to the system, when they logged on, and what information or resources were accessed.

Logic bomb | A piece of code designed to cause harm, intentionally inserted into a software system to be activated by some predetermined trigger.

Logical access control | A mechanism that limits access to computer systems and network resources.

Loop protection | Firewall rules configured to look at message addresses and denying any messages sent around an unending loop.

Loss expectancy | The amount of money that is lost as a result of an IT asset failure.

M

MAC address filter | Firewall filtering rules that filter wireless network traffic by the MAC address.

Macro virus | A type of virus that typically infects a data file and injects malicious macro commands.

Malicious add-ons | Software plug-ins or add-ons that run additional malicious software on legitimate programs or software applications.

Malicious code | Software written with malicious intent—for example, a computer virus.

Malicious software | Software designed to infiltrate one or more target computers and follow an attacker's instructions. Also called malware.

Malware | *See malicious software.*

Malware inspection | A specialized form of content inspection that looks at packet content for signs of malware.

Management control | A control that is designed to manage the risk process.

Mandatory access control (MAC) | A means of restricting access to an object based on the object's classification and the user's security clearance.

Man-in-the-middle attack | An attack in which the attacker gets between two parties and intercepts messages before transferring them on to their intended destination.

Mantrap | A physical security safeguard that controls entry into a protected area. This entry method has two sets of doors on either end of a small room.

Masking | The use of a special character (e.g., X or *) to hide some of the characters of a sensitive data element, such as a credit card number or a Social Security number.

Masquerade attack | An attack in which one user or computer pretends to be another user or computer.

Maximum tolerable downtime (MTD) | The amount of time that critical business processes and resources can be offline before an organization begins to experience irreparable business harm.

Mean time between failures (MTBF) | MTBF is the predicted amount of time between failures of an IT system during production operation.

Mean time to failure (MTTF) | The average amount of time a device is expected to operate before encountering a failure.

Mean time to repair (MTTR) | The average amount of time required to repair a device.

Memorandum of Understanding (MOU) | An agreement between two or more parties that expresses areas of common interests that result in shared actions.

Message digest algorithm (MD5) | A cryptographic hash function with a 128-bit hash value.

Meta data | A term used to refer to data about data (e.g., there are 100 entries in the database table, of the 100 entries, 99 were inputted manually and 1 was inputted automatically, etc.)

Miller test | The three-prong approach defined by the U.S. Supreme Court to decide whether to label something as obscene.

Minimum necessary rule | A rule that covered entities may disclose only the amount of protected health information absolutely necessary to carry out a particular function.

Mitigation activities | Any activities designed to reduce the severity of a vulnerability or remove it altogether.

Mobile device management (MDM) | The practice of security management for employees' mobile devices.

Mobile IP | A protocol for allowing mobile devices to transparently switch LAN segments.

Mobility | The ability to perform job functions without having to be physically confined to one office or location.

Multiprotocol Label Switching (MPLS) | A wide area network technology that operates at Layer 2 by inserting labels or tags in the packet header for creating virtual paths between endpoints in a WAN infrastructure. This is a faster method of transporting IP packets through the WAN without requiring routing and switching of IP packets.

Multipartite virus | A type of virus that infects other files and spreads in multiple ways.

Multitenancy | A database feature that allows different groups of users to access the database without being able to access each other's data.

Mutual aid | An agreement between organizations able to help each other by relocating IT processing in time of need from disaster.

N

National Centers of Academic Excellence in Information Assurance Education (CAE/IAE) | Educational institutions that meet specific federal information assurance educational guidelines.

National Centers of Academic Excellence in Research (CAE/R) | Institutions that meet specific federal information assurance research guidelines.

National Institute of Standards and Technology (NIST) | A federal agency within the U.S. Department of Commerce whose mission is to "promote U.S. innovation and industrial competitiveness by advancing measurement science, standards, and technology in ways that enhance economic security and improve our quality of life."

National Vulnerability Database (NVD) | Formerly known as the Common Vulnerability & Exposures list.

Near field communication attack | The act of intercepting at close range (a few inches) communications between two mobile operating system devices.

Need to know | A property that indicates a specific subject needs access to a specific object. This is necessary to access the object in addition to possessing the proper clearance for the object's classification.

Netcat | A network utility program that reads from and writes to network connections.

Network access control (NAC) | A method to restrict access to a network based on identity or other rules.

Network address translation (NAT) | A method of IP address assignment that uses an alternate, public IP address to hide a system's actual, internal IP address.

Network interface card (NIC) | This is the physical interface between a computer and the Ethernet LAN. It contains a unique 6-byte MAC-layer address.

Network keys | Software encryption keys used for encrypting and decrypting keys.

Network mapping | Using tools to determine the layout and services running on an organization's systems and networks.

Network operations center (NOC) | The command control center for a telecommunication service provider's backbone network and customer networks. Customer trouble calls are answered by the NOC in support of managed services and SLAs.

Network port | A hardware jack on a networking device into which a network cable is plugged, or a software construct that identifies a certain type (or class) of network messages destined for a specific type of network service.

Network reconnaissance | Gathering information about a network or system for use in a future attack.

Network separation | Firewall filtering rules that enforce divisions between networks, keeping traffic from moving from one network to another.

Nonpublic personal information (NPI) | Any personally identifiable financial information that a consumer provides to a financial institution. This term is defined by the Gramm-Leach-Bliley Act.

Nonrepudiation | Prevents a party from denying a previous statement or action.

O

Offboarding | A process when terminating interoperability relationships that defines how to transfer control of data and other assets, terminate communications, and complete any open transactions.

Onboarding | A process when setting up interoperability relationships that provides the opportunity to clearly communicate goals and expectations for all parties.

One-time pad cipher | *See Vernam cipher.*

One-way algorithm | An encryption algorithm that has no corresponding decryption algorithm.

Open ciphers | Ciphers for which source code is readily available, which makes it possible for experts around the world to examine the ciphers for weaknesses.

Open Systems Interconnection (OSI) Reference Model | An internationally accepted framework of standards that govern how separate computer systems communicate using networks.

Operating system (OS) fingerprint scanner | A software program designed to distinguish operating systems based on small variations in TCP/UDP packet replies.

Operating system fingerprinting | A reconnaissance technique that enables an attacker to use port mapping to learn which operating system and version is running on a computer.

Operational control | A control that operational personnel may implement and manage, such as physical security and incident response.

Opportunity cost | The amount of money a company loses due to downtime, either intentional or unintentional. *See also true downtime cost.*

Out-of-band key exchange | A different communication channel through which you can exchange keys from the one you use for data.

Overt act | An act carried out in the open or easily viewed by others.

Overwriting | The process of repetitively writing data to specific areas on a physical storage media to effectively replace any previous data stored in those areas.

Ownership | In authentication, this is something you have, such as a smart card, key, badge, or token.

P

Packet sniffer | A software application that uses a hardware adapter card in promiscuous mode to capture all network packets sent across a network segment.

Packet-filtering firewall | A firewall that examines each packet it receives and compares that packet to a list of rules configured by the network administrator.

Parallel tests | The same as a full-interruption test, except that processing does not stop at the primary site.

Passphrase | An authentication credential that is generally longer and more complex than a password. Passphrases can also contain multiple words.

Password Authentication Protocol (PAP) | Decentralized authentication protocol that uses cleartext usernames and passwords.

Password cracker | A software program that performs one of two functions: brute-force password attack to gain unauthorized access to a system or recovery of passwords stored in a computer system.

Patch | A piece of software or code that fixes a program's security vulnerabilities. Patches are available for many types of software, including operating systems.

Pattern- or signature-based IDS | An intrusion detection system that uses pattern matching and stateful matching to compare current traffic with activity patterns (signatures) of known network intruders.

Payment Card Industry Data Security Standard (PCI DSS) | A standard, not a compliance law, for merchants and service providers regarding safeguarding the processing, storage, and transmission of cardholder data.

Penetration testing | A testing method that tries to exploit a weakness in the system to prove that an attacker could successfully penetrate it.

Perfect forward secrecy | An approach in which each communication session setup process is unique. If an attacker compromises a current session's keys, it doesn't put any previous session keys at risk.

Personal digital assistant (PDA) | A handheld device that acts as a mobile computer device supporting cell phone, Internet browsing, and email.

Personal identification number (PIN) | A numeric password used to authenticate a user, often used as part of a two-factor authentication scheme.

Personally identifiable information (PII) | Data that can be used to individually identify a person. Examples include Social Security numbers, driver's license numbers, financial account data, and health data.

Pharming | An attack that seeks to obtain personal or private financial information through domain spoofing.

Phishing | A type of fraud in which an attacker attempts to trick the victim into providing private information.

Phreaking | The art of exploiting bugs and weaknesses that exist in the telephone system.

Physical access control | A mechanism that regulates access to physical resources, such as buildings or rooms.

Physically constrained user interface | A user interface that does not provide a physical means of entering unauthorized information.

Ping | Stands for "packet Internet groper." Ping uses the Internet Control Message Protocol (ICMP) echo-request and echo-reply communications to verify end-to-end IP connectivity.

Plaintext | Unencrypted information.

Point-to-Point Tunneling Protocol (PPTP) | A protocol to implement a VPN connection between two computers.

Polymorphic virus | A type of malware that includes a separate encryption engine that stores the virus body in encrypted format while duplicating the main body of the virus.

Popup | A type of window that appears on top of the browser window. Popups generally contain ads. Although popups are not strictly adware, many adware programs use them to interact with users.

Pop-up blocker | A web browser option that prohibits the browser from displaying pop-up windows. This can reduce exposure to accidental malware execution.

Port scanner | A tool used to scan IP host devices for open ports that have been enabled.

Port security | Firewall filtering rules that filter traffic based on ports.

Preventive control | A control that stops an action before it occurs. Preventive controls include locked doors, firewall rules, and user passwords.

Privacy | The protection of individual rights to non-disclosure.

Privacy policy | A policy that specifies how your organization collects, uses, and disposes of information about individuals.

Private (symmetric) key | Encryption cipher that uses the same key to encrypt and decrypt information.

Privately held companies | A company held by a small group of private investors.

Proactive change management | The act of initiating changes to avoid expected problems.

Procedure | A set of step-by-step actions to be performed to accomplish a security requirement, process, or objective.

Product cipher | Encryption cipher that is a combination of multiple ciphers. Each could be transposition or substitution.

Project Management Body of Knowledge (PMBOK) | A collection of the knowledge and best practices of the project management profession.

Project Management Institute (PMI) | A nonprofit international organization of project managers that promotes the field of project management.

Promiscuous mode | The mode in which sniffers operate; it is non-intrusive and does not generate network traffic. This means that every data packet is captured and can be seen by the sniffer.

Protected Extensible Authentication Protocol (PEAP) | An authentication framework running in a TLS tunnel. PEAP provides more security than EAP for authentication exchanges.

Protected health information (PHI) | Any individually identifiable information about the past, present, or future health of a person. It includes mental and physical health data.

Protocol | A list of rules and methods for communicating.

Protocol analyzer | A software program that enables a computer to monitor and capture network traffic, including passwords and data in clear-text.

Proximity reader | A device able to sense a person's nearby token or access card without requiring physical contact.

Proxy firewall | A network device or computer that serves as a firewall and an intermediary between internal computers and computers on the Internet.

Proxy server | A server that is placed on a DMZ LAN that acts as a middleman for data sharing between the outside world and a user. Proxy servers assume risks, threats, and vulnerabilities so that the workstations they're connected to don't have to.

Public (asymmetric) key | An encryption key that can be shared and does not need to be kept private.

Public key cryptography | Cryptographic algorithm that uses two mathematically related keys—one key to encrypt data and another key to decrypt data.

Public key infrastructure (PKI) | A general approach to handling encryption keys using trusted entities and digital certificates; the hardware, software, policies, and procedures to manage all aspects of digital certificates.

Publicly traded companies | Companies owned by a number of different investors, who own shares of their stock.

Qualified Security Assessor (QSA) | A certified individual qualified and authorized to perform PCI compliance assessment.

Qualitative risk assessment | A type of risk assessment that describes risks and then ranks their relative potential impact on business operations.

Quantitative risk assessment | A type of risk assessment that assigns a numerical value, generally a cost value, to each risk, making risk impact comparisons more objective.

Quantum cryptography | Cryptography that uses quantum mechanics to perform cryptographic tasks like encrypting and decrypting data or providing secure key exchange.

R

Radio frequency identification (RFID) | A technology that exchanges data through a wireless connection between a reader and a tag attached to a product to track the movement of the product.

Rainbow tables | Type of password cracker that works with precalculated hashes of all passwords available within a certain character space.

Ransomware | Malicious computer software that takes over a system, encrypting files with a secret key rendering them inaccessible to the legitimate user until he or she pays a ransom.

Reactive change management | The act of enacting changes in response to reported problems.

Real-time communications | A communication method in which messages are sent directly to the recipient immediately (in real time).

Real-time monitoring | Analysis of activity as it is happening.

Reciprocal centers | Data centers of businesses that do the same type of work but are not direct competitors and can be used as alternate processing sites in the case of a disaster.

Recommendations | Formal term for ITU-T international standards.

Reconnaissance | The process of gathering information.

Recovery point objective (RPO) | The maximum acceptable level of data loss after a disaster.

Recovery time objective (RTO) | A defined metric for how long it must take to recover an IT system, application, and data access.

Redundancy | The feature of network design that ensures the existence of multiple pathways of communication. The purpose is to prevent or avoid single points of failure.

Redundant Array of Inexpensive Disks (RAID) | A disk set management technology that gains speed and fault tolerance. RAID can provide some protection against hard drive failure, but does not protect against software or data compromises, such as virus infection.

Reference monitor | Software that provides a central point of processing for all resource access requests.

Relationships | Optional conditions that exist between users and resources. They are permissions granted to an authorized user, such as read, write, and execute.

Remediation | The act of fixing a known risk, threat, or vulnerability that is identified or found in an IT infrastructure.

Remote Authentication Dial-In User Service (RADIUS) | Popular protocol, first introduced in the early 1990s, that supports remote user authentication for large numbers of users wishing to connect to central servers.

Remote code execution | *See arbitrary code execution.*

Remote journaling | Method of recording transactions to a remote server in real time.

Remote wiping | The ability to remotely wipe or delete data on a device or storage media.

Removable storage | Storage media that can be removed and/or replaced with relative ease and without damage.

Replay attack | A type of attack in which a hacker uses a network sniffer to capture network traffic and then retransmits that traffic back on to the network at a later time. Replay attacks often focus on authentication traffic in the hope that retransmitting the same packets that allowed the real user to log into a system will grant the hacker the same access.

Report of compliance (ROC) | Defined by the PCI Data Security Standard, this is a summary of the assessment activities performed during an audit. It is included as part of the Attestation of Compliance.

Request for comments (RFC) | A document produced by the IETF, RFCs contain standards as well as other specifications or descriptive contents.

Residual risk | Risk that remains after you have installed countermeasures and controls.

Resources | Protected objects in a computing system, such as files, computers, or printers.

Retro virus | A virus that attacks countermeasures such as antivirus signature files or integrity databases.

Revocation | Stopping authorization for access to data.

RFC 1087: Ethics and the Internet | An acceptable-use policy statement as issued by the Internet Advisory Board and the U.S. government defining ethics and the Internet.

Risk | The likelihood that something, generally something bad, will happen to an asset.

Risk management | The process of identifying, assessing, prioritizing, and addressing risks.

Risk methodology | A description of how you will manage overall risk. It includes the approach, required information, and techniques to address each risk.

Risk register | A list of identified risks that results from the risk-identification process.

Rivest-Shamir-Adelman (RSA) | A digital signature algorithm that relies on the difficulty of factoring large numbers.

Rogue access points | A wireless LAN access point set up and configured by a hacker to fool users into connecting with it. The hacker may then use the connection to carry out an attack such as a man-in-the-middle attack.

Role-based access control (RBAC) | An access control method that bases access control approvals on the jobs the user is assigned.

Rootkit | A type of malware that modifies or replaces one or more existing programs to hide the fact that a computer has been compromised.

Router | A device that connects two or more networks and selectively interchanges packets of data based on predetermined routes or path determinations.

Rule-based management | Managing the security of a network by defining network device rules about what is acceptable and what is not.

S

Safeguard | Something built-in or used in a system to address gaps or weaknesses in the controls that could otherwise lead to an exploit.

Salt value | Random characters that you can combine with an actual input key to create the encryption key.

Sandbox | A strategy for separating programs and running them in their own virtual space.

Sarbanes-Oxley Act (SOX) | A U.S. federal law requiring officers of publicly traded companies to have accurate and audited financial statements. SOX also requires proper security controls to protect financial records and insider information.

Scarcity | A social engineering attack that relies on the victim's feeling that there might be a shortage (scarcity) of something or some form of access to pressure him into divulging information.

Screened subnet | A firewall device that has three NICs. One NIC connects to the Internet, the second NIC connects to the internal network, and the third NIC connects to a DMZ.

Script kiddie | A person with little or no skill who simply follows directions to carry out an attack without fully understanding the meaning of the steps performed.

Search engine optimization (SEO) | Refers to the strategies used to make a site more browser-friendly.

Secure European System for Applications in a Multi-Vendor Environment (SESAME) | A research and development project funded by the European Commission to provide Single Sign-On capability. SESAME was developed to address weaknesses in Kerberos.

Secure Hash Algorithm (SHA) | A set of cryptographic hash functions developed by the U.S. National Security Agency.

Secure LDAP | A version of LDAP that uses SSL/TLS for all messages exchanged across the network.

Secure router configuration | A collection of settings that ensure your router is only allowing valid network traffic to flow to and from valid nodes.

Secure Shell (SSH) | Commonly used protocol to set up secure login sessions to remote servers.

Secure Sockets Layer virtual private network (SSL-VPN) | A means of securing remote access to a secure website. In other words, it's a VPN that runs on Secure Sockets Layer and encrypts communications to a secure web server via a secure browser connection.

Security | A control such as a policy, procedure, and physical thing like a gate that is used to protect something from risks, threats, or vulnerabilities.

Security administration | The group of individuals responsible for planning, designing, implementing, and monitoring an organization's security plan.

Security Assertion Markup Language (SAML) | An open XML standard used for exchanging both authentication and authorization data.

Security association (SA) | The basic element of ISAKMP key management. SA contains all the information needed to do a variety of network security services.

Security awareness campaign | Specific training that aims to raise users' understanding and concern for information security.

Security awareness training | Training about security policies, threats, and handling of digital assets.

Security breach | Any event that results in a violation of any of the C-I-A security tenets.

Security control | Action an organization takes to help reduce risk.

Security gap | The difference between the security controls in place and the controls needed to address all vulnerabilities.

Security incident response team (SIRT) | Teams of people organized to identify and respond to security incidents. The SIRT is responsible for minimizing the impact of incidents and collecting any necessary evidence to analyze the incident.

Security Information and Event Management (SIEM) system | Software and devices that assist in collecting, storing, and analyzing the contents of log files.

Security kernel | The central part of a computing environment's hardware, software, and firmware that enforces access control for computer systems.

Security kernel database | A database made up of rules that determine individual users' access rights.

Security policy | A set of policies that establish how an organization secures its facilities and IT infrastructure. Can also address how the organization meets regulatory requirements.

Self-assessment questionnaire (SAQ) | Defined by the PCI Data Security Standard, this is a series of yes-or-no questions used to guide the organization toward determining their own compliance with the standard's requirements.

Separation of duties | The process of dividing a task into a series of unique activities performed by different people, each of whom is allowed to execute only one part of the overall task.

Service bureau | A service provider that has sufficient capacity to offer outsourced wholesale services to smaller customers.

Service-level agreement (SLA) | A contractual commitment by a service provider or support organization to its customers or users.

Session hijacking | A network attack in which the attacker attempts to take over an existing connection between two network computers.

Session key | A unique key for each new communication session.

Shoulder surfing | Looking over people's shoulders as they enter codes at secure devices, such as a bank cash machine or a gas pump.

Simple Network Management Protocol (SNMP) | A non-secure connectionless UDP-based protocol that is used to transmit network management data between IP devices and an SNMP data collection server

Simulation test | A method of testing a BCP or DRP in which a business interruption is simulated, and the response team responds as if the situation were real.

Single point of failure (SPOF) | A single piece of hardware or software that must operate for the larger system or network to operate.

Single sign-on (SSO) | A method of access control that allows a user to log on to a system and gain access to other resources within the network via the initial logon. SSO helps a user avoid having to log on multiple times and remember multiple passwords for various systems.

Single-factor authentication | An authentication method that uses only a single type of authentication credentials.

Slow virus | A virus that counters the ability of antivirus programs to detect changes in infected files, slowing down the detection of the virus.

Smart card | A plastic card with authentication credentials embedded in either a microchip or magnetic strip on the card.

Smartphone | A cell phone that runs mobile communications software and supports voice, Internet browsing, email, and text messaging.

Smurf attack | A network attack in which forged Internet Control Message Protocol (ICMP) echo request packets are sent to IP broadcast addresses from remote locations to generate DoS attacks.

Smurfing | A DoS attack that uses a directed broadcast to create a flood of network traffic for the victim computer.

Sniffer | *See packet sniffer.*

Sniffing | The physical interception of data communications; eavesdropping.

Social engineering | A type of attack that relies on persuading a person to reveal information.

Social media | A blanket term that describes social applications, including forums, message boards, blogs, wikis, and podcasts. Social media applications include Google+, Facebook, Instagram, and YouTube.

Software as a Service (SaaS) | A model of software deployment or service where customers use applications on demand.

Software development life cycle (SDLC) | A popular method used to describe the process of planning, developing, testing, and deploying software applications.

Software vulnerability | An error or bug in software code that can be exploited.

Spam | Unwanted email or unsolicited messages.

Spear phishing | An email or instant message spoofing fraud attempt that targets a specific organization, seeking unauthorized access to confidential data.

Spim | Similar to spam of unsolicited messages, but through an instant messaging service rather than email.

Spoofing | A type of attack in which one person, program, or computer disguises itself as another person, program, or computer to gain access to some resource.

Sprint | One of the small project iterations used in the "agile" method of developing software, in contrast with the usual long project schedules of other methods of development software.

Spyware | Software that gathers user information through the user's Internet connection without the user's knowledge.

SQL injection | A form of web application attack in which a hacker submits SQL (structured query language) expressions to cause authentication bypass, extraction of data, planting of information, or access to a command shell.

SSL handshake protocol | A process that creates the first secure communications session between a client and a server.

Standard | A mandated requirement for a hardware or software solution that is used to deal with a security risk throughout the organization.

State | Information that describes the current status of a network connection that is used by firewalls to make decisions on whether to pass or drop network packets.

Stateful inspection firewall | A firewall that examines the state of a connection as well as simple address, port, and protocol rules to determine how to process a packet.

Stateful matching | A technique of matching network traffic with rules or signatures based on the appearance of the traffic and its relationship to other packets.

Static environments | Systems that do not change very much or at all after deployment.

Stealth virus | A type of virus that uses a number of techniques to conceal itself from the user or detection software.

Steganography | The art and science of writing hidden messages.

Store-and-forward communications | The technique of relaying communications between two or more users by intermediate storage. Delivery from sender to a central storage is immediate, but the final transmission to the recipient depends upon availability and a request for the stored information.

Stream cipher | Cryptographic cipher that encrypts a single byte (or bit) at a time.

Subnet | A partition of a network defined by devices that share the same network address portion of the IP address.

Subnet mask | A network configuration parameter that defines the dividing line between the network and host addresses for IPv4 addresses. The mask is a 32-bit number that is set to all "1"s for the network bits and all "0"s for the host bits.

Subnet mask address | The complement to an IP address that defines the IP network number and IP host address.

Substitution cipher | An encryption cipher that replaces bits, characters, or blocks of information with other bits, characters, or blocks.

Succession planning | The act of planning who will step in if key personnel are incapacitated or unavailable.

Switch | A network device that connects network segments, creating a direct connection between a sending and receiving port.

Symmetric key cryptography | A type of cryptography that cannot secure correspondence until after the two parties exchange keys.

SYN-ACK | A specific network TCP message used to respond to (ACK) a request to establish a network connection (SYN). This type of message is step two in the three-step connection handshake.

SYN flood | A DoS attack that fills up a computer's connection table by sending a flood of unacknowledged connection requests. Once the connection table fills up, the computer cannot respond to any new legitimate connection requests.

Synchronous token | A device used as a logon authenticator for remote users of a network.

System infector | A type of virus that targets key hardware and system software components in a computer, and is usually associated with system startup processes.

System life cycle (SLC) | A method used in systems engineering to describe the phases of a system's existence, including design, development, deployment, operation, and disposal.

System owner | The person responsible for the daily operation of a system and for ensuring that the system continues to operate in compliance with the conditions set out by the authorizing official.

T

Tailgating | The act of following an individual closely to sneak past a secure door or access area.

Technical control | A control that is carried out or managed by a computer system.

Technology protection measure (TPM) | Technology used to restrict access to some resource.

Telephony | The field of technology that includes the development and deployment of voice communication solutions.

Telephony denial of service (TDoS) | A variation of denial of service (DoS) attacks, but launched against traditional and VoIP telephone systems. A TDoS attack disrupts an organization's use of its telephone system through a variety of methods.

Telnet | A non-secure application that supports remote terminal access in cleartext transmission.

Temporal isolation | A method of restricting resource access to specific periods of time. You may see temporal isolation more commonly described as time of day restrictions.

Temporal Key Integrity Protocol (TKIP) | An encryption method used on WPA to replace WEP.

Terminal Access Controller Access System (TACACS) | A remote access client/server protocol that provides authentication and authorization

capabilities to users who are accessing the network remotely. It is not a secure protocol.

Terminal Access Controller Access System Plus (TACACS+) | A Cisco proprietary remote access client/server protocol that provides authentication, authorization, and accounting.

Thick client | Client software that handles user I/O and most business logic (data processing), only using the server for data storage and data access.

Thin client | Client software that only handles user I/O functionality, and depends on servers to perform most business logic (data processing), data storage, and data access.

Threat | Any action that could damage an asset.

Threshold | Some value that indicates a change from normal to abnormal behavior. In the case of failed logon attempts, a threshold of five means that when a user fails to log on five times, the action should be considered abnormal.

Time of day restrictions | *See temporal isolation.*

Time-based one-time password (TOTP) | An example of HOTP, this algorithm combines a timestamp with a hashed value to reduce vulnerability to replay attacks.

Time-based synchronization system | An authentication method in which a token's internal clock is synchronized with a server's clock to generate matching values.

Timestamping | Providing an exact time when a producer creates or sends information.

Token | A physical device that transits a secret code to a user to authenticate the user. Can be a hardware-device token or a software-generated token.

Total risk | The combined risk to all business assets.

Transition functions | The transition from one state to another state.

Transitive access | Attacking the desired target system or service indirectly by first compromising a system trusted by the target.

Transitive trust | An authentication method in which the initial sign-on credentials are forwarded by request to other trusted servers.

Transmission Control Protocol/Internet Protocol (TCP/IP) | A popular suite of protocols that operate at both the Network and Transport Layer of the OSI Reference Model. TCP/IP governs all activity across the Internet and through most corporate and home networks.

Transport encryption | The process of securing communication in transit, generally done by software.

Transposition cipher | An encryption cipher that rearranges characters or bits of data.

Trivial File Transfer Protocol (TFTP) | A connectionless, UDP-based file-transfer protocol used for quick and small file transfers between two IP devices.

Trojan | A malicious software code that appears benign to the user but actually performs a task on behalf of a perpetrator with malicious intent.

Trojan horses | *See Trojan.*

True downtime cost | *See opportunity cost.*

Trust | Confidence in the expectation that others will act in your best interest, or that a resource is authentic. On computer networks, trust is the confidence that other users will act in accordance with the organization's security rules and not attempt to violate stability, privacy, or integrity of the network and its resources.

Trusted operating systems (TOS) | A type of operating system that includes additional controls to address the additional security needs of systems that handle extremely sensitive information.

Two-factor authentication | An authentication method that uses two types of authentication credentials. See also *two-step authentication.*

Two-step authentication | *See two-factor authentication.*

Typo squatting | The act of registering and "squatting" a slightly wrong URL in the hopes a user mistypes the intended URL. *See also URL hijacking.*

U

Unified communications | The integration of multiple types of enterprise communication, such as instant messaging, voice, video, and data, all on a single network.

Unified messaging (UM) | The storage of fax, email, and voice communications in a single location.

Unified threat management (UTM) | Devices used to provide filtering, plus many additional security services.

Uptime | The total amount of time the IT system, application and data was accessible.

Urgency | A social engineering attack that uses a sense of urgency or an emergency stress situation to get someone to do something or divulge information.

URL filter | Firewall filtering rules that filter web traffic by the URL, as opposed to the IP address.

URL hijacking | *See typo squatting.*

USA Patriot Act | An act passed into law in response to the terrorist attacks of September 11, 2001, which significantly reduced restrictions on law enforcement agencies' gathering of intelligence within the United States; expanded the Secretary of the Treasury's authority to regulate financial transactions, particularly those involving foreign individuals and entities; and broadened the discretion of law enforcement and immigration authorities in detaining and/or deporting immigrants suspected of terrorism and related acts.

USB token | A hardware device used for authentication that you plug into your computer's USB port. This device provides authentication credentials without the user having to type anything.

User acceptance | The last stage of software development, when users work with the software, simulating real-world use.

User assigned privileges | The most detailed authorization policy, it assigns specific privileges to the individual user.

User Datagram Protocol (UDP) | A communication protocol that is connectionless and is popular for exchanging small amounts of data or messages.

Username | The most common method to identify a user to a system. It is usually a character string that represents a person or group of people who access a computer system.

V

Vendor-neutral certification | This type of certification covers concepts and topics that are general in nature and do not focus on a specific product or product line.

Vendor-specific certification | This type of certification helps to identify professionals who possess in-depth product knowledge. Many organizations use these certifications, along with vendor-neutral certifications, when evaluating prospective employees and personnel.

Vernam cipher | The only unbreakable cryptographic cipher. Also called a one-time pad.

Video conferencing | An application that supports bridging callers and their webcam images into a common video conference.

View-based access control (VBAC) | Limiting users' access to database views, as opposed to allowing users to access data in database tables directly.

Vigenère cipher | An encryption cipher that uses multiple encryptions schemes in succession. For example, you could encrypt every fifth letter with its own substitution cipher.

Virtual LAN (VLAN) | The broadcast domain in Ethernet where all workstations are on the same logical LAN.

Virtual private network (VPN) | A method of encrypting IP packets from one end to another, as in a tunnel.

Virus | A software program that attaches itself to or copies itself into another program for the purpose of causing the computer to follow instructions that were intended by the original program developer.

Vishing | The act of performing a phishing attack by telephone in order to elicit personal information.

Voice over IP (VoIP) | A collection of communication protocols and technologies to deliver voice communication and sessions over IP networks.

VPN concentrator | Network device acting as a type of router specializing in VPN connections.

Vulnerability | A weakness that allows a threat to be realized or to have an effect on an asset.

Vulnerability assessment | A software review that identifies bugs or errors in software.

Vulnerability scanner | A software tool that collects information about any known weaknesses that exist on a target computer or network.

Vulnerability testing | A process of finding the weaknesses in a system and determining which places may be attack points.

Vulnerability window | The time between a software vendor's release of a security patch and your implementation of it.

W

Wannabe | *See gray-hat hacker.*

War chalking | The act of creating a map of the physical and geographic location of any wireless access points and networks.

War driving | A method discovering wireless networks by moving around a geographic area with a detection device.

Wardialer | A computer program used to identify the phone numbers that can successfully make a connection with a computer modem.

Waterfall model | A software development model that defines how development activities progress from one distinct phase to the next.

Watering hole attack | The act of compromising with malicious code a third-party website known to be visited by the targeted individuals or company. The attacker then must wait for the target to visit the victim site and for the planted code to aid in attacking the target systems.

Web application attacks | *See application attacks.*

Web applications | Applications that users access via a network, often the Internet, using a web browser.

Web defacement | Also called web graffiti, refers to someone gaining unauthorized access to a web server and altering one or more pages of a website on the server.

Web graffiti | Also called web defacement, refers to someone gaining unauthorized access to a web server and altering one or more pages of a website on the server.

Web security gateway | A device that performs URL-filtering, but does not examine the content of the packet.

Whaling | A phishing attack that targets the executive user or most valuable employees, otherwise considered the "whale" or "big fish." Also often called "spear phishing" as in a highly focused phishing attack.

White-box testing | Security testing that is based on knowledge of the application's design and source code.

White-hat hacker | An information security or network professional who uses various penetration test tools to uncover or fix vulnerabilities. *See also ethical hacker.*

Whitelisting | The act of maintaining a list of trusted websites. All messages and connection requests from sites not in the whitelist are ignored.

Wi-Fi Protected Access (WPA) | Current encryption for wireless networks. Much stronger than WEP, WPA is the recommended encryption for wireless use.

Wired Equivalent Privacy (WEP) | Legacy encryption for wireless networks. WEP is weak and does not provide sufficient protection for most traffic.

Wireless access point (WAP) | A radio transceiver device that transits and receives IP communications via wireless LAN technology.

Wireless Fidelity (Wi-Fi) | An alliance among wireless manufacturers to brand certified products that interoperate with wireless LAN standards. A Wi-Fi hotspot is a wireless LAN access location.

Wireless LAN (WLAN) | A LAN that uses radio transmissions to connect computers and devices instead of wires or cables.

Wiretapping | Intercepting communication sent via a wired connection.

Workstation | A desktop computer, a laptop computer, a special-purpose terminal, or any other device that connects to your network.

World Wide Web (WWW) | A collection of documents that are hyperlinked among one another and accessed using the Internet.

World Wide Web Consortium (W3C) | An organization formed in 1994 to develop and publish standards for the World Wide Web.

Worm | A self-replicating piece of malicious software that can spread from device to device.

X

Xmas attack | An old attack of sending a deliberately malformed network packet with hopes the receiving network device responds unexpectedly, e.g., rebooting or crashing. The malformed packet includes several TCP header bits set to "1," or turned on, like the lights of a Christmas tree.

XML injection | A web application attack in which the attacker injects XML tags and data into a database in an attempt to retrieve data.

XTACACS (Extended Terminal Access Controller Access System) | An extension of the TACACS remote access client/server protocol that provides authentication and authorization capabilities to users who are accessing the network remotely. It is not a secure protocol.

Z

Zero day | A new and previously unknown attack for which there are no current specific defenses. "Zero day" refers to the newness of an exploit, which may be known in the hacker community for days or weeks. When such an attack occurs for the first time, defenders are given zero days of notice (hence the name).

Zone transfer | A unique query of a DNS server that asks it for the contents of its zone.

References

Andress, Jason and Steve Winterfeld. *Cyber Warfare*. Burlington, MA: Syngress Press, 2011.

Altholz, Nancy, and Larry Stevenson. *Rootkits for Dummies*. New York: John Wiley and Sons Ltd., 2007.

Amoroso, Edward. *Cyber Security*. Summit, NJ: Silicon Press, 2006.

Aquilina, James M., Eoghan Casey, and Cameron H. Malin. *Malware Forensics: Investigating and Analyzing Malicious Code*. Burlington, MA: Syngress, 2008.

Bacik, Sandy. *Building an Effective Information Security Policy Architecture*. Boca Raton, FL: CRC Press, 2008.

Bailey, Mike et al. *Client-Side Attacks and Defense*. Woburn, MA: Newnes, 2012.

Bellovin, Steven M. *Thinking Security*. New York: Addison-Wesley Professional, 2015.

Benantar, Messaoud. *Access Control Systems: Security, Identity Management and Trust Models*. New York: Spring, 2010.

Bhaiji, Yusuf. *Network Security Technologies and Solutions (CCIE Professional Development Series)*. Indianapolis: Cisco Press, 2008.

Biegelman, Martin T., and Daniel R. Biegelman. *Building a World-Class Compliance Program: Best Practices and Strategies for Success*. New York: Wiley, 2008.

Brotby, W. Krag. *Information Security Metrics: A Definitive Guide to Effective Security Monitoring and Measurement*. Chicago: Auerbach, 2008.

Bumiller, Elisabeth. "Bush Signs Bill Aimed at Fraud in Corporations," *The New York Times*, July 30, 2002. http://www.nytimes.com/2002/07/31/business/corporate-conduct-the-president -bush-signs-bill-aimed-at-fraud-in-corporations.html?pagewanted=1 (accessed April 16, 2010).

Calder, Alan, and Steve Watkins. *IT Governance: A Manager's Guide to Data Security and ISO 27001/ISO 27002*, 4th ed. London: Kogan Page, 2013.

Carpenter, Tom. *CWNA Certified Wireless Network Administrator & CWSP Certified Wireless Security Professional All-in-One Exam Guide (PWO-104 & PWO-204)*. New York: McGraw-Hill Osborne Media, 2010.

Chabrow, Eric. "Automated FISMA Reporting Tool Unveiled," GovInfoSecurity.com, October 30, 2009. http://www.govinfosecurity.com/articles.php?art_id=1894 (accessed April 24, 2010).

Children's Internet Protection Act, The, Pub. L. No. 106-554, 114 Stat. 2763A-335 (codified in scattered sections of U.S. Code).

CISM Review Manual 2009. Chicago: Isaca Books, 2008.

Code of Federal Regulations, Title 45, sec. 160.103.

Code of Federal Regulations, Title 45, sec. 164.306.

Code of Federal Regulations, Title 45, sec. 164.316.

Code of Federal Regulations, Title 45, sec. 164.520.

Code of Federal Regulations, Title 45, sec. 164.530(f).

Code of Federal Regulations, Title 45, sec. 164.502(b).

Commission Guidance Regarding Management's Report on Internal Controls Over Financial Reporting, Code of Federal Regulations, Title 17, sec. 241.

Committee on Oversight and Government Reform, "Federal Information Security: Current Challenges and Future Policy Considerations," March 24, 2010. https://oversight.house.gov/wp-content/uploads/2012/01/20100324Fountain.pdf (accessed April 21, 2010). *See* prepared testimony of Mr. Vivek Kundra.

Consumer Sentinel Network Data Book for January–December 2012. Washington: Federal Trade Commission, 2013. http://ftc.gov/sentinel/reports/sentinel-annual-reports/sentinel-cy2012. pdf (accessed June 13, 2013).

Davis, Chris, Mike Schiller, and Kevin Wheeler. *IT Auditing: Using Controls to Protect Information Assets*. New York: McGraw-Hill Osborne Media, 2011.

Doherty, Jim. *SDN and NFV Simplified*. New York: Addison-Wesley Professional, 2016.

Douligeris, Christos, and Dimitrios N. Serpanos. *Network Security: Current Status and Future Directions*. New York: Wiley-IEEE Press, 2007.

Elisan, Christopher. *Malware, Rootkits & Botnets: A Beginner's Guide*. New York: McGraw Hill Professional, 2012.

Ernst & Young, "Emerging Trends in Internal Controls: Fourth Survey and Industry Insights," September 2005. http://www.sarbanes-oxley.be/aabs_emerging_trends_survey4.pdf (accessed April 16, 2010).

Ethics and the Internet (Request for Comments 1087). Internet Activities Board, January 1989. http://tools.ietf.org/html/rfc1087 (accessed May 22, 2013).

Faircloth, Jeremy, and Paul Piccard. *Combating Spyware in the Enterprise*. Burlington, MA: Syngress, 2006.

Federal Information Security Management Act, Title III of the E-Government Act of 2002, Pub. L. 107-347; U.S. Code Vol. 44, sec. 3541 et seq.

Ferraiolo, David et el, 2007, *Role-based Access Control*. Norwood, MA: Artech House Publishers, 2007.

Free Software Foundation. http://www.fsf.org (accessed September 17, 2010).

Freund, Jack and Jack Jones. *Measuring and Managing Information Risk*. Waltham, MA: Butterworth-Heinemann, 2014.

GNU public license agreement. http://www.gnu.org (accessed September 17, 2010).

Hampton, John J. *Fundamentals of Enterprise Risk Management: How Top Companies Assess Risk, Manage Exposure, and Seize Opportunity*. New York: AMACOM, 2014.

"Hazard Identification and Business Impact Analysis." Continuity Central (Portal Publishing Ltd.). http://www.continuitycentral.com/HazardIdentificationBusinessImpactAnalysis.pdf (accessed October 2, 2010).

Health Information Technology for Economic and Clinical Health Act (2009), Pub. L. No. 111-5, sec. 13402.

Hernandez, Steven and Corey Schou. *Information Assurance Handbook: Effective Computer Security and Risk Management Strategies*. New York: McGraw-Hill Education, 2014.

Hill, David G. *Data Protection: Governance, Risk Management, and Compliance*. Boca Raton, FL: CRC Press, 2009.

Hillson, David. *The Risk Management Handbook: A Practical Guide to Managing Multiple Dimensions of Risk*. Philadelphia: Kogan Page, 2016.

Hoopes, John. *Virtualization for Security: Including Sandboxing, Disaster Recovery, High Availability, Forensic Analysis, and Honeypotting*. Burlington, MA: Syngress, 2008.

Howard, Rick. *Cyber Fraud: Tactics, Techniques and Procedures*. Chicago: Auerbach, 2009. Institute of Electrical and Electronics Engineers (IEEE). http://www.ieee.org (accessed September 17, 2010).

Hubbard, Douglas W. and Richard Seiersen. *How to Measure Anything in Cybersecurity Risk*. New York: John Wiley & Sons, 2016.

International Information Systems Security Certification Consortium (ISC)². http://www.isc2.org (accessed September 17, 2010).

Isaca. *CISM Review Manual*, 14th ed. Rolling Meadows, IL: Author, 2016.

Krause, Micki, and Harold F. Tipton. *Information Security Management Handbook*, 6th ed. (ISC)² Press. Chicago: Auerbach, 2007.

Kundra, Vivek. "Faster, Smarter Cybersecurity," The White House Blog, April 21, 2010. http://www.whitehouse.gov/blog/2010/04/21/faster-smarter-cybersecurity (accessed April 23, 2010).

Lauricella, Tom. "Investors Hope the '10s Beat the '00s," *The Wall Street Journal*, December 20, 2009. http://online.wsj.com/article/SB10001424052748704786204574607993448916718 (accessed April 16, 2010).

Loo, Jonathan et al. *Mobile Ad Hoc Networks*. Boca Raton, FL: CRC Press, 2011.

Mandia, Kevin et al. *Incident Response & Computer Forensics*, 3rd ed. New York: McGraw-Hill Education, 2014.

Marcella, Albert J., "Electronically Stored Information and Cyberforensics," *Information Systems Control Journal*, Vol. 5 (2008). http://www.isaca.org/Template.cfm?Section=Home&CONTENTID=52106&TEMPLATE=/ContentManagement/ContentDisplay.cfm (accessed April 16, 2010).

Mason, Alex et al. *Sensing Technology: Current Status and Future Trends IV*. New York: Springer, 2014.

Meeuwisse, Raef. *Cybersecurity for Beginners*. Canterbury, UK: Author, 2015.

Mogollon, Manuel. *Cryptography and Security Services: Mechanisms and Applications*. London: Cybertech Publishing, 2008.

Moldovyan, Alex, and Nick Moldovyan. *Innovative Cryptography (Programming Series)*, 2nd ed. Rockland, MA: Charles River Media, 2006.

National Institute of Standards and Technology, SP 800-37, "Guide for Applying the Risk Management Framework to Federal Information Systems: A Security Life Cycle Approach," February 2010. http://csrc.nist.gov/publications/nistpubs/800-37-rev1/sp800-37-rev1-final.pdf (accessed May 21, 2010).

O'Toole, Darren. *Incident Management for IT Departments*. St. Albans, UK: Author, 2015.

Oriyano, Sean-Philip and Jim Doherty. *Wireless and Mobile Device Security*. Burlington, MA: Jones & Bartlett Learning, 2014.

Pearson, Brock and Tyler Wrightson. *Wireless Network Security A Beginner's Guide*. New York: McGraw Hill Professional, 2012.

"Risk Management Framework." EPCB Risk Management Consulting Services (n.d.). http:// www .emergencyriskmanagement.com/site/711336/page/248974 (accessed October 2, 2010).

Rose, Adam, and Linda S. Spedding. *Business Risk Management Handbook: A Sustainable Approach*. Oxford: Cima Publishing, 2007.

Sarbanes-Oxley Act of 2002, Pub. L. No. 107-204, 116 Stat. 745 (codified as amended in scattered sections of U.S. Code Vol. 15).

Schneier, Bruce. *Applied Cryptography*. New York: John Wiley & Sons, 2015.

Senft, Sandra et al. *Information Technology Control and Audit*, 4th ed. Boca Raton, FL: CRC Press, 2012.

Shackleford, Dave. *Virtualization Security*. New York: John Wiley & Sons, 2012.

Sikorski, Michael and Andrew Honig. *Practical Malware Analysis*. San Francisco: No Starch Press, 2012.

Stallings, William. *Cryptography and Network Security*. Upper Saddle River, NJ: Prentice Hall, 2011.

Stallings, William. *Network Security Essentials*. Upper Saddle River, NJ: Prentice Hall, 2013.

Standards for Insuring the Security Confidentiality, Integrity and Protection of Customer Records and Information ("Safeguards Rule"), Code of Federal Regulations, Title 16, sec. 314.

Stoneburner, Gary, Alice Goguen, and Alexis Feringa. *Risk Management Guide for Information Technology Systems* (NIST SP 800-30). National Institute for Standards and Technology, 2002. http://csrc.nist.gov/publications/nistpubs/800-30/sp800-30.pdf (accessed October 2, 2010).

Swenson, Christopher. *Modern Cryptanalysis: Techniques for Advanced Code Breaking*. New York: Wiley, 2008.

Tipton, Hal, Kevin Henry, and Steve Kalman, e-mail conversation with author, June 2008.

Tipton, Harold F. and Micki Krause Nozaki. *Information Security Management Handbook*, 6th ed. Boca Raton, FL: CRC Press, 2012.

Total Disaster Risk Management Good Practice. Asian Disaster Reduction Center, 2009. http:// www.adrc.asia/publications/TDRM2005/TDRM_Good_Practices/Index.html (accessed October 2, 2010).

U.S. Code Vol. 15, sec. 6801-6803.

U.S. Code Vol. 15, sec. 6801(b).

U.S. Code Vol. 15, sec. 7213m.

U.S. Code Vol. 15, sec. 7266.

U.S. Code Vol. 20, sec. 1232g.

U.S. Code Vol. 44, sec. 3542(b)(1).

U.S. Code Vol. 44, sec. 3544(a)(3)(A)(ii).

U.S. Government Accountability Office. *Federal Information System Controls Audit Manual*, 1999. http://www.gao.gov/special.pubs/ai12.19.6.pdf (accessed October 2, 2010).

U.S. Office of Management and Budget, Circular No. A-130, "Management of Federal Information Resources," December 2000. http://www.whitehouse.gov/omb/circulars_a130 _a130trans4/ (accessed April 21, 2010).

U.S. Securities and Exchange Commission, "Information Matters," February 22, 2006, http:// www.sec.gov/answers/infomatters.htm (accessed April 16, 2010).

Vacca, John R. *Computer and Information Security Handbook*. San Francisco: Morgan Kaufmann, 2013.

Valeriano, Brandon and Ryan C. Maness. *Cyber War Versus Cyber Realities*. New York: Oxford University Press, 2015.

Verizon Business, *2009 Data Breach Investigations Report*, April 15, 2009. http://www .verizonbusiness.com/resources/security/reports/2009_databreach_rp.pdf (accessed March 1, 2010).

VoIP Security Alliance. http://www.voipsa.org (accessed September 17, 2010).

Weiss, Martin and Michael G. Solomon. *Auditing IT Infrastructures for Compliance*. Burlington, MA: Jones & Bartlett Learning, 2015.

Wheeler, Evan. Security Risk Management. Burlington, MA: Syngress Press, 2011.

Whitman, M. E., and H. J. Matford *Principles of Incident Response and Disaster Recovery*. Boston: Course Technology, 2006, p. 492.

Williams, Barry L. *Information Security Policy Development for Compliance*. Boca Raton, FL: CRC Press, 2013.

Williams, Branden R. and Anton Chuvakin. *PCI Compliance*. Burlington, MA: Syngress Press, 2014.

Wood, Charles Cresson. *Information Security Policies Made Easy*. Baseline Software, Incorporated, 1997.

Wright, Craig S. *The IT Regulatory and Standards Compliance Handbook: How to Survive Information Systems Audit and Assessments*. Burlington, MA: Syngress, 2008.

Wright, Steve. PCI DSS: *A Practical Guide to Implementation,* 2nd ed. Rolling Meadows, IL: IT Governance Ltd, 2009.

Index